The *Big Book* of
CIVIL WAR SITES

*From Fort Sumter to Appomattox, a Visitor's Guide to the
History, Personalities, and Places of America's Battlefields*

INTRODUCTION BY JAMES C. BRADFORD

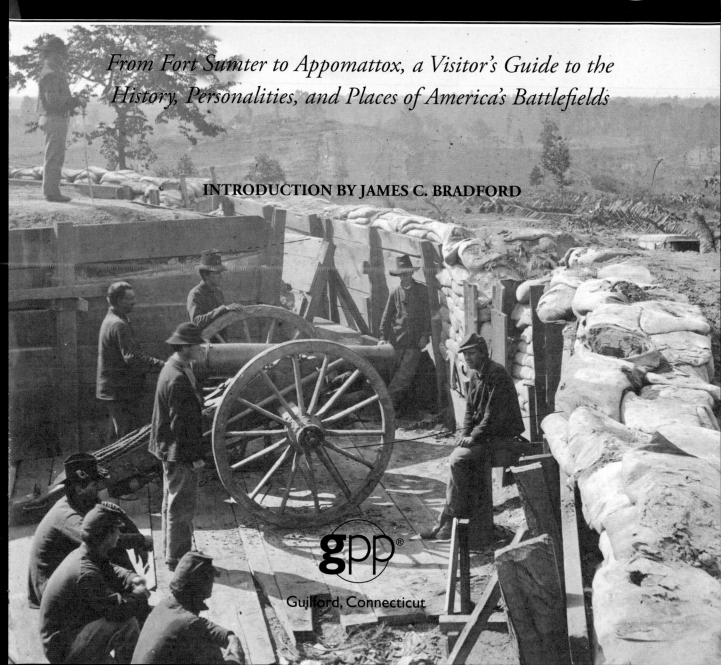

gpp®

Guilford, Connecticut

All of the information in this guidebook is subject to change. We recommend that you call ahead to obtain current information before traveling.

Introduction by James C. Bradford
Edited by Cynthia Parzych
Text contributed by John McKay, Rebeccah Pawlowski, and Eric Ethier
Unless otherwise noted, all maps and photos are courtesy of the Library of Congress.
Text design by Elizabeth Kingsbury

Library of Congress Cataloging-in-Publication Data is available on file.

ISBN 978-0-7627-5467-0

Printed in China

10 9 8 7 6 5 4 3 2 1

CONTENTS

✯ ✯ ✯ ✯ ✯ ✯ ✯ ✯ ✯ ✯ ✯ ✯ ✯ ✯ ✯

How to Use This Book

Although there have been somewhere between 75,000 and 100,000 books published about the Civil War since 1865 (depending on which source you consult), the overwhelming majority have been on the Eastern Theater (Virginia, Pennsylvania, Maryland) and the grand campaigns and huge battles fought there that have become part of the American lexicon. However, the battles and campaigns that really brought the Confederacy to a close happened elsewhere, at Vicksburg in Mississippi, at Shiloh in Tennessee, at New Orleans and Port Hudson in Louisiana, at Wilmington and Durham Station in North Carolina, at Charleston in South Carolina, and, most important, at Atlanta and Savannah in Georgia. While Gettysburg, a name known literally around the world, has long been known as "the battle" of the war, it really was just a meeting engagement followed by a three-day battle of assault and maneuver, where the Union Army hung on by its fingernails most of the battle and only grievous error (some might argue a series of errors) of judgment by Lee handed the victory to the North. In comparison, the same day that Lee's final charge up Cemetery Ridge broke the back of his own army, Pemberton in Vicksburg surrendered to Grant after a long, painful campaign that featured brilliant maneuvering on Grant's part, superb gunnery by the Confederate cannoneers guarding the Mississippi River approaches to the city, heroic though unsuccessful assaults on the ramparts of the surrounding forts by Sherman's men, six weeks of unbroken siege and heavy bombardment that resulted in the starving civilians of the city moving into caves and basements for cover, and, finally, an honorable surrender of an infantry garrison that had not been defeated in any direct assault on the city.

Similarly, although various Union armies maneuvered and fought all around the northern and eastern approaches to Richmond (their target from the very beginning) most of the four-year-long war, the city was finally taken only after Lee's decimated Army of Northern Virginia was no longer able to resist the overwhelming Union armies opposing it. On the other hand, Atlanta was an even more important target from a military standpoint than Richmond itself, having manufacturing facilities to make the weapons and uniforms impossible to import through the Union naval blockade, warehouses to store all the supplies, and three major rail lines crossing in the middle of town able to take all those needed supplies to any point of the Confederacy. Richmond's major exports were ill-advised orders and advice from the politicians and hangers-on that plagued the city like so many vermin-infested mice. Atlanta fell after fewer than four months of a brilliant, determined, and well-led campaign by Sherman, and his subsequent sightseeing trip down to Savannah really and finally cut the Confederacy in half. The loss of both supplies and transport doomed the Confederacy, itself toppling less than six months afterwards.

The first part of every chapter discusses the history and chronology of the area, with as many anecdotal stories packed in as our editors would allow, and is followed by a listing section, where basic travel information is provided. This section is by no measure comprehensive—we really saw no need to tell you about the 16 fast-food establishments parked at the entrance gate of a national battlefield, for example; nor did we feel the need to review the amenities of standardized chain motels that clog the exit ramps of freeways these days like so many sutlers' rows. We have attempted to let you know how to find these places in the rare instances it was not absolutely obvious upon arrival at a historic site. Some lodging and dining establishments were so overwhelmingly superior, however, that we felt as if we just had to bring them to your attention. We must point out that many of the areas we discuss are covered in thorough detail in other GPP publications, such as *Insiders' Guide to Atlanta, Insiders' Guide to Savannah,* and *Insiders' Guide to North Carolina's Outer Banks* (available online and at major bookstores).

Some chapters also include day trips, mostly Civil War–oriented attractions that were not really a part of whatever we were discussing in the chapter, along with some unrelated features and attractions that the average history buff should enjoy.

The Civil War and the military have a specialized language that may trip up the uninitiated. Thus a glossary at the end of the book will help you understand terms and expressions that have no plain-language equivalent.

One last caveat: This work is the product of some very opinionated and somewhat biased historians (as if there were any other kinds!). As professional historians, we have tried to lay aside biases and opinions and take fresh looks at the events that unfolded here, but as interpreting history is an entirely subjective exercise, one cannot work in the vacuum of sober objectivity. The opinions presented here are our own and do not necessarily represent the views of Globe Pequot Press, the National Park Service, the Sons of Confederate Veterans, or any other interested parties.

Before You Go

As always, it pays to make a quick phone call to the facilities at your destination, before you start out on a lengthy road trip, to confirm hours of operation and other new developments. It also pays to be aware that you will likely be subject to a search before being allowed entry to any current military facility, so it would be advisable to leave weapons or anything that might be viewed with suspicion at home. Ask at the gate if photography or videotaping is allowed at your destination.

PRICE CODES

Accommodations: Based on information available at the time of publication, we offer the following price code (average one-night charge for double occupancy rates in peak season) as a general guide. Please note that fluctuations in price and availability occur frequently. Extra charges may apply for special weekends, additional people in the room, efficiency apartments, or pets. These prices do not include local or state taxes. Unless otherwise indicated, accommodations accept major credit cards.

$	$35 to $70
$$	$70 to $100
$$$	$100 to $130
$$$$	$130 and up

Restaurants: The price code below is for a dinner entree (or lunch if dinner is not served) for one person. Appetizers, desserts, alcohol, and gratuity are additional.

$	$10 and under
$$	$10 to $20
$$$	$20 to $30
$$$$	$30 and up

Introduction

The Civil War was a watershed event in American history. Lasting four long and tragic years, it transformed the nation. Almost five million soldiers and sailors fought for one side or the other; virtually every American was caught up in the cauldron of conflict. An expensive war, it cost at least 620,000 American lives, nearly as many as all other wars combined (approximately 213,000 died in combat and another 407,000 from wounds, disease, accidents, and other causes). Thousands of civilians lost their lives as well, and military operations destroyed millions of dollars in property, laying waste to the entire economic system of the Old South.

Nearly a century and a half since the first shots were fired at Fort Sumter in Charleston Harbor, South Carolina, in April 1861, the origins of the war remain a subject of debate. Should primacy be given to disagreements over states' rights and the nature of the union, to the issue of slavery, or to other causes? Whichever factor one assigns primacy to, one thing is clear: When Abraham Lincoln was elected president on a platform that pledged to block the expansion of slavery into the western territories, seven states—South Carolina, Georgia, Alabama, Mississippi, Louisiana, Florida, and Texas—voted to secede from the United States and to form the Confederate States of America. Lincoln asserted that he had no plans to interfere with slavery where it existed, but when he called for troops to put down the rebellion and force the states of the Deep South to return to the Union, 4 states of the Upper South—North Carolina, Virginia, Tennessee, and Arkansas—joined the 7. The 11 southern states were opposed by the 23 states that remained loyal to the United States, a number that grew by 3 during the war as Nevada and West Virginia were admitted to the Union and rebellion in Tennessee was subdued by Union armies and that state was reabsorbed into the United States.

Within months of the firing on Fort Sumter, armies confronted each other along a 1,200-mile-front stretching from Chesapeake Bay and the Atlantic Ocean in the east to Missouri and Arkansas in the west. The balance of resources favored the Union. Twenty-two million people lived in the North versus nine million in the Confederacy (that included more than three million slaves, one-third of the population of the predominantly agricultural South). Most American manufacturing facilities were located in the North, which also had significantly more natural resources and raw materials, a far better developed transportation system, a functioning government, and an established navy. Southern leaders believed that a greater sense of purpose and higher morale would offset these advantages; they also believed that Southern armies were more ably led than those of their opponents.

The Confederacy was in reality independent by mid-1861, and its political and military leaders had faith that the South's ability to pursue a defensive strategy, one aimed at maintaining the status quo, gave them an advantage. Southern leaders believed that "Cotton was King," and that European dependence on the Southern staple would lead Britain and France to recognize their independence and extend material aid to the new nation. Union leaders, on the other hand, knew it was imperative that they take the offensive to reunite the nation. At the outbreak of hostilities many expected, or at least hoped for, a quick military victory and rapid reunion; others, including General Winfield Scott, believed that it would be a long war, and Scott, as commander in chief of Union armies, devised the "Anaconda Plan," a strategy designed to: 1) exert continued pressure on the Confederacy, particularly in northern Virginia; 2) blockade the southern coast to prevent the export of cotton and import of foreign manufactures, especially war supplies; and 3) subdivide the South to prevent the movement of men and material from one section to another. This strategy ultimately succeeded, and the South was squeezed to death much as its namesake, the anaconda constrictor, crushed it prey.

But this would take four years and, as the war wore on, issues that pitted brother against brother and state against state evolved. The war resulted in an end to slavery as an institution and proved that states' rights were secondary to those of the majority of Americans as expressed through the national government in Washington. The nation was reunited during the dozen postwar years commonly referred to as "Reconstruction," but many

Southerners were not reconciled to their fate until the following century.

A struggle of such magnitude brought forth leaders of heroic stature on both sides. Abraham Lincoln, consistently ranked as the greatest U.S. president and the subject of more books than any other American, regularly receives much of the credit for Union victory. The reputation of Jefferson Davis, his southern counterpart, has not fared as well, but those of Confederate generals Robert E. Lee, Thomas "Stonewall" Jackson, Albert Sidney Johnston, Jeb Stuart, and Nathan Bedford Forrest compare favorably with assessments of Ulysses S. Grant, William Tecumseh Sherman, George H. Thomas, and Winfield Scott Hancock. Historians and Civil War enthusiasts continue to debate who was the better overall commander, the better theater commander, and the most effective combat leader. Having the larger navy, the Union produced more operational heroes—for example, David Glasgow Farragut, David Dixon Porter, and Andrew Foote—than the Confederacy, but the South's Raphael Semmes and Franklin Buchanan made the most of their nation's limited naval assets, and Semmes did so with a romantic dash that matched cavalry commanders such as the Confederacy's John Singleton Moseby and the Union's George Armstrong Custer. Both sides produced controversial commanders, including George B. McClellan, who built and trained but always seemed reluctant to commit the Army of the Potomac to battle, and Joseph E. Johnston, who commanded Confederate forces and fought defensive campaigns in Virginia before ceding command in that theater to Lee and moving west to defend Atlanta against Sherman. Could his strategy of standing on the defensive, yielding ground slowly—that is, to win by not losing, a strategy followed by George Washington during the American Revolution—have succeeded in the long run, or would it merely have prolonged the agony of the South given the superior resources of the North?

The Civil War is often judged to be both the last old-fashioned war in which men charged one another across open fields to grapple hand to hand and the first modern war in which railroads, the telegraph, rifled artillery, and iron warships played significant roles. These, as well as more mundane artifacts, can be viewed at innumerable museums located throughout the nation.

When, after four long years of combat engaged on great battlefields such as Bull Run/Manassas in Virginia; Fort Donaldson and Shiloh/Pittsburg Landing in Tennessee; Pea Ridge in Arkansas; the Peninsula between the York and James River in Virginia; at Antietam in Maryland; Vicksburg in Mississippi; Gettysburg in Pennsylvania; and the Wilderness, Spotsylvania Court House, and Petersburg in Virginia; fought along the coasts at North Carolina's Outer Banks; Port Royal and Charleston, South Carolina; Mobile Bay, Alabama; and Galveston, Texas; and in operations waged on the rivers of the Mississippi Valley with Fort Henry and Island No. 10 in the north, New Orleans to the south, and Port Hudson and Vicksburg in between, plus in the Red and Arkansas Rivers; the guns fell silent, America was transformed. Factories built to supply the ready-made uniforms and shoes that clothed and shod the armies, the national currency and financial system developed to finance the war, and the rail network constructed to move men and material to the battlefields survived the war and shifted to serving the civilian population. Many of the citizen soldiers who had never ventured more than a few miles from home had their perspectives transformed; thousands moved West rather than return home permanently.

From southern Pennsylvania west to southern Missouri and in the region to the south of the Ohio River, it is difficult to drive an hour without encountering a reminder of the Civil War, be it the statue of a soldier on a county courthouse lawn, a roadside historical marker, or the site of a battlefield, many of which are preserved in state or national parks. These sites allow the traveler to revisit the nation's past, to glimpse events that laid the basis for the emergence of modern America. Reading can supply knowledge of political, social, and military aspects of the war, but nothing substitutes fully for viewing the terrain on which battles were fought. Such visits provide valuable lessons concerning the very fabric of American life. This volume is designed to help one locate the key sites of the war and to make the most of available time by guiding the visitor to the most significant parts of those sites. It can serve as the basic resource for planning forays into America's past and once on the scene of historic events, a guide to what to see and how to allocate one's time.

—James C. Bradford

WAR IN THE NORTH

Sharpsburg/Monocacy: Jump Off to the North

Darley.

The Battle of Antietam
(Sharpsburg)

*F*ought between Major General George B. McClellan's Army of the Potomac and General Robert E. Lee's Army of Northern Virginia on September 17, 1862, the Battle of Antietam was the single bloodiest day of the Civil War. Combined casualties approached 25,000—including some 3,700 dead. The battle was a tactical draw but a strategic victory for the Federals, who forced Lee to abandon his first invasion of the North. By bringing the war to the enemy, Lee had hoped to inspire peace sentiment in the North, rally recruits to his army, and—with luck—crush the Federals in a decisive battle.

Meanwhile, the world watched. A number of European nations, particularly England, relied heavily on Southern cotton, and therefore were following the American Civil War with great interest. Confederate President Jefferson Davis hoped that a convincing Southern victory on Northern soil would bring recognition and support from the South's trading partners overseas. Hoping to take advantage of disorganized Federal leadership in the wake of his victory in the Second Battle of Bull Run (August 29–30, 1862), Lee launched his offensive on September 4. Meanwhile, Lincoln reluctantly replaced Major General John Pope with Major General George B. McClellan—who had been removed from command of the Army of the Potomac earlier that summer. As meek as ever, McClellan told his wife that he had again been called upon to save the nation. "I only consent to take it for my country's sake and with the humble hope that God has called me to it," the "Young Napoleon" wrote.

Lee advanced to Frederick, Maryland, and dispatched General Thomas J. Jackson west to capture Harpers Ferry. But when the Southern commander discovered that a copy of his plans for the campaign (the famed "Special Orders No. 191") had disappeared (a Union soldier found it, wrapped around three cigars and dropped in a vacated Confederate camp), however, he was suddenly forced to contemplate retreat. Instead,

word of Jackson's imminent return (after capturing Harpers Ferry and its entire 12,000-man Federal garrison) convinced him to fight. While Confederate units stalled Federal pursuit in the gaps of South Mountain, the balance of Lee's infantry dug in between Antietam Creek and the town of Sharpsburg.

With a huge advantage in numbers (roughly 75,000 versus 40,000), McClellan should have—with proper coordination and judicious use of his manpower—been able to overwhelm his foe. Instead, he fought with caution and withheld support troops when they were most needed. The battle opened in the early morning fog of September 17, when elements of Union Major General Joseph Hooker's I Corps attacked Lee's left flank, kicking off a morning of inconclusive, bloody back-and-forth struggle through a cornfield and heavy woods. Heavy musketry mowed down soldiers and cornstalks alike—to no apparent end.

Dead soldiers in the Hagerstown Road near a cornfield after the Battle of Antietam

Meanwhile, Union General Edwin Sumner launched a poorly coordinated, two-division strike at the Confederate center, taking horrible casualties in the process. As a by-product of that misguided assault, Brigadier General William H. French found himself with some 5,700 Federals opposite a sunken road filled

Map of the Battle of Antietam showing military positions on September 17, 1862

with a bristling line of Southerners under Brigadier General D. H. Hill. Eager to break through and divide Lee's army, French attacked. For some three hours, Hill's division held its ground, as the field before them filled with dead Federals and their own cart-path turned into "Bloody Lane." Lee sent a division to support Hill. Finally, a mix-up in the Rebel line presented the Yankees with an opening: "We pressed on," a New York infantryman later wrote, "until we reached a ditch dug in the road in which the enemy lay in line, and the few who did not surrender did not live to tell the tale of their defeat." Shooting down the exposed Confederates "like sheep in a pen," the New Yorkers finally opened a gap in the Rebel lines. But neither Sumner nor McClellan chose to follow up, and the hole quickly closed.

On the Union left, meanwhile, Ninth Corps Yankees under Major General Ambrose Burnside—the round-faced Rhode Islander whose side-whiskers would inspire the term "sideburns"—had been fighting since 10 a.m. to get across a narrow stone bridge to assail the Confederate right. Shortly after noon, McClellan—looking to break the stalemate on his right—passed word through Burnside that the bridge had to be carried at all costs. Brigadier General Samuel Sturgis assigned the job to a regiment of Pennsylvanians and one of New Yorkers, and later described the action that followed:

By the time Confederate soldiers crossed Burnside Bridge, the dramatic end of the bloodiest day in American history was approaching.

They started on their mission of death full of enthusiasm, and, taking a route less exposed than the regiments (Second Maryland and Sixth New Hampshire) which had made the effort before them, rushed at a double-quick over the slope leading to the bridge and over the bridge itself, with an impetuosity which the enemy could not resist; and the Stars and Stripes were planted on the opposite bank at 1 o'clock p.m., amid the most enthusiastic cheering from every part of the field from where they could be seen.

Having finally reached enemy ground, Burnside's offensive lost its momentum as the Federals waited for ammunition to come up. By the time the blue lines reached the outskirts of Sharpsburg at around 3:30 p.m., Major General A. P. Hill's 3,300 Confederates—arriving from Harpers Ferry—had reached the field to slow them. Here McClellan might have supported Burnside with reinforcements and won the day. But he did not, and the Federals paid the price. Burnside withdrew his corps back across the creek; exhaustion and the approach of dusk prevented further fighting.

Few Civil War battles matched the fight at Sharpsburg for sheer viciousness. Even Clara Barton, who would later found the American Red Cross and who had seen her share of casualties, spoke with horror as she tended to the battle's wounded: "War is a dreadful thing. Oh, my God, can't this civil strife be brought to an end."

What might have—and should have—been a smashing Union victory ended instead in stalemate. While sickened Sharpsburg residents and soldiers began burying the dead, George McClellan sent only a small force in pursuit of General Lee's retreating army. The Federals reached Blackford's (or Boteler's) Ford—east of Shepherdstown—on the morning of the 19th, hours after Lee's tired troops had crossed. After a day of skirmishing, Union Major General Fitz John Porter's Bluecoats drove off General William Pendleton's small covering force. This inconsequential Federal pursuit ended, however, when A. P. Hill's Rebel division counterattacked the next day. McClellan's fate as an army commander was sealed; he hung on to his command until November, when President Lincoln relieved him in favor of Ambrose Burnside.

Lincoln met with General McClellan at Sharpsburg about two weeks after the battle.

While Lincoln was unsatisfied with the battle's result, Lee had been forced to retreat south and yield the battlefield to the Union—just enough positive news to compel the president to issue his Emancipation Proclamation. Scheduled to take effect on January 1, 1863, the proclamation added a moral impetus to the political struggle and spurred the recruitment of black soldiers for the first time. The roughly 180,000 black fighting men that subsequently joined Union forces gave Lincoln—and his generals—a powerful boost against Confederate armies shrinking by the day. Lincoln would later call the Emancipation Proclamation "the central act of my administration, and the greatest event of the nineteenth century."

THE BATTLE OF MONOCACY

*L*ittle known or understood, the July 9, 1864, Battle of Monocacy bought precious time for the defenders of Washington, D.C., who were squarely in the sights of Confederate General Jubal Early.

On June 18, Early bested Union General David Hunter's Federals at Lynchburg, ending Hunter's scorching drive through the upper Shenandoah Valley and sending him scampering into West Virginia. Jumping at the chance for an offensive, Early gathered some 14,000 Confederate troops and marched north, reaching Winchester on July 2. By now, Early had gotten the belated attention of the War Department and the eye of General Lew Wallace. Another of the Union's political generals, Wallace had shown flashes of potential early in the war before slipping up while commanding a division at Shiloh. Banished to the Union's little-known Middle Department, Wallace was operating out of Baltimore when Early approached. Hoping to at least slow Early's advance, Wallace raced west and deployed his tiny force of some 2,300 men in a strong position behind the Monocacy River, southeast of Frederick. The timely arrival of James Ricketts's division of the VI Corps—which Ulysses S. Grant had sent north from Petersburg—still left Wallace with, at most, 5,800 troops, and outnumbered three-to-one.

On the morning of July 9, Early's small army pushed through Frederick to find Wallace's thin line of Federals.

Early launched a total of five assaults at the Union position before Wallace pulled his men back toward Baltimore. Early's quick victory, however, cost him a full day—a precious 24 hours that brought Grant's XIX Corps reinforcements closer to the capital. He reached the northern outskirts of Washington's defensive ring on July 11, just ahead of the returning Federal VI Corps, which began filling the all-but-empty trenches around Fort Stevens.

In hindsight it seems unlikely that Early could have fought his way into Washington, even without the presence of Grant's reinforcements. But Wallace—and

Plan of the Battle of Monocacy

General Lew Wallace

many others—believed his men had saved the capital. Even Grant, whose criticism of Wallace's performance at Shiloh had all but ruined his subordinate's career, tossed Wallace a few accolades in his memoirs, which were published shortly after his July 1885 death. Regarding Early's withdrawal from Washington's doorstep, Grant offered:

> *There is no telling how much this result was contributed to by General Lew Wallace's leading what might well be considered a forlorn hope. If Early had been but one day earlier he might have entered the capital before the arrival of the reinforcements I had sent. Whether the delay caused by the battle amounted to a day or not, General Wallace contributed on this occasion, by the defeat of the troops under him a greater benefit to the cause than often falls to the lot of a commander of an equal force to render by means of a victory.*

For Wallace—who in the years following the Civil War would write the best-selling novel, *Ben-Hur,* negotiate with an outlaw named Billy the Kid (both while governor of New Mexico Territory), and serve as U.S. consul to Turkey—such praise must have been highly satisfying.

BALL'S BLUFF BATTLEFIELD AND NATIONAL CEMETERY

*T*he Battle of Ball's Bluff might have been dismissed as just one more of the Union's early-war beatings if it had not claimed the life of U.S. senator—and longtime friend of President Abraham Lincoln—Edward D. Baker.

For the men in blue, the battle was especially ugly. Since the Confederate victory at Bull Run on July 21, there had been little movement in the east. Small bodies of Union and Confederate troops watched each other from their posts on either side of the Potomac River. In October, General George B. McClellan—then hard at work assembling the Army of the Potomac—suggested that Brigadier General Charles P. Stone undertake to dislodge Confederates posted at Leesburg, just west of the river. In the early-morning darkness of October 21, Stone sent three brigades (one under the command of Oregon senator Edward Baker) across the Potomac and up a muddy rise at a roughly equal force of Rebels under Brigadier General Shanks Evans.

Supporting units entered the fray after sporadic opening shots, and the two sides exchanged fire into the afternoon. At about 4 p.m. a sharpshooter's bullet ended Baker's life; soon after, the Federal lines bent then broke, and panicked soldiers stumbled and slid back down Ball's Bluff. Rebel pursuers wounded scores of foundering Yankees as they tried to ford the river. Hundreds of other Federals were captured. The battle changed nothing. Evans lost 33 Confederates killed and another 116 wounded or missing. Stone's brigades were practically halved, with 49 Yankees killed, 158 wounded (including Oliver Wendell Holmes Jr.), and more than 700 captured or missing.

Slightly Out of the Way: Shepherdstown, West Virginia

Once known as Mecklenburg, this West Virginia (formerly Virginia) town lent its name to the two-day clash

Map of the Battle of Ball's Bluff

that occurred just to its east, along the Potomac River, on September 19–20, 1862. Wounded victims of the Battle of Shepherdstown and its massive predecessor filled virtually every building in the area. At least 100 Confederates killed outside of Shepherdstown were buried in Elwood Cemetery, where some 300 Southerners—including Stonewall Jackson's aide, Henry Kyd Douglas—now lay.

Today, visitors can walk through the cemetery as part of a day spent in town, which has been named a Historic District in the National Register of Historic Places. Shepherdstown is also the home of the George Tyler Moore Center for the Study of the Civil War. Founded in 1993, the center is now located on German Street in the Conrad Shindler House, one of countless town buildings that served as makeshift hospitals following the Battle of Antietam. The house was purchased by actress Mary Tyler Moore and donated to then-Shepherd College in 1996, as a tribute to her father George Tyler Moore, a Civil War enthusiast. For information on the center and its programs, call (304) 876-5429.

History enthusiasts will also want to visit the Historic Shepherdstown Museum, at the corner of Princess and East German Streets. Set in the restored Entler Hotel, a two-story brick holdover from the Civil War era, the museum boasts several rooms, a re-creation of a Victorian sitting room, a 1905 mail wagon, and a number of American Indian and Civil War artifacts and exhibits, among other items. The museum is open April through October. Admission is free. Further information about the museum and historic downtown Shepherdstown can be found at www.historicshepherds town.com.

HISTORIC SITES

Antietam National Battlefield
5831 Dunker Church Rd.
Sharpsburg
(301) 432-5124
www.nps.gov/anti

Today, the serene landscape of Antietam National Battlefield looks much as it did when the battle began. In recent years, the park has reacquired about 2,000 acres of the battlefield's original countryside, reforested its west and north woods, added some 8,000 feet of historically accurate fencing, and refurbished several of the park's original structures. In addition to 2½ miles of new park trails and a renovated visitor center and museum, the park is now also home to the Pry House Field Hospital Museum, an extension of the National Museum of Civil War Medicine, in Frederick. General McClellan made the house the headquarters of his Union forces, which was visited by Abraham Lincoln two weeks after the battle. Facilities are wheelchair-accessible. Located off Route 65, the park is easily accessible from any direction.

Antietam National Cemetery
Antietam National Battlefield
5831 Dunker Church Rd.
Sharpsburg
(301) 432-5124
www.nps.gov/anti

The final resting place for 4,776 Union soldiers who were killed in the battles of Antietam, Monocacy, and in other nearby conflicts, Antietam National Cemetery is now one of the 130 cemeteries that make up the National Cemetery System. At the center of the cemetery stands a 44-foot, 7-inch granite statue of a Union infantryman, facing homeward to the north to commemorate the fallen soldiers.

Ball's Bluff Battlefield and National Cemetery
Rte. 15 at Battlefield Parkway
Leesburg, VA
(703) 779-9372
www.nps.gov/nr/travel/journey/bnc.htm

Although Ball's Bluff is located in Virginia, it's just a quick drive down Route 15 from Frederick. Surrounded—much like Manassas Battlefield—by the trappings of the modern world (one must drive through a residential development to reach it), Ball's Bluff Battlefield and National Cemetery is nevertheless nicely tucked away in dense woods. A ¾-mile walking path takes visitors from the parking lot to the edge of the steep bluff down which Union troops fled at battle's end. Aside from the steep hill itself, the highlight of the battlefield is its National Cemetery, a neatly groomed, walled-in burial site containing 25 graves representing 54 of the battle's victims. Only one of these men—James Allen of the 15th Massachusetts—has been identified. Admission is free.

Barbara Fritchie House and Museum
154 W. Patrick St.
Frederick, MD
(301) 698-8992

Barbara Fritchie was immortalized in a John Greenleaf Whittier poem as the woman who challenged Confederate troops in the streets of Frederick: "Shoot if you must, this old gray head," Fritchie reportedly shouted from an upstairs window, "but spare your country's flag." This reconstruction of Fritchie's original house is open for tours by appointment.

The Kennedy Farmhouse (John Brown's Headquarters)
2406 Chestnut Grove Rd.
Sharpsburg
(202) 537-8900 (tour information)
www.johnbrown.org

Located just 6 miles from Harpers Ferry, this small farm proved to be just what John Brown needed when he went house hunting in 1859. Under the alias "Isaac Smith," Brown lived here with his followers as they prepared for their 1859 campaign to free slaves. With the help of federal funds and private donations, co-owner South Lynn spent some 20 painstaking years restoring the old farmhouse to its original appearance. Despite the historic significance of the building, which has been declared a National Historic Landmark, its maintenance and operation (still looked over by Mr. Lynn) depends on public support.

Monocacy National Battlefield
4801 Urbana Pike
Frederick, MD
(301) 662-3515
www.nps.gov/mono

The Monocacy National Battlefield Park opened a new 7,000-square-foot visitor center in 2007, transforming the occasionally overlooked park into a compelling experience for Civil War enthusiasts who want to explore the "battle that saved Washington." In addition to the new exhibits and electronic maps, the park also opened four new walking trails, making acres of the historic grounds more accessible to the public. A self-guided driving tour follows the events of July 9, 1864. Admission is free.

Mount Olivet Cemetery
515 S. Market St.
Frederick, MD
(301) 662-1164
www.mountolivetcemeteryinc.com

Francis Scott Key, Barbara Fritchie, Maryland's first governor, Thomas Johnson, and some 800 Union and Confederate soldiers lie in Mount Olivet Cemetery, which is open from dawn to dusk daily.

National Museum of Civil War Medicine
48 E. Patrick St.
Frederick, MD
(301) 695-1864
www.civilwarmed.org

The vastness of Civil War battlefields and the study of regiments, corps, and flanking movements can easily make one forget about war's human cost. For that reason alone, the National Museum of Civil War Medicine is one of those places that everyone—not just Civil War enthusiasts—should visit. The museum, which opened in 1996, filled a huge void in the field, and has since added a satellite building (the Pry House Field Hospital Museum) on the Antietam Battlefield.

Installed in 7,000 square feet of space on two floors are lifelike displays that tell the story of Civil War medicine. Boasting an unmatched collection of medical artifacts, they cover the role of the surgeon, from his own sparse training through the examination of recruits (usually superficial); the dangers of camp life (an exhibit that contains the war's only known surviving surgeon's tent); field-dressing and battlefield care; nursing; and a new exhibit on the embalming of the dead.

The National Museum of Civil War Medicine is wheelchair accessible. It also offers group tours, which take about 90 minutes and should be arranged in advance. The museum boasts a research room and a one-of-a-kind gift shop.

Rose Hill Cemetery
(301) 739-3630
600 S. Potomac St.
Hagerstown, MD
www.rosehillcemeteryofhagerstown.org

In the decade that followed the Civil War, some 2,000 Confederate soldiers killed at Antietam or South Mountain were reinterred here. Only 346 of the men were ever identified.

South Mountain State Battlefield
6620 Zittlestown Rd.
Middletown, MD
(301) 791-4767
www.dnr.state.md.us

Part of the South Mountain Recreation Area, the site of the September 14, 1862, Battle of South Mountain is now maintained and operated by the nonprofit group Friends of South Mountain State Battlefield. Only the key sections of the park—Turner's Gap, Fox's Gap, and Crampton's Gap—currently feature roadside markers, interpretive signage, or monuments. But with some financial assistance, the group hopes to add museums at the north and south ends of the battlefield.

ACCOMMODATIONS

Hill House Bed & Breakfast $$$–$$$$
12 W. Third St.
Frederick, MD
(301) 682-4111
www.hillhousefrederick.com

This circa-1870 restored Victorian town house is a great place to stay if you're looking for easy access to downtown Frederick's antiques shops and historical sites. The impeccably restored inn boasts four guest rooms furnished with original art, antiques, and period accents like four-poster and canopy beds. Guests also enjoy private bathrooms and a full southern Maryland breakfast each morning.

Hollerstown Hill $$$
4 Clarke Place
Frederick, MD
(301) 228-3630
www.hollerstownhill.com

Staying at Hollerstown Hill is much like staying in a dollhouse. Tucked away in a quiet Frederick neighborhood, the circa-1900 Victorian even boasts its own collection of antique dolls, tastefully displayed around the house in the company of other period antiques. There are four large guest rooms, each with wireless Internet, private bath, and one with its own private porch. After a busy day of sightseeing, you can wage battles of your own in a game room stocked with board games, a pool table, and even a Civil War chess set.

The Inn at Antietam Bed and Breakfast $$$–$$$$
220 E. Main St.
Sharpsburg
(301) 432-6601
www.innatantietam.com

Few people get the chance to sleep in such comfort on a Civil War battle site, especially one as important as Antietam National Battlefield. But that's just what the Inn at Antietam Bed and Breakfast offers in five distinct suites that range in price and degree of luxury. Each suite features central air-conditioning, private baths, and old-time comfort. Others

(such as the General Burnside Smokehouse Suite) also offer a fireplace, wet bar, and TV/VCR. Common areas include a small library, a parlor (with a baby grand piano), a solarium, and a wraparound porch from which residents can take in the area's unmatched scenery.

Inn at Buckeystown $$$–$$$$
3521 and 3619 Buckeystown Pike
Buckeystown, MD
(301) 874-5755
www.innatbuckeystown.com

Just south of Monocacy, this award-winning inn offers a central location from which to explore Antietam, Frederick, Harpers Ferry, and northern Virginia. Built in 1897, the historic mansion was converted to a luxurious five-bedroom guesthouse in 1981. In the rooms, you'll find sparkling chandeliers (and even working fireplaces in three of the rooms), plus glorious gardens and a wraparound porch that's perfect for savoring a glass of wine (it's strictly bring-your-own-bottle, so be sure to stop by a local winery on your way). For a late-afternoon pick-me-up, the inn also offers a delightful high tea service.

Jacob Rohrbach Inn $$$–$$$$
138 W. Main St.
Sharpsburg
(301) 432-5079
(877) 839-4242
www.jacob-rohrbach-inn.com

The Jacob Rohrbach Inn is a historical treasure, built more than 50 years before the outbreak of the Civil War. The five-bedroom inn lies within walking distance of the battlefield park and even stocks bicycles for guests who wish to explore the park on two wheels. Before you set out for the day, feast on a delicious multicourse breakfast, prepared with herbs and produce grown on the property. Although the house itself is more than 200 years old, it boasts a full suite of modern amenities like wireless Internet and cable TV, and owners Joanne and Paul Breitenbach are eager to assist with historical information, along with recommendations for sightseeing and entertainment.

Thomas Shepherd Bed and Breakfast $$$–$$$$
Corner of Duke and German Sts.
Shepherdstown, WV
(888) 889-8952
www.thomasshepherdinn.com

Those who take the quick 4-mile drive from Sharpsburg to Shepherdstown will find comfortable accommodations at the Thomas Shepherd Inn, which happens to be the only bed-and-breakfast in town. Built in 1868, the Federal-style inn is one of the few buildings in town that was not used as a hospital following the Battle of Antietam.

Located at the end of Shepherdstown's main thoroughfare, the Thomas Shepherd Inn offers convenience (within walking distance of everything in town, and driving distance of Harpers Ferry, etc.), comfort (six delightful, air-conditioned rooms, private baths), friendly service (homemade breakfast served each morning, etc.), and—considering that owners Jim Ford and Jeanne Muir have Shepherdstown's B&B market cornered—surprisingly reasonable prices.

RESTAURANTS

Blue Moon Café $$
Corner of Princess and High Sts.
Shepherdstown, WV
(304) 876-1920
www.bluemoonshepherdstown.com

The Blue Moon menu boasts just about every American staple one can imagine, including gourmet pizzas, fine dinners, hearty sandwiches and salads, and vegetarian meals. You'll take a trip around the globe just by perusing the menu: vegan chickpea curry is listed on the same page as "Jessie's Meato Escondido," a roast beef sandwich topped with feta cheese, fresh spinach, onions, and cucumbers, served on ciabatta bread slathered with herbed cream cheese. The casual environment is just as diverse, with seating in three different dining rooms and outside along the water.

Cacique $$
26 N. Market St.
Frederick, MD
(301) 695-2756
www.caciquefrederick.com

You might not think that Frederick would be a hotbed for haute cuisine, but the town has practically become a suburb of Washington, D.C., and it's attracted its share of residents with sophisticated palates. At Cacique, Spanish and Mexican cuisine sit side by side—a cultural faux pas, perhaps, but diners give a thumb's-up to Spanish dishes like paella or mussels prepared in Andalucian fashion, as well as traditional Mexican cuisine.

Captain Bender's Tavern $$
111 E. Main St.
Sharpsburg
(301) 432-5813
www.captainbenders.com

Captain Bender's is a great local gathering place. It's named for Raleigh Bender, a boatsman on the C&O Canal in the nineteenth century, who also managed a tavern on the site of his modern-day namesake. You can always count on a cold beer, a thick burger, or a generous salad, plus an assortment of panini and pizzas. The restaurant even appeals to heartier appetites with the "death dog," a foot-long hot dog topped with chili, cheese, diced onion, and sour cream.

The Cozy Restaurant $$
103 Frederick Rd.
Thurmont, MD
(301) 271-4301 (inn)
(301) 271-7373 (restaurant)
www.cozyvillage.com

Part of the historic Cozy Inn, the Cozy Restaurant is the oldest family-owned restaurant in Maryland, established in 1929. It's a good choice for groups, specializing in fine American dining in its 11 uniquely styled rooms, in addition to lavish buffet dinners and fantastic baskets of food to go. There's also a pub serving traditional bar food and Willy's Beer, prepared especially for the inn. It's just a few short miles from the famous presidential retreat at Camp David, and there's a museum on-site stocked with gifts from members of the press and visiting dignitaries.

Jennifer's $$
207 W. Patrick St.
Frederick, MD
(301) 662-0373
http://pages.frederick.com/dining/jennifers

There's something friendly and inviting about this Frederick pub, a mainstay for more than two decades. A popular draw for locals, Jennifer's decor is cozy and inviting; exposed brick walls, a large oak bar, and even a fireplace. For lunch, sample salads, sandwiches, or pizza, while dinner brings tasty creations like hot and crunchy chicken with honey-pecan butter or lamb chops. The restaurant also offers a spa menu for light eaters.

Monocacy Crossing $$$
4424A Urbana Pike
Frederick, MD
(301) 846-4204
www.monocacycrossing.com

If you feel like dining off the beaten path, you won't be disappointed with Monocacy Crossing. One of Frederick's top-rated restaurants, it delivers with fantastic food, attentive service, a well-thought-out wine list, and a gorgeous setting. Seafood creations like steamed mussels and clam chowder are fresh and perfectly seasoned, or sample the season's bounty with creations like the Eggplant Napoleon, with layers of fried slices of eggplant, roasted peppers, zucchini, and mushrooms, topped with marinara sauce. On a pleasant day, sit on the outdoor patio to dine alfresco.

The Tasting Room $$$
101 N. Market St.
Frederick, MD
(240) 379-7772
www.tastetr.com

As Frederick's first wine bar, The Tasting Room touts the most extensive, diverse wine list in Frederick—and in most of the D.C. exurbs—along with chic decor that's clearly designed with the young professional set in mind. Located on the corner of Church and Market Streets in downtown Frederick's restaurant district, the stylish restaurant and its patrons look like they'd feel right at home in Manhattan. (Even if you don't dine here, you can peer inside through its floor-to-ceiling windows.) Cosmopolitan flavors also take center stage on the menu prepared by chef and owner Michael Tauraso. Select from starters like Greek lamb, bruschetta, or tuna crudo with sesame-lime dressing, then go for a sophisticated entree like the Kobe-style Berkshire pork loin, crusted with a blend of coriander and pepper, or local rockfish.

Harpers Ferry/Winchester:
Into the Valley

Darley.

HARPERS FERRY

"*H*arpers Ferry," Indiana corporal Edmund Brown wrote after the war, "was a fitting place to begin an advance against the rebellion."

There was no doubting the area's strategic importance, located as it was on the Baltimore and Ohio Railroad line at the gateway to the vital Shenandoah Valley—a natural north-south invasion route packed with forage for man and beast. It was a town worth fighting for, even after Confederate soldiers burned its Federal arsenal and armory and dragged off its valuable gun-making machinery early in the Civil War. The town would change hands at least eight times before Major General Philip Sheridan finally secured it for the Union in 1864. By then, its once-vital armory was a blackened brick shell of its former self—almost, but not quite, lost to history.

Until October 1859, this small town located at the confluence of the Shenandoah and Potomac Rivers was known simply as the home of the historic, old arsenal, and for the stunning natural beauty that surrounded it. By then, "the Hole," as the site was first known, had its first European residents and its namesake business—a ferry service across the Potomac operated by Philadelphian Robert Harper. Authorized by President George Washington, the Harpers Ferry Arsenal opened in 1801, joining the U.S. Armory at Springfield, Massachusetts, in producing arms for the young American military. In 60 years of production, Harpers Ferry machinery turned out some 600,000 guns—including the Model 1803 flintlock and the Model 1841 percussion rifle, the nation's first. Meanwhile, sectionalism and the slavery issue tore at the United States until a grim, old Westerner marched east to transform a town and a nation.

A cold mist swirled through Harpers Ferry in the evening darkness of October 16, 1859. Outside the brick buildings of the U.S. Armory, a lone sentry named Daniel Whelan paced, unaware that revolution was unfolding in the flickering blackness around him.

In the blink of an eye, it seemed, a motley group of armed men had surrounded the startled Whelan, taken him prisoner, and forced their way into the Federal compound he guarded. Whelan listened in stunned silence as the gray-bearded leader of his assailants stepped forward and announced his presence before his god.

"I come here from Kansas," John Brown declared, "and this is a slave state; I have possession of the United States armory, and if the citizens interfere with me, I must only burn the town and have blood."

Thus began Kansas abolitionist John Brown's first step in his mission to free America's slaves. Harpers Ferry would thenceforth forever be linked—depending on one's viewpoint—with violent abolitionist extremism or with the American slave's fight for freedom.

Brown's long-planned assault on slavery was doomed almost from the start. Leading an invasion force of just 21 men, Brown had pinned his hopes for reinforcement on slaves and free blacks in the area. His raid was to be the spark that ignited a massive slave rebellion and brought about the end of the "peculiar institution." Having armed his new recruits from his own arms stores, Brown would lead them into surrounding hills to begin a guerrilla war.

None of this would happen, a fact that grizzled old "Osawatomie Brown" may have recognized after two of his minions shot and mortally wounded Shepherd Hayward—a free black employed by the Baltimore and Ohio Railroad. Hayward, who, out of curiosity, had stepped off a B&O train as it stopped on the edge of town, was shot in the back as he tried to avoid two armed strangers in the early-morning darkness of October 17.

Very little else went right for Brown's "Army of Liberation." Men dispatched to spread word of the operation and recruit volunteers returned with just a handful of mostly reluctant and confused slaves and their masters, now Brown's prisoners. The sun slowly rose as Brown waited in vain for the legions of black volunteers to appear, and as word of the raid spread. By early morning, hundreds of irate Virginians had converged on the village, guns in hand, eager to deal with the hated abolitionist invaders. Gunfire erupted; three locals fell dead, along with eight of Brown's men. Brown—now more or less trapped in the arsenal's engine room—tried unsuccessfully to negotiate for passage out of town in exchange for his hostages. No one was listening.

Map of Harpers Ferry illustrating its strategic importance on the Potomac River

At dawn on October 18, Lieutenant J. E. B. Stuart delivered to Brown a surrender request from his superior, Colonel Robert E. Lee, who had reached the site during the night with a contingent of U.S. Marines. Brown refused; marines subsequently rushed the engine house, knocked down its doors, and captured what was left of Brown's army. A handful of marines were wounded during the struggle, as was the elder Brown. One of Brown's sons was dead; a second was mortally wounded.

In a November 23 letter to a Reverend McFarland, Brown wrote:

Christ told me to remember them that were in bonds as bound with them, to do towards them as I would wish them to do towards me in similar circumstances. My conscience bade me do that. I tried to do it, but failed. Therefore I have no regret on that score. I have no sorrow either as to the result, only for my poor wife and children. They have suffered much, and it is hard to leave them uncared for. But God will be a husband to the widow and a father to the fatherless.

After a whirlwind trial through which the injured defendant remained prone on a cot, Brown was convicted of treason and murder, and was sentenced to hang.

On December 2, 1859, John Brown rode to his death sitting atop his own coffin in the back of a wagon. A brand new gallows—surrounded by 800 armed men, reporters, and curious eyewitnesses—awaited him. Without fear or apprehension, Brown mounted the gallows, and, a few minutes later, dropped to his death.

15,000 rifles from the flames, but they managed to save the machinery that turned the guns out. This they shipped to Richmond, where it was soon put to use arming Confederates.

Harpers Ferry was back in Federal hands in September 1862, when Confederate general Robert E. Lee launched his first invasion of the North. Looking to open a supply route through the Shenandoah Valley, Lee sent Stonewall Jackson west to remove the one impediment to his plan—a Yankee garrison at Harpers Ferry, now 12,500 men strong. Charged with holding the town to the last extremity was 58-year-old Union colonel Dixon Miles, a gray-bearded, elderly looking, army lifer whom events would soon prove had been caught in the wrong place at the wrong time.

John Brown walks to his death.

The approach of the Civil War magnified Harpers Ferry's importance—and its vulnerability. Dominated by high ground on three sides, it was practically indefensible.

On April 17, 1861—just three days into the war—an approaching force of Virginia militia and volunteers compelled Lieutenant Roger Jones to set the armory afire and evacuate his tiny Federal garrison. Southern troops arrived too late to claim some

Colonel Dixon Miles

Jackson—who had spent the summer defeating Union armies throughout the Shenandoah Valley—sent one column under General John Walker to take Loudoun Heights, and another under General Lafayette McLaws to deal with Federal defenders on Maryland Heights. Jackson would complete the encirclement by occupying Bolivar Heights, in the arsenal's rear.

The issue was only briefly in doubt. Walker quickly accomplished his task. McLaws's Confederates somehow managed to haul cannon and ammunition up Maryland Heights, where, on the morning of September 14, they faced off against Colonel Thomas Ford's 1,600 Bluecoats. Ford's artillerists held their own against McLaws's gunners, but his green infantry—many of whom had not yet mastered even the basics of soldiering—soon broke before the hardened Rebels. The shaken Union soldiers raced back over the Potomac and into town, ceding the heights—and, unwittingly, victory—to Jackson.

Jackson's forces opened fire and quickly forced a Union surrender. Some 1,300 Union cavalrymen managed to escape the trap, but Jackson captured everyone and everything else, including 13,000 rifles and 70 cannon. Jackson's hard-driving foot soldiers impressed their captives: "They were silent as ghosts," one Yankee recalled, "ruthless and rushing in their speed; ragged, earth colored, disheveled and devilish, as tho' they were keen on the scent of the hot blood that was already streaming up from the opening struggle at Antietam, and thirsting for it."

The town changed hands several times prior to the summer of 1864, when Union major general Philip Sheridan finally secured the Shenandoah Valley for the Union. But by then the once-prized arsenal and armory was little more than burned-out brick and mortar, valueless, save for posterity.

WINCHESTER, VA

*F*or the residents of Winchester, Virginia, any day that passed without the rattle of muskets or the thundering hoofbeats of passing cavalry was a gift. Laid out at the northern end of the Shenandoah Valley, it stood in the way of Union and Confederate armies traveling up or down the Valley Pike, or rumbling off on one of the several other roadways that passed through town. It was also home to a Baltimore and Ohio Railroad terminal. Due to its importance as a transportation hub, this small town of 4,500 changed hands more than seventy times in four years of war, and witnessed three significant Civil War battles. It was the seat of hearty Confederate support, especially after Stonewall Jackson made the town the headquarters of his Shenandoah Valley District in November 1861.

In the spring of 1862, George McClellan's Army of the Potomac trudged slowly up the Virginia Peninsula, moving inexorably toward the Confederate capital of Richmond. While Albert Sidney Johnston and then Robert E. Lee dealt with McClellan, Stonewall Jackson was left to prevent Union forces in the Shenandoah Valley from slipping west to reinforce the Yankee commander. After chasing John C. Fremont out of the valley, Jackson moved north in pursuit of Nathaniel Banks's Union army. On May 23, Jackson's men overran a small Federal force at Front Royal; two days later, Jackson assaulted Banks's army in the hills south of Winchester. Withstanding fierce resistance and devastating Federal artillery fire, Jackson sent Banks's army retreating through the town and north across the Potomac.

Even worse results befell Union major general Robert H. Milroy a year later, during Lee's second invasion of the North. Dismissing reports of Lee's rapid advance, Milroy waited until his garrison at Winchester was almost completely encircled. By the time he ordered a withdrawal, Richard Ewell's Corps was on hand to cut off his retreat and sweep up prisoners.

Confederate forces in the Shenandoah Valley continued to plague the Union until August 1864, when

*Sheridan after the Battle of Winchester,
September 1864*

Lieutenant General Ulysses S. Grant—now in overall command of Union armies—sent Major General Philip Sheridan to eliminate the problem. Sheridan was a born fighter—aggressive and opportunistic—and he hustled his 40,000-man Army of the Shenandoah into the valley in pursuit of General Jubal Early's audacious little Army of the Valley, which had threatened Washington a few weeks earlier. On September 19, Sheridan's 37,000 Federals attacked Early's 17,000, dug-in troops east of Winchester, slamming into the Confederate center and Early's left. After an afternoon of fighting, Union cavalry from the north and infantry from the east forced Early into retreating south down the pike to Strasburg. After losing again to Sheridan two days later at Fisher's Hill, Early—and the Confederates—were all but finished in the valley.

HISTORIC SITES

Harpers Ferry National Historical Park
Rte. 340
Harpers Ferry
(304) 535-6029
www.nps.gov/hafe

Visiting Harpers Ferry today is like taking a step back in time; it is a place that every American should see. Only the small engine house building in which John Brown made his last stand in 1859 (now known as John Brown's Fort) remains from the old arsenal.

Little sign remains of the army garrisons (usually Union) that were once stationed here, first to protect the arsenal and then to protect the Ohio and Baltimore Railroad that ran through town. But despite what has been lost, the town (only part of which is owned by the National Park Service) remains very much a 19th-century settlement. A house built by Robert Harper, who established a ferry service here in 1761, still stands in the lower town. Antiques and gift shops and restaurants line the quaint streets, along with historic buildings and museums. Depending on the season, costumed interpreters are on hand for demonstrations and to answer questions.

Visitors should begin their visit at the Cavalier Heights Visitor Center (which houses a small gift shop and restroom facilities), where they can park and board buses into town.

The buses are wheelchair-accessible and leave every 15 minutes. Book hounds will want to stop by the Park's Bookshop on Shenandoah Street, in the lower part of town. At nearly 3,800 beautiful acres—unhindered by the urban sprawl that threatens other parks—Harpers Ferry National Historical Park also features a number of beautiful hiking trails through the hills above town; maps for these can be found online and at the visitor center. The park also contains a library and research room, which is open by appointment.

Jefferson County Museum
200 E. Washington St.
Charles Town, WV
(304) 725-8628
jeffctywvmuseum.org

Jefferson County is proud of its Civil War heritage, and with good reason. While still part of Virginia, the county provided more troops to the Confederate cause than any other locality except for Richmond. Despite its Southern sympathies, Charles Town was also the hometown of Martin Delany, the highest-ranking African-American officer during the Civil War. The museum's most prized Civil War relic is the flag that once flew with J. E. B. Stuart's Horse Artillery. The museum is open Apr through Nov.

John Brown Gallows Site
515 S. Samuel St.
Charles Town, WV

Under the sunny, late-morning sky of December 2, 1859, a crowd of reporters, curious onlookers, and soldiers gathered in a field to witness the final moments of John Brown—the Kansas abolitionist whose raid on Harpers Ferry had further polarized a nation. Today, a private home occupies the ground on which Brown went to the gallows. But although only a historical marker outside that property remains to explain what took place on the site, it remains a solemn place worth visiting. The Jefferson County Courthouse, where Brown was tried, is also located close by.

John Brown Wax Museum
168 High St.
Harpers Ferry
(304) 535-6342
www.johnbrownwaxmuseum.com

It's hard to miss the John Brown Wax Museum, and visitors to the town definitely should not. The museum's wax figures of Brown, his followers, and the marines sent in to arrest them are eerily human, especially considering how near Brown's party once was to this site. The museum is open from mid-Mar through mid-Dec.

WINCHESTER AREA ATTRACTIONS

Civil War Orientation Center
20 S. Cameron St.
Winchester, VA
(540) 535-3543
www.shenandoahatwar.org

If you're planning to explore the Civil War sites of the Shenandoah Valley, this Orientation Center and interactive Web site will help you plan your route. Visit online at home to gather information and ideas, and then stop by the Orientation Center as you start your journey.

Fort Collier Civil War Center
922 Martinsburg Pike
Winchester, VA
(540) 662-2281
www.fortcollier.com

In 1861, Confederate general Joseph E. Johnston ordered the construction of a series of defensive earthworks around Winchester, at the northern end of the Shenandoah Valley. For three years they remained unused, until September 19, 1864, when hundreds of Union cavalrymen stormed the Confederate-filled works north of town, all but ending the Third Battle of Winchester. These fortifications—known as Fort Collier—remain a sight to see. The site is open dawn to dusk.

Kernstown Battlefield
610 Battle Park Dr.
Winchester, VA
(540) 869-2896
www.kernstownbattle.org

Now a registered National Historical Landmark, this site of two Civil War clashes (in 1862 and 1864) is now being looked after by the Kernstown Battlefield Association. Ongoing preservation efforts have led to the purchase of more than 300 acres of the battle area and the addition of road markers and interpretive signage. A small visitor center is open on weekends from May through Oct. Admission is free.

Museum of the Shenandoah Valley
901 Amherst St.
Winchester, VA
(202) 662-1473
www.shenandoahmuseum.org

This beautiful new $20 million museum opened in 2005 to tell the story of the culture and history of the Shenandoah Valley. While the Civil War isn't a primary focal point of the curriculum, it's worth a visit for anyone who's planning to explore the region in-depth. Admission varies depending on which tours you take.

Old Court House Civil War Museum
20 N. Loudoun St.
Winchester, VA
(540) 542-1145
www.civilwarmuseum.org

Built in 1840 and used as a hospital and prison during the Civil War, this building served Frederick County until 1995; in 2003 it reopened to the public as a small but interesting museum with exhibits that feature some 3,000 objects. Located in the heart of Winchester's Old Town Walking Mall, it is definitely worth a look.

✳ ✳ ✳ ✳ ✳ ✳ ✳ ✳ ✳ ✳ ✳ ✳ ✳ ✳ ✳ ✳

Stonewall Jackson's Headquarters Museum
415 N. Braddock St.
Winchester, VA
(540) 667-3242
www.winchesterhistory.org/stonewall_jackson.htm

This is another valley must-see, especially for fans of Stonewall Jackson. Lieutenant Colonel Lewis T. Moore of the 4th Virginia Infantry owned this house, which he loaned to General Jackson for use as a headquarters during the winter of 1861–1862. Maintained today by the Winchester-Frederick County Historical Society, the museum presents Jackson's office almost exactly as he left it. Many of Jackson's personal belongings—including his personal prayer table and prayer book—are on display.

Museum is open Apr through Oct. Visitors can buy a block ticket good for admission to the Jackson Museum along with the Abram's Delight Museum and George Washington's Office Museum.

TOURS

Harpers Ferry Ghost Tours
175 High St.
Harpers Ferry
(732) 801-0381
www.harpersferryghost.20m.com

With so much history afoot in Harpers Ferry, you can expect to hear a good ghost story or two. This guided walking tour is offered nightly from Apr to Oct and by reservation Mon to Sat from Nov to Mar. Tours begin at the O' Be Joyfull Center in Harpers Ferry.

Winchester Walking Tours
1360 S. Pleasant Valley Rd.
Winchester, VA
(540) 542-1326
www.visitwinchesterva.com

Stop by the Winchester Visitor Center to pick up a copy of a guide to Winchester's Civil War history, outlined in an easy-to-follow self-guided walking tour.

ACCOMMODATIONS

The Angler's Inn $$–$$$$
867 W. Washington St.
Harpers Ferry
(304) 535-1239
www.theanglersinn.com

There's no doubt that The Angler's Inn was designed with fishermen in mind, and with good reason. Harpers Ferry is located at the confluence of the Potomac and the Shenandoah Rivers, home to some of the best smallmouth bass and trout fishing in the country. But even if you're sticking to dry land, the inn is an excellent choice for an overnight or weekend stay. Located less than a mile from the national park, this 1880 guesthouse is a favorite among travelers. There are four beautiful guest rooms, each with private sitting room and private bath. Its wraparound porch is perfect for reading and for savoring complimentary cookies and soda. Another draw: one of the best breakfasts you'll ever taste, featuring entrees like omelets cooked to order, luscious waffles, and spiced bacon.

Fuller House Inn and Carriage House $$$$
220 W. Boscawen St.
Winchester, VA
(540) 722-3976
www.fullerhouseinn.com

"Location is our specialty," innkeeper Debra Johnson says of the Fuller House Inn, speaking of the downtown Winchester location of this charming inn, constructed in 1780. There are two rooms in the main house, outfitted with DVD players, refrigerators, and private baths, and guests enjoy complimentary wine and cheese and a delectable room service breakfast every morning. For extended stays, the Fuller House can also connect you with three additional properties: an 1854 Carriage House, a historic pre–Civil War house, or a downtown apartment.

The George Washington Hotel, A Wyndham Historic Hotel $$$–$$$$
103 E. Piccadilly St.
Winchester, VA
(540) 678-4700
www.wyndham.com/hotels/DCAGW/main.wnt

Wyndham Hotels took over the management of this vintage 1924 grand hotel and completed an extensive renovation in 2008. The result: a stunning 90-room historic hotel loaded with modern conveniences and genteel service befitting its elegant setting. On the premises, there's a unique Roman-bath-inspired indoor swimming pool and a popular restaurant, The Dancing Goat, featuring an open kitchen and outdoor dining in season.

The Herds Inn $$$–$$$$
688 Shady Elm Rd.
Winchester, VA
(866) 783-2681
www.theherdsinn.com

The Herds Inn stands out among the appealing B&Bs in this region, and with good reason. It's a working dairy farm that serves up a one-of-a-kind rural experience. Guests check in to a hand-built log home and watch (and join in, if they wish) the day-to-day farm activities. There's no shortage of activity; the farm is home to sheep, buffalo, goat, peacocks, chickens, turkeys, rabbits, dogs, and, of course, cows—and they're eager to interact with guests. The inn accepts only one party at a time and offers a perfect setup for families.

The Inn at Vaucluse Spring $$$$
231 Vaucluse Spring Lane
Stephens City, VA
(540) 869-0200
(800) 869-0525
www.vauclusespring.com

The Inn at Vaucluse Spring is not your typical B&B. It's a fifteen-room B&B complex, spread across a hundred rolling acres near a limestone spring. Six guesthouses make up the property, voted one of the region's most romantic inns by *Washingtonian* magazine, and there's really something for everyone. Discerning travelers can luxuriate in an elegant manor house, while outdoors enthusiasts will feel right at home in a cozy log house dating to the 1850s. The rooms and houses come equipped with fireplaces, Jacuzzi tubs, porches, rocking chairs, and common areas perfect for savoring a glass of wine or curling up with a good book.

The Jackson Rose Bed & Breakfast $$$–$$$$
1167 W. Washington St.
Harpers Ferry
(304) 535-1528
www.thejacksonrose.com

Before Thomas J. Jackson earned the nickname "Stonewall," he used this 1795 Federal-style mansion as a headquarters in spring 1861. He wrote to his wife, admiring the beautiful roses that grew in the garden outside his house. Jackson's second-story room is one of four rooms available to guests at this B&B, and for Civil War buffs, it's one of the most sought-after rooms in Harpers Ferry. Regardless of which room you check in to, you'll enjoy beautiful antique furnishings, private baths, and a to-die-for breakfast featuring entrees like vegetable frittatas, French toast, fresh-baked muffins, and scones.

Killahevlin Bed and Breakfast $$$$
1401 N. Royal Ave.
Front Royal, VA
(540) 636-7335
(800) 847-6132
www.vairish.com

Killahevlin Bed and Breakfast is located on "Richardson's Hill" in Front Royal. The house was built in 1905 by William Carson, an Irish immigrant who was largely responsible for getting Skyline Drive built. The house is on the National Register of Historic Buildings and the Virginia Landmarks Register. Two of Mosby's Rangers were hanged on the property, and although the tree from which they were hanged was cut down and its wood sold to raise money for the Confederacy, the last remaining seedling from that tree remains on the grounds. Two Civil War crucibles were recovered by Mr. Carson from the site of a forge in Riverton, and are here on the property serving duty as flower pots. Owners and innkeepers Tom and Kathy Conkey offer warm Irish hospitality in their beautiful inn. Guests relax in sumptuous whirlpool tubs and queen-size beds while taking in breathtaking views of the mountains. Downstairs, there's a private Irish pub, open 24 hours a day to guests, stocked with a delightful assortment of wine and beer—all you care to drink!

Long Hill Bed and Breakfast $$–$$$$
547 Apple Pie Ridge Rd.
Winchester, VA
(540) 450-0341
(866) 450-0341
www.longhillbb.com

Make a reservation at an inn located on "Apple Pie Ridge Road" and just try not to crack a smile. Innkeepers George and Rhoda Kriz claim that the ridge was named by Civil War soldiers who knew they could count on the Quakers who had settled in the area for food and shelter. The hospitality tradition lives on today in this three-room B&B. Rooms are charming and comfortable, equipped with whirlpool tubs, spacious closets, and other amenities. In cooperation with local historian Mac Rutherford, Mr. and Mrs. Kriz offer Civil War Driving and Civil War Walking Tour packages (in addition to a Ghost Tour package).

The Lost Dog Bed and Breakfast $$–$$$$
211 S. Church St.
Berryville, VA
(540) 955-1181
www.thelostdog.com

"We don't have any local big box stores and only a few neon signs," innkeeper Sandy Sowada says of Berryville, "so our charming main street with its barbershops, flower shop, bank, drugstore (with a soda fountain), retail stores, used book store, and restaurants all have that 1950s atmosphere."

As for her inn, Ms. Sowada says: "My bed and breakfast (circa 1884) has three distinctive guest rooms, all with private bathrooms. We serve a full country breakfast featuring local eggs, produce, and meats, but we will cook for special diets with advance notice. We are located in the heart of the historic district, and our gardens offer something in bloom throughout the growing season. And of course, opportunities for outdoor exercise and visiting Civil War battlefields abound."

RESTAURANTS

The Anvil Restaurant $$
1290 W. Washington St.
Harpers Ferry
(304) 535-2582
www.anvilrestaurant.com

Longtime visitors to Harpers Ferry and residents of the area can tell you all about the Anvil. It's a local institution, known for its fresh seafood (including West Virginia's celebrated trout), plus pastas, pizzas, and satisfying salad. The atmosphere is comfortable and casual, perhaps even a bit rustic, with an inviting outdoor patio that's perfect for relaxing after a busy day on the Civil War trail.

Battletown Inn and Gray Ghost Tavern $$$
102 W. Main St.
Berryville, VA
(540) 955-4100
www.thebattletowninn.com

This quaint Berryville inn and eatery takes home the prize for the "most Civil War–sounding restaurant name" in the Winchester region. The menu tries to balance the North and the South, serving traditional Virginia recipes as well as New American and continental cuisine. Stop in for an ice-cold beer or a refreshing iced tea while passing through town, or check into the inn for a unique overnight stay.

Brewbaker's Restaurant $$–$$$
168 N. Loudoun St.
Winchester, VA
(540) 535-0111
www.brewbakersrestaurant.com

Brewbaker's is a great choice for casual fare like zesty wings, juicy burgers, and seafood classics like crab cakes and crab balls. The kitchen shows off its playful side in creations like the "Chicken Everything": chicken simmered in olive oil, along with mushrooms, onions, broccoli, sun-dried tomatoes, and crushed red peppers, and tossed with rigatoni and parmesan cheese. Or, there are the delightful pork loins, marinated in Montreal steak seasoning and served with an apricot merlot sauce with steamed vegetables.

Cork Street Tavern $$
8 W. Cork St.
Winchester, VA
(540) 667-3777
www.corkstreettavern.com

This no-frills Old Town Winchester eatery is housed in an 1830s building that survived heavy shelling during the Civil War as the city was passed back and forth between Union and Confederate command. Locals and visitors gather here for barbecued ribs (considered the best in the Shenandoah Valley), along with tangy barbecued pork sandwiches and Reubens.

One Block West $$$
25 S. Indian Alley
Winchester, VA
(540) 662-1455
www.obwrestaurant.com

Upscale dining finds its home in Winchester in chef/owner Ed Matthews's stylish eatery, which takes its name from its location, one block west of the town's historic strip. The casual, comfortable eatery shows off the freshest flavors of the Shenandoah Valley in an inventive menu that changes daily. Matthews browses local farmers' markets for fresh ingredients like seafood, wild mushrooms, cheeses, and succulent cuts of bison, lamb, and duck. Look for delectable concoctions like caramelized sea scallops with local bok choy and grilled veal porterhouse with pancetta and sundried tomato cream.

Secret Six Tavern $$
186 High St.
Harpers Ferry
(304) 535-3044

After a long day of sightseeing, grab a table at Secret Six Tavern and soak up the breathtaking view of the town and the railroad that travels just below. True to the town's historic traditions, the restaurant takes its name from the John Brown era. A group of Northern aristocrats who called themselves the "Secret Six" silently lent their support to Brown's efforts to use force and arms to rid the nation of slavery. Included in this elite group of citizenry: the editor of the *Atlantic Monthly,* a Unitarian minister, a noted physician, an educator, and two philanthropists.

Village Square Restaurant $$$
103 N. Loudoun St.
Winchester, VA
(540) 667-8961
www.villagesquarerestaurant.com

At Village Square, chef Daniel Kalber shows his eye for fresh and local cuisine. On the menu, you'll find interesting new interpretations of classic creations like diver scallops Oscar with lump crab meat and couscous pilaf, or tequila-lime marinated duck breast with wild rice chiles rellenos and roasted corn salsa. The restaurant forms part of downtown Winchester's dining and entertainment strip.

Violino $$$
181 N. Loudoun St.
Winchester, VA
(540) 667-8006
www.violinorestaurant.com

Violino has staked out a position in the minds (and stomachs!) of Winchester-area residents and visitors for good Italian food, good Italian wine, and warm Italian hospitality. If you're lucky, you might even catch chef and owner Franco Stocco emerging from the kitchen to belt a classic aria. While regulars love the family atmosphere, first-timers are usually here for the food—and they won't be disappointed. Try the classic Italian fare or sample Stocco's original creations like the Ravioli della Nonna Emilia, filled with Swiss chard and fresh goat ricotta cheese, served in a walnut sauce; a baked portobello topped with mushroom, parmesan, and rosemary puree; or a savory rib eye prepared in a Barolo wine reduction and served with roasted potatoes.

New Market/Staunton:
The Central Valley

Darley.

Discussions of the May 15, 1864, Battle of New Market often begin and end with colorful talk of the charge of the Virginia Military Institute (VMI) Corps of Cadets, which Confederate general John C. Breckinridge had called into service and sent into battle with great reluctance. It was an electrifying moment, at a crucial time of the battle. Even Union soldiers spoke with admiration of the young, gray-coated youths' disciplined advance into galling Federal fire. Spectacle aside, the stout performance of the young cadets helped seal a Confederate victory of great strategic importance, one that bought time and resources for Robert E. Lee's hard-pressed Army of Northern Virginia.

General Ulysses S. Grant

By the spring of 1864, Union armies had been trying unsuccessfully for more than two years to wrest control of the Shenandoah Valley from the Confederacy. Now President Abraham Lincoln had given command of Union armies to Lieutenant General Ulysses S. Grant, who came east armed with a plan to end the war. His strategy called for a general advance by all Union armies. In the East, Grant would carry the brunt of the offensive against Lee in central Virginia, while Benjamin Butler marched up the James River and Franz

Sigel—hopefully—took control of the troublesome valley. Sigel, whose military résumé was dotted with failures, was a courageous fighter but a poor general. His embarrassing flight from Wilson's Creek in 1861 had cost many Union lives and sealed a Confederate victory in the war's first major battle in the west. But politicking and his popularity with the Union's thousands of German soldiers had kept him in uniform for three years, and now Grant had reluctantly assigned him a job no other Yankee general had been able to do.

Dogged by John Mosby's Confederate raiders, Sigel showed little urgency as he moved his 6,500 men south up the valley, prompting in his non-German-speaking troops "the most supreme contempt for General Sigel and his crowd of foreign adventurers." Marching north to meet him was a patched-together force under Major General John C. Breckinridge, a 43-year-old Kentuckian with a square jaw and sweeping mustache. Breckinridge lacked the formal military credentials of his Federal counterpart; he had had just a smattering of military experience during the Mexican War. But he was a capable, intelligent leader; by 1861 he had already been elected James Buchanan's vice president and served in the U.S. Senate. He was no Sigel. One aide (who happened to be the son of U.S. senator Henry Clay) called the general "the truest, greatest man I was ever thrown in contact with."

It was Breckinridge's job to protect Southern communications and transportation in the valley, while guarding the left flank of Robert E. Lee's army, now locked in mortal combat to the east with Grant's persistent Federals. That meant keeping Sigel—and any other Union force—from crossing the valley into the Blue Ridge gaps to north-central Virginia. The best way to do that, Breckinridge wisely reasoned, was to attack.

Early on May 15, Breckinridge reached the outskirts of New Market with a force of perhaps 5,000 men, including cavalry and 222 VMI cadets. After exchanging artillery fire with a few Union guns, Breckinridge pushed his two infantry brigades toward a thin Yankee line running west from the Valley Pike, north of town. The Federals were already falling back to a second position around noon when Sigel—who had been sending units up the pike piecemeal throughout the morning—finally reached the battlefield from

*Mosby's raiders in a Blue Ridge Mountain pass
above the Shenandoah*

Woodstock, 20 miles to the north. Even now his small army was incomplete.

By 2 p.m., Breckinridge had secured New Market and was on the move, northward down the pike toward the first of two battle lines laid out by Sigel. Helped by accurate artillery fire, the Confederates sent Sigel's skirmishers and then his entire first line scampering north; only some of the Bluecoats rallied at the new Yankee position. Brigadier General Gabriel Wharton's Virginians seemed about to sweep through Sigel's right when they ran into a fence planted across a rise called Bushong's Hill. The Confederates stalled, as Yankee lead poured into their ranks. As the 62nd Virginia pulled back and re-formed, a gap opened between the regiment's left and the dangling right flank of the 51st Virginia to the west. To avert disaster, Breckinridge now ordered up the anxious cadets, who had to this point been held in reserve.

In remarkable order, the boys marched forward into withering Yankee fire—slowed for just a moment—then, with cheers ringing around them, moved into the vacant slot alongside the shattered 62nd. Shortly after

this, Sigel's cavalry commander, Major General Julius Stahel, led 2,000 Yankee horsemen charging down the pike in driving rain toward the Confederate right—and into hell. What canister blasted from each side of the pike did not hit, Virginia infantrymen did. The Federal charge quickly disintegrated, and confused Yankee horsemen raced for the rear.

With the momentum of the battle suddenly changing again, a flustered Sigel decided to charge Breckinridge's left. By now, however, the VMI boys had stabilized the Rebel line east of the pike; Breckinridge, in fact, even had another regiment, the 26th Virginia, coming up from reserve. Having disposed of Stahel's cavalry, even Brigadier General John Echols's two regiments had moved up on the right. In poor order, Sigel's three regiments came forward—then one by one reversed course in the face of heavy artillery and rifle fire.

With Breckinridge's lines advancing and Yankee infantrymen and artillerists withdrawing in haste, the day's result became obvious. Only the awful weather and a brave rearguard defense offered by Captain Henry DuPont's single Federal battery saved Sigel's Bluecoats from slaughter. Meanwhile, Brigadier General Jeremiah Sullivan arrived north of New Market with two Ohio regiments too late for the battle, but in time to cover yet another shameful retreat by Sigel, who withdrew eight miles to Mount Jackson.

Sigel had matched his Kentucky counterpart in bravery, but in little else. Grant, shocked by word of Sigel's loss and retreat, now could not get rid of the German fast enough. "By all means," he wrote to Henry Halleck, "I would say appoint General [David] Hunter, or anyone else, to the command of West Virginia." The hapless Sigel was briefly reassigned to Harpers Ferry and then relieved for good on July 8.

Sigel later blamed his failure in the valley on Lee, who, he claimed, had "the advantage of a central position" that left him "always ready and able to turn the scales in his favor." But Lee—as Sigel well knew—was then locked in a death struggle with Grant and in no position to send bodies of troops anywhere. Sigel, who suggested the campaign could've been carried out in May 1864 with 20,000 troops, needed twice that by August.

Battle of Cedar Creek

General Philip Sheridan (center) and his generals

For three years, Confederate generals had run circles around the likes of Nathaniel Banks, John C. Frémont, and Franz Sigel in the Shenandoah Valley. During the past few weeks, Jubal Early had even knifed through the valley to threaten Washington. Now, on August 7, 1864, 35-year-old Major General Philip Sheridan took command of the 40,000-man Army of the Shenandoah with orders to secure the valley once and for all.

A fighting general with a strong dislike of his enemies, Sheridan quickly struck at Early's much smaller force. Sheridan's veterans whipped Early's men at Third Winchester on September 19 and again two days later at Fisher's Hill.

Convinced by early October that Early was beaten, Sheridan began to move north again—all the while burning anything that might aid his enemy. And after Union cavalry under George Armstrong Custer and Wesley Merritt smashed their Confederate counterparts at Tom's Brook on October 9, Sheridan believed he had accomplished his mission.

John C. Breckinridge

Vice President John C. Breckinridge

Only the Civil War, it seems, could have halted the political rise of John C. Breckinridge, the Kentuckian who climbed from the state legislature to the vice presidency by the age of 35. The unsuccessful presidential candidate of Southern Democrats in 1860, Breckinridge was still serving in the U.S. Senate a year later when his Southern sympathies aroused suspicion. Rather than wait for his impending arrest, Breckinridge fled south and, as he put it, exchanged "a term of six years in the U.S. Senate for the musket of a soldier."

In a Confederate uniform, Breckinridge quickly proved that some politicians, at least, could make good generals. A born leader, he quickly gained the respect of his men and peers, developing his skills on the battlefields of Shiloh and Chickamauga before taking over the Confederate Western Department of Virginia in 1864. Following his reputation-making victory at New Market, Breckinridge reinforced Lee in the Wilderness, and then served under Jubal Early during his raid on Washington and subsequent defeat at Winchester. As the war wound down, Breckinridge moved to Richmond to become Jefferson Davis's secretary of war—far too late to be of much use. This once-rising star in American politics then spent four years in exile before returning home to Kentucky, where he died in 1875.

Position of Union Army
AT CEDAR CREEK. Va.

Early's forces comprised 5 Divisions of infantry. under Pegram., Wharton, Gordon, Ramseur, and Kershaw, While Early was advancing. Sheridan quietly occupied the north bank of Cedar Creek. The Army of Western Virginia Genl Crook. held the left, its right resting on the pike. the 19th Corps. (Emory) the Centre, its left resting on the pike. The 6th Corps (Wright) the right. connecting with the 19th Corps. The 1st and 2nd Cavalry Divisions were on the extreme right. Custer being in advance in front of the 6th Corps. The line was formed from right to left across the entire valley. thus. Custer. Merritt. Wright. Emory. Crook and Powell. The cavalry of the latter picketed the whole North Fork to Front Royal. Crook and Emory had artillery in position to command the rising ground on the opposite bank of Cedar Creek. Just in the rear of Crook the Provisional Division of Kitchen were encamped. Sheridans head quarters were at a stone house 1/2 a mile in rear of the Centre.

Map of the Battle of Cedar Creek

✳ ✳ ✳ ✳ ✳ ✳ ✳ ✳ ✳ ✳ ✳ ✳ ✳ ✳ ✳

Sheridan, in fact, was absent from the army on the morning of October 19 when Early launched a surprise attack on the encamped Federals along Cedar Creek, southwest of Winchester. By mid-morning, Early's divisions had scattered much of three Union corps, and the Confederate commander was sure of victory. But Union cavalry slowed the Confederates, and Brigadier General Horatio Wright (commanding in Sheridan's absence) managed to establish a rallying point in a wood north of Middletown. Meanwhile, Sheridan—galloping at full speed from Winchester—reached the new Union line, received an update from Wright, and began preparations for a counterattack. First, though, the diminutive general rode slowly by the tightening Union ranks, reassuring each unit of success and rekindling the fighting spirit within each veteran. The awful morning was forgotten. Major Aldace F. Walker wrote later: "Cheers seemed to come from throats of brass, and caps were thrown to the tops of the scattering oaks; but beneath and yet superior to these noisy demonstrations, there was in every heart a revulsion of feeling, and a pressure of emotion, beyond description. No more doubt or chance for doubt existed; we were safe, perfectly and unconditionally safe, and every man knew it."

What at first looked like a morale-boosting victory for the South was about to end instead with Jubal Early's Confederates beaten and driven out of the Shenandoah Valley for good. Aside from some brief, afternoon skirmishing, the Cedar Creek battlefield remained quiet until 4 p.m., when Sheridan's reinvigorated army trod vigorously out of the woods west of the pike. Sheridan's right crashed into Early's left—then, along with the rest of the advancing Federal line, ground to a halt before Confederate ranks blasting away from behind stone walls. Thirty minutes into the fight, however, George Custer's division of blue-clad troopers—followed by William Dwight's infantry—slammed into Early's left and rolled up the Confederate lines. "Regiment after regiment; brigade after brigade," John Gordon later recalled, "in rapid succession was crushed, and, like hard clods of clay under a pelting rain, the superb commands crumbled to pieces." Just like that, the daylong affair turned. Where Union soldiers and wagon trains had clogged the pike heading north that morning, now the Confederates did the same, streaming south. With Early's army went Southern hopes of further use of the valley, which had supplied Lee's legions for four long years.

HISTORIC SITES

Cedar Creek Battlefield
8437 Valley Pike
Middletown, VA
(540) 869-2064
(888) 628-1864
www.cedarcreekbattlefield.org

Now part of the new Cedar Creek and Belle Grove National Historical Park, the Cedar Creek Battlefield remains under the care of the nonprofit Cedar Creek Battlefield Foundation. Founded in 1989 to stave off development on a key section of the original battlefield, the group sponsors annual reenactments to help fund ongoing preservation efforts. In recent years the group has been able to add a modern visitor center, bookshop, and exhibits to the building that houses the foundation's offices. Efforts are now focused on restoring the Solomon Heater House, around which Confederate and Union forces once swirled.

Located at the intersection of Routes 81 and 66 (Route 11—the old Valley Pike—runs through the park), the visitor center is open between Apr 1 and Oct 31 and by appointment during the winter.

New Market Battlefield State Historical Park and Hall of Valor Museum
8895 Collins Dr.
New Market, VA
(866) 515-1864
www.vmi.edu/newmarket

This 300-acre park includes the hilly ground over which Union and Confederate forces clashed on May 15, 1864; the Jacob Bushong Farm; and the Hall of Valor Civil War Museum. Travelers should begin their visit with a trip through the Hall of Valor Museum, the exhibits of which explore the war in Virginia and the Battle of New Market—especially the role of the Virginia Military Institute cadets in that fight. While exploring the battlefield, visitors will want to look over the farm, which includes two Bushong family homes; a blacksmith shop; a henhouse; a loom and meat storage house; and a bake oven among its buildings, and remains a well-preserved reminder of 19th-century life.

Stonewall Jackson Museum at Hupp's Hill
33229 Old Valley Pike
Strasburg, VA
(540) 465-5884
www.stonewalljacksonmuseum.org

This is a stop better suited for Civil War buffs with like-minded kids. Adjacent to the Cedar Creek Battlefield, the Hupp's Hill grounds offer a walking tour of Confederate entrenchments and Union gun positions, while the site's central building uses exhibits and photographs to tell the story of Stonewall Jackson and the war in the Shenandoah Valley. But the Hupp's Hill staff focuses much of its efforts on children, offering camps each summer and encouraging kids to try on uniforms, handle reproduction weapons, and learn from Civil War games and living history workshops.

The museum also has a gift shop.

OTHER POINTS OF INTEREST

Cross Keys/Port Republic

Stonewall Jackson closed out his 1862 Valley Campaign with a pair of victories in lesser-known battles, at Cross Keys on June 8 and Port Republic on June 9. Currently, there are no visitor facilities at the sites, much of which remain private property. But there are interpretive highway markers and battlefield signs in the vicinity.

Fisher's Hill Battlefield
Toms River, VA

There are no visitor facilities on the site of the September 22, 1864, Battle of Fisher's Hill, in which Union major general Philip Sheridan bested General Jubal Early's Confederates for the second time in three days. You can, however, follow a self-guided walking tour with trail markers on-site.

Gordonsville, VA
www.hgiexchange.org

Gordonville's Exchange Hotel was used as a hospital during the Civil War and now houses a small museum. You won't find the massive exhibits of larger historic sites here, but it is worth a

visit if you are in the area. Gordonsville visitors will also want to drop by the Gordonsville Presbyterian Church to see the pew in which Stonewall Jackson often prayed, and tour Maplewood Cemetery, where some 700 Southern soldiers were buried.

Shenandoah Valley/Skyline Drive
www.shenandoahatwar.org

The valley's natural beauty, inviting hiking trails, and other outdoor recreation opportunities are the reasons that most visitors visit the Shenandoah Valley. Travel on the Blue Ridge Parkway, also known as "Skyline Drive," and you're on the doorstep of more than one hundred Civil War sites. From the drive's northernmost entry point in Front Royal, you can drive past points of interest like Luray Gap, where Stonewall Jackson announced that his command had become the Second Corps of Lee's Army of Northern Virginia, and Lacey Springs, the site of a cavalry clash between Union general Custer and Confederate general Thomas L. Rosser. As you drive through the park, be sure to stop at a few of the scenic overlooks. Not only will you be rewarded with a breathtaking view of the rolling hillside, but you'll also understand the strategic importance of the towns and mountain passes during the Valley Campaigns of 1862 and 1864.

ACCOMMODATIONS

Apple Blossom Inn $$–$$$$
9317 N. Congress St.
New Market, VA
(540) 740-3747
www.appleblossominn.net

If you're traveling through New Market and like the idea of having a historic house all to yourself, the Apple Blossom Inn is just the ticket. The two-bedroom, one-and-a-half-bathroom layout is perfect for a traveling family or two couples touring the battlefields together. Built in 1806, the house comes equipped with a parlor, a full kitchen, a music room, a cozy porch with a swing, and a peaceful garden. You'll also enjoy a full cooked breakfast in the morning. The inn is the departure point for themed walking tours that bring New Market's Civil War history to life.

The Apple Blossom Inn also organizes one-and-a-half-hour walking tours of the town. Call (540) 325-9529 or log on to www.appleblossominn.net/new-market-walking-tours.html for more information.

Cross Roads Inn Bed and Breakfast $$–$$$$
9222 John Sevier Rd.
New Market, VA
(540) 740-4157
(888) 740-4157
www.crossroadsinnva.com

Larry and Sharon Smith's Cross Roads Inn is pure Virginia in its country charm and hospitality. There are complimentary hors d'oeuvres at check-in, and you can help yourself to coffee and hot chocolate from the pantry of the 1925 house at any time of day. Rates are very reasonable, and rooms feature private baths, air-conditioning, antique furnishings, and other amenities; a number of specials are offered. Guests will enjoy the six-room inn's common areas (including a fireplace in the living room), gardens, outdoor spa, and relaxing front porch. Reservations are recommended.

The Inn at Narrow Passage $$$–$$$$
US 11 South
Woodstock, VA
(540) 459-8000
(800) 459-8002
www.narrowpassage.com

The Inn at Narrow Passage is one of Virginia's longest-operating guesthouses, welcoming travelers since the 1740s. It takes its name from a dangerous nearby passage in the road, only wide enough for one wagon to cross at a time and constantly threatened by Indian attacks. During the 1862 Valley Campaign, Stonewall Jackson even checked in, using the inn as a headquarters. From here, he famously ordered Jedediah Hotchkiss to "make me a map of the valley." Today's guests can take advantage of historic guest rooms outfitted with wood floors, porches, and spectacular views of the Shenandoah River and Massanutten Mountain. A lavish breakfast is served fireside in the main dining room.

Jacob Swartz House $$$
574 Jiggady Rd.
New Market, VA
(540) 740-9208
(877) 740-9208
www.jacobswartz.com

This private two-bedroom farmhouse, built in 1852 by cobbler Jacob Swartz, is loaded with Civil War history. When Virginia seceded from the Union in 1861, Swartz enlisted in the Confederate Army. His shoe-making services were deemed invaluable, however, and he was sent back home to make boots and equipment for the Southern forces. The Battle of New Market broke out just across the river from the family's home. In December 1864, Federal troops under the command of George Custer raided the house and Swartz's cobbler shop, taking food and supplies. Today the house is a pleasant country retreat, equipped with a wood-burning stove, fully stocked kitchen, and private screened-in porch overlooking the Shenandoah River.

Piney Hill Bed & Breakfast $$$$
1048 Piney Hill Rd.
Luray, VA
(540) 778-5261
(800) 644-5261
www.pineyhillbandb.com

From the moment you arrive at Piney Hill, you'll understand why it was named one of the top B&Bs in the country by TripAdvisor. Built in the early 1800s, the farmhouse offers a luxurious respite after a busy day of touring. Sip a glass of wine as you read a book on the wraparound porch, or take advantage of the outdoor Jacuzzi and the breathtaking views of the surrounding mountains. If you're looking for more of an intimate experience, check into the Rosebud Cottage, also located on the property. It's a cozy 500-square-foot house that's perfect for a romantic getaway, outfitted with a screened-in porch and a gas fireplace; gourmet breakfast is delivered in a picnic basket to your doorstep every morning.

Rosendale Inn $$$–$$$$
17917 Farmhouse Lane
New Market, VA
(540) 740-4281
www.rosendaleinn.com

Presidential history buffs will find themselves right at home at the Rosendale Inn, located at the foot of Massanutten Mountain. Franklin Delano Roosevelt used the beautiful farmhouse as his retreat from the White House, and Mrs. Woodrow Wilson was also a guest at the B&B. Spacious rooms come furnished with period antiques and private bathrooms. Most have their own in-room fireplaces. Guests can also park themselves in rocking chairs on the veranda to soak up the picturesque scenery.

South Court Inn Bed & Breakfast $$$–$$$$
160 S. Court St.
Luray, VA
(540) 843-0980
(888) 749-8055
www.southcourtinn.com

A magnificently restored 1870s farmhouse, the South Court Inn is a popular choice among travelers who are exploring the beautiful Shenandoah Valley, its wineries, and quaint antiques shops. Perfect for a romantic escape, most of the inn's rooms feature whirlpool tubs, and innkeepers Tom and Anita Potts are happy to help you arrange in-room massages, roses, champagne, and other extras. You'll wake up to a delicious and decadent breakfast of banana-stuffed French toast, soufflés, and other treats that you wouldn't normally make for yourself. For a little more privacy, you can rent the Susie Hodges Cottage.

The Staunton Choral Gardens Bed and Breakfast $$–$$$$
216 W. Frederick St.
Staunton, VA
(540) 885-6556
www.stauntonbedandbreakfast.com

A bit south of this tour's more notable attractions, the Staunton Choral Gardens is right on the way to Lexington and within easy reach of Appomattox and other central Virginia Civil War sites. And like almost every other property in the valley, it has its own Civil War story connected to it. According to owner Carolyn

Avalos, Robert E. Lee—whose daughters attended a private school across the street—regularly boarded his horse Traveler in the inn's carriage house when he took a train from Staunton.

Naturally noted for its beautiful gardens, Staunton Choral Gardens offers warm, comfortable rooms, free high-speed, wireless Internet service, and other modern amenities. Adjacent to the inn's main building is the historic carriage house, now "a luxurious, two-story suite," Carolyn Avalos says, "very inviting and quite unique—all redone but keeping the charm." The inn is located within walking distance of all the town's attractions, which can also be reached via free trolley service.

Stonewall Jackson Inn $$$–$$$$
547 E. Market St.
Harrisonburg, VA
(800) 445-5330
www.stonewalljacksoninn.com

Civil War buffs will no doubt be attracted to an inn named after one of the war's most legendary figures. At this Harrisonburg bed-and-breakfast, each of the ten guest rooms is named for another prominent Civil War figure, from Grant to Sheridan to Pickett. The rooms are decorated with period antiques and replicas, as well as works by local artists. You'll also enjoy a private bath, wireless Internet, and cable TV in each guest room, and a scrumptious breakfast featuring Virginia ham, Virginia apples, and locally produced sausage. The circa-1885 mansion itself is architecturally unique, a combination of a Queen Anne mansion and a New England–style cottage.

RESTAURANTS

A Moment to Remember $$
55 E. Main St.
Luray, VA
(540) 743-1121
www.a-moment2remember.com

If you're staying in Luray or paying a visit to its attractions, stop for breakfast, lunch, or dinner at A Moment to Remember. Start your day with an omelet made with fresh Virginia ham or a stack of buttermilk pancakes, feast on salads or sandwiches for lunch, and enjoy a selection of seafood entrees for dinner. Or, stop by between meals for an invigorating espresso drink or a light bite.

Jalisco Authentic Mexican Restaurant $$
9403 Congress St.
New Market, VA
(540) 740-9404

You might be surprised to find authentic Mexican fare in a little town like New Market, but you won't be disappointed by the zesty flavors, generous portions, and friendly service. The extensive menu is chock-full of combination platters, grilled specialties, and vegetarian selections, which taste even better when paired with a traditional margarita (or one flavored with strawberry or peach).

Mill Street Grill $$
1 Mill St.
Staunton, VA
(540) 886-0656
www.millstreetgrill.com

If you travel as far south as Staunton, stop for a bite at the Mill Street Grill. Don't be surprised to see a waiting line at this casual pub-style eatery; it's no secret that Mill Street serves the best fall-off-the-bone ribs for miles around. Choose from baby back pork ribs, beef ribs, prime rib, or a combination of the above, expertly seasoned and served with fresh coleslaw, your choice of potato, and fresh bread accompanied by the flavored butter of the day. If you're not in the mood for ribs, you can feast on other grilled and fried creations, including chicken, seafood, steak, and more. Portions are generous, but there's also a "light side" menu with several tempting lower-calorie selections.

Mrs. Rowe's Restaurant and Bakery $$
74 Rowe Rd.
Staunton, VA
(540) 886-1833
www.mrsrowes.com

If you're traveling to Staunton and are hungry for a home-cooked meal, stop by Mrs. Rowe's for all-American classics. The menu is loaded with Southern favorites like sweet potato pie, fried chicken, meatloaf, collard greens, and other tasty dishes. If you've got a sweet tooth, you won't want to miss the homemade pies, cakes, and sweets. If you're eating on the run, order dinner to go.

Southern Kitchen $
9576 S. Congress St.
New Market, VA
(540) 740-3514

It would be hard to top Southern Kitchen for hearty American fare such as fried chicken and pie, all of which are served in generous helpings. Owned and operated by the Newland family since 1955, the diner-style eatery is a favorite of visitors to the valley. You'll find regional specialties like peanut soup and honest-to-goodness Virginia ham, plus seafood selections like flounder, rainbow trout, and fried shrimp. It's open daily from 7 a.m. to 9 p.m.

Harrisburg/Gettysburg: High Tide

What began as an ambitious undertaking in the wake of another crushing Confederate victory ended with Southern generals pondering what might have been.

The time seemed right—at least to General Robert E. Lee, commander of the vaunted Army of Northern Virginia. He and his trusted corps commanders had just engineered a stunning rout of Major General Joe Hooker's Army of the Potomac in the Battle of Chancellorsville (May 1–4, 1863).

That Union Army was on its heels, Lee felt, and surely ill prepared for a massive counterthrust. Further, a strike into Pennsylvania might loosen Major General Ulysses S. Grant's grip on Vicksburg, Mississippi, where Lieutenant General John C. Pemberton's besieged Confederate Army was on it last legs.

The potentially spectacular possibilities did not end there. An invasion of the North, Lee believed, would secure badly needed recruits from Maryland; possibly frighten Northern leaders into peace talks; and, most of all, present an opportunity to crush a Yankee army on its turf, and win European recognition for the South. Lee's indefatigable army was on a high, and eager to take the battle to the enemy. "Like the rest of the army generally, nothing gave me much concern so long as I knew Gen. Lee was in command," Edward Porter Alexander, Lee's fine artilleryman, wrote after the war. "I am sure there can never have been an army with more supreme confidence in its commander than that army had in Gen. Lee. We looked forward to victory under him as confidently as to successive sunrises."

Lee would eventually find that all was not as he thought, beginning with his opponent. In spite of his lapse at Chancellorsville, "Fighting Joe" Hooker was not about to let Lee's army waltz into the North unguarded.

The Battle of Chancellorsville

Since replacing Ambrose Burnside atop the Army of the Potomac, he had instituted a series of organizational changes that were already benefiting the army. Foremost among these changes was his restructuring of the Federal cavalry into one corps, under Major General Alfred Pleasanton. The Union Cavalry Corps, already brimming with talented young officers, would come of age during the upcoming campaign and help deal the South a terrible blow.

Major General Joseph Hooker

Lee launched his campaign on June 3, marching his Army of Northern Virginia north to Culpepper, then west into the Shenandoah Valley. Hooker sent cavalry to track him, and on June 9, Pleasanton's Federals barreled into Major General J. E. B. Stuart's camp at Brandy Station. The daylong engagement that followed left Stuart's men with the battlefield, but their commander embarrassed. The Federal cavalry had surprised him and fought him generally on even terms. No longer could Union cavalrymen be laughed off as mere pickets or messengers; they were a fighting force that Stuart would now have to deal with.

Lee, meanwhile, continued north, capturing an unprepared Union garrison at Winchester and crossing the Potomac. Hooker followed, screening Washington and Baltimore even while engaged in a battle of wills with the War Department over a perceived lack of support. On June 28—with a potentially titanic confrontation between the two armies in the offing—a frustrated Hooker offered his resignation, which was promptly accepted. His replacement was the sleepy-eyed George Gordon Meade—yet another capable corps commander seemingly set up for a great fall. Hearing of the change, Robert E. Lee remarked that "Meade will commit no blunder in my front, and if I make one, he will make haste to take advantage of it."

Lieutenant General Richard Ewell's II Corps was perched on the doorstep of Harrisburg, ready to pounce on Pennsylvania's capital when Lee received word of the Army of the Potomac's presence north

of the Potomac. Lee postponed the Harrisburg operation and consolidated his strung-out army west of Gettysburg, a small transportation hub with a population of about 2,400.

Still unsure of Meade's exact position (Jeb Stuart's cavalry, which was supposed to be screening on Lee's right, had circled far to the east and lost touch with the army), Lee allowed Major General Henry Heth to take his division into Gettysburg after a cache of shoes rumored to be stored there, although the exact reason for taking this route has been disputed. Marching southeast down the Chambersburg Pike early on July 1, Heth's men heard the popping sound of carbine fire: They had run into John Buford's two brigades of dismounted Union cavalry, screening for Meade and stretched across the pike in a defensive position. First contact had been made.

The skirmish quickly exploded into a serious fight, as Confederate reinforcements flowed toward the town from the west and north. Buford's outgunned horsemen held their ground until General John Reynolds's I Corps arrived to bolster his position. The highly respected Reynolds, however, soon fell from his horse, killed by a Rebel bullet.

Gradually the Union lines north and west of town bent, then broke, sending regiments scrambling headlong back through town. Rebel infantry charged in pursuit, as Union officers tried desperately to rally their disorganized units on high ground south of town.

Joining Major General Oliver Otis Howard (XI Corps commander) on Cemetery Hill, Major General Winfield Scott Hancock (II Corps commander) led the effort to bring order out of disaster. Here—with advantages in numbers and initiative and plenty of daylight left—the Confederates lost a crucial opportunity to seize the hills (Culp's and Cemetery) below town. "There was not an officer, not even a man, that did not expect that the war would be closed upon that hill that evening," one Confederate later wrote. But "someone made a blunder that lost the battle of Gettysburg, and, humanly speaking, the Confederate cause." Pressed to attack, Jubal Early deferred to his corps commander Richard Ewell, who was disinclined to undertake any further offensive without specific orders from Lee. But when he received a message shortly after 5 p.m. in which Lee "wished him to

Map of the field of battle at Gettysburg

take the Cemetery Hill if it were possible," he decided that it was not.

Meanwhile, newly minted army commander George Meade had been eyeing for his army an excellent defensive position to the south along Pipe Creek. Now, however, he sent word for the army to dig in where it was. Yankees spent the night felling trees, digging rifle pits, and maneuvering heavy cannon into firing positions. As the sun rose on July 2, the opposing armies had jostled into the positions from which they would fight for the next two days. Lee's forces stretched south along Seminary Ridge; five of the seven corps of Meade's Army of the Potomac were hunkered down in a classic and formidable defensive position, on high ground stretching in a fishhook shape from Culp's and Cemetery Hills south along Cemetery Ridge to a pair of hills called the Little and Big Round Tops. Rolling farmland separated the armies.

Anchoring the left end of the Union lines was the III Corps of Major General Daniel Sickles, a hot-tempered New Yorker and military neophyte fresh out of the U.S. House of Representatives. Sickles had in 1859 played the lead in one of the nation's most infamous and celebrated scandals. Catching his beautiful young wife in an elaborate tryst with the handsome U.S. Attorney Philip Barton Key—the son of Francis Scott Key, author of "The Star Spangled Banner"—the enraged Sickles chased Key down in Washington's Lafayette Square and shot him to death. In the trial that followed, Sickles's lawyer—future Secretary of War Edwin Stanton—got his client off with the first successful use of the insanity defense. Sickles then forfeited much of the public's sympathy for him by reuniting with his adulteress wife.

At Gettysburg, Sickles decided to push his III Corps forward into an angular position onto higher ground along the Emmitsburg Road, which bisected the battlefield, a position that he felt offered his men a defensive advantage. It also opened a gaping hole between his men and Hancock's II Corps to his right, an ominous fact that Meade himself pointed out to Sickles late that morning. By then it was too late to do much about it.

On Seminary Ridge, meanwhile, Lee had decided to try and capitalize on the success of July 1. If executed properly, he believed, a coordinated attack should rupture the Union lines. Lieutenant General James Longstreet—commander of I Corps and Lee's most trusted subordinate

(in the wake of Thomas J. "Stonewall" Jackson's mortal wounding at Chancellorsville)—believed otherwise. He followed his orders, but—as many of his detractors would later argue—took too long in doing so. By the time Longstreet launched his July 2 attack on the Union left, up the Emmitsburg Road, Meade's V Corps (under Major General George Sykes) had reached the area. As Sickles's divisions tumbled back under the weight of Major General Lafayette McLaws's onrushing Rebels, Sykes's men—along with Federals sent over from the right—moved forward to plug

Lieutenant General James Longstreet

the gap. Sickles fell with a shattered leg, which was later amputated. (Sickles later had his shattered leg bones preserved in a miniature coffin. They can still be seen today—with the cannonball that smashed them—in an exhibit in Washington, D.C.'s, National Museum of Health and Medicine.) Meanwhile, only heroic fighting from outgunned Maine and Pennsylvania infantrymen saved Little Round Top from falling to Texas and Alabama troops of John Hood's Confederate division. It was here that a little-known Maine professor named Joshua Lawrence Chamberlain earned everlasting fame for ordering a decisive bayonet charge as each side reached exhaustion.

The struggle for Little Round Top nearly resulted in disastrous repercussions for Meade, who responded to that emergency by stripping Culp's Hill of most of Major General Henry Slocum's XII Corps and sending it south to support his softened left flank. But the Confederates were not yet through for the day: Jubal Early nearly overran Cemetery Hill before Yankee reinforcements finally stopped him. And as dusk deepened, Major General Edward Johnson sent his division crashing up the wooded hillside of Culp's Hill—now defended by just 1,300 New Yorkers under Brigadier General George Sears Greene. Greene, an 1826 West Point graduate and renowned engineer, was a grandson of Revolutionary War hero Nathanael Greene, and a skilled fighter himself. Fighting tenaciously from behind formidable breastworks, his men held off Johnson's 5,000 attackers until Slocum's XII Corps returned in the middle of the night. The thickened Union lines shattered a follow-up assault ordered by Johnson before dawn.

As the sun rose on July 3, thousands of tired, hungry, and filthy soldiers stirred, wondering what the day would bring. Meade, after polling his corps commanders, had already decided to remain in position to receive an attack. Lee, meanwhile, was more determined than ever to break though the blue line facing him from across the fields south of town. Again overruling Longstreet's request for a turning movement south of the Round Tops, Lee ordered an attack on Meade's stretched-out center. Ordered to direct the assault, the I Corps commander told an officer: "I don't want to make this attack. I believe it will fail—I do not see how it can succeed—I would not make it even now, but that Gen. Lee has ordered it and expects it."

Nevertheless, at 1 p.m. on July 3, the hills of Adams County shook with the sound of Lee's booming cannon, some 150 guns under the direction of Lee's skilled young artillerist, Major Edward Porter Alexander. Union batteries responded for a time, then Major General Henry Hunt silenced them to conserve ammunition for a charge that now appeared inevitable. Alexander quieted his own guns some time later, passing word to Longstreet that he had barely enough shells left to support his advance. Reluctantly, Lee's husky corps commander gave the order for the assault on Meade's center—an attack soon to be dubbed Pickett's Charge.

Dashing Major General George Pickett commanded one of the attacking force's three divisions; Johnston Pettigrew and Isaac Trimble led the others. At 3 p.m., the roughly 13,000 men in gray and butternut set out to carry the heights ahead of them. It was a magnificent sight, even to the anxious Federals watching their approach. But for veterans of Fredericksburg, where hundreds of Yankees had fallen before Rebel rifles on Marye's Heights, it also meant a chance to avenge fallen friends.

The advancing Confederate lines were in no-man's-land now, too far from their target to charge, and far from the safety of the woods they had left. Now the quiet Yankee guns began to roar again—from every angle. Shells

General Pickett receiving the order for the charge on day three at Gettysburg from General Longstreet

exploded above the attackers, shredding unit flags and soldiers alike. Dressing their lines in the midst of hell, the Confederates lurched forward. Now hundreds of Yankee muskets in the center of the blue lines went off at once—filling the air with smoke and the battlefield with more dead Confederates. Union artillerists switched to canister, and ripped huge gaps in the slowing, butternut ranks. Confederates surging within feet of the ridge watched in horror as hundreds of Pennsylvanians opened up on them—en masse—from behind a stone wall. "The slaughter was terrible," one Federal recalled. Only at one point did the charging Rebels breach the Union line, led by General Lewis Armistead, who led his men forward yelling, "Boys, give them the cold steel! Who will follow me?" Within moments, Yankee reinforcements plugged the hole, and Armistead fell mortally wounded.

By 4 p.m., the sloping fields before Cemetery Ridge were filled with dead Confederate soldiers. At least two-thirds of the attacking force was a casualty. Survivors of the shattered charge were streaming back to the safety of the woods, to sporadic Union taunts of "Fredericksburg! Fredericksburg!" Even Lee's vaunted cavalry, which under J. E. B. Stuart had circled Meade's army in an attempt to attack it from the rear, had been turned back, east of town, by Federal troopers under major generals David Gregg and George Custer. Robert E. Lee now turned to his subordinates to prepare for a Union counterattack. Pickett, for one, seemed too overwhelmed to move. "General Lee, I have no division now, Armistead is down, Garnett is down, and Kemper is mortally wounded." Lee persevered: "Come now, General Pickett, this has been my fight and upon my shoulders rests the blame. The men and officers of your command have written the name of Virginia as high today as it has ever been written before." The Battle of Gettysburg was over.

Three days of fighting had produced some 50,000 casualties, including 3,155 dead Federals and 4,427 dead Confederates. The losses were especially hard for Lee, with a much smaller army, to take; they proved doubly painful for the South the next day when word of Vicksburg's surrender (to Grant) zipped over telegraph wires. Lee at least managed to preserve his remaining forces: With Meade slow to pursue, the Army of Northern Virginia slipped across the swollen Potomac River into Virginia on July 14, leaving Abraham Lincoln to fume over another lost opportunity.

Widely seen as the turning point of the Civil War, the Battle of Gettysburg did not signal the end of the Confederacy. But with Union victories in the West and Grant's ascension to command of all Union armies in March 1864, Lee would never again have the resources or freedom to strike into the North again.

HISTORIC SITES

American Civil War Museum
(formerly the National Civil War Wax Museum)
297 Steinwehr Ave.
(717) 334-6245
www.e-gettysburg.com

Opened in 1962, the museum lacks the depth and power of its counterpart in Harrisburg (see listing below), but it does a good job of re-creating scenes from the battlefield and the surrounding town with its lifelike dioramas. Visitors can immerse themselves in the battlefield action through the feature presentation in the Battleroom Auditorium, listening to battle cries and cannon fire. At the end of the presentation, you can even listen as Lincoln delivers his immortal address. The museum is open daily from Mar through Dec.

General Lee's Headquarters
401 Buford Ave.
(717) 334-3141
www.civilwarheadquarters.com

Constructed in 1834, this stone house was located at the center and rear of Lee's battle lines at the time of the battle, making it an ideal location for the Confederate officer's headquarters. It's now home to a small Civil War museum featuring artifacts and stories from the battle. The museum is open daily from Mar through Nov with extended hours in the summer.

Gettysburg National Cemetery
Baltimore Pike

Abraham Lincoln dedicated this haunting burial ground, now home to more than 7,000 soldiers and their loved ones, during his Gettysburg Address on November 19, 1863.

Gettysburg National Military Park
1195 Baltimore Pike
(717) 334-1124, ext. 8023
www.nps.gov/gett

No other Civil War battlefield is quite like the one that dominates Gettysburg, Pennsylvania. The epic proportions and importance of the July 1–3, 1863, battle is reflected today in the number of individual and unit monuments (more than 1,300) that grace its 6,000 acres. Roads provide ready access to all the park's crucial areas, from Little Round Top to Culp's Hill. Visitors can sit among the boulders of the Devil's Den, where Yankees and Rebels once stalked each other; trace the path taken by the legions of Pickett, Trimble, and Pettigrew during their fateful charge of July 3; visit the cramped home (the Lydia Leister house) in which George Meade and his corps commanders met on the night of July 2; and trace the opposing lines along Seminary and Cemetery Ridges.

Gettysburg's visitor center remains among the best of any National Military Park, and features the Gettysburg Museum of the Civil War. The museum's artifact-based displays practically burst with minié balls, cartridge boxes, bayonets, swords, uniforms, and other equipment left on the battlefield. Exhibits touch on everything from campaign life for soldiers and officers to the proper use of artillery, and they boast enough military arms to fill an arsenal. Here visitors will also find a 30-minute Electric Map program (for a small fee), a large bookstore and gift shop, and National Park Service rangers to answer questions and help arrange two-hour battlefield tours by licensed guides. The park also offers audiotapes (or CDs) for private driving tours, and private companies run bus tours.

Still one of the park's feature attractions is the Cyclorama Center, whose interior is dominated by the 360-degree, 359-by-27-foot painting of Pickett's Charge. The painting is currently undergoing restoration, and only a portion of the painting is on view. The center itself, which also offers exhibits of relics and artwork related to the Battle of Gettysburg and the Gettysburg Address, remains open. Visitors should also walk through the Soldiers' (or Gettysburg) National Cemetery, the burial site of Union soldiers dedicated so movingly by President Abraham Lincoln on November 19, 1863. (Most Confederate victims of the battle were buried in Richmond's Hollywood Cemetery.)

Today, Gettysburg National Military Park sports a new visitor center and museum—one designed to be less obtrusive by being built on ground that was not central to the battle. Meanwhile, the battlefield continues to fight off the ugly infringements of souvenir stands and convenience stores in an otherwise lovely town. Recent years have seen the removal of ugly obstructions like the 300-foot National Tower. Efforts to restore the battlefield to its original appearance (at the time of the battle) have included the removal of hundreds of acres of trees; the replanting of many more acres of trees, thickets, and orchards; and the addition of historic fencing that once divided local farms.

The park, visitor center, and Cyclorama Center are open daily.

Jennie Wade House Museum
548 Baltimore St.
(717) 334-4100
www.jennie-wade-house.com

Gettysburg native Mary Virginia "Ginnie" Wade was baking bread for Union soldiers on July 3, 1863, when a stray bullet crashed through her home and killed her. Just 20 years old, Miss Wade was the only civilian killed in town during the Battle of Gettysburg. The home today looks practically—and eerily—as it did in July 1863 (with the exception of its gift shop). Admission is charged, or you can stop by the adjacent Battlefield Tour Center (778 Baltimore St.) to purchase a combo ticket including a battlefield tour and attractions admissions.

The National Civil War Museum
One Lincoln Circle at Reservoir Park
Harrisburg, PA
(717) 260-1861
www.nationalcivilwarmuseum.org

With so much to see 40 miles south at Gettysburg, building a Civil War museum in Harrisburg once seemed, to some observers, a bad idea. True, the state capital had once been home to Camp Curtin—a Union training depot that trained and sent 300,000 soldiers into Federal armies. But no serious fighting had taken place here: The outbreak of fighting at Gettysburg forestalled General Richard Ewell's plan to attack the city, and it was never threatened again. But when it opened in 2001, this fabulous, 65,000-square-foot museum turned heads, and made Harrisburg the ideal jump-off point for an excursion to Gettysburg.

The brainchild of former mayor Stephen R. Reed—who started collecting for the museum during the mid-1990s—the National Civil War Museum boasts two floors of state-of-the-art exhibits, based on its 24,000-piece artifact collection, which dates from 1850 to 1876. (Highlights of the collection include the kepi worn by Confederate general George Pickett at Gettysburg; a Bible once carried by Robert E. Lee; one of the gauntlets Stonewall Jackson was wearing when he was shot at Chancellorsville; and Ulysses S. Grant's sword belt.) The museum strives to tell the "complete" story of the Civil War. "We wanted to tell the story, not just of the battles," Reed said, "but of the people who lived and worked, and fought and died, during the war years. And we wanted to take an unflinching look at slavery, the root cause of the conflict."

Tours of the museum's 17 exhibit galleries begin on the second floor, starting with "A House Divided." They naturally describe the military campaigns of the conflict, while also exploring "The Peculiar Institution: American Slavery," "Making of Armies," "Civil War Music," "Lincoln: War and Remembrance," and other topics. Interactive battle maps and audio posts bring each exhibit to life, and a small theater offers the 16-minute, prize-winning film, *A Nation Endures* every 20 minutes.

The museum is wheelchair accessible.

The Rupp House
451 Baltimore St.
(717) 334-1243
www.friendsofgettysburg.org

This interactive museum re-creates the culture of 19th-century Gettysburg through interactive, hands-on exhibitions and activities led by guides and volunteers in period clothing. The Rupp House (in which the museum is located) was built in 1868 to replace a lavish house that sustained serious damage during the battle. Admission is free; donations go to support battlefield preservation efforts.

Shriver House Museum
309 Baltimore St.
(717) 337-2800
www.shriverhouse.org

A welcome addition to Gettysburg and the museum community is the Shriver House Museum, a relatively new facility dedicated to telling the story of Gettysburg civilians who witnessed the epic 1863 battle. Built in 1860 by George Washington Shriver, the house was caught in the middle of the first day's fighting. Evidence of Confederate sharpshooters firing from the attic included eyewitness reports of soldiers knocking portholes in the attic's sides. Restoration efforts (which continue today) turned up bullets and stains that were recently proven to be blood. It appears certain that at least one Rebel was killed in the Shriver House attic.

The building today looks about as it did when George, his wife, Hettie, and their two small children lived there in 1861, shortly before George joined the Union cavalry. Between stops at Gettysburg's military sites, visitors should tour the restored rooms of the Shriver House (along with the nearby Jennie Wade House) to get an inkling of how civilians lived in the midst of war. Museum hours vary by season, and it is closed in Jan (except for groups by appointment).

Soldier's National Museum
777 Baltimore St.
(717) 334-4890
www.gettysburgbattlefieldtours.com

The building that now houses the Soldier's National Museum was the headquarters for Union general Oliver O. Howard during the battle. It later became the Soldier's National Orphanage and now houses a popular collection of Civil War battle dioramas and more than 5,000 artifacts. Admission is charged, or purchase a combo ticket at the Battlefield Tours depot across the street.

U.S. Army Heritage and Education Center
950 Soldiers Dr.
Carlisle, PA
(717) 245-3971
www.carlisle.army.mil/ahec

Long known simply as Carlisle Barracks, the home of the U.S. Army War College and Military History Institute and Museum is now part of the new U.S. Army Heritage and Education Center. Charged with "Telling the Army Story—One Soldier at a Time," this one-of-a-kind complex is destined to become one of the nation's most compelling historical attractions.

Founded by Englishman John Stanwix in 1757, Carlisle Barracks has since been home to a series of army schools, most notably the Carlisle Indian Industrial School, for American Indians. Here a young Jim Thorpe got his first taste of football, playing for the Carlisle Indians—once one of the nation's great football powers. The site is best known, of course, for its research facilities: anchored by a massive collection of books (some 325,000), manuscripts (11,000,000, largely unofficial papers, unit histories, and private papers), photographs (1,700,000), and maps (19,500), the Military History Institute has long been the premier site for the study of army history.

The site has opened its new Army Heritage Trail—a unique, 1-mile, outdoor walk through American military history. Fantastic re-creations along the trail address every major American war, and include a Revolutionary War redoubt, a section of the Antietam battlefield, a Civil War winter encampment, and a portion of D-Day's Omaha Beach. The trail alone makes a visit here a must. It is wheelchair accessible, and admission is free. Security is tight, however, so calling ahead is advised.

OTHER POINTS OF INTEREST

The Coster Avenue Mural and Amos Humiston Monument

Late on the afternoon of on July 1, 1863, two Confederate brigades slammed into Colonel Charles R. Coster's thin line of 1,200 Yankees on the northeastern outskirts of Gettysburg. Coster's left and right flanks collapsed, and his center regiment—the 154th New York Volunteers—was forced to follow its brother regiments in flight back through town.

One hundred twenty-five years later, a crucial moment of this struggle appeared in vivid color on the back of a warehouse at the end of a Gettysburg side street. The moving and detailed 80-foot mural was the work of Rhode Island artist and 154th New York Regimental historian Mark Dunkelman (with Johan Bjurman), who designed the image as an homage to the soldiers who fought in Kuhn's brickyard.

(A monument to the 154th New York also stands nearby.) Recently restored, the Coster Avenue mural remains one of Gettysburg's neat, little-known treasures.

Eisenhower National Historic Site
250 Eisenhower Farm Dr.
(717) 338-9114, ext. 10
www.nps.gov/eise

While there's no direct link to the Civil War, American history buffs may be interested to tour the weekend retreat of the World War II leader and president, which is adjacent to the National Military Park. The Eisenhowers lived on this estate and farm from 1961 until the former president's death in 1969. Guests must park at the National Military Park and ride a complimentary shuttle to the farm entrance.

SLIGHTLY OUT OF THE WAY: CHAMBERSBURG, PENNSYLVANIA

Although no major battles were fought here, Chambersburg likely suffered more during the Civil War than any other Northern town. The residents of this small village were still caring for soldiers wounded in the Battle of Antietam when Major General "Jeb" Stuart's cavalry looted and burned several of its buildings. Confederate raiders torched another portion of the town a year later during the Gettysburg Campaign. And on July 30, 1864, Chambersburg suffered the wrath of Lieutenant General Jubal Early, who—angered by Union devastation of parts of the Shenandoah Valley, and General David Hunter's burning of the Virginia Military Institute—sent General John McCausland's cavalry to extort reparations from the Pennsylvania town. When no money was forthcoming, McCausland evacuated the town and set it afire.

Today, visitors to the town should stop first at the Chambersburg Heritage Center, the hub of Franklin County tourism and a historic attraction in its own right. Housed in a beautifully renovated, wheelchair-accessible marble bank building built in 1915, the center is the place to go for information, travel brochures, and tips on local driving tours. It also offers a gift shop and restrooms.

Before venturing out into the town's National Historic District, visitors should also peruse the Heritage Center's extensive exhibits, which detail the town's role in the Civil War and the Underground Railroad. Serious Civil War buffs will also want to ask about the Chambersburg Civil War Seminars—an annual series of talks sponsored by the Greater Chamber of Commerce and hosted by Ted Alexander, the Chief Historian at Antietam National Battlefield.

Between Memorial Day and Thanksgiving, the Chambersburg Heritage Center is open daily. During the off-season, the center closes early and is closed on Sun. For more information call (717) 264-7101, or visit the center's Web site at www.chambersburg.org.

TOURS

From ghost walks to double-decker buses to bicycles, there are dozens of ways to tour Gettysburg—and dozens of companies ready to show you around. If you're not sure where to begin, start at the National Battlefield Park visitor center. You can arrange a private guided tour with a park ranger (two hours for up to six passengers; see www.gettysburgtourguides.org) or purchase a CD for an audio driving tour.

Companies specializing in general battlefield tours are listed below.

Gettysbike Bicycle Tours
523 Baltimore St.
(717) 752-7752
www.gettysbike.com

Gettysburg Battlefield Bus Tours
778 Baltimore St.
(717) 334-6296
(877) 680-TOUR
www.gettysburgbattlefieldtours.com

Historic Battlefield Bus Tours
55 Steinwehr Ave.
(717) 334-8000
www.historictourcompany.com

GHOST TOURS

With all of the suffering and tragedy that occurred in this historic town, it's not surprising to hear talk of hauntings. More than 200 buildings that were standing at the time of the war remain intact today, setting the perfect scene for some truly spine-tingling tales. There are many companies providing ghost tours; there's not much difference in the content, delivery, or price. If you're visiting during the busy spring and summer season, however, you may want to bear in mind that street traffic on major thoroughfares like Baltimore Street and Steinwehr Avenue may leave you straining to hear the ghastly tales.

Civil War Hauntings Candlelight Ghost Walks
237 Steinwehr Ave.
(717) 752-5588
www.cwhauntings.com

Gettysburg Convention and Visitors Bureau
571 W. Middle St.
(717) 334-6274
www.gettysburg.travel

Ghostly Images of Gettysburg
548 Baltimore St.
(717) 334-6296
www.gettysburgbattlefieldtours.com

Ghosts of Gettysburg Candlelight Walking Tours
271 Baltimore St.
(717) 337-0445
www.ghostsofgettysburg.com

Historic Farnsworth House Ghost Walks and Mourning Theater
401 Baltimore St.
(717) 334-8838
www.gettysburgshauntedaddress.com

ACCOMMODATIONS

Battlefield Bed and Breakfast Inn $$$$
2264 Emmitsburg Rd.
(717) 334-8804
(888) 766-3897
www.gettysburgbattlefield.com

Five minutes from the Gettysburg Battlefield visitor center, this 1809 farmhouse has appeared in several "Best of" lists; it's easy to see why. The inn caters to the Civil War "crowd," and guests will feel almost as if they lived in town through the battle. The eight-guest-room (each named after a regiment that fought at Gettysburg) inn is situated on 30 acres of farmland, surrounded by original campaign ground. The innkeepers host daily Civil War history presentations while staff in period costumes serve a home-cooked breakfast each morning. Each room also offers a private bath and air-conditioning. Rates are a tad higher than other local inns, but for good reason. Reservations are highly recommended.

Best Western Gettysburg Hotel $$$
One Lincoln Square
(717) 337-2000
(866) 378-1797
www.hotelgettysburg.com

We normally don't include chain hotels in this guide, but you can't stroll through downtown Gettysburg without noticing the Best Western. Established in 1797, the hotel saw its share of action in 1863, earning a listing on the National Register of Historic Places and Historic Hotels of America. At Willis House, located across the street, Abraham Lincoln penned the Gettysburg Address. The accommodations are roomy, outfitted with modern amenities like Wi-Fi and cable television.

Blue Sky Motel $–$$
2585 Biglerville Rd.
(717) 677-7736
(800) 745-8194
www.blueskymotel.com

This no-frills, old-fashioned country motel won't win any awards, but it's clean, convenient, and unbeatably affordable. Even during peak season, you'll pay less than $100 per night. The low price includes a pool, free coffee, and access to friendly, knowledgeable owners who are eager to help you plan your visit to Gettysburg's attractions.

Brafferton Inn $$–$$$$
44 York St.
(717) 337-3423
(866) 337-3423
www.brafferton.com

A bullet lodged in the mantel of one of the Brafferton's rooms tells you all you need to know about this building's history. Built in 1786, this unique residence was transformed into an inn two centuries later. Today it is one of three York Street structures that make up the Brafferton Inn. Amenities and rates vary, but all 18 rooms in the house and the adjoining carriage house reflect quiet, 19th-century comfort. Some have luxurious touches like whirlpool tubs and gas fireplaces.

The Brickhouse Inn $$–$$$$
452 Baltimore St.
(717) 338-9337
(800) 864-3464
www.brickhouseinn.com

Owners and Innkeepers Tessa Bardo and Brian Duncan stress cleanliness and convenience; their inn is within easy walking distance of Gettysburg's shops, restaurants, and attractions, and it offers off-street parking. The Brickhouse is also known for comfort and relative tranquility—despite its central location—provided in part by the inn's spacious gardens. "The Welty House—where we have five of our rooms—is a genuine historic house," the owners say. "It was occupied by Confederate forces at the end of the battle's first day and still bears bullet holes in its walls." Each room is named for one of the states represented in the battle and furnished with antiques and family heirlooms. All rooms showcase the house's original hardwood floors, and some even feature private porches with rocking chairs.

The Gaslight Inn $$$–$$$$
33 E. Middle St.
(717) 337-9100
(800) 914-5698
www.thegaslightinn.com

For another historic experience, check into this elegant nine-room inn, which dates to 1872. Each room comes with a private bath, most with Jacuzzi tubs, steam showers, and some with fireplaces. Eager to set the mood for a romantic escape, the inn will also help guests arrange special indulgences like an in-room massage, flowers, and chocolate-covered strawberries. Guests can also take advantage of personalized concierge service to help arrange sightseeing activities, dining and other diversions, and a tasty full-cooked breakfast each morning.

Gettystown Inn/Dobbin House $$–$$$$
89 Steinwehr Ave.
(717) 334-2100
www.dobbinhouse.com

Dating back to 1776, Gettysburg's oldest and most historic building overlooks the Gettysburg National Cemetery, where Lincoln delivered the Gettysburg Address. Prior to the Civil War, the house was a well-known "station" on the Underground Railroad, used to conceal runaway slaves. While many Gettysburg visitors stop here to dine at the Dobbin House, a popular colonial tavern-style restaurant, you can also spend the night at the nine-room Gettystown Inn. Rooms are comfortably furnished with antiques and old-fashioned beds. Breakfast at the adjacent restaurant is included. You can also arrange to stay at the Little Round Top Farm, a five-bedroom farmhouse set on 12 acres with a pond and a walking path to the spot where the 20th Maine infantry preserved the Union position on the hill.

Inn at Herr Ridge $$–$$$$
900 Chambersburg Rd.
(717) 334-4332
(800) 362-9849
www.innatherrridge.com

The Inn at Herr Ridge, witnessed some of the first action of the battles of Gettysburg. On the morning of July 1, Confederate forces drove the Union cavalry back toward Gettysburg along the road that passed in front of the 1815 inn and tavern. Although the inn sustained damage during the battle and during a windstorm more than a century later, the original building has been painstakingly restored to its 19th-century appearance. Owner Steven Wolf has also added 11 more guest rooms to share the experience with more travelers. There's a fine-dining restaurant, a casual tavern, and even a limited-service spa on-site as well.

James Gettys Inn $$$–$$$$
27 Chambersburg St.
(717) 337-1334
(888) 900-5275
www.jamesgettyshotel.com

Named for the town's founder, the James Gettys Inn sits in the heart of downtown Gettysburg. During the Civil War, it was known as the Union Hotel and was used as a hospital. Twenty-five years later, it hosted 250 guests for the official battle commemoration. Each spacious guest room includes a well-stocked kitchenette, private bath, and separate living area. In lieu of breakfast service, fresh pastries, juice, and fruit are brought to each guest room the night before, and rooms are equipped with coffeemakers and supplies.

RESTAURANTS

Blue Parrot Bistro $$
35 Chambersburg St.
(717) 337-3739
www.blueparrotbistro.com

Housed in a Civil War–era building, this eclectic downtown bistro serves modern American and Mediterranean fare. Start with hummus or baba ghanoush, and then sample the grilled platter: a French pork chop, lamb chop, and venison steak, served with ratatouille and garlic mashed potatoes. Or, choose a flavorful pasta dish or a juicy hamburger. Wash it down with a Pennsylvania beer.

Farnsworth House Inn $$$
401 Baltimore St.
(717) 334-8838
www.farnsworthhouseinn.com

The restored Farnsworth Dining Rooms—decorated in honor of Gettysburg commanders George G. Meade and Robert E. Lee—offer a menu filled with hearty Northern and Southern dishes, such as Virginia ham, Yankee pot roast, and Maryland-style crab cakes. Outdoor dining is also available. The Farnsworth House is also a bed-and-breakfast, and it boasts a real countrified tavern filled with memorabilia from the movie *Gettsyburg*. If you're a fan of the macabre, you may also want to check out the house's cellar stories. Ghost-seekers descend into the cellar and gather around a coffin to hear a scary litany of local ghost lore. The tavern features a number of Pennsylvania favorites.

Gina's Place $$
16 E. Hanover St.
(717) 337-2697
www.ginasplacerestaurant.com

If you're in the mood for Italian, locals will tell you that Gina's is the best in town. Don't be surprised if Gina herself greets you when you walk in the door, and then sits down with you to take your order. She's also the culinary genius behind the house-made pasta, fresh bread, and other tasty Italian creations. If you're traveling with a large group, inquire about the bountiful all-you-can-eat family-style meals.

Historic Cashtown Inn $$$
1325 Old Rte. 30
Cashtown, PA
(717) 334-9722
(800) 367-1797
www.cashtowninn.com

Also a bed-and-breakfast, and formerly a stagecoach stop—and the headquarters of Confederate General A. P. Hill—the circa-1797 building that now houses the popular Cashtown Inn still looks as if dusty riders should be tying their steeds up out front. But don't be fooled; the inn's lunch (melts, clubs, crab cakes, etc.), dinner (filet mignon, quail, seafood dishes), wine, and dessert menus are upscale and eclectic.

Olivia's $$
3015 Baltimore Pike
(717) 359-9357
www.olivias.biz

This family-owned eatery is located a few miles from Lincoln Square, but you'll find it's worth the trip. The menu blends Mediterranean classics like stuffed grape leaves, pastichio, spanakopita, and baked lasagna with innovative twists and fresh local ingredients. On a pleasant day, ask for a seat on the outdoor terrace.

First and Second Manassas: Blooded Plains

Darley.

FIRST MANASSAS

*I*f it wasn't quite the war's first battle, it was surely going to be the biggest; and thousands of gung-ho soldiers on each side expected it to be the last. Experienced military men—such as Lincoln's aging General-in-Chief Winfield Scott—knew better. Still the nation's

reigning military hero at the age of seventy-four, Scott had advocated a slow strangulation of the South, rather than a risky attempt at a quick fix. But military exigencies were no match for political and popular pressure. Newspapers across the North were already demanding that the Rebels be crushed. The *New York Tribune* was blaring the headlines: FORWARD TO RICHMOND! FORWARD TO RICHMOND! Influential publisher Horace Greeley insisted that the national army should prevent the new Confederate Congress from convening there on July 20. Equally aggressive-minded Southerners insisted that any Federal thrust be met headlong, and naturally, blunted.

Map of the First Battle of Manassas, also called Bull Run

And so on July 16, 1861, crisply uniformed, 42-year-old brigadier general Irvin McDowell set out from northern Virginia with a raw army of 35,000 with which to attack Brigadier General P. G. T. Beauregard's equally green army of 22,000 Confederates laying in wait behind a muddy Virginia stream called Bull Run. The polished McDowell was a Mexican War veteran and an 1838 graduate of West Point, where he had also spent four years teaching cadets tactics. Now he would find out if green volunteers could carry out his orders on a battlefield. Winfield Scott, for one, doubted it.

General P. G. T. Beauregard

General Irvin McDowell

McDowell's opponent was an old West Point acquaintance who had finished second, compared to his 23rd, in a class of 45.

Beauregard—who had resigned as superintendent of West Point in January before directing the Rebel attack on Fort Sumter—was already a hero across the South, and a much-hated villain in the North. Deployed to protect the vital rail junction at Manassas, Beauregard's army counted only about 21,000. Another 12,000 Confederates, however, under General Joseph E. Johnston, were within reinforcing distance in the lower Shenandoah Valley. McDowell was counting on

Major General Robert Patterson's small army to keep Johnston where he was.

Crossing Bull Run creek before dawn on July 21, McDowell opened the battle with an attack on the left of Beauregard's long lines. Each side sent in reinforcements, but the Rebel line caved in, sending Confederates south across a stream and up a rise called Henry House Hill. Blue-clad regiments followed, pressing Bernard Bee's brigade. Here, however, the Confederates stiffened, spurred on by the appearance of Brigadier General Thomas J. Jackson's supporting brigade on the hill's far side. Minutes before his own death, Bee bellowed the words that would make a legend: "Look! There is Jackson standing like a stone wall! Rally behind the Virginians!"

For two hours, McDowell's Yankees marched up Henry House Hill into the teeth of a desperate Confederate defense. Robert Patterson had not, as it happened, prevented Johnston's escape, and the infusion of his Rebel troops gradually turned the tide of battle. Late in the afternoon, Johnston and Beauregard took to the offense, launching a stunning blow against the tiring Yankees on McDowell's left flank. That was all it took. The frustrated Federals took to their heels, retreating back across Bull Run and onto the Warrenton Turnpike. Panic followed, and McDowell's army fled all the way back to Washington, D.C. The shocking victory cost the Confederates 387 killed and some 1,600 wounded. McDowell lost 460 men killed, 1,100 wounded, and another 1,300 missing.

In the wake of the debacle, Walt Whitman thought of Abraham Lincoln, whose young administration had been saddled with such crushing news, and wrote with admiration:

The president recovering himself, begins that very night—sternly, rapidly sets about the task of reorganizing his forces, and placing himself in positions for future and surer work. If there were nothing else of Abraham Lincoln for history to stamp him with, it is enough to send him with his wreath to the memory of all future time, that he endured that hour, that day, bitterer than gall—indeed, a crucifixion day—that it did not conquer him—that he unflinchingly stemm'd it, and resolv'd to lift himself and the Union out of it.

The first Battle of Bull Run

SECOND MANASSAS

The strategic situation in the east hadn't changed much 13 months later, when armies of blue and gray met at Manassas for a rematch. Early that summer, George McClellan had driven his grand, new Army of the Potomac to the gates of the Confederate capital before a change in Confederate command, heavy rains, and McClellan's own demons conspired to push his befuddled army all the way back down the Virginia Peninsula.

Exasperated with the timid and difficult McClellan, Abraham Lincoln relieved the general of his army and assigned two of its corps to Major General John Pope, a 40-old West Pointer who had made a name for himself with a couple of minor victories on the Mississippi.

Pope spent most of August awaiting the arrival of McClellan's men and shifting his own 50,000 troops around central and northern Virginia in response to Robert E. Lee's movements north. Failing to detect Stonewall Jackson's lightning march past his right flank, Pope reacted only after Jackson defeated Nathaniel Banks at Cedar Mountain, cut the Orange and Alexandria rail line at Bristoe, and sacked the Union supply base at Manassas Junction. Marching his 65,000 men northeast up the Warrenton Turnpike, Pope discovered Stonewall Jackson's 24,000 Confederates dug into an abandoned railroad bed in a wood north of Manassas. On August 29, Pope—failing to concentrate his forces properly—pitched into Jackson's in a series of attacks, all of which were repulsed. Finally, he launched Major General Fitz John Porter's command at Jackson's right, only to find James Longstreet's newly arrived corps entrenched there.

The following day, Pope renewed his attacks with the same results, until Longstreet, followed by Jackson, ordered massive counterattacks. Pope's army folded up, and in an eerie repeat of the previous year's fight here, retreated east up the turnpike behind a solid rear-guard defense. Lee's victory cost him 9,200 casualties, including

Map of the Second Battle of Manassas

Second Battle of Bull Run, August 29, 1862

nearly 1,500 killed and 7,600 wounded. Pope's losses amounted to 1,724 killed, 8,372 wounded, and nearly 6,000 missing or captured. The revolving door atop the Army of the Potomac whirled again, spinning Pope all the way to The Plains and bringing George McClellan back for another tour.

HISTORIC SITES

Ben Lomond Historic Site
10311 Sudley Manor Dr.
Manassas, VA
(703) 367-7872
www.pwcgov.org

This home was built in the 1830s and sustained considerable damage during the battles at Manassas. During the first battle, it was used as a hospital. On the walls, you'll still see graffiti messages from wounded soldiers.

Brandy Station Battlefield
19484 Brandy Rd. (Graffiti House)
Brandy Station, VA
(540) 727-7718
www.brandystationfoundation.com

The biggest cavalry battle ever fought on this continent took place at Brandy Station, Virginia, on June 9, 1863, when Major General Alfred Pleasanton's Yankee troopers piled into Major General J. E. B. Stuart's Confederate camp. Some 17,000 horsemen took part in the daylong affair, which ended in Confederate victory. Stuart, however, had been surprised and fought to a standstill—an indication of the vastly improved Federal cavalry.

Today the Brandy Station Foundation (which, along with the Civil War Preservation Trust [CWPT], owns the preserved sections of the original battle site) maintains and operates the battlefield with the help of donations, grants, and fund-raisers. A recent success here was the CWPT purchase of a small but crucial 18.9-acre section of the original battlefield.

Whether by driving tour or prearranged guided tour (Apr through Oct), there is much to see here today, starting with the Graffiti House. In this building, soldiers from each side scrawled messages or their names here while recovering from wounds. The building also serves today as a museum and park visitor center, offering exhibits, information, tours, and lectures.

The John Singleton Mosby Museum and Education Center
173 Main St.
Warrenton, VA
(540) 351-1600
www.mosbymuseum.org

The John Singleton Mosby Museum and Education Center tells the story of Colonel John Mosby and the county from the 1850s through 1880.

The building now known as Brentmoor, the Spilman-Mosby House was built in 1859 by Judge Edward M. Spilman. Spilman sold the house to former Partisan Ranger John Keith, who in turn sold it to Mosby, who had used Warrenton as a base of operations for much of the war. Mosby, in turn, sold the house to another Confederate veteran, longtime friend Eppa Hunton. The building is now on the National Register of Historic Places.

Liberia Plantation House
8601 Portner Ave.
Manassas, VA
(703) 368-1873
www.ci.manassas.va.us/index.aspx?nid=221

Once a thriving plantation with as many as 90 slaves, Liberia was used by Brigadier General P. G. T. Beauregard as a headquarters during the summer of 1861. A year later, Union major general Irvin McDowell made the building his own headquarters, driving the owners, the Weir family, away for the remainder of the war. Call ahead for information.

The Manassas Museum
9101 Prince William St.
Manassas, VA
(703) 368-1873
www.manassasmuseum.org

The 7,000-square-foot Manassas Museum is the hub of all things historical in Manassas, including a number of small Civil War sites not part of the Manassas Battlefield. Permanent and changing exhibits and videos tell the story of Northern Piedmont history, with a special focus on the Civil War and its effect on the community. The museum also contains a research library and excellent gift shop. Information about other area sites that fall under the jurisdiction of the Manassas Museum System can also be found here.

You can pick up a brochure that details a walking trail and driving trail connecting many of Manassas's Civil War sites at the museum or at the historic railroad depot, or log on to www.civilwartrails.org to view an interactive map and pick up some tips for organizing your visit. On the same Web site, you'll also find a guide to the Route 50 corridor and sites in Warrenton and Fauquier County.

The museum is open year-round and is wheelchair accessible.

Manassas National Battlefield Park
651 Sudley Rd. (visitor center)
Manassas, VA
(703) 361-1339
www.nps.gov/mana

For now, at least, only the ghosts of the men who died here occupy the battlefields of Manassas, quietly guarding the few cannon and monuments that honor their exploits. Outside these serene plains wait the land-grabbing minions of modern society, ready to spring onto this prime real estate and plant yet more strip malls and condominiums. Perhaps no major Civil War site faces the squeeze of encroaching "civilization" quite like Manassas National Battlefield does. It is surrounded by suburban sprawl, which, in places, extends to the very edge of its original breastworks.

Despite the ever-present threat outside its boundaries, this 5,000-acre park looks and feels much the same (aside from one very busy, four-lane intersection) today as it did 140 years ago. Much of it feels secluded from the 21st century. The recent removal of power lines from the Brawner Farm and partial restoration of the Henry and Thornbury Houses have helped. The park has also added a new picnic area.

Before setting out on a walking tour of the park, visitors will want to check out its small museum, which offers exhibits, a short film, and a helpful electronic battlefield map.

Manassas Railroad Depot
9431 West St.
Manassas, VA
(703) 361-6599
(877) 848-3018
www.visitmanassas.org

The depot is the town's de facto visitor center, where brochures and tourist information can be found. It is also the home of the James and Marion Payne Memorial Railroad Heritage Gallery, a combination of exhibits and artifact displays representing the town's extensive railroad history. Admission is free to the gallery.

Mayfield Earthwork Fort
8401 Quarry Rd.
Manassas, VA
(703) 368-1873
www.manassascity.org

This 11-acre site was constructed by P. G. T. Beauregard's Confederates during May and June 1861, in anticipation of Union attack. After March 1862, Union soldiers also periodically used the earthworks.

There is an interpretive trail with markers and replica "Quaker guns." The park is open daily from sunrise to sunset and is free of charge.

The Museum of Culpeper History
803 S. Main St.
Culpeper, VA
(540) 829-1749
www.culpepermuseum.com

If you're traveling southwest, continue on to Culpeper, another charming Virginia town that's brimming with Civil War history. From Manassas, it's about an hour to this town, tucked away in the scenic Blue Ridge Mountains. The Culpeper Museum offers a fantastic overview of the county's historic past. Located at the entrance to the Culpeper Historic District, this unassuming facility (which was originally known as the Culpeper Cavalry Museum) now focuses on the history of Culpeper County. In addition to impressive indoor and outdoor displays related to Native American and Colonial history, the museum boasts an entire gallery dedicated to the Civil War.

Old Jail Museum
Court House Square
Warrenton, VA
(540) 347-5525
www.fauquierhistory.com

Consisting of two structures built in 1808 and 1823, this beautifully preserved old jail now houses a series of exhibits about the Revolutionary War, Native American history, the Civil War, and local favorite John Singleton Mosby. The Old Jail Museum is free of charge, but donations are welcome.

OTHER POINTS OF INTEREST

Aldie Mill
Aldie, VA
(703) 327-9777

Located just west of Route 15 on U.S. Route 50, the small town of Aldie witnessed the passing of troops on June 17, 1863, as they marched toward Gettysburg. Mosby's men also fought near Aldie Mill in 1861. The early-19th-century mill is open for free tours on Sun, Apr through Oct. Tours are free, but donations are welcome.

Blackburn's Ford
North of Manassas off Rte. 28

Soldiers got their first taste of battle on this ford on Bull Run. On July 18, Union troops approached the ford during a reconnaissance trip only to find Confederate forces waiting. The Southern forces stood their ground, setting the tone for the major battle that was about to transpire.

Marshall, VA

Mosby's raiders fought and finally, on April 21, 1865, disbanded in this small town west of Manassas and Haymarket. Confederate loyalists silently cheered here as they watched Stonewall Jackson pass through on his way to the Battle of Second Manassas.

Piedmont Station
Delaplane, VA

It was at this train station west of Manassas that soldiers from the Army of the Shenandoah boarded a train on their way to Manassas Junction on July 19, 1861. Colonel Thomas J. Jackson was among the travelers; two days later, he would earn his nickname "Stonewall" at the First Battle of Manassas. The troops' 30-mile trip east is believed to be the first instance in which troops were moved into combat on railroad.

Rectortown, VA

Another small town in this Civil War history–rich corner of Virginia, it was here that General George McClellan was relieved of his command of the Union forces and replaced by General Ambrose Burnside in November 1862 after McClellan's failure to destroy Lee's army at Antietam.

Signal Hill
Manassas Park, VA

This small, independent town just outside of Manassas was once home to a Confederate signal station. On July 21, 1861, a Confederate signal officer named E. P. Alexander first spotted a Union cannon and forces closing in on the Confederate line. He sent a signal to Nathan "Shanks" Evans, who held the command near the Run Bridge. It is believed to be the first time "wigwag" signaling—a system of coded flag movements—was used during combat.

Thoroughfare Gap
West of Manassas, off I-66

Confederate forces led by Stonewall Jackson traveled through this mountain pass on their way to fight in the Second Battle of Manassas. Confederate General James Longstreet followed with his troops, but they were met with resistance from Union forces under the command of General James B. Ricketts. The Union forces failed to stall Longstreet's advance, thus enabling the Second Battle of Manassas to take place. You can still see the ruins of Chapman's Mill, a Confederate meat-curing and distribution center, which witnessed much of the battle.

Warrenton Cemetery
Warrenton, VA

In this cemetery, located across the street from the visitor center, there's a memorial honoring the more than 600 Confederate soldiers who died in the region's makeshift hospitals. It's also home to Mosby's grave.

ACCOMMODATIONS

Bennett House Bed & Breakfast $$–$$$$
9252 Bennett Dr.
Manassas, VA
(800) 354-7060
www.virginiabennetthouse.com

If you're looking for a place to stay in Manassas, an area increasingly threatened by urban sprawl, your options are largely confined to national and international chain hotels. For something a little more unique, however, Bennett House is your best bet. The impeccably kept bed-and-breakfast offers tranquil, home-style comfort (as well as antiques-filled rooms, central air, and in-room cable and VCRs) in the heart of Old Town Manassas. Mornings are memorable, as innkeepers Jean and Curtis Harrover offer a full country breakfast. The inn has just two rooms, so visitors should make a reservation well in advance.

Black Horse Inn $$$–$$$$
8393 Meetze Rd.
Warrenton, VA
(540) 349-4020
www.blackhorseinn.com

If you don't mind a bit of a drive from the battlefield, treat yourself to a stay at the award-winning Black Horse Inn in Warrenton, about 30 minutes west of Manassas—a town with unspoiled scenery and Civil War attractions of its own as well. The circa-1850 mansion served as a hospital during the Civil War and was frequently visited by the Black Horse Cavalry. Today, the nine-room inn is among the finest in northern Virginia. Many of its rooms are outfitted with canopy beds, gable ceilings, and Jacuzzi and antique claw-foot tubs; stables are even available for visiting horses. Breakfast and tea service is also included in the room rate.

Country Inn & Suites $$$$
10810 Battleview Pkwy.
Manassas, VA
(703) 393-9797
www.countryinns.com

We've done our best to avoid chain accommodations, but in a region where national brands hold sway, it's good to include one of the top players. Country Inn & Suites provides an exceptional value—pleasant amenities, including a complimentary and substantial breakfast, an indoor pool, and whirlpools in many of the rooms—and a great location between the Manassas National Battlefield Park and Old Town Manassas.

✯ ✯ ✯ ✯ ✯ ✯ ✯ ✯ ✯ ✯ ✯ ✯ ✯ ✯ ✯ ✯

Fountain Hall Bed and Breakfast $$$–$$$$
609 S. East St.
Culpeper, VA
(540) 825-8200
(800) 298-4748
www.fountainhall.com

While Culpeper is a bit of a drive from the sites of Manassas and Warrenton, you're in for a treat if you make the trip. Steve and Kathi Walker's Fountain Hall is truly one of a kind. Built in 1859 in the heart of Culpeper, this grand Colonial Revival, complete with glorious walnut staircase, is within walking distance of the Culpeper Museum, National Cemetery, and the fine dining offered downtown. Civil War buffs can easily walk to Brandy Station or the Cedar Mountain area, while the battlefields of Manassas, Fredericksburg, and Spotsylvania are just a short drive away. For old-fashioned relaxation, Fountain Hall features an extensive library and lawn games.

The Grey Horse Inn Bed & Breakfast $$$–$$$$
4350 Fauquier Ave.
The Plains, VA
(540) 253-7000
(877) 253-7020
www.greyhorseinn.com

Innkeepers John and Ellen Hearty welcome guests to this wonderful hunt country retreat in the town of The Plains. Confederate troops marched through the town—amid spies working for both sides—in August 1862 as they ventured to Manassas. There are six bedrooms, including one two-room suite, tastefully decorated to reflect the spirit of this 1880s-era mansion. The picturesque grounds and gardens form the perfect setting to enjoy a book or savor a cup of tea. True to its name, the inn is also popular among horse lovers who flock to The Plains for Virginia's Gold Cup steeplechase race and other equestrian events.

Poplar Springs, the INN Spa $$$$
9245 Rogues Rd.
Casanova, VA
(540) 788-4600
(800) 490-7747
www.poplarspringsinn.com

What could be more romantic than a town called Casanova? Secluded, charming, and outfitted with one of the region's most inviting spas, Poplar Springs is a fitting match for the town in which it's located. The inn is nestled on 200 private wooded acres, with hiking and biking paths that lend to exploration on foot. Because it's a popular choice for stressed-out Washingtonians eager for an escape, the inn goes overboard to help you relax: think breakfast in bed, prompt valet service, and highly attentive service. While much of the 22-room property is modern construction, the historic Manor House now houses a fine-dining restaurant known for its roaring fire, soothing piano music, and fine cuisine. Don't be surprised to see sweetbreads, venison, elk, and other unusual items on the menu.

Westfields Marriott $$$$
14750 Conference Center Dr.
Chantilly, VA
(703) 818-0300
www.marriott.com

For luxury accommodations and even a quick round of golf or spa treatment between Manassas and Dulles Airport, this AAA-Four Diamond designated Marriott property is a fine choice. Unlike many of our other recommendations, this 327-room resort is sleek and modern, equipped with modern, business-traveler-friendly amenities like wireless Internet, but also furnished with touches of art and antiques. There's a Fred Couples–designed golf course on the premises, along with a high-end spa.

RESTAURANTS

Carmello's & Little Portugal Restaurant $$$
9108 Center St.
Manassas, VA
(703) 368-5522
www.carmellos.com

It may be surprising to find one of the Washington, D.C., metropolitan area's premier Portuguese restaurants in the commuter town of Manassas, but many regional residents with discerning palates have found their way to Carmello's since it opened. On the menu, you'll find a blend of classic northern Italian pasta dishes, along with Portuguese creations like bife pimenta (filet mignon served in port wine with cracked pepper) and vierias (shrimp, scallops, lobster, and artichoke hearts sautéed in garlic and white wine sauce). Pair up your dinner with a bottle of Alvarhino or another Portuguese wine. It's located on Old Town Manassas's primary shopping street, perfect for an after-dinner stroll.

City Square Café $$

9428 Battle St.
Manassas, VA
(703) 369-6022
www.citysquarecafe.com

This family-friendly restaurant has served comfortable, casual fare to locals and visitors for more than 30 years. Owners Robert and Susana Barolin serve Mediterranean dishes like chicken parmesan and veal Marsala, along with standard American classics like prime rib and shrimp scampi. Showcasing the flavors of the Barolins's native Uruguay, you'll also find an extensive selection of South American wines on the wine list, along with empanadas on the menu.

Claire's at the Depot $$$

65 S. Third St.
Warrenton, VA
(540) 351-1616
www.clairesrestaurant.com

As the Washington, D.C., metropolitan area continues to expand to the west, once-sleepy towns like Warrenton begin to attract more urban-minded residents, along with high-quality restaurants such as this one. On the menu, you'll find eclectic, modern cuisine. The turn-of-the-century depot in which it's located shows off the flavors of the town's railroad past. Modern twists and regional classics frequently show up on the menu, like scrumptious she-crab soup and oysters served in a cornmeal crust. Dishes are flavorful, crafted with local produce and seasoned with fresh herbs grown on-site, and vegetarians won't be disappointed by the meatless selections. If you dine here in the spring or summer, ask to be seated on the glorious outdoor patio among the seasonal flowers and fountains.

Foti's Restaurant $$$

219 E. Davis St.
Culpeper, VA
(540) 829-8400
www.fotisrestaurant.com

New to the Culpeper restaurant scene, Foti's has quickly become known as one of the area's best eating establishments. This is not a restaurant to walk into straight from a battlefield; it is a first-class, fine-dining house perfect for those looking for superb food and a relaxing night on the town. Wondering about the name? It's a childhood nickname that co-owner Frank Maragos used to answer to, setting the tone for a friendly, familiar dining experience. Main courses include such flavorful creations as crispy seared

Tasmanian salmon and lamb three ways. Reservations are highly recommended.

Okra's Louisiana Bistro $$

9110 Center St.
Manassas, VA
(703) 330-2729
www.okras.com

Even discerning Cajun diners take a shine to Okra's, a colorful, friendly eatery in Old Town Manassas. Munch on appetizers like alligator bites and fried okra as you wait for your food and sip an Abita beer or Hurricane. For the main course, you can't go wrong with the jambalaya, teeming with andouille, shrimp, and tasso ham, or the zesty crawfish étoufée, flavorful and bursting with vegetables and spices. The restaurant is also a lively place for nightlife with frequent live music acts. It stays open late, too.

The Rail Stop Restaurant $$$

6478 Main St.
The Plains, VA
(540) 253-5644
www.railstoprestaurant.com

It's no wonder that railroad-themed restaurants are popular in this part of Virginia; the steel tracks played an integral role in the histories of many of the Commonwealth's small towns and cities. In the tiny hamlet of The Plains, the Rail Stop is the place to go for your urban restaurant fix—and possibly even a brush with a celebrity. (Actor Robert Duvall lives nearby and was once co-owner of the restaurant.) Stop in at lunchtime for a satisfying grilled salmon BLT topped with pancetta, arugula, and basil aioli or linger over a tantalizing dinner of pan-seared scallops accompanied by mushroom risotto and smothered in a garlic cream sauce or fresh gnocchi paired with Italian sausage, artichokes, roasted peppers, tomatoes, onions, and fresh mozzarella.

Sweetwater Tavern $$

14250 Sweetwater Lane
Centreville, VA
(703) 449-1100
www.greatamericanrestaurants.com

Locals love Sweetwater Tavern—a Fairfax, Virginia–based restaurant with a few locations in the Washington, D.C., metro area, including this one that's just north of Manassas. It's always hopping, and the food, service, and ambience are consistently good. Sample the house-made beers and munch on Southwestern creations like Tex-Mex egg rolls and spicy bean-cheese-guacamole dip, then move on to crowd-pleasing main courses like crispy chicken tenders, juicy burgers, and barbecued ribs. If you're shopping for evening entertainment, you're also likely to find live music and a crowd that appreciates it.

Virginia Barbeque $$
9952 Liberia Ave.
Manassas, VA
(703) 369-4227
www.virginiabbq.com

If you're looking for great barbecue in the town of Manassas, this is the place for it. Don't let the plain strip mall in which it's located fool you; it's well known in the area for producing fabulous meats in the Virginia, North Carolina, or Texas tradition. Because you're in Virginia, we'd steer you to the specialty: Virginia-style pulled pork, slathered in the spicy tomato-based sauce for which the Old Dominion is known. The restaurant also does an admirable job with traditional barbecue accompaniments, like tangy coleslaw, perfectly seasoned baked beans, and freshly prepared hush puppies.

Baltimore: Powder Keg

View of Baltimore in 1862

Bathed in glory by the city's defiant stand against the British in 1814, Baltimore was, by midcentury, a bustling seaport and trade center big enough to rival Washington, D.C., in status. In 1830 the brand-new Baltimore and Ohio Railroad opened, and slowly extended its reach across Maryland, through Harpers Ferry, and by 1853 all the way across western Virginia (now West Virginia) to the Ohio River. It brought new settlers to the Midwest, and returned east with trade goods.

By 1861 Baltimore was a city divided. As in that political powder keg called St. Louis, Missouri, Confederate sympathizers lived side by side with stout Unionists. The ugly riot that darkened the city in April 1861 reflected Maryland's sharply divided loyalties, and helped guide new president Abraham Lincoln in his efforts to keep the state from seceding.

Union officials had already managed to avoid trouble in Baltimore once, when the president-elect passed through the city on his way from Illinois to Washington, D.C., late on February 22. Warned of a plot to assassinate him as he switched trains in Baltimore, Lincoln reluctantly agreed, as he later put it, "to run no risk where no risk was necessary." The intelligence, after all, had come from Allan Pinkerton—founder of the Pinkerton Detective Agency—who presumably knew what he was doing. Pinkerton's agency would later gain fame on the frontier during its pursuit of the Jesse James Gang. First, however, Pinkerton would come under fire for backing George McClellan's ridiculous claims of enemy troop numbers during his brief tenure atop the Army of the Potomac.

With a heavy coat covering his shoulders and an unfamiliar soft hat on his head, Lincoln (along with Pinkerton and Ward Hill Lamon, his personal bodyguard) slipped unannounced from a special train in Baltimore in the wee hours of February 23, transferred to the

Allan Pinkerton

number of Southern governors, this was the step—they claimed—that pushed them into the Confederate camp. Eastern Maryland was home to a vocal, pro-Southern population. The arrival of Northern troops in Baltimore was bound to cause a fuss.

On April 19—100 years to the day after the Battles of Lexington and Concord—the 6th Massachusetts Militia debarked in Baltimore en route, like Lincoln a few weeks earlier, to Washington. A hostile crowd awaited them. When the inexperienced militiamen passed, angry Marylanders unleashed a barrage of stones. In return, the attackers received a volley of musketry. The exchange left four soldiers and a dozen civilians dead on the street.

Things were only slightly quieter two months later when Elisha Hunt Rhodes rolled into town with the 2nd Rhode Island Volunteers. "We arrived in Baltimore after dark and disembarked from the cars to march through the city to the Washington Depot," wrote Rhodes. "Immense crowds met us at the depot and the streets were lined with people who shouted for Jeff Davis and abused us roundly."

Warning a Maryland peace commission to "Keep your rowdies in Baltimore," Lincoln used heavy-handed persuasion to keep the state loyal. Federal authorities arrested Baltimore's mayor when he refused to pledge an oath of loyalty to the Union. A small army of Union troops deployed throughout the city while Lincoln used the media to infuse pro-Union sentiment. Baltimore calmed. Although Maryland soldiers fought for each side during the war, the state remained in the Union.

capital-bound train, and reached Washington without incident. Things took a violent turn a few weeks later, however, after Lincoln—in the wake of the Confederate attack on Fort Sumter—issued a call for 75,000 volunteers with which to suppress the rebellion. For a

---

HISTORIC SITES

Baltimore and Ohio Railroad Museum
901 W. Pratt St.
Baltimore
(410) 752-2490
www.borail.org

After a near-disastrous roof collapse that left a number of locomotives and other artifacts badly damaged, the renowned B&O Railroad Museum reopened with expanded visitor services and educational programs. The heart of the

40-acre museum complex, of course, remains its historic locomotives and its unmatched collection of railroad artifacts and ephemera dating to 1830. The combination of these marvelous old machines and recognition of their importance in the Civil War (and the expansion of the frontier) makes this museum a must-see for adults and kids.

You can also visit the B&O Railroad Museum at Ellicott City Station, the oldest surviving railroad station in America, dating to 1830. See the "Other Sites of Interest" section.

Reginald F. Lewis Museum of Maryland African American History & Culture
830 E. Pratt St.
Baltimore
(443) 263-1800
www.africanamericanculture.org

While the Civil War isn't a primary focal point of this museum, which opened in 2005 at Baltimore's Inner Harbor, it does an admirable job of recounting the contributions of Maryland's free and enslaved African Americans before, during, and after the war. It's a must-see for any African-American history enthusiast, tackling topics like family life and community bonds, labor contributions, and cultural and entertainment achievements.

USS *Constellation* Museum
Pier 1, Inner Harbor
301 E. Pratt St.
Baltimore
(410) 539-1797
www.constellation.org

The last all-sail ship built by the U.S. Navy, the *Constellation* was used to police the coast of Africa to enforce slave trading laws. During the war, it defended Union merchants from Confederate raiders. It's also the only Civil War–era ship that's still afloat. Hours vary by season.

OTHER SITES OF INTEREST

B&O Railroad Museum: Ellicott City Station
2711 Maryland Ave.
Ellicott City, MD
(410) 461-1945
www.ecborail.org

The oldest surviving railroad station in the United States, the Ellicott City Station is a nice complement to a visit to the B&O Railroad Museum. Visitors can learn about the rise of railroad transportation in the United States; there's also an exhibition that discusses the importance of the railroad to the Union during the Civil War. It's open Fri, Sat, and Sun.

Druid Hill Park
North and Madison Sts.
Baltimore
www.druidhillpark.org

The city's first large municipal park was purchased in 1860 at the height of a nationwide movement to develop parks for city dwellers. Early in the war, Union soldiers camped near the park's entrance. As the war gathered steam, the park became an organizing point for members of the U.S. Colored Troops. Admission is free.

Federal Hill
Baltimore
www.historicfederalhill.org

This park overlooking the Inner Harbor attracts visitors for more than just a postcard-perfect view. After the riot of 1861,

Union troops took command of the strategic location under the command of General Benjamin F. Butler, who led troops from Annapolis to Baltimore in the middle of the night on the B&O Railroad. Overnight, the men put up a small fort and aimed their cannons squarely at downtown Baltimore to intimidate would-be dissenters and to keep the city and the state under Union control.

Fort McHenry National Monument and Historic Shrine
2400 E. Fort Ave.
Baltimore
(410) 962-4290
www.nps.gov/fomc

Famed for its role in repelling the British attack on Baltimore during the War of 1812, Fort McHenry was garrisoned by Union troops and used during the Civil War as a prison for Confederate soldiers and sympathizers.

Lansdowne Christian Church
101 Clyde Ave.
Baltimore
(410) 242-4821
www.erols.com/lanscc

This historic church was built in 1905, a gift from Civil War veteran Charles Hull and his wife, Mary, to honor the fallen Union soldiers. The benefactors required, however, that the church hold a memorial service every May in memory of Hull's brothers-at-arms, making the church the focal point of local Memorial Day observances.

Maryland Historical Society
201 W. Monument St.
Baltimore
(410) 685-3750
www.mdhs.org

There's a small gallery in this museum that showcases Civil War artifacts recovered from the battleground border state. You can also watch a short video about the war and its effects on the region. If you're in luck, you'll catch a temporary exhibition with a Civil War theme. The museum is open Thurs through Sun.

Mount Clare Museum House
1500 Washington Blvd.
Baltimore
(410) 837-3262
www.mountclare.org

Located in the center of what was once a rich plantation, Mount Clare is a splendid example of Georgian architecture built for one of the city's most celebrated colonial residents, Charles Carroll. During the war, guns and munitions were stored on the grounds of the mansion in a position known as Camp Carroll. Union forces used the western pastures as a cavalry training facility. The mansion is open Tues through Sat.

ACCOMMODATIONS

Abacrombie Fine Food and Accommodations　　$$–$$$
58 W. Biddle St.
Baltimore
(410) 244-7227
www.abacrombie.net

Locals know this 12-room B&B best for its fine-dining restaurant, voted "Best Restaurant" by the *Baltimore Sun,* but overnight guests discover clean, comfortable, and reasonably priced accommodations that include free parking and breakfast. Rooms are furnished with antiques and replicas that reflect the history and flavor of the historic location. A word of caution: The Abacrombie is housed in a four-story row house, so be sure to pack lightly; you may be climbing steps!

Admiral Fell Inn　　$$$$
888 S. Broadway
Baltimore
(410) 522-7377
www.sterlinghotels.com

A Baltimore landmark and one of the National Trust for Historic Preservation's Historic Hotels of America, the stylistically diverse, 80-room Admiral Fell Inn fits nicely into the Fells Point Historic District. Its nicely appointed, modern rooms and suites (which offer everything from fireplaces and canopy beds to Jacuzzis) look and feel much cozier than most hotel rooms. As you might expect in a historic hotel, ghost legends abound. Curious guests can sit down for afternoon tea to learn about the spirit-residents or decide for themselves during a one-hour ghost tour of the hotel and grounds. A stone's throw from the Inner Harbor, the quietly

classy inn is central to everything in Baltimore. But if you want to stay in for dinner, the inn also boasts its own fine-dining restaurant named True.

Aunt Rebecca's Bed & Breakfast　　$$$
106 E. Preston St.
Baltimore
(410) 625-1007
www.auntrebeccasbnb.com

Situated in an 1870 brownstone town house, Aunt Rebecca's is a favorite among visitors to downtown Baltimore, and with good reason. Its innkeepers are warm and welcoming, its prices are reasonable, and the location can't be beat. The three guest rooms are large and comfortable and feature special touches like claw-foot bathtubs. Rates include free parking and a tasty, home-cooked breakfast served to all guests at 8 a.m.

Brookshire Suites　　$$$$
120 E. Lombard St.
Baltimore
(410) 625-1300
www.harbormagic.com/brookshire/brookshire_default.asp

If all of the history hunting has left you craving something a little more contemporary, check in to the Brookshire Suites. It's a sister property of historic Admiral Fell Inn, but there's a strikingly different mood at this 97-room Inner Harbor hotel. Guests enjoy a complimentary hot breakfast served in the Cloud Club, a top-floor dining room with a breathtaking view of the city and its surroundings. Local wines and beers are served by the glass—and free of charge—to guests on weekdays, while summers bring weekly bargain-priced Crab Feasts to allow guests to try out a Maryland culinary tradition. Guest rooms and suites are roomy, clean, and comfortable, and many have pleasant views of the harbor.

Celie's Waterfront Bed and Breakfast $$$$
1714 Thames St.
Baltimore
(410) 522-2323
(800) 432-0184
www.celieswaterfront.com

Located on the historic Fells Point waterfront, Celie's is sunny, comfortable, convenient, unique, and brimming with modern amenities (plus access to the inn's private rooftop deck). The inn's Harbor Front rooms are perfect for romantic getaways, outfitted with four-poster king-size beds, wood-burning fireplaces, and hydro-thermal massage tubs. The hotel also boasts two large suites equipped with pullout couches and kitchens that sleep four to six guests. In-room fridges are stocked with complimentary water and sodas, and continental breakfast is included in the room rate.

4 East Madison Inn $$$$
4 E. Madison St.
Baltimore
(410) 332-0880
www.4eastmadisoninn.com

If you prefer the authenticity of Baltimore's neighborhoods to the built-up modernity of the Inner Harbor, check into this elegant nine-room B&B in Mount Vernon. The cozy rooms are furnished with glorious antiques, ornately carved Victorian furniture, chandeliers, and even fireplaces in some rooms. Guests enjoy modern conveniences like high-speed Internet, free parking, comfortable beds, and a lavish, home-cooked breakfast.

Glenda's Bed & Breakfast $$$
2028 Park Ave.
Baltimore
(410) 383-8535
www.lodgingchannel.com

This charming two-room B&B is carved out of a three-story 1886 brick and brownstone row house with magnificent high ceilings. Although it's tempting to sleep in when you're luxuriating in a cozy bed (and perhaps even enjoying the in-room fireplace), you won't want to miss breakfast prepared by Glenda herself. You'll also be treated to afternoon tea, complete with tasty desserts, served daily 4 to 5 p.m. While it's not in the heart of the tourist district, it's a short 5- to 10-minute drive or bus trip to most points of interest—well worth it for the reasonably priced accommodations and personal service.

Inn at Henderson's Wharf $$$$
1000 Fell St.
Baltimore
(410) 522-7777
www.hendersonswharf.com

Step inside the Inn at Henderson's Wharf and you'll see why it's consistently rated one of Baltimore's top hotels. Located in Fell Point, where Baltimore dips gently into the Chesapeake Bay and where restaurants and nightclubs abound, the 38-room inn is warm and welcoming, offering friendly, knowledgeable service and even a complimentary bottle of wine upon check-in. Rooms are luxuriously outfitted with lush feather beds, flat-screen TVs, and, in some cases, exposed-brick walls. Guests can walk to the bars, shops, and restaurants in Fell Point for the evening, then wake up to a delicious breakfast spread—which can also be enjoyed in an outdoor garden patio.

Inn at 2920 $$$$
2920 Elliott St.
Baltimore
(410) 342-4450
www.theinnat2920.com

Most travelers associate B&Bs with antique furnishings and floral bedspreads, but that's not the case at this upscale, contemporary property. The five fashionably furnished rooms have fun and funky names and designs, and some come with a resident beta fish whose name matches the theme of the room. Valentino, for example, lives in the "Bordello Room," while Columbus stays in the "Room at the End of the World." Guests can luxuriate in Jacuzzi tubs and enjoy high-speed wireless Internet access and gourmet breakfast. From the Canton neighborhood, where the inn is located, it's a 20- to 30-minute walk to downtown Baltimore or a quick water-taxi ride across the harbor.

RESTAURANTS

Aldo's Ristorante Italiano $$$
306 S. High St.
Baltimore
(410) 727-0700
www.aldositaly.com

If you want to splurge on a wonderful Italian meal in an inspiring setting, Aldo's is a fine place to do it. Step inside and you'll see why it's considered the most beautiful restaurant in Little Italy. The dining room is outfitted with soaring columns, glorious high ceilings, and intricate woodwork, much of it carved by chef/owner Aldo Vitale. The chef hails from the Calabria region of southern Italy and infuses light, Mediterranean cooking traditions into many of his dishes. If you're in the mood for a little indulgence, however, look past the light and healthy seafood dishes and feast on Aldo's Tournedos Rossini, a decadent combination of grilled filet mignon, seared Hudson Valley foie gras, Italian black truffle, porcini, and wild mushroom sauce, served with four-cheese risotto. It's open for dinner nightly. Men should note that jackets are required.

Amicci's $$
231 S. High St.
Baltimore
(410) 528-1096
www.amiccis.com

This friendly, laid-back Italian restaurant lacks the formality you'll find in other Little Italy hot spots. The food is simple, fresh, and reasonably priced; there's not much on the dinner menu that's priced above $18. Choose from classic Italian favorites and comfort foods like lasagna, chicken parmigiana, and house-made gnocchi. Pastas come served with classic sauces or gussied up with sautéed chicken, shrimp, and fresh veggies. Families will also feel right at home in this kid-friendly eatery.

Della Notte $$$
801 Eastern Ave.
Baltimore
(410) 837-5500
www.dellanotte.com

A popular draw in Baltimore's renowned Little Italy neighborhood, Della Notte features classic Italian cuisine made from the finest veal, poultry, and seafood. The restaurant's diverse menu also offers hearty dishes such as filet mignon,

lamb shanks, and Chesapeake Bay rockfish. Breads and desserts are made fresh on the premises. Another bonus: Della Notte offers free parking, a rarity in Little Italy! Reservations are recommended on weekends.

Helen's Garden Café $$$
2908 O'Donnell St.
Baltimore
(410) 276-2233
www.helensgarden.com

Helen's is the place to go in the Canton neighborhood for salads, sandwiches, pasta dishes, and other light lunch fare. For dinner, you'll find a tantalizing assortment of meat dishes like curried salmon, pork chops au poivre, and Greek shrimp, with dozens of complementary wines available by the glass. The space is charming and inviting, furnished with eclectic pieces of art.

MaMa's on the Half Shell $$$
2901 O'Donnell St.
Baltimore
(410) 276-3160

If you're prowling for fresh seafood, MaMa's should be on your radar screen. While the shrimp are succulent and the crab cakes are packed with as much meat as you could hope for, the real draw is the ice-cold jumbo-size oysters. Sit outside on the patio and savor the flavors of the Chesapeake, best when washed down with a local beer. MaMa's is located in the Camden neighborhood, an easy cab ride from downtown.

Nacho Mama's $$
2907 O'Donnell St.
Baltimore
(410) 675-0898
nachomamascanton.com

For Mexican fare served in a fun, festive atmosphere, stop by this Canton bistro, which adds a Baltimore twist to southwestern classics. Quesadillas are stuffed with shrimp, artichokes, and, of course, jumbo lump crab meat. Mexican favorites like tacos, fajitas, and chimichangas are hot sellers, while other diners opt for Mama's classic meatloaf or chipotle-seasoned barbecued baby back ribs. Come during happy hour and you're likely to find a crowd of locals gathered here for after-work margaritas, munching on chips served in hubcaps.

Obrycki's Crab House and Seafood Restaurant $$$
1727 E. Pratt St.
Baltimore
(410) 732-6399
www.obryckis.com

In Baltimore, everyone's got an opinion on where you should go for crabs. While some may argue that Obrycki's house-blended seasoning isn't as tasty as the traditional Old Bay seasoning, the popularity of this Fells Point eatery among locals and visitors tells a different story. The restaurant uses only the freshest local seafood, which limits it to seasonal (Mar through Nov) operations. If cracking into a crab isn't for you, you can also feast on crab cakes and other regional specialties here.

Phillips Harbor Place $$$
301 Light St.
Baltimore
(410) 685-6600
www.phillipsseafood.com

Phillips must be doing something right. A Baltimore dining destination since 1980, you'll still find long lines packed with tourists and locals during peak season. Don't leave without tasting the specialty of the house: the famous lump crab cakes, flavored with two types of mustard and the signature house seasoning. Or, for a true seafood extravaganza, feast on the all-you-can-eat seafood buffet (adjacent to the main restaurant), which includes steamed crabs and a smattering of side dishes.

Pierpoint Restaurant $$$
1822 Aliceanna St.
Baltimore
(410) 675-2080
www.pierpointrestaurant.com

Although it's been open for more than twenty years, Chef Nancy Longo's Pierpoint Restaurant remains one of the most talked-about restaurants in Baltimore. While it's ever popular with locals, Longo's culinary creations showcase Maryland's bounty, making it a great pick for visitors, too. The Fells Point eatery is cozy and intimate; it's best to make a reservation or come on a less-crowded weeknight. There's also a spectacular open kitchen, allowing diners to watch the team in action as they craft tasty concoctions like Maryland-style cioppino, pork chops, and Moroccan lamb with mango pesto.

Samos $$
600 Oldham St.
Baltimore
(410) 675-5292
www.samosrestaurant.com

Don't judge this well-loved Greektown restaurant for its plain and simple exterior; take a look instead at the long lines of locals who have named this place one of their favorites for authentic Mediterranean fare, served in a casual setting (and equally popular for takeout). Step inside the modest eatery, and you'll be greeted by the mouth-watering smell of gyros turning on a spit and warm pita bread emerging from the oven.

Washington, D.C.:
The Capital

Darley.

Civil War–era Washington, D.C., was a city of contrasts, one part bustling metropolis and one part muddy, frontier boomtown. In its drinking establishments, robust support for both the Union and the new Confederacy was voiced. Politicians and foreign visitors gathered in the ever-popular Willard Hotel to debate the merits of the states' rights. Loud arguments occasionally degenerated into fights in the Senate and House; congressmen armed with pistols and derringers walked the streets prepared to defend their beliefs.

Would-be soldiers seeing the city for the first time had differing impressions. Poor sewage and drainage systems contributed to a rising stench from the Potomac River that summer heat only magnified. And it was hard to think of a city in which pigs roamed the streets as the national capital. (One evening that summer, an army lieutenant chasing a skulker down Pennsylvania Avenue

captured his quarry when the man tripped over a cow napping in the street.) Even the Capitol was a mess. For nearly a decade, engineers, masons, and carpenters had been busy refurbishing the building; but even now, the iron dome designed to replace the original wooden model remained unfinished. And with war clouds forming, mobilization of a national army would only add to the city's transitory appearance.

Here, on March 4, 1861, a broad mix of locals and out-of-towners packed the shoulders of Pennsylvania Avenue to catch a glimpse of the tall, lanky Westerner about to be inaugurated as president. At noon, Abraham Lincoln emerged from the Willard Hotel with his white-haired, careworn predecessor, James Buchanan, and they climbed into a carriage to make the short trip to the U.S. Capitol. It loomed up behind the gathered dignitaries as if to remind them of the important national work at hand.

From the Capitol's east portico, Lincoln delivered his inaugural address to a crowd gathered below the watchful eyes of soldiers posted atop nearby buildings. In his closing remarks, the former lawyer reached out to the South, where seven states had already seceded from the Union:

> *We are not enemies, but friends. We must not be enemies . . . The mystic chords of memory, stretching from every battlefield, and patriot grave, to every living heart and hearthstone, all over this broad land, will yet swell the chorus of the Union, when again touched, as surely they will be, by the better angels of our nature.*

The April 12 Confederate bombardment of Fort Sumter, however, shattered any remaining illusions of peace. And after a Rebel Army sent thousands of Yankees fleeing back from Manassas into the capital in July, the threat of a Confederate attack on Washington took on real meaning. Union engineers went to work constructing an elaborate defensive ring around the city—one that by 1865 would include some 160 separate forts and batteries linked by rifle pits in a 37-mile arc. Only once was this ring challenged, and then not seriously. In July 1864, Jubal Early led a force of 14,000 Confederates down (north) the Shenandoah Valley, past a hastily gathered Union force at the Monocacy River, and to the

Lincoln's inaugural procession passes the Capitol gate.

Fort Sumter

northern outskirts of the city. But Early, who was really trying to divert Union troops from Petersburg, quickly retreated back onto home ground. Panicked city residents breathed a collective sigh of relief.

War changed the District. The mud and wandering farm animals remained, but Abraham Lincoln, the man who had done so much to bind the nation back together, was gone, assassinated by John Wilkes Booth within days of Robert E. Lee's surrender. His replacement, Tennessean Andrew Johnson, would soon prove to be a shadow of his predecessor.

But with the war over, thousands of soldiers were returning home—packing up tents and vacating the vast earthworks that had turned the city into an armed, itinerant camp. Black codes were gone, the Thirteenth Amendment had been passed, and free African Americans were assuming a more visible place in Washington society. Peace and hope had returned. Even the capitol dome—long the symbol of a shattered nation—had been finished.

Civil War soldiers in Washington, D.C.

Edwin M. Stanton

"The dreadful disaster of last Sunday can scarcely be mentioned," wrote Edwin M. Stanton following the Union defeat at Manassas on July 21, 1861. "The imbecility of this Administration culminated in that catastrophe—an irretrievable misfortune and national disgrace never to be forgotten. . . . the capture of Washington now seems inevitable." The gruff Stanton, an ardent Democrat and, until a few months prior to the battle at Manassas, James Buchanan's attorney general, was one of Abraham Lincoln's harshest critics in the early days of the Civil War. Six months later he was Lincoln's secretary of war, with the two eventually becoming warm friends and ironclad partners in the war to end the Rebellion.

A lawyer by trade, the bespectacled and bearded Stanton was not an easy man to like. He preferred to have his own way, suffered opposing opinions with little patience, and was unafraid to make his own feelings clear—as Lincoln was well aware. By January 1862, he was also a close friend of George B. McClellan, the reigning Army of the Potomac commander, who would prove to be more of a thorn in the side of Lincoln than Robert E. Lee. Stanton had earned notoriety in 1859 when he defended congressman Daniel Sickles (by 1861 a Union officer) in a murder case that rocked the capital. Entering a plea of "temporary insanity"—a defense never before used successfully in the United States—Stanton won an acquittal for a man who had shot his wife's lover (U.S. Attorney Philip Barton Key, son of Francis Scott Key) in broad daylight in D.C.'s Lafayette Square.

Overriding his personal opinion of Lincoln or politics in general was Stanton's love of the Union. He quickly justified the president's faith in him by straightening out a War Department riddled with corruption and left a shambles by his predecessor, Simon Cameron, whom Lincoln had deftly made ambassador to Russia. A capable and efficient administrator, Stanton banished undedicated government employees, canceled wasteful government contracts, and moved the telegraph office into the War Department offices, where he and Lincoln spent endless hours poring over reports from the field.

Between these two former lawyers, a firm partnership formed—one based on a love of law, belief in the Union, appreciation of each other's strengths, and within months, a disdain for George McClellan. Once a member of the Lincoln administration, Stanton quickly saw his old friend for what he really was—a conniving, vacillating organizer unwilling to or incapable of leading an army. Joining the voices already raised against McClellan, Stanton urged Lincoln to replace the Army of the Potomac commander. Having learned to manage his irascible secretary, the president did—but only when the time was right.

By April 1865, the partnership of Lincoln and Stanton had overseen the final Union victory. The secretary was one of those that visited the wounded president's bedside as he lay dying on April 14 and 15. And when Lincoln passed, it was a heartfelt Stanton who uttered the immortal words: "Now he belongs to the ages."

MUSEUMS AND ATTRACTIONS

African American Civil War Memorial
U St. and Vermont Ave. NW
Washington, D.C.
(202) 667-2667
www.afroamcivilwar.org

Dedicated in 1998, this memorial honors the more than 200,000 African-American soldiers who fought to preserve the Union. The centerpiece of the memorial is "Spirit of Freedom," a 10-foot statue bearing the likenesses of young black soldiers and a sailor, created by Kentucky artist Ed Hamilton. It was the first major work by an African-American sculptor to earn a place of honor on federal land in Washington, D.C. Surrounding the statue is a granite-paved plaza encircled by walls bearing the names of the men who served. The memorial is located in the Shaw neighborhood, named for Robert Gould Shaw, the white colonel who led the 54th Massachusetts Volunteer Infantry's troops, as immortalized in the movie *Glory*. Near the memorial, the African American Civil War Memorial Freedom Foundation Museum and Visitors Center (1200 U Street NW) offers further insight into the black experience during the Civil War. Admission is free.

Clara Barton National Historic Site
5801 Oxford Rd.
Glen Echo, MD
(301) 320-1410
www.nps.gov/clba

The founder of the American Red Cross first made her mark caring for wounded soldiers of the Civil War, both on and off battlefields, earning for herself the moniker "Angel of the Battlefield." A bullet nearly ended her career at Antietam. Clara Barton National Historic Site is open for guided tours daily. Admission is free.

Donald W. Reynolds Center for American Art and Portraiture
8th and F Sts. NW
Washington, D.C.
(202) 633-1000
www.reynoldscenter.org

This magnificent Greek Revival building was constructed between 1836 and 1868 to serve as the U.S. Patent Office, developed under the guidance of then-president Andrew Jackson. One of the District's earliest "tourist traps," visitors would flock to the building to view models of new gadgets and gizmos seeking patent protection. The glorious building also played host to Lincoln's second inaugural ball. Today it's an attraction once again, housing two of the Smithsonian Institution's art collections, the National Portrait Gallery and the Smithsonian American Art Museum—both of which hold significant collections of Civil War–era art. In the National Portrait Gallery's presidential portraits collection (the only complete collection, outside of the White House), there's a photograph of Lincoln taken by Alexander Gardner on a glass negative in February 1865. The negative broke, producing a crack that crosses the crown of Lincoln's head. The crack has since been interpreted as an omen for the impending assassination. Admission is free.

Ford's Theatre National Historical Site
511 10th St. NW
Washington, D.C.
(202) 347-4833
www.fordstheatre.org

There's no American theater that's quite as historic as Ford's. On April 14, 1865, President and Mrs. Lincoln joined Major Henry Reed Rathbone and Clara Harris for a performance of *Our American Cousin*. While the president and his party were seated in the presidential box, they were surprised by Confederate activist and actor John Wilkes Booth, who shot Lincoln and stabbed Rathbone before leaping to the stage in an attempt to escape. Lincoln died at 7:22 the next morning at the Petersen House, located directly across the street. The theater closed its doors immediately after the assassination and served as a warehouse, museum, and office building for 90 years before President Eisenhower authorized its restoration in 1954. Ford's reopened in 1968 and has since functioned as a working theater known for its productions of American stage classics.

If you're not able to catch a play, it's still worth the trip to see the theater itself, largely restored to the way it looked in 1865. The lower level houses a museum packed with artifacts, including Booth's .44 caliber derringer and informative displays discussing the assassination conspirators and their trials. You can also walk across the street to tour Petersen House and see the room where Lincoln died. Ford's Theatre is open daily (except during matinee performances). Admission is free.

Frederick Douglass National Historic Site
1411 W St. SE
Washington, D.C.
(202) 426-5961
www.nps.gov/frdo

The former slave who became one of the giants of the Civil War era purchased this 21-room home in 1877. Known as Cedar Hill, the historic home is located across the Anacostia River, offering a spectacular view of Washington, D.C.'s cityscape to the north. The museum offers exhibits, interpretive programs, and a film which tells the story of Douglass's life. Reopened in February 2007 following an extensive renovation, the glorious home was restored to look as it did in Douglass's day.

International Spy Museum
800 F St. NW
Washington, D.C.
(202) 393-7798
www.spymuseum.org

There's no doubt that this high-touch, high-tech museum has a post-WWII focus, but Civil War spies like Belle Boyd and Rose Greenbow do factor into a few of its exhibitions. Time-travel forward into the 20th century to see Cold War gadgets like buttonhole cameras, lipstick guns, and cipher machines, or to take part in Operation Spy, the museum's new hour-long, immersive espionage experience. Museum hours vary by season.

Library of Congress
Independence Ave. at 1st St. SE
Washington, D.C.
(202) 707-8000
www.loc.gov/visit

While the Library of Congress is the world's largest library, it's more than just a collection of books. Housed in one of Washington, D.C.'s most spectacular spaces, the Library is a treasure trove of priceless national and international artifacts. Although the exhibited items change, the Civil War is always a theme in the Library's American Treasures gallery, and researchers find it an invaluable resource for deeper investigations into pivotal events in American history. Admission is free.

Lincoln Memorial
The National Mall at 23rd St. NW
Washington, D.C.
(202) 426-6841
www.nps.gov/linc

If you only have time to visit one memorial in Washington, D.C., make it this powerful tribute to the president who worked to keep the country together during the tumultuous war. It's symbolically located across the Memorial Bridge from Arlington National Cemetery, where Robert E. Lee's plantation home looms in the distance, representing the reunion of the two sides. In another symbolic gesture, the memorial's 36 columns represent the 36 states that

were reunited at the time of the assassination. Read a passage from the Gettysburg Address on one side of the marble temple and an excerpt from Lincoln's Second Inaugural Address on the other. Admission is free.

National Archives Building
700 Pennsylvania Ave. NW (entrance on Constitution Ave. between 7th and 9th Sts. NW)
Washington, D.C.
(202) 357-5000
www.archives.gov

While the National Archives is best known as the home of the original Declaration of Independence, the Constitution, and the Bill of Rights, the National Archives is a must-see for anyone conducting Civil War research. It's here that you'll find draft records, court-martial case files, photographs, and key pieces of correspondence, including a recently uncovered letter from Lincoln to his general-in-chief Henry Halleck in 1863 suggesting that if General George Meade could follow up his victory at Gettysburg with another defeat of Robert E. Lee and his southern troops, the war would be brought to an end. Admission is free.

National Museum of American History
14th St. and Constitution Ave. NW
Washington, D.C.
(202) 633-1000
http://americanhistory.si.edu

Also known as "America's Attic," this popular Smithsonian Institution museum houses artifacts of U.S. history, pop culture, politics, technology, and more. American military history, along with social history and presidential lore, are themes that show up in various parts of the vast collection. Admission is free.

National Museum of Health and Medicine
6900 Georgia Ave. NW
Washington, D.C.
(202) 782-2200
www.nmhm.washingtondc.museum

What's now a repository for medical artifacts, anatomical and pathological specimens, and other health-related materials started in 1862 as the Army Medical Museum, designed to help improve medical procedures and conditions during the Civil War. The museum still operates as part of the Armed Forces Institute of Pathology, but its focus has expanded beyond battlefield medicine to include civilian artifacts and exhibitions on timely medical topics. True to its roots, there's still a significant collection of Civil War relics, including the bullet that killed Abraham Lincoln and the probe used in his autopsy. You'll also find a shattered leg bone from Major General Daniel Sickles, who famously murdered Francis Scott Key's son, Philip Barton, in a crime of passion in 1859. Sickles was acquitted of the crime in the first successful application of the "temporary insanity" defense. When war broke out in the aftermath, he joined the army to clean up his tarnished reputation. He was struck by a cannonball at Gettysburg and donated his mangled leg to the Army Medical Museum. The major general reportedly visited the specimen every year on the anniversary of the amputation, and some say that his ghost continues to visit today. Admission is free.

Renwick Gallery of Art

17th St. and Pennsylvania Ave. NW
Washington, D.C.
(202) 633-7970
http://americanart.si.edu

Now one of the Smithsonian Institution's repositories of American art, the Renwick Gallery served as a supply depot for Union forces from 1861 through 1864 and as headquarters for General Montgomery C. Meigs, army quartermaster, in 1865. Magnificent paintings and crafts hang where uniforms, tents, and other essentials were once meted out to soldiers on their way to fight in Virginia.

U.S. Capitol

1st St. between Independence and Constitution Aves.
Washington, D.C.
(202) 226-8000
www.aoc.gov

During the Civil War, the Capitol was more than just a meeting place for senators and congressmen. It was used by Union forces as a barracks for about 4,000 troops, a hospital, and even a bakery where bakers made about 16,000 loaves of bread each day. Today, it's better known for its official function as a meeting, working, and debating place for members of Congress. All visitors must join a ticketed, guided tour to view the Capitol's interior. Complimentary tickets are distributed at the Capitol Guide Service kiosk (near the intersection of First Street and Independence Avenue SW) beginning at 9 a.m. Mon through Sat. Admission is free.

Washington Monument

Constitution Ave. and 15th St. NW
Washington, D.C.
(202) 426-6841

When war broke out between the States, the 555⅛-foot tall Washington Monument was nearly a third complete, although construction had begun in 1848. Demand for building supplies, funds, and able-bodied troops brought construction of the delay-plagued monument to a halt. Construction resumed in 1876, and the monument was completed in 1888, but thanks to the long delays, the marble on the bottom third of the obelisk was taken from a different level in the quarry. As a result, it's a different color. Free tickets are required to ride to the top of the monument; they are distributed beginning at 8:30 a.m. at the ticket kiosk on 15th Street. The monument is open from 9 a.m. to 5 p.m. daily, with the last tour beginning at 4:45 p.m. Admission is free.

The White House

1600 Pennsylvania Ave. NW
Washington, D.C.
(202) 456-1414
www.whitehouse.gov

At the time of the Civil War, the White House looked different than it does today. In fact, it wasn't even officially called the White House. That name was formally bestowed on the presidential residence during the Theodore Roosevelt administration. The mansion was much smaller and quite crowded with the Lincolns and their young family. Conditions were also much less sanitary; sewage emptied onto the Ellipse, fueling diseases like smallpox and typhoid, which claimed the life of Lincoln's son, Willie. The White House Visitors Center, located at 14th Street and Pennsylvania Avenue, NW, sheds some light on the building's history and its role in the Civil War. Touring the building itself requires advance arrangements; contact your Congress member up to six months in advance to inquire about tours, which are available Tues through Sat for groups of 10 or more. Admission is free.

STATUES, SQUARES, AND OTHER SITES OF INTEREST

Admiral David G. Farragut Memorial

Farragut Square
17th and K Sts. NW
Washington, D.C.

Washingtonians know Farragut Square as one of the busiest office districts, home to two bustling Metro lines. The 10-foot statue that sits at the middle of the square honors Rear Admiral David G. Farragut, whose heroics led to the Union's

✳ ✳ ✳ ✳ ✳ ✳ ✳ ✳ ✳ ✳ ✳ ✳ ✳ ✳ ✳ ✳

capture of New Orleans and Mobile Bay. Vinnie Ream Hoxie, the creator of the statue, was the first female sculptor to be commissioned by the U.S. government.

Blair House
1651-53 Pennsylvania Ave. NW
Washington, D.C.

Located directly across the street from the White House on the most protected block of Pennsylvania Avenue, Blair House is best known as the home-away-from-home for foreign heads of state and royalty on official state visits. It's not open to the public, but Civil War buffs may want to stroll past this house for its historic significance. It's here where Robert E. Lee turned down Lincoln advisor Francis P. Blair's offer to command the Union troops, vowing his allegiance to his home state of Virginia instead.

Fort Dupont Park
Minnesota Ave. and Randle Circle SE
Washington, D.C.
(202) 426-7745
www.nps.gov/nace/ftdupont.htm

Fort Dupont was established in 1861 by Union forces as a means of protecting the 11th Street Bridge, an important link between the Southeast neighborhood of Anacostia and the capital city itself. No battle was fought here, but the fort gained some notoriety as a safe haven for runaway slaves. Little remains of the fort today, but you can still see its earthworks in the 376-acre Anacostia park that shares its name. The park's Activity Center is open Mon through Fri; the park is open from sunup to sundown.

General George B. McClellan Monument
Connecticut Ave. and California St. NW
Washington, D.C.

Near Washington, D.C.'s Adams Morgan neighborhood, there's a statue of McClellan, the Union commander who faltered during the Peninsula Campaign, then emerged victorious at Antietam. Despite his victory, tactical errors caused Lincoln to question his judgment and eventually relieve him of his command. McClellan also had a mixed showing in his political career; he ran unsuccessfully against Lincoln for the presidency in 1864 but served as governor of New Jersey from 1878 to 1881. In his memorial statue, designed by Frederick MacMonnies and dedicated in 1907, he sits atop a horse, overlooking Connecticut Avenue.

General John Alexander Logan Statue
Logan Circle, Vermont Ave. at 13th and P Sts. NW
Washington, D.C.

A traffic circle in one of the District's trendiest residential areas is named for General John Alexander Logan. In the center of the circle there's a bronze equestrian statue of Logan, dedicated in 1901. Logan fought with distinction in some of the war's biggest battles—Manassas, Vicksburg, and Atlanta—before losing a bid for the vice presidency in 1884.

General Philip Sheridan Monument
Sheridan Circle
Massachusetts Ave. and 23rd St. NW
Washington, D.C.

Surrounded by some of Washington, D.C.'s finest embassies and diplomatic addresses, this equestrian statue was crafted by Gutzon Borglum, best known for his sculptures at Mount Rushmore. The Union commander led the Cavalry Corps of the Army of the Potomac in the East, pursuing Robert E. Lee and forcing his surrender at Appomattox.

General William Tecumseh Sherman Monument
Sherman Square
15th St. and Pennsylvania Ave. NW
Washington, D.C.

Sherman served valiantly under Grant at the Battle of Vicksburg and then took Grant's place as Union commander in the western theater of the war. He led troops to capture Atlanta in September 1864, ensuring Lincoln's reelection. Afterwards, his armies embarked on a devastating march through Georgia and the Carolinas. He's commemorated in a mounted statue in a small park nestled between the White House Ellipse and the Department of the Treasury.

General Winfield Hancock Scott Memorial
Pennsylvania Ave. at 7th St.
Washington, D.C.

Dedicated in 1896, this statue honors General Scott, best known for his triumph over Robert E. Lee at Gettysburg. Considered one of the most capable commanders of all time, Scott is also credited with developing the Union's Anaconda Plan, which brought down the Confederacy.

Major General George C. Meade Monument
Pennsylvania Ave. and 3rd St. NW
Washington, D.C.

George Meade is credited with orchestrating Lee's defeat at Gettysburg. By positioning his troops for defensive attacks on the left, right, and center, he successfully fended off Pickett's Charge. The marble monument, crafted by Charles A. Grafly, was dedicated in 1927.

Major General James B. McPherson Monument

McPherson Square, Vermont Ave. between 15th and K Sts. NW
Washington, D.C.

Constructed from a seized cannon by Louis Rebisso, this equestrian statue honors McPherson, Ulysses S. Grant's chief engineer, who commanded the army of Tennessee and faltered near Atlanta. It was dedicated in 1876.

The Peace Monument

Pennsylvania Ave. at 1st St. NW
Washington, D.C.

Built to honor U.S. Navy casualties in the Civil War, this 44-foot marble statue and fountain sits in front of the U.S. Capitol. It was sculpted by Franklin Simmons in 1877. Facing west, toward the National Mall, a female figure representing Grief hides her face on the shoulder of another female figure, representing History. In her hands, History clutches a stylus and tablet reading "They died that their country might live." Below Grief and History, another female figure, Victory, holds a laurel wreath and oak branch, symbolizing strength. Mars and Neptune, representing War and the Sea, sit just below. A final female figure, Peace, looks out toward the Capitol.

The Rock Creek Park Forts

Rock Creek Park
3545 Williamsburg Lane NW
Washington, D.C.
(202) 895-6000
www.nps.gov/rocr

Washington, D.C.'s vast urban playground is home to the remains of forts that once protected the capital city. At Fort Stevens (13th and Quackenbos Streets, NW), Jubal A. Early's Southern forces took on the Union defenders in 1864 as federal notables, including Abraham Lincoln, looked on. Just north of the fort, Battlefield National Cemetery is the final resting place of the 41 Union soldiers who died defending the fort. There's nothing left at Fort Reno (Belt Road and Chesapeake Street NW), but, as the highest point in the city, the grounds do open up to an incredible view. Also nearby: Ford DeRussey (Oregon Avenue and Military Road NW) and Fort Bayard (Western Avenue and River Road). You can find some parts of the forts still standing at Fort Slocum Park (Kansas Avenue, Blair Road, and Milmarson Place NE), Fort Totten (Fort Totten Drive, south of Riggs Road), and Battery Kemble Park (Chain Bridge Road, MacArthur Boulevard, 49th Street, and Nebraska Avenue).

Ulysses S. Grant Memorial

Union Square, 1st St. NW
Washington, D.C.
(202) 426-6841

Set against the backdrop of the U.S. Capitol, this striking tribute to Grant was sculpted by Henry Shrady and dedicated in 1922. The statue itself—the largest equestrian statue in the country and the second largest in the world—was modeled after a sketch that Grant drew of a soldier from Massachusetts after the battle at Spotsylvania Court House, surveying the National Mall to the west.

Washington Arsenal Site

4th and P Sts. NW
Washington, D.C.

Now home to Fort McNair, the Arsenal was used to ship supplies to battle sites in Virginia. John Wilkes Booth and his co-conspirators were brought here after Lincoln's assassination, where they were later tried and hanged.

TOURS

Cultural Tourism DC (www.culturaltourismdc.org) acts as an umbrella group for many of Washington, D.C.'s small museums and neighborhood heritage sites, many of which are listed in this guide. Walking tours and bus tours of Washington, D.C.'s Civil War heritage sites are occasionally available; you can also download a copy of Cultural Tourism DC's "Civil War to Civil Rights" walking tour route in downtown D.C.

Gray Line (www.grayline.com) offers regular day-long tours of Gettysburg departing from downtown Washington, D.C.

ACCOMMODATIONS

Adams Inn $$–$$$$
1744 Lanier Place NW
Washington, D.C.
(202) 745-3600
(800) 578-6807
www.adamsinn.com

This cheery, comfortable inn is popular with family travelers, backpackers, and even business travelers—and with good reason. The rooms are clean, neatly furnished, and very affordable. Fifteen of the inn's 25 guest rooms come with private bath, and all guests enjoy continental breakfast, high-speed Internet, and laundry privileges. The surrounding Adams Morgan neighborhood serves up some of the city's best international cuisine, along with fun and festive nightlife.

**Chester A. Arthur House Bed and Breakfast
at Logan Circle** $$$$
13th and P St.
Washington, D.C.
(202) 328 3510
(877) 893-3233
www.chesterarthurhouse.com

Civil War buffs will feel right at home at the Chester Arthur House, which is located on a circle named for Major General John Logan. An equine statue of the man credited as the inspiration behind Memorial Day overlooks the area. One may care little for Logan (who was probably the best of Lincoln's political generals) or Chester A. Arthur (the inn's namesake and the nation's 21st president), but the gracious comfort and beautiful decor of this 1883 townhouse will win anyone over. The inn's location and guest-room rates are excellent. But there are just three rooms, so call well in advance.

The Dupont Hotel $$$$
1500 New Hampshire Ave. NW
Washington, D.C.
(202) 483-6000
(800) 423-6953
www.doylecollection.com

You can't beat this hotel's fantastic Dupont Circle location. There are shops, restaurants, art galleries, and coffeehouses on every corner, along with glorious Beaux Arts buildings. The hotel was renovated, and rooms are clean, comfortable, and outfitted with all of the services you'd expect at a business hotel. It's part of the Irish-owned Doyle Collection.

The Georgetown Inn $$$$
1310 Wisconsin Ave. NW
Washington, D.C.
(202) 333-8900
(888) 587-2388
www.georgetowncollection.com

If you're coming to Washington, D.C., to soak up some history, you may want to stay in Georgetown, a neighborhood that found itself greatly divided during the Civil War. Land-holding gentry with roots in the South sympathized with their slave-holding counterparts even as federal officials struggled to hold the Union together. This 96-room inn sits in the center of Georgetown's dining, shopping, and nightlife district. Guests can expect a comfortable stay with complimentary coffee and newspaper, and valet parking.

The Hay-Adams Hotel $$$$
16th and H Sts. NW
Washington, D.C.
(202) 638-6600
(800) 853-6807
www.hayadams.com

A member of the Leading Hotels of the World, this opulent historic property is named for John Hay, Lincoln's personal assistant and secretary of state under William McKinley and Theodore Roosevelt, and author Henry Adams, a descendant of the noted political family. In 1884, Hay and Adams bought adjoining lots at 16th and H Streets on the site of the present-day hotel. The homes were later razed and, in 1927–1928, an Italian Renaissance–styled apartment hotel was constructed on the site. Outfitted with posh amenities like kitchens, elevators, and an air-conditioned dining room, the Hay-Adams House became the hotel of choice for traveling notables like Charles Lindbergh, Amelia Earhart, and Ethel Barrymore.

The Henley Park Hotel $$$–$$$$
926 Massachusetts Ave. NW
Washington, D.C.
(202) 638-5200
(800) 222-8474
www.henleypark.com

Opened in 1918 as a luxury apartment building, the Henley Park was once home to famous Washingtonians like senators and congressmen. Today, this charming Victorian inn is a favorite of European travelers. Rooms are a bit dated, but its location near the Washington Convention Center puts the Henley Park in one of the most desirable locations in town. The on-site restaurant, Coeur de Lion, is also a draw, and the adjacent Blue Bar is a sure bet for mellow live entertainment. Guests enjoy amenities like express check-in, minibars, and health club privileges. Because it's located so close to the Washington Convention Center, rates are always higher during big conventions.

Hotel Harrington $$$–$$$$
11th and E Sts. NW
Washington, D.C.
(202) 628-8140
(800) 424-8532
www.hotel-harrington.com

This no-frills, basic hotel is ideally located in the heart of downtown, just a few blocks from the National Mall, the White House, and the Penn Quarter arts and entertainment district.

Hotel Lombardy $$$$
2019 Pennsylvania Ave. NW
Washington, D.C.
(202) 828-2600
(800) 424-5486
www.hotellombardy.com

It's nothing fancy, but this inn-like hotel's central location puts it within walking distance of Georgetown, Dupont Circle, and the White House, along with a couple of Metro stations. Rooms are equipped with kitchenettes, minibars, and other amenities.

Hotel Monaco $$$$
700 F St. NW
Washington, D.C.
(202) 628-7177
(800) 649-1202
www.monaco-dc.com

The landmark 1842 Tariff Building that once housed the nation's first General Post Office is now the stunning, 183-room Hotel Monaco. Operated by the Kimpton Hotel Group, the Monaco blends the building's historic character and classic marble elements with chic, stylish, and colorful decor. During the Civil War, the hotel's Paris Ballroom is believed to have been used as an operating room for wounded soldiers; guests and event-goers have reported hearing whispered voices that linger to this day. While there's scant evidence to support these claims, there's no doubt that many a distraught bride and mother came here to await news of her loved one's whereabouts. While the building was undergoing renovation between 2001 and 2003, a construction worker reported seeing the figure of a woman in Civil War attire anxiously pacing in the building's courtyard. Like Washington, D.C.'s other Kimpton hotels, the Monaco warmly welcomes pets (and even lets you borrow a goldfish for companionship, if you like), and offers a complimentary wine hour.

Maison Orleans Bed and Breakfast $$$$
414 5th St. SE
Washington, D.C.
(202) 544-3694
www.bbonline.com/dc/maisonorleans

Just six blocks from the Capitol, Library of Congress, and many of the capital's best restaurants and attractions, Maison Orleans is a relaxing and unique oasis in the heart the city. Rates are fair and the ambience is cozy, but there are just three rooms—in addition to furnished one-bedroom and studio apartments.

The Melrose Hotel $$$$
2430 Pennsylvania Ave. NW
Washington, D.C.
(202) 955-6400
(800) MELROSE
www.melrosehoteldc.com

It's easy to feel at home here. After all, this West End hotel is another D.C. hotel fashioned out of a former apartment building. The Melrose's rooms are cheery and spacious, decorated with classic and contemporary touches. There's a Metro station right around the corner, and Georgetown and Dupont Circle are just a few blocks away.

Morrison-Clark Inn $$$–$$$$
11th St. and Massachusetts Ave. NW
Washington, D.C.
(202) 898-1200
(800) 332-7898
www.morrisonclark.com

Like its sister property, the Henley Park, the Morrison-Clark is a gracious Victorian property just blocks from the Washington Convention Center. Rooms are charming, if a little tired, and outfitted with modern amenities like free wireless Internet, data ports, and complimentary newspapers. The Morrison-Clark Restaurant is a popular choice for romantic dinners, and the hotel's garden room and courtyard are well suited for weddings.

The Willard InterContinental Washington $$$$

1401 Pennsylvania Ave. NW
Washington, D.C.
(202) 628-9100
(800) 827-1747
www.washington.intercontinental.com

There's no hotel in the nation's capital that boasts quite as rich a history as the Willard. In February 1861, representatives from 21 of the 34 states met at the Willard in an effort to avert the pending war. A plaque on the hotel's Pennsylvania Avenue entrance honors these valiant efforts. Amid countless assassination threats, Lincoln was smuggled into the hotel after his election and prior to his inauguration in March 1861. His folio is on view in the history gallery. During the Civil War, the hotel was a gathering place for both Union and Confederate sympathizers. As a guest at the hotel, Julia Ward Howe wrote the "Battle Hymn of the Republic" as she listened to Union troops march past her window, playing "John Brown's Body." Actor John Wilkes Booth also frequented the Willard, making several visits in the weeks leading up to the Lincoln assassination. Legend has it that Ulysses S. Grant coined the term "lobbyist" here, referring to the favor-seekers who bothered him as he savored cigars and brandy in the hotel lobby. Outfitted with all of the posh amenities you'd expect in a fine luxury hotel, the Willard is located next to the White House and footsteps from the National Mall.

Windsor Park Hotel $$$

2116 Kalorama Rd. NW
Washington, D.C.
(202) 483-7700
(800) 247-3064
www.windsorparkhotel.com

If the price doesn't attract you to this pleasant, family-friendly inn, the proximity to Washington, D.C.'s eclectic Adams Morgan and Dupont Circle neighborhoods should. The hotel's 43 simply furnished guest rooms come with a small refrigerator, newspaper, and complimentary continental breakfast.

Woodley Park Guest House $$$$

2647 Woodley Rd., NW
Washington, D.C.
(202) 667-0218
(866) 667-0218
www.woodleyparkguesthouse.com

Formerly known as the Connecticut-Woodley Guest House, this elegant, recently renovated district inn blends modern amenities (central air-conditioning, high-speed Web access, etc.) with the comfortable look of antiques in its 18 rooms and suites, at reasonable rates for its location. The owners also do their part to foster a sense of community; there's always someone lingering in the kitchen for a chat, and all of the works of art that adorn the walls were created by former guests.

RESTAURANTS

Ben's Chili Bowl $

1213 U St. NW
Washington, D.C.
(202) 667-0909
www.benschilibowl.com

Ben's Chili Bowl doesn't have any strong Civil War connections, apart from its proximity to the African American Civil War Memorial. Nevertheless, no Washington, D.C., dining guide would be complete without it. Opened in 1958, Ben's has weathered neighborhood riots and decay and still it manages to attract throngs of customers for its signature dish: the chili half-smoke (that's half hot dog, half sausage, served on a bun and doused in chili, onions, and mustard). Wash it down with a creamy homemade milkshake. You'll find urban hipsters, government staffers, and longtime neighborhood residents gathered here.

Bistrot du Coin $–$$

1738 Connecticut Ave. NW
Washington, D.C.
(202) 234-6969
www.bistrotducoin.com

It's nothing fancy, but locals love this lively Dupont Circle bistro. It's open every day—including Thanksgiving and Christmas—and always seems to draw an eclectic crowd of young and old, gay and straight diners from the neighborhood and beyond. Feast on steamed mussels, decadent tartines, hanger steaks, and other French and Belgian classics.

Blue Duck Tavern $$–$$$$
Park Hyatt Washington
1201 24th St. NW
Washington, D.C.
(202) 419-6755
www.blueducktavern.com

Chef Brian McBride has proven himself to be a master of regional cuisine at Blue Duck Tavern, which made a splash in the Washington, D.C., dining scene when it opened. Tasty creations like pork loin with bourbon-soaked peaches, rabbit terrine, delectable crab cakes, and thick-cut fries cooked in duck fat, and homemade desserts like hand-churned ice cream and flamed chocolate bourbon pie have made it a crowd favorite. While the food is divine, the open kitchen is enough to make any chef turn green with envy.

Brasserie Beck $$–$$$$
1101 K St. NW
Washington, D.C.
(202) 408-1717
www.beckdc.com

There's a delightful trend in many of Washington, D.C.'s top new restaurants: Notable chefs are serving exquisite food in a comfortable, casual setting at reasonable prices. Brasserie Beck is a prime example. Chef Robert Wiedmaier earned acclaim among fine dining aficionados during a stint at Aquarelle at the Watergate before opening Marcel's, his own restaurant, in the Foggy Bottom neighborhood. His second venture, Brasserie Beck, serves casual French and Belgian fare in a bistro setting. If the cuisine doesn't bowl you over—and the housemade sausages and seasoned steamed mussels likely will—then the beer menu may be your downfall. True to his French-Belgian roots, Wiedmaier has a beer sommelier on staff and serves up an ever-changing lineup of more than 50 Belgian beers.

Clyde's of Georgetown $$–$$$
3236 M St. NW
Washington, D.C.
202-333-9180
www.clydes.com

Clyde's is a Washington, D.C.–area favorite with locations in Georgetown, downtown, and in the Maryland and Virginia suburbs. You can count on consistently good American fare made from fresh, local ingredients and served in a casual, distinctly American setting. Burgers, salads, chicken sandwiches, and crab cakes are always on the menu, but you can expect lighter salads and berry-laden desserts in the summer months and heartier stews in the colder months. There's another D.C. location in Chinatown at 7th and G Streets NW.

Filomena $$$$
1063 Wisconsin Ave. NW
Washington, D.C.
(202) 338-8800
(888) FILOMENA
www.filomena.com

When you pass by this quaint Georgetown eatery, you're apt to see the "pasta mamas" at work in the window preparing fresh noodles and stuffed pastas. It's a hint of what's to come inside the restaurant—fresh Italian creations and a cozy, homelike atmosphere. Bill and Hillary Clinton were known to dine here during their White House days.

Kinkead's $$$–$$$
2000 Pennsylvania Ave. NW
Washington, D.C.
(202) 296-7700
www.kinkead.com

If you love seafood and aren't afraid to pay a little more for fine preparation, great ambience, and perhaps even some celebrity-spotting, make a reservation at Kinkead's. Though it opened more than a decade ago, Kinkead's still draws crowds. Regional delicacies like soft-shell crabs and skate wings are must-tries, and even New Englanders will appreciate Boston-born chef Robert Kinkead's take on the lobster roll.

Lauriol Plaza $$$–$$$$
1835 18th St. NW
Washington, D.C.
(202) 387-0035
www.lauriolplaza.com

Lauriol Plaza is a longtime favorite for fresh Mexican cuisine. The zesty grilled fajitas and cheesy enchiladas are consistently good and the margaritas never disappoint, but the real draw here is the huge upstairs patio. Overlooking 18th Street between Dupont Circle and Adams Morgan, it's a popular gathering spot on breezy afternoons and warm evenings.

Lebanese Taverna $
2641 Connecticut Ave. NW
Washington, D.C.
(202) 265-8681
www.lebanesetaverna.com

Lebanese Taverna is another Washington, D.C., institution. It started as a single restaurant in Washington, D.C.'s Woodley Park neighborhood but has since expanded to additional locations in Virginia and Maryland. The family-owned Middle Eastern restaurant is always a sure bet for tasty moussaka, kebabs, shwarma, and plenty of vegetarian favorites.

Martin's Tavern $$–$$$$
1264 Wisconsin Ave. NW
Washington, D.C.
(202) 333-7370
www.martins-tavern.com

History buffs love Billy Martin's Tavern, the oldest establishment of its kind in Georgetown. Opened in 1933, the Martin family is now on its fourth generation of restaurant owners. It's here that John F. Kennedy proposed to Jackie in Booth #3, while Richard Nixon preferred Booth #2. Lyndon Johnson and Alger Hiss were also regulars, as was Madeleine Albright. You won't be disappointed by the traditional American dishes nor the lively mix of tourists and neighborhood residents that pack the restaurant most nights of the week. It's open daily for lunch and dinner.

The Monocle $$$$
107 D St. NE
Washington, D.C.
(202) 546-4488
www.themonocle.com

A favorite of members of Congress and other Capitol employees, this family-owned, downtown Washington institution was the first white-tablecloth restaurant on Capitol Hill. Though new competitors have entered the marketplace, it's still a favorite, serving up traditional American dishes in an elegant dining room or more casual bar. Try the signature roast beef sandwiches; it's easy to see why John F. Kennedy would order them for special delivery to the White House.

The Occidental $$$$
1475 Pennsylvania Ave. NW
Washington, D.C.
(202) 783-1475
www.occidentaldc.com

This 100-year-old restaurant is steeped in history. Next door, there's the Willard Hotel, and the White House sits just beyond. Inside, the restaurant is decorated with black-and-white photos of the presidents, politicos, and celebrities who have dined at The Occidental throughout the century. You'd expect to find fine American fare on the menu, and you won't be disappointed . . . nor will you be bored. Chef Rodney Scruggs works wonders with natural, locally procured ingredients to make delicious dishes like duck breast served with homemade spaetzle and braised rabbit ragu.

Old Ebbitt Grill $$–$$$$
675 15th St. NW
Washington, D.C.
(202) 347-4800
www.ebbitt.com

Established in 1856, Old Ebbitt Grill owns the distinction of being Washington, D.C.'s oldest restaurant. Although it no longer operates out of its original home, its classic furnishings and location just two blocks from the White House give it a historic feel. The restaurant prides itself on offering a fantastic oyster bar, though you also won't go wrong with tasty crab cakes, trout crusted with parmesan cheese, and homemade pastas and soups. It's known as a power breakfast spot during the week.

1789 $$$$
1226 36th St. NW
Washington, D.C.
(202) 965-1789
www.1789restaurant.com

If your historical tastes run into the Federal period as well, reserve a table at 1789. Fashioned after an elegant country inn, 1789 was named for the year in which nearby Georgetown University was founded. The cozy two-story row house is intimate and romantic; don't be surprised to see a marriage proposal or an anniversary celebration happening at the table next to you. Executive chef Nathan Beauchamp, voted the metro area's top rising culinary star by the Restaurant Association Metropolitan Washington, crafts masterful American fare from ingredients like pheasant, lobster, lamb, and crabs.

Spices Asian Restaurant & Sushi Bar $$
3333-A Connecticut Ave. NW
Washington, D.C.
(202) 686-3833
www.spicesdc.com

If your travels take you to Washington, D.C.'s Cleveland Park neighborhood—and a tour of Civil War forts very well might—treat yourself to a bite at Spices. In true Pan-Asian spirit, the restaurant serves tasty sushi, tempting curries, tasty pad thai, and classic Chinese dishes, all at affordable prices.

The White Tiger $–$$$
301 Massachusetts Ave. NE
Washington, D.C.
(202) 546-5900
www.whitetigerdc.com

There's a lot to like about this Capitol Hill eatery, which fo-
cuses on northern Indian creations. Flavorful biryanis and
tandoori dishes are served on gold platters, and, as you'd ex-
pect in an Indian restaurant, there are ample vegetarian op-
tions. In the summer, diners flock to the outdoor patio, which
twinkles with white lights. One of the most attractive things
about this neighborhood favorite: the prices.

Wok 'N Roll $–$$
604 H St. NW
Washington, D.C.
(202) 347-4656
www.wokandrolldc.com

There's a good reason we're including a quirky Chinatown
restaurant with a funny name among our picks. In 1865,
Mary Surratt operated a boardinghouse in the building that
now houses Wok 'N Roll. It's here that John Wilkes Booth met
Surratt's son, John, and other conspirators in the plot to assassinate the president. Many of the restaurant's patrons
don't know the building's significance; they're here for the
extensive menu of Chinese and Japanese creations, refreshing bubble teas, and sushi during happy hour.

Northeastern Virginia: Borderland

Darley.

Union soldiers at Arlington House; Civil War photographer Matthew Brady is wearing the top hat.

In late April 1861, only the murky waters of the Potomac River separated what was left of the old Union from the fledgling Confederate States of America. From the window of his Arlington home, Robert E. Lee could look out at Abraham Lincoln's White House and ponder his own decision to turn his back on the nation he had served so long.

On April 22, Lee left his longtime home forever, and traveled to Richmond to accept command of Virginia's state forces. His wife soon followed, and as Union war preparations continued, Yankee officers turned the historic Arlington House into a headquarters building. In 1864, quartermaster General Montgomery C. Meigs authorized the burial of fallen Union soldiers on the grounds of Lee's former home—the first of some 20,000 Civil War soldiers to be buried in what became Arlington National Cemetery.

The extension of Washington's fort system into Fairfax County strengthened the Union hold on Northern Virginia territory, which was by September 1861 incorporated into the Union Department of the Potomac. A Confederate Department of Northern Virginia (incorporating the short-lived Department of Alexandria) also existed, although the Union presence south of the Potomac extended its parameters as far south as Manassas and the peninsula.

Alexandria, soon to be the home of Fort Ward, inspired particular anger among Unionists during the Federal occupation of that town on May 24, 1861. After removing a Confederate flag from the roof of the Marshall House Hotel, 24-year-old Colonel Elmer Ellsworth was shot to death by the establishment's owner. A close friend of President Lincoln's, Ellsworth was mourned as the Union's first casualty of the war.

Marshall House Hotel, Alexandria

Confederate Personality: Robert E. Lee

Few military commanders have ever inspired the kind of loyalty, even worship, that Army of Northern Virginia soldiers felt for their beloved "Marse Robert." The son of Revolutionary War hero Henry "Light Horse Harry" Lee, Robert E. Lee was born in Westmoreland County, Virginia, in 1807, grew up in Alexandria, and entered West Point in 1825. After a series of stops at U.S. Army posts, Lee got the chance (along with dozens of former classmates and future enemies) to prove his mettle on the rugged battlefields of Mexico.

General Robert E. Lee

While General Winfield Scott further cemented his American-hero status with his 1847 Mexico City Campaign, Lee established himself as perhaps Scott's finest junior officer with his daring and smarts. Lee learned much from his superior, but as he returned to the drudgery of peacetime army life, did not figure to use those lessons anytime soon. After a three-year stint as superintendent of West Point, Lee received a bump up to lieutenant colonel and command of the 2nd U.S. Cavalry in Texas. His direction of the U.S. Marines' capture of John Brown in 1859 (Lee happened to be in the nation's capital at the time) interrupted his otherwise mostly uninteresting stint on the frontier.

With civil war approaching, Lee remained in U.S. Army blue; he even accepted a promotion in March 1861 to command of the 1st U.S. Cavalry. But while Lee opposed secession, he could not bring himself to lead an army against his home state; if Virginia was for the South, then so was Lee. On April 18, he declined Scott's offer of command of Union armies; on the 20th he resigned his commission.

The man whose name would soon echo across the continent began his Confederate service on a relatively low rung, as commander of Virginia's state forces. He was serving as a military advisor to Confederate president Jefferson Davis in June 1862, when Union general George McClellan drove his Army of the Potomac to within a dozen miles of Richmond. Lee's rise to legend status began after Davis sent him into the field to replace Joseph E. Johnston following the Battle of Seven Pines.

HISTORIC SITES

Arlington House, the Robert E. Lee Memorial
Arlington National Cemetery
Arlington, VA
(703) 235-1530
www.nps.gov/arho

When Robert E. Lee resigned his U.S. Army commission to begin his service to Virginia, he left behind the family home of 30 years. Federal forces soon occupied it. Built between 1802 and 1818 by George Washington Parke Custis (or, more accurately, his slaves) to honor his stepfather, George Washington, Arlington House hosted the wedding of Custis's daughter, Mary Anna Randolph Custis, to Robert E. Lee in 1831.

The house is open for self-guided tours daily; it's best to call ahead during the renovation to ensure that it's open. One floor of Lee's old greenhouse building now houses the Robert E. Lee Museum, a collection of exhibits and artifacts related to the Confederate commander and his family. Admission is free.

Arlington National Cemetery
Arlington, VA
(703) 607-8000
www.arlingtoncemetery.org

Replacing the farmland and gardens formerly owned by Robert E. Lee, Arlington National Cemetery was created at

Union Personality: Ulysses S. Grant

Other American presidents have risen from obscure beginnings to reach the nation's highest office. None, however, had to bounce back from personal misfortunes quite as often or as late in life as did Grant, whose Missouri farm was appropriately named "Hardscrabble."

Born in Point Pleasant, Ohio, in 1822, Hiram Ulysses Grant seemed to have escaped a life as a farmer or tanner (his father's occupation) when he received a nomination to West Point in 1839. Like many other officers whose academic records at West Point offered little hint of their battlefield potential, Grant stood out in horsemanship, and little else. He graduated in 1843, and accepted his second lieutenant's commission in the infantry.

The Mexican War offered Grant (and scores of other officers destined for Civil War fame) opportunities for adventure and advancement; the Ohioan earned two brevets for gallantry, and served as quartermaster for the 4th Infantry. Groomed for command in Mexico, Grant soon found himself back in the highly competitive officer corps of the small, stagnant, peacetime army—no place for a man of exceptional ability or ambition. Bored, separated from his wife, and desperately lonely, Grant struggled on the frontier. He occasionally drank too much and feuded with his superior officer. By July 1854, he had had enough of army life; he resigned his commission and returned home to be with his family.

General Ulysses S. Grant

But civilian life proved equally challenging. After struggling as a farmer, Grant moved from Missouri to Galena, Illinois, where he clerked in his father's leather-goods shop. The Civil War saved Grant from frustration and obscurity. Given command of the 21st Illinois, Grant was bumped up to brigadier general before a near-disaster in the November 7, 1861, Battle of Belmont, Missouri. Subsequent victories at Forts Henry and Donelson, and, later, Chattanooga and Vicksburg, convinced President Abraham Lincoln to give him control of all Union armies in March 1864. Combat command brought out the best in Grant. Simply put, Southern diarist Mary Chesnut wrote, Grant had "the disagreeable habit of not retreating before irresistible veterans."

Four other Yankee soldiers (all from Ohio) went on to become president of the United States: Rutherford B. Hayes (1877–1881) was brevetted to major general, and was wounded four times; James Garfield (mortally wounded by an assassin three months after March 1881 inauguration) reached the rank of major general; Benjamin Harrison (1889–1893) was brevetted to brigadier general; and William McKinley (1897–September 1901, assassinated) served in the 23rd Ohio with Hayes, and was brevetted to major.

the urging of quartermaster General Montgomery C. Meigs, and dedicated on June 15, 1864. Civil War buffs might look for headstones etched with the word "Civilian" or "Citizen." These are the burial sites of nearly 4,000 former slaves. There's also a section of the cemetery that honors the memory of the United States Colored Troops. Residents of Freedman's Village, a refuge for runaway slaves, are buried nearby.

Arlington National Cemetery is open daily and ample parking is available. For an overview of the cemetery highlights, take Tourmobile, a narrated sightseeing vehicle that conveys you to the most popular points of interest in the cemetery, including the Kennedy gravestone, Arlington House, and the Tomb of the Unknowns.

Chantilly Battlefield
West Ox Rd. and Monument Dr.
Chantilly, VA
(703) 324-8700

The only major battle to take place in Fairfax County, the Battle of Chantilly took place on September 1, 1862, following the second battle of Manassas. Stonewall Jackson fought, and two Union generals, Philip Kearny and Isaac Stevens, both lost their lives. In the small park that marks the battle site, you can visit a monument to the two fallen generals.

Fort Ward Museum and Historic Site
4301 W. Braddock Rd.
Alexandria, VA
(703) 746-4848
http://oha.alexandriava.gov/fortward

Fort Ward explores the history of the ring of defensive forts that encircled Washington, D.C., during the Civil War. The museum offers permanent and rotating exhibits, a research library, educational programs, and artifacts that provide a snapshot of Civil War life. There's even an 1862 topographical map outlining the capital city's defenses and one of three Hale rocket launchers that are still known to exist. A full tour of the fort's trenches, bombproofs, and gun emplacements is a unique experience that Civil War buffs should not miss.

OTHER POINTS OF INTEREST

Fairfax Museum and Visitor Center
10209 Main St.
Fairfax, VA
(703) 385-8414
www.fairfaxva.gov/museumvc/exhibitions.asp

The City of Fairfax and its role in the Civil War fall into focus at this small-town museum. A permanent town history exhibition—which also includes information on the Battle of Chantilly, which was fought nearby—is staged in the museum's Hammill Gallery, while other galleries house timely and topical temporary exhibitions. The museum doubles as a visitor center, providing information on popular regional attractions. Admission is free.

Fairfax Station
11200 Fairfax Station Rd.
Fairfax Station, VA
(703) 425-9225
www.fairfax-station.org

Both sides battled for control over this critical stop on the Orange and Alexandria Railroad. Whichever side controlled it would have access to the quickest and most direct way to ferry soldiers and supplies between Alexandria and Richmond. The former train depot is now home to the Fairfax Station Railroad Museum, a quaint community museum that pays a fair amount of attention to the town's role in the Civil War. The museum is open Sun.

Lee-Fendall House
614 Oronoco St.
Alexandria, VA
(703) 548-1789
www.leefendallhouse.org

Robert E. Lee's Virginia roots are evident throughout northern Virginia, especially in Alexandria. The Lee-Fendall House was home to 37 members of the Lee family, passed down through the generations from 1785–1903. The furnishings on display show the house as it looked during the antebellum period and during the war itself. Tours are offered every hour on the hour. It's best to call ahead to confirm that the house is open; it's frequently rented for weddings and other private events.

The Lyceum: Alexandria's History Museum
201 S. Washington St.
Alexandria, VA
(703) 746-4994
http://oha.alexandriava.gov/lyceum

A trip to Old Town Alexandria is a step back in time, and there's no better place to learn about the history of this charming port town than the Lyceum. Founded in 1839, the Lyceum serves as a library, lecture room, exhibition hall, and gathering place for residents and visitors to Alexandria. The building was used as a hospital during the Civil War and, more than a century later in 1985, it was designated Alexandria's History Museum. Admission is free.

St. Mary's Church
Fairfax Station Rd. at Rte. 123
Fairfax Station, VA
(703) 978-4141
www.stmaryofsorrows.org

When war broke out, Confederate forces controlled the area surrounding St. Mary's Church and the railroad west to Manassas, but the Union's domain followed the railroad east to Burke, putting the newly constructed Catholic church in the middle of the crossfire. After the First Battle of Manassas, St. Mary's was used as a field hospital. Wounded soldiers were laid out and treated on pews taken from the church, and many that succumbed were buried on the church grounds. Clara Barton was among the volunteer nurses who traveled to St. Mary's to treat the injured soldiers. Inspired by her experience at Fairfax Station, she established a civilian society that would later become the American Red Cross. The church is still open for Sun Mass and is one of the region's most sought-after wedding venues.

Sully Plantation
3650 Historic Sully Way
Chantilly, VA
(703) 437-1794
www.fairfaxcounty.gov/parks/sully

Constructed at the end of the 18th century, Sully was established by Richard Bland Lee, Northern Virginia's first congressman and Robert E. Lee's uncle. Both sides stopped at this Georgian-style manor during the war, though the Union-sympathizing gentlemen owners were known to flee to Alexandria during the war, leaving the women in charge. The estate's slave quarters have also been restored, offering a realistic snapshot of slave life in Northern Virginia. The plantation is open every day except Tues. Guided tours of the house are given every hour on the hour. Tours of the slave quarters and outbuildings are available as well.

Northern Virginia Forts

Several earthworks forts were constructed in Northern Virginia by Union forces to bolster the defense of the Federal capital. Fort Ward boasts the most extensive remains, artifacts, and interpretation, but many of the other forts have evolved into popular parks for picnics and outdoor recreation.

Fort C. F. Smith
2411 N. Twenty-Fourth St.
Arlington, VA

Fort Ethan Allen
3829 N. Stafford St.
Arlington, VA

Fort Marcy
671 Chain Bridge Rd.
McLean, VA

ACCOMMODATIONS

Almost Heaven Bed and Breakfast $$$$
6339 Brocketts Crossing
Alexandria, VA
(703) 921-9043
(877) 418-8256
www.bedandbreakfastinnvirginia.com

Any place that claims to be "almost heaven" isn't afraid of setting its guests' expectations fairly high, and this Alexandria B&B doesn't disappoint. The beautiful private home is furnished with antiques, hardwood floors, and even an in-ground pool and Jacuzzi. Families traveling with children can take advantage of kid-friendly amenities like a pool table, darts, electronic basketball, and even an air-hockey table. On the weekends, guests enjoy homemade, fruit-filled waffles and cooked-to-order omelets for breakfast. It's just a few minutes away from Metrorail and Old Town Alexandria.

Arlington-Alexandria Bed & Breakfast Network
(703) 549-3415
(888) 549-3415
www.aabbn.com

Arlington and Alexandria are brimming with national hotel chains, but bed-and-breakfasts are somewhat of a rarity. This network connects you with several of the region's private homes that offer short-term accommodations and extended-stay leases.

Bailiwick Inn $$$$
4023 Chain Bridge Rd.
Fairfax, VA
(703) 691-2266

If you're looking for a place to stay in Fairfax with a little bit of history and charm, you can't beat the Bailiwick Inn, a lovely, Federal-style town house that boasts an inn, bakery, and fine-dining restaurant all in the same space. Even Confederate colonel John Singleton Mosby understands the appeal; he once raided it! There are 14 guest rooms, all named for famous Virginians, decorated with antiques and reproductions. Some guest rooms are also outfitted with fireplaces and whirlpool tubs, and room rates include afternoon tea and breakfast.

The Captain McGuire House $$–$$$$
Prince St.
Alexandria, VA
(703) 549-3415

Although Alexandria's charming cobblestone streets practically scream "bed-and-breakfast country," there are surprisingly few in town, thanks in part to strict real estate codes and sky-high property values. The circa-1816 Captain McGuire House is a fine exception, nestled between historic row houses a block from the shops and restaurants on King Street. There are only two rooms, one outfitted with a queen-size bed, decorative fireplace, and private bath. A third-floor bedroom has two twin beds and a private bath with a shower.

Hotel Monaco $$$$
480 King St.
Alexandria, VA
(703) 549-6080
www.hotel-ot.com

Alexandria's other Kimpton hotel tells a different story than the stately Morrison House. For years, the property operated as a Holiday Inn Select. After a $22 million renovation that brought the 241-room hotel up to four-star standards, it reopened as the sleek, stylish Hotel Monaco. Although it's loaded with 21st-century amenities, the Monaco's location in the heart of the Old Town Historic District is one of its top selling points. You can walk down to the waterfront for open-air dining or walk to the Metro to access Washington, D.C.'s most celebrated sites.

Inns of Virginia—Falls Church $$$
421 W. Broad St.
Falls Church, VA
(703) 533-1100
www.innsofva.com

There's nothing fancy about this no-frills Falls Church hotel, but you can't beat the value. It's clean, safe, and well-located near Metrorail, shops, and restaurants. Rooms were recently renovated and now boast 27-inch flat-screen TVs, free wireless Internet, free parking, and complimentary continental breakfast.

Morrison House $$$$
116 S. Alfred St.
Alexandria, VA
(703) 838-8000
www.morrisonhouse.com

While most other hotels managed by San Francisco–based Kimpton are known for their bold decor and funky furnishings, the Morrison House is decidedly demure, complementing its Old Town Alexandria location with antiques, reproductions, and other classic touches. In the boutique hotel's 45 guest rooms, you'll find two- and four-poster beds, even decorative fireplaces, crystal chandeliers, and round-the-clock butler service. It's not all about the past, however. Guest rooms are also outfitted with wireless Internet capabilities, multiline phones with free local calls, and yoga and Pilates equipment available to borrow.

Stafford House $$$$
3746 Chain Bridge Rd.
Fairfax, VA
(703) 385-9024
www.staffordhouse.net

Don't let the Stafford House's "married couples only" policy prevent you from enjoying a stay at this luxurious B&B. It's perfect for a romantic getaway or a relaxing respite after a day of intense sightseeing. Guests enjoy access to an enormous, private whirlpool bath and dry sauna and enjoy room-service breakfast. Single travelers are also welcomed, and unmarried couples are referred to other nearby B&Bs.

RESTAURANTS

Argia's $$
124 N. Washington St.
Falls Church, VA
(703) 534-1033
www.argias.com

If you're staying in Falls Church, and you're hungry for Italian, this neighborhood eatery should be at the top of your list. Argia's takes recipes handed down from chef and co-owner Adam Scott's grandmother (note the family photographs on the wall) and adds in a few modern variations. The eggplant al formaggio is a delectable take on eggplant parmesan, grilled and layered with goat cheese and tomatoes. Calamari comes lightly dusted in parmesan and flavored with fresh basil. Dishes are served as single portions or family style, designed for sharing.

Artie's $$$
3260 Old Lee Hwy.
Fairfax, VA
(703) 273-7600
www.greatamericanrestaurants.com

This family-friendly favorite serves classic American creations like crab cakes, baby back ribs, and succulent pork tenderloin glazed with a citrus-chipotle sauce and paired with parmesan potatoes. Artie's boasts one of the region's best brunches as well. Brioche French toast is decadent and sweet, and you can't miss with the egg dishes and the fresh-baked bread.

Bazin's on Church $$$
111 Church St., NW
Vienna, VA
(703) 255-7212
www.bazinsonchurch.com

The Town of Vienna's historic district is peppered with a few Civil War sites, along with a few eateries. Among them is Bazin's, a new venture for chef Patrick Bazin, who earned acclaim at the Occidental, one of D.C.'s leading historic restaurants. Inventive surf-and-turf creations abound on the menu: Mushroom-crusted rockfish is served with parmesan orzo, and filet mignon comes paired with a wild mushroom and baby spinach enchilada.

Del Merei Grille $$
3106 Mount Vernon Ave.
Alexandria, VA
(703) 739-4335
www.delmereigrille.com

Alexandria, Virginia's up-and-coming Del Rey neighborhood has emerged on the dining and nightlife map in recent years, and with good cause, thanks to places like Del Merei Grille. It's a friendly gathering place for locals and visitors who are beginning to discover that there's more to Alexandria than its 18th-century cobblestone streets. Start with an order of fried pickles—a Southern specialty—or beer-battered mozzarella served with spicy tomato sauce, and then choose something from the grill like filet mignon, shrimp, or scallops and jazz it up with the sauce of your choice: peppercorn brandy cream, blue cheese, dill cream, or barbecue sauce. If you don't want to create your own meal, there are also plenty of things to choose from. Shrimp is sautéed with mushrooms and andouille sausage and served over creamy cheese garlic grits with a Cajun cream sauce. Braised barbecued ribs are paired with collard greens and home-baked macaroni and cheese.

Five Guys $
107 N. Fayette St.
Alexandria, VA
(703) 549-7991
www.fiveguys.com

In the Washington, D.C., metropolitan area, Five Guys is synonymous with hamburgers. It's just what you want in a burger joint: juicy burgers, available in regular and "little" sizes that are large enough to satisfy most appetites. Pay a little extra to top it with bacon and cheese, then make it your own with free toppings like fried onions, sautéed mushrooms, and jalapeno peppers. Not in the mood for a burger? There are also hot dogs, veggie burgers, and gooey grilled cheese sandwiches. Split a heaping order of hand-cut fries, cooked in peanut oil and served boardwalk style or doused in Cajun spice. While this is the local chain's flagship location, you'll find other locations in Arlington, Chantilly, D.C., and elsewhere in the mid-Atlantic.

Idylwood Grill and Wine Bar $$$
2190 Pimmit Dr.
Falls Church, VA
(703) 992-0915
www.idylwoodgrill.com

It's easy to drive right past this Falls Church eatery. It's tucked into a suburban strip mall located near busy Leesburg Pike. The two-level restaurant is developing a regional reputation as a fine choice for savory Mediterranean fare. Sit down and feast on fresh flat bread, perfectly paired with fruity olive oil. While you'll likely recognize the names of many dishes on the menu, you'll be amazed by the preparations. Calamari are doused in a beurre blanc sauce, flavored with herbs and shallots. You can't go wrong with lamb dishes or hearty pastas, topped with tasty pesto- and tomato-based sauces.

Ray's the Steaks $$
2300 Wilson Blvd.
Arlington, VA
(703) 841-7297

Ask any steak lover in the region for a dinner recommendation, and they're likely to point you to Ray's. It's located in an unassuming Arlington shopping center, but it's not uncommon to find a throng of hungry customers waiting to get in. The steaks are delicious, hand-procured, butchered, and aged by proprietor Michael Landrum. While the tender meats get top billing here, it's easy to fall in love with side dishes like creamy spinach and buttery mashed potatoes. It's also easy to find an affordable bottle of wine to pair with the choice cuts of meat.

Restaurant Eve $$$
110 S. Pitt St.
Alexandria, VA
(703) 706-0450
www.restauranteve.com

Fine dining hit its stride in Old Town Alexandria when Restaurant Eve appeared on the scene. Cathal Armstrong, voted chef of the year by the Restaurant Association Metropolitan Washington and one of the country's best new chefs by *Food & Wine,* has earned acclaim for this cozy American bistro. Sign up for the five- or nine-course tasting menu in the Chef's Tasting Room or craft your own menu in the comfortable bistro. Specialties include veal sweetbreads with porcinis, new potatoes and garlic, and soft-shell crabs with tomatoes and avocado emulsion. Desserts are decadent and divine. One of the best sellers: a mini-birthday cake covered in pink frosting and sprinkles.

Southside 815 $$
815 S. Washington St.
Alexandria, VA
(703) 836-6222
www.southside815.com

If you book a table at Southside 815, there's not much chance that you'll leave hungry. The Old Town Alexandria restaurant is known for its generous servings of Southern classics served at affordable prices. Start your meal with a basket of fresh-baked buttermilk and sweet potato biscuits or an order of fried pickles, then move on to main courses like grilled pork chops smothered in apple chutney, drunken pot roast, or baby back ribs. For dessert, dive into the luscious peach pound cake topped with vanilla ice cream and warm caramel sauce.

Sunflower Vegetarian Restaurant $$
2531 Chain Bridge Rd.
Vienna, VA
(703) 319-3888
www.crystalsunflower.com

Metropolitan Washington, D.C.'s vegetarian community has fallen for the Sunflower, and with good cause. The food is delicious enough to trick carnivores into enjoying it, and the service is warm and inviting. Start your meal off with an order of edamame, seasoned with a tasty bouquet of spices and salts. Main dishes come with a serving of healthy brown rice. Some of our favorites include "Sweet and Sour Sensation," a vegetarian interpretation of sweet-and-sour pork made with soy protein, "Songbird," an interesting take on kung pao chicken, and "General Tso's Surprise," a delectable interpretation of General Tso's chicken. Wash it down with a glass of homemade lemonade, sweetened with honey. Don't understand all of the healthy ingredients on the menu? There's a glossary that sheds some light on some of the trickier terms.

Tallula $$$
2761 Washington Blvd.
Arlington, VA
(703) 778-5051
tallularestaurant.com

Arlington's Clarendon neighborhood is earning a reputation among the culinary minded, thanks to dining hot spots like Tallula. Wine plays a key role in the menu here, served in tumblers to show their colors and characteristics in the best possible light. And because many of the bottles are reasonably priced, it's a good excuse to try out New World vintages that are uncommon in other D.C. restaurants. Some of the starters are designed to be shared or relished in two-bite servings. Among the main courses, the diver scallops with braised pork belly and sweet corn puree and bison short ribs are interesting choices. If you're not a fan of meat, check out the enticing vegetarian menu.

Fredericksburg/Spotsylvania: Before Richmond

Darley.

THE BATTLE OF FREDERICKSBURG

*O*nly "Pickett's Charge" on the third day at Gettysburg compares with the horrible bloodletting that took place before Marye's Heights, above Fredericksburg, Virginia, on December 13, 1862. The Confederate shredding of one wave of blue-coated Yankees after another topped off the failure of yet another Army of the Potomac commander, this time heavy-whiskered Major General Ambrose Burnside.

The fourth commander (including two stints by George B. McClellan) of the Union's mightiest army, Ambrose Burnside inherited command from his old friend McClellan on November 7, after the latter general's mediocre performance during and after the Battle of Antietam. Hoping to strike General Robert E. Lee's Confederate Army again before the arrival of winter, the burly Rhode Islander marched his massive, 130,000-man force south to Falmouth, Virginia—lost three weeks waiting for pontoon boats to arrive—then continued toward Fredericksburg, where Lee's army was encamped. Union engineers spent December 11 stretching their pontoon bridges across the Rappahannock River (which ran northwest to southeast), while Yankee cannon lobbed shells over them and into the city, on the opposite shore. The following day, while Burnside reconnoitered and discussed with his senior commanders his plan of attack, thousands of his restless foot soldiers marched into Fredericksburg and looted it.

Union engineers constructing pontoon bridges across the Rappahannock River, December 11, 1862

Major General Ambrose Burnside

With his army stretched roughly north to south beyond the fields west of Fredericksburg, Robert E. Lee had a number of advantages: supportable interior lines, high ground, and for the men in his center, an almost-unassailable position behind a 400-foot stone wall along the crest of Marye's Heights, above the town. Having lost the initiative and any hope of surprise, Burnside would have to count on sheer numbers: he had a 2–1 edge in manpower. For the Federals on December 13, there would be no elaborate feints; no flanking movements or surprise cavalry assaults—only power.

But as at Antietam and other battlefields, the Union commander nullified his advantage through inefficient—and, eventually, suicidal—deployment. Hoping to nail down Lee's right while he hammered the Virginian's left-center, Burnside ordered left-wing commander Major General William Franklin to launch an attack. But Franklin's small-scale, early-afternoon assault petered out in the face of a vigorous Confederate response.

The attack on the Rebel positions in Fredricksburg on December 13, 1862

For the shivering, blue-garbed infantrymen of Major General Edwin Sumner's right wing, meanwhile, a hideous nightmare had begun. All afternoon, regiment after regiment filed through the streets of Fredericksburg, formed up, and trudged up the slowly ascending, half-mile of ground toward Marye's Heights. Confederate cannon blazed away. By the hundreds, astonished Confederate infantrymen lay their rifles across the stone wall and pulled triggers. It was a perfect shooting gallery. Only Brigadier General Thomas Meagher's vaunted Irish Brigade managed to stagger within shouting range of the Confederate lines. Remembering the scene years later, one Union officer, Josiah Favill, wrote "there was no romance, no glorious pomp, nothing but disgust for the genius who planned so frightful a slaughter."

Night fell. On into December 14—as thousands of bleeding and freezing Yankee soldiers lay on the hilly turf below Marye's Heights—a heartsick Burnside pondered another attack, this time with himself at its head. Finally talked out of it, he arranged for a belated truce to bury the dead and collect the wounded, and then ordered a withdrawal back across the river.

For the stunned Army of the Potomac, the headaches were not quite over. Resolving to make up for the devastating setback by surprising Lee from the rear, Burnside ordered a looping march around Lee's left across the Rappahannock. Campaigning at this time of year was hard enough with the onset of rain and snow that now swamped Burnside's army, freezing soldiers and halting the endless Union wagon trains in feet of frosty mud. Still, soldiers retained their sense of humor, even coming up with a poem about their plight:

Now I lay me down to sleep
In mud that's many fathoms deep;
If I'm not here when you awake,
Just hunt me up with an oyster rake.

Unsympathetic witnesses derided the Union columns as they struggled, shivering, down icy roads. With his doomed movement already being laughed off as the "Mud March," Burnside called it off on January 25. For his used-up troops, the long, 1862 campaigning season was at a merciful end. Two days later, so was Ambrose Burnside's reign as Army of the Potomac commander.

THE BATTLE OF CHANCELLORSVILLE

*H*aving deposed the unfortunate Burnside, Abraham Lincoln turned to Major General Joseph Hooker, a capable, hard-fighting, and hard-drinking 48-year-old veteran of corps command who had served under his predecessor at Fredericksburg. Hooker immediately replaced Burnside's unwieldy Grand Division army structure with the more-traditional corps setup, and reorganized the long-neglected Union cavalry into a single command under Major General George Stoneman. (Major General Alfred Pleasanton would replace Stoneman in June.)

Map of the Battle of Chancellorsville, May 3, 1863

Rested after a winter in camp, Hooker's Army of the Potomac opened the 1863 campaign season in stunning fashion. Sending Major General John Sedgwick and 30,000 Federals to keep Lee busy at Fredericksburg, and Stoneman's cavalry raiding to the south, Hooker crossed the Rappahannock with 65,000 men and swung around behind Lee. The surprised and shorthanded Lee (elements of James Longstreet's corps had been detached and sent south to Richmond) found himself trapped between the two halves of Hooker's massive army. On April 30, Hooker's staff confidently announced to the army:

It is with heartfelt satisfaction the commanding general announces to the army that the operations of the last three days have determined that our enemy must either ingloriously fly, or come out from behind his defenses and give us battle on our own ground, where certain destruction awaits him.

Lee was certainly not about to fly anywhere. Never afraid to try the unconventional, he divided his 53,000-man army, leaving just 10,000 to watch Sedgwick while he turned and marched 10 miles west to confront his latest Union opponent. He found Hooker's army in line 2 miles east of the forbidding Wilderness—a tangled mess of undergrowth, trees, and briars through which a man could scarcely walk. Hooker made the first move on May 1, sending elements of three corps attacking east down local roads. Lee counterattacked, and as the fighting raged just west of the village of Chancellorsville, Hooker stunningly called a halt to his assault. Ignoring the protests of his corps commanders, Hooker pulled his flanks back and centered his new position at Chancellorsville. With his army dug in behind stiff fortifications, his position was formidable. His reasons for giving up his momentum and the initiative to Lee—the clear underdog in this contest—have never been made clear. The normally aggressive army commander apparently told one subordinate that he had lost confidence in Hooker. Whatever the reason for his decision, it opened the door for the most famous flank attack of the war. After discussing it with Lee, Stonewall Jackson and 26,000 Confederates set out early on May 2 to spring a surprise attack on Hooker's right flank, which scouting Rebel cavalry had found unprotected. The absence of most of Stoneman's Yankee cavalry—still

missing to the south—was a blessing. Still, it was a risky plan; should Hooker change his colors and attack, Lee, with just 17,000 men, would be hard-pressed to escape Hooker's blue-coated hordes.

Aside from some skirmishing with a portion of Jackson's flanking party, Hooker did not attack. Neither he nor 11th Corps commander, Major General Oliver Otis Howard, seemed to be aware of what was brewing on their right. Howard found out at about 5:30 p.m., when the piercing Rebel yell filled the ears of his shocked 11th Corps men as they cooked up their rations. Bullets screamed by, followed by Jackson's divisions. Dropping their food, Yankees bolted from their camp at top speed, their pursuers hard on their heels. The fighting on the Union right continued past dusk, as Yankee reinforcements fought to stem the slowing Confederate tide.

For the Confederate Army, the good news of the day was tempered by a horrifying report that Jackson had been seriously wounded. Reconnoitering under the moonlight, the corps commander had been mistakenly shot three times by his own soldiers. He was out of the fight; cavalryman J. E. B. Stuart took command of his corps. Informed of Jackson's injuries by a junior officer, a troubled Lee replied: "Ah, Captain, any victory is dearly bought that deprives us of the services of General Jackson even for a short time."

May 3 saw Hooker's army tightening into a loop-shape with its flanks extended toward the Rapidan and Rappahannock Rivers. Hooker—knocked senseless by the concussion of an exploding shell—had little to do with the day's fighting, during which Lee, Stuart, and dominating Confederate artillery compressed the Union lines. Only the news of John Sedgwick's approach from the east stalled Lee, who detached a force to deal with the oncoming Yankees. Sedgwick, who had overrun Jubal Early's Marye's Heights defenders and chased him south, was himself now repulsed at Salem Church.

The following day, Lee led some 20,000 men east to dispose of Sedgwick, who retreated carefully north over the Rappahannock. The recovered Hooker—whose manpower advantage in the absence of Lee offered an opportunity to wipe out Stuart—did little but prepare to retreat. By noon on May 6, his army was back north of Rapidan, and the Chancellorsville Campaign was over, with Lee's Confederates—again—the clear winner. Each side had lost more than 1,600 men killed. The loss of Jackson, who after losing an arm to amputation would succumb to pneumonia on May 10, particularly stunned the South. Jackson's loss would be hard to overcome. But with conditions otherwise favorable for something audacious, Lee began to prepare for an invasion of the North.

The Rebel Yell

Of the myriad symbols and images of the old Confederacy, the rebel yell is perhaps the one most widely known yet most misunderstood. This particular battle cry was first heard at the First Manassas (First Bull Run), shortly after the war had begun. The originator of this cry was none other than the revered Brigadier (later Lieutenant) General Thomas Jonathan "Stonewall" Jackson (who earned his nickname in this very same battle). As Union infantry approached his Virginians, he rode calmly down the line of battle and gave his order: "Hold your fire until they're on you. Then fire and give them the bayonet. And when you charge, yell like furies!" Minutes later, the "weird halloo of the rebel yell" (as Shelby Foote put it) was heard for the first time, as 20,000 Confederate soldiers swept the Union Army from the field.

A Union survivor of that battle later recalled, "There is nothing like it on this side of the infernal region. The peculiar corkscrew sensation that it sends down your backbone under these circumstances can never be told. You have to feel it."

There are no known recordings of an actual full-volume rebel yell, the nearest approximation being a snippet of high-pitched "yipping" recorded on a 1920s-era movie about Civil War veterans. These men were in their 70s and 80s and obviously not in the prime of life or health anymore, so the sound was more reminiscent of a soft call to one's dog rather than a fear-inducing battle cry. One aged veteran, noting the rather weak attempt at the sound, leans toward the camera and, with a wink in his eye, explains, "That's the famous rebel yell!"

From scattered descriptions, it is apparent that the familiar "yee-haw!" heard from the stands at college football games is not the actual cry; many veterans compared it to a lusty and truly frightening version of a fox-hunter's yelp. One of the better descriptions comes from notes taken at an 1891 veterans convention in Memphis, when the widow of Admiral Raphael Semmes asked Captain Kellar Anderson (of the famed Kentucky Orphan Brigade) to let her hear a rebel yell. Anderson gave a rather lengthy reply, starting with a description of the hellish action around Snodgrass Hill at the battle of Chickamauga. Then he went on:

There they go, all at breakneck speed, the bayonet at charge. The firing appears to suddenly cease for about five seconds. Then arose that do-or-die expression, that maniacal maelstrom of sound; that penetrating, rasping, shrieking, blood-curdling noise, that could be heard for miles on earth, and whose volumes reached the heavens; such an expression as never yet came from the throats of sane men, but from men whom the seething blast of an imaginary hell would not check while the sound lasted. The battle of Chickamauga is won.

Dear Southern mother, that was the Rebel yell, and only such scenes ever did or ever will produce it.

Even when engaged, that expression from the Confederate soldier always made my hair stand on end. The young men and youths who composed this unearthly music were lusty, jolly, clear-voiced, hardened soldiers, full of courage and proud to march in rags, barefoot, dirty and hungry, with head erect to meet the plethoric ranks of the best equipped and best fed army of modern times. Alas! Now many of them are decrepit from ailment and age, and although we will never grow old enough to cease being proud of the record of the Confederate soldier, and the dear old mothers who bore them, we can never again, even at your bidding, dear, dear mother, produce the Rebel yell. Never again; never, never, never.

GRANT'S 1864 OVERLAND (RICHMOND) CAMPAIGN

The Battle of the Wilderness

Hailed by some as the Union's savior, Ulysses S. Grant returned to the East during the spring of 1864 to take command of all Union armies. His victories out West had helped secure the Mississippi River for the Union; now he had been charged with bringing Confederate General Robert E. Lee to heel. Eastern veterans grown skeptical by the repeated failure of much-ballyhooed new commanders accepted the Western hero with hope. "If he succeeds, the war is over," a Massachusetts captain wrote. "For I do assure you that in the hands of a General who gave them success, there is no force on Earth which would resist this army."

Grant's plan, basically, was to attack on all fronts. From Tennessee, Major General William T. Sherman would slash through Georgia, destroying Confederate supplies, communications, and transportation. In the East, Major General Benjamin Butler would march up the James River to pressure Richmond from the east. And while Franz Sigel (or his eventual successor Philip Sheridan) took control of the Shenandoah Valley, George Gordon Meade's beleaguered Army of the Potomac would deal with Lee. Now a lieutenant general, Grant would travel with Meade's army.

Battle of the Wilderness

Plan of the Battle of the Wilderness

Launching his Overland Campaign on May 4, Meade marched his 120,000 Yankees across the Rapidan River toward Lee's 60,000 Confederates. Grant hoped to advance through the infamous Wilderness—a hellish tangle of woods and underbrush—and strike Lee on open ground before Lee could respond. The next day, however, elements of Meade's right and Lee's left collided on the worst possible terrain for fighting. The smoke of musketry saturated the area, blotting out the sky in the middle of the day. With cavalry and artillery of little use, infantry struggled to maintain any kind of formation—even to distinguish friend from foe just a few yards away. It was, one survivor testified, a "battle of invisibles against invisibles." Another veteran remembered the "puffs of smoke, the 'ping' of the bullets, and the yell of the enemy. It was a blind and bloody hunt to the death, in bewildering thickets, rather than a battle."

The bloody, terrifying fighting in the woods continued on May 6. Lee sent Lieutenant General Richard Ewell's corps up the Orange Turnpike against Meade's right, while Major General Winfield Scott Hancock and James Longstreet dueled back and forth on the Federals' left. With no room for elaborate maneuver, the two armies slugged it out to exhaustion. Separated from their units by entangling thickets, enemy soldiers fought hand to hand with rifles and bayonets. "There wasn't a tree . . . but what was all cut to pieces with balls," one Yankee remembered, "and the dead and wounded was lying thick. It was an awful sight." Badly wounded soldiers cut off from their units could only die alone. Others suffered a worse fate after darkness fell, perishing in fires set by heavy musketry.

Aside from costing the two armies a combined 28,000 casualties, the two-day fight settled nothing.

Map of Battlefield of Spotsylvania Court House

The Battles of Spotsylvania Court House

After two days of killing in the Wilderness, George Gordon Meade—putting into practice Grant's relentless strategy—kept up the pressure on Robert E. Lee's Confederates by sliding southeast toward Spotsylvania Court House. But units of Lee's army beat him to the crossroads town and proceeded to fashion a mule-shoe-shaped line of virtually impregnable fortifications of logs, earth, and sharpened stakes that covered three sides of the town and protected the Confederates' flanks. It was the sort of defense that less-determined Union generals would have done their best to avoid.

Near dusk on May 10, 5,000 Federals charged and carried a northern section of the Rebel works, before being forced to withdraw with heavy casualties. Encouraged,

Grant sent a larger force—some 15,000 infantrymen with bayonets fixed—charging into the Rebel fortifications at 4:30 a.m. on May 12. The Confederates counterattacked from within their own lines, kicking off nearly a full day of back-and-forth struggle in a section of Lee's lines that became known as the "Bloody Angle." Under darkened skies and drenching rains, soldiers fought at close quarters: "Skulls were crushed with clubbed muskets," one of Grant's aides wrote, "and men stabbed to death with swords and bayonets thrust between the logs in the parapet which separated the combatants."

Exhausted following the nightmarish slaughter of May 12–13, the two armies continued to probe and skirmish for another week until Grant and Meade—with Lee following—stepped off to the east, then the south, again, moving inexorably toward Richmond. In two weeks, Grant had incurred some 18,000 casualties (killed, wounded, or missing) compared to Lee's 12,000, proving to some that he cared little for his soldiers and to others that he would fight until victory was won.

again barricaded behind impressive earthworks. The badly coordinated assault resulted in one of the war's bloodiest (alongside Fredericksburg and Gettysburg) repulses, and 7,000 Yankee casualties in less than an hour. Grant's month-long campaign resembled, to some, a horrific waste of life and expense. Once the Union's best hope, Grant was now decried as a "Butcher." "I do think there has been too much assaulting, this campaign!" one frustrated Federal declared. Major General Gouverneur K. Warren—a hero of Gettysburg who would later be relieved of his command—complained: "For thirty days now, it has been one funeral procession, past me; and it is too much!" Nearly four days passed as Lee and Grant haggled over the details of a truce for burial detail. Meanwhile, hundreds of suffering, wounded soldiers died on the battlefield.

Grant had learned his lesson. His next move—a lightning crossing of the James River to ensnare Petersburg—would leave both Lee and his detractors stunned.

Cold Harbor

Grant and Meade continued moving south along the railroad, occasionally testing Lee's sliding lines with little success. After several clashes along the North Anna River, Meade and Lee met at another crossroads called Cold Harbor, 10 miles northeast of Richmond. After a day of skirmishing on June 1, Grant prepared a massive frontal assault designed to exploit any weakness in Lee's lines. Nearly a month of bloody stalemate had Grant chomping at the bit and determined to smash through the armies of his nemesis.

On June 3, three Union corps attacked Lee's army,

Burial detail on the battlefield at Cold Harbor

Chatham
120 Chatham Lane
Falmouth, VA
(540) 371-0802
www.nps.gov/frsp/chatham.htm

When you visit the Fredericksburg battlefields, be sure to make time to see Chatham, a Georgian-style mansion that served as the Union headquarters during the Battle of Fredericksburg. It's also one of only three houses in the United States to have been visited by George Washington, Thomas Jefferson, and Abraham Lincoln. When war broke out, the house was owned by James Horace Lacy, a slave holder and Southern sympathizer who left his wife and children on the estate and joined the Confederate Army. Union forces took over the house in 1862, using it as a hospital to treat some of the 12,600 casualties from the disastrous defeat at Fredericksburg. Clara Barton and Walt Whitman were among the medical attendants. There's a replica pontoon boat inside, fashioned after the ones used by the troops to cross the Rappahannock River. You can also catch a free movie, which illustrates the effects of the war on residents of the area.

Cold Harbor Battlefield and Visitor Center
Route 156 (5 miles SE of Mechanicsville)
(804) 226-1981
www.nps.gov/rich

Although Cold Harbor is closer to Richmond and is part of Richmond National Battlefield Park, we've included it in this section due to its relationship to the other locations in the campaign. Cold Harbor has a visitor center that boasts an electric map program and exhibits depicting the 1862 Battle of Gaines' Mill and the 1864 Battle of Cold Harbor. The battlefield itself features original entrenchments, which can be examined from numerous interpretive walking trails.

Cold Harbor National Cemetery
6038 Cold Harbor Rd.
Mechanicsville

Also a part of the battlefield (but administered by the Veterans Administration) is Cold Harbor National Cemetery, where more than 2,000 victims of area battles lay. On the cemetery grounds, there's a masonry lodge designed by quartermaster Montgomery Meigs and monuments donated by the states of Pennsylvania and New York to honor their fallen soldiers. The Tomb of the Unknown Soldier, erected in 1877, honors the 889 unknown Union soldiers who were killed and buried in trenches in and around Cold Harbor.

Ellwood
36380 Constitution Hwy.
Locust Grove
(540) 786-2880
http://www.nps.gov/frsp/ellwood.htm

Like Chatham, Ellwood was owned by the Lacy family at the start of the war and is now part of the battlefield park. While it lacks the grandeur of Chatham, it's not without its historic significance. During the Battle of Chancellorsville, many of the wounded were treated here, including Confederate general Stonewall Jackson. His amputated arm is famously buried in the Lacy family cemetery on the house's grounds. Union troops used Ellwood as a headquarters a year later during the Battle of the Wilderness.

Fredericksburg Area Museum and Cultural Center
1001 Princess Anne St.
Fredericksburg
(540) 371-3037
www.famcc.org

This community museum located in Fredericksburg's 1816 Town Hall/Market Square building reaches beyond the Civil War to showcase the town's colonial history, its ties to the railroad, and other themes. Artifacts like Confederate currency and officers' uniforms and weapons help relate the town's role before, during, and after the war.

Fredericksburg and Spotsylvania National Military Park
120 Chatham Lane
Fredericksburg
(540) 373-6122
www.nps.gov/frsp

Second only to Chickamauga and Chattanooga in terms of size, this military park is one of the most significant: It includes four important battlefields (including the Wilderness and Chancellorsville), two visitor centers (Fredericksburg and Chancellorsville), and four historic buildings. One of these structures is now the Stonewall Jackson Shrine, the small Chandler Plantation building in which Stonewall Jackson died on May 10, 1863. In addition to numerous walking trails and driving tours (with audiotape), the park often provides guided tours. Its two visitor centers offer 22-minute films.

A number of recent changes to the park have brought

its battlefields closer than ever to their original appearance. During the summer of 2006, the National Park Service (NPS) set about restoring the "Sunken Road" and stone wall along Marye's Heights. Along this battered old road (and behind this wall), Lee's Confederates stood as they mowed down Ambrose Burnside's Federals during the Battle of Fredericksburg. The park has also managed to acquire the land over which Stonewall Jackson launched his crushing flank attack on Joseph Hooker's army at Chancellorsville, along with the site of James Longstreet's flank attack in the Wilderness.

The park is open free of admission from dawn to dusk daily. Hours for the visitor centers vary by season. (Ask about the popular Kenmore and Washington Street Tour.) Rather than visitor centers, the Wilderness and Spotsylvania Court House Battlefields feature interpretive shelters where historians are often available (during warmer months) to answer questions.

Massaponax Baptist Church
5101 Massaponax Church Rd.
Fredericksburg
(540) 898-0021
www.massaponaxbaptist.org

Massaponax Baptist Church was just four years old when Union lieutenant general Ulysses S. Grant, Major General George Meade, and their staffs stopped there on May 21, 1864, following the Battle of Spotsylvania Court House. Grant had a number of the church pews carried outside, where he and his subordinates rested and plotted their next moves. Timothy O'Sullivan, one of the war's most prolific photographers, subsequently captured the gathering in one of the war's best-known sequence of images.

Often used as officers' headquarters or as temporary shelter for passing soldiers, the church still bears visible signs (scrawled names and messages) of the soldiers' presence. It is also still open for regular services, so call ahead before stopping in.

Spotsylvania County Museum
8956 Courthouse Rd.
Spotsylvania
(540) 582-7167

The Old Berea Church, constructed in 1856, now houses the Spotsylvania County Museum. While the small collection of local artifacts and genealogical records will be of most interest to local history buffs, the church bears the marks of shots and shells from the Battle of Spotsylvania Court House, which raged nearby. Admission is free.

Spotsylvania Court House
9104 Courthouse Rd.
Spotsylvania
(540) 891-8687

Established in 1839, Spotsylvania Court House witnessed one of the bloodiest battles of the Civil War, which marked the beginning of the fall of the Confederacy. The Court House stood at the intersection of Routes 613 and 208, guarding the shortest route to Richmond. The building sustained significant damage during the Civil War and was reconstructed in 1900, using the Doric columns of the original building.

White Oak Museum
985 White Oak Rd.
Falmouth, VA
(540) 371-4234
www.whiteoakmuseum.com

Housed in a one-room schoolhouse, the White Oak Museum's collection includes a mix of Union and Confederate artifacts like reconstructed huts, bullets, belt plates, and buttons gathered from area battle sites. The museum is located on the original site of the White Oak School, which was burned and rebuilt in 1912.

TOURS

Ghosts of Fredericksburg Tours
706 Caroline St.
Fredericksburg
(540) 710-3002
www.ghostsoffredericksburg.com

Offered on select Fri and Sat evenings in season, author Mark Nesbitt's eerie tours trace the macabre past of a town considered the most haunted in America. The 80-minute tours are led by costumed guides who relate stories from Fredericksburg's colonial and Civil War past. Reservations are strongly recommended.

Trolley Tours of Fredericksburg
(540) 898-0737
www.fredericksburgtrolley.com

If you've got a short time to explore, leave your car at the hotel and climb on board the trolley. In an hour and 15 minutes, you'll get a nice overview of downtown's rich history and the nearby Civil War battlefields. The tour departs from the visitor center; hours vary by season.

ACCOMMODATIONS

Kenmore Inn $$$–$$$$
1200 Princess Anne St.
Fredericksburg
(540) 371-7622
www.kenmoreinn.com

A charming Old Town Fredericksburg inn, the Kenmore has nine rooms, all with private baths, and four with working fireplaces. The building itself dates to 1793 and claims members of George Washington's family as its former owners. Despite the historic location, the rooms are outfitted with modern amenities like wireless Internet and flat-screen TVs. Guests enjoy a tasty cooked-to-order breakfast, featuring farm-fresh eggs, pancakes, and other classics. The inn's fine-dining restaurant serves delectable American cuisine prepared by chef Josh Oleson.

La Vista Plantation Bed & Breakfast $$$$
4420 Guinea Station Rd.
Fredericksburg
(540) 898-8444
(800) 829-2823
www.lavistaplantation.com

Located just 2 miles from the Massaponax Baptist Church (where photographer Timothy O'Sullivan photographed Union generals Grant, Meade, and a host of others in May 1864), Ed and Michele Schiesser's La Vista Plantation sits in the heart of Spotsylvania Campaign ground. Follow a long driveway to the 1838 farmhouse, whose spacious rooms and common areas are meticulously and tastefully furnished with antiques. Guests enjoy gracious hospitality and a tasty breakfast made with fresh brown eggs from one of the resident hens, along with amenities like central air, satellite TV, and VCRs, working fireplaces, big canopy beds, and even refrigerators. Those guests that simply can't get enough of the Civil War can help themselves to books in the inn's library. Rooms are rented by reservation only, so call ahead.

On Keegan Pond Bed & Breakfast $$–$$$$
11315 Gordon Rd.
Fredericksburg
(888) 785-4662

This cozy B&B is a good choice for Civil War travelers who prefer more of a bucolic setting. Artifacts found on its five-acre grounds indicate that Union scouts were on the grounds during the opening sequences of the Battle of Chancellorsville. The inn's two rooms are clean and comfortable, furnished with antiques and equipped with central air, heat, and private baths.

The Richard Johnston Inn Bed & Breakfast $$$–$$$$
711 Caroline St.
Fredericksburg
(540) 899-7606
(877) 557-0770
www.therichardjohnstoninn.com

If you're looking for a historic place to stay in the heart of Old Town Fredericksburg, check into the Richard Johnston Inn. The inn's seven rooms and two suites are charming and comfortable, furnished with antiques and big, comfortable beds. The top selling point, however, is the inn's central location, with shopping, dining, and sightseeing options on its doorstep—and the visitor center just across the street.

Schooler House Bed & Breakfast $$$–$$$$
1303 Caroline St.
Fredericksburg
(540) 374-5258
www.schoolerhouse.com

If you want to mix in a little romance and elegance with your history, you can't beat the Schooler House. Built in Victorian Italianate style in the town's historic district, the house itself dates to the late 19th century. Period antiques and art decorate its two bedrooms, both of which come with private baths—and you might even happen upon a claw-foot bathtub. Period antiques are also found throughout the inn. Innkeeper Andi Gabler, an expert on local history, treats her guests to a healthy, generous breakfast spread, served on antique dishes and silver. On the grounds, you'll also find a tranquil garden with a goldfish pond and waterfall that's perfect for relaxing after a day of sightseeing.

Wingate by Wyndham $$–$$$
20 Sanford Dr.
Fredericksburg
(540) 368-8000
www.wingateinns.com

The Fredericksburg location of this growing chain (a division of Wyndham Hotels) warrants a visit for its value and convenience to the interstate. This 129-room hotel serves up a host of amenities for business travelers like a 24-hour business center and high-speed Internet, but leisure travelers will also enjoy the free local calls, indoor pool, and ample breakfast service. It's clean and comfortable, an excellent home base for exploring the battlefields in and around Fredericksburg.

WyteStone Suites $$$–$$$$
4615 Southpoint Pkwy.
Fredericksburg
(540) 891-1112
(800) 794-5005
www.wytestone.com

The 85-room WyteStone Suites is another example of a business hotel that provides a great value for tourists as well. Traveling families will especially benefit from the all-suite layout, indoor swimming pool, in-room refrigerator and microwave, and complimentary hot breakfast. There are also six wheelchair-accessible suites. It's easy to spot from I-95, and there's no shortage of quick service restaurants and shopping options nearby.

RESTAURANTS

Allman's BBQ $$
1299 Jefferson Davis Hwy.
Fredericksburg
(540) 373-9881
www.allmansbarbeque.com

Allman's unassuming exterior belies its reputation as Fredericksburg's longtime king of Carolina-style barbecue. Its vintage 1954 interior sports the look of a classic diner, but it's the food that fills barstools, and Mary "Mom" Brown's ribs and coleslaw have been doing just that for 50 years. There's a second drive-through location at 2022 Plank Rd.

Bistro Bethem $$$
309 William St.
Fredericksburg
(540) 371-9999
www.bistrobethem.com

Blake and Aby Bethem's chic, casual bistro offers an enticing seasonal menu, featuring fresh fish, wild game, and other tasty creations prepared with a Southern accent. Macaroni and cheese is prepared with Gruyère, fontina, and white cheddar and a hint of shallots. You can also nibble on housemade charcuterie plates and antipasto selections and treat yourself to heavenly desserts.

Brock's Riverside Grill $$$
503 Sophia St.
Fredericksburg
(540) 370-1820
www.brocksgrill.com

You can't beat the ambience at Brock's Riverside Grill. The comfortable, casual eatery is perched on the banks of the Rappahannock River. On the menu you'll find delectable seafood and hand-cut steaks, along with an assortment of pastas, sandwiches, and salads. If you're in the mood for dancing, stop by on a Thur, Fri, or Sat evening.

Carl's Frozen Custard $
2200 Princess Anne St.
Fredericksburg

Ice cream lovers—and especially frozen custard lovers—won't want to miss a stop at Carl's, a local favorite since 1947. While there's no food service here, you can easily make a meal of the chocolate, vanilla, and strawberry frozen concoctions churned in a 1940s-era Electro-Freeze ice-cream machine. It's open daily from mid-Feb to mid-Nov.

Eileen's Bakery and Café $
1115 Caroline St.
Fredericksburg
(540) 372-4030
www.eileensinc.com

If you're staying in Old Town Fredericksburg, stop by Eileen's for a cup of coffee and breakfast sandwich or warm mushroom popover on your way to see the sights. Or, pick up one of Eileen's gourmet sandwiches or salads for a picnic lunch. In addition to classic turkey and ham creations, you'll also find some inventive vegetarian options like a grilled asparagus sandwich served with roasted tomato mayo and curried mushrooms.

Goolrick's Pharmacy $

901 Caroline St.
Fredericksburg
(540) 373-3411
www.goolricks.com

For another retro dining experience, stop in to Goolrick's pharmacy in downtown, home to the oldest operating soda fountain in the country. If you're looking for a little nostalgia, you'll find it in a thick, creamy milkshake, fresh-squeezed lemonade, or grilled cheese sandwich served in the back of this independent drugstore.

J. Brian's Tap Room $$

200 Hanover St.
Fredericksburg
(540) 373-0738
www.jbrianstaproom.com

Charles Dickens once stayed and dined in the historic hotel building that now houses J. Brian's Tap Room. With its tall ceilings and hardwood floors, the restaurant blends in well with its historic location. Fare here is simple and satisfying: think burgers, steaks, and pizzas, perfectly paired with a beer or glass of wine.

Olde Towne Steak and Seafood $$$

1612 Caroline St.
Fredericksburg
(540) 371-8020
www.oldetownesteakandseafood.com

Established in 1981, Olde Towne Steak and Seafood is a Fredericksburg classic, consistently ranked among Fredericksburg's top eateries. The name says it all: generous platters of lobster, shrimp, and other seafood creations, along with juicy steaks, tender chicken, and "surf and turf" selections. All entrees are served with a garden salad, potatoes, and fresh-baked sourdough bread.

Ristorante Renato $$$

422 William St.
Fredericksburg
(540) 371-8228
www.ristoranterenato.com

For delicious northern Italian cuisine, pull up a chair at Ristorante Renato, where you'll find a tasty selection of home- made pastas and Mediterranean classics like gnocchi doused in veal ragu and eggplant parmesan. Finish it off with a delicious bite of tiramisu, spumoni, or cannoli. The 260-seat restaurant is ideal for parties and festive occasions, just footsteps from Fredericksburg's historic core.

Sammy T's $$

801 Caroline St.
Fredericksburg
(540) 371-2008
www.sammyts.com

If you're looking for a light and healthy dining choice, grab a table at Sammy T's. The menu is packed with creative vegan and vegetarian creations like black bean cakes, apple and cheddar sandwiches, and a to-die-for bean and grain burger topped with sautéed mushrooms, peppers, tomatoes, and onions and smothered in cheese. The building itself dates to 1804; after the Civil War, Brigadier General Darrel Ruggles (Confederate States of America) lived here as he developed new innovations for the railroad.

The Peninsula: On to Richmond!

Darley.

✯ ✯ ✯ ✯ ✯ ✯ ✯ ✯ ✯ ✯ ✯ ✯ ✯ ✯ ✯ ✯ ✯

"Our neighbors are in a very strong position," Major General George McClellan wrote of his Confederate opponents at Yorktown, Virginia, in April 1862. "I cannot turn Yorktown without a battle, in which I must use heavy artillery & go through the preliminary operations of siege." It was a letter that would have drawn angry catcalls from McClellan's opponents in Washington and hails of laughter from the few Rebels in the works opposite his own. With more than 100,000 well-trained and well-supplied Federals under his command, the wary McClellan had halted his drive for Richmond in the face of perhaps 20,000 Confederates. Instead of unleashing his considerable power, he pent it up behind massive earthen fortifications and laid siege to the town. For

a month his coiled army waited, while Major General John Magruder vacated the town under his nose.

And so began McClellan's promising Peninsula Campaign, a drive that—had it been under the control of a more aggressive officer—might have ended the war in 1862. Rather than approaching the Confederate capital from the north, McClellan convinced Abraham Lincoln to accept a more elaborate strategy (with minor modifications): He would transport his huge army south by water, and then march it up the Virginia Peninsula to threaten Richmond from the east. McClellan put his 105,000 men and equipment ashore at Fort Monroe, and in April marched north.

After his "grand victory" at Yorktown, McClellan

Map of the Union earthworks in front of Richmond, April 1862

Battle of Williamsburg, May 1862

pushed his massive and sharp-looking Army of the Potomac up the Peninsula. Lead elements of his army engaged in a sharp fight with Johnston's retreating Confederates at Williamsburg on May 5. The advance continued northeast, until McClellan was just 6 miles from Richmond. When heavy rains stranded two of McClellan's corps north of the swollen Chickahominy River, Johnston lashed out at the Federals at Seven Pines. The two sides fought to a bloody draw, but—of more importance—Johnston fell with a bullet in his shoulder. The next day, President Jefferson Davis gave Johnston's command to Robert E. Lee, who had no intention of allowing the army to remain on its heels.

Lee assigned the two corps of his Army of Northern Virginia to major generals Thomas Jackson and James Longstreet. Then, assured by his dashing cavalry commander, Major General J. E. B. Stuart, that McClellan's right flank was open, Lee left a defending force at Richmond and marched east with some 45,000 Rebels. After a brief clash at Oak Grove on June 25, Lee attacked the now-withdrawing Federals at Mechanicsville on June 26, Gaines' Mill on the 27th, then at Garnett's Farm, Savage's Station, Glendale, and Malvern Hill in succession. In this last clash, devastating Yankee artillery fire shredded waves of Confederate attackers, spurring futile requests from McClellan's subordinates to counterattack. But the commanding general, who had long since abandoned a campaign while on the brink of complete victory, was too intent on "saving" his army. After leading his army back to Harrison's Landing, McClellan was relieved of it altogether, in favor of (briefly) John Pope.

Battle of Dam No. 1
13650 Jefferson Ave.
Newport News, VA

The entrance to this battlefield park sits just behind the Newport News Visitor Center. If you're up for a good hike, it's interesting to follow the April 16, 1862, battle, where McClellan's only real attempt to break Magruder's lines was handily rebuffed by Confederate forces. The Confederate fortifications in this park are very well preserved, and a well-marked trail describes the battle action in detail. The park is open daily; a small museum on-site is open seasonally.

Berkeley Plantation
12602 Harrison Landing Rd.
Charles City, VA
(804) 829-6018
(888) 466-6018
www.berkeleyplantation.com

Although this historic plantation isn't quite on the peninsula, situated between Williamsburg and Richmond, we've included it in this chapter because it was McClellan's final stop, the supply headquarters where the troops gathered to assess the damages and triumphs of the campaign. The military bugle call "Taps" was composed here during this time. Beyond its Civil War significance, Berkeley Plantation is a must-see for any American history enthusiast. Built in the 1600s, the plantation was the site of the first Thanksgiving celebration and was the birthplace of President William Henry Harrison.

Casemate Museum
20 Bernard Rd.
Fort Monroe, VA
(757) 788-3391
www.monroe.army.mil

The largest moat-encircled masonry fort in the United States, Fort Monroe was built between 1819 and 1834 to protect the entrance to Hampton Roads and the port cities located nearby. If you're exploring the Peninsula Campaign, the Casemate Museum is a great starting point. In May 1861, mere weeks after the first shots were fired on Fort Sumter, three slaves escaped from the peninsula fortifications, to which they were assigned, to this Union fortification. Union major general Benjamin F. Butler refused to return the slaves to their owner, suggesting that the Fugitive Slave Act did not apply in a foreign country, which Virginia was claiming to be.

Prior to the war, Robert E. Lee was assigned here as the post engineer. The fort was never taken by the South during the war. As part of the Fort Monroe tour, you can also take a boat over to Fort Wool (in season), an island fort which was used by Union forces against the Confederate forts at Norfolk during the campaign. The Casemate Museum outlines the history of the fort, highlighting the area where ex-Confederate president Jefferson Davis was imprisoned after the war. Admission is free.

Congress and Cumberland Overlook, Christopher Newport Park
2500 W. Ave.
Newport News, VA
(757) 247-8523

The first major naval battle in Hampton Roads took place March 8, 1862, when the 30-gun, wooden USS *Cumberland* and its likewise wooden sister vessel, the 50-gun USS *Congress,* clashed with the CSS *Virginia*. The *Virginia* was formerly known as the USS *Merrimack,* a steam frigate whose hull was cut down to the waterline and covered with 4 inches of iron plate. The ship was also fitted with a 6-foot, 1,500-pound iron ram. The *Virginia* rammed the *Cumberland,* quickly sinking the ship and the 121 sailors aboard. Watching its cannon shot merely bounce off the ironclad ship, the *Congress* surrendered, handing the Confederate navy a fantastic victory. Interpretive plaques offer more insights into the day's events.

Endview Plantation
362 Yorktown Rd.
Newport News, VA
(757) 887-1862
www.endview.org

Endview was used first by the Confederacy and later by the Union as a hospital, but even prior to the Peninsula Campaign, it had already witnessed a fair amount of military action in the Revolutionary War and during the War of 1812. Nevertheless, the circa-1769 house was reconstructed to its appearance during the Civil War era, which remains the focus of many of its interpretive programs and living history activities. It is open for tours; hours vary by season.

Fort Norfolk
810 Front St.
Norfolk, VA
(757) 640-1720
www.norfolkhistorical.org/fort/index.html

The last of 19 harbor-front forts commissioned by George Washington, Fort Norfolk helped protect the port city during the War of 1812. In the Civil War, the fort was occupied by both sides. Confederates used its magazines to arm the *Virginia* prior to its battle with the *Monitor*. Union forces claimed the fort back later the same year and used it as a prison. Tours are free.

Hampton History Museum
120 Old Hampton Lane
Hampton, VA
(757) 727-1610
www.hampton.va.us/history_museum

Opened in 2003, the Hampton History Museum traces more than four centuries of local history through 10 fascinating galleries, including one with a special emphasis on the Civil War era. Visitors explore the importance of Fort Monroe and the nearby Battle of Big Bethel through displays and artifacts. The port of Hampton sustained considerable damage during the Civil War, burned by Confederate loyalists on August 7, 1861, to prevent it from falling into Union hands. Near the museum, St. John's Church, built in 1728, is the only building to partially survive the fire.

Lee Hall Mansion
163 Yorktown Rd.
Newport News, VA
(757) 888-3371
www.leehall.org

Confederate commanders Johnston and Magruder used this elegant 1850s mansion as their headquarters at the height of the action. The last large plantation house of its era in the region, today Lee Hall is home to a museum that interprets the actions and activities of the Peninsula Campaign. Many of the house's public rooms—including a formal dining room, music room, ladies' parlor, and two bedrooms—have been carefully restored to their antebellum glory. In the English basement, you'll find exhibits related to the campaign, such as a tablecloth recovered from the *Monitor* and artifacts recovered from nearby battlefields. The museum also serves as a starting point for bus tours of local Civil War sites; check the Web site for more information. Museum hours vary by season.

Lee's Mill Battlefield Park
180 River's Ridge Circle
Newport News, VA
(757) 247-8523

Lee's Mill was the site of the first notable exchange during the Peninsula Campaign. General George McClellan and his Union forces left nearby Young's Mill on April 5, 1862, and were met with more than 1,800 Confederate soldiers and massive earthen fortifications at Lee's Mill, prompting McClellan to lay siege to the Confederates' Yorktown-Warwick defense line. Trails and interpretive signs in the park outline each side's positions during the brief skirmish.

The Mariners' Museum & USS *Monitor* Center
100 Museum Dr.
Newport News, VA
(757) 596-2222
www.mariner.org
www.monitorcenter.org

Long one of the nation's top maritime outfits, the Mariners' Museum opened the new USS *Monitor* Center just in time to mark the 145th anniversary of the ironclad's epic battle with the CSS *Virginia*. The *Monitor*, which foundered and sank off Cape Hatteras on December 31, 1962, was discovered in 1973. While the bulk of the vessel remains on the ocean floor—protected by her status as a National Marine Sanctuary—the *Monitor*'s massive Dahlgren guns and gun carriages, turret, steam engine, propeller, anchor, and hundreds of other artifacts have been raised from the deep in recent years.

The centerpiece of the museum is the fantastic full size replica of the ironclad. The museum also offers a battle theater and state-of-the-art exhibits designed to tell the story of the *Monitor* from her birth through her discovery, recovery, and conservation. Already a must-see for history buffs, the Mariners' Museum has added a unique jewel that any Civil War buff will want to see and experience. The museum is wheelchair accessible.

Monitor-Merrimack Overlook
Anderson Park
Sixteenth St. and Oak Ave.
Newport News, VA
(757) 247-8523

Anderson Park, located on the tip of the peninsula, offers a perfect view of the site where the two legendary ironclads clashed on March 9, 1862, forever changing naval warfare. The USS *Monitor* charged into the waters surrounding Newport News in the aftermath of the sinking of the USS *Cumberland* and the surrender of the USS *Congress*. The two ironclads fired shells at each other for hours, yet neither managed to cause much damage on the other.

Nauticus and Hampton Roads Naval History Museum
One Waterside Dr.
Norfolk, VA
(757) 664-1000
www.nauticus.org

Hampton Roads's maritime history comes to life in this 120,000-square-foot science center. The Civil War is just one of the topics explored at this maritime center, whose focus ranges from sharks and aquatic life to meteorology to naval warfare. The Hampton Roads Naval History Museum, located on the second floor of the museum complex, pays careful attention to the battle of the *Monitor* and the *Virginia,* along with other Civil War exchanges. The museum is also responsible for the operations of the Battleship *Wisconsin,* docked in the harbor and considered part of the center. Admission to the Naval History Museum and the *Wisconsin* is free. Museum hours vary by season.

Portsmouth Naval Shipyard Museum
2 High St.
Portsmouth, VA
(757) 393-8591
www.portsnavalmuseums.com

Portsmouth is home to the oldest naval shipyard in the United States, the Gosport Navy Yard. Confederates took command of the yard on April 21, 1861, and used it to convert the USS *Merrimac* into the ironclad CSS *Virginia.* In later years, Gosport would also see the construction of the *Texas,* the country's first battleship, and the *Langley,* the world's first aircraft carrier. A permanent exhibition at the museum focuses on the history of Portsmouth and the Gosport Navy Yard, focusing on the country's pivotal early years, 1785–1840. Admission includes entry to the Lightship *Portsmouth.*

Seven Days' Battle Sites
(See Richmond National Battlefield Park in the Confederate Capital chapter)

The Seven Days' Battle refers to offensive action by Robert E. Lee, which forced Union troops to retreat back to the James River in June–July 1862. Many of the places that saw action—including Drewry's Bluff, Beaver Dam Creek, Gaines' Mill, Savage's Station, Glendale, and Malvern Hill—are considered part of the Richmond National Battlefield Park, due to their location between the Peninsula and the Confederate capital.

Virginia War Museum
9285 Warwick Blvd.
Newport News, VA
(757) 247-8523
www.warmuseum.org

This local museum displays more than 50,000 artifacts from wars fought on Virginia soil from 1775 to the present. With so many Civil War battles waged in Virginia, it's no surprise to find a sizable part of the exhibit space and artifacts dedicated to the war, plus the antebellum era and the aftermath. It's also a good place to check for living history programs and Civil War sites tours.

TOURS

Miss Hampton II
710 Settlers Landing Rd.
Hampton, VA
(757) 722-9102
www.misshamptoncruises.com

To truly appreciate the history that transpired in these tidewater ports, your best bet may be to see the sights from the water. From Hampton, hop on board the *Miss Hampton II,* which offers daily (twice daily during the summer) tours of Hampton Roads. The two-and-a-half-hour tour shows off the historic Chesapeake Bay and even includes a stop at Fort Wool, opposite Fort Monroe, in season (weather permitting).

ACCOMMODATIONS

Aldrich House Bed and Breakfast $$$–$$$$
505 Capitol Court
Williamsburg, VA
(757) 229-5422
(877) 745-0887
www.aldrichhouse.com

While most of the Civil War attractions listed in this section are located to the east of Williamsburg, we've included some lodging and dining options in the area. By stationing yourself in Williamsburg for a few days, you'll be within a short drive of not only the peninsula, but also Richmond and Petersburg. You'll also have access to some of southern Virginia's top accommodations, restaurants, and other historical attractions. Located just a few blocks from Colonial Williamsburg, Tom and Sue Patton's Aldrich House is a great choice for family travelers who prefer the intimacy of a B&B. There are three spacious, elegantly appointed rooms, one with its own fireplace and one with a whirlpool tub. Cat lovers (and those with allergies) should be aware that KC, the resident cat, has free rein throughout the house. Breakfast is delightful, featuring fresh fare like eggs, pancakes, and fruit salad.

Boxwood Inn $$–$$$$
10 Elmhurst St.
Historic Lee Hall Village
Newport News, VA
(757) 888-8854
www.boxwood-inn.com

This small and charming, 1896 bed-and-breakfast in the heart of Virginia's Historic Triangle offers friendly service, queen-size beds, private baths, and antique furnishings at bargain prices. Military history buffs may want to stay in the room that once played host to General John J. Pershing and other military officers stationed at nearby Fort Eustis during World War I and II. Lee Hall Mansion, used by John Magruder and Joseph E. Johnston as headquarters during the Peninsula Campaign, is just a half-mile away. The inn offers not only a continental breakfast, but an "early bird" to-go basket if you want to get an early start to a busy day of sightseeing, or a "sleepy head" breakfast for late risers. If you don't spend the night here, consider coming by for dinner. The Boxwood Inn produces a regular lineup of themed dinner shows: a plantation dinner featuring the South's finest, a 1940s-themed buffet of victory garden classics, murder mysteries, Dickensian Christmas celebrations, and more.

Cedars Bed and Breakfast $$$$
616 Jamestown Rd.
Williamsburg, VA
(800) 296-3591
www.cedarsofwilliamsburg.com

With 10 rooms and suites, Cedars is not only the biggest B&B in Williamsburg, but also one of the best in the South. The Georgian-style mansion was built in the 1930s using bricks collected by schoolchildren from the demolition of a century-old building on the nearby campus of the College of William & Mary. History buffs will love the location, a mere seven-minute walk to Colonial Williamsburg. A bountiful breakfast is served each morning, featuring entrees like eggs Florentine, blueberry French toast, and peach cobbler, and the refrigerator and common areas are stocked with snacks for midday noshing. Amenities range from central air, fireplaces, and mini-refrigerators to private baths and wireless Internet access.

Glencoe Inn $$$–$$$$
222 North St.
Portsmouth, VA
(757) 397-8128
www.glencoeinn.com

Further down the peninsula, the charming town of Portsmouth puts you in easy driving distance of Hampton and Newport News, but also within 30 miles of the inviting sandy coastline of Virginia Beach. Portsmouth's Glencoe Inn is historic and romantic, situated alongside the Elizabeth River in the heart of the Portsmouth historic district. The innkeeper, Ann McGowan McGlynn, carries a Scottish theme throughout the four-bedroom Victorian-style property. Rooms are affordably priced, outfitted with comfortable beds, private baths, and postcard-perfect views of the surrounding harbor and gardens. Some even feature kitchenettes and Jacuzzis.

Lady Neptune Bed & Breakfast $$$$
507 N. First St.
Hampton, VA
(757) 848-5877
http://ladyneptuneinn.com

This 1930s-era house was narrowly spared from demolition in 1988 when development pressures threatened the land on which it was located. Too attached to their home to watch it come down, the owners elected to have the house lifted off its foundation, placed on a large barge, and carried across the Chesapeake to its new home in Hampton. There are four clean and comfortable guest rooms, each appointed with a four-poster, queen-size bed. For breakfast, you can expect a generous buffet loaded with Southern classics like fried catfish, Chesapeake crab eggs Benedict, shrimp, grits, and eggs. The inn also puts together special packages with pampering treats for romantic getaways or theme park and attractions tickets for family vacations.

Magnolia House Bed & Breakfast $$$$
232 S. Armistead Ave.
Hampton, VA
(757) 722-2888
www.maghousehampton.com

This impeccably furnished bed-and-breakfast offers a delightful stay in historic Hampton and provides easy access to the other towns and attractions on and around the peninsula. Hosts Joyce and Lankford Blair are warm and hospitable, eager to help you with sightseeing suggestions, information, and, of course, a delicious breakfast each morning. Rooms are beautifully decorated with art and accents that match the historic character of the house, plus luxurious linens, terry robes and slippers, wireless Internet, and other amenities.

Williamsburg Inn $$$$
136 E. Francis St.
Williamsburg, VA
(757) 253-2277
www.colonialwilliamsburg.com

If you want to treat yourself to luxurious accommodations as you explore the peninsula—and you're prepared to pay prices that match—book a room at the legendary Williamsburg Inn. It's here that Queen Elizabeth II stayed during her 2007 visit to commemorate the 400th anniversary of the founding of Jamestown (and, incidentally, it's where she stayed during her 1957 visit for the 350th anniversary as well). The 62 guest rooms in the main hotel are large and tastefully decorated, featuring bathrooms with granite sinks, marble floors, and wonderful soaking tubs, plus free wireless Internet and other posh amenities. Perhaps the inn's best selling point, however, is its location in the heart of Colonial Williamsburg, and golfers will find its surrounding course to be both beautiful and challenging. If an overnight stay here isn't in your budget, however, it's also a great choice for afternoon tea service.

A Williamsburg White House $$$$
Bed and Breakfast Inn
718 Jamestown Rd.
Williamsburg, VA
(757) 229-8580
(866) 229-8580
www.awilliamsburgwhitehouse.com

Billing itself as the "Williamsburg White House," this historic B&B takes its name quite literally. Each room—even the dining room and the library—bears the name of a former commander in chief. Civil War travelers may opt for the Lincoln Suite, which features his-and-hers private baths and a king-size four-poster bed (but be wary of the adjacent Ford's Theatre sitting room). Slightly smaller rooms are named and decorated in honor of Washington, Jefferson, and Theodore Roosevelt. You're also given executive privilege to linger in the Diplomatic Reception Room, the Reagan Dining Room, or the Kennedy Library as you enjoy complimentary drinks and hors d'oeuvres in the afternoon. For breakfast, you'll enjoy decadent pastries, quiches, frittatas, and other tasty creations. Colonial Williamsburg is a quick walk away, and the peninsula Civil War sites are easily reachable with an hour's drive.

RESTAURANTS

Bill's Seafood House $
10900 Warwick Blvd.
Newport News, VA
(757) 595-4320

You won't find any seafood restaurant gimmicks here—not even a waterside location. But if you're curious where locals go to taste fresh catches from the surrounding bay, this is it. Feast on generous portions of fried flounder, homemade hush puppies, delicious crab cakes, and other fresh and flavorful classics. There's no need to dress up to dine at this comfortable family-friendly eatery, located near the Mariners' Museum.

Fat Canary $$$
410 Duke of Gloucester St.
Williamsburg, VA
(757) 229-3333
www.fatcanarywilliamsburg.com

Fat Canary consistently earns rave reviews as one of Colonial Williamsburg's top culinary attractions—and for that reason you may wish to make a reservation in advance. The menu is constantly changing to reflect what's fresh and in season, and given chef Thomas Power's diverse culinary experience, you never know what to expect. Try something unique like sea scallops in coconut curry or soft-shell crabs. The Fat Canary shares its location with The Cheese Shop, a great place to pick up a sandwich or snack to go.

Second St. $$
140 Second St.
Williamsburg, VA
(757) 220-2286
www.secondst.com

An "American Bistro" and a Williamsburg mainstay, Second St. sports the look of a converted foundry or a community brew pub—but with much better food, including a burger voted Williamsburg's best. Beyond the burgers, you'll find a menu stocked with all sorts of American classics: meatloaf, shrimp and grits, and a hearty pile of jumbo lump crab meat served with au gratin potatoes and garlic spinach. Desserts like carrot cake and sticky bun bread pudding are designed to be shared.

Shields Tavern $$
422 E. Duke of Gloucester St.
Williamsburg, VA
(757) 229-2141
www.colonialwilliamsburg.com

One of four taverns operated by the Colonial Williamsburg Foundation, Shields Tavern is a combination coffeehouse/tavern. During the day, it's a great place for a pick-me-up cappuccino or a light bite like egg custard or Smithfield honey ham biscuits. During the evening, the tavern side becomes more prominent as diners enjoy Welsh rarebit, Yorkshire beef patties, and other period classics. Hours change seasonally; it's best to call in advance.

Surf Rider Restaurant $$
1 Marina Rd.
Hampton, VA
(757) 723-9366

Although it's not easy to locate, this out-of-the-way eatery serves up some of the region's finest seafood, including delectable lump crab cakes, fried shrimp, and scallops, oysters, and soft-shell crabs in season. It's often packed with locals, which should always be a good sign that you've successfully stepped beyond the tourist scene. While the seafood is bound to please, you also shouldn't pass on their signature vegetable, a gigantic broccoli stalk, perfectly cooked and paired with hollandaise sauce. There's plenty for two or more to share. An added bonus: You can take in the glorious view of the marina through the floor-to-ceiling windows.

The Trellis $$$
403 Duke of Gloucester St.
Williamsburg, VA
(757) 229-8610
www.thetrellis.com

A longtime favorite restaurant for special occasions, The Trellis serves regional fare that changes regularly to make the most of what's in season. Look for light and flavorful salads in summer and hearty soups and roasted vegetables in winter. When it comes to main courses, you won't go wrong with a fresh seafood selection or succulent cuts of meat, best when paired with healthy side dishes like bourbon-braised peaches or saffron-infused rice. For chocolate lovers, dessert is a must; The Trellis is famous for its "Death by Chocolate" cake.

Richmond: Confederate Capital

Darley.   Bobbett fc

Ruins of Richmond, 1865

For a few months during the spring of 1861, Montgomery, Alabama, was the capital of the Confederacy. Had it remained there, the war likely would have been fought much differently. For reasons of military and political expedience, however, the Confederate government relocated to Richmond in July. From then on, the Rebel defense of that city—and Federal attempts to capture it—came to represent the Confederacy's struggle for survival. Entire Union campaigns revolved around its capture until 1864, when Ulysses S. Grant's siege of Petersburg made its fall inevitable.

One of the South's top manufacturing cities prior to 1861, wartime Richmond housed one of the nation's top makers of ammunition and railroad steel (Tredegar Iron Works) along with multiple hospital facilities (such as the massive Chimborazo Hospital) within its protective line of earthen fortifications. Its citizens suffered increasingly as the war ground on, as prices multiplied and food grew scarce. Fiercely protected for four years, Richmond fell within hours of Petersburg's capture on April 3, 1865. Shortly after, a massive fire scalded the city, leaving much of downtown an ashen skeleton of its former self. And while Washingtonians greeted news of the city's fall with wild celebrations, weary Richmond residents cringed. "The saddest moment of my life," one Virginian said, "was when I saw that Southern Cross dragged down and the Stars and Stripes run up above the capitol."

Richmond burned to the ground on April 3, 1865.

Jefferson Davis

A senator from Mississippi and a former secretary of war (under President Franklin Pierce), Jefferson Davis was also a Mexican War veteran, and he longed for a field command in the new Confederate Army. Instead, he was selected as the Confederacy's first president.

During four years of civil war, both the Union and Confederate governments suffered from internal political squabbling—the kind of infighting that affected military policy and, ultimately, success on the battlefield. Forced to handle ambitious politicians such as William Seward and Simon Cameron, Abraham Lincoln proved to have an amazingly deft political touch. Jefferson Davis had it at least as bad in Richmond, dealing with a recalcitrant Congress and cabinet while mediating constant and legendary feuds among his generals, and often between officers (such as Joseph E. Johnston) and himself. (Davis went through six secretaries of war in four years.) Cold and impersonal with anyone outside of his family, Davis lacked both the disarming charm and management skills of his Washington counterpart. "He did not know the arts of the politician," his wife Varina wrote of him, "and would not practice them if understood."

Jefferson Davis with his family

The fall of Richmond left the Confederate government on the run. Davis was eventually captured and shipped off to prison at Fortress Monroe, where he languished for two years. He was never charged with anything, however, and eventually resettled in Mississippi, where he died in 1889. Davis was buried in Richmond's Hollywood Cemetery.

HISTORIC SITES

American Civil War Center at Historic Tredegar
500 Tredegar St.
(804) 780-1865
www.tredegar.org

The American Civil War Center is a great starting point for a Civil War odyssey. It's the only facility of its kind to tell the story of the war from three perspectives: Northern, Southern, and African-American. Each side's contributions, principles, battles, and leaders are woven together in the flagship permanent exhibition, In the Cause of Liberty, housed in the 1861 Tredegar Ironworks Gun Foundry. Start your visit with an introductory film, *What Caused the Civil War?*, to brush up on the historical basics. The Richmond Civil War Visitor Center is located on the site as well.

Confederate War Memorial Chapel
2900 Grove Ave.
(804) 740-4479

Constructed in 1887 by Confederate veterans, this chapel honors fallen soldiers who fought for the Southern cause. It's now operated by the Sons of Confederate Veterans. The chapel's unusual mosaic stained-glass windows make it worth a visit for art and architecture lovers.

Hollywood Cemetery
412 S. Cherry St.
(804) 648-8501
www.hollywoodcemetery.org

The burial site of presidents James Monroe and John Tyler, beautiful Hollywood Cemetery is better known to Civil War folk as the resting place of George Pickett (and a number of Gettysburg victims), J. E. B. Stuart, Fitzhugh Lee, and Confederate president Jefferson Davis.

Monument Avenue
Harrison St. to Horsepen Rd.

Monument Avenue is the only street in the United States that's also a National Historic Landmark. Development of the avenue began in 1890, following the dedication of a monument to Robert E. Lee. Other Confederate notables honored with statues along the 5-mile street include Jefferson Davis, J. E. B. Stuart, Stonewall Jackson, and Matthew Fontaine Maury. Between the monuments, you'll also find beautiful, elaborate homes in a variety of architectural styles.

Museum and White House of the Confederacy
1201 E. Clay St.
(804) 649-1861
www.moc.org

For more than 100 years this museum has been the place to go to learn about all things Confederate, from the brief history of the Confederate nation through the fabled idea of the Lost Cause. Today the museum boasts three floors of exhibits, an unmatched collection of Confederacy-related artifacts (including the original Confederate White House located next door), a research library, and a museum store. Among the objects on permanent display here are the original oil painting, *The Last Meeting of Lee and Jackson,* and the first-ever Army of Northern Virginia battle flag.

Museum hours vary by season, and it is wheelchair accessible. Combination tickets to the museum and the White House are available at a discount.

Richmond National Battlefield Park
3215 E. Broad St.
(804) 226-1981, ext. 23
www.nps.gov/rich

There is plenty to see around Richmond, and much of it is packed into Richmond National Battlefield Park. Divided into 13 separate areas, this massive park incorporates a number of battlefield sites that could easily stand as parks on their own. Visitors should plan to spend a couple of days in the area, as the park boasts dozens of miles of original (and elaborate) field fortifications, self-guided trails, and several museums and visitor centers.

The first stop on a visit here should be at the Richmond Civil War Visitor Center at Tredegar Iron Works (490 Tredegar Street), a fantastic, three-floor collection of exhibits, artifacts, interactive displays, and machinery used by Tredegar to produce much of the South's artillery and ammunition. The center also offers maps, a CD for a Seven Days' Battle driving tour, and a park orientation film, which only the most learned Civil War students should consider passing up.

A second major highlight of the park is the Chimborazo Medical Museum (3215 East Broad Street), a facility dedicated to the history of the hospital and Civil War medicine. A collection of original surgical instruments, exhibits, and a short film are offered at this facility, where more than 75,000 Confederate soldiers received treatment during the war.

Most of the park, of course, is comprised of battlefields and other sites, including Chickahominy Bluff, Beaver Dam Creek, Gaines' Mill, Cold Harbor Battlefield and Visitor Center (5515 Anderson-Wright Drive), the Garthright House, Glendale Battlefield and Visitor Center (8301 Willis Church Road), Malvern Hill Battlefield, Fort Harrison (visitor center located at 8621 Battlefield Park Road), Drewry's Bluff, and Parker's Battery. Several of these sites have been included in other tours due to their relation to other campaigns, such as the Peninsula Campaign.

The park battlefields are open free of charge from sunrise to sunset. Visitor centers at Tredegar Iron Works, Chimborazo, and Cold Harbor are open daily. The Glendale and Fort Harrison visitor centers maintain the same hours, from June through Aug.

OTHER SITES OF INTEREST

Valentine Richmond History Center
1015 E. Clay St.
(804) 649-0711
www.richmondhistorycenter.com

If you want to learn more about the history of the Richmond region, plan a stop at this museum. The centerpiece is the 1812 Wickham House, which offers a glimpse of Richmond life in the early 19th century. Other permanent exhibits explore the sculptures of museum namesake Edward Viginius Valentine and offer a glimpse of the residents who have called Richmond home since its settlement days. The History Center also organizes regularly scheduled bus tours and walking tours that showcase Richmond history. Admission includes entrance to the History Center, Wickham House, Monumental Church, and the John Marshall House, home to the former Supreme Court chief justice. The church is open from May through Oct.

Virginia Historical Society
428 N. Blvd.
(804) 358-4901
www.vahistorical.org

There's no place in the Commonwealth that boasts a collection of Virginia artifacts quite like this one, housed in a building that was once known as "Battle Abbey." Long-term exhibits focus on Virginia history, residential life, and archaeology, but temporary exhibits occasionally focus on Civil War themes. Admission is free.

Virginia State Capitol and Executive Mansion
Capitol Square at Ninth and Grace Sts.
(804) 698-1788
www.virginiacapitol.gov

Thomas Jefferson designed the seat of Virginia's government, now home to America's oldest continuous representative assembly. During the Civil War, the Confederate legislature convened in the neoclassical building. The Capitol completed a major renovation—its first since 1906—in time for the Jamestown 400th anniversary celebration and Queen Elizabeth II's 2007 visit. Admission is free.

ACCOMMODATIONS

The Berkeley Hotel $$$$
1200 E. Cary St.
(804) 780-1300
www.berkeleyhotel.com

Follow a lamp-lit cobblestone road to this charming boutique hotel in the Shockoe Slip neighborhood, one of Richmond's most popular destinations for eclectic dining, shopping, and nightlife. While the hotel does its part to blend in with the surrounding historic neighborhood through design and decor, it was actually constructed in 1988. Its 56 rooms are quite spacious and outfitted with amenities like wireless Internet and in-room coffeemakers, along with service befitting its AAA four-diamond rating. If you haven't gotten enough exercise walking the battlefields, you can also take advantage of gym privileges at a nearby YMCA.

Grace Manor Inn $$$$
1853 W. Grace St.
(804) 353-4334
www.thegracemanorinn.com

The Grace Manor Inn takes the B&B experience to new heights. "Let us pamper you" is the motto around here, and innkeepers Dawn and Albert Schick (and their three pet Yorkies) do their part to live up to the promise. Their 1910 Victorian house, located in the Fan District, is a delightful retreat after a long day of sightseeing. They've thought of everything—even bubble bath in the bathroom. You'll be treated to a sampler of cheeses and a complimentary bottle of wine, perfect for savoring on the second-floor balcony overlooking picturesque gardens. Of course, a gourmet breakfast awaits you in the morning and fresh-baked cookies are on hand for an afternoon snack.

Jefferson Hotel $$$$
101 W. Franklin St.
(804) 788-8000
www.jeffersonhotel.com

A National Historic Landmark, Jefferson is a grand place, boasting nearly 300 rooms, a five-diamond restaurant, and top-of-the-line service. It's the best hotel in the region, hands down, and a great choice for an on-the-road splurge. The Jefferson was built in 1895 at the whopping cost of nearly $10 million by Lewis Ginter, who served in the Confederate Army, and then later made a fortune in the tobacco industry. The luxurious hotel narrowly survived a fire at the turn of the century and, after a few fashionable decades, eventually fell into disrepair in the 1950s and 1960s, closing in 1980. It reopened in 1983 following a $34 million renovation. Rooms are large and elegantly furnished to match the circa-1895 character of the hotel. Step into the lobby, and you'll be greeted by a life-size marble sculpture of Mr. Jefferson himself, carved by Richmond sculptor Edward Valentine prior to the hotel's opening. For many guests, however, the dramatic, 36-step spiral staircase is the prime attraction, reminiscent of *Gone with the Wind*. The hotel's on-site fine-dining restaurant, Lemaire, serves outstanding American cuisine, or guests can take advantage of the Jefferson's complimentary shuttle service for more nearby dining options.

Linden Row Inn $$–$$$
100 E. Franklin St.
(804) 783-7000
www.lindenrowinn.com

Located in historic downtown Richmond within walking distance of the state capitol, the circa-1840 Linden Row Inn reflects European styling while offering Southern hospitality.

The inn keeps true to its historic setting with architectural features like high ceilings, fireplaces, and elegant Victorian decor. At the same time, its 70 spacious rooms (and 7 suites) feature modern conveniences such as high-speed Internet service, newly remodeled bathrooms, complimentary continental breakfast, and premium TV channels at very reasonable prices.

West-Bocock House $$
1107 Grove Ave.
(804) 358-6174
http://users.rcn.com/brwest

The circa-1871 West-Bocock House blends the charms of the country with the conveniences of the city. You'll fall asleep on luxurious French linens in an antique four-poster bed and wake up to a plantation-style breakfast in the morning. At the same time, you're just footsteps away from Richmond's dynamic restaurant and nightlife scene. Innkeeper Billie Rees West goes out of her way to show her guests the true meaning of Southern hospitality. Rooms are comfortable and reasonably priced.

William Catlin House $$–$$$
2304 E. Broad St.
(804) 780-3746

Built in 1845, this B&B lacks the frills of some of the other properties listed in this guide, but it's clean, quiet, and comfortable, located in the Church Hill neighborhood. There are seven guest rooms, including a couple of two-bedroom suites, all furnished with antiques to match the historic setting. The Shockoe Slip neighborhood is just a few minutes away, with great shopping, dining, and nightlife options.

The William Miller House $$$$
1129 Floyd Ave.
(804) 254-2928
www.ourfanhomes.com

This cozy B&B is a fantastic find, nestled among lovely Victorian homes in the historic Fan District. Named for its first owner, the Greek-Revival-style home was built just after the Civil War. Both guest bedrooms are colorfully furnished—one with a king-size bed and one with a queen-size bed—and outfitted with a full private bathroom. Co-owner (and accomplished chef) Mike Rohde prepares sumptuous breakfast creations like orange-poppyseed waffles with blueberry sauce or scrambled eggs with Boursin cheese.

RESTAURANTS

Bank and Vault $$$
1005 Main St.
(804) 648-3070
www.bankandvault.com

What was once a turn-of-the-century Richmond bank is now home to one of the city's hottest dining destinations. The space itself—"Bank" refers to the dining section and "Vault" to the bar—is chic and stylish, with high ceilings and walls decorated with bright fabric paintings. On the menu, you'll find New American cuisine, including some new takes on Southern classics. Fried green tomatoes are served with pepper maple Boursin-style cheese and pancetta. Grilled flat-iron steak is topped with cabrales cheese and paired with piquant patatas bravas. For a satisfying main dish, try the grilled double pork chop, served atop white cheddar grits with greens on the side. The wine list focuses on value, serving interesting varietals from Spain, Italy, Australia, and California.

Caliente $$
2922 Park Ave.
(804) 340-2920
www.calienterichmond.com

If you're a fan of spicy food—be it Mexican, Cajun, or Thai—book a table at this fun, roadhouse-style Richmond eatery. Caliente lives up to its name, specializing in anything and everything that's hot and spicy. Even the decor is red, decorated with peppers and bottled hot sauces for diners in need of an extra kick. Start with a jerk chicken quesadilla or buffalo gator bites, made with fried alligator tail. Move on to main dishes like a chorizo and black bean sub, jambalaya, or coconut-crusted chicken with orange chipotle vinaigrette. Finish it off with a dessert that's cool and refreshing, like the decadent piña colada bread pudding. Whatever you choose, you can count on it being flavorful and reasonably priced, and the outdoor patio seating is an added plus in mild weather.

Comfort $$
200 W. Broad St.
(804) 780-0004
www.comfortrestaurant.com

You might not expect a hot new restaurant to have a simple name like Comfort, but you'll be sorry if you pass on this one. Comfort's menu, much like its light, airy decor, is simple and basic. At lunch, you'll find BLTs and fried catfish sand-wiches, while dinner entrees include heartier servings of meatloaf, pulled pork, rabbit, and grilled trout. For many diners, however, the side dishes are the main attractions; macaroni and cheese, baked squash casserole, black-eyed peas, and cheddar cheese grits are delectable and perfect for sharing.

Extra Billy's BBQ $$
5205 W. Broad St.
(804) 282-3949
www.extrabillys.com

A Richmond tradition for more than 20 years, Extra Billy's is named for William Smith—the 60-something Virginia politi-cian who led a brigade in Stonewall Jackson's corps before becoming governor in 1864. He would be proud of his namesake restaurant, whose ribs have been rated the area's best. A mouth-watering "Billy Burger," plate of honey-glazed ribs, or sizzling spit-roasted half-chicken will more than sat-isfy Civil War buffs fresh from the battlefields of Richmond.

The Hard Shell $$$
1411 E. Cary St.
(804) 643-2333
www.thehardshell.com

Perhaps the top seafood restaurant in all of Richmond, The Hard Shell offers a luscious selection of the freshest oysters, clams, lobster, clams, and more. But there are plenty of deli-cious items on the menu for non-seafood eaters, such as filet mignon, ribs, and even vegetarian dishes. A nice wine list complements the dinner menu, and a wedge of the restau-rant's key lime pie tops off any meal. Its location in Shockoe Slip makes it a good starting point for a night on the town.

La Grotta $$$
1218 E. Cary St.
(804) 644-2466
www.lagrottaristorante.com

If you're a fan of Italian cuisine, you won't want to miss a meal at the intimate La Grotta, a below-ground restaurant located in Shockoe Slip. A popular "special occasion" choice

for locals, don't be surprised to find diners celebrating prom night, birthdays, anniversaries, or even engagements. Nevertheless, you won't feel out of place if you didn't pack a jacket and tie. The menu is loaded with Italian favorites like gnocchi, veal scallopine, and osso bucco, served with lovely focaccia and hard-crusted Italian bread. For dessert, you can't go wrong with profiteroles or ricotta cheesecake.

Legend Brewing Company $$
321 W. Seventh St.
(804) 232-3446
www.legendbrewing.com

Beer lovers should pay a visit to Legend Brewing Company, the oldest and largest microbrewery in central Virginia. The brewery makes nine varieties of beer, including the Legend Brown Ale, the most popular variety, flavored with caramel and malt. While the handcrafted beers are the draw for beer lovers, Legend is also a good choice for a light meal. Beer-friendly appetizers range from basics like soft pretzels and bratwursts to complex pairings like barbecue strawberry duck crepes with mushroom ceviche. Choose from main dishes like ribs, burgers, crab cakes, and bratwurst paired with German potato salad, plus a full selection of classic desserts.

Millie's $$$
2603 E. Main St.
(804) 643-5512
www.milliesdiner.com

Opened in 1989, Millie's is one of Richmond's best-loved eat-eries, fashioned after a 1950s-style diner but known for its innovative, upscale cuisine prepared in an open kitchen. The restaurant is housed in the former turn-of-the-century build-ing that used to serve the workers who toiled in Richmond's tobacco fields. Menus change regularly, but you can count on fresh, seasonal fare. Summertime selections might in-clude pan-seared rockfish with zucchini gratin or spicy Thai shrimp with asparagus, shiitake, lime, and red cabbage, while heartier fare reigns supreme in the winter.

Sidewalk Café $$
2101 W. Main St.
(804) 358-0645
www.sidewalkinthefan.com

Ask a Richmond local for a restaurant pick, and they're likely to name this popular eatery in the Fan District. It's packed most nights of the week with diners savoring the Mediterranean, American, and Italian favorites. Share an order of hot fries, hummus and pita, or nachos to start, then choose from main courses like souvlaki, pasta, or scallops baked with feta which are nicely complemented by selections from the simple, affordable wine list.

The Tobacco Company Restaurant and Club $$$
1201 E. Cary St.
(804) 782-9555
www.thetobaccocompany.com

For more than three decades, The Tobacco Company has been delighting Richmond diners with casual dining in a pleasant Victorian setting. You can expect extensive brunch, lunch, and dinner menus featuring flavorful regional fare. Sample tasty selections like zesty crab croquettes, velvety she-crab soup, crab-stuffed flounder, and prime rib. The three-story restaurant is also a popular choice for late-night entertainment, with live music in its first level. Dinner reservations are required.

Zeus Gallery $$$
201 N. Belmont Ave.
(804) 359-3219

The small and cozy Zeus Gallery has drawn crowds of food-loving locals and visitors to its home in the Fan District for more than a dozen years. The menu, spelled out on a chalk-board, is fresh, funky, and ever-changing, peppered with Mediterranean flavors. Look for starters like wild mushroom and Sonoma goat cheese or shrimp and chevre-stuffed wontons and main dishes like spicy dry-rubbed pork medallions with dried cherries and apricots or porcini-dusted pan-seared salmon. There are only 12 tables, however, so you'd be wise to make a reservation.

Petersburg: Siege Warfare

Darley.

Battle of Petersburg

Located 25 miles south of Richmond, Petersburg was a massive conduit through which railroads connected the Confederate capital with Virginia's southern and western neighbors. With Petersburg in his pocket, a well-supplied and supported Union general could isolate and gradually squeeze the life out of Richmond's defenders.

That is precisely what happened. After a month of vicious combat capped by the stunning June 3, 1864, reverse at Cold Harbor, Lieutenant General Ulysses S. Grant suddenly drove south and over the James River in mid-June, putting the Army of the Potomac in place to grab Petersburg and isolate Richmond.

Between June 15 and 20, Major General P. G. T. Beauregard's Rebel defenders—helped after the 17th by Robert E. Lee's shifting army—repelled a series of Union attacks on the Petersburg fortifications. Resigning himself to a siege, Grant continued to probe and dig toward Lee's lines, attacking Lee's communications and transportation while stretching the Confederate trenches west. In July, Jubal Early's raid up the Shenandoah Valley forced Grant to detach elements of two corps to Washington, but it made little difference.

Grant's grip on their city tightened, and Petersburg residents struggled to find the bare necessities of life. Weary infantrymen dug in around Petersburg ducked shells and skirmished. Most were still trying to sleep on the morning of July 30 when Yankees lit a fuse beneath

their trenches. Minutes later, the sizzling combustible ignited four tons of gunpowder, catapulting tons of earth, sandbags, logs, and lifeless soldiers toward the sky and ripping a gap in the Rebel lines southeast of town.

While Union batteries delivered a follow-up barrage of shells, shocked Confederate officers recovered from their surprise to shift troops into the hole in their lines, which Union regiments were rushing to expand. Botched orders and shoddy leadership turned this opportunity into disaster. Federals charged straight into the huge ditch created by the explosion, and they were quickly pinned in by howling Confederates. Reinforcements of the United States Colored Troops (USCT) fought bravely, as vicious hand-to-hand fighting turned into a near massacre. Federals fell by the score.

Union troops in the trenches at Petersburg

Blame for the disastrous "Battle of the Crater" fell on Ninth Corps commander Major General Ambrose Burnside, who had developed a nasty penchant for wasting the lives of his soldiers. Meanwhile, the siege continued. Booming Union artillery drove thousands of people into the hills, where they struggled to avoid shells and find enough food to survive in makeshift bunkers. On the inland side of the city, Confederate soldiers pinned down in miles of trenches fought their own battle to survive—enemy soldiers as well as hunger. Beyond the

Rebel trenches were even more extensive Union pits, into which more men in blue seemed to pour each week.

Although Lee managed to keep Grant at bay throughout the fall of 1864, his army withered away during the winter. On March 25, 1865, Lee sent Major General John Gordon after a Union outpost to the east. Gordon briefly overran Fort Stedman, but could not hold it, and lost more than 3,000 men in the process.

By April 3, 1865, Petersburg, Virginia, was a dusty ghost town, pinned against the Appomattox River by hideously scarred landscape and Major General George Gordon Meade's Union Army of the Potomac (now more often identified with General in Chief Ulysses S. Grant, who had made it his headquarters). Nearly 10 months of dirty, dusty siege had sealed the city's fate.

On April 1, Union infantry and cavalry overwhelmed Confederate defenders west of the city at a crossroads called Five Forks. With his right flank turned, Robert E. Lee could do little when Grant attacked his lines a day later. Finally convinced of success, Grant attacked Lee's

James Longstreet

Four years of war took their toll on James Longstreet, who was severely wounded in 1864 and widely blamed for the crucial Confederate defeat at Gettysburg in July 1863. For Robert E. Lee's longest-serving corps commander, it only got worse at war's end.

Born in South Carolina in 1820 and raised in Georgia, James Longstreet graduated from the U.S. Military Academy at West Point in 1842. There he lived and studied with a number of future Civil War generals and began a lifelong friendship with Ulysses S. Grant. After service in the Mexican War and several years of frontier duty, Major Longstreet resigned from the army in May 1861. He subsequently accepted a commission as a lieutenant colonel in the Confederate States Army.

Between the June 25, 1862, clash at Oak Grove and the May 3, 1863, Battle of Chancellorsville, Longstreet and Thomas J. Jackson commanded the two corps of Robert E. Lee's seemingly invincible Army of Northern Virginia. Without Jackson, who was mortally wounded at Chancellorsville, Lee was finally beaten at Gettysburg in July 1863. The stinging defeat ended his invasion of the North and spurred charges of insubordination

General James Longstreet

against Longstreet, who had disagreed with Lee on tactics. The following May in Virginia's tangled Wilderness, a Yankee bullet knocked Longstreet from the saddle, leaving Lee without his two best subordinates in his ongoing duel with Longstreet's old friend, and now Union general in chief, Ulysses S. Grant.

By the time Longstreet returned to action in October 1864, Grant had Lee's army in a stranglehold that could only end in submission. Near Appomattox Court House, Virginia, on April 9, 1865, Union Major General George Custer approached Longstreet under a flag of truce and demanded—in the name of Major General Philip Sheridan—the Confederate Army's surrender. "I am not the commander of this army," an irritated Longstreet replied, "and if I were, I would not surrender it to General Sheridan." Later that day, Lee surrendered the army to Grant.

After the war, Longstreet's acceptance of federal Reconstruction legislation, his willingness to accept Federal employment (including an appointment by President Grant as surveyor of customs for New Orleans, and a later stint as U.S. minister to Turkey), and, especially, his defection to Grant's Republican Party, made him a prime target for ex-Confederates looking to cast blame. Longstreet's slowness, they claimed, had cost Lee time and again—especially at Gettysburg, where the corps commander had waited too long to attack the Union left on July 2.

Longstreet defended his Civil War service in his memoirs; a few friends also came to his defense. In recent years, historians have restored to a large degree the general's tarnished reputation, returning him to his place in Civil War memory as Lee's "old war-horse."

A. P. Hill

Born in Culpeper, Virginia, in 1825, Ambrose Powell Hill graduated from West Point in 1847. After stints in Mexico and on various frontier posts, Hill, in March 1861, traded his U.S. Army commission for the colonelcy of a Confederate army regiment, the 13th Virginia. Promoted rapidly up to major general, Hill established himself as one of the South's great fighting generals, with a knack for saving the day. At Antietam in September 1862, the timely arrival of Hill's division on the battlefield south of Sharpsburg prevented a disaster brewing for the Confederates. After taking command of Robert E. Lee's III Corps following the death of Stonewall Jackson, Hill fought at Gettysburg, the Wilderness, and Spotsylvania—proving to be better suited to a smaller command. In the predawn darkness of April 2, 1865, just a week before Lee's surrender at Appomattox, a Union bullet killed Hill outside the trenches west of Petersburg.

General A. P. Hill

thinly manned trenches west of the city late on April 2. Lee evacuated the remnants of his army and headed west, while Federals occupied Petersburg and, a day later, the Confederate capital. The war was all but over.

HISTORIC SITES

Blandford Church
111 Rochelle Lane
Petersburg, VA
(804) 733-2396
www.petersburg-va.org/tourism/blandford.htm

This historic church was built in 1735, but abandoned in 1806 as the congregation drifted to a new downtown location. It regained prominence in 1901 when the Ladies Memorial Association of Petersburg began to rebuild the church as a Confederate Memorial. The association turned to each former Confederate state and solicited funds to create and install a Tiffany commemorative window to honor the fallen soldiers from that state. The adjacent cemetery was the site of the first Memorial Day celebration, held in June 1866 in honor of the 30,000 Confederate soldiers buried on the hillside.

Pamplin Historical Park and the National Museum of the Civil War Soldier
6125 Boydton Plank Rd.
Petersburg, VA
(804) 861-2408
(877) PAMPLIN
www.pamplinpark.org

Pamplin Park is an absolute must-see. Since opening in 1994, this combination museum/battlefield has ranked among the nation's most visited historical sites. Continuous expansion (now 422 acres) coupled with state-of-the-art exhibits and educational programs have since made it the top Civil War attraction in the country.

The park is named for its benefactors—Robert B. Pamplin Sr. and Dr. Robert B. Pamplin Jr.—who in 1991 purchased a parcel of land that bore remnants of the Confederate earthworks overrun by Ulysses S. Grant's Union soldiers on April 2, 1865. A second purchase, of the adjacent Tudor plantation, was made in 1994; restoration of this home (once used as a headquarters by Confederate general Samuel McGowan) was completed two years later. In 1999, Pamplin Park's title grew a little longer with the opening of the National Museum of the Civil War Soldier, a fantastic, 25,000-square-foot facility that beautifully countered the park's natural features with state-of-the-art exhibits and visitor services. Even more recently, the park has opened reconstructed slave quarters on the Tudor Hall Plantation, hiking trails, the Banks House (Grant's headquarters), and a new Education Center.

Strengths of the park include its superb staff and the opportunities for visitors to learn about the Civil War in several different ways, including hands-on outdoor exhibits;

living history demonstrations; interpretive, audio-aided museum exhibits; and classes designed for all age groups. Excellent permanent exhibits include "Duty Called Me Here," "A Land Worth Fighting For," "The Battle of the Breakthrough," and "Slavery in America." Visitors with children, meanwhile, will want to consider contacting the park about its new Adventure Camp, a fun but educational introduction to soldier life for folks of all ages.

Petersburg National Battlefield
5001 Siege Rd.
Petersburg, VA
(804) 732-3531, ext. 200
www.nps.gov/pete

The ugly, daily struggle at Petersburg was unlike the fighting on any other battlefield, ensuring that its earthen remnants would found a park like no other. Stretching more than 30 miles from the Union supply depot at City Point to the Five Forks Battlefield west of the city, this remarkable park includes three visitor centers along its 13-stop driving tour. The foremost of these, the Eastern Front Visitor Center, is a mini museum, using exhibits and interactive displays to tell the military and civilian story of the nine-and-a-half-month siege.

Highlights of the park include the City Point headquarters cabin used by Grant during the siege; a massive, 13-inch seacoast mortar (like the terrifying "Dictator" used here by Federals); outstanding examples of fieldworks; the Elliott's salient entrance to the Petersburg mine shaft; the original crater site; and endless earthworks.

The Siege Museum
15 W. Bank St.
Petersburg, VA
(804) 733-2404
www.petersburg-va.org/tourism/siege.htm

The Siege Museum takes a closer look at civilian life in the town of Petersburg before, during, and in the aftermath of the Civil War. Much of the collection focuses on how the town suffered and persevered during the 10-month siege, the longest of its kind in American military history. As you tour the museum, you can also catch an 18-minute film outlining the town's involvement in the Civil War, narrated by Joseph Cotton.

ACCOMMODATIONS

High Street Inn $$–$$$
405 High St.
Petersburg, VA
(804) 733-0271
www.thehighstreetinn.com

The Queen Anne–inspired High Street Inn was built just before the dawn of the 21st century and has enjoyed quite a colorful past. Built as a residence, it was later used as a funeral home and a Veterans of Foreign War outpost before becoming a B&B more than 20 years ago. Check in to one of the six spacious guest rooms, each of which bears the name of a historic street or character in Petersburg history. You'll be treated to hospitable touches like lemonade and cookies delivered to your room and generous breakfast service.

Ragland Mansion Guesthouse $$–$$$
205 S. Sycamore St.
Petersburg, VA
(800) 861-8898
www.raglandmansion.com

Italianate in design, the grand Ragland Mansion stands out in the historic Poplar Lawn district. The antebellum mansion survived the siege and was expanded on by railroad tycoon Alexander Hamilton. Its seven rooms (plus a suite) all feature air-conditioning, private baths, queen- or king-size beds, and TV.

Walker House Bed & Breakfast $$–$$$
3280 S. Crater Rd.
Petersburg, VA
(804) 861-5822
www.walker-house.com

This circa-1815 mansion boasts four bedrooms named for the four seasons, each of which is equipped with cable TV, wireless Internet, and private bath. Each room is decorated to reflect its namesake season. Even if the inn is full, however, you'd never know that you were sharing it with four other parties. Help yourself to snacks and beverages, available 'round the clock in a second-floor kitchenette. Wake up to a breakfast of fresh waffles, sausages, and other tasty creations. The house itself is not without its own Civil War connections; it was used for the inquiry after the Battle of the Crater featured in the movie *Cold Mountain*.

RESTAURANTS

Alexander's $$
101 W. Bank St.
Petersburg, VA
(804) 733-7134

Located in historic Old Towne Petersburg, this charming and friendly little restaurant offers Italian and Greek cuisine, including gourmet sandwiches and salads and flavorful specialties like souvlaki, roasted leg of lamb, lasagna, and manicotti.

Andrade's International Restaurant $$
7 Bollingbrook St.
Petersburg, VA
(804) 733-1515
www.andradesinternational.com

Recommended by local innkeepers, Andrade's is known for serving Peruvian and Spanish fare like delicious garlic shrimp and seasoned steaks. On a pleasant afternoon, you can also sit outside and enjoy dining alfresco.

Jimmy's Grille $$
16 Goodrich Dr.
Petersburg, VA
(804) 733-3181
www.jimmysgrilleinc.com

This local favorite is tucked away from the main strip, but the rewards are worth it if you seek it out. Feast on lavish breakfasts like omelets and pancakes or lunch and dinner entrees like barbecued pork sandwiches or classics like meatloaf and fried chicken featured in the daily special.

King's Famous Barbecue $$
2910 S. Crater Rd.
Petersburg, VA
(804) 732-0975
www.kingsfamousbarbecue.com

A Petersburg institution, opened in 1946, locals and visitors know King's for its legendary barbecue, with pork, beef, ribs, and chicken constantly smoking in an open pit in the pine-paneled restaurant dining room. The meat is flavorful when served straight from the pit or seasoned with King's vinegar-flavored sauce. That's not the only thing on the menu, though; there's also southern-fried chicken, ham steak, and fresh seafood.

Nanny's $$
11900 S. Crater Rd.
Petersburg, VA
(804) 733-6619
http://nannysbbq.com

Bring your appetite to Nanny's, where you'll find one of the most generous, ample buffet spreads in town. The menu varies every day, but you can count on fried chicken, barbecued beef, pulled pork, fried fish, and other Southern classics.

Appomattox: The End

Darley.

Although his beloved, dwindling Army of Northern Virginia had been forced from its Petersburg and Richmond trenches on April 2–3, General Robert E. Lee was not quite ready to give up the fight. If his hungry army could obtain provisions and elude Union pursuit long enough to link up with General Joseph E. Johnston's army in North Carolina, the combined Confederate force could, in turn (hopefully), confront Grant's hordes and those of Major General William T. Sherman, whose three-wing army had by now scorched its way through Georgia and on through the Carolinas.

Lee had limited options and Grant had the resources to account for each. Marching west to Amelia Court House, Lee found ammunition rather than the rations he had ordered. Losing a day to foraging, he next found his path blocked by Philip Sheridan's Union cavalry. Lee skirted the trouble and continued west, hoping to find rations and transportation south at Farmville. On April 6, however, elements of Grant's army caught up with Lee's divided rear guard near Sailor's Creek, smashed in its center, and forced the surrender of some 8,000 Confederates—including Union nemesis Lieutenant General Richard Ewell.

Seventy-two hours later it was over. Leading his last 30,000 men west in a bid for the rail head at Lynchburg, Lee found Federal cavalry awaiting him at the village of Appomattox Court House. Early on April 9, Lee half-heartedly ordered a probe of Grant's encircling lines, and realized that the inevitable had finally occurred. After exchanging notes with his Yankee antagonist, Lee agreed to meet with Grant to discuss surrender terms. A comfortable meeting place was found in the home of Wilmer McLean, whom Lee and an aide encountered early in the afternoon.

Dressed in a typically dusty and informal uniform, Grant entered the McLean home at about 1:30 p.m. and shook Lee's hand. The worn-out Confederate commander looked resplendent in his best dress grays. During the afternoon, the two old West Pointers ironed out an agreement that allowed Lee's officers to retain their sidearms, and his soldiers to return home with their horses, requiring only that they agree not to take up arms again. Grant then arranged for the delivery of rations to Lee's disheartened soldiers. "I felt anything other than rejoicing at the downfall of a foe who had fought so long and valiantly," Grant recalled later, "and had suffered so much for a cause."

Lieutenant George Custer prepares for third charge at Sailor's Creek.

By late afternoon, it was all over. Although Joseph E. Johnston's small army and other Confederate units were still active, they would not remain so for long. Lee's surrender was the South's death knell. After shaking hands with Union officers, many of whom he knew well from the prewar army, Lee walked slowly outside and mounted up. Grant emerged behind, and his subordinates joined him in doffing their hats as Lee rode off, returning the salute.

The surrender at Appomattox Court House

The Wilmer McLean house, photographed in April 1865

Wilmer McLean

Following the July 21, 1861, Battle of Bull Run, 47-year-old, Manassas, Virginia, native Wilmer McLean moved his family out of town to protect them from the violence sure to come. Prior to the battle, Confederate brigadier general P. G. T. Beauregard had commandeered McLean's farmhouse as a headquarters; shortly after, a Union shell smashed through his kitchen. McLean sent his family south, and eventually purchased a home for them in the picturesque central Virginia village of Appomattox Court House.

On April 9, 1865, McLean encountered Confederate colonel Charles Marshall, an aide to Lee, who asked him to recommend a suitable meeting place for the opposing commanding generals. After some discussion, the bewildered McLean offered to open his own home to the generals. By early afternoon, Ulysses S. Grant and Robert E. Lee were sitting at small tables in McLean's front parlor.

In the wake of the historic meeting, McLean found his parlor looted—rooted through for souvenirs by excited Yankee officers (some of which, at least, they paid for). The table at which Lee signed the surrender document eventually wound up in the hands of Mrs. George Armstrong Custer, a gift from Major General Philip Sheridan, who reportedly bought it from its owner. (The Smithsonian Institution now owns it.) It has since been said that the Civil War began in Wilmer McLean's kitchen and ended in his parlor.

HISTORIC SITES

Appomattox Court House National Historical Park
VA Rte. 24 (2 miles northeast of the town of Appomattox)
Appomattox, VA
(434) 352-8987
www.nps.gov/apco

The site of Robert E. Lee's surrender to Ulysses S. Grant on April 9, 1865, the tiny town of Appomattox is now a historical village of 27 buildings spread across 1,700 acres. The gem of the park is, of course, the Wilmer McLean House, which stands near the park visitor center. The park offers tours and audio-visual programs, and also features a 70-seat theater in which two slide shows are presented daily.

Sailor's Creek Battlefield Historical State Park
788 Twin Lakes Rd.
Green Bay, VA
(434) 392-3435

Lee's army began to lose steam at Sailor's Creek, and a handful of the sites that witnessed the action and the decline are open to the public. At Hillsman House, the centerpiece of the state park, Union troops plotted their attack on the Confederates stationed across the creek. Drive through the park and listen to radio interpretations of the events of April 6, 1865. Admission is free.

TOURS

Lee's Retreat Driving Tour
425 Cockade Alley
(800) 673-8732
www.varetreat.com

Radio messages and interpretive signs at more than 25 points of interest follow the movement of Lee and his troops during the last days of action, April 2–9, 1865. As you drive through the area and spot Civil War Trails signs, tune your radio to 1600 or 1620 AM to hear commentary at sites like Namozine Church, which witnessed some action on April 3 and later served as a hospital; Amelia Springs, the site of a skirmish on April 6; and Rice's Depot, which served as Lee's headquarters in the final days. The Web site www.varetreat .com outlines the points of interest along the way.

ACCOMMODATIONS

Babcock House Bed and Breakfast Inn $$$–$$$$
250 Oakleigh Ave.
Appomattox, VA
(434) 352-7532
www.babcockhouse.com

Located just minutes from the site of Robert E. Lee's surrender of his army to Ulysses S. Grant, Babcock House is at the center of all there is to see in this historic town. Built in 1884, Babcock House retains its 19th-century looks, while offering all the modern amenities. Innkeepers Jerry and Sheila Palamar pride themselves on offering "gracious hospitality and elegant dining in a friendly and informal atmosphere." Room rates are quite reasonable, especially considering the location. If you're staying elsewhere, make the Babcock House your stop for dinner.

Ivy Creek Farm B&B $$$–$$$$
2812 Link Rd.
Lynchburg, VA
(434) 384-3802
www.ivycreekfarm.com

While Appomattox is the real attraction for Civil War buffs who visit the region, the small town is limited in its lodging and dining options. Fortunately, Lynchburg is a short 30-minute drive away, and it presents additional options for travelers looking for a place to relax after a day of sightseeing. This popular eight-acre country-estate-turned-B&B located just outside of Lynchburg features three roomy guest suites furnished with period decor. Guests are treated to a full gourmet breakfast featuring decadent treats like brioche stuffed with eggs and fresh mushrooms, pumpkin–chocolate chip muffins, and caramel-glazed biscuits. There's also an indoor pool on the property, and rooms are outfitted with wireless Internet, flat-screen TVs, and Bose sound systems.

Longacre $$–$$$$
1670 Church St.
Appomattox, VA
(434) 352-9251
www.longacreva.com

Just 3 miles from the courthouse, this Tudor-style country retreat rambles across two acres with gardens, a fish pond,

and spectacular forests. Guests can take advantage of common amenities like an indoor lap pool, a cozy tea room, a screened-in porch that's perfect for nature watching, plus hammocks for lazy afternoons. The breakfast spread is loaded with homemade goodies like pancakes, quiche, and home-baked breads, plus cereals and fruits. You can rent a room or check in to the Carriage House, which also boasts a private pool and full kitchen.

Rockcliffe Farm Retreat & Lodge $$$$
816 Walkers Ford Rd.
Concord, VA
(434) 933-4371
www.rockcliffefarm.com

This woodsy retreat is perfect for Civil War buffs who love the great outdoors and for touring groups. The three-bedroom lodge can accommodate up to 16 guests. You'll have the run of the house, including its full kitchen, library, and sunroom. Despite its rustic setting, you'll find the farm equipped with modern must-haves like wireless Internet and satellite TV. For a true outdoors adventure, ask about bicycle, canoe, and kayak rentals.

Spring Grove Farm Bed and Breakfast $$$–$$$$
3440 Spring Grove Rd.
Appomattox, VA
(434) 352-7429
(877) 409-1865
www.springgrovefarm.com

For a combination of indoor and outdoor relaxation (and the opportunity to really get away), it would be hard to top Spring Grove Farm Bed and Breakfast—a beautifully restored, 11-room (or suite), 16-fireplace, house on 200 acres of lush Virginia farmland. After wandering around the grounds or enjoying its gardens, guests can relax inside by enjoying a movie in the inn's stylish media room, playing one of its two grand pianos, or spending some quiet time with a book on a porch or walking the property with one of the property's seven dogs. Rates, which depend on the room booked, are a bit pricey, but no one could argue with the surroundings.

RESTAURANTS

Granny Bee's Restaurant $
Corner of Main and Lee Sts.
Appomattox, VA
(434) 352-2259

If you only eat one meal in Appomattox, there's a good chance it'll be at Granny Bee's. It's the best place in town for "Yummy Home Style Cooking," plain and simple. Breakfast and lunch specials can be had for just $4, and the dinner menu features country staples like baked ham and hamburger steak in addition to excellent steak and prime rib dinners.

The Huddle House $$
Route 460 and Court St.
Appomattox, VA
(434) 352-9104
www.huddlehouse.com

Georgia-based Huddle House gets our nod in Appomattox due to its "open 24 hours" status—a plus for Civil War buffs who arrive in town late after a long day of sightseeing and driving. Tourists can relax in Huddle House's classic diner atmosphere while plotting the next day's itinerary over a "Big House Platter," steak, or omelet (breakfast is served all day), all at reasonable prices.

Isabella's Italian Trattoria $$–$$$
4925 Boonsboro Rd.
Lynchburg, VA
(434) 385-1660
www.isabellasitalian.com

If it's Italian fare you're craving, drive to Lynchburg and plan a stop at Isabella's. It's not your traditional Italian fare, however; you might start with a light and refreshing Italian mojito, made with limoncello, rum, club soda, and fresh basil. You'll find inventive spins on Italian classics; a Caprese salad is prepared with grilled tomatoes, and chicken parmesan comes crusted in parmesan cheese and pepper, doused in mozzarella cream and served atop a bed of linguini with tomato and basil sauce. Garden-fresh salads come dressed up with Mediterranean accents like port wine–soaked figs or toasted hazelnuts.

WAR IN THE SOUTH

North Carolina:
Outer Banks to the
Last Great Battle

✶ ✶ ✶ ✶ ✶ ✶ ✶ ✶ ✶ ✶ ✶ ✶ ✶ ✶ ✶

At the beginning of the "secessionist crisis" after the election of Lincoln in 1860, North Carolina was not overwhelmingly in favor of leaving the Union, as opposed to the position held by its namesake to the south. Although a primarily agricultural state, there were relatively few slaves in the state, which was marked more by disparate, isolated elements mostly either neutral or outright hostile to both slavery and secession. Several meetings across the state in late 1860 only produced more evidence that if secession was inevitable, it would be done without widespread support.

As the talks raged, South Carolina declared itself free and independent on December 20, the first state to openly declare secession from the Union. In North Carolina the only large public celebration was a mass gun firing in Wilmington, a city noted for its strong support of secession. This act touched off even more heated debate across the state, the majority of citizens tending to support staying within the Union but radically opposed to any force being used to keep any state within it. In the middle of this continued crisis, the state legislature disbanded for the Christmas holidays.

With most of the politicians safely out of the way, staunch secessionists in Wilmington went into action. On December 31 the citizens of that coastal city wired Governor John Willis Ellis of North Carolina, asking permission to seize nearby Forts Caswell and Johnston, as they constituted a "threat" to access to the city via the Cape Fear River. Ellis refused, but the citizens went ahead and seized the forts based on an erroneous rumor that U.S. troops were on the way to garrison them. Ellis then immediately demanded that the Carolinians evacuate the posts and, when they had removed themselves, sent a letter of apology to President James Buchanan (Lincoln had been elected but not yet sworn in at the time).

All through the winter and early spring of 1861, Ellis continued to act in an equally conservative manner, backed up by a February 28 popular vote against a secession convention. Even the secession of six fellow Southern states and the bombardment of Fort Sumter at Charleston on April 12 and 13, 1861, did not sway Ellis from his Unionist stance. The deciding factor, however, was an April 15 letter from Lincoln asking Ellis to provide two regiments of militia to "suppress the Southern insurrection." Ellis regarded such a request as a violation of the 10th Amendment to the Constitution, which addresses the rights of the individual states, and "a gross usurpation of power" on Lincoln's part.

Ellis immediately ordered the seizure and occupation of "Federal" (or Union) installations and forts throughout the state and called for a secession convention. On May 20 the convention met and, by the day's end, had both adopted an ordinance of secession and ratified the Confederate constitution. North Carolina was officially separated from and at war against the United States government.

THE WAR IN NORTH CAROLINA BEGINS

*A*lthough General in Chief Winfield "Old Fuss and Feathers" Scott had warned at the very beginning that the war with the South would be long and bloody, most military personnel and civilians alike, North and South, scoffed at the 75-year-old general's words. The initial rush of volunteers was fueled partially by the desire to see combat "before it's all over," and 90-day enlistments of both individuals and militia companies were common on both sides.

Several small battles won by the Confederacy in the summer of 1861 seemed to indicate that the South was en route to an early victory, and both armies readied for what each thought would be a single, gigantic, and ultimately decisive battle. On July 21 these armies—28,452 Union troops facing 32,232 Confederates—met at Bull Run Creek, Virginia, in a daylong clash that ended with the whipped Union Army running in sheer panic from the field back to Washington. The First Manassas, as Southerners referred to the battle, was both a resounding major victory for the Confederacy and a signal that this was to be a long, bloody war, just as Scott, who was active only in the earliest stages of the war, had predicted.

The Battle of First Bull Run, also known as First Manassas

After getting over the shock of initial Confederate victories and the threat against Washington itself, Union Army planners settled down and devised a multiphase strategy to use against the Confederacy, ironically based on Scott's original ideas. One of the first offensive operations would be against North Carolina's eastern coast to seize the vital ports and cut the north-south supply lines from Virginia. To start carrying out these plans, Major General Benjamin Franklin Butler and Commodore Silas Horton Stringham were given the task of attacking and capturing the most important Outer Banks access to mainland ports, Hatteras Inlet.

HATTERAS ISLAND

*W*hen the war began, one of the Union strategies was to blockade the entire Southern coastline to prevent supplies from coming in and amphibious forces from going out. To counter the threat on the Outer Banks, Confederate authorities had given their blessing to a quasi-military fleet of small sailing vessels, dubbed the "mosquito fleet" by the Southerners and "privateers" or outright "pirates" by the Union, that ran supplies through the blockade, helped defend the coastline, and raided Union ships when the opportunity arose.

To back up these small ships, five strong forts and associated batteries were constructed all along the narrow coastal islands and placed under the overall command of Brigadier General Walter Gwynn and Brigadier (later Major) General Theophilus Hunter Holmes.

Battle of Hatteras Inlet

To defend the vital access to the mainland ports, North Carolina had constructed two forts on either side of the small village on the north bank of Hatteras Inlet: Fort Hatteras, mounting 12 32-pounder guns, was on the west side and closer to the channel itself, while Fort Clark, mounting 5 32-pounders, was a smaller post closer to the ocean. Commanding the Hatteras Island Garrison was Colonel William F. Martin, with about 400 men and 35 artillery pieces. With news of the approach of Union naval forces, Martin requested and received somewhere between 200 and 400 reinforcements (accounts vary significantly on this point).

Modern Times at Forts Hatteras and Clark

Due to wind, tide, and time, nothing remains of either post, save a marker near the ferry station indicating where the two forts were, now a spot in the Atlantic Ocean. A small museum at the base of the Cape Hatteras Lighthouse houses a display about the Civil War activities here.

Despite the dearth of actual Civil War sites in this area, we recommend a visit as part of a tour of eastern North Carolina; while the Outer Banks have radically changed shape and size in the past 140-plus years, you can get a good idea of the terrain and weather that both sides had to endure in this campaign.

Sailing down from Fort Monroe, Virginia, was a Union naval force of seven ships under the direct command of Stringham mounting 143 cannon, accompanied by transports carrying Colonel Rush Christopher Hawkins's 9th (Hawkins's Zouaves) and Colonel Max Weber's 20th (United Turner Rifles) New York Infantry Regiments and the 2nd U.S. Artillery Battery, under overall command of Butler. Arriving off the Outer Banks on the afternoon of August 27, Stringham spent the rest of the night getting his ships into position to begin a bombardment of the Confederate posts the next morning.

On the morning of August 28, Stringham opened a heavy bombardment of Fort Clark and landed roughly half of Weber's regiment under its cover. Weber's men easily overran the Confederate defenses after Fort Clark's defenders ran out of ammunition and retreated to Fort Hatteras. Watching the Confederates running over the sand dunes toward the westernmost fort, Stringham initially thought both posts had been abandoned. The USS *Monticello* was ordered into the inlet to give chase, only to be pounded by heavy fire from the still-ready-and-able defenders at Fort Hatteras. Ironically, the only Union casualty of the day's action was an infantryman killed by one of Stringham's guns. As the seas were rough, Stringham was forced to pull offshore, leaving Weber's small command to hold Fort Clark.

During the night, as Martin was preparing to attack and retake Fort Clark, Commodore Samuel Barron, chief of Confederate Coastal Defenses, landed with about 200 reinforcements and took over command of the operation. His first action was to cancel any offensive plans, and he spent the rest of the night repairing and building up the sand-work fort.

The next morning, August 29, Stringham sailed back into the inlet over calm seas and began a heavy bombardment of Fort Hatteras. Unusual for the time, he kept his ships moving while firing and stayed just out of range of the Confederate guns. After just three hours of intense fire, Barron was forced to surrender his post and troops.

After Hatteras

After the fall of Forts Clark and Hatteras, Confederate authorities saw that defense of the narrow Outer Banks was going to require major manpower and resources, neither of which was in abundance. Fort Morgan at Ocracoke Inlet and Fort Oregon at Oregon Inlet were quickly evacuated and just as quickly taken over by

Butler's forces, leaving just Fort Fisher at the Cape Fear River inlet to guard the outer coast.

The only other action on this part of the Outer Banks was a bizarre set of pursuits between Hatteras and Chicamacomico (now called Rodanthe). On October 5, 1861, Hawkins had advanced toward the tiny north Hatteras Island town, aiming to capture and garrison it against the threat of a Confederate overland attack. As they closed in, six Confederate gunboats suddenly appeared, as well as part of a small Georgia infantry regiment (the 3rd Georgia Volunteers). A chase ensued, with the Union force running the 20 miles back to the safety of Fort Hatteras. The next morning, the chase began again, but this time Hawkins's men pursued the Confederates all the way back to Chicamacomico. Both sides' navies joined in on the fun, running on either side of the narrow banks in support of their troops. Besides a relative handful of casualties, absolutely nothing came out of what the locals referred to as the "Chicamacomico Races."

BURNSIDE'S 1862 NORTH CAROLINA EXPEDITION

*W*ith the quick fall of all Confederate defenses on the Outer Banks, two things became glaringly obvious: First, there would be a major effort by Union forces to capture the mainland ports, and second, the only thing standing in their way was the small garrison on Roanoke Island. As the defense of the entire area was now under Confederate control, Governor Clark, who had replaced Governor Ellis after his death, had little control over the buildup of a strong defense network, which the civilian population was demanding from him. Richmond responded to his appeals by simply stating that all available trained men were urgently needed in Virginia (not coincidentally, where the officials stating this were also located) and that only newly recruited units were available.

Brigadier General Richard Caswell Gatlin was placed in command of the newly formed Confederate Department of North Carolina. Brigadier (later Major) General Daniel Harvey Hill was initially given the responsibility of defending Albemarle and Pamlico Sounds (the body of water between the Outer Banks and the North Carolina mainland), and Brigadier General Joseph Reid Anderson took command of the District of Cape Fear, based out of Wilmington. Hill was apparently less than happy with his new command and soon resigned in order to return to General Robert E. Lee's Army of Northern Virginia. To replace him, Gatlin placed Brigadier General Henry Alexander Wise in charge of the area north of Roanoke Island and Brigadier General Lawrence O'Bryan Branch in charge of the stretch from Roanoke Island to New Bern.

Exact numbers are very hard to pin down, but Wise and Branch had somewhere around 8,000 men between their commands, most with Branch in New Bern. Roanoke Island itself was guarded by a few earthwork forts; on the east (seaward) side of the island was a tiny, unnamed two-gun redoubt at Ballast Point, and in the center was Fort Russell, a three-gun redoubt having a clear field of fire over the only road. On the northwest (landward) side of the island were three small sand-work forts, Forts Huger, Blanchard, and Bartow, mounting a total of 25 guns. No posts were established on the southern side of the island, possibly because the land was marshy and difficult to build on.

The most unusual defensive position was Fort Forrest, a partially sunken ship on the mainland side of the sound that had been reinforced and mounted with eight guns. The entire Confederate garrison numbered a mere 1,434 North Carolinians and Virginians, soon placed under direct command of Colonel H. M. Shaw, after Wise became too ill to lead the defense. Shaw was intensely disliked by his own men; one source quotes a soldier remarking that he was "not worth the powder and ball it would take to kill him."

Sailing rapidly toward this unhappy situation was the largest amphibious force the United States had ever mounted to that time: 67 gunboats and troop transports under command of Commodore (later Rear Admiral) L. M. Goldsborough, carrying more than 13,000 soldiers under command of Brigadier (later Major) General Ambrose Everett Burnside, an undistinguished commander better known for his namesake whiskers than his military prowess. In his postwar memoirs, General in Chief Ulysses S. Grant said that Burnside was "an officer who was generally liked and respected. He was not, however, fitted to command an army." By February 4, 1862, the fleet had crossed Hatteras Inlet safely and prepared to sail north into combat against Confederate forces.

The Burnside Expedition landing at Roanoke Island, February 7, 1862

THE ASSAULT OF ROANOKE ISLAND

*B*urnside's fleet moved north through Pamlico Sound and arrived just off Roanoke Island on February 7, opening fire on Fort Barrow between 10:30 and 11 a.m. Out of range, none of the Confederate batteries was able to return in kind the pounding artillery barrage. The Union Navy kept up their fire all day long, and as darkness approached, Burnside began landing his infantry at Ashby's Harbor, about 3 miles south of the southernmost Confederate fortification. A scouting force of about 200 Confederates was nearby when the first Union troops came ashore, but the Southerners elected to retreat to Fort Russell without firing a shot. By midnight, more than 10,000 Union soldiers were ashore, along with several artillery batteries, and making preparations to move north at first light.

At dawn, three Massachusetts infantry regiments (the 23rd, 25th, and 27th) attacked Fort Russell, strung in a line formation across the road and into the swamps on both sides. The 400 Confederate defenders opened a heavy fire down the road, blocking the 25th Massachusetts advance, but they were soon forced to pull out when the other Union infantry appeared out of the swamps on both flanks. As the Massachusetts men entered the redoubt to take the abandoned guns, Hawkins's Zouaves (the 9th New York Infantry Regiment) burst out of the woods and ran screaming over the redoubt's walls. Hawkins claimed ever after that his men had bravely charged and taken the "heavily defended" post.

As the rest of the Union infantry regiments rapidly advanced north on the small island toward the remaining three forts, Shaw decided that any further action was futile and surrendered without firing another shot. In all, 23 Confederate soldiers, including Wise's own son, were killed in the brief action, 58 were wounded, 62 missing, and about 2,500 captured, including nearly a thousand newly landed reinforcements from Nags Head. Burnside reported his losses at 37 killed, 214 wounded, and 13 missing, including 6 sailors killed and 17 wounded by return fire from Fort Bartow.

ACTIONS IN EASTERN NORTH CAROLINA

*W*ith the Outer Banks and Roanoke Island secured and available as staging bases, Burnside turned his attention to the mainland. His overall strategy from this point on seems a little less clear-cut than the assault on the Outer Banks; his postwar writings in *Battles and*

Leaders only state that he had presented a rather vague plan to General of the Army George B. McClellan, to outfit an amphibious force "with a view to establishing lodgements on the Southern coast, landing troops, and penetrating into the interior . . ."

With the Confederate "mosquito fleet" fleeing with hardly a shot fired before the powerful Union naval task force, elements of Commandant Goldsborough's fleet set off after their base at Elizabeth City, across Albemarle Sound from the newly captured island, taking it with little resistance on February 10. Part of Burnside's infantry command joined the navy for "assaults" on other, nondefended towns off the sound; Edenton was ransacked on February 11, and Winton was burned to the ground on the 20th. Burnside and Goldsborough then turned their attention to the south, across Pamlico Sound toward New Bern and Morehead City.

To defend against the oncoming Union force, Branch had about 4,000 ill-trained and untested troops, stretched in a line from an old earthwork named Fort Thompson near the Neuse River, across the Atlantic and North Carolina Railroad track to Morehead City, and on nearly 2½ miles to the bank of the Trent River. Later Civil War doctrine called for a line this size to be held by at least 10 times this number of men. Six smaller earthwork redoubts surrounded the city, and an incomplete line of trench works and redoubts ran around the outside of Fort Thompson, all unmanned due to the manpower shortage. Branch's only real defensive advantage was the 13 guns inside Fort Thompson and the 12 scattered down the line of battle. The other forts were mounted with cannon, but none was positioned to resist a land-based attack.

On March 12 the Union fleet arrived in the Neuse River about 14 miles south of New Bern, and that night Burnside gave his orders for the attack. The men were to land the next morning, march north along the Morehead City Road, and attack the Confederate line at the earliest opportunity.

The Battle of New Bern

Branch had arranged his men in an interesting fashion, possibly due to his total lack of experience or training as a military officer (he was a lawyer turned politician turned politically appointed general). From the fort to the railroad track, he placed four regiments, Major John A. Gilmer's 27th, Lieutenant Colonel Thomas L. Lowe's 28th, Colonel James Sinclair's 35th, and Colonel Charles C. Lee's 37th North Carolina Infantry, with Colonel Clark Avery's 33rd North Carolina Infantry Regiment just behind them in reserve. To the right (west) of the railroad, he placed Colonel Zebulon B. Vance's 26th and Colonel R. P. Campbell's 7th North Carolina Infantry Regiments. In the middle, at the critical point in his line pierced by the railroad, he placed the least able of his men, the newly recruited, still un-uniformed and mostly shotgun-equipped Special Battalion, North Carolina Militia, led by Colonel H. J. B. Clark.

On the morning of March 13, Burnside's troops waded ashore unopposed, the entire force able to join on land by 1 p.m. It had begun raining, and by the time the Union troops started moving north, the roads had become a quagmire of mud. Burnside said later it was "one of the most disagreeable and difficult marches that I witnessed during the war." It took until dark to move north to the Confederate picket line, where it was decided to bivouac for the night and attack the next morning. Without tents or shelters of any kind, the night must have been a most difficult one for the rain-soaked infantrymen.

As dawn approached on the 14th, Burnside split his command into three brigades: Brigadier General John Gray Foster's 1st Brigade was to attack on the right, Brigadier General John Grubb Parke's 3rd Brigade the center, and Brigadier General Jesse Lee Reno's 2nd Brigade was to roll up the extreme left. As dawn broke, the three Union brigades moved out.

Burnside had camped for the night much closer to the Confederate line than he had thought, and the lead brigade, Foster's 1st, was in action almost immediately. Branch ordered the landward-facing guns of Fort Thompson to open up, which was answered by return fire from Union gunboats sailing in support up the Neuse River. Foster's men were caught in the crossfire, suffering heavy casualties, and were soon forced to withdraw. Seeing the attack was bogging down on his right and spotting the break in the Confederate line at the railroad track, Reno led the four regiments under his command into the breach, the 21st Massachusetts Infantry in the front.

Map of the Battle of New Bern, March 14, 1862

With the Union infantry storming down the road toward their position, the militiamen broke and ran, most without firing a single shot. With the line to their right caving in, the 35th North Carolina soon followed suit. The only reserve regiment, the 33rd North Carolina, quickly moved up to plug the hole in the line and, between their volley fire and that of the 26th North Carolina to the right, soon broke up the Union attack and hurled it back. Reno moved further to his left and prepared to attack once again.

By this time, the third Union brigade, Parke's, had moved into position, and all three brigades launched a renewed attack on the Confederate line at nearly the same time. This time the attack was successful, with Union infantry pouring through gaps in the line and raising their battle flags on the ramparts of the Confederate defenses. Branch, seeing his entire command caving in, ordered everyone to disengage and move back into New Bern. Once there, apparently believing Burnside was hot on his heels when in fact the Union assault had stopped for a rest within the breastworks, Branch ordered New Bern to be immediately evacuated and his headquarters moved to Kinston, 40 miles farther east.

When Burnside's men moved into town on the afternoon of the 14th, all Confederate troops had fled, and the town was taken without further incident. Rather than trashing and burning the place, as was the Union custom, Burnside decided to garrison the town and use it as a supply and headquarters station for raids into the rest of North Carolina. Union troops held the town for the rest of the war. The short campaign had cost Burnside 90 killed and 380 wounded and another 4 sailors wounded, while Branch lost 64 killed, 101 wounded, and 413 captured or missing.

Beaufort and Morehead City

With New Bern newly secured, Burnside had only one task left to bring the entire central and eastern coasts under Union control—the seizure of Fort Macon on Bogue Banks, just across Bogue Sound from Beaufort just 33 miles to the southwest, guarding the only inlet left in Confederate control along the Outer Banks. With this post under Union control, the port of Morehead City would be open to Union troop and supply shipments to use in the planned invasion of central and southern North Carolina.

Fort Macon was named for Nathaniel Macon, who was Speaker of the House of Representatives and a U.S. senator from North Carolina. The five-sided structure was built of brick and stone with outer walls 4.5 feet thick with more than 9.3 million locally produced bricks, and it mounted 54 artillery pieces of various calibers. At the beginning of the war it was seized, in a scene repeated all over the coastal South, by local militia who demanded the post from the single ordnance sergeant who manned it.

At the time of Burnside's expedition, Fort Macon was commanded by Lieutenant Colonel (later Colonel) Moses J. White of Vicksburg, Mississippi, with a garrison of about 450 (some accounts say 480 to 500) infantry and artillerymen.

THE BATTLE FOR FORT MACON

With the Union Navy already under way to lay siege to the fort, Burnside ordered Parke to take his 3rd Brigade, with about 1,500 men fit for duty, south along the road through Morehead City and to lay siege to the Confederate outpost by land. Parke left New Bern on March 18 and walked into Morehead City without resistance five days later. After taking Beaufort the next day, also without resistance, Parke immediately and politely requested Fort Macon's surrender; White, also politely, turned down his request. White knew that, without reinforcement or resupply, his post was doomed, but he was determined to fight it out as long as possible.

Over the next month the Union Navy landed men and supplies on Bogue Banks west of the fort and constructed a series of artillery redoubts and firing pits that gradually extended closer and closer to the fort. White's men could only stand and watch and fire at the occasional ship or redoubt that came too close. By April 22 Parke had managed to emplace heavy cannon and siege mortars within 1,200 to 1,400 yards of the fort's walls. Parke once again asked for surrender and was once again turned down.

The Union land batteries opened fire at dawn on April 25, and the Navy joined in a little after 8 a.m. White's were high-velocity, flat-trajectory guns unable to hit the well-entrenched redoubts, but they raked the Union ships with a murderous fire, causing them to break off and retreat in less than one hour. Parke kept up an accurate and heavy fire for nearly 11 hours, helped in no small part by a Union signal officer in nearby Beaufort who watched the impact of each round and signaled corrections to the artillerymen. With his help, about 560 of the 1,100 rounds fired landed inside the fort, an amazingly high statistic for the time.

By 4 p.m. White had suffered enough and signaled that he was ready to ask Parke for a truce. The firing stopped immediately. The next morning, White went aboard the schooner USS *Alice Price* and surrendered his post and his command. By noon the 5th Rhode Island Infantry Regiment marched inside the fort's walls and raised the Stars and Stripes once again. Losses on both sides were quite light for such a heavy bombardment; 7 Confederates were killed and another 18 wounded, while Parke suffered the loss of 1 dead and 3 wounded.

AFTER THE BATTLE

Beaufort served as a supply station for the Union Army and Navy for the rest of the war, despite several rather weak attempts to recapture it. With all eastern water accesses of the state now under Union control, Confederate authorities prudently pulled their overmatched forces back into the interior and north to support Lee's army in Virginia. By springtime Union troops had marched in and taken Plymouth and Washington, North Carolina, without opposition.

With the exception of a continuous series of Union and Confederate raids that produced nothing for either side, no major offensive was launched in North Carolina for nearly three more years. The major battles had shifted away from the supply and farming region of eastern North Carolina to the heart of the Confederacy in Tennessee, Mississippi, and Georgia, and to the seemingly endless struggle around Richmond, Virginia.

Wilmington, 1864–65

After Burnside's successful 1861–62 campaign in the eastern portion of the state had cut off Confederate supply and transport routes into Virginia, Wilmington inherited a vital role as the most important safe port for blockade-runners. The supplies they managed to sneak past the Union fleet were then transferred to trains on the Wilmington & Weldon Railroad and sent north to Lee's army. Lee remarked on several occasions that he would not have been able to fight on so long without this steady flow of supplies. Two other railroads carried some supplies to the western portion of the state and then on to Tennessee and Georgia, and down to Charleston and Columbia in South Carolina.

Wilmington had a very favorable and easily defended location 26 miles inland on the wide and deep Cape Fear River, whose twin entrances from the Atlantic Ocean were well fortified. Also to the Union Navy's grief, it was very nearly impossible to sail into the river inlet without the use of local, firmly Confederate guides to show the way through the treacherous Frying Pan Shoals.

To guard against even the remote possibility of a Union attempt to assault the city by water, there were no less than six forts. The two channels into the Cape Fear River are separated by Smith's Island (now called Bald Head Island), the location of Fort Holmes. On the west bank of the river above the island were Forts Johnston (later renamed Pender) and Anderson, while the lesser-used Old Inlet was guarded by Fort Caswell and Battery Campbell. To guard the much more heavily used New Inlet, a massive sand-work fortification called Fort Fisher was constructed on Federal Point starting in the summer of 1861. Fisher was not a fort in the classic sense, as it did not have encompassing walls. Instead, it was L-shaped, with the longest side facing the expected avenue of attack, the Atlantic Ocean. Several earthwork redoubts and batteries surrounded each fort, adding to an already impressive amount of available firepower.

The Union blockade fleet had initially considered Wilmington an insignificant port, ignoring it at first and then placing only a single ship, the USS *Daylight,* off the coast in July 1861. By late 1864 its importance was clear even to Union planners in Washington; by that time more than 50 blockade ships lay just offshore.

Fort Fisher

Even with this tight noose around the supply lanes, blockade-runners managed to slip through up until the time of the battle itself.

THE BATTLES FOR WILMINGTON

While Grant was tied up in the months-long battle around Petersburg, he realized that in order to bring the stalemated fight to a successful conclusion, he was going to have to cut Lee's supply lines. Until the only remaining port supplying the Army of Northern Virginia, Wilmington, could be cut off or taken over, this was not going to be possible. Grant ordered General Benjamin Franklin Butler and Rear Admiral David Dixon Porter to take their forces south to capture the city. Butler had two divisions of infantry—Brigadier General Adelbert Ames's 2nd of the XXIV Corps and Brigadier General Charles Jackson Paine's 3rd of the XXV Corps—as well as two batteries of artillery, with a grand total of nearly 8,000 men. Porter commanded the largest force of ships ever assembled at that time in the United States under one command, nearly 60 ships mounting a total of 627 guns.

As attack on the port city was likely at some point, Confederate president Davis sent General Braxton Bragg to take over command of the defenses in December 1864. The previous area commander, Major General William Henry Chase Whiting, was a competent officer well liked by both his troops and the local citizens, and Davis's choice of the notoriously inept Bragg to replace him (he was actually placed over Whiting, who stayed on to directly command the garrison) was loudly protested. The size of the command then around Wilmington is highly debatable, but it can be safely assumed that Bragg initially commanded somewhere around 3,000 men.

Lee was fully aware of the critical and vulnerable nature of the port city and warned Davis that, if the city fell, he would be forced to pull back and abandon Richmond itself. When the Virginia general learned of Butler and Porter's advance down the coast, he sent Major General Robert Frederick Hoke's division to help defend the vital port, adding another 6,000 men to the line.

The First Battle for Fort Fisher

Butler, considered by many on both sides to be Bragg's equal in ineptness, was determined to open the Cape Fear River by reducing its strongest defense, Fort Fisher. On December 20, 1864, the Union fleet began arriving off the Wilmington coast in the midst of a severe storm, taking nearly three days to get organized. Finally, on the night of December 23, with nearly all his command present and ready to assault, Butler sprang his "secret weapon" on the unsuspecting Confederates.

Butler had decided that a ship loaded to the gills with gunpowder, floated to the outer defenses of Fort Fisher and then exploded, would reduce at least one wall of the sand-work post to dust and allow his troops to pour in through the opening. Amazingly, he managed to sell Porter on the idea and got Grant's grudging approval to go ahead. (Butler and Grant were mortal enemies, and the supreme Union commander had simply wanted to fire Butler rather than allow him another chance to screw up, but could not due to Butler's political connections.)

At 1:45 a.m. on December 24, an unnamed "powder ship" loaded with 215 tons of gunpowder was sailed to within 200 yards of the fort and then exploded. The resulting massive blast failed to even superficially damage the well-constructed fort, and the sleepy defenders peered out, wondering if one of the Union ships had just suffered a boiler explosion or something of a similarly innocuous nature. Despite the failure of his secret weapon, Butler ordered the planned attack to proceed.

As dawn crept over the horizon, Porter's gunboats began a heavy bombardment of the fort, while Butler ordered his troops ashore to the peninsula just north of the Confederate stronghold. Capturing two small batteries and pushing back Confederate skirmishers, the Union troops had made it to within 75 yards of the fort by the morning of Christmas Day. Butler learned that General Hoke's division was then only 5 miles away and moving in fast. Panicking, Butler ordered his troops to break off and return to the troop transports, which he in turn ordered to hoist anchor and sail away so fast that more than 600 infantrymen were left stranded on the beach. Porter, who had no idea what Butler was up to, was forced to send his own ships and sailors to the beachhead under fire from the defenders of Fort Fisher to rescue the stranded troops. Butler reported a loss of 15 wounded and 1 killed in action (by drowning), while the Confederates suffered about 300 killed, wounded, and captured, as well as the loss of four precious artillery pieces.

A furious Grant immediately fired Butler, damning the political consequences, and hurriedly assembled another, stronger assault force under Major General Alfred Howe Terry. He sent Porter a message: "Hold on, if you please, a few days longer, and I'll send you more troops, with a different general." Porter pulled about 25 miles offshore, to the general line of the Union blockade fleet, to await Terry's arrival.

The Second Battle for Fort Fisher

Porter did not have long to wait. Terry left Bermuda Landing, Virginia, on January 4, 1865, with a total of 8,000 soldiers. Joining Porter's squadron just off Beaufort, the force sailed once again for the Cape Fear River, again through a strong storm, arriving late on the afternoon of January 12.

Whiting had received word that the Union force was en route to try again and, fearing that this attempt

would be much stronger, personally led 600 North Carolina troops from the garrison at Wilmington to reinforce Colonel William Lamb's garrison of 1,200. Hoke's newly arrived command deployed on the peninsula north of the fort, in case the second assault followed Butler's attempted route.

A few hours after the Union fleet arrived, Porter ordered all guns to open fire on the Confederate fort while the infantry landed north of Hoke's line. Terry spent the next two days carefully bringing his total force ashore and deploying them in a semicircle around the fort. One Union brigade under Colonel Newton Martin Curtis was sent to the western end of the peninsula, capturing a small redoubt and digging in close to the fort.

At dawn on January 15, Porter's ships once again opened up a massive bombardment, lasting more than five hours, until Terry signaled his men to advance. Riflemen from the 13th Indiana Infantry Regiment led the assault, dashing forward under fire to dig in less than 200 yards from the fort and then rake the parapets with a deadly accurate fire.

While this rifle fire kept the Confederate defenders' heads down, Terry ordered forward Curtis's brigade, now reinforced with Colonel Galusha Pennypacker's brigade, against the western face of the fort. As the Union troops cut through the wooden palisades and dashed up the sand walls, Lamb's men rose out of their shelters and met the Union soldiers with fixed bayonets and drawn swords.

As the western wall defenses broke down into a massive hand-to-hand melee, 2,200 sailors and marines from Porter's command sprang forward to assault the northeastern corner of the fort. There, the Confederate defenders were able to return a disciplined fire, killing or wounding more than 300 of the naval command and forcing them to quickly retreat.

The Union's Terry left the rest of his command before Hoke's Confederate line, and Hoke never sent any of his men to help relieve the fort's defenders at Bragg's direct order. About 10 p.m., after hours of unrelenting and vicious hand-to-hand combat and the commitment of the last Union reserves, the seriously wounded Lamb finally surrendered his post. The exact numbers of dead and wounded Confederates are difficult to assess, as records of this fight are spotty and highly debatable as to accuracy, but somewhere between 500 and

Map of the Second Battle for Fort Fisher

700 were killed or wounded and another approximately 2,000 captured. The South's Whiting himself was mortally wounded during the assault, dying less than two months later. Terry reported Union losses of 184 killed, 749 captured, and 22 missing, including the seriously wounded Curtis, who was shot three times while leading the way over the ramparts, while Porter reported the loss of 386 in addition to the casualties in his marine assault force.

As a morbid postscript to the hard-fought battle, on the morning of January 16 two drunk sailors (sometimes identified as U.S. Marines) were walking around, looking for something worth stealing, when they came to a heavy bunker door. Opening it, they lit a torch and stuck it in the dark opening. The resulting explosion of about 13,000 pounds of gunpowder killed 25 more Union soldiers, wounded another 66, and killed an unknown number of wounded Confederate prisoners in the next bunker.

The Fall of Wilmington

With the main defense post now in Union hands, Bragg wasted little time mounting any sort of renewed defense. The next day Fort Caswell's garrison was withdrawn and the walls blown up, followed in quick order by most of the rest of the forts, batteries, and redoubts. Fort Anderson was left manned to cover Bragg's withdrawal. This post stayed until February 20, when Major General Jacob Dolson Cox's XXIII Corps moved upriver and forced them out without much of a fight. The next day Hoke's troops were finally withdrawn and escaped north with the last remnants of Bragg's force to Goldsboro. On February 22, Mayor John Dawson of Wilmington rode out to surrender his city to the Union invaders.

THE LAST OF THE ARMY OF TENNESSEE

As the campaign to take Wilmington wound to a close in February 1865, Confederate operations in the Deep South were rapidly coming together near the eastern North Carolina town of Goldsboro. Bragg's defeated force was withdrawing there to regroup (and for its commander to figure out whom to blame for his latest disaster); Sherman was pounding through South Carolina, driving what was left of the Confederate Army of Tennessee and various attached militias before him toward Goldsboro; and the newly appointed U.S. Department of North Carolina commander, Major General John McAllister Schofield, had been directed to move in from New Bern and take Goldsboro under Union control.

Desperately seeking some way out of the disastrous conclusion now looming before him, Davis finally came to a long-overdue decision and appointed Robert E. Lee as general in chief of all of the combined Confederate armies. One of Lee's first acts was to place General Joseph Eggleston Johnston once again as commander of the Army of Tennessee and almost incidentally as commander of the Confederate States of America (CSA) Department of the Carolinas, with an aggregate total of about 45,000 men of widely varying skill and training levels. Bragg was reduced to command of a division under Johnston, a move that no doubt humiliated him but delighted his many political enemies.

Johnston promptly ordered most of his command to concentrate with him in the central portion of the state, to make a stand against Sherman's oncoming force. From reports filtering up from South Carolina, where Sherman was advancing without any real resistance, he knew that the Union commander was arrayed in a column four corps abreast in a nearly 60-mile-wide front. Johnston planned to concentrate his forces so as to hit Sherman from one flank and then attack each corps's flank and defeat each in turn.

The Battle of Wyse Fork

*A*s Wilmington had been effectively, if hastily, abandoned by Bragg's troops, Schofield found no wagons or trains there available to move his Union troops rapidly inland. Undeterred, he ordered his forces under Cox in the longer-held base at New Bern to also move inland, and by late February two great Union columns were heading west. Bragg had pulled some of his troops safely out of Wilmington and now had about 8,500 men under Hoke near Kinston to protect his headquarters at Goldsboro. Johnston had sent a few green troops under Hill to reinforce Hoke's line, including a unit known as the "North Carolina Junior Reserves," consisting mostly of completely untrained teenage boys.

On the morning of March 8, as Cox rather blandly moved up the Kinston Road toward Southwest Creek, Hoke and Hill moved out of the trench line in a well-timed attack and assaulted the Union column on both flanks. Several thousand surprised and horrified Union soldiers either ran or surrendered on the spot, while Cox hastily ordered the remainder to dig in and fight back. Sporadic fighting lasted the rest of the day and into the next, while some Union reinforcements came up to replace the scattered force. By nightfall on March 9, Cox had about 12,000 men in his trench line.

At dawn on March 10, Hoke swung around and hit the Union left flank while Hill struck the right flank, forcing a few troops to pull back or run, but both Confederate commands were forced to withdraw after a relatively short fight.

Seriously weakened by the three-day battle, Hoke and Hill were forced to withdraw back into Kinston and then almost immediately pull out as Cox's stronger force approached. Cox entered the city on March 14, as Bragg pulled what was left of his forces back into Goldsboro.

Sherman's Advance

*S*herman had stormed through South Carolina without any real resistance and by the first of March was approaching Cherhaw, near the North Carolina border. After evacuating Charleston, also without a fight, Beauregard had directed Lieutenant General William Joseph Hardee to take his corps (with two divisions and 8,000 men) to Cherhaw and delay Sherman's advance while everyone else got into some kind of order. Johnston determined that he should concentrate his forces near Fayetteville in order to best strike at Sherman's flank, no matter if he went south toward Goldsboro or north toward Raleigh.

Schofield and Sherman agreed that they should link up their respective commands at Goldsboro before moving on Raleigh to cut the main Confederate supply line there; Johnston determined to strike hard at Sherman's column and was maneuvering his forces to hit before that linkup could be accomplished.

Hardee wisely pulled his infantry steadily back from Sherman's advance, leaving most of the fighting up to Major General Joseph Wheeler's Cavalry Corps, who kept up a running battle with Sherman's cavalry chief, Brigadier General Judson Kilpatrick, most of the way to Fayetteville. Sherman's infantry moved steadily forward, reaching Fayetteville on March 12. There he rested his troops for three days before starting out again.

The Battle of Averasborough

As he had in Georgia and South Carolina, Sherman had arranged his force of four corps into two great columns covering a 60-mile front; on the left were the XIV and the XX Corps, collectively referred to as the Army of Georgia, under Major General Henry Warner Slocum. On the right were the XVII and XV Corps under one-armed Major General Oliver Otis Howard, collectively referred to as the Army of Tennessee. On March 15 the great Union Army marched out of Fayetteville northeast toward Goldsboro and an expected linkup with Schofield's army.

Hardee had pulled back to a strong defensive position near the tiny settlement of Averasborough, on the Raleigh Road, atop a ridgeline between a swamp and the Cape Fear River. On the afternoon of March 15, not long after leaving Fayetteville, Kilpatrick's Cavalry Corps, attached to Slocum's Corps, ran into the line of Confederate defenses and immediately tried to ram their way through them. Hardee's men held fast, forcing Kilpatrick to withdraw and request infantry support. Slocum deployed his men during the night and at dawn on March 16 assaulted Hardee's line.

Hardee's only task was to delay the Union force, and he did an outstanding job here. Alternately pulling back and counterattacking, Hardee's fewer than 6,000 men forced Slocum to deploy his entire XX Corps and then order up the XIV Corps for reinforcements late in the afternoon. By nightfall, well over 25,000 Union soldiers were engaged or deployed for battle, while Sherman's lines were starting to become unstrung, just as Johnston had hoped. Rather than turn and support Slocum's fight, for some unknown reason, Howard's right wing kept moving forward, separating the two armies by more than a day's march by the morning of March 17.

As darkness fell, Hardee broke contact and moved his small force rapidly back toward Johnston's line outside Goldsboro, no doubt pleased that his actions had delayed the Union left wing by at least two days. About 600 Union soldiers were killed or wounded, while Hardee reported a loss of about 450.

The Battle of Bentonville, Day One, March 19, 1865

Unknown to Sherman and Slocum, Johnston was massing his available forces just 20 miles north, outside the tiny village of Bentonville and hidden in the woods on the north side of the Goldsboro Road. Howard's right wing was advancing down the New Goldsboro Road about 4 miles to the southeast and was well down the road by the time Slocum got his troops reorganized and on the road again. Sherman was convinced that Johnston, the defensive genius, was entrenching around Raleigh at that very moment. With Hardee's corps still advancing up the road from Averasborough, the Confederate commander could muster about 21,000 men, as opposed to the 30,000 in Slocum's command alone.

As Brigadier General William Passmore Carlin's 1st Division, the lead elements of Slocum's XIV Corps, moved up the Goldsboro Road early on the morning of March 19, his skirmishers started engaging what they thought were local militia. Instead, they were running straight into Hoke's newly reinforced command arrayed across the road, fresh up from the battles around Wilmington. Slocum ordered an envelopment movement to his left, which instead had his men running straight into the middle of Johnston's main line of battle.

As the battle started unfolding, Major General Lafayette McLaw's division, the vanguard of Hardee's command, finally arrived. Johnston, responding to panicked requests for reinforcements from Bragg, sent the road-march-weary soldiers over to the far left of his lines to join Hoke, arriving only to see the Union troops retreating in disarray. Johnston's tactical plan had been to stop and break up the Union column and then spring a strong attack into their flank from his wooded position as soon as possible. Thanks to Bragg's continued ineptness as a battlefield commander, the chance to do this with McLaw's troops was lost.

While the rest of Hardee's command moved into position and Johnston prepared to attack, Slocum had his men hastily dig in and sent word for his XX Corps to move up as soon as possible. The Union commander also sent word to Sherman that he had found Johnston's army and requested Howard's army be moved north into the rapidly growing battle.

Just before 3 p.m., with all his forces now in place and ready, Johnston gave the order to start what became the last major Confederate offensive of the war. Led by Hardee, Johnston's combined force swept out of the woods and thundered down on Carlin's seriously outnumbered division. In minutes the Union line fell apart, and Johnston's screaming men ran down the road toward the next Union division coming into the line, Brigadier General James Dada Morgan's 2nd Division.

Morgan had ordered his men to quickly construct a log breastwork soon after encountering Hoke's men, and this hastily built barricade broke up the Confederate assault. Under heavy fire, Hardee's men hit the ground and returned fire, while Hoke was ordered out of his trench line into the assault. Soon, every reserve Johnston could muster was thrown into the fight, while Slocum's XX Corps made it into the line in time to withstand the assault. As darkness fell, Johnston ordered his men to break contact and pull back to a strong defensive position near Mill Creek, while Sherman ordered Howard's entire Army of Tennessee north into battle.

The Battle of Bentonville, Days Two and Three, March 20–21, 1865

Very little fighting occurred during the day of March 20, with Johnston strengthening his position around Mill Creek and Howard's two corps moving into the line of battle. As day dawned on March 21, both armies stood static in their defensive lines, with Johnston trying to keep his force intact and Sherman simply wondering when his Confederate opponent would withdraw and allow him to proceed to his rendezvous with Terry and Cox at Goldsboro.

By the middle of the afternoon, hot-headed Major General Joseph Anthony Mower grew impatient and ordered his division to advance, totally without orders from either Slocum or Sherman. Moving west along a narrow path along Mill Creek, Mower's men blew past pickets set up in the rear of Johnston's line and soon advanced to within 600 feet of Johnston's headquarters. Commanding a hastily assembled counterattack, Hardee personally led a Texas cavalry unit into Mower's left flank, followed in short order by cavalry and infantry attacks on every flank of the Union command. Mower was soon forced out of the Confederate lines with heavy losses, but his division managed to inflict the ultimate blow on Hardee. Private Willie Hardee, his son, was a member of the very Texas cavalry brigade the general led into battle and was mortally wounded in the heavy exchange of fire.

Johnston had had enough. During the night of March 21, he pulled the remnants of his command out of the line and headed back toward Raleigh. The ill-conceived stance had cost him 2,606 men killed, wounded, captured, or missing, while Sherman's forces suffered a loss of 1,646. The only objective Johnston managed was the delay of Sherman's march for a few days, while nearly destroying his own army in the attempt. With hindsight, it is clear that even if Johnston had managed the unlikely result of totally destroying Slocum's Army of Georgia, he would have still faced the 30,000-plus-strong Army of Tennessee shortly thereafter.

Postscript

Johnston had once commanded a powerful, relatively well-equipped, and extremely well-trained Army of Tennessee, 42,000 strong, before Sherman's grinding "total war" tactics had reduced it to a pitiful shell of its former glory. "High" Private Sam Watkins, of the Maury Grays, 1st Tennessee Infantry Regiment, had marched for the South as part of this great army since the very beginning. In his postwar memoirs he remarked that his regiment had once numbered 1,250 men, had received about 350 replacements, and had joined with other regiments throughout the war, bringing it to a grand total of about 3,200 men, but after the Battle of Bentonville, it was reduced to just 65 officers and men.

Sherman rather halfheartedly moved on to Goldsboro on March 23, where he met up with Terry's and Cox's commands newly arrived from the coast, then moved north to take the abandoned city of Raleigh. There he received word on April 16 that Johnston wanted to discuss

Bennett Place, where generals Sherman and Johnson met

surrender terms. The two generals met at Bennett Place between Durham and Hillsborough, where very generous terms were offered to the courtly Confederate general after two days of talks. Both generals had just learned of Lincoln's assassination on April 14, which no doubt added some haste to their efforts to end the fighting.

Grant traveled south to tell his old friend Sherman that these terms were not acceptable to the new administration in Washington and that he would have to insist the Confederates accept the same terms offered to and accepted by Lee on April 9. Jefferson Davis, newly arrived in Goldsboro in flight from the Union armies, rudely ordered Johnston, his political enemy, to break away from Sherman's armies and join him in flight to the south. Johnston quietly ignored him and, as Davis continued his escape attempt southward, met again with Sherman to discuss the surrender. After agreeing to the new, harsher terms, Johnston surrendered his once-great army on April 26, 1865.

Reasoning with Hurricane Season

Since our first research trips into this area, no fewer than seven major hurricanes have either hit this area or passed close by. The resulting floods and damage to roads, buildings, and beaches meant that many businesses had to shut down to undergo repairs. Most reopened, but next year will undoubtedly play host to another major hurricane season. Weather experts say that hurricane seasons peak and ebb in relative strengths and numbers of major hurricanes and that the East and Gulf Coasts can expect high levels of both for the next eight years or so. It is strongly suggested that you call ahead just before your trip to make sure that the roads are passable and your hotel is open, and it pays to monitor weather conditions during the hurricane season (roughly June through November, peaking in late August and September).

POINTS OF INTEREST

Averasborough Battle Sites

The Battle of Averasborough was fought a few miles northeast of Fayetteville, just off I-95 between Fayetteville and the intersection with I-40 near Benson. Very little of the battlefield remains untouched, but the initial point of contact is well marked. Take exit 65 off I-95 onto NC 82, and go north toward Godwin. About 1.2 miles past the US 301 intersection is a large historic marker on the left in a curve on the road. This marks Hardee's initial position, and the battle moved more or less northwest from this point about 2 miles.

About another half-mile north on NC 82 is Lebanon, one of a handful of period structures in the area, which was used as a Confederate hospital during the brief battle.

Bellair Plantation and Restoration
1100 Washington Post Rd.
New Bern, NC
(252) 637-3913

The last and largest brick plantation country house of the 18th century in North Carolina, the Bellair Plantation (circa 1734) is a majestic three-story brick building approached from NC 43 North by two long driveways, one lined by lavish old cedars. Georgian handcrafted woodwork greets visitors at the imposing eight-paneled door and continues through the main rooms. Original family furnishings are still in the house, probably because Bellair was specifically guarded from harm during the Civil War by order of Major General Ambrose Burnside of the North. The written order, dated March 20, 1862, still hangs on the wall at Bellair. The basement holds the cooking fireplaces with tools and ironworks of the period. Forty-five-minute tours are offered on weekdays by appointment. Group discounts offered.

Bentonville Battleground State Historic Site
5466 Harper House Rd.
Four Oaks, NC
(910) 594-0789
www.nchistoricsites.org/bentonvi

A small museum houses a few artifacts collected from the battlefield, and across the road is a set of reconstructed trenches. The museum has a set of maps that depict fairly well how the battle unfolded, and a short film presentation gives a good account of the fight here. A special high-tech battlefield map uses 3,500 small lights to illustrate the movement of soldiers in coordination with a recorded battle description. This museum reopened in August 1999, after its first renovation since 1965. This site hosts the popular Bentonville Reenactment every five years on the third weekend in Mar. The next reenactment will be on Mar 20 and 21, 2010. The reenactor Web site is: www.bentonville145.com.

Next door to the museum is the Harper House, used as a Confederate hospital and partly restored to its wartime condition. It is kept locked, but the site manager will open it up for a tour on request. For those into the occult, we should mention that we have heard quite a few ghost stories about this house from the reenactor community; quite frankly, the image we have of what this place must have looked like as a wartime hospital, filled with amputees and other seriously wounded soldiers, is eerie enough.

In the woods behind the trench line is a portion of surviving earthworks constructed by Slocum's men; a small path leads back to them. The museum has both a free driving-tour map and a book for sale about the battle; either (or both) are recommended in order to travel down the country roads east of the museum to find the actual battle-site markers (this site is on the extreme western edge of the actual battlefield). Be aware that most of the battlefield is now private property and not open for walking. In fact, this battlefield has been named as one of the most endangered from development in the nation.

Admission is free, but donations are accepted (and encouraged).

Bodie Island Lighthouse and Keeper's Quarters
West of NC 12, between Nag's Head and Oregon Inlet
Whalebone Junction, NC
(252) 441-5711
www.nps.gov/caha

This black-and-white beacon with horizontal bands is one of four lighthouses still standing along the Outer Banks. It sits more than a half-mile from the sea, in a field of green grass. The site is a perfect place to picnic.

In 1870 the federal government bought 15 acres of land for $150 on which to build the lighthouse and keeper's quarters. When the project was finished two years later, Bodie Island Lighthouse was very close to the inlet, stood 150 feet tall, and was the only lighthouse between Cape Henry, Virginia, and Cape Hatteras. But the inlet is migrating away from the beacon, and the current lighthouse is the third one to stand near Oregon Inlet since the inlet opened during an 1846 hurricane. The first light developed cracks and had to be removed. Confederate soldiers destroyed the second tower to frustrate Union shipping efforts.

Wanchese resident John Gaskill served as the last civilian lightkeeper of Bodie Island Lighthouse. As late as 1940,

he said, the tower was the only structure between Oregon Inlet and Jockey's Ridge. Gaskill helped his father strain kerosene before pouring it into the light. The kerosene prevented particles from clogging the vaporizer that kept the beacon burning.

Today the lighthouse grounds and keeper's quarters offer a welcome respite during long drives to Hatteras Island. Wide expanses of marshland behind the tower offer enjoyable walks through cattails, yaupon, and wax myrtle. You can stick to the short path and overlooks if you prefer to keep your shoes dry.

The National Park Service added new exhibits to the Bodie Island keeper's quarters in 1995. The visitor center there is open daily. The lighthouse itself is not open, but you can look up the tall tower from below when National Park Service employees are present to open the structure. Even a quick drive around the grounds to see the exterior is worth it.

Brunswick Town State Historic Site/Fort Anderson
8884 St. Phillips Rd. Southeast
Winnabow, NC
(off NC 133, Southport, NC)
(910) 371-6613
www.nchistoricsites.org/brunswic/brunswic.htm

At this site stood the first successful permanent European settlement between Charleston and New Bern. It was founded in 1726 by Roger and Maurice Moore (who recognized an unprecedented real estate opportunity in the wake of the Tuscarora War, 1711–13), and the site served as a port and political center. Russelborough, home of two royal governors, once stood nearby. In 1748 the settlement was attacked by Spanish privateers, who were soundly defeated in a surprise counterattack by the Brunswick settlers. A painting of Christ presented to the People (*Ecce Homo*), reputedly 400 years old, was among the Spanish ship's plunder and now hangs in St. James Episcopal Church in Wilmington. At Brunswick Town in 1765, one of the first instances of armed resistance to the British Crown occurred in response to the Stamp Act. In time, the upstart upriver port of Wilmington superseded Brunswick. In 1776 the British burned Brunswick, and in 1862 Fort Anderson was built there to help defend Port Wilmington. Until recently, occasional church services were still held in the ruins of St. Philip's Church. The other low-lying ruins and Fort Anderson's earthworks may not be visually impressive, but the stories told about them by volunteers dressed in period garb are interesting, as is the museum.

Admission to the historic site is free. Closed Sun and Mon. From Wilmington, take NC 133 about 18 miles to Plantation Road. Signs will direct you to the site (exit left), which lies close to Orton Plantation Gardens.

Cape Fear Museum
814 Market St.
Wilmington, NC
(910) 798-4350
www.capefearmuseum.com

For an overview of the cultural and natural histories of the Cape Fear region from prehistory to the present, the Cape Fear Museum, established in 1898, stands unsurpassed. A miniature re-creation of the second battle of Fort Fisher and a remarkable scale model of the Wilmington waterfront, circa 1863, are of special interest. The Michael Jordan Discovery Gallery, including a popular display case housing many of the basketball star's personal items, is an interactive natural history exhibit for the entire family. The Discovery Gallery includes a crawl-through beaver lodge, Pleistocene-era fossils, and an entertaining Venus flytrap model you can feed with stuffed "bugs." Children's activities, videos, special events, and acclaimed touring exhibits contribute to making the Cape Fear Museum not only one of the primary repositories of local history, but also a place where learning is fun.

Museum hours vary by season; wheelchair accessible.

Cape Hatteras Lighthouse
1401 National Park Dr.
Manteo, NC
(252) 473-2111
www.nps.gov/caha

The nation's tallest brick lighthouse, this black-and-white-striped beacon is open for free tours from early spring through the fall and is well worth the climb. It contains 268 spiraling stairs and an 800,000-candlepower electric light that rotates every 7.5 seconds. Its bright beacon can be seen more than 20 miles out to sea.

The original Cape Hatteras Lighthouse was built in 1803 to guard the area known as the "Graveyard of the Atlantic," but it was poorly designed with an underpowered light. One sea captain dubbed it the "worst light in the world." Standing 90 feet tall and sitting about 300 yards south of its current site, the first lighthouse at Cape Hatteras was fueled with whale oil, which didn't burn bright enough to illuminate the dark shoals surrounding it. This was an invitation to disaster, as just off this eastern edge of the Outer Banks, the warm Gulf Stream meets the cold Labrador Current, creating dangerous undercurrents around the ever-shifting offshore shoals. Erosion weakened the structure over the years. Finally, in 1861 retreating Confederate soldiers took the light's lens with them, denying the Union Navy the light's harboring safety but also leaving Hatteras Island in the dark.

The lighthouse that's still standing was erected in 1870 on a floating foundation and cost $150,000 to build. More than 1.25 million Philadelphia baked bricks are included in the 180-foot-tall tower. A special Fresnel lens that refracts the light increases its visibility.

During the summer of 1999, the National Park Service moved the lighthouse 1,500 feet inland, at a cost to the federal government of $12 million. This move was in the nick of time, as multiple hurricanes shortly thereafter seriously eroded the coastline near the old location.

Staffed entirely by volunteers, the Cape Hatteras Lighthouse is open all the way to the outdoor tower at the top. The breathtaking view is like looking off the roof of a 20-story building. And the free adventure is well worth the effort. The climb is strenuous, so don't attempt to carry children in your arms or in kid carriers. Climbing is permitted from mid-Apr through Columbus Day. The visitor center, museum, and grounds are open year-round. Tickets to the lighthouse tour are sold on a first-come, first-served basis, and tours begin every 10 minutes, with a limit of 30 persons per tour. Children under 12 must be accompanied by an adult. Hours are subject to change, so call first. Nearby structures originally housing the lightkeepers and their families now house a fascinating museum of the history of both the lighthouse and Cape Hatteras itself.

Carteret County Historical Society/The History Place
1008 Arendell St.
Morehead City, NC
(252) 247-7533
www.thehistoryplace.org

In 1985 the Carteret County Historical Society was given the old Camp Glenn School building, circa 1907, which had served the community first as a school and later as a church, a flea market, and a print shop. The society moved the building from its earlier location to Wallace Drive, facing the parking lots of Carteret Community College and the Crystal Coast Civic Center, just off Arendell Street in Morehead City. The members renovated the building and created a museum to show visitors and residents how life used to be in Carteret County.

There are rotating exhibits with emphasis on the area's Native American heritage, schools, businesses, and homes. The museum houses the society's research library, including an impressive Civil War collection, that is available to those interested in genealogy and history. The museum conducts occasional genealogy workshops. Monthly exhibits feature area artists, and there is a gift shop. Admission is free.

Cedar Grove Cemetery
Queen St. and National Ave.
New Bern, NC

If you're one of those people who loves wandering through old graveyards, you'll not want to miss this one. Statuary and monuments beneath Spanish moss–draped trees mark burial traditions from the earliest days of our nation. One smallish obelisk lists the names of nine children in one family who all died within a two-year time span. The city's monument to its Confederate dead and the graves of 70 soldiers are also here. The cemetery's main gate features a shell motif, with an accompanying legend that says if water drips on you as you enter, you will be the next to arrive by hearse.

Dixon-Stevenson House
609 Pollock St.
New Bern, NC
(252) 514-4900
(800) 767-1560
www.tryonpalace.org/dixonhouse.html

Erected in 1828 on a lot that was originally a part of Tryon Palace's garden, the Dixon-Stevenson House epitomizes New Bern's lifestyle in the first half of the 19th century, when the town was a prosperous port and one of the state's largest cities.

The house, built for a New Bern mayor, is a fine example of neoclassic architecture. Its furnishings, reflecting the Federal period, reveal the changing tastes of early America. At the rear of the house is a garden with seasonal flowers, all in white. When Union troops occupied New Bern during the Civil War, the house was converted to a regimental hospital.

First Baptist Church
411 Market St.
Wilmington, NC
(910) 763-2471
www.fbcwilmington.org

This is Wilmington's tallest church. The congregation dates to 1808, and construction of the redbrick building began in 1859. The church was not completed until 1870 because of the Civil War, when Confederate and Union forces in turn used the higher steeple as a lookout. Its architecture is Early English Gothic Revival with hints of Richardson Romanesque in its varicolored materials and its horizontal mass relieved by the verticality of the spires, with their narrow, gabled vents. Inside, the pews, galleries, and ceiling vents are of native heart pine. Being the first Baptist church in the region, this is the mother church of many other Baptist churches in Wilmington. The church offices occupy an equally interesting

building next door, the Conoley House (1859), which exhibits such classic Italianate elements as frieze vents and brackets and fluted wooden columns.

First Presbyterian Church
400 New St.
New Bern, NC
(252) 637-3270
www.firstpresnewbern.org

The oldest continually used church building in New Bern, First Presbyterian was built in 1819–22 by local architect and builder Uriah Sandy. The congregation was established in 1817. The Federal-style church is similar to many built around the same time in New England but is unusual in North Carolina. Like that of nearby Christ Episcopal Church, the steeple on First Presbyterian is a point of reference on the skyline. The church was used as a Union hospital and lookout post during the Civil War, and the initials of soldiers on duty in the belfry can still be seen carved in the walls. Visitors are welcome to tour the church between 9 a.m. and 2 p.m. weekdays.

Fort Caswell
100 Caswell Beach Rd.
Oak Island, NC
(910) 278-9501
www.fortcaswell.com

Considered one of the strongest forts of its time, Fort Caswell originally encompassed some 2,800 acres at the east end of Oak Island. Completed in 1838, the compound consisted of earthen ramparts enclosing a roughly pentagonal brick-and-masonry fort and the citadel. Caswell proved to be so effective a deterrent during the Civil War that it saw little action. Supply lines were cut after Fort Fisher fell to Union forces in January 1865, so before abandoning the fort, the Caswell garrison detonated the powder magazine, heavily damaging the citadel and surrounding earthworks. What remains of the citadel is essentially unaltered and is maintained by the Baptist Assembly of North Carolina, which owns the property. A more expansive system of batteries and a seawall were constructed during the war-wary years from 1885 to 1902. Fort Caswell is open for self-guided visits. Drive-throughs of the property are free. The fort is closed to tours from Memorial Day to Labor Day.

Fort Fisher State Historic Site
1610 Fort Fisher Blvd. S.
(off US 421, south of Kure Beach, NC)
(910) 458-5538
www.nchistoricsites.org/fisher

✷ ✷ ✷ ✷ ✷ ✷ ✷ ✷ ✷ ✷ ✷ ✷ ✷ ✷ ✷ ✷

Fort Fisher was the last Confederate stronghold to fall to Union forces during the War between the States. It was the linchpin of the Confederate Army's Cape Fear Defense System, which included Forts Caswell, Anderson, and Johnson and a series of batteries. Largely due to the tenacity of its defenders, the port of Wilmington was never entirely sealed by the Union blockade until January 1865. The Union bombardment of Fort Fisher was the heaviest naval demonstration in history up to that time.

Today all that remains are the earthworks, the largest in the South. The rest of the fort has been claimed by the ocean. However, a fine museum, uniformed demonstrations, and reenactments make Fort Fisher well worth a visit. Don't miss the Fort Fisher Aquarium. Thirty-minute guided tours allow you to walk the earthworks, and slide programs take place every half-hour. The Cove, a tree-shaded picnic area across the road, overlooks the ocean and makes an excellent place to relax or walk. However, swimming here is discouraged due to dangerous currents and underwater hazards.

Since Fort Fisher is an archaeological site, metal detectors are prohibited. Museum hours vary by season. Admission is free (donations are requested). The site, about 19 miles south of Wilmington, was once commonly known as Federal Point. The ferry from Southport is an excellent and time-saving way to get there from Brunswick County.

Fort Johnston
Davis and Bay Sts.
Southport, NC
(910) 457-7927

The first working military installation in the state and reputedly the world's smallest, Fort Johnson was commissioned in 1754 to command the mouth of the Cape Fear River. A bevy of tradespeople, fishermen, and river pilots soon followed, and so the town of Smithville was born (renamed Southport in 1887). During the Civil War, Confederate forces added Fort Johnson to their Cape Fear Defense System, which included Forts Caswell, Anderson, and Fisher. Fort Johnson's fortifications no longer stand, but the site is redolent with memories of those times. The remaining original structures house personnel assigned to the Sunny Point Military Ocean Terminal, an ordnance depot a few miles north.

Fort Macon State Park
2300 E. Fort Macon Rd. (NC 58)
Atlantic Beach, NC
(252) 726-3775
www.ncparks.gov/Visit/parks/foma/main.php

Fort Macon State Park, at Milepost 0 on the east end of Bogue Banks, is North Carolina's most visited state park, and with around 1.4 million visitors each year, it is the Crystal Coast's most visited attraction. Initially the fort served to protect the channel and Beaufort Harbor against attacks from the sea. Today the danger of naval attack is remote, but during the 18th and 19th centuries this region was very vulnerable. The need for defense was clearly illustrated in 1747, when Spanish raiders captured Beaufort, and again in 1782, when the British took over the port town.

Construction of Fort Dobbs, named for Governor Arthur Dobbs, began here in 1756 but was never completed. In 1808–09 Fort Hampton, a small masonry fort, was built to guard the inlet. The fort was abandoned shortly after the War of 1812 and by 1825 had been swept into the inlet.

The fort was deactivated after 1877 and then regarrisoned by state troops in 1898 for the Spanish-American War. It was abandoned again in 1903, was not used in World War I, and was offered for sale in 1923. An Act of Congress in 1924 gave the fort and the surrounding land to the state of North Carolina to be used as a public park. The park, which is more than 400 acres, opened in 1936 and was North Carolina's first functioning state park.

At the outbreak of World War II, the army leased the park from the state and, once again, manned the fort to protect a number of important nearby facilities. In 1944 the fort was returned to the state, and the park reopened the following year.

Today Fort Macon State Park offers the best of two worlds: beautiful, easily accessible beaches for recreation and a historic fort for exploration. Visitors enjoy the sandy beaches, a seaside bathhouse and restrooms, a refreshment stand, designated fishing and swimming areas, and picnic facilities with outdoor grills. A short nature trail winds through dense shrubs and over low sand dunes. The park is abundant with wildlife, including herons, egrets, warblers, sparrows, and other animals.

The fort itself is a wonderful place to explore with a self-guided tour map or with a tour guide. A museum and bookstore offer exhibits to acquaint you with the fort and its history. The fort and museum are open daily year-round. Fort tours are guided through late fall. Reenactments of fort activities are scheduled periodically from spring to fall. Talks on the Civil War and natural history and a variety of nature walks are conducted year-round.

Frisco Native American Museum
NC 12
Frisco, NC
(252) 995-4440
www.nativeamericanmuseum.org

This fascinating museum on the sound side of NC 12 in Frisco is stocked with unusual collections of Native American artifacts gathered over the past 65 years, plus numerous other fascinating collections unrelated to native peoples. Opened by Carl and Joyce Bornfriend, the museum boasts one of the most significant collections of artifacts from the Chiricahua people and has displays of the work of other Native American tribes from across the country, ranging from the days of early man to modern time. Hopi drums, pottery, kachinas, weapons, and jewelry abound in homemade display cases with hand-lettered placards.

Many visitors are astonished at the variety, amount, and eclectic appeal of the displays in the museum. The Friends of the Museum group has a small shop located beyond the museum book room that is called Collector's Corner. It is a separate section, clearly labeled as a benefit shop for the museum. It has lots of collectibles, including some military items, political memorabilia, and Wedgwood, and all proceeds go to the museum. Native craft items made by about 40 artisans from across the country are also available for sale.

The book section and natural history center have recently been expanded. With advance notice, the Bornfriends will give guided tours of their museum and lectures for school and youth groups. Call for prices. The museum property also includes outdoor nature trails through three acres of woods, with a screened-in pavilion, a large pond, and three bridges on the land. Museum hours vary by season.

The *Monitor*
Off Cape Hatteras, in the Atlantic Ocean

Launched January 30, 1862, the *Monitor* is one of the nation's most famous military ships. Its watery grave is the first National Underwater Marine Sanctuary. Divers sanctioned by the National Oceanic and Atmospheric Administration have spent years retrieving items from the ironclad boat, which rests upside down in 230 feet of water about 17 miles off Cape Hatteras.

The *Monitor* was owned by Union forces and was their counterpart to the Confederate ship *Virginia* during the Civil War. The *Virginia* was the world's first ironclad warship, built from the hull of the Union frigate *Merrimac,* which Southern forces captured and refitted. On Mar 8, 1862, the pup tent–shaped steamer *Virginia* cruised out of Norfolk to challenge a blockade of six wooden ships. By day's end, the *Virginia* had sunk two of those Union ships and damaged another.

Built by Swedish-American engineer John Ericsson and appropriately dubbed the "Cheesebox on a Raft" because of its unusual design, the *Monitor* was a low-slung ironclad that included a revolving turret to carry its main battery. This strange-looking ship arrived in Norfolk on March 9 and soon battled the *Virginia* to a draw. Retreating Confederates eventually destroyed the *Virginia*. The *Monitor* was ordered to proceed farther south.

The New Year's Eve storm of 1862 caught the Union ironclad off Cape Hatteras, far out in the Atlantic. The *Monitor* sank completely, taking its crew with it. Its whereabouts were unknown until university researchers discovered the *Monitor* in 1973.

Federally permitted scuba divers have brought many artifacts off the *Monitor*'s waterlogged decks, including bottles, silverware, and china pieces. In 1983 they even brought up the ship's distinctive four-blade anchor. During the summer of 2002, the U.S. Navy successfully recovered the distinctive turret, which now is undergoing preservation at Virginia's Mariners' Museum.

Orton Plantation Gardens
9149 Orton Rd. SE
Winnabow, NC
(910) 371-6851
www.ortongardens.com

This property represents one of the region's oldest historically significant residences in continuous use. The family names associated with it make up the very root and fiber of Cape Fear's history. Built in 1725 by the imperious "King" Roger Moore, founder of Brunswick Town, the main residence at Orton Plantation underwent several expansions to become the archetype of Old Southern elegance. It survived the ravages of the Civil War despite being used as a Union hospital after the fall of Fort Fisher. Thereafter it stood abandoned for 19 years until it was purchased and refurbished by Colonel Kenneth McKenzie Murchison of the Confederacy. In 1904 the property passed to the Sprunt family, related to the Murchisons by marriage, and the plantation gardens began taking shape. In 1915 the family built Luola's Chapel, a Doric structure of modest grandeur available today for meetings and weddings. The property is closed Dec through Feb.

Outer Banks History Center
1 Festival Park Blvd.
Manteo, NC
Roanoke Island Festival Park
(252) 473-2655
www.obhistorycenter.ncdcr.gov

Next to the *Elizabeth II*, across from the Manteo Waterfront on Ice Plant Island, the Outer Banks History Center is the most remarkable repository of northeastern North Carolina chronicles collected in any place. More than 25,000 books, 4,500 official documents of the U.S. Coast Guard and the U.S. Life Saving Service, 25,000 photographs, 1,000 periodicals, 700 maps, and hundreds of audio and video recordings are housed in this state-supported cultural site. Special collections include the David Stick Papers, the Frank Stick Collection, the Cape Hatteras National Seashore Library, the Cape Lookout National Seashore Oral History Collection, and the Aycock Brown Tourist Bureau Collection of 17,000 photographs. There are maps of the area more than 400 years old here.

Opened in 1988 on the right-hand side of the *Elizabeth II* visitor center building, the Outer Banks History Center includes a comfortable reading room with long tables for research and a gallery with rotating exhibits that are free to the public. North Carolina natives will enjoy exploring their own history here. Visitors will find the Outer Banks legacy equally enchanting.

Most of the collections included in this library belonged to Outer Banks historian David Stick, who died in May of 2009. The author of many books on the Outer Banks, Stick gathered much of the information during his years of research and writing. Stick's father, also David Stick, helped found the Cape Hatteras National Seashore as part of the National Park Service.

Staffers at the history center are knowledgeable and happy to help anyone access the facility's vast resources. Journalists, history buffs, students, archaeologists, writers, and even interested tourists will find the stop well worth their time. The history center is open year-round. The history gallery is open seven days a week; closed Jan through Mar.

Outer Banks Visitors Bureau
1 Visitors Center Circle
Manteo, NC
(252) 473-2138
(800) 446-6262
www.outerbanks.org

The Outer Banks Visitors Bureau is located in a 10,000-square-foot facility near the eastern terminus of the Croatan Sound Bridge. The bureau houses both the Outer Banks Welcome Center and administrative offices, and it offers a sizable collection of brochures, maps, and promotional materials about area attractions. Staffers can also supply information on local demographics and business opportunities. The center features a rest area, toilets, and an RV dump station. Hours vary by season.

Pea Island National Wildlife Refuge
P.O. Box 1969
Manteo, NC
(north end of Hatteras Island, both sides of NC 12)
(252) 987-2394
www.fws.gov/peaisland

Pea Island National Wildlife Refuge begins at the southern base of the Herbert C. Bonner Bridge and is the first place you'll come to if you enter Hatteras Island from the north. The beach along this undeveloped stretch of sand is popular with surfers, sunbathers, and shell seekers. On the right side of the road, heading south, salt marshes surround Pamlico Sound and birds seem to flutter from every grove of cattails.

With 5,915 acres that attract more than 365 observed species of birds, Pea Island is an outdoor aviary well worth venturing off the road, and into the wilderness, to visit. Few tourists visited this refuge when Hatteras Island was cut off from the rest of the Outer Banks and people arrived at the southern beaches by ferry. But after the Oregon Inlet bridge opened in 1964, motorists began driving through this once-isolated outpost.

Four miles south of the Bonner Bridge's southern base, at the entrance to the new portion of NC 12, the Pea Island Visitor Center offers free parking and easy access to the beach. If you walk directly across the highway to the top of the dunes, you'll see the remains of the more than 100-year-old federal transport *Oriental*. Her steel boiler is the black mass, all that remains since the ship sank in May 1862.

Poplar Grove Plantation
10200 US 17
North Wilmington, NC
(910) 686-9518
www.poplargrove.com

The 1850 Greek Revival house was the focus of this 628-acre plantation that was supported by as many as 64 slaves prior to the Civil War. Today costumed guides lead visitors and recount its history. Skills important to daily 19th-century life, such as weaving, smithery, and basketry, are frequently demonstrated. A restaurant and country store add to Poplar Grove's attraction, as do the many events held here throughout the year, including Halloween hayrides and the Down Home Antique Fair in May. Listed on the National Register of Historic Places, Poplar Grove Plantation is 8 miles outside Wilmington on US 17 at the Pender County line.

Weirs Point
North end of Roanoke Island, NC
off US 64/264

At the Roanoke Island base of the bridge to Manns Harbor, Weirs Point is an attractive, easily accessible public beach on Croatan Sound. Free parking is available at the turnoff on Roanoke Island just before the end of the bridge. The brackish water is warm and shallow here. Sandy beaches are wide enough to picnic, sunbathe, or throw a Frisbee across.

Picnic benches, a Dare County information kiosk, and restrooms are provided at Weirs Point. Watch for stumps and broken stakes in the water. The tide also creeps up quickly, so beware of needing to move beach blankets away from its encroaching flow.

Whalebone Welcome Center
2 NC 12
Nags Head, NC
(252) 441-6644
(877) 629-4386

Operated by the Dare County Tourist Bureau, this wooden visitor center sits just south of the Whalebone Junction intersection on NC 12. It's open daily from Mar 1 to Dec 31, closed in Jan and Feb. The staff can answer all kinds of questions about southern destinations along the Outer Banks. The public restrooms are some of the few you'll find on this remote stretch of NC 12.

Wrightsville Beach Museum of History
303 W. Salisbury St.
Wrightsville Beach, NC
(910) 256-2569
www.wbmuseum.com

A recent attraction on Wrightsville Beach, this museum is housed in the Myers Cottage, one of the oldest cottages on the beach (built in 1907). The museum presents beach history and lifeways through permanent exhibits featuring a scale model of the oldest built-up section of the beach, photos, furniture, artifacts, a slide show, and recorded oral histories, plus rotating exhibits on loggerhead turtles, surfing, the Civil War, shipwrecks, hurricanes, and beach nightlife at such bygone attractions as the Lumina Pavilion. The museum closed Dec through Feb. Admission is free. Upon crossing the drawbridge, bear left at the WELCOME TO WRIGHTSVILLE BEACH sign; the museum is on the right near the volleyball courts beyond the fire station.

DAY TRIPS

Bennett Place
4409 Bennett Memorial Rd.
Durham, NC
(919) 383-4345
www.nchistoricsites.org/bennett/bennett.htm

You don't have to be a Civil War buff to appreciate the significance of what occurred on the farm of James and Nancy Bennett in April 1865. It was in the Bennetts' home that two battle-fatigued adversaries—Joseph E. Johnston and William T. Sherman—met to work out a peaceful settlement. Their original agreement was nixed in the wake of hostilities surrounding Abraham Lincoln's assassination, but their talks continued and eventually resulted in Johnston's surrender. It was the largest troop surrender of the Civil War, ending the fighting in the Carolinas, Georgia, and Florida.

The Bennett grandchildren lived on the farm until 1890. A fire destroyed the farmhouse and kitchen in 1921. The present buildings were reconstructed in the 1960s from Civil War sketches and early photos. To get to Bennett Place, take the Hillsborough Road exit off US 15/501 Bypass or I-85, and follow the signs. Call about extended summer hours. Admission is free, and you can picnic on the grounds.

North Carolina Museum of History
5 E. Edenton St.
Raleigh, NC
(919) 807-7900
www.ncmuseumofhistory.org

This elegant building opened in 1994 across the street from the capitol. It contains four grand display areas for North Carolina historical collections. You can visit the state's Sports Hall of Fame, a collection on North Carolina women, another on folk life, and a fourth that is a chronological history of the state. The museum also has a gift shop filled with items from North Carolina, most of them made in the state. The museum's open, spacious rooms make popular spots for government receptions. The collections include more than 350,000 artifacts, photographs, and videos, and the museum offers hands-on activities for children. Admission is free.

ACCOMMODATIONS

Rates vary dramatically from one area of the Outer Banks to another, from oceanfront rooms to those across the highway, between in- and off-season times, and especially depending on the amenities offered with each unit. In general, however, fall, winter, and early spring prices are lower than midsummer rates. The most expensive season, of course, is between mid-June and mid-Aug.

As this is a major resort and vacation area for the entire mid-Atlantic coastal region, finding hotels and motels is absolutely no problem. Nearly every major national and regional chain has at least some presence here, located conveniently on NC 12, which runs the length of the Outer Banks.

Many hotels and motels honor AARP and other discounts, and children stay free with paying adults in many of these accommodations.

Beaufort and Morehead City

Although Fort Macon directly guarded and is just across the sound from Beaufort, the closest amenities accessible by land are in Morehead City. There is a choice of several chain motels, all offering the usual amenities, on Arendell Street, the "main drag" of the business district there.

Bentonville

As there are few, if any, amenities in Bentonville or the surrounding immediate area, we suggest you look for food and lodging in Raleigh, 35 miles northwest, which gives you the added benefit of being in the area of Bennett Place (see the Day Trips on page 162).

Best Western Raleigh North $–$$
2715 Capital Blvd. (junction of US 1 bypass, US 64, and US 401
  at the Beltline)
Raleigh, NC
(919) 872-5000
www.bestwestern.com

This hotel maintains clean and efficient service. Popular with traveling businesspeople because of its reasonable rates, it is close to a number of restaurants, including the authentic Mexican El Dorado, and is close to the Highwoods business park. It has a pool and 139 rooms, complimentary breakfast, and a manager's reception on Tues and Wed evenings. It sits across the highway from the Parker Lincoln office building.

Courtyard Raleigh Crabtree Valley $–$$
3908 Arrow Dr.
Raleigh, NC
(919) 782-6868
www.summithospitality.com

The Courtyard Raleigh Crabtree Valley offers rooms with refrigerators, coffeemakers, and other amenities. Some rooms have whirlpool baths. A weekday stay in any room gets you a full breakfast buffet and free van service to and from the airport. An outdoor pool provides a means for exercise and relaxation.

Sheraton-Raleigh Hotel $$$$
421 S. Salisbury St.
Raleigh, NC
(919) 834-9900
www.starwoodhotels.com/sheraton

The interior of this 17-story downtown hotel is one of the most elegant of any in the city, and its 350 rooms make it among the largest. It is located next to and is connected through the underground parking lot with the city's Civic Center and the BB&T York-Hannover skyscraper. It is a block from Memorial Auditorium and the City Market. It has a heated indoor pool and a Jacuzzi, and the Raleigh Plaza has business meeting facilities for groups up to 400.

Hatteras Island

Cape Hatteras Motel $$$
46556 NC 12
Buxton, NC
(252) 995-5611
(800) 995-0711
www.capehatterasmotel.com

When you arrive in Buxton, you'll see the Cape Hatteras Motel situated on both sides of the road. Owners Carol and Dave Dawson maintain this motel. The motel rooms and units with kitchens are popular with anglers, surfers, and folk who just plain enjoy Hatteras Island's beaches. Windsurfers especially like this facility because it is near some of the best windsurfing conditions on the East Coast at nearby Canadian Hole.

Most of the units with kitchens sleep up to six comfortably and offer double as well as queen- and king-size beds. The newer, more modern town houses are located on the ocean. The motel has an outdoor swimming pool and spa. The motel's position at the north end of Buxton is not only convenient to pristine uncrowded beaches but also is near restaurants and services.

Most of the units rent weekly during the season, but nightly rentals also may be available, depending on supply. Book reservations early.

Croatoan Inn $$
46854 NC 12
Buxton, NC
(252) 995-5968
(800) 635-6911
www.thecroatoaninn.com

The Croatoan Inn offers some of the best prices for accommodations on the Outer Banks. The traditional Outer Banks–style rooms here appeal to family-oriented guests who appreciate moderate prices, accommodations with character, and the peaceful environment of Hatteras Island. The Croatoan is known for its attention to detail, which is apparent in the clean, well-maintained rooms and grounds.

The spacious rooms have a light, airy feel and include cable TV with HBO. Many rooms have refrigerators and microwaves. Some have wooden deck chairs on a wide, covered porch. Park right outside your door.

Guests have use of the swimming pool and boat ramp as well, and you'll find a shaded picnic area with barbecue grills amid mature oak trees, away from the road. The landscaping includes martin and bluebird houses and planted shrubs and flowers that attract the local bird population. Don't miss seeing the osprey platform on the sound-side area beyond the trees.

The Croatoan Inn is located in the heart of Buxton within easy walking distance of several shops and restaurants. The beach is a short walk away.

The apartments generally rent on a weekly basis, but rooms are usually available anytime. The motel is open from Mar 1 through Dec 31. Pets allowed.

New Bern

All hotels and bed-and-breakfasts accept most major credit cards.

Hilton New Bern/Riverfront $$$$
100 Middle St.
New Bern, NC
(252) 638-3585
(800) 695-8284
www1.hilton.com

With a total of 153 rooms and 18 suites, the five-story-tall Hilton is not only New Bern's largest hotel but also one of its nicest. Modeled in the style of the old Southern grand hotels, the grounds are immaculately gardened, an adjacent marina provides a scenic view of the Trent River waterfront, and an in-house restaurant offers both fine dining and a decent wine list. All the expected amenities of a truly grand hotel are present, updated to include such niceties as an exercise room and a jogging/nature trail through the extensive landscaped grounds.

Palace Motel $
1901 Dr. Martin Luther King Blvd.
New Bern, NC
(252) 638-1151

A basic, no-frills establishment, the low-cost Palace Motel sits a bit off from the "main drag." There are 66 rooms here, all of which have the usual amenities, and a small but clean pool.

Roanoke Island

The Elizabethan Inn $$–$$$
814 US 64
Manteo, NC
(252) 473-2101
(800) 346-2466
www.elizabethaninn.com

The Elizabethan Inn is a year-round resort facility with spacious shaded grounds, country manor charm, and Tudor architecture that reflects the area's heritage. Only 7 miles from the beach, the hotel consists of three buildings providing 78 rooms, efficiencies, and apartments, plus conference facilities, a health club, a gift shop, and a restaurant. Nonsmoking and wheelchair-accessible rooms are available. All rooms have cable TV with HBO, refrigerators, and direct-dial phones. Rooms are available with a king-size bed or two queen-size or standard double beds, and two rooms have whirlpool baths. All rooms are comfortable and well suited for a quiet, Roanoke Island–style vacation.

The inn's Nautics Hall Health and Fitness Complex, the largest and most complete health club in the area, is available for guests of the inn. Guests may also use the small outdoor pool and a heated, competition-size indoor pool. Another nice touch: Guests have free use of bicycles to tour the nearby village or travel the paved bike path.

Inquire about special rate packages. The inn is open year-round.

Wilmington and Vicinity

Best Western Coastline Inn $$–$$$$
503 Nutt St.
Wilmington, NC
(910) 763-2800
(800) 617-7732
www.coastlineinn.com

An unusually pleasant establishment, the Coastline Inn has 53 rooms, each with a view of the waterfront. Amenities include wireless Internet connections and coffeemakers in each room, and a nice touch is the continental breakfast placed outside your room in a basket each morning. There are several decent restaurants within a short walking distance, and a waterfront bar and lounge offers a pleasant way to end the day.

Cabana Suites $$–$$$$
222 Carolina Beach Ave. N.
Carolina Beach, NC
(910) 458-4456
(800) 333-8499
www.oceanfrontcabana.com

Decidedly more upscale than the usual "beach" motel, Cabana Suites is really built more along the lines of attractive condominiums, with one- or two-bedroom suites available, all with kitchen facilities. The usual amenities are present, some rooms have unobstructed ocean views and private balconies, and decent restaurants and shopping are a short walk away.

Ocean Crest Motel $$–$$$$
1417 E. Beach Dr.
Oak Island, NC
(910) 278-3333
www.ocean-crest-motel.com

Another very nice, clean, and decent oceanside motel, with one- and two-bedroom suites with kitchen facilities and private balconies facing the ocean. All the usual amenities are present, and a fishing pier is right next door.

RESTAURANTS

Just as with the hotel situation, finding a meal on the Outer Banks is not difficult at all. Although the area is seriously crowded during the school vacation months of summer, and many of these establishments close up completely during winter, there is still quite a variety to choose from at any time of year. It is also comforting to note that the fast-food and midlevel chains have made little headway on the Outer Banks, where the independent and mom-and-pop establishments still rule. Here are a few places we recommend.

Beaufort and Morehead City

Nearly all the usual fast-food and midlevel dining establishments are clustered together in Morehead City on Arendell Street. Besides these, we can recommend one locally owned establishment.

Bistro by the Sea Restaurant & Banquet Room $$$
4031 Arendell St.
Morehead City, NC
(252) 247-2777
www.bistro-by-the-sea.com/home.htm

Bistro by the Sea, a favorite of locals for both food and hospitality, opened in its current location (in front of Hampton Inn) in 1997. The Bistro celebrates its space, like moving into a dream house, after five cramped years in the restaurant's old 1,000-square-foot area. Chef-owner Tim Coyne serves reliably wonderful dinner entrees using very fresh vegetables, seafood, and tasty cuts of beef. Seafood entrees vary nightly according to freshness and availability. Other than seafood specialties, we also recommend the chargrilled filet mignon or rib eye, liver in orange liqueur, or stir-fried chicken with rice and wontons. We also like the pasta creations, such as seafood-and-cheese-filled pasta shells, eggplant Parmesan, and capellini with pesto, vegetables, and scallops. Sandwiches are available along with a tempting selection of desserts. Bistro by the Sea has all alcohol permits and a piano and vodka bar.

Bentonville

Big Ed's City Market $
City Market
Raleigh, NC
(919) 836-9909

Fresh vegetables from the farmers' market make this restaurant's country cooking truly down-home. Leftovers are donated to the Raleigh Relief Rescue Mission daily.

Captain Stanley's Calabash Seafood $$
3333 S. Wilmington St.
Raleigh, NC
(919) 779-7878

If you're willing to wait in line, sometimes a very long line, this is the place for inexpensive seafood. Calabash seafood, named for a North Carolina coastal town, is dipped in batter and then deep-fried.

Five Eighteen West $$–$$$
518 W. Jones St.
Raleigh, NC
(919) 829-2518
http://518west.com

This culinary addition to downtown Raleigh opened with the established reputation of its sister restaurant, 411 West in Chapel Hill, preceding it. The former warehouse has been beautifully renovated to resemble a Roman piazza with terrazzo floors, wrought-iron balconies, and a trompe l'oeil–sky ceiling. The menu offers Italian contemporary cuisine with fresh seasonal pastas, seafood, vegetarian dishes, and pizzettes, individual wood-fired pizzas. Desserts are made daily in-house, and weekly specials are available. Reservations are accepted. Arrive early to enjoy a drink and the atmosphere at the handcrafted cherry bar before eating.

Hatteras Island

Down Under Restaurant & Lounge $$–$$$
25920 NC 12
Waves, NC
(252) 987-2277
http://downunderrestaurant.com

Water views are spectacular at this Australian-style restaurant. You can sit at the bar in this warm and friendly eatery and watch the sun set over the sound. Or you can enjoy your meal in the dining room and see the pelicans glide over

Atlantic waves or the moon rise over the dark sea. Decorated with authentic Australian art and memorabilia, Down Under is one of a kind on the Outer Banks. Lunch specialties include soups, salads, wraps, and paninis. The Great Australian Bite, similar to an Aussie burger, is made with hamburger, a fried egg, grilled onions, cheese, and bacon. Spicy fish burgers, Vegemite sandwiches, and marinated chicken sandwiches are good authentic options too. Kangaroo, a delicious meat and very popular at Down Under, is imported from Australia for 'roo stew, 'roo burgers, and kangaroo curry.

Dinner selections include Down Under shrimp stuffed with jalapeño peppers and cream cheese and wrapped in bacon. We also enjoy a side order of the foot-high onion rings and a Foster's lager. Parents will appreciate the children's menu, and kids will appreciate the extraordinary decor. Everyone will enjoy the view.

Sonny's Waterfront Restaurant $$–$$$
57947 NC 12
Hatteras Village , NC
(252) 986-2922

This casual, family-run eatery serves breakfast and lunch year-round, and dinner as well from Apr until late Nov. Breakfast begins at 6 a.m. for fishermen and includes hash browns, grits, western omelets, ham-and-cheese omelets, and hotcakes—just a few of Sonny's specialties. Sonny's stops serving dinner after Thanksgiving and is closed for a few days during the Christmas season.

Regular menu items range from steaks to seafood to pasta. Alcoholic beverages aren't served here, but you're welcome to bring your own. Sonny even will provide frosty beer mugs and wineglasses for you. Senior citizens' and children's menus are offered. Reservations are accepted for large parties.

New Bern

The Chelsea $$$
335 Middle St.
New Bern, NC
(252) 637-5469
www.thechelsea.com

The Chelsea is exactly the kind of restaurant we are always looking for—in a building with an interesting architecture or history (in this case it's a circa-1912 brick building that housed the drugstore where Pepsi-Cola was invented) with a well-trained head chef who likes to experiment with eclectic cuisine. "Eclectic" is the operative term here, showing influences of French, German, Cajun, and Asian traditions, fused with traditional American fare. The wine list runs a bit too much toward the lighter (weight and quality) Californias, but any place that keeps Guinness, Bass, and Newcastle Brown on tap can't be all bad! We heartily recommend the Chelsea, to the point that it would be worth driving out of your way to enjoy.

Roanoke Island

Big Al's Soda Fountain & Grill $$–$$$
100 Patty Lane
US 64/264
Manteo, NC
(252) 473-5570
www.themefifty.com

You can't miss Big Al's, across from the Christmas Shop in downtown Manteo. Owners Vanessa and Allan Foreman were originally planning to open a little ice-cream parlor, but the concept expanded into a full-blown soda fountain and family restaurant. It's definitely a place to take the kids. With '50s decor and memorabilia, Big Al's is a great place to kick back and enjoy some good ol' American food and fountain treats. Children's meals are available, and kids can check out the game room, with a pinball machine, video games, and a jukebox.

Weeping Radish Eco Farm and Brewery $$–$$$
6810 Carotoke Hwy.
Manteo, NC
(252) 491-5205
www.weepingradish.com

Located next to the Christmas Shop on the main highway in Manteo, this large Bavarian restaurant includes an outdoor beer garden, separate pub, children's playground, and two-story dining room. A European flavor prevails throughout. Traditional German meals are served, and continental cuisine also is available.

The restaurant's name comes from the radish served in Bavaria as an accompaniment to beer. Cut in a spiral, it's sprinkled with salt and packed back together. The salt draws out the moisture and gives the radish the appearance of weeping. Beer isn't served with radishes here except by special request, but the brews are certainly the best part about this place. A microbrewery opened at the Weeping Radish in 1986, offering pure, fresh-malt German brews without chemical additives or preservatives. You can watch this "nectar of the gods" being brewed on-site. Or take home a pint or small keg to enjoy later. The Weeping Radish is open seven days a week in summer. Call for off-season hours.

Wilmington and Vicinity

Big Daddy's Seafood Restaurant $$
206 K Ave.
Kure Beach, NC
(910) 458-8622

A huge building (it can seat about 500) houses this local institution, which offers primarily seafood prepared in a variety of ways. A decidedly casual establishment, Big Daddy's tends to attract large numbers of local families with children, drawn by the Low Country, family-style dining; an inexpensive all-you-can-eat salad bar; and the 1950s-style Surf and Turf Supreme (beef tenderloin with split Alaskan king crab legs). Although this is an independent establishment, the entrance to the restaurant is through a Cracker Barrel Restaurant–style gift shop offering novelties and candy. Big Daddy's is almost impossible to miss, located at the only stoplight in Kure Beach.

Elijah's Restaurant $$–$$$
2 Ann St.
Wilmington, NC
(910) 343-1448
www.elijahs.com

In a beautiful location on the Cape Fear River waterfront, Elijah's offers genuine Low Country fare as well as Cajun-style seafood and steaks. There are really two restaurants in this one location: the outside oyster bar, which features alfresco deck seating, and the more formal inside dining room. Seafood, poultry, pasta, and beef dishes are all available, although we recommend simply selecting whatever is offered as the special of the day.

Front Street Brewery $$
9 N. Front St.
Wilmington, NC
(910) 251-1935
www.frontstreetbrewery.com

As you may note in this guide, we have a weakness for microbreweries, and Front Street turned out to be one of our favorites. A distinctly German-flavored establishment, the food ranges from light bar-food, such as sandwiches and salads, to very well-prepared steaks and seafood. As with any microbrewery, the beer is the main attraction, and the quality of the products here is excellent. Although there is a changing variety of seasonal and fest beers, the house brews include a Wurzburg-style unfiltered Hefe Weissbier, a hoppy and slightly bitter Dusseldorf Ale, and a wonderful Irish-style malt stout.

South Carolina: First to Fight

Darley.

A contemporary cartoon shows one interpretation of the Secession Movement, with South Carolina in the lead.

For many people, the Civil War in South Carolina means one thing: Charleston. And in one sense they are quite correct. While South Carolina was the first to secede and one of the last to be brought under the Union Army's control, only two relatively small battles were fought in the state outside the immediate Charleston area. In all, most of the combat in the state primarily revolved around the struggle for control of Charleston and the relatively weak resistance to Sherman's 1864 march through the middle part of the state. Ironically, less fighting occurred in this most politically radical of the Confederate states than did in Florida, an oft-forgotten "backwater" theater of the war.

BACKGROUND TO THE WAR IN SOUTH CAROLINA

*I*t can be (and is) endlessly debated whether the Civil War was fought over the issue of slavery, primarily or otherwise, but the fact is that this divisive issue was at least a motivation for the earliest efforts at secession. John Caldwell Calhoun of South Carolina, while a U.S. senator from 1832 to 1843 and again from 1845 to 1850, agitated constantly for "nullification," the right of individual states to declare null and void and subsequently ignore any federal law, rule, or regulation that conflicted with their original agreement to join the Union. This was a widely popular stance in the South, whose slave-holding major landowners felt constantly threatened by abolitionist movements in the northern, "free" states.

The argument that "the Civil War was about freeing the slaves" doesn't adequately explain what was going on politically in the United States before 1860. A thorough discussion of this would fill many volumes; for a well-researched and reasonable presentation, we suggest reading *Battle Cry of Freedom* by James McPherson. The first

This sheet music cover celebrates the South Carolina state convention, held on December 20, 1860, where the state seceded from the Union. The cover illustration shows some of the 169 delegates who gathered to sign the secession documents.

300 pages give a good overview of this very complex time and introduce the major issues and personalities.

In oversimplified terms, the South as a whole was obsessed with the idea that the 10th Amendment to the Constitution (among other documents) gives the individual states ultimate control over most acts of the federal government, and this control includes the right to declare itself separate from the Union if its citizens so desire. The North as a whole was equally obsessed with the idea that the federal government reigns supreme over acts of the individual states and that the Union as an entity was inviolate; once entered, it could not be exited without, at a minimum, the express consent of the federal government. This line of argument had been going on in one form or another since shortly after the United States became a sovereign nation, reaching an early peak in the federalist versus anti-federalist arguments of Alexander Hamilton and Patrick Henry.

Whatever the base cause, tensions were running so high by 1860 that the election of Abraham Lincoln was reason enough for South Carolina politicians to start calling for secession, literally within hours of the vote. A secession convention was called for in short order, meeting on December 18 and unanimously passing an Ordinance of Secession on December 20. The two-day delay in passing this measure was not due to any real opposition to the document but was necessary so that each of the 169 delegates could stand up in turn and bombastically grandstand about the "Yankee outrages."

———————— ————————

"THE UNION IS DISSOLVED"

*M*inutes after the signing, the *Charleston Mercury* newspaper published a special edition proclaiming the new independence of South Carolina and expressing the hope that its Southern brethren would soon follow. The same thought occupied the Northern politicians, and Union military officials moved quickly to protect forts and installations around the Southern coastline.

Garrison commanders in Florida and South Carolina reacted swiftly to the War Department order (to protect their posts as best as possible, preferably without igniting a shooting war), gathering up their men in the strongest and easiest-to-defend of their forts and preparing for what could be a long siege. In Charleston, Major (later Major General) Robert Anderson abandoned the low-walled Fort Moultrie on Sullivan Island and moved his small Northern command to still-unfinished Fort Sumter, in the middle of the cold night of December 26. Before leaving, he "spiked" the guns of Fort Moultrie, rendering them unable to fire and useless, and burned most of the remaining supplies and equipment. As a final act of defiance, he ordered the post flagpole to be chopped down so that any of the assorted flags of secession would not fly from it.

Once inside Fort Sumter, Anderson was faced with a serious tactical situation; only 48 guns had been mounted in the 140 gun positions, and 27 of these guns were mounted *en barbette* atop the upper ramparts, where their crews would be exposed to hostile fire. In addition, he only had 84 officers and men to run the post and was responsible for housing and feeding another 43 civilian workers still attempting to complete construction of the fort. On the positive side, he had enough rations and supplies to last more than four months, even if he could not be resupplied.

The night after Anderson made his move, a group from the 1st Regiment of Rifles, one of the Charleston militias under Colonel (later Brigadier General) James Johnson Pettigrew, rowed out into Charleston Harbor and seized Castle Pinckney, one of the batteries that guarded Charleston Harbor. The only Union soldier present, Lieutenant Richard K. Meade, protested the invasion verbally and then got in his own rowboat and went off to Fort Sumter in a dark cloud over his "treatment" by Pettigrew. This was the first seizure of U.S. property by a seceded state and coldly indicated that this was not to be a happy separation. Meade tendered his resignation from the U.S. Army soon thereafter and joined the Confederate Army as an engineer. Pettigrew went on to greater glory in the Confederate Army of Northern Virginia, leading a brigade under Major General Henry Heth and then taking over this division in charging Cemetery Ridge on the third day at Gettysburg (the so-called Pickett's Charge). He was wounded in this disaster and again wounded 10 days later at the Battle of Falling Waters, that time mortally.

The Lull before the Storm

*T*hrough the rest of the winter of 1860–61, things were relatively quiet in Charleston. Confederate and Union forces alike worked to build up their defenses, the South Carolinians constructing, reinforcing, or re-arming some 60 forts, batteries, and redoubts all around the harbor. Anderson worked on completing his post as best as possible with what workers and materials he had on hand—the U.S. government had entered into an uneasy agreement not to reinforce or resupply any of its besieged garrisoned forts in the South if they were in turn left unmolested.

Fort Sumter was a five-sided fort, 300 feet wide by 350 feet long, with walls about 40 feet high made of locally procured brick; it was built on an artificial island in the middle of Charleston Harbor. Construction began about 1828 on the main post to guard this major harbor. No natural land was sufficient upon which to build

Fort Sumter pictured with the Confederate flag still flying

a strong fort upon in the harbor itself, so more than 70,000 tons of rock were dumped on a low sandbar to form a firm foundation. Construction progressed at a glacial pace; the post was still unfinished and most of the guns still unmounted when Anderson was forced to withdraw within its walls in December 1860.

THE OPENING SHOTS OF THE WAR

As the first months of 1861 faded away, Anderson and his men worked to mount what guns they could and waited for their masters in Washington to figure out how to get them all out of this mess. While talks were going on, the USS *Star of the West* tried to slip into the harbor and resupply the garrison. As the Union supply ship sailed past the Confederate batteries on Morris Island on January 9, batteries manned by cadets from the nearby Citadel college opened fire. Moments later, two shots slammed into the ship's wooden hull, prompting the captain to do an immediate about-face and head for safety. Some historians regard this as the true opening act of the military phase of the war.

Little happened for the next three months, until early April. Anderson's garrison was running dangerously low on rations, the U.S. government seemed befuddled by the continued declarations of secession by the Southern states, seven in all by this time (in chronological order: South Carolina, Mississippi, Florida, Alabama, Georgia, Louisiana, and Texas). Newly appointed commander of Confederate forces in Charleston, Brigadier General (later full General) Pierre Gustave Toutant Beauregard, knew that Anderson's situation was growing critical and, with the full blessing of the new Confederate government, decided to take advantage of it. He also knew that a heavily armed U.S. Navy squadron was en route with supplies for the fort, prepared to blast its way in if necessary, and he would have to act quickly.

On April 11, 1861, Beauregard sent Anderson, his friend and old artillery instructor at West Point, a formal request for surrender of his post. Anderson replied politely, asking if he could wait until April 15 to surrender. Beauregard knew that the navy ships were due to arrive on the 14th and in turn refused. He further sent word to Anderson that he would fire on the fort if not surrendered by midnight. At 3:30 a.m. on Friday, April 12, Beauregard sent one last message to Anderson, stating that he intended to open fire in exactly one hour. Anderson then ordered his men down into the deepest and best-protected casements.

At 4:30 a.m., Captain George S. James yanked the lanyard of a 10-inch mortar mounted in Fort Johnson on James Island, sending an 88-pound shell arcing high over the dark harbor for 20 long seconds, which finally exploded with a bright flash and dull roar in the middle of the fort's parade ground, a perfect shot. This was the signal for which every Confederate artilleryman around the harbor had been waiting for weeks. Within minutes, 30 guns and 17 heavy mortars opened fire as well, aiming at the darkened target only 1,800 to 2,100 yards away.

Anderson kept his men in the casements until dawn and then allowed them to man their guns, under strict orders not to man those on the upper, exposed parapets. Captain Abner Doubleday took the honor of yanking the lanyard to fire the first return shot. As each gun facing toward the Confederate-held fortifications came on line and began a disciplined return fire, Sergeant John Carmody snuck upstairs under heavy incoming fire and loaded up and fired a few of the barbette guns. As the fort had not been given a full load-out of ammunition before the secession crisis hit and had not been resupplied since, Anderson's guns soon burned up what was left in the magazines. By late afternoon, only six smaller-caliber guns were able to keep up a steady fire.

Beauregard kept up a pounding fire for 34 straight hours, seriously damaging the fort's three-story outer wall and raking the upper gun deck with hot shot and shrapnel. Noting that some of his hot-shot guns had set a few interior buildings ablaze, Beauregard ordered more guns to start firing the heated shells, quickly turning the fires into a massive blaze that threatened the otherwise-protected gun crews. Finally, after more

Confederate General Pierre Gustave Toutant Beauregard

Two generations of Southern men are saddled with the middle name "Beauregard" in tribute to this immortal man; perhaps no other single Confederate officer so completely epitomized the aristocratic "gentleman officer." Beauregard was born in St. Bernard Parish, Louisiana, on May 28, 1818, a true Creole who could speak French before English. He graduated second in his class at West Point in 1838, going on to help build the system of fortifications along the Gulf Coast and various command positions in and around New Orleans. During the Mexican-American War he served with a conspicuous flair, winning two promotions for gallantry as well as suffering two slight wounds. Immediately before the outbreak of hostilities, he was appointed superintendent of West Point but lost the post a few days later when he made it clear that he was not about to turn his back on a seceding Louisiana.

Confederate General Pierre Gustave Toutant Beauregard

Upon resigning his U.S. Army commission in February 1861, he was almost immediately given a Confederate brigadier general's commission and shortly placed in command of the Charleston defenses. There, on April 12, 1861, he directed the "opening shots" of the war against Fort Sumter, commanded then by Major Robert Anderson of the U.S. Army, Beauregard's close friend and artillery instructor at West Point. His next command was over the Confederate forces in northern Virginia near Manassas Junction, where he commanded the main battle line in a great victory over superior Union forces on June 1. One of five brigadier generals subsequently promoted to full general (the others being Samuel Cooper, Albert Sydney Johnston, Robert E. Lee, and Joseph Eggleston Johnston), he was soon sent west after feuding with both President Jefferson Davis and his War Department.

At Shiloh, Beauregard served as second-in-command to A. S. Johnston, assuming command of the Confederate Army of the Mississippi upon Johnston's death. A few months later, too ill to command, he turned over his command to General Braxton Bragg while he recovered, but Davis personally blocked his return to command later. He spent most of the rest of the war in command of the Carolinas and Georgia coastal defenses, briefly serving alongside Lee at Petersburg, and ended up serving under J. E. Johnston in his last stand in the Carolinas.

So great was Beauregard's reputation here and abroad that he was offered command of both the Romanian and Egyptian armies, both of which he refused. He lived out the rest of his life in Louisiana, working in several administrative posts, and died in New Orleans on February 20, 1893.

than 4,000 well-aimed rounds had slammed into his post, Anderson signaled his surrender, at 1:30 p.m. on April 13.

It is almost beyond belief that not a single man on either side had been seriously wounded or killed in the day-and-a-half exchange of heavy and very accurate artillery fire; even more incredibly, the subsequent single Union casualty occurred as Anderson's gun crews were firing a last salute before leaving their post. Private Daniel Hough of Battery E, 1st U.S. Artillery, was killed when his ammunition pile exploded while firing the 50th round of a planned 100-gun salute, becoming the first known casualty of the war. Two others in his crew were wounded, one later dying of his injuries. Anderson stopped the salute rounds and quietly began his command on a steamship bound for New York. Fort Sumter now belonged to the state of South Carolina.

★

THE CONFEDERATE OCCUPATION OF FORT SUMTER

*F*ort Sumter quickly became a symbol of the rebellion, both in the North and South, and both sides were equally determined to possess it. Literally the moment Anderson left, South Carolina troops moved in and started repairing some of the damage from the intense bombardment. The Confederates held Fort Sumter for the next 27 months, nearly to the end of the war, although there were no fewer than 2 direct assaults and 11 major bombardments against its garrison. Over the course of almost two years, as many as 46,000 shells (approximately 3,500 tons of metal) were fired at the island fort.

The First Attack

On April 7, 1863, the Union Navy mounted the first attempt to take back their fort. A squadron of eight

The First Shot

There is an ongoing controversy over who fired the "first shot" of the war. Most general histories rather blandly state that widely admired Virginia secessionist Edmund Ruffin fired this shot, usually accompanied by a really great photo of the irritable agitator sitting with his rifle, staring a hole in the camera. Ruffin was a member (probably honorary, as he was 67 years old at the time) of the Palmetto Guards and was supposedly present at Stevens Battery on Charleston Harbor that night (but even this point is open to debate).

The "official" invitee to pull the lanyard for the first shot was supposed to be congressman (later Brigadier General, even later Private when he resigned his commission and joined Lee's army as a scout) Roger Atkinson Pryor, the former U.S. congressman from Virginia, who had endlessly preached not only for secession but for bombardment of Fort Sumter as well. "Strike a blow!" was his endless call to war, at least before he was actually given the chance. Pryor declined the invitation to fire the signal round, simply stating quietly, "I could not fire the first gun of the war." Captain George S. James stepped forward as commander of the battery and without ceremony yanked the lanyard.

At least one source, possibly hoping to preserve the old legend, suggests that Ruffin fired the first "actual" shot from Stevens Battery after James fired the "signal" for him to do so. In opposition to all this, Shelby Foote, famed novelist-historian of the Civil War, repeats the Ruffin story in his mostly reliable and superbly written *The Civil War: A Narrative.*

This whole argument is simply a subset of the line of arguments that consume and delight historians. Where were the true "first shots" fired: at Fort Sumter, at Fort Barrancas in Pensacola Bay a few hours beforehand, at the USS *Star of the West,* elsewhere? Then, of course, there is an even bigger argument over where the first battle was fought. As you can see, historians tend to consume themselves at times over what are in all reality rather trivial points.

Edmund Ruffin

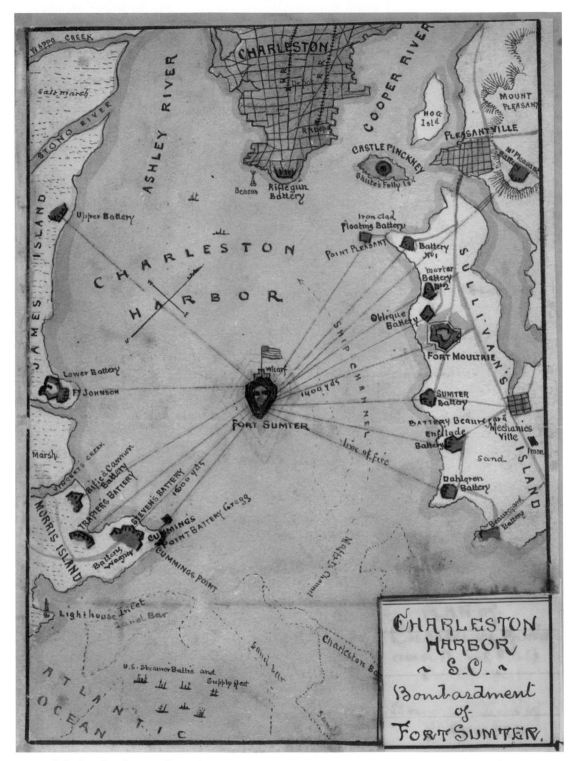

Map of the bombardment of Fort Sumter

ironclad monitors and the capital ironclad battleship USS *New Ironsides,* a 3,500-ton, 20-gun frigate under Rear Admiral Samuel Francis Du Pont, attempted to blast past the defenses of Fort Sumter and force open an entrance to the harbor. In what was supposed to be a coordinated and mutually supporting attack, Major General David Hunter had his troops loaded on transports just offshore, preparing to land on Folly, Cole's, and North Edisto Islands.

The "battle," as it was, did not take long. Du Pont's small fleet sailed into the harbor, guns blazing on Confederate batteries at Fort Sumter and Sullivan Island, to no real effect. Beauregard's batteries returned a galling fire, pounding the ironclads with well-aimed shot and shell from at least nine separate gun emplacements. The USS *Keokuk* would sink the next day, struck by more than 90 shots and her armored hull breached. Other ships in his squadron had suffered a total of 351 hits from the cannoneers of Fort Sumter, while only returning a grand total of 55 ineffective hits on the masonry fort. Du Pont was unable to push past Fort Sumter and soon turned back to sea, at the cost of 22 of his sailors killed or wounded. Hunter never even attempted to land his troops. Beauregard suffered the loss of 14 killed and wounded in the brief attack.

A Second Attempt

By early September 1863, with the situation improving for Union forces besieging the islands surrounding Charleston Harbor, Admiral John Adolph Dahlgren, commanding the Union blockade fleet at Charleston, somehow got the idea that Beauregard was pulling out of Fort Sumter and relayed this bit of "intelligence" to area commander Major General Quincy Adams Gillmore, who advised Dahlgren to send a force in to retake the fort.

Once again, the attack didn't last long. The fort had not been abandoned but was instead fully manned and commanded by Major (later Brigadier General) Stephen Elliott, whose home in nearby Beaufort was being used as a Union headquarters at the time. About 1 a.m. on September 9, 1863, a force of about 400 U.S. sailors and marines rowed up to the fort's landing, only to be greeted by heavy and accurate rifle fire from the parapets. Some Confederate defenders even tossed down small cannon shells mounted with lit fuses, an early and crude version of hand grenades.

The Union sailors and marines were totally overwhelmed, having been told not to expect any resistance at all. Within a few minutes 21 were killed or wounded, another 100 or so captured, and the rest were rowing like mad for the safety of Union-held islands. Elliott reported that he had not suffered a single casualty in the assault.

A Last Union Attempt

Realizing that direct assault on the well-protected post was rather unhealthy and that it was absolutely impossible to simply sail by its defenses, Gillmore determined the best course of action was to simply reduce both Fort Sumter and the city of Charleston to rubble by a heavy and prolonged artillery fire. With Morris Island now under Union control (see Battery Wagner later in this chapter), Gillmore ordered batteries to be set up and to begin firing as soon as possible. The first shots rang out on the morning of August 17, 1863, continuing unabated night and day until August 23. Other batteries gradually came into line, bombarding both the fort and the city more or less continually until both were evacuated in early 1865.

One famous siege gun was the "Swamp Angel," an 8-inch Parrott rifled gun weighing more than eight tons and mounted on a special carriage able to "float" on the swampy soil of Morris Island. It fired a 175-pound shell with deadly accuracy, but typical of this class of artillery piece, its barrel burst on the 36th round.

Although the heavy bombardment gradually leveled the fort's three-story walls down to a single story of casements, Confederate engineers simply used the rubble to reinforce this lowest tier, making it even more resistant to artillery fire. The fort never surrendered its garrison; with the approach of Sherman's grand army in February 1865, both it and the city were evacuated.

SECESSIONVILLE

$\mathcal{D}$uring the buildup of defenses around Charleston Harbor early in 1861, a small mud redoubt was constructed on James Island near a small settlement called Secessionville. This redoubt, later dubbed Battery Lamar, was soon manned by a 500-soldier garrison, who thought that they were left out on the fringe of any action at their remote location.

General Hunter had placed two Union divisions under Brigadier General Henry Washington Benham on the southeastern portion of James Island early in June 1862, planning to use them to assault Charleston by land along the Stono River, having just learned that Beauregard had abandoned some of his outer defenses. Hunter gave strict and very specific orders to Benham not to take his force and try to assault either the city or nearby Fort Johnson until more infantry could be brought up.

Major General John Clifford Pemberton, newly appointed commander of the Confederate Department of South Carolina, Florida, and Georgia, noted the increased Union movements south of Charleston and ordered defenses there to be bolstered. Brigadier General Nathan George Evans was given command of the James Island defenses and directed to build additional earthworks and redoubts to meet the expected attack.

Battery Lamar was given a new commander, Colonel T. G. Lamar, and 350 additional artillerymen and infantry for its defense, and an additional three regiments of infantry were placed in a central location less than two hours march from any of the new defenses. Battery Lamar now mounted an 8-inch Columbiad, a 24-pounder rifled gun, another 24-pounder smoothbore cannon, and an 18-pounder smoothbore. Two 24-pounder smoothbores were placed in another redoubt on the north side of the small fort for flank protection and to act as a reserve.

During the night of June 15, Benham decided to ignore his orders and directed his divisional commanders to ready for an immediate assault on Battery Lamar.

At 5 a.m. on the 16th, four regiments moving at the double-quick abreast burst out of the muddy cotton fields and quickly overran the Confederate pickets. Lamar had worked his men through most of the night trying to improve their post, and they were caught asleep when the attack began. By the time the gun crew stumbled out of their quarters and manned their guns, the Union line was less than 200 yards away.

Lamar ordered all guns to immediately open fire. The Columbiad, loaded with a canister charge, was the first to cut loose, tearing a gaping hole in the blue ranks. Soon the other guns were firing, joined by infantry coming into line on the ramparts. On the fort's left face, three Union regiments made it to the top of the ramparts before Confederate infantry racing into position forced them back with a staggering volley fire. On the fort's right face, the 79th New York Infantry, famous for their early-war Scottish Highlander kilt uniforms, actually made it over the ramparts and attacked the gun crews. A fierce hand-to-hand combat was broken up when Union artillery batteries zeroed in on that section of the fort, killing some of their own men and forcing the rest to withdraw.

Two more assaults proved no more successful, and Benham finally withdrew his troops a little after 9 a.m. Benham was forced to report to a furious Hunter that he had lost 685 killed, wounded, or missing. He was subsequently brought up on charges for disobeying orders and reduced in rank, which was restored later on the personal order of Lincoln. Lamar reported 204 killed, wounded, or missing in the brief action.

MORRIS ISLAND

$\mathcal{B}$y the summer of 1863, capture and control of the low-slung sandbar called Morris Island was viewed as the only way Union forces were ever going to be able to batter down the defenses of Charleston. As the city was well situated at the north end of a harbor and surrounded

Gillmore ordered more troops landed later that same day and set up siege artillery to try to reduce the fort before another assault. Twenty-six heavy artillery pieces and 10 large mortars were manhandled into place and began firing on the fort by the afternoon of July 12, supported by heavy fire from Dahlgren's ironclads.

Federal battery on Morris Island

THE 54TH REGIMENT

*I*n what was considered a radical experiment at the time, an all-black regiment led by white officers had been formed in Boston soon after Lincoln issued his Emancipation Proclamation—the 54th Massachusetts Infantry Regiment. Its commander, Colonel Robert Gould Shaw, was the son of a prominent and wealthy abolitionist, and two of Frederick Douglass's sons marched in the ranks. After a rather prolonged period of training and fitting out, obstructed in no small part by widespread racism within the Union Army command structure, the 54th moved out to join Gillmore's command in South Carolina.

by mile after mile of swampy lowlands, the Union Army had been unable to penetrate close enough overland to establish siege gun emplacements within range, and the Union Navy had been severely beaten back when it tried to ram its way through the waterborne defenses.

On July 10, a well-coordinated attack on Morris Island began, with Dahlgren's ironclad squadron successfully landing Brigadier General George Crockett Strong's 1st Brigade (1st Division, X Corps) with about 3,000 troops on the southern tip of the island, supported by artillery batteries stationed on nearby Folly Island. Advancing under heavy fire from the island's main fortification, Battery Wagner, Strong's men advanced to within rifle range of the sand-work fort during the night. At dawn on July 11, he personally led an assault on the fort, with his 7th Connecticut Infantry managing to gain the ramparts, but they were soon forced back with the loss of 339 men. The 1,200 Confederate defenders of the 27th South Carolina Infantry, 51st North Carolina Infantry, and 1st South Carolina Artillery under Brigadier General William Booth Taliaferro lost only 12 men in the failed assault.

Shaw's regiment received their baptism of fire on Sol Legare Island on July 16, 1863. Confederate forces under Brigadier General Johnson Hagood swept down James Island, determined to attack the Union forces gathering on Folly Island on their flanks and drive them away from Morris Island. The 54th was standing a picket line that morning on the northernmost end of the Union line, when Brigadier General Alfred Holt Colquitt's brigade charged across the causeway. Shaw ordered the rest of his men up, and a vicious hand-to-hand brawl erupted while Brigadier General Alfred Howe Terry struggled to get the rest of his division up to support them.

The Union forces were gradually pushed completely off James Island, with the 54th remaining engaged and acting as a rear guard the whole way. By nightfall all the Union troops were on Folly Island and preparing to move over to Morris Island.

General Gillmore's works in front of Fort Wagner in July 1863

Battery Wagner

By July 18, Gillmore decided that the massive artillery barrage had reduced the fort's defenses down to the point where a strong assault would be successful. Brigadier General Truman Seymour's 2nd Division was brought up in whole to take the fort, with the brigades of Strong and Brigadier General H. S. Putnam to lead the assault. The 54th was selected by Strong to be the spearhead regiment, to be followed closely by two other infantry regiments, with Putnam's brigade of three regiments close behind them.

The reason for the single-regiment frontal assault was simple: The only access to the fort, which spread nearly completely across Morris Island, was down a narrow strip of sand between the ocean and a swamp and then across a water- and abatis-filled moat before the men could even approach the walls.

Just before dusk on July 18, the 54th formed up in ranks and moved off down the beach toward the fort. The weeklong artillery barrage had failed to significantly damage the Confederate fort, however, and as the Union infantry approached, Taliaferro's men swarmed out of their bomb-proofs and manned their guns.

The assault was an unqualified disaster. Although a few of Shaw's men managed to fight their way through the outer defenses and gain the ramparts, they soon were shot down and the rest of his regiment hurled back. Shaw was killed in the assault, as well as nearly half his men. The rest of Strong's brigade fared no better; no other regiment managed to gain the ramparts, and five of the six regiment commanders were killed or wounded. Seymour himself was seriously wounded, and Putnam was killed in the attempt. In all, the Union forces suffered a total of 1,515 casualties out of the 5,300-man assault force. Taliaferro, reporting the loss of 174 killed and wounded in the attack, still held the fort.

Taliaferro and his men stayed in the sand-work fort, trading artillery fire with the Union Army and Navy, until September 1863, when Union reinforcements landing nearby made it clear the fort was about to be taken at any cost. Taliaferro then abandoned his post and moved his men back into Charleston. The battered remnants of the 54th were eventually refitted and reinforced, and the regiment stayed in service through the rest of the war, fighting primarily in Florida. The question as to whether African-American men could fight had been decisively answered, though at a terrible cost.

THE END FOR CHARLESTON

After the fall of Savannah in December 1864, Sherman wasted little time in turning his attention northward. Entering South Carolina with 63,000 men arranged in four great columns in late January 1865, almost no Confederate force was available to stand up against him. A single division under Major General Lafayette McLaws did their best at the Salkehatchie River Bridge east of Allendale, but all they managed to do was hold up one Union corps for a single day, at the cost of 170 men killed or wounded.

As Sherman's "bummers" ravaged through the middle of the state, Lieutenant General William Joseph Hardee, now in command of Confederate forces around Charleston, determined that he would have to immediately evacuate his troops or risk having them cut off and trapped between Sherman and the Union Navy. On the night of February 17, 1865, with the bulk of Union forces still several days away, burning Columbia, Hardee ordered Fort Sumter abandoned and marched out of the city heading for Cherhaw to support General Joseph Eggleston Johnston's Army of Tennessee, now in North Carolina and preparing for last-ditch defenses.

Sherman never moved toward Charleston, instead moving his grand army slowly northeast toward North Carolina, meeting almost no resistance along the way. Charleston's mayor surrendered the city a few days later to a handful of Union officers who had ridden up from Beaufort. The "grand affair," which had started out with so much grand talk and excitement less than four years before, came to a quiet end.

POINTS OF INTEREST

The Battery

One can argue that Charleston's White Point Gardens, which most people know as The Battery, shouldn't officially be called an "attraction," like a museum or a fort. On the other hand, it's a darn good bet that no first-time visitor to the city ever left here without making it a point to walk there or at least drive by.

In a city where almost every other building or street holds some historical significance, few sites afford a better view of Charleston's 300-year-long parade of history than The Battery.

That seaside corner of land at the end of East Bay Street, where it turns and becomes Murray Boulevard, is now a pleasant park with statues and monuments, long-silent cannon, and spreading live oak trees. There's even a Victorian bandstand that looks as if it could sport a uniformed Sousa band any Sun afternoon. But the atmosphere on The Battery hasn't always been so serene.

The Battery has been a prominent feature in Charleston since the earliest days of the English settlement. Then it was known as Oyster Point because it was little more than a marshy beach covered in oyster shells—bleached white in the Carolina sun.

At first, it was mostly a navigational aid for the sailing vessels going into and out of the harbor. The peninsula was still unsettled, and the first colonial effort was farther upstream on the banks of the Ashley River at what is now called Charles Towne Landing. Later, when the settlement was moved to the much more defensible peninsula site, the point was a popular fishing area, too low and too easily flooded to be much of anything else. Charts used during the years 1708 to 1711 show only a "watchtower" on the site and just a few residences built nearby.

Remember, Charles Towne was still a walled city at that time, the southernmost wall being several blocks north, near what is now the Carolina Yacht Club on East Bay Street. The point was definitely a "suburban" location. The area took a decidedly higher public profile about a decade later, when pirate Stede Bonnet and some 40 or 50 scalawags like him were hanged there from makeshift gallows. The local authorities must have gotten the right ones, as they were apparently quite effective in bringing an end to the pirate activity that had plagued the Carolina coast.

The first of several real forts built on the site came along as early as 1737. This and subsequent fortifications were crudely built, however, and none lasted long against the tyranny of the sea. By the time of the American Revolution, White Point was virtually at the city's door and no longer considered a strategic site for defense.

Hurricanes in 1800 and again in 1804 reduced whatever fortification remained there to rubble. Another fort, this version constructed for the War of 1812, apparently gave White

Point a popular new name: The Battery. At least, the new name appears on maps beginning about 1833.

The seawall constructed along East Battery (the "high" one) was built after a storm in 1885. Storms and repairs have traded blows at the seawall for many years: in 1893, 1911, 1959, and, of course, with Hugo in 1989.

The area's use as a park dates back to 1837, when the city rearranged certain streets to establish White Point Gardens. It was from this vantage point that Charlestonians watched the battle between Confederate fortifications across the river and the small band of Union troops holed up in Fort Sumter on April 12, 1861. Once the war had started, this peaceful little garden was torn up and convulsed into two massive earthwork batteries, part of Charleston's inner line of defense. And while one of these battery sites housed a Blakely rifle (a 3.50 caliber rifled cannon that fired a variety of specially flanged shot and shell in the 12-pound range), neither battery ever fired a shot in anger. (Some incoming artillery rounds landed here during the extended bombardment of the city from late 1863 until Charleston fell in February 1865.)

The end of the Civil War was the end of The Battery's role in Charleston's military defense, although several subsequent wars have left poignant souvenirs behind for remembrance. Today no fewer than 26 cannon and monuments dot The Battery's landscape, each of which is described on a nearby plaque or informational marker.

Battery Wagner
Morris Island, SC
www.morrisisland.org

Of all the forts and battlegrounds that dot the Low Country landscape and pay quiet tribute to the area's military history, perhaps the most muted one is Battery Wagner. The story is a brief one in the long struggle of the Civil War, but it is a significant one that is especially poignant today. In 1989 the story of Battery Wagner was portrayed in the acclaimed film *Glory*, which starred Matthew Broderick, Denzel Washington, and Morgan Freeman.

Time and tides have long since removed all traces of Battery Wagner. Today Morris Island is vacant and uninhabited. It was annexed by the City of Charleston and is expected to one day be developed to become a vital part of the ever-growing metropolitan area surrounding the city. Although a monument at Battery Wagner is planned, the site remains remarkably overlooked by the public at large. But whatever its future may hold, the story of Morris Island will always include the story of Battery Wagner and the 54th Massachusetts Regiment.

The Charleston Museum
360 Meeting St.
Charleston, SC
(843) 722-2996
www.charlestonmuseum.org

Directly across Meeting Street from the Visitor Reception and Transportation Center is one of Charleston's finest jewels: the Charleston Museum. Because it is the first and oldest museum in America, having been founded in 1773, the museum's collection predates all modern thinking about what should be kept or discarded in preserving the artifacts of a culture. The Charleston Museum operates three facilities: the Main Museum, the Heyward-Washington House, and the Joseph Manigault House.

The main museum's scope is the social and natural history of Charleston and the South Carolina coastal region. Objects from natural science, cultural history, historical archaeology, ornithology, and ethnology are presented to illustrate the importance each had in the history of this area. The Charleston Silver Exhibit contains internationally recognized work by local silversmiths in a beautifully mounted display. Pieces date from colonial times through the late 19th century.

Visitors will see what the museum's many archaeological excavations have revealed about some of the city's best and worst times. Some artifacts date from the early colonial period, while others are from the Civil War years. Some exhibits focus on early Native Americans who lived in this region. Others trace changes in trade and commerce, the expansive rice and cotton plantation systems, and the important contributions made by African Americans.

Children will be intrigued by the KidStory exhibits, with amazing things to touch, see, and do. They'll see toys from the past, games children played, the clothes they wore, furniture they used, and more. The photographs, ceramics, pewter, and tools reveal a very personal portrait of Charlestonians from the past.

The two houses operated by the Charleston Museum give visitors two examples of fine homes and furnishings during various times in American history.

For those wishing to visit two or more of the sites, discounted adult admission is available.

Fort Johnson
South Carolina Department of Natural Resources
217 Fort Johnson Rd.
Charleston, NC
(843) 953-9300
www.dnr.sc.gov/marine/mrri/ftjohnson.html

Fort Johnson is another Charleston-area fortress steeped in history and adaptively reused for modern needs. Since the early 1970s, the waterfront James Island site has been the home of the South Carolina Marine Resources Research Institute, which researches and promotes the state's marine industries. But military buffs know Fort Johnson in another role. Like Fort Moultrie, this site has military significance that dates back several hundred years.

No trace now exists of the original Fort Johnson that was constructed on the site in about 1708. It was named for Sir Nathaniel Johnson, proprietary governor of the Carolinas at the time. A second fort was constructed in 1759, and small portions of that structure remain as "tabby" ruins there today. (Tabby is an early building material made from crushed lime and oyster shell.)

Records show the fort was occupied in 1775 by three companies of South Carolina militia under the leadership of Lieutenant Colonel Motte. During the American Revolution, the fort remained in colonial hands until 1780, when the British forces advancing on Charleston reported finding it abandoned. A third fort was built in 1793, but a hurricane destroyed it in the 1800s. Some work on Fort Johnson was done during the War of 1812, but the following year another storm destroyed that progress. Shortly afterward, Fort Johnson was dropped from official reports of U.S. fortifications.

During early 1861, South Carolina state troops erected mortar batteries and an earthwork of three guns on the old fortress site. The signal shot that opened the bombardment of Fort Sumter and marked the beginning of the Civil War was fired from the east mortar battery of Fort Johnson on April 12, 1861.

All throughout the Civil War, building activity increased until Fort Johnson became an entrenched camp mounting 26 guns and mortars. However, apart from routine artillery firing from the site, the only major action at the fort occurred on July 3, 1864, when its Confederate defenders repulsed two Union regiments totaling about 1,000 men. The Union forces sustained 26 casualties and lost 140 men as captives. The Confederate loss was 1 killed and 3 wounded. On the night of February 17, 1865, Fort Johnson was evacuated during the general Confederate withdrawal from Charleston Harbor.

After the Civil War, Fort Johnson became a quarantine station operated by the state and the city of Charleston. It continued to be used in that capacity until the 1950s. Today's inhabitants at the site (the Marine Resources folks) do not prohibit exploration, so you might find this history-drenched spot worth a visit.

Fort Moultrie
1214 W. Middle St.
Sullivan's Island, SC
(843) 883-3123
www.nps.gov/fosu/historyculture/fort_moultrie.htm

From the earliest days of European settlement along the eastern seaboard, coastal fortifications were set up to guard the newly found, potentially vulnerable harbors. In this unique restoration, operated today by the National Park Service, visitors to Fort Moultrie can see two centuries of coastal defenses as they evolved.

In its 171-year history (1776 to 1947), Fort Moultrie defended Charleston Harbor twice. The first time was during the Revolutionary War, when 30 cannon from the original fort drove off a British fleet mounting 200 guns in a ferocious, nine-hour battle. This time, Charleston was saved from British occupation, and the fort was justifiably named in honor of its commander, William Moultrie. The second time was during the long Union siege of Charleston.

Today the fort has been restored to portray the major periods of its history. Five different sections of the fort and two outlying areas each feature typical weapons representing a different historical period. Visitors move steadily back in time from the World War II Harbor Entrance Control Post to the original, palmetto log fort of 1776.

Groups should make reservations for guided tours. Pets are not allowed inside the building, but are allowed on the grounds with a leash. A family rate is available.

From Charleston, take US 17 North (Business) through Mt. Pleasant to Sullivan's Island and turn right on Middle Street. The fort is about 1½ miles from the intersection.

Fort Sumter National Monument
Charleston Harbor, SC
(843) 883-3123
www.nps.gov/fosu

Today Fort Sumter is a national monument administered by the National Park Service of the U.S. Department of the Interior. It is still accessible only by boat, and the only public tour of this tiny man-made island and world-famous fort is offered through Fort Sumter Tours. You can board the Fort Sumter tour boat at either Liberty Square in downtown Charleston or Patriot's Point Naval and Maritime Museum in Mt. Pleasant (across the Cooper River). The two-and-a-quarter-hour tour consists of approximately 35 minutes of narration while cruising the historic Charleston Harbor, one

hour at Fort Sumter, and then 30 minutes of narration on the return trip.

The trip affords delightful views of Charleston's waterfront and the tip of the peninsula from an ocean voyager's perspective. (There's a separate, one-and-a-half-hour tour that does not stop at the fort and includes a cruise under the Cooper River bridges on up to the vast facility that until recently was the U.S. Naval Base in North Charleston.) The specially built sightseeing boats are clean and safe and have onboard restrooms.

Once you're at Fort Sumter itself, you can walk freely about the ruins. There's a museum on-site with fascinating exhibits of the fort's history. National Park Service rangers are there to answer any questions you may have.

You'll need to check in for your tour at least 25 minutes early for ticketing and boarding. Departure times vary according to the season and the weather, so call for departure information (843-722-2628 or 800-789-3678). During the busy summer season, there are usually three tours a day from each location. Wheelchair access is available only at the Liberty Square departure location. Group rates are available, but advance reservations for groups are encouraged.

Magnolia Cemetery
70 Cunnington St.
Charleston, SC
(843) 722-8638
www.scocr.org/Links/MagnoliaCemetery.htm

One of the most telling places in all Charleston has to be the remarkably distinctive 19th-century cemetery at the north end of the peninsula, not far off East Bay Street/Morrison Drive.

Not on any contemporary beaten path and clearly not a tourist destination, Magnolia Cemetery is the quiet, final resting place of many important Charlestonians and other players in the city's long-running and colorful drama. It is also an intriguing collection of Southern funerary art in an almost unbearably romantic setting, yet another eloquent expression of Charlestonian pride and prejudice.

The site was originally on the grounds of Magnolia Umbria Plantation, which dates back to 1790. Rice was the principal crop here in the first half of the 19th century. By 1850, however, a 181-acre section of that land had been surveyed for a peaceful cemetery, dedicated on November 19, 1850, on the edge of the marsh. From that time on (even to the present), many of Charleston's most prominent families chose Magnolia as the place to bury and commemorate their loved ones.

Many of the city's leaders, politicians, judges, and other pioneers in many fields of endeavor are interred beneath the ancient, spreading live oaks of Magnolia. Among them are five Confederate brigadier generals. There is a vast Confederate section, with more than 1,700 graves of the known and unknown. Eighty-four South Carolinians who fell at the Battle of Gettysburg are included.

There are literally hundreds of ornate private family plots, many of which bear famous names. You will find the monument of Robert Barnwell Rhett—"Father of Secession," U.S. senator, attorney general of South Carolina, and author. There's also the grave of George Alfred Trenholm, wealthy cotton broker who served as treasurer of the Confederacy and organized many a blockade run for the cause. Trenholm is thought by many to be the man on whom Margaret Mitchell's Rhett Butler was based for *Gone with the Wind*. Among the famous artists and writers buried in Magnolia are Charleston's Alice Ravenel Huger Smith and John Bennett.

To find Magnolia, drive north on East Bay/Morrison Drive and turn right at the traffic light onto Meeting Street/SC 52. Turn right at the first opportunity onto Cunnington Street; Magnolia's gates are at the end of the street. Call for current hours before a visit.

Powder Magazine
79 Cumberland St.
Charleston, SC
(843) 722-9350
www.powdermag.org

Only a couple of blocks from the bustling market area is, quite simply, the oldest public building in the Carolinas. And yet, as Charleston attractions go, the Powder Magazine is relatively unknown to tourists and to some locals as well.

Perhaps the site is overlooked because it's dramatically upstaged by Charleston's sumptuous house museums and romantic streetscapes. And in truth, the utilitarian Powder Magazine actually predates Charleston's legendary aesthetics. It was built for a time when the still-new English settlement was predominantly interested in self-defense and basic survival.

In the early years of the 18th century, Charles Towne was still threatened by Spanish forces, hostile Indians, rowdy packs of buccaneers, and an occasional French attack. It was still a walled city, fortified against surprise attack.

In August 1702 a survey of the armament in Charles Towne reported "2,306 lbs. of gunpowder, 496 shot of all kind, 28 great guns, 47 Grenada guns, 360 cartridges, and 500 lbs. of pewter shot." In his formal request for additional cannon, the royal governor requested "a suitable store of shot and powder ... (to) make Carolina impregnable." And so in 1703 the Crown approved and funded such a building, which was completed in 1713 on what is now Cumberland Street.

The Powder Magazine was the domain of the powder receiver, a newly appointed city official entitled to accept a gunpowder tax levied on all merchant ships entering Charleston Harbor during this period.

The building served its originally intended purpose for many decades. But eventually, in an early colonial version of today's base closings, it was deemed unnecessary (or too small) and sold into private hands.

This multi-gabled, tile-roofed architectural oddity was almost forgotten by historians until the early 1900s. In 1902 it was purchased by the National Society of Colonial Dames of America in the State of South Carolina. It was maintained and operated as a small museum until 1991, when water damage, roof deterioration, and time had finally taken too high a toll. What the Powder Magazine needed to survive at all was a major stabilization and restoration—something beyond the resources of the owners.

In an agreement whereby Historic Charleston Foundation did the needed work under a 99-year lease, the Powder Magazine underwent a $400,000 preservation effort, its first ever. This included a temporary roof over the entire structure, allowing the massive walls to dry out before necessary repairs could even begin. Much-needed archaeological and archival research was also done on the site.

The Powder Magazine opened to the public in the summer of 1997. Inside, an interactive exhibit interprets Charleston's first 50 years, a time when it was still a relatively crude colonial outpost of the British Empire.

Secessionville
Fort Lamar
James Island, SC
(803) 734-3893
www.csatrust.org/secessionville.html

While the small settlement has disappeared without a trace (the area is now a subdivision called Secessionville Acres), the earthwork fort is now a South Carolina Heritage Preserve and is undergoing preservation and restoration efforts by volunteers. A reenactment of the Battle of Secessionville is held annually.

To get to the site, drive south out of Charleston on US 17, and turn left onto Folly Road (SC 171) just past the Ashley River Bridge. Turn left onto Grimball Road, right onto Old Military Road, and almost immediately left again onto Fort Lamar Road. The preservation site is about 1¼ miles down the road on the left. Hours are one hour before dawn to one hour after dusk. Free admission. See the Web site www.battleofsecessionville.org for upcoming events and reenactments.

ACCOMMODATIONS

As nearly all the significant Civil War sites are in and around Charleston, we have limited our suggestions for hotels/motels and restaurants to this city.

A friendly word of advice: Charleston attracts droves of visitors year-round, and we strongly recommend that you make reservations well in advance. For major events like Spoleto and holiday weekends, it's advisable to think up to six months in advance.

Charleston Place Orient Express $$$$
205 Meeting St.
Charleston, SC
(843) 722-4900
(888) 635-2350
www.charlestonplace.com

In terms of size, the former Omni is the granddaddy of Charleston hotels, with 444 units sprawling across a massive complex in the shopping district. The hotel, with its impressive lobby and reception area, opens into the walkway of a mini-mall that includes such famous stores as Godiva, St. John's, and Gucci. The on-site spa is open to hotel and day visitors and offers an indoor-outdoor rooftop swimming pool, fitness equipment, and a children's splash pool. Under the auspices of Orient Express, the rooms at Charleston Place are taking on the aura of Europe in the 1930s. Expect to find marble bathtubs and gold fixtures in the roomy baths. And notice the little touches in the rooms like art deco lighting and the subdued use of color. It adds just that much more romance to your lodging experience.

Several superb dining options are available right under the Charleston Place roof. Foremost among them is the Charleston Grill, tucked away among the shops and boutiques.

Doubletree Guest Suites at Charleston–Historic District $$$$
181 Church St.
Charleston, SC
(843) 577-2644
www.doubletree.com

Located in The Market area, Doubletree Guest Suites is a comfortable courtyard hotel consisting of oversize suites. Units have "the Charleston look" and include complete kitchens, separate bedrooms, and living rooms. Life is made easy with a complimentary breakfast buffet, and for those who enjoy burning the calories they consume, there's a fitness center in the courtyard that seats at least 12 comfortably (great for relaxing while gazing at the stars). When energy levels diminish, the hotel's VCR tape library is available to complement your cable television service.

Mills House Hotel $$$$
115 Meeting St.
Charleston, SC
(843) 577-2400
(800) 874-9600
www.millshouse.com

The original structure was built in 1853 and was also the site for the funeral of Horace Hunley, the Confederate marine engineer who designed early submarines. The structure burned in the Great Charleston Fire of 1861, but was rebuilt. The original balcony remained and is still part of the hotel's outer decor today. This full-service hotel is not only filled with history, but also fine dining and an art gallery for guests' enjoyment.

RESTAURANTS

Hyman's Seafood, Aaron's Deli, Hyman's Half Shell $$
215 Meeting St.
Charleston, SC
(843) 723-6000
www.hymanseafood.com

A casual seafood dining experience for lunch or dinner, Hyman's offers a large selection of fresh-caught fish and a wide variety of shellfish. A raw bar and lounge are upstairs. Hyman's fries in 100 percent soybean vegetable oil. Try the fried okra or the Low Country gumbo, even if you have always shied away from the vegetable. The she-crab soup is award-winning. We suggest parking in the Charleston Place garage.

Tommy Condon's Irish Pub and Seafood Restaurant   **$–$$**
160 Church St.
Charleston, SC
(843) 577-3818
www.tommycondons.com

The most authentic Irish pub in Charleston, Tommy Condon's has "live" Irish entertainment and serves a wide variety of imported beers and ales such as Bass and Newcastle Brown. The menu is a mixture of Irish and Low Country items including shrimp and grits, seafood jambalaya, and fresh fish of the day. There is a covered deck for outside dining, and patrons are welcome for lunch or dinner any day of the week.

Nashville and Franklin: Destruction of the Confederate Armies in Tennessee

On a short list of all the boneheaded maneuvers during the Civil War, General John Bell Hood's invasion of Tennessee for the Confederacy in late 1864 without a doubt ranks at or near the very top. Possibly influenced by his reported use of large doses of laudanum as a pain reliever for his serious injuries from Gettysburg and Chickamauga, Hood concocted this plan after being thoroughly trounced by Major General William T. Sherman's three grand armies around Atlanta in the late summer of 1864.

Maintaining to his death that the only way to defeat Sherman was to draw him into battle on terrain of his own choosing (possibly true), Hood decided to take what was left of his Army of Tennessee and march north out of the Atlanta area, "forcing" Sherman to follow and then defeating him by parts as the Union armies marched after him.

General Joseph Eggleston Johnston

BACKGROUND TO THE BATTLE

𝓘n May 1864 three grand armies with a total of 110,123 men and 254 cannon under Sherman marched south out of their winter quarters at Chattanooga, Tennessee, aiming for the heart of the Southern Confederacy, Atlanta. Standing in their way was General Joseph Eggleston Johnston with a single army of 54,500 men and 144 artillery pieces. Within four months, Sherman tore a path through northwest Georgia, resoundingly defeated the Confederate Army in nearly every battle, besieged Atlanta, and finally took the city when the last defenders slipped out during the night of September 1.

Johnston was a defensive genius, probably delaying the inevitable far longer than any other Southern general could have. His primary handicaps, ironically, had nothing to do with his overt enemy, Sherman, but lay in the enmity of President Jefferson Davis's military advisor, General Braxton Bragg, and one of his own corps commanders, Hood. Both conspired against Johnston behind his back to Davis, making

outrageous charges that he was "reluctant to fight" and that his tactics would lead to ruin. Davis was all too willing to listen; although Bragg had proved a disaster as an army commander, and even General Robert E. Lee warned that Hood was out of his league above a corps command (and others warned he wasn't particularly good at that position, although a capable and outstanding divisional commander), Davis held a grudge against Johnston. The exact reason for this enmity is open to debate, but most likely it resulted from political infighting at the very beginning of the Confederate government.

When Johnston was finally forced south of the Chattahoochee River just north of Atlanta, Davis mocked outrage at this act of "incompetence" and promptly fired him. Placed in his stead was Hood, who promised to go on the offensive, and whose appointment dashed the morale of the men he was to lead. Johnston had been their hero, a man they trusted and who trusted in them as well, who had placed their lives above holding property, and who had been forced to withdraw nearly a hundred miles but had done it without leaving behind any command or even a single artillery piece.

Braxton Bragg

Perhaps one of the most hated and vilified men in the entire Confederate Army, Braxton Bragg's greatest advantage as a military commander was his close friendship with President Jefferson Davis. Born on March 22, 1817, in North Carolina, Bragg graduated high in his class at West Point in 1837 and served with Davis in the Mexican War before resigning from the army to start a plantation in Louisiana.

When the war began, Bragg served first as a high-ranking officer in the Louisiana militia before being tapped for duty as a Confederate general officer in charge of part of the Gulf Coast defenses. Soon promoted to major general, he was transferred to A. S. Johnston's command at Corinth and commanded a corps at Shiloh. Thanks to his close friendship with Davis, Bragg was soon promoted to full general and given command of the Army of Tennessee. Despite his earlier heroics (mostly in the Seminole and Mexican-American Wars) and his relative competence as a corps commander, Bragg was a near unmitigated disaster as an army commander. Serious defeats followed his invasion of Kentucky, the fights at Perryville and Stones River, and his actions during the Tullahoma Campaign. A resounding victory at Chickamauga can be traced not strictly to his battlefield strategy, but more to the timely arrival of Major General James Longstreet's corps and a simultaneous Union defensive blunder.

Just after the battle at Chickamauga, Bragg returned to his usual form, refusing against strong protest to pursue the crushed Union Army (he was deathly afraid of running headlong into a possible Union ambush) and allowing it time to regroup. A subsequent and complete defeat at Chattanooga finally resulted in his loss of command for good; his actions there were so incompetent that Davis could no longer overlook them. His removal from command brought great celebration in the ranks, reinforced when the beloved J. E. Johnston was placed in his stead. Davis placed Bragg as his chief of staff, where he continued to plague the Confederate armies with a series of interfering moves, unnecessary commands and directives, and political retaliations. At the very end of the war, he returned to combat duty and served as a divisional commander under J. E. Johnston at the Battle of Bentonville.

Bragg's postwar life was no more successful than his wartime life. He served briefly as the chief engineer for the state of Alabama before moving on to Galveston, Texas. He died there on September 27, 1876, suddenly struck by a stroke while walking down the street. Few postwar memoirs have the slightest positive comments about him—other than proclaiming his devotion to the Confederate cause; perhaps the kindest comments are that he was an able and effective organizer and staff officer. His defenders admit to a person that his battlefield accomplishments were few and far between but point out that he suffered from chronic migraine headaches and was often ill, sometimes quite seriously, from other causes during his campaigns.

Hood, on the other hand, was well known for his "battlefield heroism," actions that played well in the press but tended to get a lot of his own men killed for no real gain. His charges at Devil's Den at Gettysburg in July of 1863 had lost him the use of an arm, and his charge on the second day at Chickamauga a little more than two months later cost him his right leg. He carried this same flair for dashing off into the face of the enemy into his leadership of the Army of Tennessee, which he ordered on the offensive the same day he assumed command, July 17, 1864.

Hood at Atlanta

On July 20, 1864, Hood ordered an assault at the Battle of Peachtree Creek, just north of Atlanta. Two days later he tried another assault at the Battle of Atlanta, actually a few miles east of the city, and on July 28 he tried yet another at the Battle of Ezra Church, west of Atlanta. The only result in three actions was to reduce his fighting force to fewer than 37,000, with a few thousand Georgia militiamen thrown in for good measure. A final series of battles at Jonesboro shattered his own army, and Hood promptly abandoned Atlanta. Sherman's armies walked in unmolested on September 2.

Battle of Jonesboro

Davis "encouraged" Hood to attack Sherman and recapture the city, but that overwhelming task daunted even the "attack at all costs" Texan. Instead, he proposed to march north of the city to strike and cut Sherman's supply line from Chattanooga, which, hopefully, would force the Union Army out of the city and north in pursuit. Although neither Hood nor Johnston had yet decisively defeated Sherman in a major pitched battle the entire campaign, with the Southern army intact, he now convinced the Confederate president that by choosing his defensive terrain carefully, he could defeat a well-armed, well-equipped, and relatively fresh force four times his size. Amazingly, Davis bought the idea and approved the plan.

Hood Moves North

With three corps in his command, led by Major General Benjamin Franklin "Frank" Cheatham, Lieutenant General Stephen Dill Lee, and Major General Alexander Peter Stewart, a cavalry corps commanded by Major General Joseph "Fighting Joe" Wheeler, and a separate cavalry division commanded by Brigadier General William Hicks "Red" Jackson, Hood moved out of his last Atlanta base of Lovejoy on September 18, swinging wide around the western flank of the Atlanta defenses, and headed north. Sherman had anticipated the

maneuver and had already sent Brigadier General George Henry Thomas (the "Rock of Chickamauga") with three infantry divisions back to Chattanooga to prepare.

Hood moved relatively slowly, crossing the Chattahoochee River near Campbellton on October 1. He continued north for two days, finally encamping near Hiram. Stewart was ordered to move east and attack and cut the Western & Atlantic Railroad line at Big Shanty (now Kennesaw), Acworth, and Allatoona.

The Attack at Allatoona Pass

Stewart's men surprised and captured about 170 Union troops at Big Shanty on October 4 and then quickly moved north and captured a larger garrison at Acworth. Flushed with these easy successes, Hood personally ordered Major General Samuel G. French to take his division on up the tracks to capture and destroy the bridge and railroad cut at Allatoona Pass in Georgia. Hood was under the impression that the pass was only lightly held, as the two previous rail stops had been. However, Sherman had made the tiny settlement on the south side of the deep railway cut into a central base of logistical operations, had it heavily fortified, and had ordered another division under Brigadier General John M. Corse forward to garrison it. On both peaks over the 90-foot-deep railroad cut, heavily reinforced emplacements had been built. The westernmost set of peak defenses was dubbed the Star Fort, because of the arrangement of railroad ties surrounding it.

French divided his force and approached Allatoona from the north, west, and south. Once all were in position, he rather arrogantly sent Corse a terse message:

Sir: I have the forces under my command in such positions that you are now surrounded, and, to avoid a needless effusion of blood, I call upon you to surrender your forces at once, and unconditionally. Five minutes will be allowed for you to decide. Should you accede to this, you will be treated in the most honorable manner as prisoners of war.

Corse was somewhat less than impressed, and 15 minutes later he replied, "Your communication demanding surrender of my command, I acknowledge receipt of,

Allatoona Pass

and respectfully reply, that we are prepared for the 'needless effusion of blood' whenever it is agreeable with you."

French wasted no time in sending Brigadier General Francis M. Cockrell's Missouri Brigade and Brigadier General William H. Young's (Ector's) Brigade to assault from the west. Both pushed through the first line of defense, then the second, and then through a third line of defense, all the while fighting hand to hand with clubbed rifles and bayonets. Advancing to within a few feet of the Star Fort, the fighting rapidly intensified, with the Confederate advance finally being stopped before it could overrun the fort. With warnings coming from outposts that a Union force had been spotted moving rapidly toward the battle area, French disengaged and marched his depleted force west to rejoin Hood.

All through the daylong battle, a Union signal post at Kennesaw Mountain sent a message to Corse: "General Sherman says hold fast; we are coming." This message,

which popularized the expression "hold the fort," was nothing more than a morale booster, for Sherman did not order any additional infantry to the area until the next day, and none arrived until two days later. The forces spotted by the Confederate side were apparently just cavalry on a scouting mission.

Casualties in this little-remembered battle were exceptionally high, with Corse reporting 706 dead and wounded, and French also reporting 706 (including 70 officers), about 30 percent of either side's total force. Young himself was wounded just outside the fort and captured shortly afterward. Corse reported in a message to Sherman that he, too, had been wounded: "I am short a cheek bone and an ear but am able to lick all hell yet!" When Sherman came up later, he was unimpressed with the severity of his wounds and said, "Corse, they came damn near missing you, didn't they?"

Getting to Allatoona Pass

The battlefield is accessible from I-75 north from Atlanta. Take exit 283 (Emerson-Allatoona Road), turn right (east), and go about 2 miles to the pass area. On the way you will cross over a set of railway tracks, which are the modern relocation of the tracks the soldiers were fighting over.

Nearly all the area covered by the battle is today heavily overgrown or equally heavily developed, and the east side of the battlefield is under the murky waters of Lake Allatoona. The dug railroad gap is heavily overgrown, and it is difficult to get a clear picture of the tactical situation, but at least one period structure remains. The Mooney House, the yellow-and-white tin-roofed structure in the sharp curve in the road at the pass entrance, was used as a field hospital during the battle and can be seen in a famous photograph of the area by George M. Barnard taken just after the battle.

There is a small parking area with two historic markers across the street from the Mooney House, which indicate quite well the 1864 layout and tactical situation. One contains a fair reproduction of the Barnard photo, which pictures landmarks still visible today. The Star Fort is still present, although overgrown and in deteriorating condition on top of the left peak of the railway cut. A warning: Both the fort and the Mooney House are private property and not open to the public. Please be respectful and observe them from the parking lot. The eastern redoubt, on top of the right peak, is on U.S. Army Corps of Engineers property and can be accessed by a steep, partially overgrown path just inside the entrance to the pass walking north.

The Armies Advance in Opposite Directions

Following the decisive loss at Allatoona Pass, Hood elected to continue north, moving west around Rome through Cedartown, Cave Springs, and Coosaville, while Sherman moved north after him with a force of 40,000 men (55,000 in some accounts), a partial vindication of Hood's audacious plan. Wheeler's cavalry joined the campaign at this point, screening his movement from Sherman's force, while Jackson's cavalry stayed below Rome near the Coosa River. Attacks at Resaca on October 12 and 13 were failures, but Lee's and Cheatham's corps were able to capture the railroad north of Resaca the next day. In one of the only real successes in north Georgia, the 2,000-man Union garrison at Dalton was forced to surrender, but with Sherman hot on his heels, Hood was unable to hold the city.

Hood moved west again toward northwestern Georgia near the Alabama state line, setting up a line of battle near LaFayette on October 15. Hood's strategy here is uncertain, as he was moving away from the mountainous terrain he had claimed would be to his advantage. There are mountains here, and rugged ones in places, but this was the same area in which Sherman had already demonstrated an ability to operate. The northeastern mountains were not specified in Hood's plans but were his most likely original destination. If his plan was to keep Sherman bottled up in northern Georgia, it both succeeded and failed.

When Hood slipped away after the Union troops deployed for battle at LaFayette on October 17, Sherman remarked that Hood's tactics were "inexplicable by any common-sense theory . . . I could not guess his movements as I could those of Johnston." After a total of three weeks of chasing the now fast-moving Confederate Army of Tennessee, Sherman ordered his forces to return to Atlanta and prepare for a march to the south.

Warned by Grant that Hood was taking his army north into Tennessee to threaten his supply lines, Sherman remarked, "No single force can catch Hood, and I am convinced that the best results will follow from our defeating Jeff Davis's cherished plan of making me leave Georgia by maneuvering."

At the same time, Davis was begging Hood "not to abandon Georgia to Sherman but defeat him in detail before marching into Tennessee." Hood replied that it was his intent to "draw out Sherman where he can be dealt with north of Atlanta." In his postwar memoirs, Hood clung to this unrealistic stance and hopes of defeating both Sherman and Thomas's powerful force in Tennessee:

> *I conceived the plan of marching into Tennessee . . . to move upon Thomas and Schofield and capture their army before it could reach Nashville and afterward march northeast, past the Cumberland River in that position I could threaten Cincinnati from Kentucky and Tennessee . . . if blessed with a victory (over Sherman coming north after him), to send reinforcements to Lee, in Virginia, or to march through gaps in the Cumberland Mountains and attack Grant in the rear.*

It was whispered by not a few members of the Army of Tennessee that Hood was half mad from his injuries—a shot in the arm at Gettysburg and a leg shot off at Chickamauga shortly thereafter. Widely viewed as a gallant fighter, his leadership did not impress those under him in the sense that his tactics killed a lot of his men. Private Sam Watkins said, "As a soldier, he was brave, good, noble and gallant, and fought with the ferociousness of the wounded tiger, and with the everlasting grit of the bull-dog; but as a general he was a failure in every particular."

Hood continued his march north, and Sherman, upon hearing the news, couldn't have been happier, saying, "If he will go to the Ohio River, I will give him rations." He sent Major General John M. Schofield's Army of the Ohio, consisting of Major General David F. Stanley's IV and Brigadier General Jacob B. Cox's XXIII Corps, to Thomas to defend Tennessee and then turned his attention to his March to the Sea.

Hood in Alabama

The Confederate Army of Tennessee reached Decatur, Alabama, on October 26, where Hood met General Pierre Gustave Toutant Beauregard, commander of the Division of the West. Beauregard approved Hood's plan to invade Tennessee but made him give up Wheeler's

cavalry, which was sorely needed in the coming campaign against Sherman in south Georgia. In exchange, Major General Nathan Bedford Forrest's Cavalry Corps was moving down from eastern Tennessee to provide coverage.

While waiting for Forrest to arrive, Hood moved his force west, retaking and fortifying Florence, Alabama, and Corinth, Mississippi, and repairing the railroad line between the cities to shuttle his supplies as needed. Forrest took nearly three weeks to arrive, finally appearing on November 17.

To counter Hood's move west, Thomas sent Stanley's corps, reinforced with one division from Cox's corps, to Pulaski, Tennessee, directly astride the Nashville & Decatur Railroad that he expected Hood to advance on. On November 14 Schofield arrived in Pulaski to establish his headquarters and detail the defense against Hood's army. At that time Schofield commanded an army of 25,000 infantrymen and 5,000 cavalry, while Thomas had another 40,000 troops scattered between Nashville and north Georgia, nearly all relatively fresh and well supplied. With Forrest's arrival, Hood had about 33,000 infantrymen and 6,000 cavalrymen, all tired, battle-weary, and poorly supplied.

Hood Marches North

On November 19 Hood at long last moved out on his great campaign, led by Forrest's cavalry and Lee's corps. Rather than following the railroad as Schofield expected, Hood moved along three parallel roads to the west of the small town of Pulaski, heading toward Columbia, 31 miles to the north. The weather was wretched—a cold rain mixed with snow and sleet turning the muddy roads to ice, which cut and burned the bare feet of most of the tattered infantrymen.

Recognizing the danger of his flank being turned, Schofield hustled all but one brigade of his army to Columbia, arriving and fortifying the bridges over the Duck River by November 24. Hood's army closed in on the town on the morning of November 26. That night he outlined yet another strategy to his three corps commanders. He told them that Nashville was an "open city" and a ripe prize to be easily taken. To do so, they had to move fast toward the capital city, bypassing what

Union forces they could and overwhelming those they could not.

Once again, it is difficult to see just what Hood's overall intent was. Originally moving north to draw Sherman out of Atlanta, he succeeded but then ran into Alabama rather than finding suitable terrain to fight from. Once in Alabama, he ignored Davis's pleas not to abandon Georgia completely and convinced Beauregard that he could defeat Thomas's forces in Tennessee piecemeal, recover the state for the Confederacy, then either help reinforce Robert E. Lee's army in Virginia or invade Ohio. To do either he had to eliminate any Union threat from his own base of support by defeating Thomas, or at the very least by forcing him to retire from Tennessee. Yet, when literally given the opportunity to challenge parts of the Union Army with a superior force, at Pulaski and now at Columbia, he chose to outflank them and continue north.

Home

One company of Hood's army had arrived back home after nearly four years of combat—Captain A. M. Looney's Company H of the 1st Tennessee Infantry Regiment, the "Maury County Grays." One surviving original member, Private Sam Watkins, was overcome with emotion at what had happened to his friends and comrades:

> *The Maury Grays . . . left Columbia, four years ago, with 120 men. How many of these 120 original members are with the company today? Just twelve. Company H has twenty listed. But we twelve will stick to our colors till she goes down forever, and until five more of this number fall dead and bleeding on the battlefield.*

Spring Hill

Realizing early on that Hood had no intent of forming a direct assault at Columbia, and possibly was going to try to envelop him to the north, Schofield sent Stanley's corps reinforced with additional infantrymen and artillery to the smaller city. The Union corps arrived at Spring Hill about 2 p.m.

Hood had sent Forrest to the north to bypass the Union defenses north of Columbia, and they arrived at Spring Hill at nearly the same time Stanley did. Both sides skirmished to no real gain on either side until just before dark. Lee's corps had stayed outside Columbia to "make a racket" while Hood moved Cheatham's and Stewart's corps around to the east to Davis Ford on the Duck River, crossing through pastures, woods, and creeks before remerging on the Rally Hill (Franklin) Turnpike toward Spring Hill just at dark on November 29, neatly flanking Schofield in the maneuver.

Arriving just at dark, part of Cheatham's corps came up and helped push the Union force back into town. Stanley managed to hold the town and keep the road to Columbia open. Hood's army was exhausted by the rough marching and combat action, however, and nearly immediately lay down in the mud on either side of the road to catch some badly needed sleep.

As the Confederate infantry slept, Schofield slipped out of Columbia and passed through a mere 200-yard-wide gap between the two Southern corps without being detected, making it to Spring Hill without incident. When Hood found out, a huge fight between him and Cheatham erupted in which he blamed Cheatham for the escape and requested that Richmond send a replacement, while Cheatham complained he had not been specifically ordered to take and cut the road. While the rest of the Southern generals joined in the fun and argued through the night, Schofield and the rest of his corps moved out of Spring Hill and on toward Franklin, reaching the outer defenses by dawn on November 30. Once there, Schofield discovered he was not going to be able to move his men and heavy supply trains into the city until his engineers rebuilt the bridges and fords destroyed by Forrest's raids. He ordered his men to hastily throw up earthwork defenses on the south edge of town in case Hood was following too closely. He planned on withdrawing back across the river after dark and then to move on up to Nashville during the night.

★

FRANKLIN

*H*ood was indeed following closely. After withdrawing his request for Cheatham's replacement and making a few last rude comments, he got his army moving north again, chasing after Schofield. The vanguard of the Southern force arrived atop a low range of hills just south of Franklin just before 3 p.m., and Hood immediately gave orders to attack the Union lines they could clearly see being constructed. The three corps commanders were incredulous. Dusk was only a bit over two hours away, the army was still in a column formation with parts of it still hours away, and the Union troops clearly had a superior and fortified position well protected by artillery batteries.

This is when Hood threw another one of his fits. He had habitually considered anyone who disagreed with him an enemy and was loath to change any plan he had created, even in the face of overwhelming evidence that it was a poor one. In addition, he had often remarked since taking command that the men and officers loyal to former Army of Tennessee commander Johnston were "soft" and too prone to retreating in the face of the enemy. He insisted that they were to march right down there and take those works, even at the cost of their own lives, almost as a punishment for daring to disagree with him.

The Battle of Franklin

After 3 p.m., the two Confederate corps present started forming in lines of battle, Cheatham's corps on the left, Stewart's corps on the right. At the same time, the bridge and ford work had been completed, and Schofield was getting ready to pull his forces back north across the river. At 3:30 p.m. the signal trumpets blew, and a mass of butternut-clad infantry charged across the open ground toward the Union emplacements. Major General John Calvin Brown's and Major General Patrick Ronayne Cleburne's Confederate divisions briefly overran Brigadier General George B. Wagner's division,

Battle of Franklin

which was left out on the road south of the main defense belt in an ill-thought-out move.

Mounting a strong counterattack, Colonel Emerson Opdyke's 1st Brigade (Wagner's Division), which had been the rear guard all day and was taking a well-deserved rest at the river, leapt back over the defense wall and charged Cleburne's men. A furious fight erupted with point-blank shots and hand-to-hand combat all along the line. One of his officers, Major Arthur MacArthur, father of the World War II hero Douglas MacArthur, managed to slash one Confederate regiment's color bearer with his sword and take the prize, even though he was shot three times in the process.

All along the rest of the line, individual regiments and brigades reached the second Union line of defense, but none was able to pierce it. The field behind them now raked by constant canister and shot from the Union batteries, there was no place left to retreat either. Both sides stood just yards apart for hours, pouring musket and artillery fire into each other's ranks, without either side giving way.

The slaughter finally stopped about 9 p.m., well after dark, when gun by gun, the firing slowly petered out. Surviving Confederate regiments literally crawled back across the dead-strewn field to the safety of their original positions. Schofield promptly abandoned the field, leaving his dead and wounded behind, and immediately marched back to Nashville, arriving about noon on December 1.

Hood's casualties were almost unfathomable. Of the 26,000 he had sent into battle, 5,550 were dead or wounded, with another 702 missing. Thirty-two regimental and brigade battle flags had been taken. No less than 54 regimental commanders were killed, wounded, or missing. The worst loss was that of six generals: Cleburne, Brigadier General John Adams, Brigadier General Otho French Strahl, Brigadier General States Rights Gist, Brigadier General John Carpenter Carter, and Brigadier General Hiram Bronson Granbury. Of the other six generals on the battlefield, one had been captured and only two were left unwounded and fit for service.

Schofield's casualties, although heavy, were still lighter than Hood's. Of the 28,000 men Schofield had on the line that afternoon, 1,222 were killed or wounded, while 1,104 were captured or missing.

The March to Nashville

*H*ood's army was in no shape to fight after the beating at Franklin, but nothing would deter Hood from his determination to take the Tennessee capital back. Schofield's forces had quit the field at Franklin immediately after the battle, and Hood followed suit. Ordering his men up and at 'em, the depleted Confederate Army of Tennessee stood outside the defenses of Nashville by December 2.

Once again, we face the question of what Hood was planning to do. He admitted himself after the war that he knew his army was too depleted to assault the Nashville emplacements and that Schofield was well placed and well supplied and had reinforcements on the way. By no stretch of the imagination could one follow or endorse his plan (as outlined in his postwar memoirs, *Advance and Retreat*): wait outside for Thomas's combined army to come out and attack his own fortifications and hope that promised reinforcements (which probably did not even exist) of his own could manage to travel from Texas in time to help him.

Thomas, on the other hand, was quite comfortable and in no mood to hurry into a fight. Major General Andrew Jackson Smith arrived with his three divisions of XVI Corps by the time Schofield came in from Franklin, and Major General James Blair Steedman brought up a division of 5,200 men detached from Sherman's command the next day. By December 4, Thomas had a total of 49,773 men under his command, some of whom were well rested and had not seen combat recently, while Hood could muster (on paper) only 23,207 tired, cold, and demoralized troops. This figure did not take into consideration the large number of desertions of battle-hardened veterans the South's Army of Tennessee was beginning to experience.

The Battle of Nashville

Under growing pressure from Grant to go into action, Thomas made preparations to decisively defeat the weaker Confederate Army and gain "such a splendid and decisive victory as to hush censure for all time." Finally, at 6 a.m. on the foggy morning of December 15, his army moved out. Thomas planned to hit both of Hood's flanks with a coordinating attack that would destroy his lines of battle in a matter of minutes. Thomas had no desire to simply push Hood away from Nashville; he was determined to destroy that Confederate army once and for all.

Steedman started the attack at 8 a.m. on Hood's right, the coordinated plan falling apart immediately due to the poor weather and bad roads. Two hours later Smith's corps hit Hood's left flank, followed by Wood and Schofield over the next few hours. Hood was steadily pushed back, but his lines held fast and pulled together to form a tight, straight line of battle. By nightfall, Hood had been pushed back about a mile, where he formed a new line of battle that stretched between Shy's Hill and Overton Hill.

At dawn on December 17, Thomas's forces started probing the new Confederate line for weakness. At 3 p.m. a strong attack was made against the defense atop Overton Hill, followed a half-hour later by initial actions against Shy's Hill. By 4 p.m. the attack on Hood's right had been repulsed with heavy losses, but the attack on Shy's Hill succeeded in routing the

Hood's army photographed during the Battle of Nashville

Confederate defenders and effectively bringing the battle to an end.

The Confederate Army of Tennessee was at long last broken. All semblance of order broke down as many soldiers either ran for the rear or allowed themselves to be taken prisoner. Many more simply dropped their rifles and returned home, too defeated to fight anymore. Hood pulled what was left south out of Nashville and marched through a brutal winter landscape all the way back down to Tupelo, Mississippi. Once there, Hood quietly asked to be relieved of command on Friday, January 13, 1865.

Hood insisted that his losses were "very small," but he was not the sort to admit defeat or desertion of his own men. Various sources give wildly disparate figures, but a rough guess is that Hood lost about 1,500 killed and wounded in the battle, with another 4,500 captured. He lost a grand total of nearly 20,000 men in the whole failed campaign. Thomas reported losses of 387 killed, 2,562 wounded, and 112 missing in the battle.

Even after this shattering defeat, the end of this great army was not yet at hand. Reorganizing yet again, the Army of Tennessee was reunited with its beloved commander, General Joseph Eggleston Johnston, and moved back east to confront Sherman once again, this time in his march through the Carolinas.

POINTS OF INTEREST

Belle Meade Plantation
5025 Harding Pike
Nashville, TN
(615) 356-0501
www.bellemeadeplantation.com

Relive a bit of the Old South at Belle Meade Plantation, the 1853 mansion known as the "Queen of the Tennessee Plantations." The Greek Revival mansion was once the centerpiece of a 5,400-acre plantation known the world over in the 19th century as a thoroughbred farm and nursery. In 1807 John Harding purchased a log cabin and 250 acres of land adjacent to the Natchez Trace from the family of Daniel Dunham. Harding and his wife, Susannah, enlarged the cabin as their family grew. In the 1820s they began construction of the present-day Belle Meade (a French term meaning "beautiful meadow") mansion, originally a two-story, Federal-style farmhouse.

Harding, who built a successful business boarding and breeding horses, continued to add to his estate. In 1836 his son, William Giles Harding, established the Belle Meade Thoroughbred Stud. William Giles Harding made additions to the mansion in the 1840s and in 1853. The Hardings also maintained a wild deer park on the property and sold ponies, Alderney cattle, Cotswold sheep, and cashmere goats. During the Civil War, the Federal government took the horses for the army's use and removed the plantation's stone fences. Loyal slaves are said to have hidden the most prized thoroughbreds. The mansion was riddled with bullets during the Battle of Nashville.

After the war, William Giles Harding and his son-in-law, William H. Jackson, expanded the farm. It enjoyed international prominence until 1904, when the land and horses were auctioned. The financial crisis of 1893, an excessive lifestyle, and the mishandling of family funds led to the downfall of Belle Meade, which in the early 1900s was the oldest and largest thoroughbred farm in America. The stables housed many great horses, including Iroquois, winner of the English Derby in 1881. The mansion and 24 remaining acres were opened to the public in 1953 under the management of the Nashville Chapter of the Association for the Preservation of Tennessee Antiquities. For more information on Belle Meade, read *Belle Meade: Mansion, Plantation and Stud* by Ridley Wills III (1991: Vanderbilt University Press, Nashville). Wills is the great-great-grandson of William Giles Harding and the great-grandson of Judge Howell E. Jackson.

The beautifully restored mansion is listed in the National Register of Historic Places. It is elegantly furnished with 19th-century antiques and art of the period. The site also includes the 1890 carriage house and stable filled with antique carriages; the 1790 log cabin (one of the oldest log structures in the state); and six other original outbuildings, such as the garden house, smokehouse, and mausoleum. Guides in period dress lead tours of the property, offering a look back at the lifestyles of early Nashville's rich and famous. The shaded lawn is a popular site for festivals. The last tour starts daily at 4 p.m.

Carnton Plantation
1345 Carnton Lane
Franklin, TN
(615) 794-0903
www.carnton.org

This 1826 antebellum plantation was built by Randal McGavock, who was Nashville's mayor in 1824 and 1825. The late-neoclassical plantation house is considered architecturally and historically one of the most important buildings in the area. In its early years, the mansion was a social and political center. Among the prominent visitors attending the many social events there were Andrew Jackson, Sam Houston, and James K. Polk.

On November 30, 1864, after the bloody Battle of Franklin, the home was used as a hospital. Wounded and dead soldiers filled the house and yard. The Confederates lost 10 generals during the battle to death, injury, or capture. The bodies of five of the generals were laid out on the mansion's back porch. At that time, Carnton was the home of McGavock's son, Colonel John McGavock, and his wife, Carrie Winder McGavock. In 1866 the McGavock family donated two acres adjacent to their family cemetery for the burial of some 1,500 Southern soldiers. The McGavock Confederate Cemetery is the country's largest private Confederate cemetery.

Carter House
1140 Columbia Ave.
Franklin, TN
(615) 791-1861
www.carterhouse1864.com

This 1830 brick house was the center of fighting in the Battle of Franklin in 1864, one of the bloodiest battles of the Civil War. The house, built by Fountain Branch Carter, was used as a Federal command post while the Carter family, friends, and neighbors hid in the cellar during the battle. Among the dead in the battle was Captain Tod Carter, the youngest son of the Carter family, who fought for the South and died at the home 48 hours after being wounded.

The Carter House is a registered National Historic Landmark. A video presentation, access to the visitor center museum featuring Confederate artifacts and photos of soldiers, and a guided tour of the house and grounds are included with admission to the attraction. Hours vary by season.

Oaklands Historic House Museum
900 N. Maney Ave.
Murfreesboro, TN
(615) 893-0022
www.oaklandsmuseum.org

One of the most elegant antebellum homes in Middle Tennessee, this house began around 1815 as a one-story brick home built by the Maney family. The family enlarged the house with a Federal-style addition in the early 1820s and made more changes in the 1830s. The last addition was the ornate Italianate facade, completed in the 1850s.

Oaklands was the center of a 1,500-acre plantation. Union and Confederate armies alternately occupied the house during the Civil War. On July 13, 1862, Confederate brigadier general Nathan Bedford Forrest led a raid here, surprising the Union commander at Oaklands. The surrender was negotiated here. In December 1862 President Jefferson Davis of the Confederacy boarded at Oaklands while visiting nearby troops. There is a gift shop on the property.

Sam Davis Home Historic Site
1399 Sam Davis Rd.
Smyrna, TN
(615) 459-2341
www.samdavishome.org

This Greek Revival home, built around 1820 and enlarged around 1850, sits on 169 acres of the original 1,000-acre farm that was the home of Sam Davis. Davis, called the "Boy Hero of the Confederacy," enlisted in the Confederate Army at the age of 19. He served as a courier, and while transporting secret papers to General Braxton Bragg in Chattanooga, he was captured by Union forces, tried as a spy, and sentenced to hang. The trial officer was so impressed with Davis's honesty and sense of honor that he offered him freedom if he would reveal the source of military information he was caught carrying. Davis is reported to have responded, "If I had a thousand lives I would give them all gladly rather than betray a friend." He was hanged in Pulaski, Tennessee, on November 27, 1863. The home is a typical upper-middle-class farmhouse of the period. A tour of the property also includes outbuildings. Several annual events take place here. Hours vary by season.

Stones River National Battlefield
3501 Old Nashville Hwy.
Murfreesboro, TN
(615) 478-1035
www.nps.gov/stri

One of the bloodier Civil War battles took place at this site between December 31, 1862, and January 2, 1863. More than 83,000 men fought in the battle; nearly 28,000 were killed or wounded. Both the Union Army, led by Major General William S. Rosecrans, and the Confederate Army, led by General Braxton Bragg, claimed victory. However, on January 3, 1863, Bragg retreated 40 miles to Tullahoma, Tennessee, and Rosecrans took control of Murfreesboro.

The Union constructed a huge supply base within Fortress Rosecrans, the largest enclosed earthen fortification built during the war. The battlefield today appears much as it did during the Battle of Stones River. Most of the points of interest can be reached on the self-guided auto tour. Numbered markers identify the stops, and short trails and exhibits explain the events at each site. Plan to spend at least two hours to get the most out of your visit, and stop first at the visitor center. An audiovisual program and museum will introduce you to the battle. A captioned slide show is available, too. Pick up a brochure guide or recorded guide to use on the self-guided auto tour.

During summer, artillery and infantry demonstrations and talks about the battle are scheduled. The park is administered by the National Park Service. Admission is free. (See the Other Tennessee Battlefields chapter for a complete description of this battle.)

Tennessee State Capitol
Charlotte Ave. between Sixth and Seventh Aves.
Nashville, TN
(615) 741-0830
www.tnmuseum.org

The Greek Revival–style building was begun in 1859. Its architect, William Strickland of Philadelphia, began his career as an apprentice to Benjamin Latrobe, architect of the U.S. Capitol in Washington, D.C. Strickland died before the Tennessee State Capitol was completed and, per his wishes, was buried in the northeast wall of the building, near the north entrance. Strickland's son, Francis Strickland, supervised construction until 1857, when Englishman Harvey Akeroyd designed the state library, the final portion of the building.

The capitol stands 170 feet above the highest hill in downtown Nashville. On the eastern slope of the grounds is the tomb of President and Mrs. James K. Polk and a bronze equestrian statue of President Andrew Jackson. During the

Civil War the capitol was used as a Union fortress. In the 1930s the murals in the governor's office were added. Various restoration projects have taken place over the years. In 1996 a bronze statue of Andrew Johnson was erected so that all three U.S. presidents from Tennessee are commemorated on the capitol grounds.

Guided tours are conducted and a brochure is available for self-guided tours. Admission is free.

ACCOMMODATIONS

As a major metropolitan area and convention destination, Nashville and the surrounding area are filled with chain motels and hotels, mostly clustered near the airport and around the interstate highway exits.

The Old Marshall House Bed and Breakfast $$–$$$
1030 John Williams Rd.
Franklin, TN
(615) 791-1455
www.oldmarshallhouse.com

This two-story farmhouse was built in 1867 by Joseph Kennedy Marshall, who was released in 1865 after 16 months as a Confederate prisoner in Rock Island Prison. The home is now a bed-and-breakfast, with rooms in the main house as well as the on-site log cabin (The Cat's Meow) that served as the original owner's home during the building process. The house is located near Carter House and Carnton Plantation.

RESTAURANTS

F. Scott's Restaurant and Jazz Bar $$–$$$
2210 Crestmoor Rd.
Nashville, TN
(615) 269-5861
www.fscotts.com

Casually elegant, warm, and inviting, F. Scott's is considered by many to be one of the best restaurants in Nashville. This is a place where the sophisticated feel comfortable, but it's not necessary to dress up to the hilt; you'll fit in, whether you're in jeans or coat and tie. F. Scott's serves American bistro-style food. The menu changes seasonally, but there is always plenty of pasta, chicken, duck, lamb, pork, and fresh fish. F. Scott's has three dining rooms and a jazz bar with live entertainment six nights a week. In addition to a wonderful dining experience, this is a very pleasant place to stop for a drink. F. Scott's is open only for dinner, and reservations are recommended.

Hog Heaven $
115 27th Ave. N.
Nashville, TN
(615) 329-1234
www.hogheavenbbq.com

This is a good time to apply the "don't judge a book by its cover" rule. Hog Heaven doesn't look like much—it's a tiny white cinder-block building tucked in a corner of Centennial Park behind McDonald's—but once you taste their barbecue, you'll know why they attached the word "heaven" to the name. This is some good eatin'. Hog Heaven's hand-pulled pork, chicken, beef, and turkey barbecue is actually pretty famous among Nashville's barbecue connoisseurs.

The menu is posted on a board beside the walk-up window. After you get your order, you might want to hop on over to Centennial Park and dig in, since the only seating at the restaurant is two picnic tables on a slab of concrete right in front of the window. You can order barbecue sandwiches, barbecue plates that come with two side orders, and barbecue by the pound. The white barbecue sauce is just right on top of the chicken, and the regular sauce comes in mild, hot, or extra hot. Quarter-chicken and half-chicken orders are available, and Hog Heaven has spareribs, too. Barbecue beans, potato salad, coleslaw, turnip greens, white beans, green beans, and black-eyed peas are among the side dishes. The homemade cobbler is a heavenly way to end a memorable Hog Heaven meal. Hog Heaven delivers to areas nearby.

Sunset Grill $$–$$$
2001-A Belcourt Ave.
Nashville, TN
(615) 386-3663
www.sunsetgrill.com

Sunset Grill is one of Nashville's favorite restaurants. It serves new American cuisine in a casually elegant atmosphere. Any night of the week you're apt to see customers in jeans dining next to a group in tuxedos.

The Voodoo Pasta is a menu staple. It has grilled chicken, bay shrimp, and andouille sausage in spicy Black Magic tomato sauce with fresh egg fettucini pasta. The Vegetarian Voodoo Pasta has eggplant, spinach, and mushrooms, in a spicy Black Magic tomato sauce with egg fettuccini pasta. Other menu favorites include blackberry duck and lamb dijonnaise. There is a good selection of vegetarian dishes. The desserts are beautiful and extensive in choice, but don't worry, you can also order a large dessert trio or half-portions. If you want to go all out, order the dessert mirror, 10 full portions of various desserts served on a mirrored tray.

Sunset Grill has an excellent wine selection—one of the best in town—with more than 200 wines, 60 available by the glass. The Tuesday-afternoon wine-tasting classes have become quite popular; seating is limited for these, so make a reservation if you don't want to miss out. Sunset Grill is one of the few places in town that has a late-night menu.

Chattanooga:
The Battle above the Clouds

Darley.

In the late afternoon of September 20, 1863, following the disaster at Chickamauga (see chapter on Chickamauga), Union troops streamed back in a near panic to their stronghold at Chattanooga. Many abandoned both arms and equipment in their haste to escape the Confederate force they thought would surely pounce at any moment. Amid them (and in front of a great number of them) rode their dispirited commander, Major General William Starke Rosecrans, no doubt wondering how to tell his bosses that earlier dispatches predicting victory in the north Georgia battle were premature at best.

Although his able lieutenant, Major General George Henry Thomas, the "Rock of Chickamauga," still held his ground at the northern end of the battleground, Rosecrans was in near hysterics on hearing (untrue) rumors that 20,000 or more Confederate troops under Lieutenant General Richard S. Ewell were on their way from Virginia. In quick succession, Rosecrans telegraphed Washington begging for "all reinforcements you can send hurried up," and he sent other telegrams stating he could stand and fight and others that claimed he would soon have to withdraw north. To complete his rushed and distracted set of actions, he ordered Thomas to retreat and join him in Chattanooga, and that small outposts atop Lookout Mountain be abandoned as "undefensible."

Chattanooga had first fallen into Union hands in early September 1863, the Confederate force under General Braxton Bragg pulling out without a shot being fired when Rosecrans's three columns—including 60,000 men moving south—threatened to cut the rail line to Atlanta. At the same time, Major General Ambrose Burnside's Union Army of the Ohio, divided into four columns including 24,000 men, swept down on the smaller Confederate garrison at Knoxville, also forcing it to abandon the city without a fight. The two Confederate forces combined under Bragg in northwest Georgia, just below the Tennessee line. For all practical purposes, Tennessee was then under complete Union control.

BACKGROUND TO THE BATTLE

Problems in the Armies

Strangely enough, at this time both forces were closely matched in both troop strength (56,359 Union to 65,165 Confederate) and the controversial nature of their sometimes simply incompetent commanders. Bragg was intensely despised by both officers and ordinary soldiers and kept his rank and position primarily by way of his personal friendship with President Jefferson Davis. Private Sam Watkins of the Maury Grays, 1st Tennessee Infantry, said, "None of General Bragg's soldiers ever loved him. They had no faith in his ability as a general. He was looked upon as a merciless tyrant."

Bragg also was noted for his personal vendettas against his "enemies," those fellow Confederate officers who disagreed with him on one point or another. In the midst of renewed Union offenses in the summer of 1863, Bragg chose instead to pay more attention to his conspiracies against outstanding generals such as major generals Benjamin Frank Cheatham and John McCowan and Lieutenant General William J. Hardee.

Major General George Henry Thomas, known as the "Rock of Chickamauga"

Rosecrans, on the other hand, was considered a dangerous tactician by his Confederate foes, but while loved by his men and admired for his generalship in most battles, his own peers thought him unstable and prone to panic under stress. Lincoln later remarked that Rosecrans had acted "confused and stunned like a duck hit on the head." In the midst of Rosecrans's rushed preparations for the retreat to Chattanooga, one glaring problem escaped his notice—his own supply lines. Confederate forces had cut his northern rail access, steep and nearly impassable mountains surrounded him on three sides and were soon to be manned with Confederate artillery and infantry emplacements, and a low-water situation combined with adjacent Confederate outposts on the Tennessee River flowing past his command prevented resupply by riverboat. To add to his woes, most of a more than 800-hundred-wagon supply train coming in on the one inadequate road was captured on October 2 by Major General Joseph Wheeler's cavalry raiders. Rations at this point were estimated at a mere 10 days' worth, and ammunition existed for only about two days of fully involved combat. Instead of a fortified redoubt, Rosecrans's muddled planning had placed them in an isolated prison.

General Braxton Bragg

On the Confederate side, things were hardly better. At Chickamauga, to the outrage of his senior commanders, Bragg refused to allow them to press on after the rapidly retreating routed majority of Union forces, ordering instead a concentration of effort on Thomas's sparse force holding fast to Horseshoe Ridge. Even after Thomas's men slipped away after nightfall on September 20, Bragg refused to allow a pursuit, believing the noises the retreating Union forces were making indicated they were preparing for an assault the next morning. Not until two full days later did Bragg move forward to Missionary Ridge, only to see the Union forces already well entrenched within Chattanooga below.

After some patrol and light skirmishing action on September 22 showed the extent of the Union Army's fortifications, Bragg settled down to try to starve out the besieged city garrison. Within a few days, Union rations were reduced by half, then to one-quarter. Even with some supplies coming in through a torturous 65-mile mountain route constantly under attack by Wheeler's cavalry, it became nearly impossible to maintain even this inadequate ration. Guards were posted to prevent soldiers from stealing the feed of the most essential horses; another 15,000 horses and mules simply died of starvation.

After heavy rains washed out the only bridge on their own supply line, Confederate men were reduced to the same meager rations as their Union foe. With the infantry obviously dissatisfied with Bragg's tactics and personal vendettas, as well as the bleak supply situation, President Davis decided to make a mid-October visit to the battlefield to shore up morale. It didn't work as planned, as Sam Watkins describes:

Tell old Bragg for God's sake not to let the Yanks whip him as he usually does when this army gains a victory . . . If the armies of the West were worth a goober we could soon have piece [sic] on our own terms.

—Private W. C. McClellan of Lee's Army of Northern Virginia, in a letter to his father in northern Alabama, as quoted in Bell Irvin Wiley's *Life of Johnny Reb*

And in the very acme of our privations and hunger, when the army was most dissatisfied and unhappy, we were ordered into line of battle to be reviewed by Honorable Jefferson Davis. When he passed by us, with his great retinue of staff officers and play-outs at full gallop, cheers greeted them, with the words, "Send us something to eat, Massa Jeff. Give us something to eat, Massa Jeff. I'm hungry! I'm hungry!"

Battle of Chattanooga

Sherman to the Rescue

Unknown to either side at Chattanooga, at least at first, once word of the situation reached Washington, four divisions of General William T. Sherman's Army of Tennessee set out from Vicksburg and two corps under Major General Joseph Hooker set out from Virginia. On October 30 the forward elements of Hooker's corps reached Bridgeport, Tennessee, and Rosecrans made plans to assault and seize the closest ferry point, Brown's Ferry, just west of Lookout Mountain itself. Before all could be made ready, Rosecrans was relieved

Lookout Mountain

of command and replaced by Thomas. Major General U. S. Grant himself arrived with reinforcements from Vicksburg on October 23, and both commanders agreed to continue with Rosecrans's plans.

Led by Lieutenant Colonel James C. Foy of the 23rd Kentucky Infantry, hastily gathered pontoons and other flatboats floated quietly downriver on the night of October 27 and captured Brown's Ferry with hardly a shot being fired by the small Confederate outpost. While engineers and pioneers hastily assembled a pontoon bridge to bring reinforcements across, Foy had his men entrench for the attack that was sure to come.

The only Confederate troops nearby did soon mount an attack, but only about one-half of a regiment under Colonel William C. Oates could be summoned for the assault. In a 20-minute fight, Oates's men were routed by both Foy's men and other Union units hastily brought across the still-unfinished bridge. The key to Bragg's entire strategy—Brown's Ferry—had been guarded by a tiny, unsupported percentage of the men under his command.

On October 28, with Bragg and Lieutenant General James Longstreet personally observing from atop Lookout Mountain, Brigadier General John West Geary's 2nd Division of Hooker's 12th Corps crossed the newly finished pontoon bridge and entered Lookout Valley, stopping at the Wauhatchie rail junction. At midnight that same night, Brigadier General Micah Jenkins's Division of Longstreet's corps attacked Geary, now reinforced by two other brigades. The three-hour fight resulted in both Jenkins's being thrown back and a complete Confederate withdrawal out of the valley and up onto the slopes of Lookout Mountain, leaving all the good supply lines into the city in Union hands. The Confederates still held all the high ground surrounding the city, and Bragg remained confident that this was the only advantage he would really need.

THE FIGHT BEGINS: ORCHARD KNOB

With the Union situation improving by the day with fresh men and supplies coming in, and the Confederate supply problems mounting, Bragg amazingly decided to concentrate on his own personal vendettas once again. Blaming Longstreet for the Union successes at Brown's Ferry and Wauhatchie, Bragg ordered him and two other generals to prepare for an all-out assault on the strong Union positions in Lookout Valley. Longstreet duly reported for the three of them that such an attack would be "impracticable."

Viewing this sensible report as a personal affront, Bragg decided Longstreet's attitude was unacceptable. In a letter to Jefferson Davis, Bragg complained that Longstreet was "disrespectful and insubordinate" and reported that he planned to send him off with his corps to the renewed campaign around Knoxville. On November 4, Longstreet left by rail with nearly a third of Bragg's entire force.

Sherman's forces finally began arriving on November 21, and with this encouraging news, Grant ordered attacks to begin as soon as possible. His first target was a small, steep hill in front of Missionary Ridge called Orchard Knob. On the morning of November 23, three Union brigades led by brigadier generals William B. Hazen, August Willich, and Samuel Beatty stormed the lightly held outpost, capturing the knob in about five minutes of heavy fighting. The surviving Confederates fled back to the entrenchments at the base of Missionary Ridge, and almost before they knew it, the Union held one of the best strategic observation posts for the coming battle. The cost was very high, though, with Hazen alone losing 167 men.

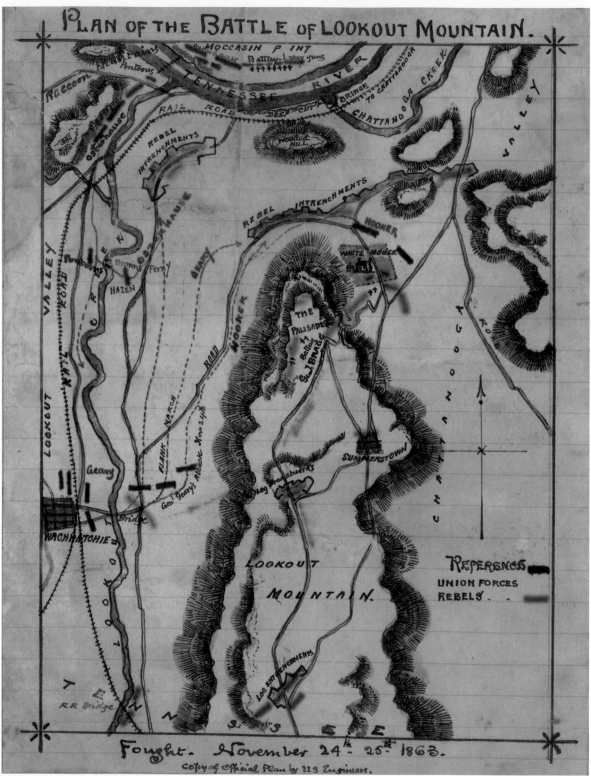

Map of the Battle of Lookout Mountain

LOOKOUT MOUNTAIN: CRAVENS HOUSE FIGHT

*E*arly the next morning, with Sherman's forces fully across the river (but mistakenly out of position to strike at Missionary Ridge), Hooker was ordered to make a "demonstration" against Lookout Mountain, to draw attention away from the main assault on Missionary Ridge. With a low fog enveloping the mountain and obscuring the view of Confederate artillery and infantry outposts atop the mountain at Point Lookout, Geary's division supported by Brigadier General Walter C. Whitaker's brigade moved quietly up the flank of the rough, boulder-encrusted mountainside, aiming not to take the upper crest (which Hooker thought was completely immune to direct assault) but to capture the middle and lower reaches of the mountainside. When they at last encountered a line of Confederate entrenchments and emplacements manned by Brigadier General Edward C. Walthall's brigade, they found to their joy that

The Cravens House

the Confederate force was positioned to repulse a direct assault up the slope, not from across the steep mountainside. In less than 15 minutes of furious fighting, the Confederate force was driven out and sent fleeing back to its main line of defense at the Cravens House.

Storming around the mountain after the fleeing Confederates, the Union forces, led now by the 60th and 137th New York Regiments, advanced through a furious cannonade toward the white farmhouse, close behind Walthall's retreating Confederates. They closed in so tight that a two-gun battery at the Cravens House itself was unable to fire upon them, for fear of hitting its own troops, and the house was soon overrun and captured. More Confederate forces arrive to shore up the trench lines of the tiny battleground, but they were soon routed and sent fleeing down the mountain by Whitaker's reserve brigades coming onto the field.

POINT LOOKOUT

*G*eary sent word to Hooker of their achievement and asked for resupply so that they could advance farther. Amazed and almost upset that this "demonstration" had gone so far, Hooker ordered Geary and Whitaker to entrench and stay put. With the Confederate forces above and around them in the woods keeping up a steady fire and even rolling large boulders down the mountainside at them, the Union forces manned their enemies' previous breastworks and waited.

Bragg, alerted to his plight on Lookout Mountain by the sound of heavy Union artillery being placed atop it, made a fatal decision. Convinced that this action constituted a major assault on his commanding position, he ordered the withdrawal of all units from atop and on Lookout Mountain, and the valley below as well, to concentrate his forces on Missionary Ridge. By sunrise on November 25, Hooker had complete command of the entire mountain, at least by default. As a final act, men of the North's 8th Kentucky and 96th Illinois

Infantry Regiments climbed the nearly sheer rocky cliffs to plant their flags on the abandoned emplacements.

The oft-remarked "battle above the clouds" in fact never really occurred; at best, it could be accurately called the "battle within the fog." Grant himself grumbled over the brief fight's wide exposure and exaltation in the press, stating that it had hardly even constituted a skirmish. In his postwar memoirs he remarked, "The Battle of Lookout Mountain is one of the romances of the war. There was no such battle and no action even worthy to be called a battle on Lookout Mountain. It is all poetry."

Missionary Ridge

With reinforcements from the withdrawn positions around Chattanooga coming in line, Bragg had a strong position on Missionary Ridge. Aside from the natural defense of the steep mountain terrain, he had positioned his men in two main defensive bands. The first line of defense was a set of interlocking rifle pits at the mountain's base and the second was a set of strongly reinforced breastworks nearly atop the ridgeline, reinforced by artillery emplacements.

Turning attention immediately toward his main objective, Grant ordered Sherman to attack the far right of the Confederate line on Missionary Ridge early on the morning of November 25. Moving forward on the afternoon of the 24th, Sherman discovered too late that the hill his men were already assaulting, Billy Goat Hill, was not continuous with the ridgeline but separated by a steep and wooded ravine. With his typical bullheadedness, Sherman attempted to push through the ravine and hit the far right of the Confederate line anyhow, only to be halted by Major General Patrick R. Cleburne's still entrenching troops. Even with a near seven-to-one advantage, the Union forces could not push through the strong Confederate position. Even worse, a counterattacking downhill bayonet charge by Cleburne's men at a part of the ridge called Tunnel Hill pushed the Union line back to the base of the hill and captured nearly a whole Union brigade's worth of men after an incredibly fierce hand-to-hand fight.

With Sherman stuck on the Union left, Grant ordered Hooker to cross the valley and strike on the low ridges on the right, with Thomas's men, to make a "demonstration" from Orchard Knob toward the middle of the Confederate line. As planned, this center attack would force the Confederates to shift their men away from the flanks, giving Sherman and Hooker the edge they needed to take the flanks.

The Infantry Assault on Missionary Ridge

Once more, the "demonstration" became the battle centerpiece. About 3:30 p.m., Thomas's men moved forward with orders to engage the first set of rifle pits and halt. Charging across the nearly half-mile of open ground, under inaccurate and ineffective Confederate artillery fire all the while, the Union troops quickly took over the Confederate rifle pits, earlier ordered to be abandoned when attacked in a serious tactical blunder by Lieutenant General William J. Hardee. Under heavy and accurate fire from above, Thomas's men realized that to stay in this exposed position was sheer suicide. Ignoring his orders, Lieutenant Colonel William P. Chandler of the 35th Illinois Infantry leapt to the top of the breastwork and, with a cry of "Forward!," led his men up the steep hillside.

This was all the motivation that the rest of Thomas's command needed, and company by company, roaring at the top of their lungs, soon all were in full assault uphill. Atop Orchard Knob, Grant was horrified at the sight. With the memory of Sherman's men in full flight down Tunnel Hill still very fresh, he had a terrible vision of Thomas's men being chewed to pieces and routed. Turning in anger, he demanded of his corps commanders who had ordered that charge. Thomas and Major General Gordon Granger both calmly answered, truthfully, that they had not. Grant turned back to watch the scene unfolding, muttering that if that attack failed, someone would pay dearly. One does get the impression that he was not referring to the infantrymen.

Sweeping like a wildfire up the mountainside, the uncoordinated attacks all along the center of the Confederate lines could not be stopped. About 5 p.m., the 32nd Indiana and 6th Ohio Infantry Regiments reached the crest at Sharp's Spur, right in the center of Colonel William F. Tucker's Mississippi Brigade. Quickly capturing one 12-pounder Napoleon

Map of the Battle of Missionary Ridge

Sam Watkins

Sam Watkins was born near Columbia, Tennessee, in 1839, and was attending college there when the war broke out. He immediately quit school and joined Company H, 1st Tennessee Infantry Regiment of the Confederate Army, afraid that the war would soon end and he would not see any action. Self-described "High-Private" Watkins served until the end of the war and amazingly survived in the midst of some of the fiercest fighting in the Western Theater. His unit, soon joined by the 27th Tennessee Infantry Regiment and another independent battalion, fought from just after the First Manassas (First Bull Run) until the surrender of General Joseph Eggleston Johnston's Army of Tennessee at Greensboro, North Carolina, in April 1865. Although his combined regiments counted some 3,200 men in their ranks throughout the war (by his own estimation), Watkins was one of only 65 original members still standing after four years of fighting, and one of only seven survivors of the original 120 men of Company H.

Although Watkins was in the first line of battle in most of his unit's engagements, he managed to survive nearly unscathed—seriously wounded only once. He lived to tell about his experiences in one of the greatest memoirs of the Civil War, *Company Aytch Or, A Side Show of the Big Show,* published in 1882. Originally written in serial form for the *Columbia Herald,* the book is an emotional and quite philosophical journey through the heart and mind of a combat infantryman separated from all he knows and loves and forced into brutal savagery simply to survive. Watkins took an ironic and somewhat humorous view of "what I saw as a humble private in the rear rank of an infantry regiment," and his memoir is distinctly different from the legions of other, more self-aggrandizing memoirs and diaries published after the war.

Watkins's view of the war was from the trenches, and throughout the book he commented that he was not aware of and did not care about the grander strategies; he just marched where he was led and fired when he was told. However, his observations of those mostly vain and self-serving men who led his regiment and army stand out as piercingly accurate. He saw General Braxton Bragg as a "merciless tyrant" that no one in the ranks "ever loved or respected." About the best thing Watkins could say about Bragg was a simple postwar observation, "But he is dead now." Watkins thought General John Bell Hood a "failure in every particular" as a general and leader, but "brave, good, noble and gallant," although he stated that Hood was both mentally and physically incompetent for command.

Johnston was held in much higher regard by Watkins and most of his men and is also well thought of by most modern historians. Watkins said, "He was loved, respected, admired; yea, almost worshipped by his troops. . . . The veriest coward that was ever born became a brave man and a hero under his manipulation." While Johnston did not have the support of the higher Confederate command and authorities, his men loved him because he "made us love ourselves," and Watkins mentioned time and again how they would have followed the little general literally anywhere. Watkins's own regimental commander, Colonel Hume R. Field, was equally admired; Watkins said that he was the "bravest man, I think, I ever knew" and that the War Department should have placed him in charge of whole armies instead of a mere regiment. Watkins's view of officers in general, however, was more practical: "I always looked upon officers as harmless personages," and on the battlefield, "I always shot at privates."

Watkins went on after the war to marry his beloved Jennie, who was mentioned throughout his memoir, and to raise eight children. He died in Columbia in 1901.

of Captain James Garrity's Alabama Battery, the Ohio men forced the Confederate gunners at bayonet point to fire on their own retreating men.

Other Union regiments soon reached the crest and fanned out to both sides, with Confederates making only token resistance before pulling back. With strong attacks now coming from three points atop the ridge, Bragg gave hasty orders to retreat. Mostly in ragged groups and as individual soldiers, some in quickly organized defensive postures, the Confederates streamed back toward Georgia. Hooker was ordered to give chase. Cleburne was ordered to save what was left of the army and to protect their retreat at the north Georgia town of Ringgold.

The Fight at Ringgold

*R*eceiving these orders just before the Union advance elements arrived, Cleburne elected to set up his defensive position just south of the small town atop two small hills on either side of the rail line. With only a little more than 4,000 men and two small artillery pieces, he knew that he could not withstand a direct assault by Hooker's 12,000 troops.

Hooker's men passed through the small town nearly uncontested on the morning of November 27 and immediately set out along the south rail line, led by the 13th Illinois Infantry. Waiting until the Union men were less than 150 yards away, Cleburne ordered both cannon to open fire with both solid shot and canister.

The resulting carnage was extreme, with the 13th Illinois being shot to pieces within minutes, and the flanking regiments on either side of the gap suffering equally immense casualties.

Cleburne kept up his defensive position until shortly after noon, when Union artillery finally arrived on scene. Less than an hour later, he had his men and both artillery pieces safely off the hilltops and heading back toward Dalton. At a cost of 110 casualties, he had both stopped the Union advance and bloodied Hooker to the tune of at least 500 casualties. Many of Hooker's own men grumbled that this official figure was far too low.

Grant arrived in town later that same day and ordered Hooker to stop the pursuit. Intending to sit out the winter in relative comfort in Chattanooga, he ordered Hooker to stay put for a few days, and then withdraw to the north. Hooker finally left on November 30, burning the small Georgia town in his wake. The bitter fight for control of the gateway city to the Deep South finally came to an end, ironically with a Confederate tactical victory.

Chattanooga Today

Chattanooga is a rapidly growing major city (only one Georgia county along the 100-plus-mile I-75 corridor is not within either metropolitan Chattanooga or Atlanta), and its Civil War heritage stands front and center in its images and advertisements. Curiously, there is relatively little remaining untouched of the most fought-over battleground, Missionary Ridge, and it and some of the other major landmarks are very poorly marked and somewhat hard to find. Due to the city's growth alongside the meandering Tennessee River, streets are laid out in a confusing array, and it is a bit difficult to find your way around town at first.

Looming over the city like a great granite guardian angel is Lookout Mountain, the focal point for most Civil War–related activities. However, even this obvious landmark suffers from having its only real battleground (the Cravens House) barely marked and easily overlooked. On the positive side, the original Confederate artillery emplacements at the mountain's crest are still in place, encompassed by a small but tidy park run by the National Park Service. Although no skirmish transpired here, one can get a magnificent view of the city and on clear days see all the major battle landmarks in the area.

Three major interstate highways meet in Chattanooga (I-24, I-59, and I-75), giving easy access to the area from all directions. The suggested route, if convenient, is I-75 north from Atlanta, turning onto I-24 northbound and exiting at exit 178 (Broad Street/Lookout Mountain). An abundance of signs at the end of the ramp will guide you to whichever site or area you wish to visit first.

Take the Battlefield Parkway exit off I-75 (GA 2, exit 141) and travel west about 5 miles, then head south on US 27 about 1 mile to the park. The visitor center is just inside the north entrance and is very well marked.

To follow closely the track that Rosecrans's retreating army took from Chickamauga to Chattanooga, from Chickamauga stay on US 27 North about 3 miles to a large ridgeline bisecting the state line. This

(continued on page 215)

Battle at Ringgold

is the left flank of the Confederate Missionary Ridge line. A right turn onto Crest Road will take you across what was once the second and highest set of emplacements, nearly on top of the highest point of the mountain ridge, all the way to the far right flank where Crest Road meets Campbell Street. Please note that nearly all of this avenue is private property, even where historic markers and cannon monuments abound. Also note that this road is narrow and twisting, and parking is difficult to find in most places. A good choice if you are physically able is to park at the Sherman, DeLong, or Iowa Reservations (very few parking slots are at each) and walk along the route.

Today most of the area of operations of this short campaign has been altered or covered up by the rapidly growing city of Chattanooga. The most significant battlegrounds are now federal property, with the National Park Service preserving and operating several separate areas around the city. The largest continuous preserved area consists of Point Park and Lookout Mountain and includes the Cravens House, Point Lookout, and much of the northwest face of the large ridgeline. A very small, 1-city-block-square park encompasses the highest elevation of Orchard Knob, and several small "reservations" dot the top of Missionary Ridge.

We strongly suggest you visit at least the visitor center of Chickamauga Battlefield (see our chapter on Chickamauga for a complete description), which the National Park Service operates as the centerpiece of the two-state Chickamauga and Chattanooga National Military Park.

ACCOMMODATIONS

Chanticleer Inn Bed & Breakfast $$$$
1300 Mockingbird Lane
Lookout Mountain, GA
(706) 820-2002
www.stayatchanticleer.com

Th Chanticleer, which sits atop Lookout Mountain on a beautiful plateau that borders Tennessee, Georgia, and Alabama, is merely minutes from downtown Chattanooga and mountain attractions such as Ruby Falls and the Incline Railway. A full home-made breakfast is included and desserts are offered in the afternoon.

Chattanooga Choo Choo $$$$
1400 Market St.
Chattanooga, TN 37402
(423) 266-5000
(800) 872-2529
www.choochoo.com

At the Chattanooga Choo Choo hotel complex you can sleep onboard one of its 48 authentic and beautifully restored Victorian train cars or opt to bunk in a more standard-type room. There are restaurants and shopping nearby as well as soothing gardens, swimming pools, and one of the world's largest working "HO" gauge model railroads.

RESTAURANTS

Niko's Southside Grill $$–$$$
1400 Cowart St.
Chattanooga, TN
(423) 266-6511

The fresh ingredients and flavors of the Mediterranean influence Southern-American cuisine at Niko's Southside Grill, which offers grilled meats, fresh fish, and vegetarian fare.

Sticky Fingers $–$$
2031 Hamilton Place Blvd.
Chattanooga, TN
(423) 899-7427

Tuck into a rib platter or a combo plate and choose from pulled pork or chicken, hickory-smoked wings, grilled chicken breast, and more. Sticky signature sauces and rubs are also available online.

Shiloh:
The Bloodiest Days of 1862

Darley.

---- ✦ ----

THE CONFEDERATE SITUATION

Johnston's newly organized Army of Mississippi, based in the important rail center of Corinth, Mississippi, steadily built up strength through March 1862. Major General Leonidas Polk, Brigadier General (and former U.S. vice president) John C. Breckinridge, and Major General William J. Hardee brought the remnants of their corps down from Kentucky; Major General Braxton Bragg brought most of his corps north from Pensacola, Florida; and Brigadier General Daniel Ruggles's division marched east from New Orleans. Other commands scattered around the Deep South detached individual regiments and brigades, which arrived in the northern Mississippi town all through the last two weeks of March. By April 1, Johnston had a roughly organized, ill-trained, and mostly inexperienced force of about 45,000 officers and men under his command.

---- ✦ ----

THE UNION SITUATION

After taking Fort Henry in the north-central region of Tennessee, Flag Officer Andrew Hull Foote sailed his small gunboat fleet down the Tennessee River nearly unmolested all the way to Florence, Alabama, decisively demonstrating just how vulnerable the South was to invasion via the river systems. One of the very few attempts at a Confederate resistance to his mission was on March 1, when Gibson's Battery of the 1st Louisiana Artillery Regiment, mounted on a bluff just downstream from Savannah, Tennessee, lobbed a few shells at the fleet as they passed. Colonel Alfred Mouton's infantry from the adjacent 18th Louisiana Infantry joined in, ineffectively shooting up the side of the armored gunboats. Foote returned fire, and the shelling soon stopped.

Two weeks later, Union forces started moving south under the overall command of Major General Henry Wager Halleck with two missions: Take control of and repair roads through middle Tennessee, and clear the area of any Confederate forces they encountered. Once all of his forces were concentrated at Savannah, Halleck intended to move

Andrew Hull Foote

farther south, into Mississippi, and destroy the rail junctions in Corinth, Jackson, Humbolt, and Iuka. To accomplish this mission, Halleck had two grand armies: Major General Ulysses S. Grant's Army of Tennessee and Major General Don Carlos Buell's Army of the Ohio, with a combined total of just under 63,000 men on the march south.

A heavy reconnaissance force under Brigadier General Charles Ferguson Smith (promoted one week later to Major General) arrived in Savannah on March 13, charged by Halleck to seize and hold or at least cut the Memphis & Charleston Railroad at Corinth without engaging the Confederate forces rumored to be gathering in the area. Brigadier General William Tecumseh Sherman arrived from Kentucky the next day, and Smith promptly sent him off toward Eastport, Mississippi, to see if he could cut the railroad there. As he sailed south on the Tennessee River aboard Lieutenant William Gwin's gunboat, *Tyler,* Gwin pointed out the location of their earlier skirmish with the Confederate artillery battery. Alarmed at the close presence of the enemy to his intended target, Sherman sent word back to Smith that this location should be occupied in force as soon as possible. Smith agreed and immediately dispatched Brigadier General Stephen Hurlbut's 4th Division to occupy the small bluff, Pittsburg Landing, about 3 miles northeast of a tiny settlement called Shiloh Church.

Plan of the Battle of Shiloh

⭐

THE BUILDUP

$\int$herman soon returned from his reconnaissance, after finding Confederates were present in force at his intended target, and joined Hurlbut at Pittsburg Landing. Scouting the area, he reported back to Smith that the area was "important" and easily defended by a relatively small force, although the ground provided a good encampment space for several thousand troops. The few settlers at the landing had fled with the arrival of Union gunboats, and the only "locals" remaining were small-plot farmers scattered about the county. The small Methodist meetinghouse, Shiloh Church, was described by one source as a "rude one-room log cabin, which would make a good corncrib for an Illinois farmer." Sherman urged Smith to relocate the majority of forces to this small landing, the northernmost road link to their intended target of Corinth, Mississippi.

Shiloh Church

General Grant arrived in Savannah on March 17 to take over direct command of the Tennessee River operation from Smith, setting up his headquarters in the Cherry Mansion on Main Street. He soon ordered his (roughly) 35,000-man force to deploy on the west side of the river, save a small garrison in Savannah, with five divisions to join with Sherman at Pittsburg Landing, and Brigadier General Lewis "Lew" Wallace's 2nd Division to occupy Crump's Landing, 6 miles north of Sherman's position.

Another major Union army, Major General Buell's Army of the Ohio, was on the way south from Nashville with another 30,000 men (both this figure and Grant's total command size are wildly disparate in differing accounts). Grant planned to rest his men and wait for Buell's arrival before starting his operation against Corinth. Although he was aware that the Confederates were present in force just 20 miles away, he believed that they would simply entrench around Corinth and have to be forced out. An attack on Pittsburg Landing was, quite literally, the last thing he expected the Confederates to do.

The Deployment

It took well over a week to transport all the Union forces south to the new position, and the divisions moved inland and encamped in a loose semicircle south of the landing and across the Corinth Road as they arrived. Sherman's own 5th Division headquarters was just to the west of the Corinth Road. Colonel John A. McDowell's 1st, Colonel Ralph P. Buckland's 4th, and Colonel Jesse Hildebrand's 3rd Brigades deployed from Owl Creek left (east) to just south of Shiloh Church. Colonel David Stuart's 2nd Brigade of Sherman's division encamped separately about 2 miles farther east, at the far left and southernmost of the combined Union line, just above Locust Grove Branch at the Hamburg-Savannah Road. Hurlbut's 4th Division encamped to the left (due east) of Sherman's main line, with Colonel Nelson G. Williams's 1st, Colonel James C. Veatch's 2nd, and Colonel Jacob G. Lauman's 3rd Brigades arrayed across the intersection of the Corinth and Hamburg-Savannah Roads.

Major General John A. McClernand's 1st Division deployed behind (north of) Sherman's. Colonel Abraham M. Hare's 1st, Colonel C. Carroll Marsh's 2nd, and Colonel Julius Raith's 3rd Brigades encamped along the Corinth Road as it ran due west to the Hamburg-Purdy Road intersection. Smith's division stayed close to Pittsburg Landing itself, Colonel James M. Tuttle's 1st, Colonel Thomas West Sweeny's 3rd, and Brigadier General John McArthur's Brigades encamped just north of the end of the Corinth Road and west to Snake Creek. Brigadier General Benjamin M. Prentiss's newly organized 6th Division landed and moved the south to the right (west) of Stuart's Brigade. Colonel Madison Miller's 2nd and Colonel Everett Peabody's 1st Brigades made camp to Sherman's southeast, in the woods across and to the west of the Eastern Corinth Road.

By March 19, all six divisions were in place and comfortably making camp. Smith had been injured while jumping from one boat to another during the landing and was soon forced to hand over command of his 2nd Division to Brigadier General William Harvey Lamb Wallace. Smith died on April 25 of an infection in his foot from the wound.

The Confederate Advance

Johnston was well aware of Grant's presence to the north of his headquarters and received a message on April 2 that Buell's force was nearby as well. Still waiting in Corinth for the last of his assigned forces to arrive, Johnston decided that he would go ahead and attack the gathering Union force before Buell's addition could make it stronger. The orders he issued were simple: March north and engage the enemy between his encampments and the river, turning their left flank and forcing them away from their line of retreat until they were forced to surrender.

Beauregard planned out the tactical details of the coming attack and issued orders to move out on the morning of April 3. Confederate units scattered across upper Mississippi and lower Tennessee were to converge by April 4 at Mickey's farmhouse, 8 miles south of Pittsburg Landing, where final preparations for the attack would begin. Hardee's and Bragg's corps would march north from Corinth, along with one division of Polk's corps, along the parallel Bark and Pittsburg Landing Roads. Breckinridge's corps moved north from Burnsville and Polk's other division (Major General Benjamin Franklin Cheatham's) would move southeast from Purdy, Tennessee, to join at the rendezvous farm.

The march took much longer than Beauregard had planned due to poor preparation and a steady rain that turned the dirt roads into mud quagmires. It was late in the evening of April 5 before everyone was in position at the junction of Corinth and Bark Roads, with Hardee's corps arrayed in the front only a half-mile from the Union picket line. Union cavalry patrols had engaged with forward elements of each column on both April 4 and 5, leading Beauregard to ask Johnston to call off the attack. He stated that his carefully scheduled attack plan was now "disrupted" and that with the cavalry attacks, surely all aspects of surprise were long gone. Johnston was adamant about continuing the attack, telling Beauregard, Polk, and Bragg, "Gentlemen, we shall attack at daylight tomorrow." Moments later, he remarked to one of his staff officers, "I would fight them if they were a million. They can present no greater front between these two creeks than we can, and the more men they crowd in there, the worse we can make it for them."

The Night of April 5

All through the dark, damp night, Confederate soldiers lay in the woods, listening to Union bands playing patriotic tunes just yards away. Union soldiers had listened to the Confederates advancing into position all evening and had sent a slew of frantic messages up the chain of command, warning of their presence. Amazingly, all these warnings were ignored by Grant's staff, who believed they amounted to nothing more than reconnaissance patrols. Grant was still firmly convinced that Johnston's men were continuing to entrench heavily at Corinth and was only concerned with how difficult it was going to be to "root them out."

To top off the Union Army's lack of combat preparedness, Halleck had ordered Grant not to be pulled into a fight that would distract him from his goal of taking Corinth, and Grant followed suit by ordering no patrolling of his own forces, for fear they might engage the enemy "patrols" and create a general battle. His brigade commanders farthest south were growing increasingly nervous, passing on report after report to headquarters that their men were spotting more and more Confederate cavalry, infantry, and even artillery. Their frantic requests for reinforcement, or even for permission to mount their own scouting missions, were denied; their division commanders only reiterated Grant's orders.

Finally, as darkness fell on April 5, Peabody decided it would be better to beg forgiveness if he was wrong than to ask permission again and gave orders for a combat patrol to go out as early as possible the next morning. At 3 a.m. on April 6, Major James Powell led his 25th Missouri and the 12th Michigan Infantry Regiments, with a total of 250 men, out into the predawn blackness, heading south toward the Corinth Road. They marched southwesterly down a narrow farm lane only about a quarter-mile before running into Confederate cavalry vedettes. Both sides exchanged fire briefly before the Confederate cavalrymen suddenly broke contact and withdrew. Just before 5 a.m. Powell deployed his men into a line-abreast skirmish line and continued southeast, toward Fraley's cotton field.

THE FIRST DAY, APRIL 6, 1862: THE BATTLE BEGINS

*P*owell's men moved into the cotton field and soon came under fire. Major Aaron B. Hardcastle's 3rd Mississippi Battalion had observed the Union troops entering the field and waited until they closed within 90 yards before opening fire. The Union soldiers hit the ground and returned a heavy volume of fire. The exchange lasted until 6:30 a.m., both sides suffering moderate casualties, until Powell observed Hardcastle's men suddenly disengaging and moving back into the woods. Believing they were retreating, Powell ordered his men up and was preparing to move out again when, to his horror, a mile-wide mass of Confederate soldiers suddenly appeared at the wood line before him—9,000 men of Hardee's corps on their way north.

The Confederate force was fully up and moving, their surprise attack only slightly tripped up by Powell's tiny force. Behind Hardee was Bragg's corps, also in a near-mile-wide line of battle, followed by Polk's corps in route-march formation (columns of brigades) on the Corinth Road. In the rear, and also in columns of brigades, was Breckinridge's reserve corps. The whole formation was T-shaped, almost a mile wide, and more than 2 miles long, all moving forward at a quick-time march toward the Union encampments.

Before he was killed and his small patrol force scattered, Powell managed to get word back to Peabody about the general attack. Peabody immediately moved his brigade south to try to aid Powell. Hardee was having a tough time moving his large force north—the Union patrol and skirmishers delayed his general movement, and the terrain was not conducive to moving such a large mass of troops and equipment very quickly. As the two forces moved toward each other, Prentiss rode up to Peabody and began berating him for sending out the patrol and "bringing this battle on." After a few minutes of argument, Peabody set his men up in a line of battle near his original encampment, while Prentiss set his force up on the left, making ready to engage the oncoming Confederates.

The time was 7 a.m., and the sun was dawning on what looked like a beautiful, cloudless day.

Shiloh National Cemetery Wikipedia Kbh3rd

Hardee's Assault

Hardee's corps had broken up into the individual brigades, which spread out to engage the Union encampments in an almost 2-mile front. At Spain Field on the Eastern Corinth Road, Brigadier General Adley H. Gladden's brigade burst out of the wood line directly across from Prentiss's line, the field itself swept with heavy artillery fire from both sides. A galling fire came from the Union line that staggered the Confederates. Able to stand for only a few minutes, the brigade retreated to the wood line, dragging with them the mortally wounded Gladden, who died later that same day.

Over on the left, at about the same time, Brigadier General Sterling A. M. Wood's brigade hit Peabody's right flank, pushing the Union infantry out of their line and back. Johnston, no longer able to stand being out of the line of fire, turned over operations in the rear to Beauregard and rushed forward to lead the battle from the front. Arriving just in time to see Wood's success and Gladden's repulse, he ordered all four brigades now up on the line to fix bayonets and assault the Union line at the double-quick, and 9,800 men ran screaming forward into the Union lines.

As his command withered under the assault, Peabody rode forward to rally his men and was hit four times in a matter of minutes by rifle fire as he moved down the line. Finally, in front of his own tent, watching the butternut-clad ranks closing in on him from two sides, Peabody was shot from his saddle, dying instantly. His command completely crumbled, followed shortly by Prentiss's own men. Even as William Wallace's and Hurlbut's brigades moved south to reinforce them, most of the Union infantry had had enough of this fight and retreated toward Pittsburg Landing.

Bragg's Assault

As the Union men broke and ran, the victorious Confederate infantry raced into their just-abandoned encampment and fell over the piles of fresh food and good equipment. Exhortations from their officers to return to the fight did no good, as the brigades and regiments dissolved into a rabble, pillaging the camps. Beauregard and Johnston had to take several precious minutes getting the men back under control and reorganizing them

to renew their attack, while the Union line stopped its headlong retreat and fell into new positions for defense.

Johnston ordered Bragg's corps into the growing battle, splitting his five brigades between the left and right of Hardee's men and ordering Bragg to take command of the assault on the right flank. On the right, Brigadier General John K. Jackson's and Brigadier General James R. Chalmers's brigades briefly joined the rout of Prentiss, while on the left Colonel Preston Pond's and Brigadier General Patton Anderson's brigades joined Brigadier General Patrick Ronayne Cleburne's brigade, which was steadily advancing on Sherman's position at Shiloh Church. Colonel Randall L. Gibson's brigade continued straight northeast, in between the two ongoing major assaults, to try to break the Union center and turn Sherman's left flank. In an attempt to bring the strongest force on his right flank and force the Ohio general's division away from the river, Johnston brought up Polk's corps and sent his four brigades into the line alongside Bragg. Hardee was instructed to take direct command of the left flank and to hammer hard on Sherman's position.

The Second Union Line

By 9 a.m., 13 Confederate brigades were fully engaged along a nearly 3-mile front, steadily pushing back Union forces. Sherman was soon reinforced by McClernand's division, while the newly arriving commands of Hurlbut, William Wallace, and McArthur joined in a hastily organized line along with what was left of Prentiss's brigade to Sherman's left over to the Hamburg-Savannah Road. Wallace was particularly well positioned along a narrow wagon trace, hardly even a road, that was concealed in an oak forest atop a low ridgeline with a good field of fire before him across the open Duncan field. This position in the center of Grant's defense line was later referred to as the Sunken Road.

A little after 10:30 a.m., just after Grant finished his visit with Sherman, Polk initiated a gigantic attack on Sherman's and McClernand's positions with 10 reinforced brigades, more than two-thirds of the entire Confederate force on the field. The Union lines reeled under the massive attack and soon broke, falling back almost three-quarters of a mile to Jones Field before regrouping. Ironically, this attack produced the exact opposite of what Johnston wanted: It drove the Union line back, but the Union right flank rather than the left, and moved it toward Pittsburg Landing.

The Hornets' Nest

At the same time, a smaller attack on the Union left flank by Chalmers's and Jackson's brigades slammed into McArthur's and Stuart's brigades, wounding both Union commanders and forcing them to retreat. By 11 a.m. a strong Union line was forming, centered on William Wallace's and Prentiss's position, hidden along the Sunken Road. Several Confederate attacks on this position were thrown back with heavy losses before Bragg realized what a strong force was concentrated there. As Gibson's brigade attacked through a dense thicket just east of Duncan Field toward the Sunken Road, Union artillery canister fire and infantry rifle fire raked through the brush. The bullets and canister balls ripping the leaves apart reminded the Confederate infantrymen of a swarm of angry hornets, and they named the place the Hornets' Nest.

Gibson's Brigade charging Hurlbut's troops in the Hornets' Nest

To the left (west) of the Hornets' Nest, Bragg once again displayed his irritated impatience and ordered attack after attack around or across Duncan Field on the well-positioned Union line, each one being broken and thrown back in turn. (There is some controversy about the exact nature of this series of attacks; traditionally, the story holds that these attacks went straight across the wide-open field itself, while some more recent research seems to indicate that the attacks actually went down the relatively concealed roads on either side of the field.) To add to Bragg's problems, Sherman and McClernand managed to regroup their scattered forces and counterattack Hardee's and Polk's forces, briefly regaining their own original camps. To reestablish his gains, Beauregard threw his last reserves in the lines, which stopped the Union counterattack. A fierce battle raged between the two armies in Woolf Field, near the Water Oaks Pond just north of the Corinth Road, for just under two hours before the Union troops were once again thrown back to Jones Field.

The Peach Orchard

On the right of the Hornets' Nest, multiple attacks against Hurlbut and McArthur had been repulsed with heavy losses, until at last some of the Confederate soldiers refused to mount another assault. Riding forward at about 2 p.m., Johnston announced that he would get them going and told the battered force that he would personally lead the next attack. Riding down the line of infantry, he tapped on their bayonets and said, "These must do the work. Men, they are stubborn; we're going to have to use the bayonet." He then turned, and with a shouted

Clearing the battlefield: burning the dead horses in the Peach Orchard

command for them to follow him, he headed toward the Union left flank. The line of infantry rose with a scream, and four brigades followed Johnston into battle.

At this same time, Stuart's brigade, which was directly in front of where Johnston was headed, had nearly completely run out of ammunition, and Stuart ordered a retreat. With Johnston's men sweeping forward, both Hurlbut's and McArthur's flanks were exposed and caved in. Both Union brigades retreated north to the upper end of Bell's field, near a small peach orchard. Returning a heavy volume of fire on the advancing Confederate force, newly opened peach blossoms fell like snow on the ground as bullets and shot sprayed through the trees.

As Johnston watched the battle unfolding a little after 2:30 p.m. from across the Hamburg-Savannah Road at the southeast corner of Bell's Field, a bullet ripped through his right leg just below the knee. It probably was fired by one of his own men (the ball came in from the rear); the wound, amazingly, went almost unnoticed by Johnston. Years earlier, Johnston had been struck in the same leg during a duel, which damaged the nerves and possibly numbed the leg to the point that he couldn't feel a gunshot wound. Minutes later he nearly tumbled from his horse but was caught by his aide, Governor Isham Green Harris of Tennessee, and placed on the ground in a nearby ravine. No medical help was immediately available, as Johnston had sent his personal surgeon out a few minutes earlier to check on some wounded Union prisoners. Harris frantically tore open Johnston's uniform looking for a significant wound, but dismissed the leg wound as minor. Unfortunately, the leg wound had opened up a major artery, dumping blood into the general's knee-high boot, and Johnston bled to death within minutes. A tourniquet was later found in the general's pocket, the quick application of which would have saved his life.

Beauregard Assumes Command

At about 3 p.m. Beauregard was informed that Johnston was dead and took over command of all the Confederate forces in the field. Responding to the growing sounds of battle around the Hornets' Nest, he ordered most of his left flank to shift over to the right (east) to reinforce

the attack there. By doing so he committed two major mistakes. First, his assault that threw back Sherman's counterattack had been highly successful, pushing the Union right flank far back across the north end of Jones Field and on across the Tilghman Branch, seriously decimating the Union ranks. A follow-up attack could well have split the Union line of battle, sending Sherman and McClernand north and west away from Pittsburg Landing, precisely as Beauregard had originally planned.

Second, the growing battle on his right flank was due to a continued hammering at a relatively small Union force well positioned at the Sunken Road forest area, but which was isolated from retreat, resupply, or reinforcement. Bypassing this position would have undoubtedly resulted in a surrender of the entire command by nightfall and could possibly have led to a successful capture of the steamboat landing itself. Instead, not only did Beauregard order a continued hammering at the isolated Union position, but the shift of units from other isolated fights on the battlefield relieved pressure on other Union units, which were then able to withdraw and reestablish a line along the Hamburg-Savannah and Corinth-Pittsburg Roads, protecting Pittsburg Landing as a landing place for Buell's rapidly approaching command.

The lack of control Beauregard, or any other high commander, had over the spread-out Confederate forces became painfully obvious in the fight around the Hornets' Nest; even if Beauregard had not ordered a concentration of forces there, it most likely would have occurred anyway. Individual regiments and brigades that were not already engaged elsewhere and that had rookie or undisciplined commanders started following what Shiloh park ranger Stacy D. Allen called the "make yourself useful policy," drifting over toward the sound of battle without specific orders to do (or even not to do) so.

Bloody Pond

With news of the death of Johnston, Bragg shifted over and took direct control of the Confederate right. Hurlbut had established a new line on the north end of the Peach Orchard (which was what Johnston was observing when shot), and despite having an unsupported left flank, he was making things hot for the assaulting

Confederates. Just behind his position was a small, shallow pond that had the only fresh water available on this part of the battlefield. Wounded and parched infantrymen and horses alike crawled over to its shores to get a cool drink; many men were too badly wounded to raise their heads once in the pond and drowned in the foot-deep water. Dozens of blue-clad infantry were piled up in heaps of the dead and dying all around the water, their wounds dripping into the damp ground, staining the pond a deep crimson. When Confederates advanced past the ghastly scene, someone remarked what a "bloody pond" it was; the name stuck.

About 4 p.m., Hurlbut's line finally caved in under the intense Confederate fire, and he retreated up the Hamburg-Savannah Road. Jackson's and Chalmers's brigades, now supported by Clanton's Alabama Cavalry Regiment, rushed through the hole left by Stuart's and McArthur's collapse and began advancing north to the east flank of the Hornets' Nest. About the same time, the seventh direct assault against the Hornets' Nest was hurled back; bleeding and battered troops of Florida, Louisiana, and Texas pulled back to try to reestablish their ranks.

The Surrender of the Hornets' Nest

Brigadier General Ruggles had seen enough. Gathering up as many artillery batteries and individual gun crews as he and his staff could locate, by 4:30 p.m. he had 53 guns parked axle to axle on the west border of Duncan Field, 400 to 500 yards directly across open ground from Wallace's and Prentiss's position in the Hornets' Nest. This was the largest assembly of artillery arrayed against a single target ever seen in the Western Hemisphere at that time. Given the order to fire, the entire line of artillery opened up with a thunderous roar. Ruggles had ordered a mixed load of shot, shell, and canister fired as rapidly as possible. For nearly a half-hour the artillery kept up a fire that averaged three shots per second going into the Union position.

When at last the murderous fire lifted, another Confederate assault charged the Union lines led by Wood, this time sweeping all around both flanks and meeting at the junction of the Hamburg-Savannah and Corinth Roads north of the Hornets' Nest. As the assault came down upon them, both Wallace and Prentiss ordered a retreat, trying to break out of their position before being surrounded. While leading an Iowa brigade north to the Corinth Road, Wallace was struck on the head; he lived a few more days and died in his wife's arms in nearby Savannah. With the death of Wallace and the impossibility of his situation painfully obvious, Prentiss finally surrendered what was left of the two brigades—himself and 2,250 men—a little after 5:30 p.m., the largest surrender to date in the war.

Grant's Last Line of Defense

While the remainder of his forces were slowly dissolving away to the west and south, Grant hurriedly brought up as much artillery and as many men as he could scrape together to guard the critically important landing. By the time the last survivors of the Hornets' Nest surrendered, Grant had about 70 cannon and 20,000 infantrymen in line for defense. His 1¼-mile-long last-ditch defense line started at Dill Branch on the left flank (east), where it entered the Tennessee River just south of the landing, ran due west to the Hamburg-Savannah Road, then turned north along the road to just north of Perry's Field. The majority of artillery was placed just below the crest of the low, rolling hills above the landing, obviously intended to be used for point defense should an evacuation prove necessary.

As the last artillery batteries pulled into position, the vanguard of Buell's Army of the Ohio finally appeared across the river from the landing. Hastily transported across the river, Nelson's division had to force their way through several thousand Union soldiers desperately trying to flee the battlefield. As they fell into place, one last Confederate charge came up the hill at them.

The Last Charge of April 6

About 6 p.m., Jackson's and Chalmers's brigades moved through the Dill Branch ravine, aiming straight at the hill above Pittsburg Landing. The mass of Union artillery opened fire on them, joined by the Union gunboats *Lexington* and *Tyler* with their 8-inch guns. As these two brigades struggled through the flooded branch and rugged ravine, the remnants of Anderson's, Stephens's, and

Wood's brigades joined in the attack without overall coordination, a mere 8,000 Confederates attacking uphill and across rugged terrain without artillery support into a strongly fortified Union position manned by at least 10,000 infantry, studded with nearly 40 artillery pieces, and with reinforcements hustling down the road to join in.

Within minutes the Confederate assault petered out, the butternut-clad infantry slipping away in squads and companies to find shelter as the early spring sun set on the horizon. Only Chalmers's and Jackson's infantrymen managed to briefly get within rifle range of the Union line; most of them were out of ammunition by that point, intent on closing and using the bayonet.

Beauregard sent word to all his commanders to suspend the attack for the night and pull back to the captured Union encampments. One by one, guns fell silent as the Confederates moved out of range. Units were in serious disarray on both sides, and the long night would be needed just to restore some semblance of order. Some Confederate units had not slept more than naps in two days, and most had not eaten since the day before. Although warned that Buell was nearby, Beauregard disregarded the threat and decided along with Bragg, Polk, and Hardee that the best plan was to rest and wait until daylight to get the army back into proper organization and to renew the assault. All felt that the only task remaining was to sweep up Grant's

The gunboats Tyler *and* Lexington *support Federal troops at Shiloh.*

line and force him to retire north, a task that should not take more than a few hours.

Losses on both sides were very high in the daylong battle, with both sides suffering near-identical casualties—almost 8,500 dead, wounded, and missing. The critical factor in these losses, however, was that Grant had reinforcements on the way, while Beauregard was on his own, without hope of relief.

THE NIGHT OF APRIL 6–7, 1862

*J*ust as fighting was ending for the day, Lew Wallace's division finally arrived on the battlefield. It was only 6 miles away when sent for at 11 a.m.; a march that should have taken about two hours had taken more than seven. Grant was livid, but mistakes in navigation had simply tied up the men all day and left them wandering around muddy country roads north of the battlefield while Wallace tried to find the right one to lead him to Sherman's support. Grant used Wallace's tardiness later as an excuse to blame away some of the Union Army's disaster of April 6, but if he had shown up on time where he was headed, his division would have entered the brunt of the fighting around Shiloh Church and most likely would have been routed as Sherman and McClernand had been. Wallace, the postwar author of *Ben-Hur,* lived with this series of mistakes the rest of his life, dying with the thought on his mind that his errors may have killed Union soldiers.

As the two battered armies settled down for a fitful rest, clouds gathered and a heavy, cold rain started to fall shortly after 10 p.m. Grant wandered around his headquarters, reluctant to go inside, as the building had been converted to a hospital, and the shrieking wounded and charnel-house atmosphere were simply unendurable. Sherman, wounded again in the shoulder during the afternoon, finally found him under a large oak tree, holding a lantern and smoking one of his ever-present cigars. "Well, Grant, we've had the devil's own

William Tecumseh Sherman

Just the mention of this Union general's name is enough to raise the blood pressure of many a loyal Southerner. In 1998 a land transaction in South Carolina was completed under a number of rather unusual conditions, including that no one named Sherman or whose name could be unscrambled to spell out Sherman could ever be permitted to purchase that property.

Born in Lancaster, Ohio, in 1820, Sherman was sent from his home to live with the family of Senator Thomas Ewing after his own father died in 1829. Nicknamed "Cump" by his boyhood friends, Sherman was appointed to West Point by his foster father, graduating in 1840 ranked 6th out of 42. His first assignment as a brevet 2nd lieutenant was to the 3rd Artillery, and through the 1840s and early 1850s he was assigned to posts in Florida, South Carolina, Georgia, and California. During the Mexican War he saw very little action, assigned as an aide to Captain Philip Kearny and Colonel Richard B. Mason. Assigned to a post in California after the war, he resigned his commission as a captain and went to work in the banking industry there. In 1857 he moved to Fort Leavenworth, Kansas, and opened a law and real estate practice, moving on to become superintendent of the Louisiana State Seminary of Learning and Military Academy in 1859. He remained in that capacity until Louisiana seceded in 1861.

With the outbreak of war, Sherman was quickly recommissioned, this time at the rank of colonel, and placed in command of the 13th Infantry Regiment. Rapid promotions being the norm in the early, confused months of the war, he was soon promoted to command of a brigade in Brigadier General Irvin McDowell's army, defeated in battle shortly thereafter at the First Manassas. Sherman was soon promoted to brigadier general and sent to Kentucky as second in command to Brigadier General Robert Anderson. When Anderson became too ill to lead a short time later, Sherman assumed command. Sherman was never what one would describe as a temperate or politic man, and when the press questioned him endlessly about his plans (similar to today's braying mob at press conferences), his irritated, snappish responses caused the newspapers to start rumors that he was "off in the head," a charge that would haunt him throughout the war. Various sources report that Sherman suffered a mild mental breakdown during this period.

The Union high command, affected by the news stories and showing a lack of leadership common throughout the war, reassigned Sherman, who was doubtlessly relieved to be out of such a bad situation. He was sent to command the 5th Infantry Division of Major General Henry West Halleck's army in Missouri, which was building up to invade western Tennessee and northern Mississippi. In April 1862, as part of Major General Ulysses S. Grant's corps, Sherman's division was encamped near Shiloh Church, 23 miles north of their target of Corinth, Mississippi, when they were suddenly attacked by 25,000 men of General Albert Sydney Johnston's combined Confederate Army of the West. Although wounded in the early phases of the battle, Sherman stayed in the field and helped organize a successful counterattack.

When Grant replaced Halleck in command of all the western armies, Sherman, now promoted to major general, stayed with him, commanding a corps. Sherman successfully fought guerrillas at Memphis and in the grand land-water campaign at Vicksburg, before being sent to relieve the besieged forces at Chattanooga. In March 1864 Grant was recalled east to take over as commander in chief of all Union armies, leaving his friend Sherman in command of the western armies. Building up his Army of Tennessee in Chattanooga over the winter and spring of 1863–64, Sherman unleashed the 100,000-man force on northern Georgia in May. Slowly pushing his Confederate opponent (and friend), General Joseph Eggleston Johnston, back toward the defenses of Atlanta, Sherman did not receive a real break until Johnston was replaced by Lieutenant General John Bell Hood at the end of July. Five weeks later, the campaign came to a close, with Sherman firmly in control of Atlanta and northern Georgia. With this, the war in the Western Theater was for all practical purposes over.

Sherman's reputation today largely stems from his March to the Sea, the Georgia campaign where he brought 60,000 men from Atlanta to Savannah, but truthfully, this wasn't much of a military campaign. Resistance was almost nonexistent, consisting of one small battle and a handful of skirmishes. Sherman's biggest problem on the march was feeding his vast army off the depleted countryside. However, the behavior of his "bummers" through this march and the subsequent one through the Carolinas, encouraged by the "total war"–thinking commander,

(continued on next page)

gave him his reputation as a thief and firebug. He ordered that anything of military value be taken or burned, and his men applied this order very liberally. Leaving only 10 percent of the buildings standing in their wake in Atlanta, his army burned and looted their way across a 40- to 60-mile-wide swath through central and south Georgia and an equally wide, depleted path in South and North Carolina. The destruction was so complete that certain buildings in those areas today are celebrated for their survival.

After accepting Johnston's surrender of the Western Theater armies in April 1865, Sherman turned to fighting and rounding up Indians in the far West. When his old friend Grant was elected president, he appointed Sherman a full general and placed him as commander in chief of the army. He finally retired from the service in 1886 and died in New York in 1891. One of the pallbearers at his funeral was none other than his friend and ancient nemesis, Joseph Johnston.

day, haven't we?" remarked the fiery Ohioan. Grant, far from demoralized, replied simply, "Yes. Lick 'em tomorrow, though."

Grant ordered the gunboats stationed in the Tennessee River to keep up a steady bombardment all night, but their shells mainly burst among the Union wounded still left out in the killing fields. The Confederates had pulled back to the former Union encampments and were comfortably housed in their enemies' tents while they feasted on the abundant supplies. Cleburne, sitting in a tent and watching the shells burst around the bodies of the Union dead and wounded, remarked, "History records few instances of more reckless inhumanity than this."

As the night wore on, Buell's Army of the Ohio traveled south from Savannah and crossed over into Grant's line; by 8 a.m. on April 7 more than 13,000 fresh, well-equipped troops stood ready to renew the fight. Beauregard had no reinforcements to bring up but remained optimistic. Upon hearing a false report that Buell's force was actually moving on Decatur, Alabama, he fired off a report to Richmond that he had "won a complete victory" that day and would finish off Grant's force in the morning.

As morning approached, Grant had about 45,000 men ready for an assault on the Confederate positions, most of them well rested and spoiling for a fight, while Beauregard could field only about 28,000 (some accounts say 20,000) tired men not yet reformed into their brigades, or even completely resupplied.

THE SECOND DAY, APRIL 7, 1862

*J*ust before dawn on Monday morning, April 7, 1862, Grant ordered his combined armies to move out. Buell's fresh troops moved nearly due south, toward Hardee's and Breckinridge's lines, while Grant's resupplied and reinforced army moved southwest in two lines of battle toward Bragg's and Polk's lines. Led by heavy artillery fire from the massed Union guns, the sudden dawn attack caught their Confederate opponents completely by surprise, turning the tables from the day before.

No organization existed; the Confederate infantry had simply dropped in place the night before at whatever camp was handy, and few had bothered to resupply their depleted cartridge boxes from the piles of captured Union ammunition boxes scattered everywhere. Most likely believed that, if Grant were smart, he would leave the field during the night rather than suffer another "lickin'."

To top off Beauregard's problems, Polk had withdrawn his corps nearly 4 miles to the south, to the site of his previous night's encampment, and it took nearly two hours after the Union's initial attack to locate him and get his corps moving. Once in the line, none of the four corps commanders actually commanded his entire corps as the units intermingled and were confusingly arrayed in the haste to mount a defense.

The Confederate Defense

With great effort, the four Confederate corps commanders managed to form a meandering defense line in the face of the Union attack, roughly running northwest to southeast from the Jones Field across Duncan Field south of the Hornets' Nest to just about the place of Johnston's death the day before, on the Hamburg-Savannah Road. They managed to hold this line under great pressure until about 11 a.m., when a general pullback in order was called. The line moved back intact about a half-mile on the left and extended another half-mile on the right to counter increased pressure from Buell's forces on its right flank.

By noon the Confederate line had again pulled back under pressure to a line centered on Shiloh Church. Union units all along the line kept up a steady artillery and infantry fire; Grant's plan was to simply roll south using his fresh troops to grind up the tired Confederate infantry. The plan worked quite well; several counterattacks by Hardee, Breckinridge, and Bragg were absorbed and thrown back with heavy casualties.

The Confederate Retreat

By 1 p.m. it was obvious to Beauregard that not only were they not going to be able to win this battle, but he was also in danger of being swept in pieces from the field. He hesitated for nearly an hour, however, before finally passing orders down the line for his commands to break contact and retreat to Corinth. Several artillery batteries repositioned at Shiloh Church, along with Colonel Winfield S. Statham's and Colonel

---

Getting to Shiloh

Shiloh is in a relatively remote part of Tennessee, very close to the common border of Tennessee, Alabama, and Mississippi. The nearest city with access to an interstate highway is Jackson (I-40 between Memphis and Nashville), 52 miles to the northwest via US 64 and US 45. The nearest large cities are Memphis, 113 miles west on US 64, and Chattanooga, 204 miles east via US 64 and I-24.

As we came in to Shiloh from the east, we took I-24 north out of Chattanooga to exit 134 (Monteagle), turning west on US 41 Alternate through Sewanee and turning west/south on US 64 just outside Winchester. US 64 is a pleasant but long journey through southern Tennessee about 140 miles to Savannah. This small town lies just 10 miles northeast of the national military park. Continue on US 64 until you cross the Tennessee River into Crump, and then take the first major road intersection to the left, TN 22, which runs straight through the park.

Shiloh today is a quiet, wooded, and serene place little changed overall from 1862. The surrounding towns are larger, and instead of steamboats on the adjoining Tennessee River, there are pontoon boats and fishermen. It is just as remote, though, and one can easily imagine the reaction of Grant's inexperienced troops placed in such a "crude and hostile environment," as one Ohio private wrote. The majority of the original battlefield has been preserved as a national military park and is operated by the National Park Service.

The original little wooden Shiloh Church is long gone, but the congregation is still present and meets every Sunday in a brick-and-stone sanctuary built on the same spot in 1949. A replica of the original church has recently been constructed near this site. The surrounding graveyard has some gravestones that were present when Sherman made his stand here, and most of the roads both armies walked down are still in existence, albeit now paved and improved.

Be aware that the weather in this area tends to be extremely hot during summer; snow and ice are not unknown during the winter, and violent weather (including tornadoes) is often a feature of springtime. Visits to some of the battlefield areas involve quite a bit of walking, so make sure to dress appropriately and carry sufficient water with you during hot weather.

Robert P. Trabue's brigades of Breckinridge's corps, to act as a heavy rear guard.

Cavalrymen were ordered to hastily destroy all the Union equipment and supplies that the retreating infantry weren't able to carry off with them. As the piles of broken tents and wagons blazed into the stormy afternoon, Breckinridge broke off contact and withdrew in good order at the rear of the long Confederate column. As the Confederate line moved south about 5 p.m., Grant's exhausted infantry was simply too tired to follow. Breckinridge stopped for the night and redeployed at the intersection of Bark and Corinth Roads. No Union force challenged their rest, and at dawn he moved south into Corinth.

Grant had won a magnificent victory, but at a heavy price. Of his 65,000-man combined army (with Buell's),

1,754 were killed, 8,408 wounded, and 2,885 captured or missing in action—a fifth of his whole command. The tattered remnants of his proud regiments were too shot up and exhausted after two solid days of combat to pursue the retreating Confederates, who made it back into Mississippi without resistance.

Beauregard suffered worse; in addition to losing the beloved army commander Albert Sidney Johnston, he had to report losses of 1,728 killed, 8,012 wounded, and 959 missing or captured. This loss of 10,699 soldiers constituted nearly a fourth of all the men he had helped bring into the campaign. Once back in Corinth, he ordered the town prepared for defense against an attack by Grant and set about turning nearly the entire small community into one vast hospital for his thousands of wounded.

POINTS OF INTEREST

Cherry Mansion
265 Main St.
Savannah, TN
(731) 925-8181 (Hardin County Tourism)

This 1830 two-story house was used by Grant as his headquarters immediately before and after the battle. Tours are offered by appointment only. The grounds are open for strolling, and a nearby monument commemorates Grant's stay here.

Shiloh National Military Park
1055 Pittsburgh Landing Rd.
Shiloh, TN
(731) 689-5696
www.nps.gov/shil

This 3,960-acre park covers all but a small fraction of the original battlefield and contains all the significant sites. A very nicely appointed visitor center graces the hill just above Grant's last line of defense, containing a small but well-presented set of artifacts, a friendly and quite knowledgeable staff, and a 25-minute film, *Shiloh—Portrait of a Battle,* shown every 90 minutes. We recommend it for its good description of both the battle and events that led up to it.

Just across the parking lot is the bookstore, run by a private concessionaire, Eastern National, which has made

a great effort to provide a well-stocked and well-selected choice of books, maps, and some nice souvenirs. An unusual item we noticed was small ceramic replicas of some of the state monuments scattered around the park. Eastern National has earned our gratitude for resisting promotion of the "anything with a rebel flag on it" school of souvenir shop. Behind the bookstore is a selection of soft drink and snack machines, restrooms, and a pay phone.

Make sure you pick up a copy of the driving tour brochure in the visitor center, and we recommend arming yourself with a copy of Trailhead Graphics' "Shiloh National Military Park" battlefield map, available in the bookstore. The driving tour will get you around the major sites in a reasonable amount of time, while Trailhead's map lists the exact location of every one of the 151 monuments, 600 or so unit position markers, and 200 artillery pieces. A very nice adjunct to these maps is the *Guide to the Battle of Shiloh* by Jay Luvass, Stephen Bowman, and Leonard Fullenkamp, part of the excellent U.S. Army War College "Guides to Civil War Battles" series. This battle was a very large, confusing, and widespread campaign, and this book was our constant companion when trying to understand certain movements and actions—although as it is meant for professional historians and military officers, it, too, tends to be confusing and hard to understand in places! It is available in the park's bookstore.

Directly adjacent to the bookstore is the Shiloh National Cemetery, the final resting place of 1,227 known and 2,416 unknown Union dead from this battle and others nearby. A unit of the national cemetery system, it also contains remains of veterans from later wars. Grant's headquarters was located in the middle of this field and is marked by a vertical cannon barrel.

All across the battlefield are mass graves of the Confederate dead, hastily buried and mostly unmarked by the Union troops, who stayed on the field for another six weeks. Five of the mass graves have been located and marked; one is on the driving tour. Admission to the park gets you a dashboard card for your car at the visitor center, which is valid for seven days. Closed Christmas.

Tennessee River Museum
495 Main St.
Savannah, TN
(731) 925-2364
(800) 552-FUNN (3866)
www.tourhardincounty.org

Housed in the chamber of commerce building next to the county courthouse, this small museum has set a daunting task for itself, which has partially been fulfilled: to chronicle the life and times of the Tennessee River Valley from prehistoric times to today. Still obviously under development, several exhibits tell the story of the Native American mound builders, the Trail of Tears, the Golden Age of Steamboats, and the river gunboats used during the battle here.

ACCOMMODATIONS

The closest cities with a selection of services are Savannah, about 10 miles north of the park via TN 22 and US 64, and Corinth, Mississippi, about 23 miles south via TN 22 and US 45.

The small settlement of Shiloh, just outside the south park boundary at the intersection of TN 22 and TN 142, has exactly one service station/convenience store, one restaurant, and one souvenir shop.

There are very few accommodations in the immediate area of the battlefield park, but the usual array of chain establishments are in Savannah to the northeast and Corinth to the south; of the two, Corinth is farther away but has a larger selection.

RESTAURANTS

There is nothing available in the park besides soft drink and candy machines, so you will have to drive either north or south on TN 22 for anything more substantial. As with the accommodation situation, the usual array of fast-food and lower-end sit-down chains are available either way, but a wider array of offerings is in Corinth.

The Catfish Hotel $–$$
1140 Hagy Lane
Shiloh, TN
(731) 689-3327
www.catfishhotel.com

The Catfish Hotel was once just a little shack built in 1825 by a family who farmed and fished the surrounding land. It was later occupied by Union soldiers during the Battle of Shiloh. It is located just north of the Shiloh Battlefield Visitor Center and offers great meals as well as fantastic views of the Tennessee River while dining.

Other Tennessee Battlefields

Darley. Bobbett sc.

The 16th state to be admitted to the Union (1796), Tennessee was the last to secede and join the new Confederacy and did so, ironically, partly as a reaction to a request by President Lincoln for troops to put down the "insurrection" in other states. Parts of the state were heavily pro-Union, most notably the far-eastern, mountainous sections that were part of the one-time separate state of Franklin. Some of the largest battles in the Western Theater were fought here, although the Union controlled most of the state for most of the war. As a final irony, even Lincoln's September 1862 Emancipation Proclamation did not apply to Tennessee; by that time it was fully under Union control and no longer "presently in rebellion."

It is tempting to note that Tennessee was also the first state to be brought back under Union control, as is so often claimed, but the rather "fuzzy" situations in Maryland and Kentucky raise some doubts here. Kentucky was proclaimed by its legislature to be officially neutral, and several of Maryland's most influential legislators were arrested by Federal authorities to prevent a vote of secession, but both were slaveholding states with very strong ties to the Confederacy. Both supplied combat troops and supplies to the South, even though both were ruled by what has been referred to as a "hostile foreign government," i.e., the United States.

Battles, skirmishes, and raids occurred across the entire length and breadth of Tennessee, although the largest occurred in the central and southern portions of the state. Outside the major battles that are discussed in other chapters, these actions can be divided into three broad categories: the campaigns for Knoxville, the Battle of Stones River, and the struggle for control of the northwestern rivers. Smaller actions ranged all through the state largely as a result of Major General Nathan B. Forrest's and Colonel John Hunt Morgan's cavalry raids for the South.

THE CAMPAIGN FOR KNOXVILLE

*T*oday the third-largest city in Tennessee, during the Civil War Knoxville was a strong Confederate outpost in an otherwise remote area that was heavily pro-Union. It also was the key communication and transportation point between the Confederate armies in Tennessee and Virginia.

President Abraham Lincoln had a personal interest in the Unionists in Knoxville; like him, they were small-plot farmers strongly opposed to slavery and secession and strong advocates of the Republican stance. For this, their pro-Confederacy neighbors persecuted them, sometimes to the point of torture and murder. Early in 1863 Lincoln directed his western armies to take Knoxville as soon as possible to "relieve" the Unionists in the area.

Background to the Campaign

The combined Union armies in the west had had their fill of fighting since shortly after the war began, and for nearly two years had been unable to mount an offensive in force into the eastern reaches of the Confederate heartland. Major General Ulysses S. Grant, on siege outside Vicksburg in May and June of 1863, had been urging his fellow Union army generals to launch an offensive in central Tennessee in order to cut off General Joseph Eggleston Johnston's attempts to relieve the embattled Confederate garrison there. Major General William Stake "Rosy" Rosecrans, comfortably encamped with his Union Army of the Cumberland in Murfreesboro, Tennessee, finally and reluctantly agreed to mount an offensive. On June 23 his army moved out and slogged southward through a cold rain toward the Confederate force at Tullahoma.

General Braxton Bragg had sent a good portion of his Confederate Army of Tennessee to Mississippi and was at that time in no shape to stand up to Rosecrans.

During the nine days it took the Union force to arrive, Bragg withdrew all of his remaining men and most of his supplies south to Chattanooga, where he heavily entrenched. Rosecrans took Tullahoma without a shot being fired, and then he did nothing for the next eight weeks while Bragg reinforced both his army and his fortifications at Chattanooga.

With increasing pressure from Lincoln, Rosecrans finally moved out eastward to retake the strongly pro-Union east Tennessee from Confederate control. Rosecrans was to take the vital rail and manufacturing center at Chattanooga, while Major General Ambrose Everett Burnside's Army of the Ohio was to march from their base in Cincinnati to take Knoxville.

Getting to Knoxville

Knoxville is in the eastern reaches of Tennessee, accessed by I-75 from the north and south and I-40 from the east and west. Nashville is 175 miles west on I-40, Chattanooga is 112 miles south on I-75, Asheville is 107 miles east on I-40, and Lexington, Kentucky, is 173 miles north on I-75. US 441 goes southeast about 30 miles to Pigeon Forge and Gatlinburg, directly adjacent to the Great Smoky Mountains National Park, a nice addition to tours in the area.

All the defense works around Knoxville, including Fort Sanders, long ago disappeared. Most of the city then is on what is today the University of Tennessee at Knoxville campus, near the intersection of US 11/70 and US 129. A few of the older buildings on campus were used as barracks for both armies during their occupations.

The university has a marker commemorating Fort Sanders in front of Sophronia Strong Hall, unfortunately located 2 blocks south of the actual location. The United Daughters of the Confederacy have placed a monument at the actual location, the hill nearest the corner of 17th Street and Laurel Avenue.

The Capture of Knoxville

The Confederate Department of East Tennessee was commanded at the time by Major General Simon Bolivar Buckner, newly sent up from Mobile to prepare for Burnside's threat to the region. In Knoxville was a single infantry brigade and two cavalry brigades—all told, only 2,500 men. The northern approach to the city, Cumberland Gap at the Kentucky state line, was guarded by only a single brigade under the command of Brigadier General John W. Frazer, with 2,000 men and 14 pieces of artillery in total.

Major General Simon Bolivar Buckner

Before Burnside could even get a good start southward, Rosecrans was threatening Chattanooga, and Buckner was ordered to withdraw from Knoxville to help defend the river and rail center to the west. Leaving Frazer in place at Cumberland Gap and one infantry brigade just east of Knoxville, Buckner left town with all the rest of his infantry and cavalry on August 16.

Cumberland Gap had been taken and lost three previous times by Union forces, and Burnside knew better than to directly confront Frazer's strong defensive position there. His Army of the Ohio

Brigadier General John W. Frazer

then consisted of Brigadier General Robert Brown Potter's IX and Major General George Lucas Hartsuff's

XXIII Corps, with about 24,000 men total. Sending one division of the advance brigade of the IX Corps to "demonstrate" against Frazer's command, Burnside moved the rest of his force several miles to the west, crossing the Cumberland Mountains at Winter's Gap and Big Creek Gap.

Burnside's command entered Knoxville unopposed on September 3, welcomed by a large crowd of local Unionists. The single Confederate infantry brigade still present prudently declined to engage the overwhelmingly superior Union force and quietly slipped out of the area to join Buckner in Chattanooga. Burnside detached two brigades to confront Frazer's entrenched Cumberland Gap position from the south; faced with strong Union forces on either side of the gap, Frazer surrendered his command without a fight on September 9.

The Occupation of Knoxville

Burnside, the Union general better known for his namesake facial hair than his military prowess, set up his headquarters in newly captured Knoxville with the intent of using it as a base to raid western Virginia. So intent was he on this task that he ignored a number of requests for help from Rosecrans, first as the fight at Chickamauga was going badly and again when Chattanooga was besieged.

As Bragg made his plans to break back into Union-held Chattanooga in late 1863, he committed a grievous tactical error and ordered Lieutenant General James "Old Pete" Longstreet to take his corps (nearly a third of Bragg's entire army) to the east and retake Knoxville. Bragg, a personal friend of President Jefferson Davis but an erratic commander and occasionally poor judge on the battlefield, had a personal feud with the South Carolinian and sent him east mainly just to be rid of him.

Longstreet's 10,000-man force consisted of Major General Lafayette McLaw's and Brigadier General Micah Jenkins's division (of Lieutenant General John Bell Hood's corps) and Colonel Robert Porter Alexander's and Major Alexander Leyden's Artillery Battalions (35 guns total), along with Major General Joseph "Fighting Joe" Wheeler's Cavalry Corps with 5,000 men. The

Confederate task force moved out of the Chattanooga line on November 5, riding on trains so old and tracks so worn out that nearly everyone had to get off and walk up each hill. It took eight days to cover the first 60 miles and another three to finally reach the Tennessee River 30 miles west of Knoxville. Wheeler's cavalry had been sent ahead to probe around the city and find an undefended high spot to set up artillery.

The Defense of Union-Held Knoxville

Burnside had not been idle in the intervening months, setting up a ring of strong earthwork forts and redoubts around the hilly city. Wheeler was soon forced to report back to Longstreet that there was no undefended high ground from which to launch an attack. While Longstreet made ready to cross the Tennessee River and pondered just how to launch his attack, Burnside decided to take the offensive.

Burnside was well known in the Union Army as being a poor battlefield commander, which he would be the first to admit, and the decision to leave the strong defenses of Knoxville and personally lead a 5,000-man force west to directly confront the oncoming Confederate troops was a poor one, indeed. The lead elements of both forces first encountered each other at the Tennessee River between Loudon and Lenoir City. All the bridges and ferries there had been burned in an effort to further slow down Longstreet's advance.

Longstreet was delighted. With Burnside out of the city, all he needed to do was find a quick ford and race around him, cutting the Union force off from its home base. Wheeler reported in short order that a suitable crossing was only a-half-mile to the south, at Huff's Ferry. Longstreet quickly rerouted his army there and crossed a still-under-construction pontoon bridge just after noon. Burnside was still unaware that Longstreet had drawn so close and was caught completely by surprise when the first elements of the Confederate force engaged his pickets in Lenoir City just at dusk.

Rapidly backpedaling, Burnside managed to hold off the ineffective assaults and withdrew his forces intact through Concord, heading for Campbell's Station (today known as Farragut). The Union forces left Lenoir City at dawn on November 16, "temporarily abandoning the valley of the Tennessee south of Loudon," according to Brigadier General Orlando M. Poe of the North, and making all speed back to the fortifications under construction in Knoxville. Longstreet realized that if he could reach the crossroads at Campbell's Station first, he could cut off Burnside's force from the main body in Knoxville and defeat both in turn. Almost a footrace ensued, with both armies racing up parallel roads toward the small crossroads settlement.

Campbell's Station

Burnside's troops, led by Colonel John F. Hartranft's 2nd Division, won the race, but just barely. Hartranft deployed his men facing west on the Kingston Road just before noon to cover the baggage train that continued east toward Knoxville without stopping. The rest of Burnside's combat troops formed a second line about a half-mile behind Hartranft's. About 15 minutes later, the vanguard of Longstreet's force, McLaw's division, arrived and immediately assaulted the Union line still forming up.

McLaw's attack was at first successful, driving the left of the Union line back and forcing it to re-form to the rear. Jenkins had been ordered to simultaneously strike the Union right, but his maneuver was ineffective and the line held. With two more Union divisions now in place and ready just behind him, Hartranft broke contact just after noon and withdrew to the new Union line of battle.

Longstreet's men stayed in close contact, assaulting the Union line on the right and center just as Hartranft fell into position, again without any gain. As the attacks continued, Burnside ordered his force to fall back under pressure to a ridgeline about three-fourths of a mile to their rear. The Union withdrawal was brilliantly executed, the troops keeping up a steady fire while slowly moving back to the higher ground. McLaw and Jenkins kept the pressure on, one attacking head-on while the other attempted maneuvers to turn the Union flank, all to no avail. As darkness fell, the Union line held and the Confederates ceased their assaults. Burnside ordered his troops to march through the night farther east, into the defenses of Knoxville, arriving there by dawn on November 17.

The running battle produced a surprisingly small number of casualties for so many hours of contact—approximately 400 Union and 570 Confederate.

The Second Defense of Knoxville

While Burnside had gone west to confront Longstreet, his remaining force had not been idle. Ten hilltop fortifications and miles of trench lines now ringed three-fourths of the city, the fourth side protected by the Holston River (now called the Tennessee River). The most prominent fortification was Fort Sanders, on the northwest corner of the defense belt and manned by about 440 troops with 12 artillery pieces. This strong fortification was surrounded by a dry ditch 12 feet wide and 8 feet deep, and the walls rose almost vertically 15 feet above the ditch. Although the designer, Poe, was worried that the hilltop post stuck too far forward of the main defensive belt

Fort Sanders

and thus presented an inviting target to the oncoming Confederates, he relocated his cannon to be able to fire straight down the ditch and added a new type of defense feature.

Poe had his engineers string telegraph wire about 1 foot off the ground between stumps and stakes just outside the ditch, weaving a densely knotted pattern several feet wide that would slow down and break up the line of any attacking force. This "trip foot" is now a common military defense feature, and Knoxville is the first place it is known to have been used in battle. Longstreet brought his forces up close to the Knoxville defenses and then halted. Although the weather was turning bitterly cold and some of his barefoot soldiers were literally freezing, he decided to wait until reinforcements arrived to make his move. Scouting the Union defense line while he waited, Longstreet determined that the only spot he had a real chance of taking was Fort Sanders, sited atop a low hill but just 200 yards away from a thick tree line that would cover and conceal his troops.

Brigadier General Bushrod R. Johnson arrived with 2,600 men in Colonel John S. Fulton's and Brigadier General Archibald Gracie's brigades on the night of November 25, along with Brigadier General Danville Ledbetter, Bragg's chief engineer for the Army of Tennessee, who scouted the Union emplacements along with Longstreet. Based primarily on Ledbetter's assessment of the situation, Longstreet modified his plans and ordered the assault to begin just before dawn on Sunday, November 29. With his newly arrived reinforcements, the Confederate commander had nearly 20,000 troops at his disposal to counter the estimated 12,000 of Burnside's force.

> Today, April 14, 1882, I say, and honestly say, that I sincerely believe the combined forces of the whole Yankee nation could never have broken General Joseph E. Johnston's line of battle, beginning at Rocky Face Ridge, and ending on the banks of the Chattahoochee.
>
> —Corporal Sam Watkins of the Confederacy, in Co. Aytch

The Battle for Fort Sanders

The night of November 28 was freezing cold, with a misty rain turning to ice and sleet as the hours wore on. Longstreet assigned three brigades to make up the assault force: Brigadier General Benjamin G. Humphreys's Mississippi, Brigadier General Goode Bryan's Georgia, and Colonel S. Z. Ruff's (Wofford's) Georgia, all of McLaw's division. Brigadier General G. T. Anderson's Georgia Brigade of Jenkins's division was ordered to "demonstrate" at their left flank against the northernmost wall of the fort.

About 11 p.m. skirmishers were ordered forward to capture the Union rifle pits before the fort; this action also alerted the Union defenders that action was imminent. For the rest of the night, small firefights broke out between pickets and skirmishers of both sides, joined in occasionally by canister rounds from the fort. Longstreet's assault troops lay on the frozen ground atop their guns, trying to keep them dry and catch a little sleep. Fires had been forbidden, as they were too close to the Union line, and the freezing drizzle undoubtedly made everyone miserably cold.

At the first sign of light on the eastern horizon, three signal guns of Alexander's artillery fired arcing red flares that exploded over the fort. With this the mass of Confederate infantry sprang to their feet and charged the ramparts of the earthwork redoubt. Twelve guns of Alexander's artillery fired as rapidly as possible for a few minutes and then ceased firing so as not to strike the onrushing infantry.

Poe's trip wire broke up the mass charge, but in quick order the assault troops gathered themselves and rushed onward, firing as they went. In the confused darkness, under rifle and artillery canister fire from the fort and stumbling through the outer defenses, all three brigades accidentally merged into one mass, meeting at the northwest bastion of the earthwork fort. Their massed fire at that point caused the Union guns to go silent, leading Longstreet and Alexander alike to believe the fort's defenses had already been reduced. Casualties to this point had been extremely light, and a massive wave of butternut-clad troops pushed into the ditchwork defenses.

No scaling ladders had been constructed, as the walls were not thought to be unusually steep, but both

Ditchwork defenses at Fort Sanders

the reality of the construction and the ice-covered ground brought the assault to a sudden halt. As Union defenders stayed down, occasionally raising an unaimed rifle over the rampart to fire at the massed infantry, men formed human ladders to gain the heights, standing on each other's shoulders and passing their fellow soldiers on up. As dawn slowly brought light to the fort, officers and color bearers began planting the Georgia and Mississippi battle flags on the parapet.

As the first Confederates gained the top of the walls, the Union troops inside opened fire with every gun available. Nearly as soon as a color bearer planted a flag, he was shot down, and officers lifting their swords to urge on their troops were equally swiftly gunned down. One after another the fallen bloodred "damned flags of the rebellion" were lifted up by an infantrymen and then fell as he, too, was gunned down by the determined Union infantry and artillery gunners. As the Confederate troops came too close to the Union line to fire their cannon, Lieutenant Samuel N. Benjamin, commander of Company E, 2nd U.S. Artillery, within the fort, had his men light the fuses of cannon shells and throw them over the walls like hand grenades, exploding more than 50 of the lethal devices in the very faces of the Confederates in the ditch.

As the full light of dawn revealed the hopelessness of taking even one bastion of the fort, Longstreet reluctantly recalled his troops. As the first wave was withdrawing, Anderson ordered his men forward, unaware that his attack had also been canceled. The scene repeated itself, with the Georgians thrown back with heavy losses after a 40-minute pitched fight atop the ramparts.

Aftermath

As Jenkins was preparing for yet a third assault, word came to Longstreet that Bragg had been decisively defeated at Chattanooga and his help was urgently needed in Dalton. The attempt to regain Knoxville came to a sudden end as Longstreet immediately pulled out of the battle and marched south.

Longstreet quickly learned that Rosecrans had sent Sherman with two full corps to break his siege of Knoxville and now stood between him and Bragg. Reluctantly he abandoned his plans to march into Georgia and turned up toward northeastern Tennessee, hoping that Sherman would pursue him there and relieve the pressure on Bragg's Army of Tennessee. Sherman probably saw right through that idea and shortly returned to Chattanooga, leaving two divisions behind to reinforce Burnside should Longstreet backtrack and try again. Longstreet spent a miserable winter with the remains of his command in Greenville, Tennessee, and returned to General Robert E. Lee's Army of Northern Virginia in the spring.

Left behind, atop, and around Fort Sanders were the bodies of 129 killed and many of the 458 wounded from Longstreet's ill-conceived assault. Ruff, Colonel H. P. Thomas, and Colonel Kennon McElroy all lay dead on the parapet next to a number of their color bearers. Confederate losses for this entire campaign were 198 dead, 850 wounded, and 248 missing, with Burnside losing 92 dead, 393 wounded, and 207 missing.

a total of just over 44,000 men. Major General Thomas Leonidas Crittenden's left wing moved straight down the Nashville & Chattanooga Railroad tracks, while Major General Alexander McDowell McCook's right and Major General George Henry Thomas's center wings marched to his right down the McLensville Turnpike and part of the Franklin Turnpike.

Bragg had plenty of warning from both his scouts and Wheeler's cavalry, still operating between his command and Nashville. He spread his forces out into a 32-mile-wide front from Triune through Murfreesboro itself to Readyville, covering any possible approach from the north. The ill-tempered Confederate commander had two corps at his disposal: Lieutenant General William J. Hardee's corps on the left and Lieutenant General Leonidas Polk's corps on the right. Wheeler's cavalry both slowed down the Union advance and protected the army's flanks; all told, about 32,000 men were available for combat.

Bragg's scouts soon reported the exact approach route and composition of the Union force, and he pulled his troops into a tight semicircle just north and west of Murfreesboro, astride the West Fork of the Stones River. Ironically, Rosecrans himself was blind to the Confederate movements and strength, having sent his own cavalry north and west, chasing off after Forrest and Morgan. About 3 p.m. on December 29, without any warning, Crittenden's corps made

Troop positions on December 29, 1862

contact with the Confederate forces of Major General John Cabell Breckinridge's 2nd Division (of Hardee's corps) along the Stones River bank, northwest of Murfreesboro. A small skirmish erupted, ending shortly when both forces moved back a bit to await orders on how to proceed.

While Rosecrans hastily brought up the rest of his force to concentrate on what he believed, for some unknown reason, to be a Confederate force in full retreat, Wheeler sprang into action. Riding in a giant arc through the Union rear, he captured about 1,000 prisoners, burned more than a million dollars' worth of ammunition and medical supplies, and caused a general panic that nearly turned into a rout back to Nashville.

Both Sides Prepare for Battle

Unprepared to immediately launch into battle against the strong Confederate position before him, Rosecrans hesitated through most of the day of December 30, finally meeting with his top lieutenants to hammer out a plan of action in the afternoon. Together they agreed that the Confederates' weakest point was on the right of their line, where Breckinridge stood to the far north of the line of battle. While units were shifted north to prepare for an assault the next morning, McCook's men were directed to light a large number of campfires on the far right of the Union line to fool their adversaries into thinking that units were being shifted for an attack coming from that angle, instead.

McCook's wing was arrayed, from right to left, by Brigadier General Richard W. Johnson's 2nd, Brigadier General Jefferson C. Davis's 1st, and Brigadier General Philip H. Sheridan's 3rd Divisions. In the center of the line was Brigadier General James S. Negley's 2nd Division of Thomas's wing, and on the left was Brigadier General John M. Palmer's 2nd and Brigadier General Thomas J. Wood's 1st Divisions of Crittenden's wing, which extended the Union line all the way to the river. Two other divisions were in an assembly area behind the lines, readying for an assault scheduled for 7 a.m. on December 31. Rosecrans had passed orders down that his men were to finish their breakfast before the attack began.

All through the day of December 30, Bragg expected a Union assault on his lines and shifted his troops to better meet the Union formation. Late in the afternoon, noting the Union troop movements and fooled by the fake campfires, he was convinced that the main attack would come from that direction, onto his left flank. He ordered his troops to be shifted to meet the perceived threat and readied for his own attack on what he thought was the mass of enemy, on the Union right. The attack was to begin at first light, a little after 6 on the morning of December 31.

Corps Confusion

The Army of the Cumberland under Rosecrans was officially designated the XIV Corps (formerly Buell's Army of the Ohio) on its creation on October 24, 1862. Although the army as a whole was far larger than the traditional corps, the true corps-level organizations under its command were designated "wings" instead. This confusing mess was finally rectified on January 9, 1863, when the wings were redesignated the XXI, XIV, and XX Corps.

Breckinridge stayed in position on the right, while the other two divisions of Hardee's corps swung around to Polk's left. The left of the Confederate line consisted of Major General John Porter McCown's and Major General Patrick Ronayne Cleburne's divisions of Hardee's corps. The center consisted of Major General Jones Mitchell Wither's division of Polk's corps, with Major General Benjamin Franklin "Frank" Cheatham's division just to the rear as a reserve. Brigadier General John A. Wharton's Cavalry Brigade took up the far left flank of the Confederate line.

The Confederate Assault Begins

At 6:22 a.m. 4,400 butternut-clad and battle-hardened troops of McCown's division stormed out of the gray, misty predawn twilight into the right of the Union line, catching totally by surprise the Northern soldiers leisurely eating breakfast, shaving, and getting dressed.

Most of McCook's regiments still had their weapons at stack arms and unloaded as they were routed or shot to pieces where they stood.

Cleburne's division, advancing behind and in support of McCown's, found itself alongside their fellow division in the front line, as the Union army hastily retreated to the north and west, dragging the Confederate assault behind them. As their assault slowed, mainly from the rough terrain and exhaustion, Cheatham's division entered the attack and helped push the Union line farther north. Davis's and Sheridan's divisions managed to hastily assemble a sufficiently strong line of battle and put up a strong resistance that slowed the Confederate advance. About 9:30 a.m. Sheridan even managed to mount a limited counterattack, which pushed back Cheatham long enough to allow a more orderly retreat. By 10 a.m. the Union line was compacting into a strong position just west of and running parallel to the Nashville Pike.

Although the morning had gone very well for Bragg, casualties were appalling; Hardee and Polk had both lost about one-third of their men and were begging for reinforcements. Bragg had none to send.

Rosecrans Responds

The Union line had formed, "bending back their line, as one half-shuts a knife-blade," according to Colonel David Urquhart of Bragg's staff, with the sharp angle forming a salient in a four-acre patch of woods called the Round Forest, which the troops soon renamed "Hell's Half-Acre." Rosecrans ordered his remaining uncommitted units, originally tasked to assault the Confederate right, into this salient for a last-ditch defense. Brigadier General Horatio Philips Van Cleve's 2nd and Brigadier General Thomas John Wood's 1st Division got into position in the woods just in the nick of time.

Bragg ordered what he thought would be a final assault into the Union position in the small patch of woods, led by Brigadier General James Ronald Chalmers's 2nd Mississippi Brigade. These men were some of the freshest available, having just spent the previous 48 hours lying in shallow trenches on the far right of the line, awaiting an attack that never came.

One regiment, the 44th Mississippi, went into the assault with most of the men unarmed; their rifles had been collected up a few days earlier to distribute to units thought more in danger of attack, and just before going into the line of battle, they were reissued what the brigade ordnance officer declared as "refuse guns." Most either could not be fired at all or had to be reassembled after each shot.

Chalmers's brigade "moved forward in splendid style," according to one of their opponents, Colonel Thomas Sedgewick of the 2nd (U.S.) Kentucky, but almost immediately began receiving murderous fire from the well-positioned 2nd Kentucky and 31st Indiana Regiments. The Confederates withered under the intense fire, but then recovered and closed to within 150 feet of the Union troops, where they exchanged fire for nearly 30 minutes before retreating with heavy losses. Chalmers himself was seriously wounded, and some regiments lost as many as eight color bearers in the brief assault.

As the last of Chalmers's men retreated, at about 9:30 a.m., a brief lull fell over the fighting. Fresh Union regiments were brought into the salient, while another Confederate attack was organized. Brigadier General Daniel Smith Donelson led his Tennessee Brigade into the same sector about 10 a.m., this time successfully breaching the Union line to the right (west) of the Round Forest, taking prisoners and capturing some artillery pieces. As the Confederate attack successfully progressed, more and more units were fed into the line by commanders of both sides, both determined to take and hold this critical position.

The fierce battle for possession of the wooded salient raged on for more than two hours before the Confederates were forced to withdraw. "Appalling casualties" is hardly an apt description of what the Tennesseans endured; Colonel W. L. Moore's 8th Tennessee Infantry Regiment, which had advanced far beyond any other unit, coming close to the turnpike itself, finally retreated, leaving behind 301 dead and wounded of the 440 troops it had advanced with, including Moore himself. This loss, 68 percent casualties, was the worst suffered by a Confederate regiment in any single battle of the entire war.

Getting to Stones River

Stones River Battlefield is in Murfreesboro, about 30 miles south of Nashville on I-24. Take exit 78B, which will connect you directly with US 96 East. Stay on this highway until the intersection with US 41/70, turn left (north) on US 41/70 to Thompson Lane (just a short distance north on the highway), and turn left (west) onto Thompson. Follow this road to the turnoff onto the Old Nashville Highway, and the plentiful signs in the area will take you into the battlefield proper.

After the battle, the Union troops stayed busy constructing one of the largest forts of the war, a 200-acre post surrounded by 14,000 feet of earthworks, soon named Fortress Rosecrans. Grateful men of Hazen's brigade built a large memorial to him and their comrades lost in the vicious fight before leaving later in 1863; this is considered the oldest intact monument of the war.

Today most of the battlefield is taken up by the urban sprawl of rapidly growing Murfreesboro. A small portion of the original 4,000-acre battlefield is preserved and protected by the National Park Service, which also oversees the inclusive Stones River National Cemetery. Only Union soldiers (and veterans of subsequent wars) are buried here; more than 2,000 of the Confederate dead are buried in a mass grave at nearby Evergreen Cemetery. Only 159 of this number are known and so marked. The remainder of the Confederate dead were buried in unmarked, now-lost mass graves by Rosecrans's men, who stayed in and around the battlefield for another five months.

The Afternoon Battle of December 31

With the failure of the morning assaults, the battlefield grew quiet for another few hours. At about 4 p.m. the last four Confederate brigades that had not yet seen action assaulted the Round Forest position once again. Brigadier General Daniel Weisiger Adams's 1st and Brigadier

General John K. Jackson's brigades were repulsed with heavy losses. Colonel Joseph Benjamin Palmer's and Brigadier General William Preston's brigades were sent in for the same results.

With the attacks over for the day with the approaching darkness, the Confederates held most of the field, now covered with dead and wounded soldiers of both sides. Rosecrans considered withdrawing back to Nashville but decided to stay and attack again—that is, if his opponent Bragg did not. Bragg returned to his headquarters in Murfreesboro and, somehow convinced that his army had been totally successful in the assault, telegraphed Richmond that "God has granted us a happy New Year."

Neither side attacked the next day, January 1, 1863, Rosecrans ordering his men to heavily entrench. Bragg took the quiet along the line, for some unknown reason, to indicate that the Union soldiers were on retreat back to Nashville. Wheeler's and Wharton's cavalry spent the day harassing the Union supply lines, with some moderate success. Bragg decided to assault the high ground to the left of the main Union line, hoping to find a place he could mount artillery and pour enfilading fire down on the rest of the Union line. Breckinridge was given the task of taking this position the next afternoon.

January 2, 1863

Breckinridge was horrified by his orders. Acting on his own, he had ordered a reconnaissance of the very area Bragg was proposing to attack. On his return from the dangerous scouting mission, Captain W. P. Bramblett of H Company, 4th Kentucky, the Orphan Brigade (so called because Kentucky was occupied by Union forces and the men could not go home until the war was over), had remarked that not only was this position already strongly held, but that more Union regiments were moving in, and it looked like "Rosecrans was . . . setting a trap" for Bragg to fall into.

Traveling to Bragg's headquarters, the Kentuckian presented his findings and requested the attack be canceled or moved. Bragg, ever intractable when told his ideas were faulty, insisted that the attack go ahead as scheduled, and set the hour of assault for 4 p.m., one hour before the winter sun set. Breckinridge angrily returned to his

command, proclaiming to some of Bragg's staff officers that he was carrying out the attack under protest and fully expected it to fail.

As Breckinridge's men moved slowly into position, word was passed to drop their packs (which infantrymen were loath to do, rightfully worried that a rapid retreat would mean the loss of their personal possessions) and prepare for a rapid assault. Hanson rode down his regiments forming up, stopping before each and ordering the regimental commander, "Colonel, the order is to load, fix bayonets and march through this brushwood. Then charge at double-quick to within a hundred yards of the enemy, deliver fire, and go at him with the bayonet." As the men aligned themselves, a cold, wet sleet started coming down hard, numbing bare hands and feet and soaking what threadbare clothes they had left.

At exactly 4 p.m., a signal round went off from an artillery battery, and the assault force fixed bayonets and moved forward at the double-quick. Leading on the left was Brigadier General Roger Weightman Hanson's 4th Brigade, with Brigadier General Gideon Johnson Pillow's 2nd Brigade to his left, followed about 150 yards to the rear by Colonel Randall Lee Gibson's 1st and Preston's 3rd Brigades—all told, about 4,500 men.

The first 900 yards of the assault went well. Although almost immediately coming under fire from Union positions on the hilltop, Hanson's and Pillow's brigades advanced without seriously disturbing their formation, brushing aside the Union skirmishers in front of the main line of battle with hardly a casualty. Colonel Samuel Beatty Price's 3rd Brigade of Van Cleve's division, atop and just in front of the targeted hill, held their fire until the Confederates were nearly upon them.

With the onrushing Kentuckians only 60 yards away, Price ordered his command on their feet to fire a volley into the butternut-clad ranks. The men of the Orphan Brigade never slowed down. Returning their own volley, the men let out their weirdly high-pitched battle yell and charged the Union line, bayonets glistening in the late-afternoon rain and sleet. The Union troops fired one last ragged volley and then bugged out, leaving the hill to the assaulting Confederates. As Hanson's men jumped over the abandoned Union breastworks, a Union artillery shell hit the general in his leg. Breckinridge, riding up to assess the success of his assaulting units, jumped off his horse and frantically tried to stop the bleeding, but to no avail. Although an ambulance soon arrived and Hanson was soon in the care of a surgeon, he died minutes later.

Storming over the hill and into the valley below, the Confederate assault continued unbroken to the east banks of Stones River itself. No doubt recalling how artillery had broken the Union ranks at Shiloh's Hornets' Nest a few months previous, Major John Mendenhall of the Union, Crittenden's artillery officer, had hastily assembled every available artillery battery and positioned them on a rise overlooking the west bank of the river. Fifty-eight guns commanded the river approach with unobstructed fields of fire onto both banks. As the Confederates boiled out of the wood line and ran to the river, running over a small rise next to the riverbank, Mendenhall ordered his batteries to open fire.

The explosion of artillery shattered the Confederate assault. More than 100 shots per minute rained down on the assault force, blowing apart whole regiments in a matter of minutes. The attack almost instantly turned into a matter of holding what they had gained; within minutes it turned into just getting out alive. No order given, the Southern soldiers simply retreated as best they could, dragging behind them a counterattack that ended up regaining all the Union losses of the afternoon. Confederate losses amounted to more than 1,700 of the best men on the field, nearly half of what had started out.

His attacks muted, his offense stalled, and his ranks shattered, Bragg stayed on the field one more day without contact with the Union forces, and then quietly withdrew during the night of January 3 south of Murfreesboro to Shelbyville. Rosecrans's force was too spent to pursue, staying in the area another five months before resuming any offensive operations. Neither side could really claim victory, both being mauled to the point where their armies were rendered nearly useless for many months, but Rosecrans's army held the field at the end, and Bragg failed in his attempt to retake Nashville. Rosecrans lost a total of 12,906 dead, wounded, and missing; Bragg, a total of 11,740.

RIVERS CAMPAIGN

Background to the Campaign

After Lincoln's election and the parade of Southern states seceding from the Union, it was not at first thought that any grand scheme or strategy for defeating the strong Confederate armies would have to be devised. General Winfield Scott, aged commander in chief of all Union armies, suggested early on a plan that would cut off trade and supply to the South, effectively starving it into submission. This so-called Anaconda Plan was initially rejected by Northern politicians, who in the manner of politicians everywhere and throughout history, demanded a "quick 'n' easy" solution to a complex and deadly problem. Their idea, which was unfortunately happily carried out by the army, was to simply march out and "show the grand old flag," and the Southerners would run screaming from the field.

Southerners proved a bit more intractable than the Northern politicians had predicted. With the Union disaster at the First Manassas (First Bull Run to the Yankees), realization set in that this was not going to be any sort of "90-day war" and that a real, workable strategy would have to be adopted. Based on Scott's plan, a three-part strategy was approved and adopted: first, a tight naval blockade of the entire Southern Atlantic and Gulf Coasts to cut off supplies and trade with foreign nations; second, an invasion of Virginia as soon as possible, with the goal of capturing the Confederate capital of Richmond; and third, the capture and control of the major river systems in the heartland of the Confederacy, the Mississippi, Cumberland, and Tennessee Rivers.

The naval blockade was effectively put into place on more than 3,500 miles of Southern coastline by July 1861, but Major General George Brinton McClellan's feeble attempts to take Richmond proved much less successful. To carry out the third portion of the grand plan, Brigadier General Ulysses S. Grant and Flag Officer Andrew Hull Foote (various sources list him as

Joseph Eggleston Johnston

One of the most beloved of all Civil War generals, second only to Lee in this regard, Joseph Eggleston Johnston was born in Farmville, Virginia, in 1807 and was appointed to West Point in 1825. He graduated 13th in his class of 46 in 1829 and was initially assigned to the 4th Artillery, seeing service during the Blackhawk War, on the western frontier, and during the Seminole War in Florida. He resigned his commission in 1837 to work as a civil engineer in Florida, only to run into further combat situations with hostile Indians while working with John Wesley Powell's expedition. Although seriously wounded in the head, Johnston rallied a defense and successfully moved the party to a safer area.

In 1838, partly in recognition of his exploits with Powell, Johnston was recommissioned in the engineering corps of the army and promoted to captain. He served under General Winfield Scott during the Mexican War, was wounded five times in combat, and led the final charge at Chapultepec.

Johnston resigned his U.S. Army commission on April 22, 1861, and was almost immediately commissioned as a major general of Virginia and brigadier general of the Confederacy (mixed commissions like this were common in the Confederacy). He commanded the combined Confederate forces at the opening major battle at Manassas and was subsequently one of four promoted to the highest rank of full general (along with Robert E. Lee, Albert Sydney Johnston, and Samuel Cooper). Johnston did have a personal fault of occasionally complaining about things of little consequence, and his comment that he should have been given seniority over Lee in this set of four, based on his rank and position in the prewar U.S. Army, served only to irritate President Jefferson Davis of the Confederacy, turning him into a lifelong enemy. Davis had several personal faults as well, and his thin skin and inability to stand criticism were his worst. Soon afterward, Johnston was seriously injured at the battle of Seven Pines and was relieved from duty. When he returned to service in November 1862, he was placed in charge of the newly formed Department of the West, theoretically in command over General Braxton Bragg's Army of Tennessee and Lieutenant General John Clifford Pemberton's Department of Mississippi, Tennessee, and East Louisiana, although he was given no support by Davis in having his orders and directives obeyed.

After Pemberton had lost Vicksburg and Bragg lost Tennessee, partly as a result of the conflicting orders given by Johnston and Davis, Bragg was relieved of command, promoted to military chief of staff, and replaced with Johnston in December 1863. There Johnston reversed a number of Bragg's draconian rules and regulations, such as having men who stayed too long on leave shot for desertion, refusing to issue many leaves in the first place, issuing reduced rations when plenty were available, and requiring two and even three roll calls a day to catch anyone who might dare try to sneak away. Command of the Army of Tennessee was both Johnston's finest hour and where his natural abilities flourished. He honestly loved and cared for his men, and they returned his love with a devotion that lasted to their own deathbeds. One of the privates in the ranks of his army, Sam Watkins of Columbia, Tennessee, had this to say about the day Johnston assumed command:

A new era had dawned; a new epoch had been dated. He passed through the ranks of the common soldier's pride; he brought the manhood back to the private's bosom; he changed the order of the roll-call, standing guard, drill, and such nonsense as that. The revolution was complete. He was loved, respected, admired; yea, almost worshipped by his troops. I do not believe there was a soldier in his army but would have gladly died for him. With him everything was his soldiers, and the newspapers, criticizing him at the time, said, "He would feed his soldiers if the country starved."

We soon got proud; the blood of the old Cavaliers tingled in our veins. We did not feel that we were serfs and vagabonds. We felt that we had a home and a country worth fighting for, and, if need be, worth dying for. One regiment could whip an army, and did it, in every instance, before the command was taken from him in Atlanta.

Johnston rebuilt his army just in the nick of time to face an army twice his size under Sherman, invading northern Georgia in May of 1864. Johnston was a past master at the running defense, as Sherman was a master at maneuver warfare, and his first priority was maintaining his force. Starting with the battles around Dalton, Johnston slowly gave ground before Sherman's juggernaut, making sure the Union armies bled heavily for every inch they gained. Whenever possible and prudent, the Confederate commander launched counterattacks, thinning the Union ranks at New Hope Church and Pickett's Mill. In other places, he set up defenses so strong that the Union ranks bled nearly dry trying to take them, at Rocky Face Ridge, Resaca, and Kennesaw Mountain.

Although Johnston managed to keep his army intact and in fighting trim and lost not a single artillery piece in the long retreat from Dalton, criticism of him and his tactics reached a fever pitch after he pulled south of the Chattahoochee River, just outside Atlanta. Johnston's plan all along had been to force a costly campaign on Sherman, then pull into the nearly impenetrable defenses of Atlanta and allow the Union force to batter itself to pieces there. However, President Davis's enmity toward Johnston reached a breaking point as he pulled back to Atlanta, and Davis fired the beloved commander on July 17, replacing him with one of his own corps commanders, the fiery and ill-tempered Lieutenant General John Bell Hood. To paraphrase what Sam Watkins said so well, let us close the book on that sad chapter after Hood's promotion; agonizing as it is to consider, suffice to say only that the once proud and able Army of Tennessee suffered the torture of misuse after misuse, before at last expiring on the ramparts around Nashville six months later. Sherman, incidentally, was delighted with the replacement, remarking that while Johnston was a dangerous foe, Hood was fairly predictable, and "I was never so nervous with him at my front."

Johnston was reappointed command of the pitiful remnants of the Army of Tennessee on February 23, 1865, and ordered to resist Sherman's march once again, this time in the Carolinas. Still more concerned about the lives of his men than the fate of the obviously doomed Confederacy, Johnston led them into only one more major battle, at Bentonville, North Carolina, on March 19. Reasonably successful in their first assault into the flanks of one of Sherman's four columns, Johnston wisely retreated before his Union nemesis could gather his own forces and crush him. Johnston opened surrender talks with Sherman shortly thereafter, the talks becoming more urgent after word reached them of Lincoln's assassination. Although Jefferson Davis, passing through the area on his flight from Richmond, rudely ordered Johnston to break contact with Sherman's force and retreat south with him, the courtly general instead signed the surrender documents on April 26.

After the war, Johnston worked in the insurance business in Savannah and Richmond and then served two terms in Congress as a representative from Virginia. He and Sherman became close friends after the war, and Johnston served as one of his old Union nemesis's pallbearers at his funeral. Going bareheaded during the ceremony, on a cold, misty day in 1891, Johnston developed pneumonia and died just weeks later. His aide had tried to get the aged general to at least wear a hat, but Johnston's only reply was, "He [Sherman] would not wear one if he was in my place."

a captain, commodore, or admiral at this point in time) were given the mission of opening up the great Southern rivers to Union control. Together they decided to concentrate initially on taking control of the Tennessee and Cumberland Rivers in northern Tennessee.

The Union Army-Navy Plan

Grant and Foote agreed to start their campaign on the Cumberland River at Fort Donelson, near the Tennessee-Kentucky border, which would open up a river corridor to Nashville. Foote had overseen the construction of a new class of navy craft specifically designed for such interservice operations, the ironclad riverboat. These boats were relatively small, 75 feet long and 50 feet wide on average, shallow-draft craft with protected midship paddle wheels for propulsion, ironclad either entirely or at least protecting the gun decks, with rectangular casements covered by sloping iron armor with a small opening for cannon.

Early on, most of these gunboats were simply modified civilian riverboats, with widely varying sizes and gun capacities. One carried only four 8-pounder guns, while others carried guns as heavy as 42 pounds and mounted as many as 12 guns. Foote commanded three unarmed boats and four ironclads in the opening battles, manned by a rather motley assortment of 500 sailors who were formerly riverboat crewmen, Maine lumber-boat sailors, New England whalers, New York ferrymen, and some only described as "Philadelphia sea-lawyers."

On the army side, Grant had about 15,000 soldiers organized into two divisions with five brigades. Brigadier General Charles Ferguson Smith took charge of three brigades, while Brigadier General John Alexander McClernand had two brigades under his command.

The Confederate Plan

In overall charge of the South's defense of the Mississippi River and its approaches was Major General Leonidas

Cover of sheet music for a patriotic song dedicated to Lincoln's secretary of the navy, Gideon Welles, in which Uncle Sam rides a "ram," or ironclad steam vessel, down the Mississippi River.

Major General Leonidas Polk, photographed in his bishop's robes

Polk, an Episcopalian bishop who was quite frankly more at home in the ministry than the military. He was convinced that the main Union attack would move down the Mississippi and accordingly placed most of his men and material in the buildup of fortifications at Columbus, Kentucky, for the defense of Memphis. He refused several requests for manpower and supplies to build up defenses on the Tennessee and Cumberland Rivers, believing that these were "backwater accesses with no real strategic value."

Governor Isham G. Harris of Tennessee, more concerned about the loss of the middle of his state than Polk was, personally ordered General Daniel S. Donelson of the Confederate Army to construct fortifications on these two rivers at the Kentucky border, where they are only 12 miles apart. Donelson chose a very poor site for the post guarding the Tennessee River; later named Fort Henry, it was placed on a floodplain that frequently flooded and was commanded by high ground across the river. The Cumberland River post was much better; later named Fort Donelson in his honor, the earthwork fort consisted of 2½ miles of fortifications surrounding two heavily entrenched artillery emplacements atop a 70-foot bluff overlooking the river.

> *The right of revolution is an inherent one. When people are oppressed by their government, it is a natural right they enjoy to relieve themselves of this oppression, if they are strong enough, whether by withdrawal from it, or by overthrowing it and substituting a government more acceptable.*
>
> —Lieutenant General Ulysses S. Grant, Union Army, from his memoirs

Interior of Fort Henry on the morning after its capture, from a sketch by H. Lovie, artist with Commodore Foote's expedition

The Battle of Fort Henry

Grant and Foote agreed to start their campaign by capturing Fort Henry. Foote started up the Tennessee River with his seven gunboats closely followed by Grant's force loaded on transport barges. Grant's plan was to land his force on either side of the fort, to prevent escape of the garrison, and march overland toward an assault while Foote's gunboats weakened the Confederate defenses by continuous bombardment.

Inside Fort Henry, things were getting soggy. The river was flooding again, and water was standing 2 feet deep in parts of the fort. Brigadier General Lloyd Tilghman, post commander, was disgusted; calling the fort's condition "wretched," he sent most of the 2,500-man garrison to nearby Fort Donelson and kept only a single 60-man artillery company to man the 17 guns.

On February 6, 1862, with Grant's troops landed and on their way over muddy, flooded roads, Foote sailed his gunboats nearly to the ramparts of the fort and opened fire. With the fort continuing to flood, Tilghman's gunners returned a telling fire, disabling two gunboats and killing or wounding nearly two score of their crew. The fort's crew fared little better, with four guns flooded out or disabled by enemy fire and 20 men killed or wounded. After less than two hours of bombardment, Tilghman surrendered his post before Grant had a chance to close in. The fort was so flooded by that point that the Union officers accepting the surrender floated in the main gate by boat. Lost in the brief confrontation were 11 killed, 31 wounded, and 5 missing for the Union force; Tilghman reported his losses at 20 killed or wounded and the rest made prisoner.

The Battle for Fort Donelson

The day after the fall of Fort Henry, the commander of the Western Theater, General Albert Sydney Johnston, ordered the abandonment of Columbus and Bowling Green, Kentucky, and the movement of most of his armies south of the Cumberland River. To facilitate this movement and make safe his new positions, he ordered that Fort Donelson be reinforced and held.

Battle of Fort Donelson

Fort Donelson originally held a garrison of 5,000 troops, soon reinforced to a total of 18,000 (as few as 12,000 by some accounts) but burdened with a weird command structure where three generals shared the responsibility: Brigadier General John Buchanan Floyd, Brigadier General Gideon Pillow, and Brigadier General Simon Bolivar Buckner. To add to the unworkable situation of having three commanders, Buckner and Pillow were bitter political enemies back home in Kentucky; Pillow was a lawyer with no formal military training and a bad case of arrogance; Buckner was the only professional soldier of the three; and Floyd was a weak-willed politician who had been Buchanan's secretary of war. Floyd took over as senior commander strictly by virtue of his earlier date of commission.

> *While you were eating your good dinner we soldiers would have been glad to have the crumbs that fell from your table. I will tell you what our meals were this day: Breakfast, rice and beef. Dinner, rice. Supper, beef and rice. Rice is our favorite dish now.*
>
> —William Henry, 101st Illinois
> Infantry Regiment of the Union Army

The Advance to Fort Donelson

Grant waited several days before marching on Fort Donelson, building up his forces to as many as 27,000, with about 15,000 ready for an immediate investment of the Confederate stronghold. On the afternoon of February 13, the Union troops were in position to the south and west of the fort, with Foote on the way upriver with his gunboats and more troops to land on the north side of the fort. The day was clear and sunny, with quite a warm temperature for a winter's day, leading many of the Union soldiers to ditch their heavy overcoats by the side of the road as they marched in.

The night of February 13 a winter storm blew in, dropping the temperature down to 10 degrees and setting off a raging blizzard on the unprotected troops. Campfires had been forbidden, as any light brought a barrage from Fort Donelson's guns. A brief skirmish earlier in the day had resulted in numerous Union wounded, many of whom froze to death during the long night.

The Gunboats Enter the Action

Late in the afternoon of February 14, Foote arrived and swung into action. His four heavily armored gunboats

Getting to Forts Henry and Donelson

Forts Henry and Donelson were located quite close to each other in an area of Tennessee now known as the Land Between the Lakes (or simply LBL to the locals). To get there from Clarksville, which is located just off I-24 northwest of Nashville, take US 79 for about 40 miles. Fort Donelson National Military Park, directly on US 79, is 3 miles west of the small town of Dover. The site of Fort Henry is on, appropriately, Fort Henry Road, about 6 miles farther west on US 79.

Time and river floods have rendered invisible the ramparts of Fort Henry, now indicated only by a single historic marker and a hiking trail around the riverbank area. There are no amenities, restaurants, motels, or basically anything else at this location. The nearest town of any size is Dover, roughly 10 miles east on US 79.

Some of Fort Donelson has been preserved and protected by the federal government, which also located a National Cemetery at the site. The Cumberland River is no longer recognizable from its Civil War days, having been dammed up to form Lake Barkley. Very little survives today from the Civil War period, the local attraction being the massive Land Between the Lakes recreation area, toward which most of the few local businesses are oriented.

closed to within 400 yards of the fort, exchanging heavy fire with the Confederate artillery crews until darkness set in. Foote was decisively defeated, his gunboats raked with heavy cannon fire until rendered useless, and most of his sailors aboard killed or wounded. Foote himself was seriously injured aboard his flagship, the *St. Louis,* ultimately dying 16 months later of complications caused by the wound.

Although the Confederate force had been quite successful resisting the waterborne assault, it was obvious that they would not be able to make much of a stand against Grant's land-based assault, sure to come in the following days. The three generals agreed to break out

toward the east and rejoin the rest of Johnston's force in Nashville. Launching a strong attack on the Union lines across the Nashville Road at daybreak, Pillow and Buckner managed to force the road open by noon. Unbelievably, though, Pillow ordered a retreat back into the fort on hearing a report that the Union troops in the area might be receiving reinforcements. Floyd, still in the fort, supported Pillow, and all the Southern soldiers who had forced the breakout were smartly marched back into the besieged garrison.

Pillow later claimed that he ordered the return to the fort because of a "confusion over orders," stating that he thought the men were to go back, pack their belongings, and presumably tidy up the place before leaving. Once back in the fort, he insisted that his men needed food and rest before embarking on such a long march, and Floyd timidly backed him up against the violently agitated Buckner, who rightfully insisted they had to leave immediately for any hope of escaping the Union envelopment. As they stood arguing, Grant launched his own attack.

Correctly assessing that as the attack had come from the Confederate left, their right must be weaker, he ordered an assault on that part of their line. General Charles Ferguson Smith led his division in a strong assault against the Confederate trench lines, now held only by a single regiment of infantry. Buckner immediately moved his men back to counterattack, but Smith was able to capture and hold the outer line of defenses on that side of the fort before darkness brought an end to the day's fighting.

The Surrender of the Fort

The three Confederate generals again conferred, Pillow and Floyd in a sheer panic at their own capture and Buckner disgusted with their amateurish attempts at command. Floyd passed command of the post to Pillow, who immediately passed it to Buckner, who had made it clear that the only choice available was surrender. As Buckner made ready to end his resistance, Floyd and Pillow commandeered a steamboat and got themselves to safety across the river, along with a few hundred soldiers of Floyd's command. Newly appointed cavalry officer Lieutenant Colonel Nathan Bedford Forrest, disgusted with Buckner's intention to surrender, received his permission to escape through the surrounding swamps with as many men as possible.

On the morning of February 16, Buckner sent a message across to Grant asking for his surrender terms. Grant replied in a famous message, "No terms except unconditional and immediate surrender" (from which his nickname "Unconditional Surrender" came). Meeting at the Dover Inn later that afternoon, Buckner surrendered his command and the post. Casually discussing the action later with his prewar friend Grant, Buckner mentioned that he must have been disappointed not to have captured Pillow and Floyd as well. Well aware of Pillow's alleged "abilities" as a battlefield commander, Grant remarked that had he captured Pillow, he would have immediately released him, as Pillow was more a danger to the Confederacy than an asset!

Numbers of those engaged, casualties, and prisoners vary wildly from source to source, but somewhere in the neighborhood of 27,000 Union and 21,000 Confederate troops were involved in the action, with Grant losing about 2,800 dead, wounded, or missing. The Confederate

force lost about 2,000 dead or wounded and had about 14,500 made prisoner, the rest escaping with Forrest or bugging out on their own.

Confederate soldiers searching for the wounded by torchlight after the capture of Fort Donelson

---

POINTS OF INTEREST

Confederate Memorial Hall
3148 Kingston Pike
Knoxville, TN
(865) 522-2371
www.knoxvillecmh.org

Formerly known as Bleak House, for the Charles Dickens novel, this slave-built brick house was constructed in 1858 and was used as Longstreet's and McLaw's headquarters during the brief siege operation. The tower was used as a sniper post during the Confederate operations; Brigadier General William Price Sanders of the Union's Army, the fort's namesake, was killed by a shot from this tower while standing on the lawn of the still-existent Second Presbyterian Church on November 16, 1862. The house was damaged by Union artillery fire and reportedly still has bullets embedded in the walls.

The house is now owned by the United Daughters of the Confederacy and is preserved and open to the public as a museum, with many period furnishings and decorations. It is open Wed, Thurs, and Fri. The last tour begins at 3:15

p.m. Group rates are available. The house is closed the entire month of Jan. The house has a gift shop that contains books about the history of the house as well as other educational items.

Fort Donelson National Battlefield
US 79 West
Dover, TN
(931) 232-5348, ext. 0
www.nps.gov/fodo

This 90-acre park features a small museum with a small collection of artifacts, as well as a 15-minute film about Grant's river campaign. Occasional ranger-led demonstrations of rifle and cannon firing are presented, mainly in the summer months, and brochures for a self-guided driving tour are available at the information desk. Several emplacements and river batteries are well preserved and give a good feel for what it was like here during the siege.

Don't miss the Confederate monument, which is rumored to be placed over a mass grave of Southern dead.

After the fight, hastily buried Union dead were reinterred in what became a National Cemetery on the property, while the mass graves of Confederates were left undisturbed. As they were never marked, these final resting places lie scattered about the property, forgotten and lost. The National Cemetery contains 655 Union dead, only 151 of which are known. Soldiers from later wars are laid here as well, swelling the population to about 1,500.

Admission is free, but donations are accepted and strongly encouraged.

The Museum of East Tennessee History
601 S. Gay St.
Knoxville, TN
(865) 215-8824
www.easttnhistory.org

This nicely laid out museum in the 1870s-era U.S. Post Office building displays a collection concentrating on the general history of the Knoxville area. There is a new permanent exhibit, Voices of the Land: The People of East Tennessee, with a Civil War section that includes a well-presented collection of uniforms and weapons. Admission is free for all on Sun.

Oaklands Historic House Museum
900 North Maney Ave.
Murfreesboro, TN
(615) 893-0022
www.oaklandsmuseum.org

Once the center of a 1,500-acre plantation, Oaklands was built in 1815 and is the best preserved of several existing antebellum mansions in the area. The plantation was the site of both the surrender of Murfreesboro to Forrest on July 13, 1862, and where President Jefferson Davis stayed when he visited the troops in December of the same year.

The house has been restored to its early Civil War splendor, with a beautiful sweeping main staircase and intricate fleur-de-lis wallpaper.

Stones River National Battlefield
3501 Old Nashville Hwy.
Murfreesboro, TN
(615) 478-1035
www.nps.gov/stri

The 450-acre park includes only the portion of the battlefield involved in the first Confederate assault on December 31 and a section to the east close to the Round Forest area. The visitor center has a small but nicely presented collection of battlefield artifacts and a nine-minute orientation film about the battle, as well as a very nicely stocked bookstore. A self-guided driving tour audiotape is available (and recommended), as well as limited information about portions of the battlefield not on the property. Admission is free, but please do leave a donation in the box at the visitor center entrance. During summer, ranger-led tours are offered, as well as occasional living-history exhibitions.

ACCOMMODATIONS

Knoxville

Knoxville has a good selection of both independent and chain hotels and motels, as well as a sprinkling of bed-and-breakfast inns. For a complete listing and current information on local festivals and events, contact the Knoxville Tourism and Sports Corporation, (865) 523-7263, www.knoxville.org.

Maplehurst Inn Bed and Breakfast $$–$$$
800 W. Hill Ave.
Knoxville, TN
(865) 523-7773
(800) 451-1562
www.maplehurstinn.com

This small inn has one big advantage: It is very close to the Civil War sites at the University of Tennessee campus. Eleven rooms and a penthouse are available. They all feature cable TV with movies, and some have Jacuzzis. The adjoining restaurant serves breakfast only.

Murfreesboro

Murfreesboro is a fair-size city, with plenty of food and lodging choices. For a complete listing, as well as information on local events, contact the Rutherford County Chamber of Commerce at (615) 893-6565 or (800) 716-7560; www.rutherfordchamber.org.

✴ ✴ ✴ ✴ ✴ ✴ ✴ ✴ ✴ ✴ ✴ ✴ ✴ ✴ ✴ ✴

Carriage Lane Inn Bed and Breakfast $$–$$$
337 E. Burton St.
Murfreesboro, TN
(615) 890-3630
(800) 357-2827
www.carriagelaneinn.com

This inn is a collection of properties, all with private bath and elegantly appointed furnishings. It sits on what used to be the carriage lane to the Maney family home, which is now Oakland Historic House Museum. Historic sites, antiques shopping, and restaurants are all within walking distance.

Doubletree Murfreesboro $$–$$$
1850 Old Fort Pkwy.
Murfreesboro, TN
(615) 895-5555
(800) 222-8733
www.murfreesboro.doubletree.com

A beautiful, open, and spacious hotel, with a nicely laid out and decorated atrium lobby and 168 rooms and suites. A fitness center, restaurant, bar, and pool are on the property.

RESTAURANTS

Knoxville

Copper Cellar Cumberland $$–$$$
1807 Cumberland Ave.
Knoxville, TN
(865) 673-3411
www.coppercellar.com

Close to the university campus, this high-end establishment specializes in steak and prime rib plus fresh fish and seafood dishes. Portions are huge, as are the desserts, and the best thing is that you most decidedly will not go away hungry. No dress code is posted or apparently enforced, but this is not a blue jeans sort of place. Lunch is crowded, with a lot of corporate suits present; supper seems a bit more relaxed.

Patrick Sullivan's Steakhouse & Saloon $$–$$$
100 N. Central Ave.
Knoxville, TN
(865) 637-4255
www.patricksullivans.com

This well-appointed tavern, built in 1888, is an upscale eatery in the best sense of the word, serving chicken, pork, fish, and pasta dishes prepared in several unusual ways. Some of the current menu choices are pan-seared pepper steak, prime Colorado beef, jumbo shrimp, and a tasty pasta creation. The burgers and blue plate specials are widely acclaimed. Thanks to the wooden floors and bare brick walls, the noise level can be quite high; there is a balcony level usually available where the seating is a bit quieter. Hours can fluctuate, so call ahead.

Murfreesboro

Demo's Restaurant $$
1115 N.W. Broad St.
Murfreesboro, TN
(615) 895-3701
www.demosrestaurants.com

A local favorite, Demo's specializes in spaghetti dishes and offers several varieties of other pastas, steaks, and seafood and a few Mexican dishes. The dining room is nicely decorated in dark green, with period-style lighting fixtures.

Forts Henry and Donelson

There are no facilities worthy of mention in the immediate vicinity of Forts Henry or Donelson, as this is a rather rural section of the state that attracts very few tourists. The nearest town with adequate facilities is Clarksville to the east. There you will find the usual array of chain fast-food and mid-range restaurants, as well as a selection of chain motels, mostly clustered around US 41 on the north side of town. Nearby Fort Campbell drives the local economy here, which leans heavily toward the sort of businesses young soldiers support, especially north of town to the Kentucky border. (Fort Campbell is actually in both states, and the entrance gates sit on either side of the state line.)

Chickamauga:
The Rock and the Angel of Death

Darley.

Map of the Battle of Chickamauga

Following an unsuccessful campaign in Kentucky and failure to push back Major General William Starke Rosecrans's Union Army of the Cumberland at Stones River, Tennessee, in January 1863, General Braxton Bragg withdrew his still-intact Army of Tennessee back to Tullahoma to attempt a stand. Charged with protecting the vital transportation center of Chattanooga, Bragg intended to let Rosecrans bleed his army to death in frontal assaults on the Confederate position along the Duck River rather than trying another offensive himself.

Months went by without action. Rosecrans had nearly wrecked his own army at Stones River and needed time to refit. Finally, under pressure from President Abraham Lincoln, the Army of the Cumberland moved south, bursting through multiple gaps south of Tullahoma on June 24 and taking Bragg completely by surprise. His own line of retreat in danger of being cut off, Bragg hastily withdrew his entire force into Chattanooga with barely a shot being fired.

BACKGROUND TO THE BATTLE

*B*ragg had no idea of the actual position of the advancing Union columns. Believing that they still intended to envelop Chattanooga somewhere to the east from Knoxville, he spent several days fretting and giving conflicting orders. The Confederates reestablished their lines in the small mountain town by the Tennessee River, but when Union forces crossed unopposed at three points below the city, the Confederates again were ordered to withdraw south without a fight—this time completely out of Tennessee and on to the northwest Georgia town of LaFayette. Without a firm grasp of the situation and in a nervous frustration over what to do about it, Bragg missed several excellent opportunities to strike the separate Union columns as they exited the Lookout Mountain passes. On September 9, as the last of Bragg's army left, the vanguard of Rosecrans's entered the city from the north.

At about the same time, Major General Ambrose Burnside's Army of the Ohio divided into four columns with 24,000 men and forced the Confederate garrison at Knoxville to abandon the city, again without a major fight. These forces joined Bragg's column in the general retreat south into Georgia. The Confederate commander was determined to protect the vital industrial center of Atlanta and to regain control of Chattanooga if possible, so he tried an interesting tactic to draw Rosecrans's forces into battle on his own terms.

Paying too much attention to planted "deserters," who convinced Rosecrans that Bragg was in full,

Army of the Cumberland in front of Chattanooga

panicked retreat, the Union commander placed his 60,000-man force in three widely separated columns in order to cut him off and force the Confederate Army into battle, where it could be destroyed once and for all. One column led by Major General Thomas L. Crittenden passed through Chattanooga and went on to Ringgold, Georgia. Another, led by Major General George H. Thomas, passed through Bridgeport, Alabama, and with some difficulty crossed Sand Mountain to approach LaFayette. The third column, led by Major General Alexander McDowell McCook, went another 40 miles to the southwest of Chattanooga through northern Alabama toward Summerville, Georgia.

As the Union forces moved to his north and west, Bragg sent urgent requests for reinforcements and gathered his forces for battle.

TWO ARMIES AT CHICKAMAUGA

𝓑ragg knew that to protect Atlanta, retake Chattanooga, or even hold on for long in the north Georgia mountains, he would need reinforcements, plentiful and soon. In addition to the men from the Knoxville garrison, two divisions were sent from Major General Joseph Eggleston Johnston's army in Mississippi. General Robert E. Lee agreed, reluctantly, to allow Lieutenant General James Longstreet to go to Bragg's aid with two divisions of his corps (the third, Major General George E. Pickett's division, was still combat ineffective after Gettysburg). All these reinforcements would bring the Confederate force to a higher available manpower than the Union's, an exceedingly rare event at any point during the war.

With help on the way, Bragg became impatient to go into offensive action. Between September 10 and 13, with Rosecrans's forces widely separated and cut off from mutual support, Bragg grabbed the tactical advantage and ordered divisional-size attacks at several points. Mysteriously, not a single attack was carried out; each

divisional commander found one reason or another not to assault. Rosecrans shortly received word from spies and scouts about both the fizzled attacks and the incoming reinforcements and ordered his columns to pull together just west of Chickamauga Creek. By September 17 the columns were in close proximity, and Rosecrans ordered them forward to concentrate in the vicinity of Lee and Gordon's Mill on Chickamauga Creek.

Engagements at the Bridges

On that same day, Bragg's forces were in place from near Reed's Bridge over Chickamauga Creek in the north to opposite Lee and Gordon's Mill in the south. With the leading elements of Longstreet's corps just arriving by train and still a few hours' march away, the order for attack was given. Bragg's strategy was to sweep forward and take control of the LaFayette road, hitting the Union forces from the east, cutting them off from a line of retreat back into Chattanooga, and hopefully driving them back toward Alabama. Brigadier General Bushrod R. Johnson's brigade was ordered to start the offensive by seizing and crossing Reed's Bridge, followed by movement forward all along the nearly 5-mile line.

Confederate artillery opens fire on Union calvary on September 18, 1863, near Reeds Bridge.

Johnson moved forward early on the morning of September 18, but his and the other brigades' advances were slowed by a combination of bad roads and miscommunication. Colonel Robert Minty's 1st Brigade (2nd Cavalry Division) made the first contact with the advancing Confederate force, skirmishing about a mile east of Reed's Bridge before being pushed back to the creek itself. Before withdrawing, Minty ordered the bridge burned, further delaying the Confederate assault. Johnson's men did not actually cross the creek until late in the afternoon. By that time the leading element of Longstreet's corps, Major General John Bell Hood's division, arrived and took command of the column.

Just to the south at Alexander's Bridge, another contact was made at about 10 a.m. between Colonel John T. Wilder's 1st Brigade (Mounted Infantry, 4th Division, XIV Corps), supported by the 18th Indiana Artillery, and Brigadier General St. John R. Liddell's Confederate division. Holding the line for most of the day, Wilder was forced to withdraw at about 5 p.m. when his right flank was turned by newly arriving elements of Major General William H. T. Walker's corps, who had crossed the creek farther downstream. Pulling back toward Lee and Gordon's Mill, Wilder was soon reinforced and managed to halt the sputtering Confederate advance after a fierce night attack.

Day Two, September 19, 1863, Morning

On Saturday morning, after a long night of shifting his forces about to meet the developing Confederate threat, Thomas's XIV Corps arrived at Kelley's field on the LaFayette road, and he ordered Brigadier General John M. Brannon's 3rd Division eastward to make contact with the Confederate force. About 7:30 a.m. they suddenly encountered dismounted troops in the vicinity of Jay's Mill and both sides opened fire. There was no opportunity for either side to get organized, and the fight rapidly turned into a confused melee, with men firing every which way and seeking whatever cover they could in the surrounding forest. A few minutes into the fight, none other than Brigadier General Nathan Bedford Forrest himself came charging up, pistol in one hand, saber in the other, and began bellowing orders. The dismounted troops were part of his cavalry corps, detailed to protect the northern flank of the Confederate lines. Quickly, his men got into line, lying down in the damp grass side by side and returning a disciplined fire into the Union ranks. Casualties were high, nonetheless, for the legendary cavalry commander, who lost almost 25 percent of his men in the first hour alone.

Both Forrest and Brannon quickly called for reinforcements, and shortly Colonel John M. Connell's 1st and Colonel Ferdinand Van Derveer's 3rd Brigades (of Brannon's 3rd Division) arrived to shore up the Union line, while Walker and Liddell brought their divisions to Forrest's aid. The fight grew almost by itself; very soon additional units began pouring into the rapidly growing battle, extending the lines a few hundred yards to each side, then a half-mile, a mile, and then finally a nearly 4-mile-wide solid front of combat existed over the fields and forest from near Lee and Gordon's Mill all the way up to well north of Jay's Mill. Throughout the early afternoon, assault after assault pushed one side back a bit, then the other, neither side gaining any real ground or advantage. Both lines were in close contact the entire time, with appallingly high casualties piling up by the minute.

From that point on through the end of the day the battle was a "soldier's fight," as the thick woods and disordered array of combat units made it nearly impossible for commanders on either side to make informed tactical decisions. Both lines overlapped at several points, and hand-to-hand combat was commonplace across the fields.

Day Two, Midday

Starting a little after noon, Thomas began shifting his forces north to oppose Confederate forces coming on line against his left flank. This opened up a hole in the main Union line that was quickly exploited by three brigades of Major General Alexander Stewart's division. Attacking straight across the LaFayette road at the Brotherton farm, they succeeded in breaking the thin Union line. Following his lead, just to the left at the nearby Viniard Field, brigadier generals Jerome B. Roberton's and Henry L. Benning's brigades (of Hood's division) stormed across the LaFayette road and pushed the Union forces out of their entrenchments and back about 200 yards.

Ghost Stories

It doesn't take much traveling about in Civil War history circles until you start encountering ghost stories. Nearly as ubiquitous as tinny renditions of "Dixie," rebel flags, and poorly made "authentic" kepis, ghost stories are sort of a peripheral industry in and of themselves, with pricey ghost tours, books, and hallowed traditions of sightings, usually in places that were peripheral to the war itself. The litany of the tour guide is often the giveaway that a "real" story from somewhere else has been borrowed to spice things up: ". . . and here in the window of this upstairs bedroom, the ghostly image of Sally Jane Beauregard is often seen at midnight on the third of the month during a full moon, staring out down the lane as if pining away for her lover who left, never to return . . ." We have often wondered what would happen if Sally Jane Beauregard really did show up one night.

Despite all the crass commercialization of the supernatural in certain areas, there seems to be a widespread and firmly held belief that something not of the flesh is present in any number of places—throughout our travels over the years, we have had all sorts of sober, serious historians, park rangers, and reenactors broach the subject with us without prompting, telling us of sights, sounds, and even smells they have experienced in the places blood was shed. Author John McKay admitted to a rather eerie encounter while a young soldier at Fort Campbell, Kentucky, in the 1970s. He saw what appeared to be a group of horsemen carrying a battle flag and crossing the road about a quarter-mile ahead of his jeep; they disappeared from sight in a large empty field on the other side.

A few places seem obvious to have encounters of this sort—the battlefield at Gettysburg, Pennsylvania, has produced enough sightings to fill two books on that subject alone, and nearly the entire ranger staff at Andersonville National Historic Site had at least one or two stories of encounters to relate. Rangers and even some visitors at Shiloh had some stories, most of which seemed to circulate around the Bloody Pond section of the battlefield. One volunteer at the Castillo de San Marcos National Monument in St. Augustine (known as Fort Marion during the war) told a hilarious tale about the layers of "haints" around the 17th-century castle, where one is not certain if the ghost one encounters is Spanish, English, Native American, Confederate, or Union!

One story that has circulated around the reenactment community for years (and has been told to us as happening to "a friend of a friend" by no less than two dozen people) involves an incident one night at the Pickett's Mill battlefield, just west of Kennesaw Mountain near Marietta, Georgia. The details in the various retellings vary somewhat, but the gist is that two reenactors showed up after dark one night before the annual living-history exhibition on the battlefield (this is not unusual, for reenactors sometime travel hundreds of miles to events, not leaving until the workweek is done). Rather than go crashing through the thick, dark woods to the encampment site, they decided to sleep in their car in the visitor center parking lot, which is only feet from the Confederate lines during the battle. During the night they were awakened by the sound of masses of people moving around on the other side of the center, followed by "rebel yells" and (in some retellings of the story) the sounds of muskets discharging. Deciding that some of the other reenactors supposedly on the site were just out having a little moonlit fun, they stayed in their car and went back to sleep. The next morning upon rising and looking around for their compatriots, they discovered that the encampment area had been changed to one off-site and that no one except themselves had been on the battlefield all night.

Another story was related to us about an adjoining battlefield, New Hope Church, where an eminent artifact collector and historian from Atlanta was out with a companion walking the old battleground on the afternoon of May 27, 1964. A sudden spring thunderstorm blew in over the field, causing the two men to seek shelter in a nearby toolshed. Our source did not know what they encountered next, but the historian and his friend soon departed the field quickly, through the midst of the driving rain. Coming up to a nearby farmhouse, they sought shelter with the old farmer, who berated them for being out on the battlefield that day. "Don't you know that nobody goes down in there on this day?" he asked. It was 100 years to the day after that terrible battle was fought, also during the midst of a driving thunderstorm.

These are the sort of stories that are delicious to read about, but the real rising-hair-on-the-neck feeling can only come from hearing them firsthand in the places they happened. Don't hesitate to ask your guide or available rangers about what they may have seen, heard, or felt—it does give an exquisite flavor to the experience.

In all seriousness, there is something very different about the places we write about in this book. We have found the battlefields, ironically, to be some of the most peaceful places we've ever visited, as if all the energy has been sucked out of the area by the enormity of what happened there so long ago. As we have stood by the Peach Orchard at Shiloh, atop Snodgrass Hill at Chickamauga, on the ramparts of Fort McAllister near Savannah, on the porch at the Carter House in Franklin, in front of the row upon row of stark white tombstones at Andersonville, and in the open fields of Bentonville, there is an almost perceptible hush, as if the wind itself is reluctant to disturb the rest of those who are buried there. As we clambered through the overgrown trenches at Nickajack Ridge outside Atlanta and the thick woods near Griswoldville, we had the feeling that those who fell there have waited patiently for someone to tell of their sacrifice. These may not be ghosts in the proper sense, but the spirits of those who fought in those places are there all the same, and in some very real ways their bones are as well, given the "plant them where they fall" burial practices of the day. Tread lightly and allow them their well-deserved peaceful slumber.

At that point the Confederates had nearly split the Union forces in half and controlled their main line of communication to Chattanooga. Worse for Rosecrans, the momentum of their attack was carrying them straight toward his headquarters, across Brotherton Field at Widow Glenn's cabin.

With the breach made, reinforcements would be all that was needed to completely break the Union lines and carry the day. Resistance in the retreating Union units was stiffening, and the breakthrough was bogging down after a few hundred yards' advance. Benning requested not only infantry reinforcements but artillery as well, to counter the batteries directly in front that were shattering his ranks. Stewart's division fared a little better, with Union batteries exhausting their loads of canister before his own attack drew too close.

Rosecrans sent word to his units to hold "at all costs," and they responded well, putting up a solid wall of resistance even while their own ranks were blown apart. Several witnesses mentioned that whole companies simply ceased to exist in the rain of lead balls and iron shot. In typical Bragg fashion, however, no reserves were ordered in to exploit the situation. Without fresh men and ammunition, the breakthrough halted before any serious gain was made. As darkness fell, Hood's brigades held their line, to be relieved later in the night, while Stewart's men stayed put and hastily dug in just west of the LaFayette road.

Rosecrans and Bragg at the Battle of Chickamauga

Day Two, Evening

Just after sunset, Major General Patrick R. Cleburne's division (Lieutenant General Daniel H. Hill's corps) was sent in from its reserve position up to the right of the rebel line and immediately swung into battle with its three brigades. Hitting Thomas's units in the process of shifting positions, another fierce hand-to-hand combat ensued across nearly a mile-wide front, pushing the Union line back nearly three-quarters of a mile. Within an hour, however, it was too dark to see anything except the brilliant muzzle flashes seemingly coming from all directions, and both sides broke contact and pulled back after again suffering high casualties. The long day of fighting finally drew to a close without either side having gained any significant advantage.

The Union lines were now compacted into a 3-mile-wide continuous front, and all night long the men dug in and waited for the coming onslaught. Thomas's men constructed a mile-long series of heavily reinforced, aboveground log emplacements, rather than entrenchments, during the night, along and just to the west of Alexander's Bridge Road. Longstreet himself finally arrived at Bragg's headquarters with the rest of his men about 11 p.m. Bragg divided his forces into two corps, giving Longstreet command of the left and Lieutenant General Leonidas Polk (an Episcopalian bishop in civilian life) command of the right.

All through the night both sides shifted their positions in preparation for the next day's action. The Union right moved back away from the Viniard Field to the Glenn Field at Crawfish Springs Road, "refusing" the Confederate line, which stayed near the LaFayette road all night. On the north end of the line, Cleburne's division was reorganized and reinforced by Breckinridge's division to the right, extending the line to Reed's Bridge Road and facing due west. Forrest's cavalry had confirmed that the line outflanked the Union defenses and stayed to the right to guard their own flank.

Bragg gave orders that night for Polk's corps to attack at daybreak in force on the extreme right, to be followed by attacks all down his line, and then followed in the same manner by Longstreet's on the left. Both corps were to hit the Union line with every man they had, no reserves were to be kept back, and the attack was to be maintained until the Union line broke.

> *A reckless and unprincipled tyrant has invaded your soil. Abraham Lincoln, regardless of all moral, legal and constitutional restraints, has thrown his abolition hosts among you, who are murdering and imprisoning your citizens, confiscating and destroying your property, and committing other acts of violence and outrage too shocking and revolting to humanity to be enumerated.*
>
> —General Pierre Gustave Toutant Beauregard of the Confederacy, in a proclamation to the people of Virginia

Day Three, September 20, 1863, Morning

Sunday morning dawned with a bloodred sun through the fog and battle haze, but no sounds of gunfire reached Bragg's headquarters. Riding forward to reconnoiter the ground personally, the only sounds he heard were axes chopping and trees falling within the Union lines a few hundred yards away as they continued to strengthen their positions. Continuing on, he found the troops on the right flank drawing their rations and not even close to being ready for battle. No doubt throwing one of his famous temper tantrums, Bragg sent for Polk and his corps and divisional commanders.

Reading the naturally self-serving after-action reports of "who said what" and "when I received my orders," it was nearly impossible to ascertain with any degree of accuracy exactly what had caused the delay. The divisional commanders all stated that they had received their final orders at 7:25 a.m., but Hill claimed this was the first he had heard of any attack order. It is known that there was some serious infighting among the Confederate high command, and that a rift over who was senior to whom had developed between Polk and Hill. Bragg himself was one of the most widely despised officers in the entire Confederate Army, hated and distrusted by officer and enlisted man alike, which only increased the communication problems. The only certainty was that no attack went off at dawn, and the Union line gained in strength by the hour.

At about 9:30 a.m. the attack finally got under way (this time and subsequent ones are also disputed in different reports). Breckinridge's division led off with a three-brigade front. Moving forward about 700 yards, Brigadier General Benjamin H. Helm's rebel brigade was the first to make contact, with the 2nd and 9th Kentucky and 41st Alabama Infantry Regiments storming the barricades held by Brigadier General John H. King's 3rd Brigade (Brigadier General Absalom Baird's 1st Division, Thomas's XIV Corps). As each brigade advanced, the next in the line should have moved into position for support, but for some unknown reason, no brigade came up on Helm's left to support him, allowing enfilade fire to hit him from the Union forces now to his left.

The assaulting regiments were nearly torn to pieces, and the Union lines held fast. Helm, Mary Todd Lincoln's brother-in-law, was mortally wounded and died later that day. What was left of his brigade, along with brigadier generals Daniel W. Adams's and Marcellus A. Stovall's brigades, moved farther to the right and around the long line of fortifications, where they ran headlong into and captured a two-gun artillery battery and pushed back the extreme left of Baird's division. Stovall's brigade finally halted just to the Union left and rear at the LaFayette road (near the present-day visitor center), and Adams's moved up to his right in the Kelly Field.

Day Three, Midday

Acting against specific orders, Polk had sent in his units one at a time rather than as a united front and had held back Walker's corps in reserve. To try to shore up this failed attack, Walker was sent in at about 11 a.m. with orders to attack the same set of fortifications. Once again each brigade was thrown into the battle as it came into line, rather than as divisional- or corps-size assaults, and once again the attack was halted and repulsed. Another brigade commander was killed during the action, Colonel Peyton H. Colquitt.

A little to the south and the left, at about 10 a.m., Cleburne's division was ordered into the fight. Ordered to "dress" on Breckinridge, who was already heavily engaged, he instead moved too far to the left, and his units milled about getting organized for some time before committing to battle. Rather than pushing back Breckinridge's command, his three divisions stormed the heavily defended ramparts held by Major General

John M. Palmer's 2nd Division (Major General Thomas L. Crittenden's XXI Corps), but they were thrown back with very heavy losses.

This piecemeal advance of regiments and brigades continued on down to the left of Polk's command, but while inflicting heavy casualties on the Union defenders, it proved unable to bring enough force at any one point to break the strong line of emplacements. Throughout the morning, Thomas shifted his units around to meet each newly developing threat, and so far Polk's tactics had not been able to counter this.

At about 10 a.m. Captain Kellogg of Thomas's staff was riding from his location to Rosecrans's headquarters. As he passed by Brannon's assigned position just north of the Brotherton farm, for some reason he failed to see the men in their entrenched position. Kellogg reported this to Rosecrans a few minutes later, who believed without confirmation that this meant that a hole existed in his lines and promptly issued orders for Brigadier General Thomas J. Wood to move his 1st Division from in front of the Brotherton cabin north to link up with Major General Joseph J. Reynold's 4th Division and close this supposed gap.

Rosecrans had been having just as many infighting problems with his top commanders as Bragg, and Wood

Brotherton cabin

happened to have been personally and profanely berated by Rosecrans for failure to promptly obey orders only an hour previous. Wood knew full well that Brannon was exactly where he was supposed to be, and despite the warnings of his own staff officer that such a move would be disastrous, he decided to follow his orders to the letter. Wood's division moved out at 11:15 a.m., opening up a nearly 1,500-foot-wide undefended gap in the lines in the process.

Just on the other side of the LaFayette road at the Brotherton cabin, the spot Wood's men had just left, stood 16,000 men of Longstreet's corps drawn up in line of battle.

Longstreet's Breakthrough

Longstreet's men had moved up into position during the night, and it took several hours to get them fed and resupplied for the coming assault. It was not until just before 11 a.m. that he was able to advise Bragg that he was fully in position and ready to step off. Bragg then gave the go-ahead, and Longstreet moved forward into one of the luckiest accidents in military history.

Fully expecting to run headlong into the same strongly defended line of emplacements that had tied up Polk all morning, Longstreet had arrayed his main assault force into a powerful, compact formation. Surviving elements of three divisions had been rearranged into three divisions of eight brigades total, commanded as a corps by Hood. Directly adjacent to the south stood another division commanded by Major General Thomas C. Hindman, with three brigades arrayed two forward, one in reserve. Another division (Brigadier General William Preston's) stood in reserve to Hindman's left and rear.

No more than five minutes after Wood's division moved out of its position, four brigades assaulted side by side in a 3,500-foot-wide front (from left to right, those of brigadier generals Arthur M. Manigault, Zach C. Deas, John S. Fulton [Johnson], and Evander McNair) across the LaFayette road, the right two

brigades smashing immediately through the just-abandoned breastworks. Raising their rebel yells, the leading regiments brushed aside what little resistance was left in the Union trenches and plunged ahead, passing on either side of the Brotherton cabin and heading for the tree line several hundred yards ahead at the double-quick.

The left two front brigades (Hindman's division) moved forward at the same time but ran into well-defended log breastworks after about 300 yards. Moving at the double-quick, Deas's and Manigault's brigades assaulted the works without faltering, driving Brigadier General William P. Carlin's 2nd Brigade (Davis's 1st Division, XX Corps) out of their trenches and back in wild disorder. For the Union, Major General Philip H. Sheridan's 3rd Division had also been shifting north just behind Carlin's position, but it was also driven off the field by the fury of Hindman's attack.

Brannon's men soon found themselves under attack from three sides and pulled back to the north. Wood's division, turning to go back to its original position, was pushed back also from the brunt of McNair's men advancing up the Dyer Road. One after another, Union regiments on line abandoned their positions under pressure from the massive Confederate attack until the right side of the line completely collapsed.

The rout of most units in this part of the field became complete. With his headquarters under threat of capture and a wild confusion of men and horses swirling around him running to the rear, Rosecrans himself joined the flight of roughly half his army (his headquarters was only about a half-mile directly behind the Brotherton cabin). Abandoning the field with him was his aid, Brigadier General, and later President, James A. Garfield. Rosecrans headed dejectedly back to Chattanooga, believing that Thomas's men had been routed as well and the field already lost. Garfield accompanied his commander north to the outskirts of Chattanooga and then he turned back to try to help save the rest of his army.

STAND AT SNODGRASS HILL

$\mathcal{T}$homas realized that with Rosecrans abandoning the field, all hope for victory was gone and the best he could do was fight a rear-guard action to save as much of the army as possible. Leaving his men still successfully holding off Polk in the entrenchments along the LaFayette road, he moved his headquarters and what was left of units from the right flank back to Snodgrass Hill. With the broken and shattered remains of 19 regiments and 2 artillery batteries, he set up a line of defense around the top of Snodgrass Hill and the adjoining Horseshoe Ridge under the direct command of Wood and Brannon. All were terribly low on ammunition, and no resupply or reinforcement was thought possible.

Fast on Thomas's heels, Longstreet knew if he could throw him off the small hill then he could cut up the Army of the Cumberland piecemeal as it fled back to Chattanooga. He sent Bragg an urgent request for all available reserves, so to finish the battle as quickly as possible. Bragg replied that there were no available reserves, as everyone on the field was now committed with either his corps or Polk's, and Polk's men were "too badly beaten" to be shifted to Longstreet.

About 1:30 p.m., Longstreet's attack opened up again with Brigadier General Joseph B. Kershaw's division (McLaw's) attacking up the slope of Snodgrass Hill from the southeast. His force nearly gained the crest of the hill before being violently thrown back. Kershaw was followed in rapid succession by a continuous series of assaults all along Snodgrass Hill and Horseshoe Ridge, each one being beaten back with increasingly heavy casualties on both sides.

About 3:30 p.m., with Longstreet's assaults nearly piercing his lines at several points and his line of men becoming dangerously low, Thomas turned to look to the north and his line of retreat, wondering if the time had come to leave. Just then he spotted a column of infantry heading his way. Knowing that there were no reserves that could be sent his way, he prepared what defense against them that he could hastily muster, when

their colors finally caught the breeze. It was Major General Gordon Granger with two brigades of his reserve corps, coming up from their position at Rossville, Georgia. Granger had observed Longstreet's men piling into Thomas, and in a great fury he violated his specific orders from Rosecrans and moved some of his reserves up to relieve Thomas's beleaguered post.

Going immediately into action, they shared the ammunition they had brought with Wood's and Brannon's men and jumped into the line of entrenchments just in time to meet another Confederate assault. It, too, was beaten back, along with the next, and the next. As sunset approached, almost everyone along the Union line had completely run out of ammunition, and the Confederates were massing for another assault. Granger gave the order to fix bayonets.

Three more assaults were thrown back at the very crest of the hill in fierce hand-to-hand combat. At 5:15 p.m., in the midst of yet another Confederate attack, Thomas received word from his absent commander Rosecrans, now safely in Chattanooga, for him to take charge of remaining forces and move them in a "threatening" manner to Rossville. He immediately passed the word along to the other commanders and made preparations to pull out at sunset.

Just as the sun was setting and Thomas's men started to pull out of their positions, another strong Confederate charge sent Longstreet's men up over the crest of both Snodgrass Hill and Horseshoe Ridge, into the midst of the retreating regiments. Massive confusion erupted, with many whole Union companies and regiments being made prisoner and others managing to slip away without harm. Their men exhausted but with "their dander up," Longstreet and Polk both begged permission to chase after the retreating Union Army, but Bragg refused.

Terribly shaken by his own severe casualties and typically fretting over what he should do next, Bragg instead did nothing. Thomas slipped away unmolested back to Rossville with the remnants of his command, and Rosecrans began organizing his shattered army within the strong fortifications of Chattanooga. Not until September 22 did Bragg finally move the Army of Tennessee up to Missionary Ridge overlooking Chattanooga, only to find it was far too late to finish what had started off so well.

THE COST OF THE BATTLE

*T*he Angel of Death was ever present during the two days of vicious fighting. Chickamauga was one of the bloodiest battles of the entire war, with more than 16,000 casualties among the 58,000 Union soldiers and 18,000 casualties among the 66,000 Confederate troops. Only the three days at Gettysburg produced a higher casualty figure. Dozens of officers on both sides were killed in the close fighting, including one Union and three Confederate generals.

Most of the dead were buried in unmarked trenches dotted around the battle areas, but one private lies today in the only marked grave on the battlefield. John Ingram, who had lived with his family in this area before the war, was a close friend of the Reed family, whose house stood nearby. Finding his body among his fellow slain of the 1st Georgia Infantry Battalion, they buried him near where he fell and maintained his grave for many years.

The Union Army was terribly affected by their defeat here, but in their despair they found a true hero. Thomas's efforts were widely publicized by Northern newspapers desperate for some good news from Chickamauga; they dubbed him the "Rock of Chickamauga" for his stand at Snodgrass Hill. Rosecrans fared less well, relieved of his command soon after for his continued displays of sheer incompetence in favor of Thomas.

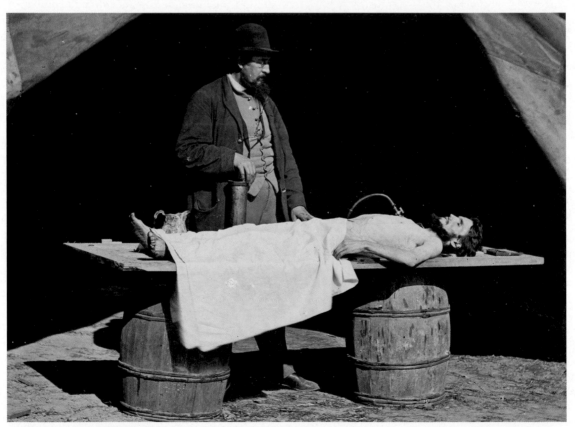

Embalming surgeon at work on soldier's body

POINTS OF INTEREST

The Chickamauga and Chattanooga
National Military Park
Fort Oglethorpe, GA
(706) 866-9241
www.nps.gov/chch

Today the Chickamauga portion of the Chickamauga and Chattanooga National Military Park is one of the best-preserved and -marked battlefields of the war. Operated by the National Park Service, this was the first and largest of four parks established between 1890 and 1899 by Congress (the others being Shiloh, Gettysburg, and Vicksburg), largely as a result of efforts by brigadier generals Henry Van Ness Boynton and Ferdinand Van Derveer, veterans of the Union Army of the Cumberland. This park was officially dedicated in a three-day ceremony starting on September 18, 1895, the 32nd anniversary of the battle. Nearly all the 1,400-plus signs and monuments on the 5,500-acre park were personally located by Boynton and other veterans of the battle.

At the time of the dedication, very little had changed in these fields since the great battle, so little restoration work was required outside of clearing undergrowth and new forests. The National Park Service has done a superb job in maintaining the area, with improvements added to accommodate increasing numbers of tourists and to better interpret the action, while not detracting from the original look and feel of the grounds.

Just inside the north main gate is a large and well-appointed visitor center that houses a small collection of paintings and general artifacts, an excellent bookstore, and very informative displays on the battle. A special feature is one wing devoted to the Fuller Collection of American Military Shoulder Arms, a donated 335-piece collection of infantry small arms centering on Civil War pieces. A 150-seat multimedia theater presents a dramatic 23-minute film about the battle at Chickamauga and the subsequent establishment of Chattanooga National Military Park. There is no admission charge for the film, and it is shown at the top of the hour year-round. Outside the newer portion of the restored and renovated 1935 building is a well-presented collection of the major types of artillery used during the battle.

The park is quite large, and it will take several visits to study the battle in real detail, but a well-marked, eight-stop, 7-mile auto tour will take you to most of the significant areas in two to three hours—depending, of course, on how often you pop out to read markers and view the monuments! A two-hour audiotape-guided tour is also available from the bookstore. Be sure to stop by the information desk and ask for a map of the tour.

For the serious student of military history, this place is absolute nirvana. There are about 700 cast-iron markers dotting the fields and woods, detailing exactly who fought at that point and what they did. Blue-lettered signs detail Union movements; the red-lettered ones detail Confederate movements. Small cast-iron signs mark houses that stood during the battle, small piles of cannonballs mark army and corps headquarters sites, and eight large pyramids of cannonballs mark the deaths of brigade commanders. In addition, more than 600 monuments and 250 cannon mark other significant sites. Quite a few sites throughout the battlefield feature modern maps, photos, and even audio descriptions of the events that transpired. Miles of hiking trails wind all through the woods; maps and guides are available from the information desk in the visitor center.

An interesting note is the number of monuments with acorns as part of their design. These indicate units and positions of Thomas's XIV Corps, which "stood like an oak tree" atop Snodgrass Hill.

Be aware that a great deal of action occurred on either side of the LaFayette road, which is the old US 27 today. A modern "bypass" highway has reduced traffic levels inside the park. Please also be aware that the entire battlefield is for all practical purposes a graveyard. The standard practice throughout the Civil War was to bury the dead either where they fell or very close by, and here they were buried in shallow mass trenches that were never marked. No one knows where these graves are located, so please tread lightly.

Admission to the Chickamauga battlefield and Cravens House is free. There is a small entrance fee to Lookout Mountain Battlefield at the Point Park unit. The park is open between sunrise and sunset.

ACCOMMODATIONS

Hotels and motels are available in limited quantity in Fort Oglethorpe, in Chattanooga to the north, and scattered all along I-75. For a central spot to tour both the Chattanooga and Atlanta campaigns, we suggest you stay in or near Dalton, east off I-75 at exits 333 and 336. For more information on Dalton, visit www.daltoncvb.com.

There is one very interesting hostelry we can highly recommend here—a former headquarters and hospital now open as a bed-and-breakfast.

Gordon-Lee Mansion B&B $$–$$$
217 Cove Rd.
Chickamauga, GA
(706) 375-4728
(800) 487-4728
www.fhc.org/gordon-lee

One of the very few period structures on the battlefield itself that survived the war is in the adjacent Chickamauga Village. Used as Rosecrans's headquarters just before the battle, it became the center of seven large Union hospitals on its grounds during the battle. Some of the downstairs rooms were used for surgery, with wagons placed just under the windows for amputated limbs to be thrown onto. Originally built in 1847 by James Gordon, it is open now as a bed-and-breakfast.

RESTAURANTS

Both US 27 and GA 2 immediately outside the north gate of the park have just about any type of fast food you may care for; for finer dining, travel US 27 to Chattanooga 20 miles north. Check at the Chattanooga Visitor Center at 2 Broad St. (follow the signs to the Tennessee Aquarium; it is directly adjacent; www.chattanoogafun.com) for suggestions and directions.

DAY TRIPS

We strongly recommend that you follow your visit to Chickamauga with one to Chattanooga to see where these actions finally ended. See the chapter on Chattanooga for a full description of sites and directions.

Close by to the east is where the Atlanta Campaign of 1864 started, and we recommend a visit to Dalton, Rocky Face Ridge, and Resaca, all well within an hour's drive. Please see the next chapter for details and directions.

Dalton to Jonesboro:
The Atlanta Campaign

Darley.

In the early spring of 1864, after three years of increasingly bitter fighting throughout the Southern states, Major General William Tecumseh Sherman saw that Georgia, and Atlanta specifically, held the key for the Union to bring the war to an end. There is a military axiom that states that while amateurs study strategy, generals study logistics as the crucial element of battle. General Robert E. Lee's forces in Virginia, the main focus of the war to that point, were able to hold the Union forces away from Richmond largely as a result of the supplies that flowed steadily up from the transportation and logistical center of Atlanta.

To complicate the picture, President Abraham Lincoln was facing a fierce election campaign against the former commander of the Union Army of the Potomac, Lieutenant General George B. McClellan, a War Democrat who nonetheless agreed with the Copperheads and Peace Democrats who saw the war as unwinnable and endless. There was a real possibility that if Sherman became bogged down in the same sort of stalemated combat that Lieutenant General Ulysses S. Grant faced in Virginia, the Northern Democrats who had pledged to end the war by peaceful means could very well take the White House that fall. "Peaceful means" meant armistice and, in reality, a Confederate victory.

was that this "scorched earth" policy would horrify and subdue the populace, who might otherwise engage his forces in guerrilla warfare or other harassing actions.

With General Ulysses S. Grant's blessings, Sherman set about building an overwhelming force from his headquarters in Chattanooga. Other Union commands were asked to supply what men they could spare, and by late April 1864, three grand armies with more than 98,000 men stood ready to invade Georgia. A steady stream of reinforcements brought this force to more than 112,000 by June.

General William Tecumseh Sherman

THE UNION COMMANDER

Sherman was a very modern general, not given to paroling prisoners or other gentlemanly considerations. He held a burning, very personal antipathy toward Georgia, which meshed well with his ideas about "total war." Literally years of seeing the words ATLANTA DEPOT stenciled on the sides of captured supply wagons and containers convinced him that the small city represented just as much a threat to his army as any military force. In his mind, the road to and from Atlanta needed not only to be taken but also laid to waste so that it could never again be used against the Union. An added benefit

---

THE CONFEDERATE COMMANDER

To oppose Sherman stood General Joseph Eggleston Johnston with but a single grand army of just two corps' strength, numbering just under 50,000 men. Reinforcements from Alabama, including Major General Leonidas K. Polk's entire corps and other commands not then under direct siege, bolstered his total strength to three corps, with just under 65,000 men by late June.

Johnston faced a very serious situation. His own combatant forces would be required to protect the railroads leading to and from Atlanta and keep their own supply lines intact, while being both undermanned and underequipped. One key factor lay in their favor: Johnston was a master of defensive strategy, rarely overwhelmingly successful in the advance but almost supernatural in his ability to know the exact moment to withdraw—just at the point where fierce resistance to the usually superior numbers had delayed or disrupted his enemy's plans the most, while keeping his own forces as intact as possible. Very unusual for a combat commander, he was also a humanist who deeply cared about his men and sought to minimize casualties even at the advantage of the enemy.

Johnston had one other serious disadvantage—the enmity of President Jefferson Davis, who blamed him for the loss of Vicksburg the previous summer, and all too readily listened to whomever had a complaint about his tactics.

Both commanders were highly experienced, experts in their own ultimate strategies, well versed in the latest military tactics developed over the previous three years, and very highly motivated to accomplish the goals that had been handed them. This was the campaign of the grand masters, unfolding almost like a dance, with each grand army moving in both opposition and concordance, swirling together in battle, only to separate intact and move with both purpose and grace to the next stage. Ironically, or perhaps not, after the war Sherman and Johnston became the best of friends.

THE OPENING BATTLES

A casual examination of a map makes it appear that Dalton, Georgia, was very nearly a natural fortress, but Sherman was no casual observer. He had explored most of this area while on detached duty in Marietta in 1844 (and not coincidentally unsuccessfully courting a certain Miss Cecilia Stovall of Etowah Heights near Allatoona at the time), and he had the remarkable ability to recall the lay of the land in great detail. He saw that Johnston's army could be trapped before the rocky ridge that was then their refuge if his own forces could get into the level, open ground between them and Atlanta. To this

end, he sent two of his armies to distract Johnston by a strong direct assault at the northernmost gap, Mill Creek, while his third army slipped through the southernmost gap, Snake Creek, and cut off Johnston's retreat route at Resaca.

Johnston similarly was not a casual observer; anticipating that Sherman would merely feint toward Dalton and then break south to try to cut his army off from the rail line to Atlanta, he ordered preparation of defensive works on "good ground" 17 miles south, just north and west of Resaca. In addition, he ordered preparation of a series of "military roads" between the two positions so that he could rapidly shuttle his troops into the prepared positions when Sherman made his move.

On May 8, 1864, having received notice from his cavalry scouts that Sherman's forces were on the march toward him, Johnston set Lieutenant General John Bell Hood's army corps in position to the north of Dalton, with his men arranged on top of the ridgeline and across Crow Valley to Pickett Top and "refused" southward over Hamilton Mountain to the direct north of Dalton. Hardee's army corps took up position to his left, just to the west of the city and directly on top of the impressive ridgeline. The Confederate line snaked along roughly 5 miles of hill and valley, forming an almost fishhook shape, with Rock Face Ridge as the shank and Dalton just below the point. A detached division guarded the railway just to the northeast of Dalton, and a smaller detachment took up post above Dug Gap, 2 miles below the city.

Sherman Moves Out

Major General George H. Thomas's Union Army of the Cumberland moved down the railway from Ringgold on May 8 and took up position just to the west of Mill Creek Gap, while Major General John M. Schofield's Army of the Ohio moved in from the north and took up position across Crow Valley. Aided by these highly visible movements and the screening ridgeline between them and the Confederate positions, Major General James Birdseye McPherson's Union Army of Tennessee quickly marched south through Snake Creek Gap.

Later that same day, two relatively small initial diversionary attacks were mounted by the Union troops against

Position of Union troops near Dalton, Georgia, May 8–9, 1864

the very strong Confederate position just south of Mill Creek Gap and against the weaker position at Dug Gap. The attack at Mill Creek nearly turned into a full-force battle, with part of Howard's IV Army Corps actually making it to the top of the northern end of the ridgeline before being violently repulsed. Both attacks were ultimately unsuccessful, though the attack at Dug Gap degenerated at one point into literal hand-to-hand combat—a comparatively rare event during the war—and featured the Confederates rolling large boulders down the steep mountainside toward the onrushing Union force.

Early in the morning of May 9, McPherson's men emerged from the gap and marched quickly toward Resaca, but the sight of Confederate cavalry and infantry troops along with the well-prepared roads gave him pause. Afraid that he would be caught on the open ground and unsure just how strong a force he was facing (actually less than one division of infantry and a few cavalry), McPherson became unusually cautious and elected to withdraw and entrench at the mouth of Snake Creek Gap. Sherman considered this act to be one of the major mistakes of the campaign; if McPherson had gone ahead and moved into Resaca at that time, Johnston would have been caught off guard and surrounded, and the campaign might well have been over for all practical purposes.

As McPherson made his move toward Snake Creek Gap, Thomas and Schofield both launched strong attacks on the Confederate line, reinforcing the previous day's assault directly against Mill Creek Gap and down the eastern slope of Rocky Face Ridge in Crow Valley. Multiple assaults over the next three days were successfully repulsed, leading Sherman to order a gradual withdrawal of forces from the fight, planning to follow McPherson's route down to Resaca. Johnston fully expected the move; by the afternoon of May 11, with the battle still fully under way, he began ordering his units to also gradually break off and march to their prepared positions outside Resaca. By midnight on the 12th, nearly all his army had broken off contact and moved south, staying intact as fighting units and taking all of their supplies with them. It was this sort of "fighting retreat" that Johnston specialized in, utilizing what resources he had to their maximum.

The Battlefield

Examination of this terrain shows the two weaknesses in Johnston's defensive position: First, his lines were stretched between the Union lines and the Oostanaula River, making a hasty withdrawal nearly impossible. Second, the rail line he had to defend lay nearly underfoot and all along the Confederate line, again limiting his chances for tactical maneuver. To his advantage was a "tight" line of battle, with his forces in proximity and the two flanks well placed directly on the banks of the river.

Sherman placed his forces in a semicircle anchored by the river on the right and curving around to face the northernmost Confederates directly. His position had little direct advantage over the Confederate line but was built up quickly by units traveling through Snake Creek Gap from the Dalton area.

Johnston's plan to defend the river and rail line from heavily fortified positions was clear, but Sherman's intent was less so. Starting early on the afternoon of May 13, uncoordinated and seemingly random attacks were made against the Confederate left, right, center, and the right again on the morning of the 15th. Most of these assaults were slowed and their lines broken up by the incredibly rough terrain immediately before the Confederate lines. Two divisions, Brigadier General Henry M. Judah's 2nd (Major General John M. Schofield's XXIII Army Corps) and Brigadier General Absalom Baird's 3rd (Palmer's XIV Army Corps) were involved in a three-corps'-strength attack on the afternoon of May 14 on the "bend" of the Confederate line. The two divisions were nearly annihilated by coordinated artillery and long-range rifle fire before they could even get their men together through the muck, losing more than 600 in a few minutes' time. Judah was kicked out of the army four days later for his alleged incompetence during the battle.

The Union assaults were ultimately unsuccessful in much more than getting quite a few of their own men killed and failing to push back the Confederate line at all. Several divisions of Hood's army corps stepped out in the late afternoon of May 15 to counterattack the Union left but were withdrawn after Johnston learned of the only real Union success of the battle. Brigadier General Thomas W. Sweeney's 2nd Division (of Major General Grenville M. Dodge's XVI Army Corps) had crossed the Oostanaula River a few miles south at Lay's Ferry and threatened to cut the rail line and the Confederate line of retreat. Within hours Johnston evacuated his forces intact across the river and marched south toward Cassville, destroying all the bridges as soon as his forces made it across. The last, the railroad bridge just below Resaca, was set afire at 3:30 a.m.

✶

THE RETREAT TO THE ETOWAH

Johnston, ever the wily strategist, came up with a unique plan while pulling back from Resaca on the night of May 15: to send Hardee's army corps with most of the supply wagons and ambulances straight through Adairsville to Kingston, 15 miles down the main road, while sending Hood's and Polk's army corps down a little-used route to the small town of Cassville, just 10 miles away. To give Hardee a little more time to ensure the safety of the supply train, Major General Ben F. Cheatham's division was placed across the road about 3 miles north of Adairsville. Hood and Polk were ordered to march rapidly and "tightly," to give the appearance that only a small force had passed down their path, and to be ready to launch a sudden counterattack when the unsuspecting Union forces appeared.

Cassville

Sherman followed Johnston south, delayed by the long river crossings necessary for his large force and by an almost comical spat between major generals Joseph Hooker and Schofield over which one had the right-of-way on the narrow roads. The Union forces had not paused to regroup after taking the Resaca battle-ground and headed south with McPherson's Army of Tennessee wide to the Union right, Thomas's Army of the Cumberland marching straight down the railway, and Schofield's Army of the Ohio (also known as and consisting only of the XXIII Army Corps) wide to the left. Expecting Johnston to make a stand at Adairsville, he ordered his widely separated columns to close together just north of the small crossroads town. The large Union force arrived in Adairsville after a brief but spirited skirmish with Cheatham's division on the morning of May 18.

Sherman was apparently deceived by the Confederate diversionary tactic. Eager to engage Johnston before the Confederate force reached a good defensive ground south of the Etowah River, he hastily pushed all his units except Hooker's XX and Schofield's XXIII Army Corps down the single road to Kingston. These two corps were ordered down the road to Cassville to protect the flank of the main Union column.

Just to the west of the main Union line of advance, a single infantry division commanded by Brigadier General Jefferson C. Davis (the 2nd Division, Union XIV Army Corps) and supported by Brigadier General Kenner Garrard's 2nd Cavalry Division marched in and captured the important industrial center of Rome on May 18 after a one-day battle with Major General Samuel G. French's Confederate division. Johnston's willingness to give up Rome without much of a fight, and in effect, most of northwest Georgia and northeastern Alabama, in order to preserve his fighting force, would later be used as "evidence" of his alleged incompetence.

At Cassville, Johnston ordered Polk to set his corps across the road about a half-mile northeast of the town square, with Hood's corps positioned about 1 mile east and parallel to the road, so as to hit the Union flank as they approached. On the morning of May 19, just as Schofield's corps was walking into the trap, a small unit of Union cavalry led by Brigadier General Edward M. McCook stumbled into Hood's troops from the east, and a brief skirmish erupted. Fearful that McCook was supported by infantry columns, Hood suddenly, and against orders, pulled back from his ambush position to reposition facing east, to gain support from Polk's right. Johnston soon felt that the chance for surprise was lost and ordered both corps to a low range of hills southeast of the town before a full-force battle could develop.

Hood defended his overreaction to the end of his life, insisting that he had infantry to his rear and that he would have been unable to launch his attack on the main column of Union troops on the Cassville road. Surprisingly enough, he was partly correct; close behind McCook were two brigades of Union infantry supported by a single battery of horse artillery wandering around lost, looking for a road leading into the east side of Cassville when they ran into the rear column of Hood's corps.

On the Confederate left, Hardee put up stiff resistance against the massed Union forces near Kingston, but shortly after the Cassville disaster, and at the urging of Hood and Polk, Johnston ordered all forces to disengage and withdraw south of the Etowah River into the Allatoona Mountains. He finally halted about 11 miles southeast of Cassville and set up a strong defensive position around the railroad gap at Allatoona Pass, just northwest of the small town of Acworth. As usual, Johnston ordered the railroad bridge across the Etowah burned as they retreated. Sherman moved in and occupied Cassville and Kingston, giving his men a few days to rest while he studied the ground ahead.

THE APPROACH TO DALLAS

*S*herman had ridden the area around Allatoona extensively as a young officer assigned to Marietta, and he knew the potential for making the gap into a natural fortress. Changing his usual frontal assault tactics, he abandoned his line of march straight down the railroad and moved westward toward the small town of Dallas. It is not clear whether he was trying to pull Johnston behind him into more open terrain (doubtful) or whether he was trying to take a more western approach into Atlanta. The real danger for Sherman was that by abandoning the railroad he was lengthening his own supply column, making it more vulnerable to a rear attack by Johnston's troops and cavalry.

Ordered up and out by buglers on the morning of May 22, the three grand Union armies moved out of camp at Cassville and Kingston in their usual three columns. Thomas and Schofield headed nearly due south while McPherson swung far to the right in

order to eventually turn and approach Dallas from due west. The huge columns of massed Union infantry in a front nearly 20 miles wide were hard to conceal, and the move west was soon discovered by scouts from Major General Joseph Wheeler's cavalry corps. By the afternoon of May 23, Johnston ordered Hardee to a good defensive ground just east of Dallas and Polk to a tiny crossroads nearby called New Hope (some maps label it New Hope Church). Hood remained entrenched at Allatoona Gap overnight and was then ordered to New Hope when Johnston realized that all the Union forces were headed toward Dallas. On his arrival, Polk shifted his men slightly to the west, tying in with Hardee and forming a strong defensive line nearly 4 miles long from directly south of Dallas to 1 mile east of New Hope in the vicinity of a small community called Pickett's Mill.

THE BATTLE OF
NEW HOPE CHURCH

*H*ood settled into line just before the forward Union skirmishers and scouts came into view. For the South, Major General Carter L. Stevenson's division set up on the right, Major General Thomas C. Hindman's division in the slightly higher ground on the left, and Major General Alexander P. Stewart's division deployed directly in front of the small log New Hope Church in the center. Just before 10 a.m. on May 25, Confederate skirmishers about a mile in front of their own lines encountered the forward elements of Hooker's XX Army Corps rapidly marching toward New Hope. They attempted to burn a bridge over Pumpkinvine Creek to set up a delaying action, but they were quickly overrun by Brigadier General John W. Geary's 2nd (Union) Division.

Warned that action was imminent, Stewart deployed his men in line astride the crossroads, ordering them to dig in as rapidly as possible. Stovall's Georgia Brigade was positioned on an open hilltop in the midst of the church's graveyard and was unable or unwilling to dig in at all, but Brigadier General Henry D. Clayton's and Brigadier General Alpheus Baker's Alabama Brigades in the center and right of the line threw up hasty but strong works of felled trees and earthen embankments. Sixteen guns from Captain McDonald Oliver's Eufaula Alabama Battery and Captain Charles E. Fenner's Louisiana Battery were massed within Stewart's roughly half-mile front.

Sherman ordered Hooker to push through what he believed was a small force and march directly to Dallas, remarking, "There haven't been twenty rebels there today." Just before 4 p.m. a severe thunderstorm blew in over the battleground. Marching steadily on through the mounting wind and pounding thunder came Geary's 2nd Division, with Major General Daniel Butterfield's 3rd Division to his left and Brigadier General Alpheus S. Williams's 1st Division on his right, all spread across a half-mile front in column formation and bearing down directly on the massed Confederate front of Stewart's division. The natural earth- and timber works, combined with the very thick underbrush, served to conceal the strength of the Confederate line from the Union attackers.

Just after 5 p.m., as Geary's skirmishers drove back Hood's, Union buglers sounded out the call to go forward double-quick. Stumbling and falling through the thick brush and unable to see what lay ahead, the men from Ohio, Pennsylvania, and New York hoped to brush straight through what they believed was a weak line of Confederate militiamen and detached infantry brigades. Just as the monsoon-force rains began, Williams's men broke out of the thickest part of the woods and rushed straight for the Confederate line.

Stewart had wisely ordered the artillery to load with double canister and positioned his 4,000 men nearly shoulder to shoulder on a very tight front, anticipating quite accurately that Hooker would be packed in heavy infantry formations on his approach. As lightning crackled all around and sheets of rain poured down, the shouting mass of more than 16,000 blue-coated infantry burst into sight less than 100 feet in front of his lines. Immediately the Confederate line opened up and disappeared again in a thick cloud of bluish-gray rifle and cannon smoke. Williams's men took the brunt of the concentrated fire, losing most of his more than 800 casualties in the first 10 minutes of battle.

For more than three hours this one-sided slaughter went on into the dark and stormy evening. Geary, Butterfield, and Williams all ordered assault after assault, trying to break through what was more and more obviously the main Confederate Army line, only to be thrown back each time by murderous artillery and rifle fire. Stewart's Confederate forces started running out of ammunition, the 60-round-per-man standard issue being depleted in as little as 30 minutes in some cases. Stewart brought his reserve forces in line primarily for their ammunition supply, and runners searched the wounded and dead for any extra cartridges. The Union's Hooker finally admitted defeat at about 7:30 p.m., pulling his men back a short distance to dig in for the night, while rebel yells and catcalls greeted their retreat.

Throughout the long night, as Union men dug in with shovels, bayonets, tin cups, or bare hands, sporadic rifle and artillery fire broke out, but no further assaults by either side were mounted. Hooker's command had lost more than 1,600 men in the short fight (most references back up this figure, but one source claims fewer than 700), while Confederate losses amounted to "between 300 and 400" as reported by Stewart. One bitter Union infantryman remarked that Hooker had sent them into a "hell hole"; the name sticks as a common reference to the brutal fight there and at Pickett's Mill.

PICKETT'S MILL

*A*fter the pasting he received at New Hope Church, Sherman returned to his standard tactic of rapid flanking maneuvers, and ordered three divisions under the direct command of Howard to the far left in an attempt to turn the Confederate right. Johnston soon learned of the flanking attempt and ordered two divisions to shift to the right of Hood's line, covering the probable Union line of attack. To the far right of the newly extended Confederate line was one of Johnston's best, Major General Patrick R.

Cleburne's division, which took up position on a hilltop overlooking Pickett's Mill.

Although his scouts reported fresh earthworks and Howard himself rode forward and observed gray-uniformed troops reinforcing them on the hill before them, the Union commander was somehow convinced that he had reached the flank, or rear, of the Confederate line of battle and possibly believed that only a small picket outpost was entrenching. His uncertainty was obvious in a message sent at about 3:30 p.m.: "I am now turning the enemy's right flank, I think." Just after noon on May 27, Howard brought his three divisions in line of attack on a hilltop just north of the small mill community, again forming the men into the same narrow, deep, heavy infantry formations that had failed so miserably two days earlier at New Hope Church.

At this point, the Confederate line curved to the east following the ridgeline atop a low rounded hill overlooking a steep, densely overgrown ravine. As the battle unfolded, two brigades of Cleburne's force were shifted to the far right of the line, refusing at right angles to the line so as to prevent any possibility of being flanked.

At 4:30 p.m. the Union line, or at least most of them, stepped off into the thick, entangling underbrush. There were very serious communication and land navigation problems, and one brigade ended up marching completely away from the growing sounds of battle "to get rations." That particular brigade's commander, Brigadier General Nathaniel McLean of Kentucky, was a political enemy of Howard's, and on that day chose a particularly poor way of demonstrating his contempt.

Howard's leading brigade, commanded by Brigadier General William B. Hazen's 2nd Brigade (of Brigadier General Thomas J. Wood's 3rd Division, Howard's IV Army Corps), easily drove away the Confederate pickets and moved into the ravine. The growth was so thick that the colors had to be encased to prevent them from being torn to pieces, and Hazen was forced to resort to his compass to keep moving in the right direction. Emerging suddenly in an open field, his troops first encountered a weak skirmish line of about a thousand dismounted cavalrymen from Brigadier General John Kelly's and Brigadier General William Hume's Confederate cavalry divisions, whom they mistook for unentrenched infantry. Steadily overpowering the cavalrymen, Hazen's men rushed cheering across the open

ground upward to what they thought was an undefended rocky ridgeline. Just before gaining the heights, Brigadier General Hiram M. Granbury's Texas Brigade suddenly appeared in view and began pouring a galling fire into the face of the onrushing Union line.

Hazen's men kept up the pressure, although suffering appalling casualties from a two-gun battery to their right at the point of the ravine (part of Captain Thomas J. Key's Arkansas Battery) and from two more regiments rushing in to support Granbury, Colonel George Baucum's 8th/19th Arkansas Consolidated Regiment to his left and Brigadier General Mark P. Lowrey's Alabama-Mississippi Brigade to his right. Hazen managed to stay in the fight for about 50 minutes before being forced to withdraw, leaving his more than 500 wounded and dead in place in the open ravine.

As Hazen withdrew, Colonel William H. Gibson's 1st Brigade advanced over nearly the same ground and met the same fate. Far from hitting a weakened Confederate line, as Brigadier General Thomas J. Wood (3rd Division commander) had hoped, Gibson's men advanced as far as the Confederate line itself before being thrown violently back. Roughly an hour of combat resulted in nothing more than an additional 687 Union casualties. Another brigade, Colonel Frederick Knefler's 3rd, was sent in at about 6:30 p.m. in order to cover Gibson's retreat and to recover as many wounded as possible. They too were subjected to intense, nearly point-blank fire from the Confederate positions as soon as they entered the entangled ravine and withdrew in short order.

The major assaults ended by 7 p.m., but occasional firefights erupted until 10 p.m., when Granbury was ordered to "clear his front." The Texans fixed bayonets and, with wild rebel yells, charged forward into the darkened ravine, killing or capturing many of the remaining Union troops. The remaining Union troops either "skedaddled" or "retreated in good order, with no pursuit [by the Texans] even being attempted," depending on whose account you read. Both sides encamped in place for the night after the firing died down at about 11 p.m., their attention still fixed on the body-strewn battleground eerily lit by dead pine trees set afire during the hot exchange.

Union losses for the day's action totaled 1,689 killed, wounded, captured, or missing, while Cleburne reported only 398 killed or wounded. This failed action so upset Sherman that he apparently completely "forgot" it in both his official report and his postwar memoirs.

The following day, May 28, 1864, Sherman finally decided that this westward flanking movement was getting him nowhere quick. Short on rations, his lines stretched nearly to the breaking point, trying to hold the entire 5-mile line of battle from south of Dallas to northeast of Pickett's Mill, as well as the lines of communication necessary to protect their supply line back to the railroad north of Allatoona. He ordered a gradual shifting motion of the line east toward Kennesaw and Marietta and sent his cavalry to capture Allatoona Gap itself. Johnston soon learned of this movement and ordered an attack on the Union right, straight toward Dallas itself, but was repulsed with no positive effects on the Union movement and at the cost of more than 600 casualties.

Lost Mountain

THE KENNESAW LINE

*B*y the first of June, Sherman had begun massing his armies at Big Shanty (now called Kennesaw) and made preparations to strike straight for the Chattahoochee River. In between stood the twin peaks of Kennesaw Mountain and Johnston's entire combat force. Johnston initially arranged his 65,000 troops in a thin, 10-mile-long line of battle that stretched from Brushy Mountain on the east to Lost Mountain on the west, about 3 miles northwest of Kennesaw Mountain itself. This line was known as both the Lost Mountain and First Kennesaw line.

In the late morning of June 14, 1864, Johnston, accompanied by Hardee, Polk, and several other general officers, climbed to the crest of Pine Mountain, in the rough center of the line. While observing the Union positions as related to their own lines, they were spotted by a Union artillery battery posted less than a half-mile away, which immediately opened fire. The first round scattered the distinguished crowd; poor old, fat, and slow General

Leonidas K. Polk, the Louisiana Episcopalian bishop, was struck directly in the chest by the second Parrott shot and died instantly.

After heavy attacks on June 14, 15, and 17, Johnston realized his men were spread much too thinly and withdrew 2 miles to the southeast quietly during the pitch-black night and heavy rains of June 18. There he heavily entrenched from the railroad to the right, up across Kennesaw Mountain, Little Kennesaw Mountain, and Pigeon Hill, and left over a low ridge later known as Cheatham Hill. This strong, compact 6-mile-long Kennesaw or Second Kennesaw line was reinforced by artillery batteries placed on the heights, and cavalry placed on both flanks. One Union officer noted that the natural barricade of the mountain seemed purposefully made to stop any attacking army. The sides facing the Union troops were steep and boulder-strewn, and most of the rest was covered with thick scrub brush. Confederate engineers cleared the peaks of trees and brush to serve as signal and artillery stations. The main entrenchments were dug at the proper military crests, with a series of screening entrenchments and rifle pits before them at the mountain base.

Cannon were hauled by hand up the steep slopes, 100 men per gun pulling, tugging, and cursing all the way. Eventually, two four-gun batteries were established on Pigeon Hill, one four-gun battery on the north end of Big Kennesaw (nearest present-day US 41), another nearly on the peak, and nine guns atop

Little Kennesaw. Before they were even completely emplaced, firing erupted between them and newly arriving Union batteries.

As soon as each of his Union forces moved up into position, Sherman ordered constant probing and skirmish actions, trying to keep the pressure on until a weakness was revealed. One spot in the Kennesaw line, a small hilltop called Bald Knob, lay just outside the main Confederate defensive position between Pigeon and Cheatham Hills, held by a Kentucky unit of the Orphan Brigade, famous for its ferocity in battle, perhaps because their home state was held by the Union and they were unable to return there on leave throughout the war. After repeated assaults throughout much of the morning and early afternoon of June 20, two brigades of Major General David S. Stanley's 1st Division (Howard's IV Army Corps, Union Army) managed to wrest control of the small outpost. In a rather bizarre move, later that evening, one brigade was withdrawn when its commander thought that a relieving force had arrived. The Kentuckians quickly realized what had happened and moved back into their old positions, just as the Union troops realized their mistake and hastened back to the same spot. Just as the Union men jumped down into the trenches, the Kentuckians popped up and began shooting at point-blank range. A few minutes of swirling, confused carnage, which resulted in possibly more than one instance of "friendly fire" casualties, and the hill was left in Confederate control once again.

Johnston's near-supernatural ability to "read" Sherman's intentions came to his aid once again; through a pounding thunderstorm on the night of June 21, Hood's entire corps marched from the far right of the line to the far left, consolidating and entrenching across the path of the approaching Union troops on Powder Springs Road.

As the Union troops prodded and advanced down that road on the afternoon of June 22, the South's Hood suddenly decided to abandon his fairly strong defensive position to risk it all on a full-force assault. Hindman's division into the north and Stevenson's division on the left suddenly burst out of the thick woods into an open plain near Kolb's Farm, heading straight into the massed fire of more than 40 Union artillery pieces. The attack gained nothing, falling apart before coming within rifle range of the hastily dug Union lines. The shattered remnants of Stevenson's division attempted to take refuge in a shallow creekbed, where they were continuously raked by artillery fire until able to pull back after dark.

This attack further strained relations between Hood and Johnston, which had not been very healthy to begin with. Johnston issued a sharp reprimand for attacking without orders, which Hood responded to with yet another letter to Jefferson Davis, complaining about the strategy being used. Strangely, reprimands were issued on the Union side as well, for Hooker reported that during the short battle "three entire corps are in front of us," Johnston's entire force strength at that time. Sherman was not amused by this report, and it didn't help that Hooker and Sherman got along no better than their Confederate counterparts.

THE FIGHT AT KOLB'S FARM

mpatient as ever, Sherman saw that his probing actions were gaining nothing, so once again he returned to his classic flanking moves. Hooker's XX and Schofield's XXIII Army Corps were both sent on a sweeping movement to the south of the Kennesaw line to attempt to gain Marietta and cut off the Confederate line of retreat.

ACTION ON THE MOUNTAIN

ith his probing actions indecisive and his flanking maneuver halted at Kolb's Farm, Sherman chose yet another tactic. Tiring of the way Johnston constantly slipped out of his flanking attacks, and possibly hoping to destroy the Confederate Army of Tennessee in one

Artist Alfred R. Waud's drawing of the bombardment on Kennesaw Mountain, June 27, 1864

Thomas chose to concentrate his attack against a salient in the Confederate line nearly 3 miles south of Pigeon Hill, later famous as the "Dead Angle." Believing that one mighty push would drive out the heavily entrenched Confederates of Cheatham's and Cleburne's divisions, he decided on the little-used heavy infantry formations. The five attacking brigades (from the Union right to left) were: Colonel John G. Mitchell's 2nd and Colonel Daniel McCook's 3rd—both of Davis's 2nd Division, XIV Corps; and Brigadier General Charles G. Harker's 3rd, Brigadier General George D. Wagner's 2nd, and Brigadier General Nathan Kimball's 1st—all of Brigadier General John Newton's 2nd Division, IV Corps). They spread out across a 200-yard front (1,500 to 2,000 yards was more normal) with about 10 yards between each brigade. The overwhelming fire from the Confederate line proved so intense that the 10-yard interval gradually closed until all five brigades ended up attacking as a single mass, 12 ranks deep. An absolute slaughter ensued as every artillery piece and rifle within range concentrated on the 1,000-yard front line. One Confederate observer atop Kennesaw Mountain mentioned that as the massed Union troops approached the entrenchments, they "seemed to melt away, or sink to the earth, to rise no more."

With so much fire coming within such a confined area, soon the dead leaves and underbrush were set afire, threatening to burn alive the wounded. Just to the right of the salient, Colonel William H. Martin of the South's 1st/15th Arkansas Regiments ran to the top of a breastwork and, waving a white flag, shouted that he was proposing a cease-fire while the fire was put out and the wounded moved. In what was surely a bizarre scene, Union and Confederates laid down their arms and worked side by side for a few minutes. Several reports mention that the Confederates "moved" whatever Union guns and ammunition they could get ahold of as well. With the fire out and the wounded safely moved, both sides returned to their weapons, and the slaughter renewed.

By nightfall, most Union units had been completely thrown back; those few left under some protection of the hilly terrain would stay within rock-throwing distance for the next six days and keep up a constant sniping harassment. Private Sam Watkins, a self-described "high-private" with the 1st/27th Tennessee Infantry Regiment

huge battle, he issued the order for a direct assault on the entrenchments of the Kennesaw line itself, to begin at 8 a.m. on June 27. McPherson was ordered to attack the southern side of the mountain, Thomas was ordered to attack south of the Dallas road in support of McPherson, and Schofield was directed to feint south of Kolb's Farm as a diversion.

At 9 a.m. on the hot morning of the 27th, three brigades of McPherson's corps stepped up onto the steep slopes of Pigeon Hill, straight into the rocky fortifications. Surprisingly, some made it far enough up the hill through increasingly heavy fire to engage in hand-to-hand combat atop the entrenchments before being forced back under heavy artillery fire. Union losses in this futile attack were more than 850, with Confederate losses described as "about 250."

(the Maury Grays) at the Dead Angle, described his feelings when the last Union attack of the day was finally repulsed:

> *I never saw so many broken-down and exhausted men in my life. I was as sick as a horse, and as wet with blood and sweat as I could be, and many of our men were vomiting with excessive fatigue, over-exhaustion and sunstroke; our tongues were parched and cracked for water, and our faces blackened with powder and smoke, and our dead and wounded were piled indiscriminately in the trenches. There was not a single man in the company who was not wounded or had holes shot through his hat and clothing.*

The only gain of the entire day's action, ironically, was Schofield's diversionary attack to the south, which managed to get between Johnston's line and the Chattahoochee River while the Confederate forces were distracted by the main attack. Sherman was enraged over the failure to break the Confederate lines, however, and seriously contemplated ordering further attacks the next day. Thomas brought him back to reality by informing him that "one or two more such assaults would use up this army." Sherman finally relented and reported in a cable to Washington that night that his attack had failed and that he had suffered "about 3,000

casualties." Several reports dispute this figure, placing it closer to 7,000 or even 7,500. Included in this number were Brigadier General Harker and Colonel McCook, both killed in the assault on the Dead Angle, along with the death or wounding of nine other Union brigade and regimental commanders at this small place. Confederate losses for the day were placed at just under 1,000.

THE CHATTAHOOCHEE RIVER LINE

After his stunning defeat at Kennesaw Mountain, Sherman required more than a week just to regroup and resupply his demoralized soldiers. On July 1 he abandoned for good his frontal assault tactics on entrenchments and planned another flanking maneuver to the south and east to try once again to bypass Johnston and gain Marietta. Once again, Johnston's scouts observed the huge army getting under way before any real progress could be made. With no real natural defensive barrier to help stop the numerically superior Union Army, Johnston decided to abandon Marietta and fall back across the wide, shallow Chattahoochee River, burning or destroying whatever supplies and equipment Sherman might find useful along the way.

General Sherman and his troops at Kennesaw Mountain

THE GEORGIA MILITIA ENTERS THE FIGHTING

By the afternoon of July 2, Johnston set up a new line of defense at the small town of Smyrna, just northwest of the Chattahoochee, while his main body crossed to the south bank. This line collapsed in less than a day of heavy skirmishing with forward elements of the Union line, and by the next afternoon Johnston pulled back to his last line of entrenchments north of the river.

Governor Joseph E. Brown of Georgia had repeatedly offered both his militia and his own "private army," the Georgia State Line, to Johnston for front-line service. Accepting them in May, just after the New Hope Church battle, both units had proven capable fighters in the line, although very unpolished. Private Sam Watkins gave a vivid description of their arrival:

> By way of grim jest, and a fitting burlesque to tragic scenes, or, rather, to the thing called "glorious war," old Joe Brown, then Governor of Georgia, sent in his militia. It was the richest picture of an army I ever saw . . . Every one was dressed in citizen's clothes, and the very best they had at that time. A few had double-barreled shotguns, but the majority had umbrellas and walking sticks, and nearly every one had on a duster, a flat-bosomed "biled" shirt, and a plug hat; and to make the thing more ridiculous, the dwarf and the giant were marching side by side; the knock-kneed by the side of the bow-legged; the driven-in by the side of the drawn-out; the pale and sallow dyspeptic, who looked like Alex. Stephens, and who seemed to have just been taken out of a chimney that smoked very badly, and whose diet was goobers and sweet potatoes, was placed beside the three hundred-pounder, who was dressed up to kill . . .

After failing to hold the line at nearby Smyrna, Johnston was desperate to get his forces intact across the Chattahoochee, into the northern fringes of Atlanta, and to escape the overpowering Union frontal assault. He ordered the few thousand men of the Georgia Militia under General Gustavus Smith to dig in on his left at hastily constructed trench lines on a steep hillside just below Smyrna, on the north bank of the Chattahoochee, near the small Nickajack Creek. This near-suicidal and expendable position directly confronted the full-corps–strength vanguard of Sherman's army. With the Union forces bearing down rapidly, the 1st Regiment of the Georgia State Line under Colonel Edward M. Galt was sent in to reinforce the line on July 4. Relieving the militia at the forward primary fighting

positions, the State Line troopers barely got into place before forward elements of Palmer's XIV Army Corps began their assault.

Palmer soon reported fierce resistance in this line, but Sherman was convinced that it represented a token rear-guard action while Johnston retreated across the river. Believing the line could be easily brushed aside, he ordered Palmer to "fiercely assault" the line with everything he had, nearly 20,000 men at that point. The total combat-effective manpower available to the State Line by this time was about 300, with the 2,000- to 4,000-strong Georgia Militia acting as reserves (most were not quite fit for even that duty) and one four-gun battery of artillery for support. Palmer's men assaulted and skirmished with the troopers all through the day of July 5 without result, until Sherman personally came up to reconnoiter.

Upon seeing the strength of the State Line's redoubts, he called off the attack, stating later that it represented "the best line of field entrenchments I have ever seen." Impressed with the fighting resistance of Joe Brown's Pets and worried that to continue the frontal attack would result in another disaster like Kennesaw Mountain, Sherman instead sent part of his army far to the left to cross the river at an unguarded site.

ROSWELL

*F*inding nearly all the ferries and pontoon bridges out due to the high water caused by weeks of heavy rains, and what bridges remaining either heavily defended or burned, Sherman was hard pressed to find a crossing that wouldn't result in losing most of his army in the muddy water.

Garrard's 2nd Division Cavalry (of Brigadier General Washington Elliott's Cavalry Corps, Schofield's XXIII Army Corps) rode about 15 miles to the north and quickly captured the small town of Roswell, overlooking the Chattahoochee River. He found the bridge there burned but identified several spots nearby where the river could be safely forded. He was ordered to keep watch for Confederate movements and to stay concealed until the main force arrived. With Major General George Stoneman's cavalry division ranging as far south as Sandtown, McPherson's corps feinting to the right, and Thomas's corps keeping the pressure on the river line, Schofield's corps quickly moved upriver on July 8 to find the best crossing site.

Roswell was a small but productive mill town, making uniforms, blankets, and other textile goods for the Confederacy. Even as word of approaching Union troops caused townspeople to leave in a panic, work continued in the mill. The wealthy and prominent Barrington King family, now headed at high speed away from the town, conferred the "ownership" of the property on the shoulders of one Theophilus Roche, a French citizen and relatively new employee of the mill. One story holds that Roche was in fact the mill's janitor. As the lead scouts of Garrard's cavalry approached, Roche ordered the Confederate national flag hauled down and replaced with the French tricolor.

Details on what happened next are poorly documented, but it is clear that this attempt to claim foreign ownership of what was obviously a Confederate-supporting mill failed to impress the Union officers on the scene. Claiming they were acting on direct orders from Sherman (a point somewhat in dispute), the mostly women and children employees of the mill were arrested as traitors and sent under guard of a cavalry attachment to Marietta, while the mill and associated buildings were burned to the ground. Underscoring what must have been a horribly frightening and humiliating action for the women, several sources quote the Union cavalrymen escorts commenting on the "fine good looks" of the Roswell women, as pointedly different from the "fearfully homely" women they had seen elsewhere in northern Georgia. Once at Marietta, these women and children were grouped with other evacuees from the destroyed mill town of New Manchester and placed on northbound trains, ending up in Ohio and Indiana. Some records claim these women were placed in Northern prison camps in those states, while other records claim that they were "dumped out by the side of the [railroad] tracks," while still other records indicate that Northern families ended up taking in most or all of them.

Sherman Crosses the Chattahoochee

By nightfall the entire division was across, and with the news of the Union Army on the south bank, Johnston decided his only recourse was to once again retreat. Abandoning the river line to Sherman, Johnston pulled his forces back south of Peachtree Creek, on the very doorstep of Atlanta itself. In a little more than 60 days, the hardened rebel force had been forced back from no less than eight strongly prepared defensive lines by Sherman's flanking movements and made to surrender all of northern Georgia.

Without further resistance to his river crossing, Sherman paused only long enough to rebuild pontoon and railroad bridges before striking south again. On July 11 McPherson was sent eastward toward Decatur and Stone Mountain with orders to cut the railway between Atlanta and Augusta. Sherman's greatest fear at this point was that Johnston would receive reinforcements by rail from Lee's Army of Northern Virginia. Thomas was sent south toward Peachtree Creek with Schofield marching just to his right, headed toward Buckhead.

Johnston carefully noted the Union approach and planned to wait until close contact was established and then to attack the gap between Thomas and Schofield before they were deployed for the fight. Before he could carry out this attack, Jefferson Davis fired Johnston in one of the worst decisions of the war. Late in the afternoon of July 17, Hood was promoted to general and given command of the entire Army of Tennessee. Just 33 years old and considered a hotheaded division-level commander who was already out of his league as high as the corps level, the move delighted no one more than Sherman. In his postwar memoirs he mentioned, "I was always anxious with Johnston at my front." He knew Hood was rash and prone to ordering ill-timed and poorly planned movements, and was anxious for him to do so before Atlanta. It would be much better to destroy the Confederate forces in the field and then easily take the vital transportation and supply center than to be forced to assault heavily fortified defenses.

Least happy of all were the Confederate soldiers, who had loved Johnston for his humane treatment of them and feared Hood would kill them all off in ill-considered battles. Private Sam Watkins said Johnston's removal was "like the successful gambler, flushed with continual winnings, who staked his all and lost. It was like the end of the Southern Confederacy."

✯

ADVANCE TO PEACHTREE CREEK

*T*he day after Hood took command, Union infantrymen of Palmer's XIV Army Corps advanced through heavy resistance by Wheeler's cavalry to the northern banks of Peachtree Creek, near Howell Mill Road. At just about the same time, Garrard's cavalry supported by McPherson's infantry reached the Georgia Railroad and captured the railroad depot at Stone Mountain, 15 miles east of Atlanta. On July 19 three brigades of Palmer's XIV Army Corps forced a crossing of Peachtree Creek toward Moore's Mill, followed by other crossings under fire by elements of Howard's IV Army Corps

near Peachtree Road and Hooker's XX Army Corps near Collier Road. By nightfall the Union forces formed a solid line of blue-coated infantry on the south banks of Peachtree Creek itself, facing due south toward the Confederate line arranged atop low hills about a half-mile away.

The Battle

Pleased with the progress of his subordinates, Sherman ordered Thomas to cross Peachtree Creek and engage Hood, Schofield to capture Decatur, and McPherson to advance toward Atlanta, tearing up the railroad tracks along the way. Obsessed with detail, Sherman sent word on exactly how he wanted the tracks torn up: "Pile the ties into shape for a bonfire, put the rails across and when red hot in the middle, let a man at each end twist the bar so that its surface becomes spiral." Hood had a reputation as a battlefield brawler, and he wasted little time going on the offensive. A general attack was ordered at about 1 p.m. on July 20, intended to drive the dug-in Union infantry back across the creek and as far as the banks of the Chattahoochee River. Before the attack could commence, Hood ordered the entire line to shift a little less than 1 mile to the east, to protect his right flank from counterattack. Despite the fact that

Federal picket just before the Battle of Atlanta, July 22, 1864

Sherman's men tearing up railroad tracks near Atlanta

this movement threw the whole line into disarray and caused a general confusion as to exactly where they were to advance, he ordered the attack to begin at 4 p.m.

At about 2:45 p.m., Major General William W. Loring's division (Stewart's corps) stepped off, almost immediately encountering Union infantry and mistakenly initiating battle action in the center of the line. Major General William B. Bates's division of Hardee's corps, ordered to begin the general assault from the extreme right of the Confederate lines, didn't actually move out until nearly a half-hour later. The rest of the 2-mile-long line followed in piecemeal, advancing more in small groups and masses than in well-formed lines, a result of the uneven terrain and thick underbrush.

The only real success of the entire assault was made by Brigadier General Thomas M. Scott's brigade (Stewart's corps) of mostly Alabama troops, who advanced through the Tanyard Branch and Collier Road vicinity, attacked, drove off, and captured the Union flag of Colonel Patrick H. Jones's 33rd New Jersey Infantry Regiment (Geary's 2nd Division, Hooker's XX Army Corps) as well as a four-gun artillery battery. Scott's men were soon forced to withdraw, as no other unit was able to break through to support them on either flank.

No other unit achieved even that modest of a success, and the entire attack was over with and all units back in their original positions by 6 that evening. The well-positioned Union forces had handed the advancing Confederates quite a mauling. Although the numbers engaged were fairly even—21,450 Union to 18,450 Confederate—casualties were much more one-sided: 1,780 Union to 4,800 Confederate. Hood's first outing as an army commander was an unqualified disaster.

To add insult to injury, shortly before noon on July 20, Union soldiers led by Captain Francis DeGress set up four 20-pounder Parrott rifles and soon began firing the first of thousands of artillery shells into the Gate City itself. The first shell exploded at the intersection of Ivy and East Ellis Streets, killing a young girl who had been walking with her parents past Frank P. Rice's lumber dealership on the northwest corner. Shelling continued for several weeks at the rate of one round every 15 minutes, more as a harassment and reminder of the siege conditions than as a real destruction attempt. The DeGress battery would soon be the very object and center of fighting for the city.

Death of General James B. McPherson at the Battle of Atlanta

THE BATTLE OF ATLANTA

*B*efore the fighting died down at Peachtree Creek, Sherman was massing his forces for the next assault. McPherson's three corps were set in motion down the Georgia Railroad to attack Atlanta from the east, while Thomas and Schofield were ordered to close up and keep as much pressure on the Confederates as possible. By late in the day on July 20, forward elements of Major General Frank P. Blair's XVII Army Corps had engaged Wheeler's dismounted cavalry on a small hilltop 2 miles to the east of Atlanta. Heavy combat erupted as the two lines collided, until the overwhelmed Southern cavalrymen withdrew about midnight.

Leggett's Hill

Realizing the tactical importance of a ridge known as Bald Hill, in the early morning of July 21, Blair sent in

Brigadier General Mortimer D. Leggett's 3rd Division and Brigadier General Giles A. Smith's 4th Division against Cleburne's division, which had replaced the decimated cavalrymen. Cleburne's men had spent the night reinforcing the hilltop position but were unable to stop the Union assault. The Confederates withdrew slightly and then spent most of the rest of the day attempting to retake the hill. While the battle raged on, Blair ordered up his artillery and set his guns into newly reversed entrenchments, bringing Atlanta itself within good artillery range for the first time. In honor of his heroics, the hilltop was renamed Leggett's Hill, a moniker that some maps still bear today.

The Night March through Atlanta

Hood had no intention of pursuing the same sort of well-planned-out, plodding, and slow retreat defense that Johnston utilized, and he saw an opportunity for offensive action against McPherson. Withdrawing Stewart's corps and the Georgia Militia to the strongly fortified positions in the outer ring of defenses around Atlanta, he ordered Hardee's corps on an all-night forced march. Moving due south down Peachtree Street through the middle of town (and panicking the civilians, who believed their entire army was deserting them), they swung eastward toward Decatur, attempting to get behind Blair's corps lines before moving north into the line of battle. Cleburne's division withdrew with some difficulty from the Leggett's Hill action and joined Hardee's march. At the same time, two divisions of Wheeler's cavalry were sent around the Union left flank to attempt a strike at their supply wagons in Decatur.

To the lowly infantryman, this brilliant plan must have lost some of its luster. Having been in action off and on for more than two months, they had pulled back time after time only to spend hours in backbreaking labor—digging in and reinforcing when they arrived at new positions, for "spades is trumps," as the men said. Then, after doing this again and again with inadequate rest and dwindling supplies, they were ordered up on the line of battle only to be violently thrown back with heavy losses. Within hours of battle once more the order was given to withdraw and now to go immediately into an all-night march. Without a doubt this was nearly

more than the poorly supplied, hungry, and thirsty men could endure.

Brigadier General Daniel C. Govan of Cleburne's division, Confederate Army, was equally unimpressed, deathly worried that "the loss of another night's rest was a heavy tax upon their powers of endurance." Hundreds of soldiers simply plopped down on the side of the road, unable to go any farther, until at last a two-hour rest was called. Hood intended for the attack to begin at daylight, but it became apparent that any possible attack could be launched no earlier than noon.

Unknown to the Confederates, McPherson was worried that they would attempt this exact movement and ordered his lines extended and turned to the south. Dodge's XVI Army Corps was ordered in to Blair's left, facing southeast and entrenching as had become the norm. At McPherson's urging, Blair's men heavily entrenched and blocked lanes of approach before them.

By the morning of July 22, Hardee's men had trudged down the McDonough Road south of Atlanta and then turned to the northeast on the Fayetteville Road toward Decatur. Still trying to make up time lost on the rest stops, Hardee ordered Cleburne's and Brigadier General George E. Maney's divisions to begin deploying to the left when they reached Bouldercrest Road (now Drive), while Bates's and Major General William H. T. Walker's divisions continued on up the road before turning left on what is today called Wilkinson Drive. Both of these moves into line were short of their original goals.

Presently running into a large millpond their guides had repeatedly warned them about, Walker's and Bates's divisions wandered around through the thick forest for nearly an hour, trying to sort themselves out and get into the line of battle. As Walker roundly cursed their guides, grumbling that they must be "traitors" to allow him to get himself in such a fix, he raised his field glasses to try to figure out his next move. A nearby Union picket spotted Walker and killed him with a single, well-aimed shot.

Fighting in East Atlanta

Walker's place was taken over by Brigadier General Hugh W. Mercer, and the planned dawn attack commenced after more confusion and shifting troops at about 12:15 p.m. On advancing to the planned line of departure near the present-day intersection of Memorial Drive and Clay Street, the Confederates discovered to their horror that, far from being in the Union rear, they were advancing straight into a heavily invested front-line position. Pressing forward under intense fire from Sweeney's 2nd Division (Dodge's XVI Army Corps), they were immediately raked by fire from two well-sited artillery positions: one six-gun, 12-pounder Napoleon battery (Lieutenant Andrew T. Blodgett's 1st Missouri Light Battery) and one six-gun, 3-inch ordnance rifle battery (Captain Jerome M. Burrows's 14th Ohio Light Battery, noted as being replaced in command by Lieutenant Seith M. Laird in a few accounts).

About 30 minutes later, Cleburne's and Maney's divisions launched their attack to the left of the ongoing fight, straight into the "bend" of the Union line held by Giles Smith's 4th Division (Blair's XVII Army Corps). This attack was much more successful, driving the Union line all the way north to Leggett's Hill and capturing an entire infantry regiment (Lieutenant Colonel Addison H. Sander's 16th Iowa) and eight artillery pieces.

McPherson had been eating lunch with his staff and corps commanders less than a mile away when he heard the sudden crash of artillery fire. He hastily mounted his horse and rode south with a small group of officers to check on the situation, pausing atop a nearby hill. From there he could see that Sweeney's division was holding up well, but he couldn't see the situation on the other end of the line. Striking out immediately for the spot between the two Confederate assaults, he realized that his line was not continuous in that area and quickly ordered up more troops to fill the gap. Riding through the unmanned gap toward Giles Smith's position, his party suddenly burst out of the heavy forest into a clearing, coming face-to-face with the advancing 5th Confederate Regiment (Captain Richard Beard's Tennessee). The Confederates called on him to surrender, but in an attempt to escape, he wheeled his horse around, raised his hat in salute, and galloped off toward the tree line. A single shot fired by Corporal Robert F. Coleman tore through McPherson's lungs, killing him instantly.

Hood finally realized that the Union left flank was engaged, not the rear as planned, and ordered Cheatham's corps out of the east Atlanta defense line and in to assault the entrenched Union main line. At

A marker on the spot where General McPherson was killed

the same time, Maney's division was ordered to break off and move to Cleburne's left, where they could support Cheatham's attack. Maney's division started their assault at about 3:30 p.m. Cheatham's corps moved out a half-hour later, possibly due to a confusion over orders. Once again Leggett's Hill was in the center of much of the action, but the repeated Confederate assaults failed to regain control of it.

The general assault found a weak spot at the Union position held by Brigadier General Joseph Lightburn's 2nd Brigade (Brigadier General Morgan L. Smith's 2nd Division, Logan's XV Army Corps). Brigadier General Arthur M. Manigault's brigade (of Cheatham's corps) led the rebel assault, pushing through the railroad cut (near the present-day Inman Park MARTA Station) and capturing the infamous DeGress's 1st Illinois Light Battery H, consisting of four 20-pounder Parrott rifles that had been cutting them to pieces for hours. They then turned left and scattered four Ohio regiments (the 47th, 54th, 37th, and 53rd, in turn). More Confederate units poured through the opening, capturing another two-gun artillery battery and forcing a total of four Union brigades to retreat from a now nearly half-mile-wide breakthrough.

Sherman, observing from his headquarters in the Augustus Hurt House a little less than a mile to the northwest, ordered Schofield to mass all his artillery (20 guns) at the Confederate breach and Logan to collect eight brigades to fill in the breach. Between the massed artillery and Logan's strong counterattack, the Confederates were soon forced back into their original positions at a heavy loss.

Wheeler's cavalry strike at Decatur met with more success, driving back two regiments of infantry and capturing 225 men and an artillery piece, but the troop was ordered back to the west to support Hardee in his attempt to capture or destroy the Union supply train, his main goal.

The day was another unqualified disaster for the Confederate Army of Tennessee. Total casualties ran more than 5,000 (Sherman claimed more than 8,000, but this was no doubt exaggerated) for no gain other than 12 briefly captured artillery pieces that could not even be withdrawn in the retreat, as all the caisson horses had been killed in the action. The Union Army of Tennessee fared little better, giving up no territory but losing 3,722 killed, wounded, or missing.

THE BATTLE OF EZRA CHURCH

*F*our days after the indecisive Battle of Atlanta, on July 26, Major General Oliver O. Howard of the North took over McPherson's Army of Tennessee and immediately began moving out to the west along the northern arc of Atlanta's defenses. His targets were the last two open railroads leading into the besieged city, the Macon & Western and the Atlanta & West Point.

Hood soon learned of the Union movement and decided, once again, that it would be a good opportunity to launch an offensive action. He sent his old corps, now under command of Lieutenant General Stephen D. Lee, along with Stewart's corps, west down Lick Skillet Road (now Gordon Road) to confront Howard at the small crossroads where Ezra Methodist Church stood, before the Union troops could reach the vital railway.

In itself not a bad plan, the only problem was that Howard's corps had already reached the crossroads, was aware of Hood's intent, and was entrenching before Lee's corps ever left the city. As his corps marched out of the Atlanta defenses at about 10 a.m. on July 28, Lee was unaware of the new developments. Brigadier General John C. Brown's and Major General Henry D. Clayton's divisions led the Confederate column line. Within a mile or so, Brown encountered elements of Brigadier William H. Jackson's Cavalry Division, who informed him of the entrenched Yankee lines ahead. Lee made a very poor decision and ordered Brown's and Clayton's men to move straight ahead and to assault without wasting time waiting for additional support to come up.

Brown's division hastily formed in line of battle directly opposite more than three Union brigades of Morgan Smith's 2nd Division (Logan's XV Army Corps) and moved forward about 12:30 p.m. Clayton's division lagged a bit behind, moving through thick forest over to Brown's right flank, and formed up and moved forward about 10 minutes later, also into about four Union brigades. Both Confederate divisions were assaulting uphill into a barricaded, entrenched line of heavily supplied infantry (the Union troops had been issued 100 rounds per man before the battle, about 40 percent more than usual), and were being thrown into the headlong fight piecemeal as they arrived on scene. To top off the list of problems, the forest in this area was so thick that the assaulting Confederates couldn't see the Union entrenchment until they were nearly on top of them.

Only one unit managed to break through the Union barricade, Colonel William F. Brantley's Mississippi brigade over on the extreme left of the Confederate line of assault, but it was soon pushed back by a strong counterattack. The rest of the Confederate line melted away under rifle fire so intense that "no mortal could stand," as put by Colonel Hugo Wangelin (3rd Brigade Commander, Smith's 1st Division, Logan's Corps, Union Army).

Stewart's corps fared no better on their attempt. Leading the way was Major General Edward C. Walthall's division moving at the quickstep over the same ground Brown had charged through. Stumbling over the dead and wounded Confederates in the thick forest, his line was repulsed in quick order, and his dead and wounded now laid side by side with his predecessors'. Sporadic skirmishing and sniper fire continued until dark, when the Confederates withdrew into the Atlanta defenses, carrying as many wounded as the exhausted men were able to drag behind them.

Part of the Confederate defenses of Atlanta

For the third straight time in less than 10 days, Hood had wrecked a significant part of his once hardened and capable army by sending them against superior forces who were well-entrenched and better supplied. Total casualty figures for the brief attack are very difficult to accurately assess, as few Confederate records exist, but the Confederates ended with somewhere between 2,500 and 5,000 killed, wounded, or missing, compared to the Union loss of about 600.

Both sides gained and lost something as a result of the 10-day, three-battle campaign around the Atlanta defenses. Sherman failed to take the city proper but did inflict serious damage on the Confederate Army of Tennessee. Hood failed to cripple or even drive back any of the three Union grand armies before him, but he did manage to hold both the city and two of the four railroads supplying it.

THE "GREAT RAID"

*F*ollowing the battle at Ezra Church, Sherman turned to his cavalry corps to try to cut Hood's supply line. On July 27 McCook's 1st Division Cavalry with about 3,500 horsemen moved around the western flank of Atlanta's defenses, bound for Lovejoy Station about 25 miles south of the city. Later that same day, Garrard's 2nd Division Cavalry and Stoneman's cavalry division moved around the eastern line of defense toward the same destination with about 5,000 horsemen. The plan was to tear up the last remaining railroads supplying Atlanta along with their accompanying telegraph lines, then proceed to the Macon and Andersonville prisoner-of-war camps to release the more than 30,000 Union prisoners.

Sherman didn't have to wait long for word of his "great cavalry raid." On July 30 McCook's division was thoroughly routed near Newnan by two cavalry brigades under Wheeler's personal command, assisted by several infantry units. McCook's retreat north has been aptly described as "pathetic," poorly planned, and poorly executed. He managed to both lose most of the prisoners they had captured and be led by other prisoners into ambush after ambush. The fact that the Union cavalrymen would actually ask their Confederate prisoners to act as guides seems almost beyond comprehension, but it did indeed happen, to McCook's sorrow. The Union commander was finally reduced to calling his commanders together and ordering them to scatter in an "every man for himself" headlong flight back toward the Union lines. McCook and about 1,200 men, the remnants of 10 cavalry regiments and artillery batteries, finally made it back to Marietta six days later.

The next day, Stoneman's entire force was captured, killed, or scattered at Sunshine Church just north of Macon. Stoneman not only failed to liberate the Union prisoners at Macon and Andersonville, but he also suffered the ignobility of joining their ranks at Macon's Camp Oglethorpe. Garrard never even left the

Atlanta area, where he skirmished with a detachment of Wheeler's around Flat Rock, 15 miles southeast of Decatur, until pulling back to the main Union line on July 29.

The "great raid" was not only a spectacular Confederate victory, but so many cavalry horses were captured that an entire infantry brigade (Brigadier General Joseph H. Lewis's Kentucky Orphan) was able to be mounted later in the fall by the Confederacy. Sherman, noted for his extravagant prose in victory, was somewhat more terse in defeat, saying, "On the whole the cavalry raid is not deemed a success."

UTOY CREEK

Sherman grew more and more frustrated with his inability to pound or starve Hood's troops out of the city and ordered yet another attack on the remaining railroad tracks to try to force the Confederates out in the open where they could be destroyed once and for all. On August 4 Schofield's XXIII and Palmer's XIV Army Corps were ordered to swing around to the southwest and strike toward the two remaining railroad tracks near East Point. Another squabble between officers—this time between Palmer and Schofield over who was the senior officer—delayed the movement for nearly two full days.

Hood got word of the Union movement on August 5 and ordered a new line of emplacements built along the Sandtown Road (now called Cascade Road) and manned by Bates's division of Hardee's corps reinforced by a two-gun artillery battery, a brigade of the Georgia Militia, and Brigadier General Lawrence S. Ross's Texas Cavalry Brigade.

At dawn on August 6, after Sherman harshly reprimanded Palmer for his attitude and the delay it caused (he later stated, "I regard the loss of time this afternoon as equal to the loss of 2,000 men"), Brigadier General Jacob D. Cox's 3rd Division (Schofield's XXIII Army Corps) advanced with a 2,500-man front against the now heavily entrenched Confederate left. This attack got within 30 yards of the Confederate line before being broken up by severe losses and thrown back. Several other multi-brigade assaults were attempted with the same result and nearly 400 casualties.

In the midst of all this action, still upset over his argument with Schofield and stinging from Sherman's rebuke, Major General John M. Palmer tendered his resignation and quit his command. Brigadier General Richard W. Johnson hastily took over command and ordered an immediate assault on the right of the Confederate line. They were no more successful, suffering 200 more casualties for no gain. Total Confederate losses for the day were about 200 and included those captured in their forward skirmish positions in the early part of the battle. Sherman tersely described the action as "a noisy but not bloody battle."

Frustrated with his inability to cut the rail lines, Sherman pondered his next move. A direct assault on the Atlanta fortifications was completely out of the question. Two, and in some places three, interlocking rings of artillery batteries and infantry parapets surrounded the city a little over a mile out from its center, reinforced by as many as four rows of abatis and long lines of chevaux de frise. These were manned with the tired, hungry, and undersupplied but highly experienced Confederate Army of Tennessee. Planned by Georgia's chief military engineer, Captain Lemuel P. Grant, and constructed using slave labor from nearby plantations, the fortress city was "too strong to assault and too extensive to invest," according to Sherman's own chief of engineers, Captain Orlando M. Poe. Sherman decided to bombard the city into submission.

On August 1 Sherman had ordered Schofield's artillery to increase their rate of fire, and after the disaster at Utoy Creek, he sent for large artillery guns and plenty of ammunition. Two 30-pounder Parrott rifles were brought in from Chattanooga, specifically for building destruction, and eight huge 4.5-inch siege guns were brought in and mounted by August 8. On August 9 Sherman ordered every battery within range to open fire "and make the inside of Atlanta too hot to be endured." That day alone more than 5,000 shells slammed into the city's heart.

JONESBORO

Sherman kept up the intense bombardment for more than two weeks, gradually wearing away the strength and endurance of the hollow-eyed soldiers within the city fortifications. Then, suddenly, on August 25 all the guns fell silent. Hood hoped for a moment that Sherman had given up and was withdrawing, but his hopes were dashed when word came of yet another Union flanking attempt. Thomas's entire Army of the Cumberland and Howard's Army of Tennessee moved around the right of Atlanta and swept down on the Atlanta & West Point Railroad 9 miles southwest of East Point. Hood could not hope to muster any sort of force to stop them but pulled nearly his entire army out of Atlanta to try to protect the last remaining railway, leaving Stewart's corps and Smith's Georgia Militia to hold the city lines.

THE FINAL BATTLE
FOR ATLANTA

Realizing that Sherman intended to strike at Jonesboro and cut the railway, after dark on August 30 Hood ordered Hardee's and Lee's corps to move hastily to defend the small town. Encountering Union pickets at about 3 a.m. and not wanting to risk a night battle, the two Confederate corps moved slightly to the east, not arriving in line at Jonesboro until just after noon on the 31st. Hood was almost frantic to defend his railroad, sending Hardee message after message to attack "as soon as you can get your troops up."

At 3 that afternoon, the order came: fix bayonets, up and at 'em, and drive the Yankees from their trenches. The two-corps-wide Confederate assault advancing through open fields and concentrated artillery canister fire into the Union-fortified positions never made it closer than 60 yards at any point before withdrawing. Losses were staggering—one-sided—at least 1,700 Confederates versus a mere 179 Union killed or wounded.

At the same time, Schofield's Army of the Ohio, reinforced by Major General David S. Stanley's IV Army Corps, moved around the southern Atlanta defenses and struck the Macon & Western Railroad near Rough & Ready (now called Mountain View). Quickly overwhelming the small dismounted cavalry unit stationed there, the Union troops quickly ripped up the tracks and moved north toward East Point.

At 6 that evening, Hood ordered Lee's corps back north to help defend Atlanta against the new attack, leaving Hardee alone in Jonesboro facing three full Union corps. At midnight Hardee sent a message by courier to Hood (the telegraph wire having been cut about 2 p.m.) advising that the attack had failed and Atlanta should be abandoned. Through the rest of the long, hot night his forces shifted around to cover the gaps left by Lee's departure and to dig in as best they could. All knew their real job was to hold the main Union armies long enough for Hood to get the rest of their forces out of Atlanta.

The last Union attack began at 4 p.m. on September 1, led by two brigades of Brigadier General William P. Carlin's 1st Division (Brevet Major General Jefferson C. Davis's XIV Army Corps) and quickly followed by brigade after brigade, division after division, until all three corps were engaged in the assault. Amazingly, although one side of his line caved in and 865 prisoners and two full batteries of artillery were captured, Hardee managed to hold until the attack ended after nightfall. About midnight he withdrew his three remaining divisions south to Lovejoy Station, leaving behind about 1,400 dead and wounded. The Union force fared little better, losing a total of 1,272, but finally taking and cutting the last railway they had sought for so long.

On the morning of September 1, having received Hardee's dreadful message, Hood at long last ordered the evacuation of the doomed city. With the railway cut, it would be impossible to take much in the way of supplies with them, so warehouses were ordered opened up for the civilians. Stewart's corps and Smith's militia began marching out around 5 p.m., with the rear guard, French's divisional pickets, withdrawing about 11 p.m.

Sappers and engineers hastily prepared the abandoned military supplies for destruction. Around midnight a thunderous roar announced the end of a large ammunition train that Hood was unable to withdraw. Sherman heard the blast 15 miles away in his headquarters at Jonesboro and knew he now had the city.

✯

THE END OF THE ATLANTA CAMPAIGN

*O*n September 3, 1864, Sherman telegraphed Major General Henry W. Halleck in Washington, "So Atlanta is ours, and fairly won."

Hood managed to slip away with his forces more or less intact, what remained of them, after blowing up his large ammunition train and abandoning warehouses full of supplies. No complete records exist, but somewhere close to 30,000 tired, starving, and ill-equipped troops were left to carry out Hood's desperate plan to strike at the Union rear. Well over 81,000 troops were still available to Sherman, who decided not to follow and finish off the badly mauled Confederate force but to simply rest and resupply within the fortifications of Atlanta.

> *The President [Jefferson Davis] never visited the army without doing it injury; never yet that it was not followed by disaster. He was instrumental in the Gettysburg affair. He instructed Bragg at Murfreesboro. He has opened Georgia to one hundred thousand of the enemy's troops and laid South Carolina liable to destruction. I charge him with having almost ruined the country, and will meet his champion anywhere to discuss it.*
>
> —Congressman H. S. Foote of Tennessee, Confederate States of America, December 1863

Union soldiers with captured guns in the fortifications around Atlanta

Ruins of Atlanta, 1864

Between Dalton and the gates of Atlanta lie the graves of 4,423 Union and 3,044 Confederate soldiers. The Union had 22,822 wounded and the Confederates 18,952 during the four-month campaign, and a total of 17,335 from both sides were captured or simply disappeared.

Sherman rested until mid-November, and then, leaving one corps behind to garrison the city and guard against the still-roaming Confederate Army of Tennessee, he divided his forces into two great columns and began his advance to Savannah and the sea. Almost as a parting gift to the vanquished rebels, he ordered every building "of military value" to be put to the torch; his troops broadly interpreted this order, burning all but about 500 of the 5,000 or so buildings left standing after the long campaign.

Both sides knew that with the fall of Atlanta and its surrounding factories and railroads, the war was, for all practical purposes, over.

POINTS OF INTEREST

Atlanta

The Atlanta Battlefield

The area of battle on July 22 ranged around the area of Moreland Avenue and I-20, just east of the immediate downtown area. Nothing remains of the Atlanta battleground in the way of entrenchments or preserved area. Leggett's Hill was bulldozed to make way for I-20 and Moreland Avenue expansions in the 1980s. A memorial marks the site where Walker died; it is an upturned cannon on the corner of Wilkinson Drive and Glenwood Avenue, directly adjacent to the north side of I-20. Close by is another upturned cannon marking the site of McPherson's death at the corner of McPherson and Monument Avenues just off Maynard Terrace. A stone church building on DeGress Avenue off DeKalb Avenue (1 block north of I-20) stands where the center of battle swirled that day; a marker notes that this was where the famed Troup Hurt House stood. Sherman's headquarters was in the Augustus Hurt House; the marked site is now on the grounds of the Carter Presidential Center on Copenhill Avenue off Moreland Avenue.

The Atlanta Cyclorama
800 Cherokee Ave.
Atlanta, GA
(404) 658-7625
www.atlantacyclorama.org

The Cyclorama is an old favorite and comes close to tying with the Atlanta History Center as our favorite place to visit. The displays center around what they call "the world's largest painting," 42 feet tall and 385 feet around, weighing more than nine tons and with sculptures in front that give a very real three-dimensional feeling to the work. This painting is of a two-hour span of time, focusing just after 3 p.m. on July 22, 1864, as seen from a vantage point near the Troup Hurt House during the Battle of Atlanta.

The level of detail is amazing; we were astonished to discover recently that a detail portrays the charge of the obscure 1st Georgia State Line near the railway cut. A very well-produced short film narrated by James Earl Jones introduces the setting in a small, separate theater before you enter the main display theater. A 185-seat theater arranged in bleacher fashion slowly revolves in front of the painting and a taped historian narrates the action, complete with related spotlighting of the painting. A special treat is when one of the museum guides takes you on another spin around, highlighting some of the more-obscure elements of the work; this happens more often during the winter off-season than during the peak visiting time.

Downstairs in the main entrance is the famed locomotive Texas, one of the heroes of the Andrews Raid, along with a few other displays and an excellent bookstore. Upstairs is a good collection of artifacts, along with an excellent collection of contemporary Civil War artwork.

Atlanta History Center
130 W. Paces Ferry Rd.
Atlanta, GA
(404) 814-4000
www.atlantahistorycenter.com

Located just off the northeastern fringes of the Peachtree Creek battlefield, the Atlanta History Center is the crown jewel of Civil War museums in the South, and perhaps the nation. We were awestruck by the new buildings and displays on the many aspects of Atlanta history, but the Civil War display was simply beyond compare. Built around the large Beverly M. DuBose general artifact collection and the huge Thomas Swift Dickey ordnance collection (we bet you didn't know anyone actually collected old shells!), both donated permanently to the center, changing exhibits keep the displays fresh and invite even the casually interested visitor back time and again. Located on 33 acres in the heart of

Buckhead, the history center includes one of the Southeast's largest history museums; two historic houses, Swan House and Tullie Smith Farm; Centennial Olympic Games Museum; historic gardens; and the Kenan Research Center. The history center also includes the Margaret Mitchell House, located at the midtown campus.

The Civil War display, Turning Point, leads you through the stages of the war, with artifacts carefully chosen and displayed as appropriate and accurate for each year. Multimedia use is extensive, with four films, several sound displays, and many small scenes and dioramas. A unique display is the sole remaining Union supply wagon. As one curator mentioned, everyone wanted to save the unusual items, but they have a hard time finding the mundane.

The center hosts annual Civil War encampments, which provide a better-than-average display of the camp and battle life of the common soldier, around the circa-1845 Tullie Smith Farm. Recent encampments have featured rifle and artillery demonstrations, cavalry and infantry maneuvers, and even mail call and food ration distributions.

This is our absolute favorite museum, and we have returned quite a few times simply to enjoy the high quality of both artifacts and displays. A side benefit for the long-suffering Civil War buff's "widow" is the extensive collections present in other exhibits of everything from folk art to the 1996 Olympics.

The Ezra Church Battlefield

As in most of the rest of the battlegrounds in Atlanta itself, nothing remains of the vast majority of the original emplacements but historical markers. Mozley Park, on Martin Luther King Jr. Drive just north of the I-20 intersection, was in the center of the fighting but is poorly marked and a bit difficult to find. Nearby Westview Cemetery (1680 Ralph David Abernathy Blvd. SW) does contain a short section of preserved Confederate trenches.

In the cemetery, atop a low hill close by the trench line, is one of the very few monuments erected by the Confederate veterans themselves (most were funded by either the states or the United Daughters of the Confederacy). Standing guard over the now nearly forgotten graves of his comrades stands a lone concrete picket, with an inscription that talks mostly of peace: "Nation shall not rise up against Nation . . . Neither shall they learn war anymore."

Georgia Department of Archives and History
5800 Jonesboro Rd.
Morrow, GA
(678) 364-3700
www.georgiaarchives.org

Not a museum, but a true gold mine of information for the hard-core buff or serious researcher, the Georgia Archives house a huge number of records ranging from muster and pension files to original letters and diaries. A large, comfortable "search room" houses an extensive number of reference works and is manned by staff members who will retrieve any other documents you may need.

The now-retired curator of Georgia's Civil War document collection, Charlotte Ray, was an invaluable source of information and inspiration in our research into other Civil War projects, and her influence is still felt at every level. The staff is polite, polished, and highly professional, and they have proven over and over that they can work miracles in finding just the obscure document you might need! There is no charge for admission.

Georgia's Stone Mountain Park
US 78
Stone Mountain, GA
(770) 498-5690
www.stonemountainpark.com

This 3,200-acre park, originally intended as a permanent Confederate memorial, is built around the world's largest outcropping of granite and features the world's largest carving on the mountainside. Larger than Mount Rushmore, the 90-foot-by-190-foot figures of Jefferson Davis, Robert E. Lee, and Stonewall Jackson took nearly 60 years to carve. Two large museums in the park—the Stone Mountain Museum at Memorial Hall and the Antebellum Plantation and Farmyard—are a bit dated, but do contain impressive displays of artifacts, paintings, and dioramas.

The park has become "the official playground of Atlanta," according to one source. On sunny weekends it can become hard to get around past all the hikers, bikers, picnickers, and sun worshipers, but it does have a large number of restaurants and attractions for the non–Civil War buff, including a laser light show, riverboat cruises, train, and skyrides.

The park is open year-round 6 a.m. to midnight. Attraction hours vary by season—call for current prices or check online. Some attractions are seasonal.

Peachtree Creek Battlefield

Today this entire battlefield is in the middle of heavily urbanized Buckhead. The only remaining portion in more or less original condition is Tanyard Branch Park on Collier Road, scene of the most intense fighting. Several markers give a good idea of the layout of battle in this area, and a few cannon and embankments add to the flavor. Collier Road runs between Peachtree Road, about 2 miles north of I-85, and

Howell Mill Road (which intersects I-75 1 mile to the west). At the corner of Collier and Peachtree is Piedmont Hospital, which has a large stone marker commemorating the battle. Another marker nearby indicates the spot where the Confederate assault began.

On the eastern flank of the battlefield is Peachtree Road, and the main entertainment district of Atlanta (Buckhead) is a short drive north. Be aware that the area around Peachtree, Pharr, and Paces Ferry Roads is simply crawling with bars (literally stacked on top of one another in some places!), which attracts large and nearly equal numbers of obnoxious young drunks and irritable police officers on weekend nights. "DUI check" roadblocks are common after dark, as are run-over pedestrians. Some upscale chain restaurants (Cheesecake Factory, Bone's) are in the area, along with mid-scale retro (Johnny Rockets) and low-rent cheap fare (Waffle House, IHOP). For spouses who aren't Civil War fans, a good distraction is the twin upscale shopping malls another mile north on Peachtree: Lenox Square and Phipps Plaza. A good scale to judge the quality of shops here (and matching prices) is the fact that the Ritz-Carlton Buckhead hotel sits between the two malls.

Utoy Creek Battlefield

The Utoy Creek battlefield is centered in what is today the Cascade Springs Nature Preserve, off-limits to the public. The only extant structure in this area is the small Utoy Church, used as a hospital during the battle (now known as the Temple of Christ Pentecostal Church). Take I-20 west out of downtown Atlanta, exiting onto Martin Luther King Jr. Drive (exit 17). To the right (northeast) is the Ezra Church battle area. Turn to the left (southwest) and immediately left again on Ralph David Abernathy Boulevard. On your right is Westview Cemetery, a major burial site for Confederates killed in the battles around Atlanta. Continuing on Abernathy Drive, turn right onto Cascade Avenue. Travel 1½ miles, and then turn left onto Centra Villa; travel another half-mile and turn left onto Venetian Drive. Drive less than a half-mile, and turn left onto Cahaba Drive; Utoy Church is on the corner.

Dalton

General Joseph Eggleston Johnston Statue
Intersection of Crawford and Hamilton Streets
Downtown Dalton, GA

Usually we would not recommend a special trip just to view a statue, but this is a must-see exception. A rather large,

impressive bronze representation of Johnston in a pensive stance, the statue was commissioned in 1912 by the United Daughters of the Confederacy from Nashville artist Belle Kinney. Although we consider Johnston to be perhaps the finest battlefield commander in the Western Theater, his reputation suffered from both Davis's enmity and his own rather abrasive personality. As far as we have been able to establish, this is the one and only statue of the Virginia native.

Jonesboro

Jonesboro Battlefield

Jonesboro battlefield lies entirely within the present-day city limits of Jonesboro and almost entirely within the central business district. The town was almost completely destroyed during the battle, but a handful of period structures still exist. The center of action is well marked and can be found in Jonesboro's historic district, on US 41/19 (also called Tara Boulevard. Yes, that Tara). The heavy commercial buildup in this area can make finding the individual sites and structures difficult. We strongly encourage you to check with the Clayton County visitors center at 104 North Main St., www .visitscarlett.com, for some excellent maps and directions.

Kennesaw

Kennesaw Mountain National Battlefield Park
900 Kennesaw Mountain Dr.
Kennesaw, GA
(770) 427-4686, ext. 0
www.nps.gov/kemo

Kennesaw Mountain today is a National Battlefield Park, stretching from just north of Big Kennesaw Mountain about 5 miles south to Kolb's Farm, 3 miles north and west of Marietta. There are a multitude of hiking and equestrian trails throughout the large complex, which has become more or less a playground for the surrounding affluent community, as well as the third-most-visited battlefield park in the nation. The major combat areas are well marked with maps, photos, and explanatory markers, and Union and Confederate state memorials dot the open fields. The 11,900-square-foot visitor center houses an excellent relevant book selection and a film about the battle, as well as a very helpful and knowledgeable staff. Park hours are dawn to dusk. Admission to the park and parking are free. There is a small admission charge to ride the shuttle bus to the top of the mountain. On weekends the road is closed to foot travel, so visitors must ride the shuttle.

Southern Museum of Civil War and Locomotive History
2829 Cherokee St.
Kennesaw, GA
(770) 427-2117
www.southernmuseum.org

Housed in an old cotton gin, and home of the famed locomotive of the Andrews Raid, the General, this museum run by the city of Kennesaw does a very credible job of using its small collection of artifacts to best advantage. A short film about the Andrews Raid relates the story of the botched Union guerrilla attempt that started less than 100 yards away, and the museum has a good book collection for sale.

Wildman's Civil War & Relic Shop
2879 S. Main St.
Kennesaw, GA
(770) 422-1785
www.wildmans-shop.com

Across the street from the tracks and museum is another local institution, Wildman's Civil War & Relic Shop, which is a dusty and rambling building housing equal parts assorted books and artifacts for sale and museum. Be forewarned: This store has a very strong racial and "unreconstructed" feel, and there are many modern books, posters, and stickers exalting the Ku Klux Klan and the local gun laws. Kennesaw gained fame in 1982 by passing the first city ordinance in the nation requiring local residents to own firearms and ammunition, largely as a result of Dent "Wildman" Myers's efforts (this gun ordinance was in response to another town's antigun ownership ordinance). This said, we consider Mr. Myers to be one of the better sources of information on the Kennesaw Campaign, and his contributions over the years to writing the local history have been invaluable.

Resaca

The Confederate Cemetery at Resaca

One of the very few high-profile remnants of the battle is the small Confederate cemetery just north of the small crossroads town. Leave I-75 at exit 320, go east about a half-mile to the intersection with US 41, and turn left. Go north on US 41 about 2 miles, and then slow and look for a small sign pointing out the cemetery to your right down Confederate Cemetery Road.

This small cemetery houses the remains of about 420 soldiers, the vast majority of whom are unknown. Local Sons of Confederate Veterans and United Daughters of the Confederacy camps frequently maintain the cemetery, giving it a very parklike appearance. Ironically, these graves may prove to be the pickets that guard the only remaining preserved part of this battlefield. This cemetery rests on what was part of Major General Alexander P. Stewart's division (Hood's corps), and a look around at the terrain makes it apparent that a good position would have been on the low hills just above the cemetery. Like so much else around this battlefield, unfortunately, these hills are on private property and not open to the public.

Sope Creek

In the early afternoon of July 9, finding a 300-yard-wide, relatively shallow spot over a submerged fish dam near Sope Creek (Soap Creek on some maps), Colonel Daniel Cameron's 103rd Ohio Infantry (Union Army) swam across to establish a beachhead. Encountering no opposition, Schofield then ordered a crossing in force at 3:30 that afternoon. Led by a combat amphibious assault by the 12th Kentucky Regiment under Lieutenant Colonel Laurence H. Rousseau, part of Colonel Robert K. Boyd's 3rd (Kentucky) Brigade (the same brigade that had "withdrawn for rations" at Pickett's Mill), the crossing was an outstanding success. The only Confederates in the area were part of a small picket outpost, who only got off a single volley before running away.

The single spot remaining in more or less original condition is Sope Creek, part of the Chattahoochee River National Recreation Area. Ruins of a paper mill burned by Union cavalry scouting for crossing sites are still visible, as well as the nearby shallow ford across the river. Take I-75 to exit 261 (Delk Road), and travel east to Powers Ferry Road. Turn right, go about a half-mile, and turn left onto Terrell Mill Road. About 1½ miles down Terrell Mill is Paper Mill Road; follow the signs to the park from there. The park is in a residential area with no amenities of any kind.

ACCOMMODATIONS

Atlanta

Atlanta is a major tourist and convention destination, and the hospitality industry in Fulton County alone employs more than 115,000 workers and pays more than $215 million in taxes to the local governments. Needless to say, just about any chain hotel or motel in every price range is readily available; the Downtown Connector, the merging of I-75 and I-85 through downtown Atlanta, is the major corridor to all the listed amenities, and a short drive in any direction on the three highways (including I-20) is the best bet for lower-priced chain establishments at nearly any exit. The following recommendations are a tiny sampling of what is available in the downtown area itself.

Evergreen Marriott Conference Resort at Stone Mountain Park $$$
4021 Lakeview Dr.
Stone Mountain, GA
(770) 879-9900
(888) 670-2250
www.marriott.com

This Marriott property is located in Stone Mountain Park and is the nicest of the lodging choices at Stone Mountain. Each room offers either a private balcony or veranda to highlight the views of Stone Mountain Park. This lodging property offers an on-site spa and is convenient to Stone Mountain's golf course.

Four Seasons $$$$
75 14th St.
Atlanta, GA
(404) 881-9898
www.fourseasons.com

Formerly the Continental Grand, this Four Seasons hotel has retained all that was grand. In the three-story lobby, light from the 10-foot-high Baccarat chandelier plays across the rose-colored Spanish marble walls around the broad grand staircase. A lounge on the mezzanine serves cocktails and afternoon high tea. Park 75 is a sit-down, white-tablecloth restaurant that serves breakfast, lunch, and supper from early morning until 11 p.m. every day. The menu is "new American with global influences and Southern accents." The Ballroom showcases a skyline view from its 6,000-square-foot open terrace. There is an on-site spa, and its gorgeous indoor lap pool suggests a Roman bath.

Marriott's Stone Mountain Inn $$$
1058 Robert E. Lee Dr.
Stone Mountain, GA
(770) 469-3311
(888) 670-2250
www.marriott.com

The Inn is a carefully preserved replica of a 19th-century plantation. The rooms are not as luxurious as those at the Evergreen Marriott, but are very spacious and many offer a sofa bed for extra sleeping accommodations. It is the quieter of the two Stone Mountain properties. Southern-style food is served in the Mountainview Restaurant.

The Village Inn Bed and Breakfast $$–$$$
992 Ridge Ave.
Stone Mountain, GA
(770) 469-3459
www.villageinnbb.com

This property was originally built in 1820 as a roadside inn, and it is the oldest structure in historic Stone Mountain Village. It survived Sherman's fiery torch due to the fact that it was used as a Confederate hospital during the Civil War.

Westin Buckhead Atlanta $$$–$$$$
3391 Peachtree Rd. NE
Atlanta, GA
(404) 365-0065
(866) 716-8128
www.westin.com/buckhead

The Westin is patterned after the elegant fashions of modern Europe: sleek and smooth with curving lines and sweeping expanses of glass. The interior art is spectacular and belies the rather uninteresting exterior. Each of the 365 guest rooms in the 22-floor property has wireless high-speed Internet as well as phone service with voice mail, cable TV with HBO, bathrobes, and a hair dryer. The hotel's health club has an indoor pool.

Dalton

Dalton is today a major shopping mecca for both the Atlanta and Chattanooga metropolitan areas, due to its reputation as a major manufacturing center of carpets and as the host to a number of outlet shopping centers, most of which are tied to the local carpet industry. However, the majority of motels and restaurants are of the lower-middle range of chains, and there is little of note in the city itself related to the war. The best selection of the usual chain restaurants and motels can be found at exits 333 and 336 off I-75; exit 333 also features a large outlet mall.

Kennesaw

This area is a heavily built-up suburb of the Atlanta metropolitan area and has nearly any amenity you could think of within a short drive. Just to the north of the battlefield park is Barrett Parkway; turn right and a major shopping and entertainment district is a very short drive to the east. In the vicinity of where Barrett Parkway intersects I-75 is a major regional mall (Town Center), several large strip shopping centers, an unusual bowling alley/microbrewery combination (U.S. Play), a good dozen chain hotels and motels, and every low- to mid-range chain restaurant present in the Atlanta market.

Roswell

Roswell is an upscale suburb of Atlanta and in fact sits in the midst of the "richest zip codes" in the Southeast (based on per-capita income of the area). The Roswell square has gentrified into a boutique and antiques-store zone, as have so many other small Southern towns, but has an unusually high percentage of decent restaurants and other amenities nearby. The northbound road through the square, Alpharetta Highway (US 19), leads to both fast-food heaven and very upscale shopping zones. Both Holcomb Bridge and Mansell Road running to the east of Alpharetta Highway just north of the square will take you to just about any chain restaurant you could imagine, as well as the usual array of chain hotels and motels near the intersections with GA 400 (about 1 to 2 miles east). Just east of GA 400 on Mansell Road is the major regional North Point Mall, as well as associated strip malls and "big box" stores.

RESTAURANTS

Atlanta

The Cyclorama (earlier in the Atlanta section) is painted from the vantage point of a person standing at a spot on Moreland Avenue about a mile north of I-20, just where the railroad tracks cross over the road. Do not be alarmed if you see a lot of strangely dressed people walking around here; this is the area known as Little 5 Points (locals call it L5P) and is the so-called "hippie" district. One block north of the railroad tracks on Moreland is the center of commerce for the area, where you can find any manner of macrobiotic food, incense, leather clothing, or artwork, and where you can get tattooed and pierced to your heart's content. We recommend Urban Tribe (1131 Euclid Ave.) or Sacred Heart Tattoo (483 Moreland Ave.) for the latter.

There is a distinct lack of the usual fast-food places in this area, which is actually a blessing. This area and the nearby Virginia-Highlands district (2 miles north on Moreland Avenue, west on Ponce de Leon Avenue, then immediately right onto Highland Avenue) are blessed with a large number of truly fabulous restaurants. Unfortunately, both districts suffer the Atlanta disease of quick open-and-shut doors; we recommend that you look for the bright green newspaper boxes and pick up a copy of *Creative Loafing*

(free). Its main restaurant reviewer is Cliff Bostick, and we have never gone wrong with one of his recommendations. Be aware that he leans very heavily toward Vietnamese and other Asian cuisine.

Bacchanalia $$$$
1198 Howell Mill Rd.
Atlanta, GA
(404) 365-0410
www.starprovisions.com

This is, without a doubt, our favorite serious foodie Atlanta restaurant; in fact, it would fit very nicely alongside the finest that New Orleans or San Francisco can offer. This former Buckhead restaurant took a bold step and relocated to a renovated factory closer to downtown, in a neighborhood that is in transition, but most delicately can be described as "interesting." However, the crowds who love the eatery's delectable fixed-price menus, which change with the passing seasons, are still putting their names on the reservation list. Along with an extensive wine list, you'll find plenty of seafood selections and updated American classics. There's plenty of on-site parking.

Canoe $$$
4199 Paces Ferry Rd. NE
Atlanta, GA
(770) 432-2663
www.canoe-atl.com

On the banks of the Chattahoochee River in northwest Atlanta, Canoe is housed in a barrel-vaulted brick building once known as Robinson's Tropical Gardens. It's said that many a young romance bloomed at this riverfront restaurant and nightspot in the golden post–World War II years. Today wedding parties have been known to arrive in canoes for a luscious reception.

In accordance with its goal of offering delicious, healthful food for today's diner, Canoe's fare includes Laughing Bird shrimp dumplings, baby arugula salad, and slow-roasted Carolina rabbit. There's also an assortment of beef and seafood. You can call ahead for reservations or take advantage of any waiting time to stroll riverside. Valet parking is available. Reservations are recommended.

La Grotta Ristorante $$$$
2637 Peachtree Rd. NE
Atlanta, GA
(404) 231-1368

Ravina Center
4355 Ashford Dunwoody Rd. NE
Atlanta, GA
(770) 395-9925
www.lagrottaatlanta.com

Fine Italian cuisine here includes pasta dishes and favorites such as ravioli, fettuccine, and herb-crusted fillet of salmon. The current menu features a "Stimulus Menu" and "Bail Out Menu." Dinner is served Mon through Sat at the Peachtree Road location, very close to the Peachtree Creek battlefield site, and reservations are suggested. The Ravina location, open for lunch and dinner, is more airy and modern than the Buckhead restaurant, with a wonderful view of the hotel's gardens from huge glass windows.

Manuel's Tavern $
602 North Highland Ave. NE
Atlanta, GA
(404) 525-3447
www.manuelstavern.com

Manuel's Tavern has been an in-town gathering place since 1956 when Manuel Maloof founded it. Maloof was politically active his entire life (at one time he was CEO of DeKalb County), and today the walls of his tavern are covered with beer signs and pictures of sports heroes, Democratic Party leaders, and icons who frequent the place. Through the years, the Atlanta Press Club has held meetings and debates here, and the *New York Times* has described it as "Atlanta's quintessential neighborhood bar." Regulars roam from the main room to the "ballroom" (really the dining room), from bar to booth to table, catching up on all the latest while enjoying Manuel's wings, sandwiches, burgers, and salads. Most Atlanta cops, firefighters, and paramedics consider this "the" place to unwind after their shift, so expect to see quite a few uniforms at any given time. It can get hectic on a busy night, but the atmosphere is friendly and inviting.

Dalton

The Dalton Depot $$
110 Depot St.
Dalton, GA
(706) 226-3160
www.thedaltondepot.net

One exception to the rule about Dalton eateries is this wartime railroad depot, in its original use until 1978 and now a mid-scale restaurant. This is the place where Johnston arrived to take over command of the Army of Tennessee, as well as the site of the celebrated arrival of Lieutenant General James Longstreet's corps, en route to the battle at Chickamauga. During the Andrews Raid, better known as the Great Locomotive Chase, the pursued and the pursuers raced by the station, the following train slowing down long enough to drop off a messenger boy to give an update to the depot's telegraph office.

The Depot specializes in steaks, pasta dishes, and premium hamburgers and has a full bar. The menu, outside of a handful of specials, is very similar to what one would find in the Applebee's and Chili's chains, but the atmosphere is much more pleasant here.

Marietta

Pappadeaux Seafood Kitchen $$$
2830 Windy Hill Rd.
Marietta, GA
(770) 984-8899

5635 Jimmy Carter Blvd.
Norcross, GA
(770) 849-0600

10795 Davis Dr.
Alpharetta, GA
(770) 992-5566
www.pappadeaux.com

This Cajun seafood house always draws a crowd; even at lunch, the wait can be more than 45 minutes! But it's worth it: The portions are large, the selection vast, and the tastes delectable. The wait passes quickly at the enormous bar. In addition to Cajun favorites, there are grilled, broiled, and baked items, and soups and salads. The setting is casual and noisy (no one will notice the kids' chatter in the large dining room). Pappadeaux's does not take reservations.

Shillings on the Square $$
19 N. Park Sq.
Marietta, GA
(770) 428-9520
www.shillingsonthesquare.net

This casual restaurant and bar has anchored a corner of the Marietta square for 20 years, hard by the Civil War–era Kennesaw House. The Streetside Grill is a favorite of locals looking for sandwiches, salads, and soups late into the night or during a short lunch break.

For those with more elegant tastes, Top of the Square is an 80-seat fine dining room, with white tablecloths, candles, and soft piano tunes putting diners in a relaxed mood. Entrees include steaks, seafood, lamb, and chicken.

Atlanta to Savannah:
The March to the Sea

Darley.

Map of Sherman's March to the Sea

Sherman's Georgia campaign, another name given for his famed March to the Sea, can be viewed as simply an extension of his Atlanta campaign, which began in the northwestern mountains in May 1864. His original goal—cutting the critical transportation and manufacturing center of Atlanta off from the rest of the Confederacy—having been met by early September 1864, Sherman pondered what to do next. One of his earliest thoughts was to strike southwest toward LaGrange and West Point while Union forces stationed in Mobile and Pensacola marched north to meet him, opening the Chattahoochee and Appalachicola Rivers to Union control.

Another considered, then rejected, plan was to strike toward the state capital at Milledgeville, and then turn on Macon, Augusta, and "sweep the whole State of Georgia," but concern over the still-undefeated Confederate Army of Tennessee just outside Atlanta gave him serious pause. His primary concern was that his supply line snaked through a relatively narrow corridor from Atlanta more than 100 miles to the north in Chattanooga and from there another 130 miles north to the main Union base at Nashville. Both the Confederate Army of Tennessee under Major General John Bell Hood and Major General Joseph Wheeler's cavalry corps up in Tennessee threatened to cut off this supply route at any given time.

Researching population and agricultural records for every county in Georgia, Sherman finally concluded that his 60,000-plus men could live off the land for a short time if they set off cross-country to join a Union army somewhere along the Atlantic Coast. Under great pressure to send his army south to rescue Union prisoners at the notorious Camp Sumter prisoner-of-war camp near Andersonville, Georgia, Sherman admitted that going down the Flint River to accomplish this would probably be the safest course of action. However, he had objectives other than simple, safe military maneuvers.

Occupied Atlanta

Sherman's grand army had simply walked into the contested city of Atlanta after Hood had abandoned it during the night of September 1, 1864. Hood, in one of his many rash decisions, had sent his entire cavalry force north to strike at the Union supply lines in Tennessee, leaving him without scouts to report on what his Union opposite was up to. Sherman, learning of the poor tactical decision, took advantage of the situation by shifting part of his forces to the south of Atlanta, near Jonesboro, and cut the single remaining railroad supply line into the city. Hood, left without means of supply or reinforcement and faced with the prospect of a protracted siege, took what opportunity was left and snuck his remaining combat forces out of the city under cover of dark.

Rather than face the small but combat-hardened group of veterans from Hood's army at their new defense lines near Lovejoy Station, Sherman elected to march his army into the city and take over the strong belt of fortifications himself. Hood, faced with the prospect of bleeding his army dry against the very fortifications they had built, decided instead to take his army north, cut the Union supply line, and try to starve Sherman out.

The Civilian "Problem"

Sherman had some interesting problems to deal with in Atlanta in addition to the roaming Confederate Army at his gate. The extensive line of fortifications built by Confederate engineers and slaves around Atlanta was simply too large for even his huge army to fully man, so he ordered his own engineers to tighten it down to a smaller ring of artillery emplacements defended by trenches for infantry. The nearly 30,000 civilians still within the city troubled him, for he did not wish to "waste" any of the mountains of supplies flowing down from Chattanooga on the noncombatants.

On September 8, Sherman gave one of his most controversial orders of the war: "The city of Atlanta, being exclusively required for wartime purposes, will at once be evacuated by all except the armies of the United States." All civilians would be transported under flag of truce 10 miles south to Rough and Ready and then unceremoniously dumped in the unprepared area without provision for shelter or food.

Atlanta citizens wait to get passes from the provost's office to leave the city on Sherman's orders.

Needless to say, this act provoked a howl of protest from Confederate civilian and military authorities. Hood stated in a letter to Sherman, "Permit me to say that the unprecedented measure you propose transcends, in studied and ingenious cruelty, all acts ever brought to my attention in the dark history of war." Mayor James M. Calhoun of Atlanta protested that the majority of citizens left (mostly women and children) could not stand up to the coming winter without shelter or food. In a letter to Sherman, he wrote that the act was "appalling and heartrending."

Sherman was not impressed. In a lengthy reply to Hood's letter, he reiterated his intentions and blasted Hood for suggesting it was anything truly unusual:

> *In the name of common sense, I ask you not to appeal to a just God in such a sacrilegious manner. You, who in the midst of peace and prosperity have plunged a nation into war, dark and cruel war, who dared and badgered us into battle, insulted our flag,*

seized our arsenals and forts that were left in the honorable custody of a peaceful ordnance sergeant, and seized and made prisoners of war the very garrisons sent to protect your people against negroes and Indians . . . Talk thus to the Marines, but not to me . . . if we must be enemies, let us be men, and fight it out as we propose to do, and not indulge in such hypocritical appeals to God and humanity.

Sherman had no intention of changing his orders, and on September 10 the first wagonloads of civilians left Atlanta. Hood was beside himself with the barbarity of Sherman's actions and just couldn't leave it be without a parting shot. "We will fight you to the death!" he wrote back to Sherman. "Better die a thousand deaths than submit to live under you. . . ."

SHERMAN MAKES HIS DECISION

By October 1, Sherman finally made up his mind where to go next. Ordering Major General George H. Thomas back to Chattanooga with two corps to defend Tennessee, he stripped down his remaining army to a handpicked fighting force of 55,255 infantry, 4,588 cavalry, and 1,759 artillerymen, with 68 guns organized into four army corps. Writing a series of letters to his friend and commander, Lieutenant General Ulysses S. Grant, back in Washington, he outlined his planned offensive. "Until we can repopulate Georgia (with Unionists), it is useless for us to occupy it; but the utter destruction of its roads, houses, and people will cripple their military resources . . . can make this march and make Georgia howl." He further advised that he was sending his wounded and unfit soldiers back up to Tennessee, "and with my effective army, move through Georgia, smashing things to the sea."

Sherman's only real worry was that the few good roads and frequent stream and river crossings in southern

Georgia could allow the remains of Hood's army and small bands of Georgia militia and home guards to delay his advance to an unhealthy degree. Unwittingly, Hood himself helped relieve some of this concern, with a renewed offensive against Sherman's rear.

THE BATTLE OF ALLATOONA PASS

*R*ealizing that there was no way his battered army could ever hope to take Atlanta back by force, Hood, with President Jefferson Davis's blessings, marched his troops out of camp near Palmetto northward, hoping to cut Sherman's supply lines north of Atlanta and force him to turn and fight him there. Crossing the Chattahoochee River near Campbellton on October 1, he continued north for two days, finally encamping near Hiram. Major General Alexander P. Stewart was ordered to move east to attack and cut the Western & Atlantic Railroad line at Big Shanty (now Kennesaw), Acworth, and Allatoona.

Like much in the war, this small but important battle had never been part of the Confederate war plan. Also like many other Confederate victories, it happened as the result of quick action, good luck, and stealth but, ultimately, led to disaster. After Stewart's men surprised and captured about 170 Union troops at Big Shanty on October 4, he quickly moved north and grabbed a larger garrison at Acworth.

Excited over what he considered easy victories, Hood ordered Major General Samuel G. French to march his division up the tracks to Allatoona Pass, where they were to take and destroy the railroad bridge. French brought along three battalions commanded by brigadier generals Sears, Cockrell, and Young. Because the two prior rail stops had been lightly protected, Hood believed Allatoona would be a similar easy mark. Unknown to the Confederates, however, was the fact that Sherman had made the tiny settlement into

a logistics base, heavily fortified it, and had ordered Brigadier General John M. Corse's division forward to garrison it. On both sides of the deep rail cut, Union forces had built stout defensive reinforcements. On the west side of the cut was a defense called, for its shape, the Star Fort, which was surrounded by railroad ties.

Approaching Allatoona from north, west, and south, French sent a short message to his adversary Corse:

> *Sir: I have the forces under my command in such positions that you are now surrounded, and, to avoid a needless effusion of blood, I call upon you to surrender your forces at once, and unconditionally. Five minutes will be allowed for you to decide. Should you accede to this, you will be treated in the most honorable manner as prisoners of war.*

Corse was not cowed: "Your communication demanding surrender of my command, I acknowledge receipt of, and respectfully reply, that we are prepared for the 'needless effusion of blood' whenever it is agreeable with you."

From the west, French sent in Brigadier General Francis M. Cockrell's Missouri Brigade and Brigadier General William H. Young's (Ector's) Brigade. Pushing through one defensive line after another, fighting hand to hand with clubbed rifles and bayonets, fighting advanced to within a few feet of the Star Fort. Fighting rapidly intensified, with the Confederate advance being stopped before it overran the fort. Soon came warnings that a Union force had been spotted moving rapidly toward the pass. French pulled back his troops and marched his to rejoin Hood in the west.

Throughout the all-day fight, a Union signal post at Kennesaw Mountain repeated to Corse: "General Sherman says hold fast; we are coming." Popularizing the expression, "hold the fort," the message was meant mainly for morale; no additional infantry arrived until two days later. It seems that forces spotted by the Confederate scouts were simply Union cavalry on a scouting mission.

Though barely remembered this century and a half later, casualties were exceptionally high, even for the Civil War. Corse reported 706 dead and wounded; French also reported 706 casualties (including 70 officers), about 30 percent of each side's total force. Young was wounded and captured shortly afterward. In his report to Sherman, the battle-hardened Corse reported that he, too, had been wounded: "I am short a cheek bone and an ear but am able to lick all hell yet!" Later, when Sherman came up to inspect the aftermath, he was apparently unimpressed with Corse's wounds: "Corse, they came damn near missing you, didn't they?"

> *This morning the enemy attacked our pickets. They planted their artilry so they had good range of us. They drove us out of our rifel pits about 11 a.m. and we fell back in the fort and then we held them and fought them until nearly 4 p.m. The timber is laying full of dead and some wounded. The wounded in our company Henry Hockman in left leg, J Garman fnger shot off, E Kahley shot in back, J Humpfrey in the side, [unidentified words], H C Carl through the breast, J Stewart slight in leg, Danil Dauber slightly in arm. Killed Simon [last name unidentified].*
>
> —Private Thomas Jefferson Moses, 93rd Regiment, Illinois Volunteers, Union Army, description of battle of Allatoona Pass, October 5, 1864 (all spelling original, from his diary entry)

THE ARMIES ADVANCE IN OPPOSITE DIRECTIONS

Following the decisive loss at Allatoona Pass, Hood elected to continue north, hitting the Union garrisons at Rome, Resaca, Dalton, and Tunnel Hill before turning west into Alabama. Sherman initially sent a force of some 40,000 men chasing after him but soon wearied of the endless pursuit. Hood's strategy here is uncertain, but if it was to keep Sherman bottled up in northern Georgia, it both succeeded and failed. When Hood slipped away after the Union troops deployed for battle at LaFayette

(just south of the Chickamauga battlefield) on October 17, Sherman remarked that Hood's tactics were "inexplicable by any common-sense theory . . . I could not guess his movements as I could those of Johnston." After a total of three weeks of chasing the fast-moving Army of Tennessee, Sherman ordered his forces to return to Atlanta and prepare for a march to the south.

Warned by Grant that Hood was taking his army north into Tennessee to threaten his supply lines, Sherman remarked, "No single force can catch Hood, and I am convinced that the best results will follow from our defeating Jeff Davis's cherished plan of making me leave Georgia by maneuvering."

At the same time, Davis was begging Hood "not to abandon Georgia to Sherman but defeat him in detail before marching into Tennessee." Hood replied that it was his intent to "draw out Sherman where he can be dealt with north of Atlanta." In his postwar memoirs, Hood clung to this unrealistic stance and his hopes of defeating both Sherman and Thomas's powerful force in Tennessee:

> *I conceived the plan of marching into Tennessee . . . to move upon Thomas and Schofield and capture their army before it could reach Nashville and afterward march northeast, past the Cumberland River in that position I could threaten Cincinnati from Kentucky and Tennessee . . . if blessed with a victory (over Sherman coming north after him), to send reinforcements to Lee, in Virginia, or to march through gaps in the Cumberland Mountains and attack Grant in the rear.*

It was whispered by not a few members of the Army of Tennessee that Hood was half-mad from his injuries, shot in the arm at Gettysburg and having a leg shot off at Chickamauga shortly thereafter. Widely viewed as a gallant fighter, his leadership did not impress those under him in the sense that his tactics killed a lot of his men. Private Sam Watkins said, "As a soldier, he was brave, good, noble and gallant, and fought with the ferociousness of the wounded tiger, and with the everlasting grit of the bull-dog; but as a general he was a failure in every particular."

Hood continued his march north, and Sherman, upon hearing the news, couldn't have been happier. "If he will go to the Ohio River, I will give him rations." Just before Hood's eastward-ranging cavalry cut the telegraph lines, Sherman sent one last message to Grant:

> *If I start before I hear from you, or before further developments turn my course, you may take it for granted that I have moved by way of Griffin to Barnesville; that I break up the road between Columbus and Macon good and if I feign on Columbus, I will move by way of Macon and Millen on Savannah; or if I feign on Macon, you may take it for granted I have shot toward Opelika, Montgomery and Mobile Bay. I will not attempt to send couriers back, but trust to the Richmond papers to keep you well advised. I will see that the road is completely broken between the Etowah and the Chattahoochee, and that Atlanta itself is utterly destroyed.*

Content with his plans, happy about Hood being more than 100 miles to his rear, and with his army primed and ready for action, Sherman had but one task left before turning his attention on gaining the sea before winter set in.

THE BURNING OF ATLANTA

Planning to begin his march out of Atlanta southward on November 16, Sherman issued orders that anything of military value in the city be destroyed before they departed. Giving the task over to his chief of engineers, Captain Orlando M. Poe, Sherman intended to render useless anything even remotely related to manufacturing, transportation, or communications. Poe took this order and applied it quite liberally, without any objection from Sherman. Starting on the afternoon of November 11, block after block was set afire, the contents being pillaged and looted beforehand by large gangs of drunken Union soldiers and sober Southern citizens alike.

North of Atlanta, Sherman gave orders that anything of "military value" be destroyed by his troops gathering for the march south. Rome, Acworth, and Marietta were all consigned to the torch, and soon little was visible of the once-pretty small towns but heaps of smoldering ruins and lonely chimneys standing like pickets.

> *An authentic [hardtack] cracker could not be soaked soft, but after a time took on the elasticity of gutta-percha.*
>
> —John D. Billings, in his book, *Hardtack and Coffee*

To conduct his destruction more efficiently, Poe had devised a new machine consisting of a 21-foot-long iron bar swinging on chains from a 10-foot-high wooden scaffold. With a gang of soldiers to move and swing it, it was a devilishly clever way to knock down whatever struck his fancy. The railroad roundhouse, factories, warehouses, residences, and masonry buildings of all description were soon reduced to piles of rubble. Under other buildings Union soldiers piled stacks of mattresses, oil-soaked wagon parts, broken fence rails, and just about anything else that would burn. Atop everything they piled artillery shot and shells abandoned by Hood's retreating army. In a touch of irony, sentries were then posted to prevent "unauthorized" acts of arson.

Finally ready to move out of Atlanta, Sherman ordered Poe to start the fires late on the afternoon of November 15. Within a few minutes the "authorized" fires had been set, at first confined to factories and warehouses containing Hood's abandoned supplies. An early evening wind soon built up the fires, and spraying sparks and burning cinders in every direction, the fires spread like, well, wildfire. Pleased by the sight of the soon out-of-control fires raging through the city, Sherman was moved to remark only that he supposed the flames could be visible from Griffin, about 45 miles to the south.

As a sort of explanation to his staff, who were starting to view the wanton destruction with unease, Sherman remarked,

> *This city has done more and contributed more to carry on and sustain the war than any other, save perhaps Richmond. We have been fighting Atlanta all the*

time, in the past; have been capturing guns, wagons, etc. etc., marked Atlanta and made here, all the time; and now since they have been doing so much to destroy us and our Government, we have to destroy them, at least enough to prevent any more of that.

As the huge fire built and built, block after block literally exploded into flame, the thick smoke choking the Union soldiers who clapped and danced with glee among the ruins, barely waiting until the flames died down to start their looting and drunken revelry once again. What initially escaped the "authorized" fires did not escape these undisciplined wretches, who helped spread the flames by burning homes and businesses to cover up their crimes. In the midst of the chaotic riot, the 33rd Massachusetts Regimental Band stood, calmly and righteously playing "John Brown's Soul Goes Marching On." Major George Ward Nichols, Sherman's aide-de-camp, remarked without a hint of sarcasm that he had "never heard that noble anthem when it was so grand, so solemn, so inspiring."

Other Union soldiers and officers viewed the destruction differently, remarking that the burning and looting of private property was not necessary and a "disgraceful piece of business." Another summed up the view more widely held by their Confederate opponents: "We hardly deserve success."

As the flames died down overnight, dawn on November 16 revealed that more than 4,100 of the 4,500 buildings in town, including every single business, had been leveled by the flames and rioting Union troops. Sherman mounted his horse, Sam, and slowly led his men out of the ruined city, bound for Savannah and the Atlantic Ocean.

"THE WILD ADVENTURE OF A CRAZY FOOL"

With the "business" in Atlanta taken care of, his men up and ready, and prospects of an easy adventure before them, Sherman ordered the march out of the city to begin. The 60,598 Union soldiers were deployed in two huge columns, sometimes called "wings." On the morning of November 15, Brigadier General Alpheus Williams's XX Corps headed off due east through Decatur toward Augusta. General Peter Osterhaus's XV Corps and General Frank Blair's XVII Corps formed the right column under overall command of Major General Oliver O. Howard and moved southward toward Macon. Early on the morning of November 16, Major General Jefferson C. Davis's XIV Corps moved out behind Williams's corps. The two-pronged attack was designed to fool Confederate defenders into thinking that Augusta and Macon were the targets of the separate wings, forcing them to divide their already inadequate forces while the two columns swung south and east and converged on Milledgeville, which was then the capital of Georgia.

To oppose the Union juggernaut was a pitiful handful of mostly irregular troops: Major General Gustavus W. Smith's (combined) Georgia Militia, the battered remnants of the Georgia State Line—freshly arrived after leaving the march north with Hood's army; a few home guard and hastily organized local militia groups; and the remnants of Major General Joseph Wheeler's cavalry corps. All told, fewer than 8,000 men were available to try to stop Sherman, most of whom had never fired a rifle in combat before.

About 7 a.m. on the morning of November 16, Sherman rode his horse slowly out of the bombarded, burned-out hulk of a once-thriving city along with the vanguard of his XIV Corps, down the dirt road leading toward Decatur and Stone Mountain. Stopping briefly, he turned to take another look at the scene of his greatest triumph and some of his greatest sorrows. From his vantage point he could barely make out the copse of trees where his beloved friend, Major General James Birdseye McPherson, had been shot and killed on July 22. Setting his battered hat back on his head and unwrapping another cigar to chew on along the way, he set his horse to a walk and left the city without uttering a word to anyone. In his memoirs, he remarked,

Then we turned our horses' heads to the east; Atlanta was soon lost behind the screen of trees, and became a thing of the past. Around it clings many

a thought of desperate battle of hope and fear, that now seem like the memory of a dream . . . There was a "devil-may-care" feeling pervading officers and men, that made me feel the full load of responsibility, for success would be expected as a matter of course, whereas, should we fail, this march would be adjudged the wild adventure of a crazy fool.

MARCHING THROUGH GEORGIA

*B*oth columns moved out of Atlanta, one proceeding initially almost due east and the other south, with almost no opposition. Following Sherman's orders to the letter and spirit, nearly everything of any value that they encountered was confiscated or burned, and assigned work gangs destroyed most of the railroad tracks. The rails were lifted and the cross-ties pulled out from under them and piled high and set afire; then the rails were held over the burning ties until they glowed red hot and twisted and bent into unusable pretzel shapes called "Sherman's bow-ties."

The only Confederate opposition to the first part of the march was a series of small to moderate-size skirmishes between Rough and Ready (10 miles north of Jonesboro; now called Mountain View) and East Macon, with elements of Wheeler's cavalry.

Milledgeville

The skirmishers and foraging parties created a nearly 60-mile-wide path of destruction as they went across Georgia. Slocum's left wing moved like a blue buzz saw through Stone Mountain, Lithonia, Conyers, Social Circle, and Madison before encountering any resistance to speak of. At Buckhead (a small town, not the Atlanta suburb), Confederate sharpshooters caused a handful of casualties before being driven

off; Sherman ordered the town totally burned to the ground in reprisal.

Howard's right wing had moved in a southeasterly direction, hoping to give the impression that Macon was their destination. Moving through McDonough and Locust Grove, Howard ordered a turn more to the east at Indian Springs, to close in tighter with the left wing and head more directly to Milledgeville. By November 20, the closest flanks of both wings were within 10 miles of each other and just a day's march from the Georgia capital.

EAST OF MACON

From the start of the march, Brigadier General Judson Kilpatrick's 3rd Cavalry Division had ridden to the far right of Howard's massed columns. He had been ordered to travel south—as close to Macon as he dared—and to tear up the railroad tracks as he went. He was then to close up again near Milledgeville. On November 20, he had a brief skirmish with Wheeler's cavalry just east of Macon, quickly driving the Confederates back into the line of entrenchments surrounding the city.

The next day, a single regiment, Captain Frederick S. Ladd's 9th Michigan, was sent to assault the small industrial town of Griswoldville, 10 miles east of Macon. Moving in without resistance, the cavalrymen soon destroyed most of the buildings in town, including the railroad station, a pistol factory, and a candle and soap factory. As they mopped up, Colonel Eli H. Murray's 1st Brigade settled in for the night about 2 miles to the east.

The Capital City

As the right wing set up just to their south, Slocum's left wing made ready to enter Milledgeville, the Georgia capital. By November 19, it became obvious that the capital was Sherman's real target, and pandemonium erupted. The Georgia legislature was then in session, and upon hearing of the danger promptly sprang into action. A law was quickly passed requiring every physically able male citizen to join in the armed resistance to the Union invasion, exempting only themselves and sitting judges from the noble sacrifice. Turning to issues of a more immediate nature, they then authorized expenditure of $3,000 in public funds to hire a train to carry themselves, their families, their furniture, and their baggage to safety.

Governor Joseph Emerson Brown, second from right, in a political cartoon of the period

Georgia's governor, Joseph Emerson Brown, acted in an equally heroic manner. Stripping the governor's mansion of everything that wasn't nailed down (and a few things that were), he fled Milledgeville at a high rate of speed. Not far behind was the trainload of politicians from the legislature, who left with scarcely more dignity, actually pausing long enough to announce they were heading "for the front" before setting off in the opposite direction.

Civilians were equally panicked, but most lacked access to tax money to use to flee the city. A. C. Cooper, a local resident who had left Atlanta on Sherman's approach in July, later wrote about the effect of Sherman on the horizon:

> *Reports varied; one would be that the enemy would be upon us ere long, as a few bluecoats had been seen in the distance, and we women were advised to pack up and flee, but there was blank silence when we asked, "Where shall we flee?" . . . Hurry,*

> *scurry, run here, run there, run everywhere. Women cried and prayed, babies yelled . . . dogs howled and yelped, mules brayed.*

Late in the night of November 21, the first Union cavalry scouts entered the city, followed the next afternoon by the vanguard of the Union left wing, both without encountering the slightest act of resistance. Moving down Greene Street, officers of the XX Corps ordered the men into parade march, and with the bands playing selections of Northern patriotic tunes, made their way to the steps of the capitol building. With the bands sarcastically playing "Dixie," a large U.S. flag was raised on the building's tall flagpole.

As their men fanned out to see what they could steal in the city, officers amused themselves by occupying the recently deserted seats in the state legislature. In a high-spirited debate, the issue of secession was once again bandied about and promptly voted down. Sherman, who rode into town the next day, said that he "enjoyed the joke."

Griswoldville

As Sherman's officers were amusing themselves playing politician in the legislative chambers, things were a bit more subdued just to the south. At dawn on November 22, Wheeler's cavalry suddenly struck Murray's encampment. A short but furious fight ensued, ending when reinforcements from Colonel Charles C. Walcutt's 2nd Brigade (Union) rushed to Murray's aid. Together they pushed the Confederate cavalrymen back through the burned-out town of Griswoldville before breaking contact and returning to their original positions, where they heavily entrenched atop a small, wooded ridge.

The previous day Lieutenant General William J. Hardee, commander of the Confederate forces facing Sherman, had become aware that the Union forces were bypassing his location at Macon and made the assumption that they were heading toward the critical supply and manufacturing depot at Augusta. A hastily assembled force was pieced together around Major General Gustavus Woodson Smith's four regiments of the Georgia Militia and ordered to move out posthaste to protect the river city.

Besides the four brigades of Georgia Militia, the small task force contained Major Ferdinand W. C. Cook's Athens and Augusta Local Defense Battalions; Captain Ruel W. Anderson's four-gun Light Artillery Battery; and the decimated ranks of the combined two regiments of the Georgia State Line under Lieutenant Colonel Beverly D. Evans. With the exception of the State Line, which had been in nearly continuous combat since May 29, the overwhelming majority of the command were the archetypal "old men and boys," this force representing the bottom of the barrel for reinforcements.

By Hardee's direction, Colonel James N. Willis's 1st Brigade, Georgia Militia, left early on the morning of November 22 along with Cook's command, bound for Augusta via the road to Griswoldville, to be followed later that same day by the remaining commands. Hardee left at the same time for Savannah to help prepare its defenses, and Smith elected to remain in Macon to do administrative chores, leaving command of the task force to the senior officer present, Brigadier General Pleasant J. Philips. As the Confederates left Macon, quite a few in the ranks remarked about how much Philips had been seen drinking that morning.

As Philips's command moved out, Howard's entire right wing was also on the move, swinging a little more to the south and heading straight toward Griswoldville.

THE BATTLE

Philips left Macon with the main part of his command and marched steadily on, arriving at the outskirts of Griswoldville just after noon. There he found Cook's defense battalions drawn up into a defensive perimeter, having spotted the well-entrenched Union lines just up the road.

Despite his explicit orders from both Hardee and Smith not to do so, Philips ordered preparations for an attack. Arranging his men perpendicular to the railroad tracks on the east side of town, Brigadier General Charles D. Anderson's 3rd Brigade, Georgia Militia, was placed on the left, just north of the tracks. Brigadier General Henry K. McKay's 4th Brigade was placed on Anderson's right, just south of the tracks, and Philips's own 2nd Brigade (now commanded by Colonel James

N. Mann) moved in reserve to the rear of McKay. Evans's State Line troopers moved forward in the very center as skirmishers, and Cook's small battalions took the extreme right of the line. Anderson's battery set up just north of the tracks near the center of the line.

Facing Philips's small command was Walcutt's strong 2nd Brigade, 1st Division, XV Corps, consisting of no fewer than seven reduced-strength infantry regiments (the 12th, 97th, and 100th Indiana; 40th and 103rd Illinois; 6th Iowa; and 46th Ohio), two cavalry regiments (5th Kentucky and 9th Pennsylvania), and Captain Albert Arndt's Battery B, 1st Michigan Artillery. In all, about 4,000 mostly ill-trained and poorly equipped Georgia troops faced about 3,000 well-armed, well-entrenched, and combat-hardened veteran Union troops.

About 2:30 p.m. Philips ordered an all-out assault, and the ragged force began moving smartly across the open field toward the Union entrenchments. Major Asias Willison of the 103rd Illinois wrote in his after-action report what happened next:

> As soon as they came within range of our muskets, a most terrific fire was poured into their ranks, doing fearful execution . . . still they moved forward, and came within 45 yards of our works. Here they attempted to reform their line, but so destructive was the fire that they were compelled to retire.

While most of Philips's militiamen were being blown apart behind them, the State Line charged up the slope toward the Union position, only to be thrown back to the wooded base. The State Line charged several more times, meeting the same result, until Evans was seriously wounded and all retired from the field.

Most of the militiamen never got closer than 50 yards to the Union position but bravely held their ground and returned fire until dusk. Philips then ordered a retreat off the field, and the shattered ranks limped slowly back into Macon. Left behind were 51 killed, 422 wounded, and 9 missing. The Union lines were never in any real danger of being breached, but losses amounted to 13 killed, 79 wounded, and 2 missing in the brief fight. Walcutt himself was among the wounded and had to be carried off the field during the engagement, to be replaced by Colonel Robert F. Catterson.

SHERMAN DRIVES ON

*W*ith the pitiful remnants of Philips's command safely back inside Macon's defense by 2 a.m. on November 23, there was literally nothing standing between Sherman and any path he might choose to take next. That morning he issued new orders for all four corps to march east, the southern wing to head straight down the Georgia Central Railroad tracks toward Millen (near Buckhead Creek), while the northern wing and attached cavalry were to follow roads on the north side of the tracks. Their target was Camp Lawton, sometimes called Magnolia Springs, to rescue the estimated 11,000 Union prisoners recently brought there from Andersonville.

Early on the morning of November 24 the grand march resumed. Strangely, Milledgeville was left relatively intact, although all the government buildings, libraries, and some churches were ransacked and desecrated, and, once again, anything of value went along with the blue-suits.

Confederate resistance to this part of the march was nearly nonexistent, and those who did show up were grossly outnumbered. A good example is the defense of the Oconee River bridge near Oconee, where a force of exactly 186 men, the remnants of three separate commands, stood ready to keep Sherman from crossing. Even with nearly 1,000 cavalrymen from Wheeler's command backing them up, more than 30,000 Union soldiers moved like a blue tidal wave down the road to crush them. Fortunately, cooler heads prevailed, and the tiny command was withdrawn before it made contact.

Sherman still today has a reputation as a thief and firebug in certain parts of Georgia, and this section of the grand march is where it was earned. All along, "authorized" foraging parties had scoured the countryside, collecting food for both soldiers and animals, and "jes' a lil' " booty for themselves while they were at it. With military opposition nearly nonexistent, and no doubt with the blessings of many veteran officers, roving gangs of "bummers" roamed the countryside, casually stealing or destroying whatever caught their fancy. A 40-mile-wide path between Milledgeville and Millen was stripped down nearly to the roots; one traveler who crossed this area shortly after Sherman's passing remarked that everything down to and including fence posts had either been taken or burned.

The destruction the Union troops were creating started to disturb many Union officers, although Sherman himself wasn't among them. His attitude was that the Georgians had "forced" him to sponsor such actions by virtue of their secession and that he only regretted that he "had" to do such acts. The situation deteriorated so much at one point that even Sherman's blindly admiring aide, Major Henry Hitchcock, noted in his memoirs that "I am bound to say I think Sherman lacking in enforcing discipline."

Millen

Major General Blair's XVII Corps arrived in Millen completely without resistance on December 1. Brigadier General Judson Kilpatrick's 3rd Cavalry Division, moving rapidly to the north on Sherman's personal order, arrived at the site of Camp Lawton on November 27, after a fierce resistance by Wheeler's cavalry, only to discover that the Union prisoners had been moved again, this time to a rude camp near Blackshear, 10 miles northeast of Waycross and the Okefenokee Swamp in deep southeastern Georgia.

Sherman entered Millen on December 3 with the rest of his army. Deeply angered that he had been unable to rescue the POWs, he issued orders to march directly on Savannah beginning the next morning, and took out his wrath on the small town as they left. In a classic understatement, he mentioned in his memoirs, "I caused the fine depot of Millen to be destroyed, and other damage done . . . "

THE LAST OF THE MARCH

*L*eaving Millen on the morning of December 4, all four corps marched directly toward Savannah and

Map showing the investment and siege of Savannah, December 1864

arrived nearly unmolested on the outskirts of the city between December 10 and 12. Along the way, two separate Confederate defenses were mounted with what remained of the Georgia Militia and the Georgia State Line supplemented by Wheeler's cavalry and some local defense forces. On both occasions their commanders elected to withdraw in the face of such overwhelming Union opposition.

Savannah's defenses were formidable, stretching more than 13 miles from the Savannah River to the Little Ogeechee River and manned by just under 10,000 men—the bare remnants of every militia and state defense force that could be scraped together. In addition, more than 50 artillery pieces with a fair supply of ammunition sat in the ring of strong earthwork fortifications.

Sherman had a serious problem by this time; his supplies of food and clothing were running critically low, and there was nothing much in the surrounding salt marshes and swamps that he could send foraging parties out for. He desperately needed to make contact with the Union Navy, lying just off the coast, but the two possible river approaches were both guarded by powerful Confederate fortifications. Needing the supply line open and open fast, he personally ordered Brigadier General William Babcock Hazen to take his 2nd Division (XV Corps) down to the Ogeechee River 14 miles below Savannah, assault and take the Confederate fort there, and open the river to the Union Navy.

Fort McAllister

Fort McAllister, on Genesis Point guarding the entrance to the Ogeechee River, had been designed by Major John McCrady, chief engineer for the state of Georgia, in the late spring of 1861. Ordinarily, a massive masonry fort like Fort Pulaski or Jackson east of Savannah would be desirable, but these were time-, money-, and manpower-intensive projects, and McCrady had none of those resources.

Instead he settled on a star-shaped, four-gun emplacement earthwork fort with walls 20 feet tall and 17 feet thick, originally intended to be equipped with four 32-pounder smoothbore cannons. The walls originally only faced the river, and a large earthen bombproof stood behind the gun emplacements to serve

Fort McAllister on the Ogeechee River, photographed in 1864

as a hospital. On June 7, 1861, the DeKalb Rifles, Company A, 1st Georgia Infantry Regiment under Lieutenant Alfred L. Hartridge was sent in to build and man the structure.

Having an infantry company build and man an artillery post strikes one as an odd move, but the relatively few trained cannoneers were needed at posts where actual combat was expected. At backwater posts like Fort McAllister, infantry companies were customarily sent in to while away the war years.

Hartridge's men did a very good job, clearing away the thick forest for a mile behind the fort site to provide clear lanes of fire and almost immediately setting about building up and improving the design.

FORT McALLISTER IN COMBAT

By the time of Sherman's arrival, the earthwork fort had been tripled in size and assaulted without success some seven separate times by Union gunboats. The DeKalb Rifles had long since departed for hotter action to the north, and a new commander had taken over, Major George W. Anderson. The garrison now consisted of about 230 men of the Emmet Rifles and the Georgia Reserves, along with real artillerymen of Captain Nicholas B. Clinch's Georgia Light Artillery Battery.

The post by this time looked quite different, having been expanded into a five-sided fort 650 feet long and 750 feet wide, with a dry ditch studded with sharpened stake abatis surrounding it. More and heavier artillery had been brought in; two 32-pounder rifled guns, three 10-inch Columbiads, and three 8-inch Columbiads guarded the river approaches. To guard against expected infantry attacks, a rear wall slightly smaller than the front wall had been built and 12 field artillery pieces mounted atop it. To complete the armament, a 10-inch Tredegar Seacoast Mortar was mounted just outside the main defense walls.

The reluctant decision to make the post an earthwork arrangement proved most fortuitous. Fort Pulaski, a few miles to the north and long regarded as an impregnable guardian of the northern approaches to Savannah, had been breached by heavy rifled cannon fire on April 11, 1862, and surrendered after a mere 30 hours of shelling. The earth walls of Fort McAllister were nearly impervious to incoming fire, the walls either deflecting or swallowing up the Union artillery fire. Even if a shell buried deep in the earth before exploding, repairing the crater was a simple matter of shoveling a few wheelbarrow loads of dirt back in it. The thousand-year era of the heavy masonry fort had come to an end.

HAZEN'S APPROACH

Sherman's choice of the West Point graduate's division to assault the Confederate fort was not a random one; not only had Hazen proven to be a capable and brave battlefield commander, but the 2nd Division was the same that Sherman had commanded at Vicksburg and Shiloh, one in which he "felt a special pride and confidence." Hazen was ordered to take the fort as soon as possible, and he left the morning of December 13, marching rapidly down the old Hardwicke Road (now GA 144).

Shortly after noon, Hazen reached the causeway leading out to the fort and promptly captured the lone Confederate sentry posted there, Private Thomas Mills. After his capture, Mills revealed that his unit had placed "torpedoes," or buried shells that exploded when stepped on, all along the soft sand causeway. Hazen ordered his men to immediately search for and dig up the land mines, delaying his approach to the fort.

By the time the road was made safe and the rest of his command came into line, it was after 4:30 p.m. Leaving nine regiments behind as reserves, Hazen moved the other nine regiments forward until they were arrayed in a semicircle around the isolated post, but no closer than 600 yards out. Confederate guns opened up, but with little effect. Union skirmishers ran forward, closing to within 200 yards of the fort, and began a damaging fire on the gunners. One of the fort's major weaknesses was the fact that all the guns were mounted en barbette, or up on top of the ramparts, leaving the gunners exposed to rifle fire.

One of the "big guns" on the ramparts of Fort McAllister

THE BATTLE FOR FORT McALLISTER

Sherman, watching the action from atop a rice mill across the river, was nearly beside himself with impatience. As the afternoon wore on and dusk approached, he had a signal sent over to Hazen: "You must carry the fort by assault tonight, if possible." A few minutes later a reply came back: "I am ready and will assault at once!" At 4:45 p.m. Hazen ordered a general assault to begin.

As the Union infantry sprang to their feet and began moving toward the fort at the double-quick, a furious rain of fire came from both sides. Moving up close to the ramparts, the Union men had almost entered the outer defense bands when huge explosions rocked the earth; more torpedoes had been buried all around the fort in the soft sand, making them nearly impossible to spot. Forcing their way forward despite the deadly mines and deafening cannon fire to their front, the 47th Ohio quickly gained the west wall and began running down it, looking for an opening to enter the fort. At the far northwestern corner, they discovered that the line of abatis stopped above the high-tide mark (it was then low tide), and they quickly ran through the opening and up onto the ramparts.

Almost at the same moment, the 70th Ohio and 111th Illinois Regiments pushed through the tangle of fixed defenses and appeared atop the ramparts nearby, and the fight quickly escalated into a vicious hand-to-hand brawl. The Confederate garrison refused to surrender, even in the face of such overwhelming odds. As each artillery position was overrun, the cannoneers continued to resist with ramrods swung as clubs and even just their fists, until bayoneted or beaten to the ground by the swarming blue masses. Each bomb-proof emplacement had to be taken individually, and the fight ended only when every last Confederate was killed, wounded, or beaten into submission. Hazen stated in his after-action report that "the line moved on without checking, over, under and through abatis, ditches, palisading and parapet, fighting the garrison through the fort to their bomb-proofs, from which

they still fought and only succumbed as each man was individually overpowered."

Although the whole action took only 15 minutes to complete, the fight was somewhat more than the Union soldiers had expected. The resistance of Captain Nicholas B. Clinch, commanding Clinch's Light Battery, which was stationed on the landward side of the fort, was typical:

> When [Clinch was] summoned to surrender by a Federal captain [Captain Stephen F. Grimes of the 48th Illinois], [he] responded by dealing a severe blow to the head with his sabre. (Captain Clinch had previously received two gunshot wounds in the arm.) Immediately a hand-to-hand fight ensued. Federal privates came to the assistance of their fellow officer, but the fearless Clinch continued the unequal contest until he fell bleeding from eleven wounds (three sabre wounds, six bayonet wounds, and two gunshot wounds), from which, after severe and protracted suffering, he has barely recovered. His conduct was so conspicuous, and his cool bravery so much admired, as to elicit the praise of the enemy and even of General Sherman himself.

Anderson had to know that his position had no hope of reinforcement from Hardee's troops inside Savannah, nor did he have any real chance of stopping Hazen's men from taking his post. However, in the archaic Southern fashion, he stood his ground and resisted until there was no one left standing. In his after-action report he noted, "The fort was never surrendered. It was captured by overwhelming numbers."

With the fall of Fort McAllister, the March to the Sea for all practical purposes ended. By 5 p.m. Sherman was able to signal the route was clear to a navy steamer already coming up the river with badly needed supplies. Losses were high for such a short fight, with Hazen losing 24 killed and 110 wounded and Anderson losing 17 killed, 31 wounded, and all the rest made prisoner.

SAVANNAH

As soon as news reached Hardee of the fall of Fort McAllister, he knew that holding onto Savannah would be futile and began making preparations to evacuate his army into South Carolina. His engineers immediately set about making a series of pontoon bridges from the foot of West Broad Street, across the network of tidal rivers, to Hardeville on the South Carolina border. This escape route ran along the narrow top of Huger's Causeway (roughly the route that US 17 follows today). A thick layer of rice straw was put over the wooden planks of the bridges to deaden the sound of wagon and gun carriage wheels. All was ready by December 19, and everyone impatiently awaited Hardee's order to leave.

Meanwhile, back on the siege line, Union gunners had kept up a steady drumbeat of fire on the city since setting up on December 10. Sherman's engineers built a series of large, well-fortified gun emplacements for the large siege cannon they expected to receive via the navy in short order, and most began settling in for what was expected to be another long stand. On December 17 Sherman sent a rather harsh note to Hardee demanding his immediate surrender, warning that he had plenty of large guns and ammunition and that unless quarter was given he would "make little effort to restrain my army burning to avenge the great national wrong they attach to Savannah and other large cities which have been so prominent in dragging our country into civil war."

Hardee, obviously bidding for a little more time, replied the next morning that he refused to surrender, and indicated that if Sherman carried out his threats to ignore the conventions of war and carry out unrestrained rape and pillage, then Hardee would "deeply regret the adoption of any course by you that may force me to deviate from them in the future." For the time, this was a rather crude and uncivilized exchange of threats. Both men knew it—and neither was fully prepared to back them up.

To cover up his planned movement, Hardee requested what help was available from the Confederate

Navy and sent three regiments of infantry to reinforce Wheeler's cavalry up on the line. Late on the afternoon of December 20, the Confederate ironclad *Savannah* steamed upriver a bit and began lobbing shells at the Union positions. As darkness fell, every heavy artillery position began shooting up what was left of their ammunition supply, heavy shells raining down with some accuracy on the Union positions for more than two hours.

While the shot, shell, and canister rounds kept the Union troops' heads down, Hardee began his retreat out of the city. All the field guns that could be moved left first, while work gangs set the remaining boats afire at their moorings. When the big guns' ammunition ran out, their crews spiked the barrels and watered down the remaining gunpowder in the magazines. Major General Ambrose R. Wright's division was the first to leave at about 8 p.m., followed by Major General Lafayette McLaw's division two hours later and Smith's Georgia Militia at 11 p.m.

Acting as the rear guard, the Georgia State Line, now under command of Colonel James D. Wilson, stayed in their skirmish line and, along with Wheeler's cavalry, kept up a steady fire toward the Union lines. When a signal rocket flared up about 1 a.m., both commands gradually ceased fire, and one company at a time left the trenches and quickly moved across the bridges into South Carolina. The bridges were then sunk in place or cut loose from their moorings by engineers, the last link setting adrift at 5:40 a.m. on December 21.

Union Troops Enter the City

When all firing ceased about 3 a.m., forward skirmishers of a dozen different Union regiments cautiously moved forward and dropped into the newly abandoned Confederate positions. Sending word back of their discovery, a general advance was soon ordered, and Sherman's "bummers" began moving east into the city itself. The advance was led by Brigadier General John W. Geary's 2nd Division (XX Corps). About 4:30 a.m., as the last of Hardee's men were filtering across the river to the north, Colonel Henry A. Barnum of the 3rd Brigade, Geary's division, encountered Mayor Richard D. Arnold of Savannah near the intersection of Louisville and Augusta Roads. There the mayor handed

★ ★ ★ ★ ★ ★ ★ ★ ★ ★ ★ ★ ★ ★ ★ ★

the Union colonel a formal letter of surrender of the city, addressed to Sherman:

Savannah, Dec. 21, 1864

Maj. Gen. W. T. Sherman, Commanding U.S. Forces near Savannah:

Sir: The city of Savannah was last night evacuated by Confederate military and is now defenseless. As chief magistrate of the city I respectfully request your protection of the lives and private property of the citizens and of our women and children. Trusting that this appeal to your generosity and humanity may favorably influence your action, I have the honor to be, your obedient servant,

R. D. Arnold
Mayor of Savannah

Barnum's men continued into the city, where, as the rosy light of dawn appeared over the horizon, the Stars and Stripes were once again raised over the U.S. Customs house. Two brigades moved on east to take the newly abandoned post at old Fort Jackson. As they entered and raised the national banner on the ramparts,

> The last state to be rid of its military occupation by the Union Army was Georgia, in February 1870.

the *Savannah,* retreating downriver, lobbed a few shells their way. Union batteries returned fire, but these last shots of the campaign had no real effect on either side.

Sherman had been at nearby Hilton Head Island conferring with navy officers on the next plan of action and did not return to the city until late on the night of December 21. Making his headquarters in the large, comfortable Green-Meldrin House at Madison Square (still existent), he sent a telegram from the parlor to President Lincoln the next day:

Savannah, Ga., Dec. 22, 1864

His Excellency President Lincoln,

I beg to present to you, as a Christmas gift, the city of Savannah, with 150 heavy guns and plenty of ammunition, and also about 25,000 bales of cotton.

W. T. Sherman
Major General

Sherman entering Savannah, December 21, 1864

✯   ✯   ✯   ✯   ✯   ✯   ✯   ✯   ✯   ✯   ✯   ✯   ✯   ✯   ✯   ✯

POINTS OF INTEREST

For places to visit in and around Atlanta, see the recommendations in our chapter on Dalton to Jonesboro. We emphasize the near necessity for anyone even remotely interested in the war to visit the Atlanta History Center in Buckhead and the Atlanta Cyclorama at Grant Park.

Confederate Memorial

Located in Forsyth Park (on Bull Street between Gaston Street and Park Avenue) is the large, rather imposing monument honoring the area's Civil War dead. This is claimed to be the largest such memorial in the South and was the most expensive by a long shot. When unveiled in 1875, the original monument showcased two statues: *Judgment* and *Silence.* The public reaction to the gaudy original was harshly negative, and the monument quickly underwent a multithousand-dollar renovation, unveiled again in 1879 with only a simple sculpture of a soldier on top. Used as a Union encampment during the occupation, today the park is the setting for quite a number of festivals and events.

Fort Jackson
1 Fort Jackson Rd.
Savannah, GA
(912) 232-3945
www.chsgeorgia.org

Located 2½ miles from the center of town on the (only) road out to Tybee Island, this is the oldest standing brick fortress in the United States, built in 1808. The 20-foot-high walls contained five 32-pounder smoothbore cannon, one 32-pounder rifled gun, two 8-inch Columbiads, and one 12-pounder mountain howitzer, all manned during the war by the 22nd Battalion of Heavy Artillery commanded by Major Edward Clifford Anderson (later the mayor of Savannah). A small museum inside houses displays centering on the Confederate naval history of the area, including several about the CSS *Georgia,* whose watery grave is marked by a red buoy about 300 yards away in the Savannah River.

The only action here during the war came in a brief 1862 skirmish with two Union gunboats and when it was fired upon by the CSS *Savannah* as Union troops raised their flag atop it in December 1864. E-mail for current prices before a visit, at oldfortjackson@dnsgeorgia.org.

Fort McAllister State Historic Park
3894 Fort McAllister Rd.
Richmond Hill, GA
(912) 727-2339
www.gastateparks.org/FtMcallister

This 1,700-acre park between the Ogeechee River and Red Bird Creek has two alluring identities: It's the site of the earthen fort that guarded the southern approach to the Savannah area, and it's a recreational area with amenities for campers and picnickers. These two attractions once existed as Fort McAllister State Historic Park and Richmond Hill State Park; in 1980 they were combined, and today the Georgia Department of Natural Resources operates the site.

Fort McAllister is one of the best-preserved earthwork fortifications built by the Confederacy during the Civil War. The site was once owned by Henry Ford, who began an extensive restoration in the late 1930s. The fort eventually fell into the hands of the state of Georgia, which restored it to near its 1863–64 appearance.

You can wander around the walls and through the interior of the fort and look inside its central bomb-proof, but be careful not to climb on these earthen structures, which are extremely susceptible to erosion from foot traffic. Take the self-guided tour of the fort and check out a 32-pounder smoothbore gun that fired red-hot cannonballs and the furnace where these projectiles were heated; the reconstructed service magazine, which held shells, powder, and fuses for the rebels' 32-pounder rifled gun; and the fort's northwest angle, where the 47th Ohio Infantry Regiment placed the first U.S. flag planted on the parapets.

The fort site also has a Civil War museum and gift shop containing Civil War shells and weapons; implements such as those used in the construction of the fort; artifacts from the Confederate blockade-runner *Nashville,* which was sunk in the Ogeechee by the Union ironclad *Montauk;* a diorama of the assault on the fort; and a display depicting life at the fort as experienced by its 230 defenders.

For day-trippers, the main attraction of the recreational area is the tree-filled picnic ground running along a high bluff overlooking the Ogeechee River. Tall pines and hardwoods make this a shady, serene spot for walking or sitting in a glider-type swing and watching the river flow by. You'll find 50 sites with picnic tables and grills, a fishing pier that extends out over the river, and plenty of rustic-looking playground equipment for the kids in this area, which borders the main road leading to the fort.

If you plan on making your visit to Richmond Hill–Liberty County last longer than a day and you like roughing it, consider staying at the park's Savage Island Campground, which has 65 campsites—50 for recreational vehicles and 15 with tent pads—all with water and electrical hookups, grills, and tables. Two comfort stations provide campers with toilets, heated showers, and washer/dryers, and the campground also has a playground, nature trail, and dock and boat ramp on Red Bird Creek.

Georgia's Old Capital Museum

Statehouse Square, on campus
* of Georgia Military College*
210 E. Greene St.
Milledgeville, GA
(478) 453-1803
www.oldcapitalmuseum.org

This imposing Gothic-style building is considered to be the oldest public building in the nation built in such a style. Begun and first used in 1803, the building served as the State Capitol until 1863. The original structure was severely damaged in several post–Civil War fires and was restored to nearly original condition in 1943. Another restoration was completed in the fall of 2001.

The Gothic-style gates at the north and south entrances to the campus were constructed just after the war from bricks salvaged from the arsenal and powder magazine blown up by Sherman's troops.

Green-Meldrim House

St. Johns Church
14 W. Macon St.
Savannah, GA
(912) 233-3845

Built in Gothic Revival style in 1853 for wealthy cotton grower Charles Green, the house was offered to Sherman for his headquarters by the owner. Green was concerned that if Sherman did not use the structure, another Union general would, and he would "suffer the indignity of such a situation." The famous "Christmas gift" telegram was sent to Lincoln from the front parlor, where Sherman also learned of the death of his infant son Charles, born during the long Georgia Campaign. Sherman never saw his son alive.

Today the home is owned by its neighbor, St. Johns Church, and serves as the parish house. The home is open for tours. Prices are subject to change; call before visiting.

Milledgeville Visitor Center

200 W. Hancock St.
Milledgeville, GA
(478) 452-4687
(800) 653-1804
www.milledgevillecvb.com

We suggest a visit here for a copy of the excellent map and guide for a walking tour of the old part of town. Trolley tours are available here, as well as information on the series of festivals held throughout the year.

Old Governor's Mansion

120 S. Clark St.
Milledgeville, GA
(478) 445-4545
www.gcsu.edu/mansion

Built in the Greek Revival style in 1839, this was the home of 10 Georgia governors, including Joseph Emerson Brown, who was arrested here by Union authorities in May 1865. Sherman rolled out his bedroll on the bare wooden floor downstairs to spend the night on November 23, remarking good-naturedly how rude it was of Brown to have left before such a distinguished visitor had arrived! Group tours are available.

Savannah Visitor Center & History Museum

301 and 303 Martin Luther King Jr. Blvd.
Savannah, GA
(912) 944-0460
(912) 651-6825
www.savannahvisit.com
www.chsgeorgia.org

Housed in the old Central Georgia Railroad Station, the visitor center is large and rather imposing, with a very helpful staff and a moderate selection of maps and brochures of local attractions. A large museum houses a nicely presented, small selection of artifacts from every phase of this city's long history, including uniforms and equipment belonging to Savannah's own regiments, as well as Forrest Gump's park bench. A short film, *Savannah the Survivor,* gives a breathless overview of the area history but hardly touches on the Civil War period. A small bookstore and no fewer than two gift shops round out the offerings, and several tour companies load up just outside the side entrance.

ACCOMMODATIONS

Atlanta

Atlanta is a major tourist and convention destination, and the hospitality industry in Fulton County alone employs more than 115,000 workers and pays more than $215 million in taxes to local governments. Needless to say, just about any chain hotel or motel in every price range is readily available. The Downtown Connector, the merging of I-75 and I-85 through downtown Atlanta, is the major corridor to all the listed amenities, and a short drive out in any direction on the three highways (including I-20) is the best bet for lower-priced chain establishments at nearly any exit.

Savannah

Savannah is a city of great diversity, and that characteristic holds true when it comes to the accommodations it offers its visitors. Savannah has several hotels that are large and contemporary and others that are medium-size and quaint. It has motels that are moderately priced but comfortable and others where, for a few dollars more, you'll be awash in amenities. Many of the hotels and motels offer suites in addition to rooms with the standard two double beds or one king-size bed, and a couple of establishments have nothing but suites.

Each of the hotels and motels listed here accepts major credit cards and is wheelchair-accessible. Almost all have nonsmoking rooms, and most do not allow pets. All establishments have color cable TV; if you're looking for premium channels, a phone call might be in order.

The in-season generally runs from mid-Mar through Oct. Some establishments decrease their rates during the hot summer months, and others jack them up on weekends, so call in advance to ascertain how much you'll have to spend. If you're planning to stay here on St. Patrick's Day weekend, expect to fork out considerably more than you would at any other time of year, and make reservations months in advance.

Best Western Promenade Hotel in the
Historic District $–$$
412 W. Bay St.
Savannah, GA
(912) 233-1011
www.promenadesavannah.com

This motel has been accommodating visitors to Savannah since the early 1970s. Once you arrive at the Best Western Historic District, you can park your car and leave it for the rest of your stay, according to the folks who run the 143-room motel. The Best Western fronts Bay Street, and the motel's rear building is on the western end of River Street, placing the three-story establishment about a block from the shops and restaurants along the river and in City Market. It's within walking distance of much of the historic district. If you want to do your sightseeing while riding, hop on a tour bus or trolley at the motel's front door. There is a complimentary continental breakfast and a fenced-in pool for swimming and sunning on the River Street side of the property. Eighty-seven of the rooms have two full-size beds, and the rest have kings.

The Confederate House $$$
808 Drayton St.
Savannah, GA
(912) 234-9779
(800) 975-7457
www.theconfederatehouse.com

One of the most romantic inns in Savannah, this 1854 Greek Revival home overlooks Forsythe Park.

Courtyard Savannah Midtown $$$$
6703 Abercorn St.
Savannah, GA
(912) 354-7878
(888) 832-0327
www.marriott.com

The Marriott's Courtyard Savannah Midtown stands between two of the city's busiest thoroughfares, Abercorn Street and White Bluff Road, but the three-story motel's beautifully landscaped grounds will give you a feeling of being away from the madding crowd. The centerpiece of the motel is the tree-filled courtyard with its quaint gazebo and swimming pool. Just off the pool is an enclosed whirlpool surrounded by lots of space for lounging, and a recently renovated fitness room near the lobby sports all-new exercise equipment. The Courtyard's large dining area, the Courtyard Café, is open for breakfast, with a full meal and continental servings available. There are 132 newly renovated rooms, including 12 suites, and all have sleeper sofas. Rooms on the upper floors open onto balconies. There are two meeting rooms, each of which can accommodate 24 persons seated at tables. Free parking is available.

Hilton Savannah DeSoto $$$$
15 E. Liberty St.
Savannah, GA
(912) 232-9000
(800) HILTONS
www1.hilton.com

This 15-story hotel stands in the midst of the historic district, and the views from rooms on the upper floors, particularly those with balconies, are spectacular. The concierge floor—the 13th, numbered as such by hotel officials apparently unconcerned with superstition—offers what staff members call the "skyline view." You'll pay extra to stay there, but you'll get the view, a room featuring deluxe amenities such as the Hilton's trademark terry-cloth bathrobes, and the use of a private lounge serving continental breakfast in the morning and drinks and hors d'oeuvres in the evening. Step out on the balcony of the lounge and enjoy a panoramic look at the graceful Eugene Talmadge Memorial Bridge and Savannah's riverfront. If you really want to stay in style, request a "corner king"—a room with a king-size bed, balcony, two large corner windows, and a bathroom equipped with a double vanity. You can dine on the premises at Beulah's, which serves breakfast, lunch, and dinner Southern-style, and you can unwind at the DeSoto Grille, newly renovated and offering Southern cuisine. Beulah's serves coffee, breakfast dishes, sandwiches, and salads.

The Hilton was built in 1968 on the site of the DeSoto Hotel, which was constructed in 1890 and was a Savannah landmark for decades. A sitting room off the lobby of the Hilton affords guests a glimpse of the old hotel—the walls are covered with memorabilia, including framed banquet programs from visits by several U.S. presidents. There is also a limousine shuttle service. Pets are allowed.

RESTAURANTS

Atlanta

As a primary travel destination and a large, well-populated urban center all in one, Atlanta has more than its fair share of eating establishments. More than 7,500 exist in the 10-county metro area; with so many newly built restaurants opening nearly daily, the five major newspaper reviewers admit regularly that they can't keep up. A fair warning, though: Nearly as many close just as quickly, which makes the eating-out scene here quite dynamic. Again, the following is a bare sample. For the best and most recently updated listings, look for a copy of the Fri or Sat edition of the *Atlanta Journal-Constitution,* or (preferably) a copy of *Creative Loafing* (free), which shows up in green-colored newspaper racks on Wed. The price range in each restaurant listing gives the cost of dinner for two, excluding cocktails, beer or wine, appetizer, dessert, tax, and tip.

Atkins Park $–$$
794 N. Highland Ave.
Atlanta, GA
(404) 876-7249
www.atkinspark.com

With a liquor license first issued in 1927, Atkins Park has the distinction of being the oldest bar in Atlanta. It hearkens back to the age of dark, wood-paneled, beery neighborhood bars. A perennial favorite of the Virginia-Highlands neighborhood, Atkins Park offers a changing menu, including specialties such as Southern-fried chicken and Wild Georgia Shrimp and Grits, as well as pasta and burgers.

The Varsity $
61 North Ave.
Atlanta, GA
(404) 881-1706
www.thevarsity.com

The one and only, the Varsity is a long-beloved Atlanta institution. At the corner of Spring Street and North Avenue, the original Varsity (there are Junior Varsitys in the Cheshire Bridge Road area of Atlanta, in Norcross, and in Athens) is just across the North Avenue bridge from Georgia Tech. It opened in 1928 and claims the distinction of being the world's largest drive-in. Every day, this single restaurant serves up to 2 miles of hot dogs, a ton of onion rings, and 5,000 fried pies. Friendly, sometimes eccentric carhops will bring your food out to your car, or you can eat inside in one of several "TV rooms." The serving counters here are a bee-hive of activity; the slogan is "Have your money in your hand and your order in your mind." The onion rings may just be the best on the planet. The Varsity does not serve alcohol.

Savannah

Your taste buds will be glad they came to Savannah—but your waistline might not be. The city offers a quantity and variety of restaurants completely out of proportion to its size. The local specialties lean heavily toward seafood, natu-rally, with shrimp fresh off the boats a particular favorite.

Crystal Beer Parlor $
301 W. Jones St.
Savannah, GA
(912) 349-1000
www.crystalbeerparlor.com

We go to the Crystal for the onion rings and the burgers, which are made from fresh sirloin ground in the beer parlor's kitchen, but there are many other selections on the menu—crab stew, shrimp-salad sandwiches, chili-dog platters, hot roast beef sandwiches, and baked stuffed flounder.

The Crystal is a local landmark, having been a favorite of Savannahians since it opened in 1933. With its high-back, padded booths and dark-wood paneling, the restaurant re-tains the feel of the 1930s. If you want to get an idea of what Savannah and its people were like 40 or 50 years ago, take a look at the Crystal's walls, which bear enlarged photographs depicting those times.

Reservations aren't required, but they're taken and are recommended for groups of 10 or more.

Spanky's Pizza Gallery & Saloon $
317 E. River St.
Savannah, GA
(912) 236-3009

308 Mall Way
Savannah, GA
(912) 355-3383

200 Governor Treutlen Rd.
Pooler, GA
(912) 748-8188

1605 Strand Ave.
Tybee Island, GA
(912) 786-5520
www.spankys.tv

Ansley Williams, Alben Yarbrough, and Dusty Yarbrough opened the first Spanky's on River Street in 1976, intend-ing to bring pizza to the area. They also served burgers and chicken sandwiches at the restaurant, which is housed in what had been a cotton warehouse. According to Williams, the chicken breasts used for the sandwiches were too large for the buns on which they were served, so the restaurants sliced off the excess chicken. Not wanting to be wasteful, they battered and fried the strips of meat and sold them as "chicken fingers." Their concoction was a hit with locals and has become a mainstay of eateries throughout southeast Georgia and the rest of the country.

The success of the River Street location led to the open-ing of Spanky's restaurants in other parts of the state, and lo-cally on the Southside near Oglethorpe Mall, in Pooler, and on Tybee Island (that one's called Spanky's Beachside). Williams and the Yarbroughs eventually went their separate ways, with Williams retaining ownership of the Spanky's on River Street and the Yarbroughs remaining involved with the others.

Andersonville:
The Worst Place on Earth

Darley.

Confederate officials searching for a place to hold thousands of Union prisoners as the war intensified in late 1863 found what they thought was a perfect place, on the Georgia Southwestern Railroad track at what they called Station Number 8, and the tiny adjacent village inhabitants called Andersonville. Captain William Sidney Winder, the officer in charge of the search, apparently had no intention of creating a hellhole when he chose this location. On the contrary, in his official report he mentions the "plentiful food" and water available, easily accessible transportation, and location far from the battle lines as the makings for a fine location.

THE PRISONER-OF-WAR SYSTEM

*U*ntil well into the second year of the war, the old European tradition of exchanging and "paroling" prisoners prevailed. After a given battle, equal numbers of prisoners from both sides were released, and those left were allowed to sign an oath that they should not take up arms again and were sent home. In theory this system worked rather well for the holding side; by allowing the prisoner to go home, you no longer had to feed, house, or guard him, and by virtue of his oath he had become a noncombatant.

This system required the mutual cooperation and honesty of each side, which did exist in the early part of the war. What makes the study of the Civil War so fascinating to many researchers is this very period, when war was conducted almost on a medieval model. Officers exchanged salutes before battle, quarter was given when requested, and opponents were addressed with the same honor and courtesy as fellow officers and men. General Robert E. Lee took this concept to a high level; throughout the war he was noted for his refusal to refer to the Union Army or any member of it as the "enemy," preferring the terms "those people over there" or "our friends opposite us."

Prisoners, and in particular officers, were usually quite well treated during the brief period they spent in captivity. It was routine for relations on opposite sides to "look each other up" if in the same area; tobacco, whiskey, and rations were often exchanged between inmates and guards; and even newspapers, debating societies, dances, and other parties were organized at some prisons. No one expected to have to house and feed prisoners for any serious length of time.

Both sides were so unprepared to deal with any real number of prisoners in the beginning, in fact, that some were held in local jails along with murderers, thieves, and other riffraff. The North began using old coastal fortifications and the South old factory buildings to hold the rapidly increasing numbers. Even with exchanges and paroles, the administrative bottlenecks soon caused overcrowding in each side's prisons.

The situation finally became critical after July 1863, when the exchange system collapsed because it became increasingly obvious that while Northern POWs honored their parole and went home to stay, the Confederates either went back to their units or joined another one. Numbers of POWs on both sides rapidly climbed, helped in no small part by the increasing number and severity of battles then taking place. The North attempted to control the problem by appointing a central authority over all the prison camps. Colonel William H. Hoffman (who had been a POW himself at the beginning of the war) set up a vast bureaucratic network of regulations, inspections, and standards for his camps. The South followed suit by appointing Brigadier General John H. Winder to a similar position, putting him in charge of all the Richmond POW camps, where nearly all the Union prisoners were being held at first.

Life in the Prison Camps

Again in theory, the system should have worked to encourage both sides to treat prisoners in a relatively humane manner, but unfortunately neither side lived up to its charge. Both in the North and in the South, camps became crowded very rapidly, and space to house prisoners and build more camps became harder to find. By early 1864 both sides resorted to building simple

Map showing the specifics of the stockade that was known as Andersonville Prison

wooden enclosures with no interior housing to "corral" the prisoners—in short, building nothing more than concentration camps.

At that time the South was barely able to feed its own army and citizens, and despite the efforts of camp commandants, most Union prisoners barely subsisted on diets of rough corn bread occasionally supplemented by half-rotted and spoiled meat. This was frequently what the camp guards and staff were eating as well. Rail routes were being decimated by Union attacks, and what little food was being produced often rotted in warehouses for lack of transportation.

News leaking out of the South about these conditions was seized on and amplified by the Northern press. Indignant articles about the Southern "abuses" of POWs enraged the public, which demanded that "justice be done" and that the Confederate prisoners be treated the same. Some Union officers were more than happy to satisfy this misplaced lust for vengeance; at war's end, Hoffman returned $1.8 million to the federal treasury (roughly equivalent to $38 million in today's dollars), bragging that this was money he had saved by cutting prisoner rations.

More than 150 prison camps wcrc built on both sides during the war. Almost all were filthy, disease-ridden hellholes fit for no man. Many prisoners vomited uncontrollably on entering the gates of Andersonville or its Northern counterpart, Elmira; the overpowering stench of open sewers, dead bodies, and rotting flesh hung like a cloud over the open field. At most prisons, "fresh fish" (new prisoners) had to be shoved through the doorway, where they would stand for hours at first, trying not to touch or sit on anything. The walls and floors of prison buildings were normally covered with thick layers of greasy slime, dirt, mold, dead lice, and other vermin.

The prisoners themselves were nearly universally filthy, lice- and flea-infested, and covered with open sores and rashes. Many became despondent, not caring what happened to themselves or others, and quit bothering to use the slit latrines to relieve themselves or even to cover up the mess afterwards. Diarrhea, dysentery, and typhoid fever ran rampant, killing many more prisoners than starvation or failed escape attempts.

Boredom was an equally lethal killer; by the height of the war many camps were so crowded that it could take literally hours to walk from one side to another, and most activities were forbidden for security reasons. Sitting in the same spot day after day, too hungry to sleep and too tired to talk, with the noise from dying and delirious fellow prisoners ringing in their ears day and night, wearing encrusted and filthy clothes, and with all hope for release or exchange gone, some prisoners finally chose suicide as a means of escape. Andersonville became notorious during the war for its "deadline," a small wooden fence 20 feet inside the main stockade wall, where guards could and usually did shoot anyone who ventured inside it (actually, most open prisons on both sides had this feature). Some prisoners "went over" just to end their suffering.

The filth that these prisoners existed in on both sides cannot possibly be overstated. Several prisoners wrote in their journals that their skin actually changed color from the layers of grime; and a Northern surgeon testified that it took months of bathing to completely remove the encrusted dirt. Most prisoners were not allowed to bathe for most or all of their incarceration; many reported that if they were allowed a bath, it would be six months or longer before another.

Andersonville Prison as it was photographed on August 17, 1864

Comparative Ratios of Prisoner Deaths

By the third year of the war, vast numbers of prisoners were falling into Southern hands, times were tough for everyone as a result of the Union naval blockade and the cutting of railroads throughout the Confederacy, and few were in the mood to deal kindly with the "Northern invaders." However, although this chapter deals specifically with the most notorious prison of all, it is important to note that the North did not treat their prisoners much better.

Roughly 29 percent of Andersonville's 45,000 prisoners died in captivity, where conditions were wretched for all concerned, but 24 percent of the 12,123 Confederates held at Elmira, New York, died in captivity as well. Elmira suffered from many of the same supply and environmental problems Andersonville faced, but there is a great deal of evidence that at least part of their prisoners' suffering was deliberately induced. The evidence is much stronger for this deliberate retaliation at other notorious Union prisons—Camp Douglas (Chicago) and Rock Island, Illinois; and Camp Morton, Indiana—all of which had relatively high prisoner mortality rates.

CAMP SUMTER

*C*onstruction of the new camp near Andersonville was delayed for a few months after the initial scouting report, both by local opposition to the project (fear of vindictive escaped prisoners) and a general shortage of labor. By the time work crews started on the new facility, in early January 1864, shortages of money and rapidly increasing numbers of Union prisoners caused the Confederate government to order a strong fence built, without any interior buildings to house the POWs. Under pressure to have the facility ready at the earliest opportunity, the workmen simply stripped the entire area of all but two trees, using the tall pines to build a 15-foot-high double wall of roughly shaved logs butted closely together. Guard towers, known as "pigeon roosts," were built against the outside of the interior wall and spaced every 30 feet.

A "star fort" (a simple fort built with protruding artillery redoubts, which from above looks like a four-, five-, or six-pointed star) on the southwest corner and six other earthwork emplacements guarded against any Union cavalry attempt to free the prisoners, and inward-facing cannon guarded against prisoner uprisings. A smaller enclosure called Castle Reed located a half-mile west housed the officer prisoners sent to this area until they were transferred to Macon's Camp Oglethorpe in May 1864. Afterwards, only enlisted prisoners languished in Camp Sumter.

The first prisoners moved in on February 25, 1864, even before the stockade walls were completed. Within a week the first escape attempt was mounted, when prisoners climbed the stockade wall using a rope handmade of torn shirts and blankets. All

Andersonville Prison at Camp Sumter, drawn by Thomas O'Dea from memory, as it appeared on August 1, 1864, when 35,000 prisoners were incarcerated there

were caught within a day or two, but their attempt inspired construction of the ill-famed deadline.

Lacking even the crudest sort of structure to protect themselves from the elements, the first arrivals were able to use leftover scraps of wood to build rude huts. Later prisoners built "shebangs" by digging shallow pits in the red clay ground and covering them with some sort of tarp. Others simply sat out in the open—totally exposed to the sun, wind, and rain.

The Camp's Unbeloved Commander

The commandant of the camp in early 1864 and through most of the early buildup was Colonel Alexander W. Persons, replaced by General Winder (Captain Winder's father) on June 17. By that date the prison already held more than twice the number it was designed for. Many of the arriving prisoners had been held at other Confederate POW camps and arrived already filthy, weak, sick, and diseased. The stage was set for a real disaster to take place, the responsibility for which would be placed on the next arrival, Winder's subordinate, Captain Henry Wirz.

Wirz was not only not a Southerner—he was not even American. A native of Switzerland, he had immigrated to the United States and was living in Louisiana when the war broke out. Wounded during the Battle of Seven Pines in the spring of 1862, he was promoted and assigned as adjunct general to General Winder in Richmond. Given various tasks after that, including a strange "secret mission" to carry documents to Confederate agents in Europe, he was eventually assigned as keeper of the inner stockade of Camp Sumter in March 1864.

Wirz had a disagreeable personality and no real flair for command. Some of his more outrageous orders and comments were later used as "evidence" against him in his war crimes trial. Many prisoners attempted to escape by tunneling under the walls, digging in the open under the pretense of digging wells for water (there also were some legitimate wells dug by the prisoners). Wirz decided at one point that the Union prisoners were "covering up" this digging with their shebangs, so he ordered that no prisoner build or inhabit any sort of overhead shelter. This insane command was soon overturned.

There were also quite a few reports that Wirz habitually walked around the stockade with pistol in hand and that he personally shot several prisoners (although this last point is the object of heated debate). Camp Sumter's best-known inmate, Private John Ransom (author of *Andersonville Diary*), certainly was no great fan of Wirz:

Overcrowding and little if any shelter led to disastrous conditions at Andersonville.

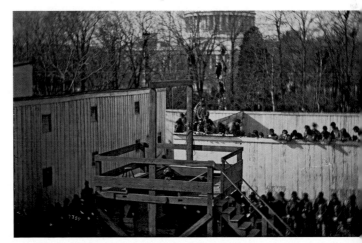

The execution of Captain Wirz for war crimes, November 1865

May 10.—Capt. Wirtz [sic] very domineering and abusive. Is afraid to come into camp anymore. There are a thousand men in here who would willingly die if they could kill him first. Certainly the worst man I ever saw.

The Decline and Fall of Andersonville

By the end of the summer of 1864, Camp Sumter's population reached 33,000, making it the fifth-largest city in the entire Confederacy. One thousand three hundred prisoners occupied each acre of land within the compound, and things went from bad to worse. Atlanta was under siege, and Sherman's cavalry was ranging all through the northern half of Georgia and Alabama, laying waste to railroads and warehouses. Rations started to get short and then nearly disappeared. Salt was the first to go, then what few fresh vegetables that had been available, and then meat totally disappeared. Most prisoners started to subsist on rough cornmeal delivered only four days a week and turned to eating rats and even birds that the stronger men were able to catch.

Some of the less-enlightened guards started amusing themselves by dropping bits of food over the wall into the mass of prisoners, just to laugh at the riot that would ensue. A few of the nastier ones would drop food within the deadline, just to get the opportunity to kill a prisoner.

A very small stream runs through the stockade site; when the camp opened, it was the only source of drinking, bathing, and toilet water in the entire facility. Needless to say, it became overwhelmed and contaminated in short order, and no other source of decent water was to be had. When a violent thunderstorm in August 1864 reopened an old spring that had been covered up by construction debris, the prisoners insisted that God himself had opened the spring with a lightning bolt and named the spot Providence Spring.

The number of prisoners dying from diarrhea and dysentery skyrocketed soon after the camp opened, claiming more than 4,500 in just a five-month period. Deaths were so common that some prisoners managed to escape by pretending they were dead, waiting until after they were carried outside the walls to the rude "death house" to make their escape. By the end of the war, exactly 12,914 had died and another 329 had escaped. Largely through the work of a single prisoner, Private Dorence Atwater of the 2nd New York Cavalry, only 460 of the graves are marked as "unknown." Atwater was assigned the responsibility of recording the names of all those who died at the camp, and fearing the loss of this record in the Confederate archives, he painstakingly handwrote another, which he kept in hopes of notifying the families of the deceased.

Prisoners were also stalked by some of their own number. A group of thugs known as the "Mosby Raiders" beat, robbed, terrorized, and even murdered their fellow prisoners quite openly for many months. Led by a particularly unpleasant character, Private William "Mosby" Collins of Company D, 88th Pennsylvania Infantry, they were finally brought down by another group of prisoners. With Wirz's cooperation, the Raiders were subjected to a trial by the prisoners themselves, and six were hanged. Three others were later beaten to death by their former victims. The six hung are buried in a special part of the cemetery, away from any other prisoner by the prisoners' request.

After the fall of Atlanta in September 1864, many prisoners were quickly relocated to other camps, farther away from the action. Only the sickest 8,000 remained by the end of September; all but about 1,300 of that number died by the end of November. The camp stayed open with a much-reduced number of prisoners, operating mainly for the sick and dying until war's end.

PLACES OF INTEREST

Andersonville National Historic Site
496 Cemetery Rd.
Andersonville, GA
(229) 924-0343
www.nps.gov/ande

Camp Sumter today would be unrecognizable to the more than 45,000 Union prisoners who passed through its gates. The original burial site of prisoners who died in camp was established as Andersonville National Cemetery on July 26, 1865, just after the end of the war, primarily to preserve and honor the graves of 12,914 who died in the adjacent POW camp over a 14-month span. Initially there was no attempt to preserve or mark the site of the notorious camp and stockade site, but the land was finally purchased in December 1890 by the Georgia Department of the Grand Army of the Republic, a Union Army veterans group. This group was unable to properly care for or maintain the property and shortly after sold it for $1 to the Women's Relief Corp (WRC), the national ladies' auxiliary of the Grand Army of the Republic (GAR).

The WRC proved good caretakers, making many improvements and keeping the grounds in good shape until donating the entire site to the U.S. government in 1910. The War Department and subsequent Department of the Army took care of the site until 1970, when the National Park Service was given the responsibility. Both the GAR and the army were primarily concerned with the national cemetery, and it wasn't until the Park Service took over that real efforts were made to preserve the stockade site and initiate education programs about it.

Today the site has a triple charge; in addition to protecting the National Cemetery and stockade site of Camp Sumter, construction began in 1996 on a new National Prisoner of War Museum, which is charged with preserving the memory and telling the story of all American prisoners of war throughout our many conflicts. This museum, opened in an emotional ceremony on April 9, 1998, is designed from the ground up as a powerful reminder to each visitor of the intensity of the stories it holds.

Walking toward the building from the parking lot, you are forced to walk in single file through a narrow passage between two brick buildings reminiscent of guardrooms. This, plus the black entry gates, gives the proper sense of foreboding and tension that a real prisoner would have faced. Once inside, the atmosphere is lightened by the high ceiling and skylights (make sure to notice the painted murals above), but the stark hallways of the exhibit corridors seem far too peaceful to hold the pictures and stories that seem almost to explode off the wall. A quiet place for reflection is provided under two small sunlit towers.

In back of the museum, on the side facing the stockade site, is the Commemorative Courtyard with a small brick-lined stream flowing past brick and bronze statuary. A short pathway takes you from the courtyard to the partially reconstructed northeast corner stockade wall of Camp Sumter.

The entire site is haunting and disturbing, as it should be. On entering the grounds you drive through a quiet woods and then turn right into the National Cemetery. The closely packed, militarily straight, and in proper file and rank tombstones seem almost like formations of ghostly infantry drawn up in some vast line of battle. It seems impossible to comprehend that so many thousands of dead actually lie in such a small space; men were buried shoulder to shoulder without a coffin in long trench-like graves and covered with about 3 feet of earth. These are not true mass graves, as each man was buried more or less independently and properly interred by the Confederate work details, not just hastily dumped in a hole.

Driving the short distance over to the stockade site, we were struck by how peaceful and quiet the vast open space is; similar to the site of many violent battlefields, it is as if all the energy was sapped from the very ground by the overwhelming suffering and carnage that took place here. A few state memorials dot the northwest corner, and white stakes placed every 50 feet or so show where the stockade wall and deadline were. Except for these and two short sections of reconstructed walls, the place is utterly empty.

A narrow paved road allows one to do a driving tour of the 26-acre site. A small memorial building built after the war by grateful ex-POWs houses Providence Spring, and the star fort and most of the earthworks are still intact. Several markers on the roadway contain photos of what the scene looked like during the war, and in most places the contrast between that period and the modern one is startling.

The National Cemetery is still active, with veterans of all the American wars (including the American Revolution) interred here, and about 150 burials take place each year. Please be respectful if you visit during a ceremony.

The visitor center and museum has a 20-minute orientation film, narrated by Colin Powell, introducing both Andersonville and the general topic of POWs. It also contains an excellent small bookstore and research library as well as the before-mentioned exhibits. Admission is by donation, and the grounds are open year-round. Water and restrooms are available, and picnicking is permitted in a designated area, but no food is sold on the grounds.

ACCOMMODATIONS

There is a single small bed-and-breakfast in the Civil War village of Andersonville, A Place Away Cottage (109 Oglethorpe St.; 229-924-1044; $). Peggy Sheppard is the innkeeper. The village also features one restaurant, Andersonville Restaurant, with an adjacent RV park; call the visitor center to check on hours and availability at the park (229-924-2558). The nearest hotels and motels are in Americus, 10 miles to the southwest on GA 49, such as the Windsor Hotel (125 West Lamar St., Americus, GA; 229-924-1555; www.windsor-americus .com; $$$–$$$$). Several chain motels and the usual fast-food restaurants are on GA 49 as you enter town and US 19 as you leave to the west. Going back to I-75, you have a wide range of chain hotel, motel, and restaurant choices clustered around Cordele (exits 101/102), Vienna (exit 109), Perry (exits 135/136), Fort Valley (exit 142), and Byron (exit 149).

Andersonville village is worth visiting after leaving the historic site. The hamlet contains a seven-acre pioneer farm, several antiques and craft shops, and the Drummer Boy Civil War Museum (109 Church St.), which has garnered praise for its high-quality private collection. Right smack in the middle of town is a 45-foot-tall obelisk memorial to Captain Henry R.

Wirz, the last commandant of Camp Sumter. This may be the only monument to a convicted war criminal in this country and has inscribed upon it the "unreconstructed" view of Wirz and the POW situation. After the war there were quite a number of people who refused to accept that the Confederacy had been finally and decisively defeated. There are still folks around who believe that the Lost Cause was a spiritual one as well as a political and military one, and that at some point in the future, "The South will rise again," to quote frequently seen bumper stickers. For more information on Andersonville village, see www.andersonvillegeorgia.com.

DAY TRIPS

We highly recommend a trip to Columbus, about 60 miles west of Andersonville, while you are in this part of the state. Take GA 49 through Americus and turn right on US 280. This will take you straight into Columbus, with the side benefit of going through Plains, the birthplace, residence, and historic site of President Jimmy Carter. Just before you enter Columbus you will drive through Fort Benning Military Reservation, which contains an exquisite collection of Civil War artifacts in its excellent National Infantry Museum (1775 Legacy Way, Fort Benning, Columbus, GA; 706-685-5800; www.nationalinfantrymuseum.com). Admission is free, but there is small charge for the theater and other attractions.

US 280 is called Victory Drive within Columbus, and 2 miles before it goes over the Chattahoochee River into Alabama is the National Civil War Naval Museum, which houses the remains of the never-finished 224-foot iron-clad ram CSS *Jackson* and the 130-foot wooden gunboat CSS *Chattahoochee,* as well as a nice collection of models, weapons, and artifacts of the Confederate Navy. A warning: Although there are a few signs pointing the way, it is easy to get confused about where to enter the parking lot for this museum due to the very heavy traffic and urban blight of Victory Drive. Turn left off Victory Drive at the large sign marking south commons, the Columbus Civic Center, and then go through the large parking lot to the right until you see the museum building. The museum is located at 1002 Victory Dr., Columbus (706-327-9798; www.portcolumbus.org).

Another interesting day trip is to Jefferson Davis Memorial Historical Site near Irwinville, the site of the

Confederate president's capture by Union troops at the end of the war. Take I-75 south to GA 32 (exit 78), and travel east approximately 15 miles into town. Turn left onto Jeff Davis Park Road; the site is about 1 mile on the left. Run by the state of Georgia, the 13-acre park contains a small museum and a few markers commemorating the event. The major attraction here is an impressive 12-foot-tall granite monument with a bronze bust of Davis on top, depicting his capture.

Unfortunately, the carved scene hints at one of the sillier myths of the war—that Davis was captured wearing women's clothing. Davis had been traveling west through southern Georgia to Texas or possibly Mexico, to try to continue the war from the Trans-Mississippi Theater. A unit of Union cavalry was in hot pursuit, and just before dawn on May 10, 1865, they suddenly raided his camp. In the confused skirmish, two columns of Union cavalry started firing on each other, killing two troopers before realizing their mistake.

Hearing the gunfire, Davis jumped up and threw on his wife's cloak by mistake in the darkened tent, ran outside, and tried to mount his horse to escape. A Union officer drew down on him, as his wife, Varina, ran up and threw her arms around him to shield him from being shot. Union soldiers in a very high spirit after his capture exaggerated the event, claiming that Davis had on bloomers and even a hoopskirt!

You can find the site and the museum at 338 Jeff Davis Park Rd., Fitzgerald, GA (229-831-2335; www.gastateparks .org/jeffd). Admission to the park is free.

Mobile Bay: Damn the Torpedoes

Darley.

Mobile, Alabama, lies at the southernmost point in the state, at the northwestern tip of a 36-mile-long and 18-mile-wide bay that allows the state its only sea access. With a population of just over 29,000 when the war started, it was one of the largest cities in the state and second only to New Orleans as a port for international trade. Although never a city noted for strong secessionist feelings, no doubt due to the strong ties with Northern traders, Mobile was proposed by local boosters as the first capital of the Confederacy. Some radical secessionists felt that the Confederacy was bound to eventually include Mexico and some or all of the Caribbean islands, so it would be in a favorable central location.

After Lincoln's election in 1860, secession fever swept the state, and Governor Andrew B. Moore soon moved to provide for military defense. On January 3, 1861, several days before a state convention met to formally declare Alabama free from the Union, he ordered local companies of the 1st Alabama State Troops to seize and man forts and arsenals around Mobile Bay. The next day, two companies moved to take Forts Morgan and Gaines, while several other companies went 30 miles north to seize the Mount Vernon Arsenal. Seven days later, on January 11, 1861, Alabama formally declared secession.

FORTRESS MOBILE

*M*obile not only had a valuable and large deepwater port to help supply the newly formed Confederacy, it also had a series of fortifications to protect it, thanks to the U.S. Army Corps of Engineers. At the east side of the entrance to the bay stood massive Fort Morgan, supported by Fort Gaines and Fort Grant across the ship channel on Dauphin Island. Mobile itself was protected by a series of small forts and artillery batteries on both shores of the northern end of the bay, as well as a series of trench lines surrounding the city on the west (landward) side.

Within days of Alabama's secession, a massive project was under way to clean up and improve the still-unfinished forts. With volunteer citizens and slaves provided by local planters, all available guns were mounted, living quarters for the garrisons built up outside the walls, wells cleaned out, and sloping glacis constructed. In March, when the Confederate government took over responsibility for area defense from the state, Colonel (later Lieutenant General) William Joseph Hardee was named commander of Fort Morgan.

Hardee, the author of the then-standard text on infantry tactics, was only in command at Mobile for three months, but he managed a near whirlwind of action. The untrained militia and local guard infantrymen were properly trained, artillerymen were trained and readied to repel the inevitable naval attack, and Hardee's own command was soon expanded to the entire Mobile Bay area. In addition, he was placed in command of the "Mobile Navy," the revenue cutter *Lewis Cass,* soon augmented by a grossly inadequate ironclad, the CSS *Baltic.* Later, after Hardee had departed, this "navy" was expanded to include two ironclad rams, the CSS *Tennessee* and CSS *Nashville;* two ironclad "floating batteries" (gunboats similar to the rams), the CSS *Huntsville* and CSS *Tuscaloosa;* and three side-wheeler gunboats, the CSS *Morgan,* CSS *Gaines,* and CSS *Selma*—all at the time of the major last battles under the command of Admiral Franklin Buchanan. The CSS *Tennessee,* Buchanan's flagship, was typical of the large, powerful Confederate-designed ironclads—209 feet long with a 48-foot beam, covered with 4 to 6 inches of armor plating and mounting two 7-inch and four 6.4-inch Brooke rifled guns.

FORT MORGAN

*T*he centerpiece of Mobile's defense against naval attack was a massive, five-sided masonry post at the very tip of Mobile Point, Fort Morgan, supplemented by two other smaller forts across the ship channel on Dauphin Island. The three-story-high brick fort still under construction when hostilities broke out in 1861 had replaced earlier defense posts dating back to a French outpost in 1699 at the site. However, it was only after the Spanish concession of Florida to the fledgling United States in 1813 that any attempts were mounted for strong, permanent fortifications on the two narrow barrier islands guarding Mobile Bay.

Fort Gaines on Dauphin Island, named for General Edmund Pendleton Gaines (best known for commanding Fort Erie with great skill during the War of 1812), and Fort Morgan on Mobile Point (named for General Daniel Morgan, Revolutionary War) are of the Third System of Fortification planning period of the 1830s and 1840s. A continuous series of strong masonry forts was planned to guard ports, towns, and strategic locations along the entire eastern seaboard and Gulf Coast. First proposed in 1821, Fort Gaines was still unfinished when the war began, described as a "shell of masonry" by one visitor. Although mounting few guns and for all practical purposes nearly unmanned early in the war, it still posed an impressive defensive obstacle, with a five-sided outer wall 22½ feet tall and 4½ feet thick. Unlike so many other Gulf Coast fortifications, Fort Gaines possessed gun emplacements well situated to defend against attacks from either land or water. By 1864 the garrison under Colonel Charles D. Anderson consisted of about 800 infantry and artillerymen, about half poorly trained local militia, and 26 heavy guns. Some of the garrison were of the Pelham Cadets, boys as young as 14 who ended up fighting about as well as any other irregular unit there.

> *[The Civil War] was a fearful lesson, and should teach us the necessity of avoiding wars in the future.*
>
> —Lieutenant General Ulysses S. Grant, Union Army, from his memoirs

Fort Morgan was a star-shaped pentagon of similar construction begun in 1819 and completed in 1834, although with a particular design feature that proved seriously hazardous during the battle. A three-story-tall, 10-sided barracks building in the center of the fort known as the "citadel" stuck up well above the surrounding parapet, lending both a perfect aiming point for Union gunners and providing a shrapnel hazard if hit during battle. To help protect the fort's gunners, wooden traverses across the side and rear of the casements as well as sand-work glacis all around the exterior masonry walls were planned, although little work was completed before the Union attacks commenced. At the time of the last battle for control of the bay, Brigadier General Richard L. Page commanded a garrison of 400 regular army and artillery troops, and the fort mounted 45 guns of various sizes and calibers.

A third major defensive point centered around Fort Powell, a smaller earthwork redoubt named for the former commander of Fort Morgan, Colonel William Llewellyn Powell, who had died on duty in September of 1863. Guarding (and formally named for) the westernmost approach to Mobile Bay, Grant's Pass, the post only mounted eight heavy guns and contained at its peak only 140 troops under Lieutenant Colonel James M. Williams, but it was able to stand up against repeated Union attacks with little damage.

Perhaps the most famous, and certainly one of the most effective, defense arrangements was the stringing of a series of "torpedoes" across the bay from Fort Morgan to Fort Gaines. The floating mines were built to explode when touched by a ship or gunboat and had enough power to shatter an armored ironclad's hull. By the third year of the war, every water approach to Mobile Bay had at least one line of torpedoes across most of the passage, and the main ship channel was guarded by no less than 180 in three rows that covered the entire channel up to within 700 feet of Fort Morgan.

BACKGROUND TO THE BATTLE OF MOBILE BAY

*F*ollowing the Union Navy's largely successful tight blockade of eastern Confederate-held ports, the Union Army campaigns in the Carolinas and Florida, and the utter failure of the weak Confederate Navy to do much more than snipe at the Union blockade, only the ports of Wilmington, North Carolina, and Mobile, Alabama, were left open to receive the critical supplies brought in by blockade-runners by the third year of the war. Wilmington was able to supply, barely, General Robert E. Lee's Army of Northern Virginia, with a trickle of supplies sent westward to Lieutenant General Braxton Bragg's Army of Tennessee. Mobile was the only remaining open port by 1864 still able to bring the majority of supplies in to the Western and Trans-Mississippi Theater armies.

Even more important than Mobile's port to the supply and reinforcement of the Army of Tennessee was the city's railroad network. After the loss of the rail center at Corinth, Mississippi, following the Shiloh-Corinth Campaign in the summer of 1862, Mobile became the only rail link between Confederate forces in the Eastern and Western Theaters. Its importance was underscored in early July 1862, when Major General John Porter McCown's division moved through the city from Tupelo, Mississippi, en route to Chattanooga, Tennessee, to reinforce the garrison there. By later July, the rest of General Bragg's 25,000-strong Army of Mississippi followed McCown's route, abandoning northern Mississippi in order to try to save Chattanooga.

Despite the extreme value Mobile posed to the Confederacy as both a rail center and port, neither side made any serious early moves to take or protect it. The series of Confederate Western Theater commanders in the first years of the war consistently looked to Forts Morgan and Gaines to provide the majority of protection for the city, supplemented by small infantry and artillery redoubts and emplacements in and around the city to guard against the "unlikely" event of a land-based attack. Major General Benjamin Franklin Butler and Flag Officer (later Rear Admiral) David Glasgow Farragut determined to concentrate their Northern forces initially on New Orleans and the Mississippi River, leaving Mobile (and Pensacola) for a later attack.

A few months after Confederate troops had abandoned Fort Massachusetts on nearby Ship Island, Butler and Farragut moved to seize the strategically positioned island. On December 3, 1861, 1,900 Union soldiers stepped ashore to take back possession of the post 12 miles off the shore of Gulfport, Mississippi, providing the Union Army and Navy an ideal base from which to threaten the entire Gulf coastal region of eastern Florida, Alabama, Mississippi, and Louisiana. However, Mobile remained securely in Confederate hands for nearly three more years, with Farragut busy along the Mississippi River and the land forces concentrating on Vicksburg and the Mississippi interior. Prior to the 1864 battle, the only serious attack was a weak attempt by Commander David D. Porter to force a passage into Mobile Bay in the summer of 1862, easily repulsed by the rebels without any immediate Union follow-up.

Naval Attacks on Mobile Bay

Due primarily to its isolated location, well south of any other major city or supply depot, any military action at Mobile was probably going to be either purely naval or an amphibious landing heavily supported by naval gunfire. This was confirmed by the first action, in December 1861, when the part-ironclad (armor only protected the boilers, leaving the gun deck open and exposed to enemy fire) CSS *Florida* sailed out from Fort Morgan's pier to engage the blockade steamer USS *Huntsville* near Sand Point. Typical for early-war encounters, naval or otherwise, both sides withdrew after firing a relatively few ill-aimed shots that did little or no damage, and subsequently both sides claimed victory.

In April 1862 the Mobile Bay naval commander, Captain Randolph, ordered the newly readied wooden gunboats CSS *Morgan* and CSS *Gaines* to sail out and try to break through the Union blockade "fleet," which consisted of only two ships at the time. Even with this weak enemy force to attack, the two Confederate gunboats only fired a total of about a dozen shots before retreating at high speed back to the safety of their harbor. In the next two years, five other such small naval actions against the blockade fleet or the Confederate forts were mounted; all had the same negative results.

The most serious attack during this period, although actually only a feint to draw attention away from a Union Army attack toward Meridian, Mississippi, had Farragut sailing four gunboats and six "mortar schooners" (wooden small ships mounting heavy mortars that could stand off from the main action a bit and lob shells inside a fort's walls) into Grant's Pass. Over the course of

★ ★ ★ ★ ★ ★ ★ ★ ★ ★ ★ ★ ★ ★ ★ ★

five days of bombardment in February 1864, his ships fired about 2,000 shots and shells into the earthwork fort, killing one man and wounding five, including post commander James Williams. In exchange, the fort stood nearly intact with the little damage done being repaired in one day, and one of Farragut's own mortar schooners was hit by Confederate gunners and nearly sunk. Although the channel had been seeded with torpedoes, and Union gunboats struck several, none exploded as expected. An after-action inspection revealed that marine worms had infested the wooden casks and rendered the triggers inoperative.

THE BATTLE OF MOBILE BAY

*W*ith most of the Gulf Coast and Mississippi River now under Union control, Farragut's next objective was to shut down the port of Mobile once and for all. Using his assembled naval force, his primary objective was to neutralize the three main Confederate forts and completely cut off the blockade-runners from a safe port. A separate army force under Major General Gordon Granger would land on Dauphin Island with about

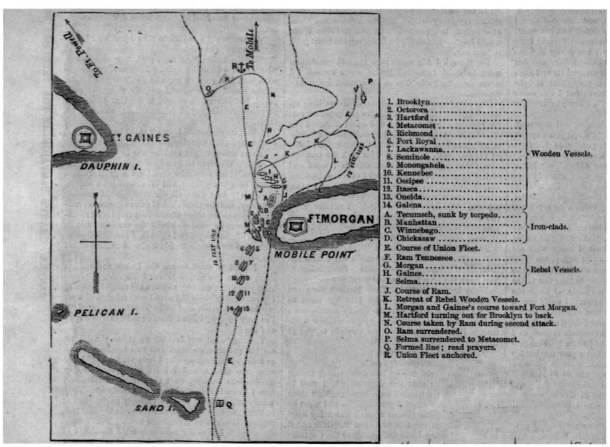

Battle of Mobile Bay

1,500 men and attack the two forts there. To oppose the assault, Commander Page (3rd Brigade, District of the Gulf) could muster about 1,040 men in the three forts and their surrounding batteries.

At dawn on August 5, 1864, Farragut began his attack. Fourteen wooden, lightly armored gunboats and four ironclad monitors sailed toward the main ship channel in a tight formation, the gunboats lashed together in pairs with the better-protected monitors alongside starboard (eastward) to protect them from Fort Morgan's artillery fire. Well aware of the torpedoes strung across the channel, Farragut deliberately ran his small fleet close to Fort Morgan, attempting to sail through the narrow space between the fort and the first line of torpedoes, although at a terrible risk from near point-blank Confederate fire. At about 7 a.m. Farragut ordered his point vessel, the USS *Tecumseh,* to open fire, which was followed in short order by a concentrated fire from Page's guns. For the next 45 minutes both sides kept up a blistering fire, but amazingly, although they were literally only a few yards apart, very little damage was done to either side.

One of Farragut's major objectives was the sinking or disabling of the CSS *Tennessee.* As his fleet sailed past Fort Morgan, the USS *Tecumseh* swung slightly west to engage the Confederate ironclad awaiting her near the middle of the ship channel but almost immediately struck a torpedo, shattering her hull and sending her quickly to the bottom. Only 21 of her 114-man crew managed to escape. The wooden gunboat USS *Brooklyn,* next in line to the USS *Tecumseh,* slowed and started turning away from the lethal minefield back toward Fort Morgan. Confederate gunners cheered, then quickly loaded their guns with grapeshot and canister, preparing to rake the enemy decks as soon as they moved within range.

Farragut, lashed by his crew into the rigging of his flagship, USS *Hartford* (to keep him from being killed from falling to the deck if wounded while in his high observation post), allegedly screamed out to his helmsman, "Damn the torpedoes! Drayton! Ahead, full speed! Hard astarboard; ring four bells! Eight bells! Sixteen bells!" (there is much debate over whether he really said this famous quote) and thus ordered his own ship to take the lead. Moving at near maximum speed, the small Union fleet pushed through the torpedo

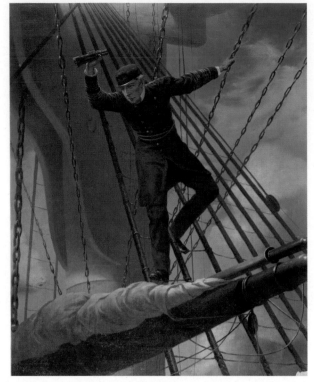

Lashed to the shrouds—Farragut passing the forts at Mobile, in his flagship, Hartford

belts without setting off any more, although several officers reported hearing fuses firing as their ships hit the floating mines.

For the South, Buchanan's own fleet opened fire as soon as their guns were unmasked to the onrushing Union gunboats. While their shots raked the Union ships for several minutes before they were able to return fire, the Confederates definitely got the worst of the exchange. Within a few minutes the CSS *Gaines* was sinking from multiple shots below the waterline, the CSS *Selma* was run down by the USS *Metacomet* and forced to surrender, and the CSS *Morgan* soon broke contact and fled east to the safety of her namesake. Only the CSS *Tennessee* remained by 8 a.m. to threaten Farragut's assault, and the Union fleet now safely past the forts quickly turned on the powerful but slow and ungainly ironclad.

The CSS *Tennessee* moved in for her own attack, but Farragut's ships surrounded her and began maneuvering for ram attacks. At 9:25 a.m. the USS *Monongahela,* the USS *Lackawanna,* and Farragut's own ship rammed the Confederate ship in turn, inflicting little damage but disrupting the gun crew's ability to fire. Buchanan suffered a broken leg when an 11-inch solid shot struck the after port cover he was standing next to. In the meantime, the three surviving Union ironclad monitors had moved up alongside the CSS *Tennessee* and had begun hammering fire on her armored decks. At 10 a.m., with his steering gear shot away and his gun crews no longer able to return fire, Captain James D. Johnston surrendered his ship.

The short naval action resulted in 12 Confederates killed, 20 wounded, and 280 captured. Farragut reported a loss of 145 killed, 170 wounded, and 4 captured.

Forts Powell and Gaines

At the same time Farragut was racing through the main ship channel, Lieutenant Commander George H. Perkins aboard the USS *Chickasaw,* along with three other gunboats, moved up Mississippi Sound toward Grant's Pass and opened fire on Fort Powell. Williams's gunners returned fire, but once again, neither side suffered in the short exchange. The USS *Chickasaw* withdrew, along with the other gunboats, but returned alone just before noon and again late in the afternoon. This time her gunners were more effective, raking the fort's exposed parapets with a hot fire and penetrating the bomb-proof. Convinced that a renewed bombardment the next day would result in his magazine being penetrated and exploded, Williams ordered his men to evacuate to nearby Fort Gaines during the night, setting fire to and destroying his post as he left.

Granger landed his troops on Dauphin Island late in the afternoon of August 3, and Page immediately requested reinforcements from the Mobile garrison. About 200 local militia and Confederate marines managed to slip past the Union fleet lying close by and get into the fort before Granger's attack commenced. By midnight on August 4, the Union landing force had closed in enough to set up their artillery batteries and opened fire on Fort Gaines's water battery as Farragut's

fleet sailed through the channel. Anderson ordered his own guns to open up on the Union battery, but with no apparent success.

Just after noon on August 6, the USS *Chickasaw* moved within range and began pounding the fort's masonry walls. Little damage was suffered, but several patients in the post hospital were killed by flying debris. Before the infantry or even other Union gunboats could get involved in the fight, Anderson decided he had had enough. Showing a sad lack of leadership, Anderson first signaled Page over in Fort Morgan for instructions, consulted with two of Page's staff officers, and was then presented with a petition signed by most of his own officers imploring him to surrender rather than fight on. With Page frantically signaling him to hold his post, Anderson raised a white flag and requested terms from Granger and Farragut. Into Union captivity went 864 officers and men, as well as 26 artillery pieces, a large amount of ammunition, and a year's supply of food.

The early surrender of both forts caused a storm of protest in both Mobile and the Confederate high command. Area commander Page said publicly that the surrenders were a "deed of dishonor and disgrace to its commander and garrison," and both Williams and Anderson were crucified in the Mobile press. Williams was quickly removed from command, although some responsibilities were gradually restored later. In all fairness, these officers faced a near impossible defensive position, bombarded from the sea, threatened by infantry by land, and cut off from any hope of continued resupply or reinforcement. When the CSS *Tennessee* surrendered, the last best chance for a naval victory was surrendered with her.

Infantry Attacks

With the western approaches to Mobile Bay now secured, Granger and Farragut turned their attention on Fort Morgan. Granger's heavily reinforced command, now numbering some 5,500 infantry and artillerymen, landed just east of the isolated Confederate fort uncontested on August 9. Page pulled his infantry inside the fort, obviously outmatched in an open land battle, and prepared for a long siege. Just before noon the Union fleet moved in and began shelling the fort; a few hours later a note was

Fort Morgan just after the surrender, August 23, 1864

delivered demanding the unconditional surrender of the last Confederate outpost. Page adamantly refused, and Granger ordered his troops to close in on the fort.

Rather than a headlong assault, Granger decided to slowly move his troops forward, building heavy artillery emplacements and siege entrenchments as they went. Farragut's sailors had repaired the CSS *Tennessee*'s steering gear and, along with the three surviving ironclad monitors, began a heavy bombardment of the fort on August 13. Two days later the now close-in Union infantry and their heavy siege artillery joined in on the bombardment and sniping. For some unknown reason, Page refused his gunners permission to return fire, except for occasional, short barrages toward the Union infantry encampment.

Granger continued to bring in more heavy artillery, and by the morning of August 21 he was able to report 25 heavy artillery pieces and 16 siege mortars mounted and ready for action. That afternoon his gunners, joined by every Union monitor and gunboat, opened up a massive, pounding barrage on Fort Morgan. Page reported later that the barrage soon "disabled all the heavy guns save two . . . partially breached the wall in several places, and cut up the fort to such an extent as to make the whole work a mere mass of debris." Although the heavy barrage lifted somewhat during the night, it resumed in full force at dawn the next day. Page was forced to admit that his command could not hold out much longer. He ordered what ammunition remained destroyed and his guns spiked, and he sent a message offering unconditional surrender to Granger. The formal surrender was signed on the afternoon of August 23.

Despite the rather heavy fighting that took place at Fort Morgan, Page reported only very light casualties: 3 killed and 16 wounded, with more than 600 marching into captivity.

The Defense of Mobile

While Page had fought off both Farragut and Granger for a few weeks, Major General Danny Herndon Maury, District of the Gulf commander headquartered in Mobile, hastily prepared the city for the coming invasion. He urgently requested reinforcements from Bragg and conscripted every available male in the city. Even with his officers rounding up anyone who could tote a rifle, by August 9 Maury still only had about 4,000 troops in entrenchments and batteries all around the city, a pitifully small force to resist the attack that all were sure was coming in days, if not hours.

However, neither Farragut nor Granger was in any particular hurry to attack Mobile. A waterborne reconnaissance on August 15 revealed to the Union admiral that the harbor defenses were far too strong for him to bring up his fleet within gun range and that an attack on the city would have to be primarily a land-based one. The Union commanders returned to Fort Morgan and sent word to Washington that they would need a serious number of reinforcements to overcome the Confederate defenses and take Mobile.

> *It is well that war is so terrible, lest we grow too fond of it.*
>
> —General Robert E. Lee to Lieutenant General James Longstreet, both of the Confederate Army, December 13, 1862

Maury sent word that he, too, badly needed large numbers of reinforcements, but he knew that his prospects for getting them were slim. He spent the next few months fortifying the city as well as possible, centering the defenses around a series of fixed and floating batteries, rebuilt or reinforced entrenchments and redoubts, and even building up and improving an old Spanish fort on the eastern shore of the bay, known, appropriately, as Spanish Fort. Outside of ordering out a handful of naval and land-based raids and skirmishes on the Mobile defenses, both Farragut and Granger seemed perfectly content to wait in Fort Morgan until reinforcements or other orders arrived.

★

THE RENEWED MOBILE CAMPAIGN

*L*ate in 1864, the commander in chief of all Union armies, Lieutenant General Ulysses S. Grant, was not at all convinced that Mobile was worth the intense manpower needed to take it, but he wanted Granger to move his force north and take Selma and Montgomery. These two cities brought under Union control would help a planned cavalry raid through Alabama and Georgia by Major General James Harrison Wilson, even then on his way south through Tennessee. Granger was promised more troops and ordered to bypass Mobile if a short campaign was insufficient to take it.

After many delays, Granger's reinforcements finally arrived in mid-March 1865, and shortly after that the Union columns moved out. Major General Edward Richard Sprigg Canby moved north with about 32,000 troops from the base at Fort Morgan on March 25. A second column led by Major General Frederick Steele marched out of Fort Barrancas at Pensacola, Florida, on March 20 with about 13,000 troops. At this time on the Confederate side, Maury could muster a total of about 9,000 soldiers, militia, conscripts, and sailors to man the 209 artillery pieces and miles of trenches and redoubts around the city and upper bay.

As soon as he was notified of the Union columns' route of approach, Maury moved all his infantry to the eastern shore, into Spanish Fort and nearby Fort Blakely. Brigadier General Randall Lee Gibson took over command of Spanish Fort, with a garrison consisting of his own Louisiana Brigade, with about 500

men, another 950 infantrymen from the Alabama reserves, and about 360 artillerymen to man the 6 heavy guns, 14 field guns, and 12 Coehorn mortars. Brigadier General St. John Richardson Liddell at Fort Blakely was in a slightly better position, with a peak force of about 2,700 troops manning a 3,000-yard-long line of entrenchments and redoubts.

Spanish Fort

Canby came on fast, approaching Spanish Fort early on the morning of March 27. To give his engineers a little more time to improve their emplacements, Gibson ordered Lieutenant Colonel Robert H. Lindsay to take about 500 men and hit the Union column before they could deploy for battle. Lindsay assaulted through the Union vanguard, but he withdrew when the column's forward regiments began deploying in line of battle. His delaying tactic worked, however, forcing Canby to delay several hours, getting his forces reorganized and moving again. By nightfall Canby's men were starting to establish siege lines only 1,000 yards from the fort, with some forward skirmishers less than 300 yards from Gibson's line.

Most siege operations during the war tended to be all-artillery affairs, with infantry on both sides primarily just trying to dig in deep enough not to be hit. However, from the morning of March 28 on through the end of the siege, Union sharpshooters kept up a steady and accurate fire inside the fort's walls, small infantry attacks were launched by both sides on the other's trench lines, and Canby's men steadily extended their line of entrenchments until they were nearly to the walls of the Confederate fort itself. The artillery kept up a steady barrage through it all, with one massive two-hour barrage on April 4 coming from no less than 40 heavy siege guns and about 12 siege mortars.

The worst bombardment of all came on April 8 at sundown, when 53 Union heavy siege guns, joined by 37 field guns and mortars and Union gunboats just offshore, started a concentrated fire directly on the fort. Ironically, Gibson had planned his own barrage for that same date and time, but his gunners were only able to crank off a few rounds before the

The Confederate Flag

The first Confederate flag, or Stars and Bars, incorporated two horizontal red stripes separated by a white stripe. It included seven white stars in a blue field. This flag was adopted in March 1861 and raised over the Confederate capitol, then in Montgomery, Alabama, by the granddaughter of former U.S. president John Tyler. But this flag caused confusion at the Battle of First Bull Run in Virginia because it looked very much like the Union's Stars and Stripes. Following the battle, General Pierre Gustave Toutant Beauregard designed a battle flag for the Confederate Army of Northern Virginia. This flag, erroneously referred to today as the Confederate Stars and Bars, was a red square with a blue St. Andrew's cross and 13 superimposed white stars (representing the 11 seceded states, plus the "enemy-held" states of Kentucky and Maryland).

A variation of this flag was used by armies in the Western Theater, being the same basic design but rectangular rather than square. This same flag was used by the Confederate Navy and called the "Naval Jack." This is what many still call the Confederate flag, and most historians refer to as the "Southern Cross." In May 1863 the Confederacy adopted a new national flag to replace the first Stars and Bars. It was white with the more-familiar battle flag in the upper left corner.

This flag is sometimes referred to as the "Stonewall Flag," as one of its first uses was to drape Lieutenant General Thomas Jonathan "Stonewall" Jackson's casket after he was mortally wounded following the Battle of Chancellorsville. Also known as the "Stainless Banner," this flag showed mostly white unless flying in a stiff breeze and was frequently mistaken for a flag of truce or surrender, so a new design in 1865 added a red bar on the flag's white edge. This last flag design came about too late in the war to see much actual service. Today, however, the Army of Northern Virginia's battle flag (or the western variation) is the one most people identify as the "Confederate flag."

Confederate flag surrounded by battle scenes

Union barrage drove them to their shelters. During the heavy barrage, troops from Colonel James L. Geddes's 3rd Brigade leading Brigadier General Eugene Asa Carr's 3rd Division (of Major General Andrew Jackson Smith's XVI Corps) assaulted the left of the Confederate line. Overrunning the first line of entrenchments, they were nearly to the fort itself when a rebel counterattack led by Lieutenant Alfred G. Clark with about 100 men stopped the assault before it could overrun the parapet walls.

Clark was killed in the counterattack, but his small command managed to stop the Union assault. Aware that he was not going to be able to hold against a renewed attack, Gibson ordered his gunners to spike their guns and gradually withdrew his command out of the fortification walls. During the night the remnants of his force worked their way across the marshes to Fort Blakely, then were transferred by steamboat across the bay into Mobile. While he was able to take most of his 395 wounded out with him, he left behind 93 dead and about 750 missing or captured.

Fort Blakely

While Canby advanced on and laid siege to Spanish Fort, Steele moved north in a feint on Montgomery, then west to attack Fort Blakely. Early on April 1 his vanguard, Lieutenant Colonel Andrew B. Spurling's 2nd Cavalry Brigade, encountered Captain J. B. Hart's 46th Mississippi Infantry Regiment, deployed about 5 miles east of Fort Blakely as skirmishers. Spurling's cavalry immediately charged, driving the small Confederate command nearly the whole way to the fort, and captured 74 of the 100 men as well as the regimental colors. Their charge was only halted by concentrated fire from another regiment posted outside the fort, fewer than 100 Missourians from Colonel James McCown's (Cockrell's) brigade.

Throughout April 1 and 2 Steele's advancing command came into line and launched into a running fight with Liddell's advance guard, gradually pushing them to within a half-mile of the fort, where both sides dug in for another protracted siege. The next week was spent beefing up the lines and launching isolated attacks, none of which gained any territory from the other. When Spanish Fort fell on the night of April 8, Canby moved his infantry north and ordered Steele to join in a general attack the next day. At 5:30 p.m. on April 9, four Union divisions jumped out of their trench line, leading a mass assault of more than 16,000 infantrymen on the small Confederate fort. Within a few minutes they completely overran Fort Blakely, capturing 3,423 Confederate soldiers in the process.

The siege at Fort Blakely broke the back of the entire Confederate command at Mobile. Casualty reports are apparently missing, but fewer than 200 Confederate soldiers escaped into the bay and the relative safety of the remnants of the Mobile fleet. All three generals present were captured, while Canby and Steele's command lost a combined total of 113 killed and 516 wounded.

The last two batteries remaining under Confederate command, Battery Huger and Battery Tracy, remained, blocking any Union advance toward Mobile until nightfall on April 11. Their ammunition exhausted, Maury's last artillerymen spiked their guns and then escaped by steamboat back to Mobile, where they joined the retreat north toward Montgomery. These were the last shots fired in the last battle of the Western Theater; final commander of the Department of East Louisiana, Mississippi, and Alabama, Lieutenant General Richard "Dick" Taylor, met with Canby at Citronelle, Alabama, on May 2 to discuss surrender terms. The last 4,500 Confederate soldiers under his command formally surrendered on May 4, 1865 (some sources state May 8), nearly a month after Lee had surrendered in Virginia and more than a week after Johnston had surrendered in North Carolina. Only General Edmund Kirby Smith held out longer, surrendering his Trans-Mississippi Department on May 26, ending all formal military action in the war.

THE TOUR

Mobile

Mobile is at the extreme southwestern corner of Alabama, just a few miles from the Mississippi state border. I-10 connects Mobile with Biloxi and New Orleans to the west and Pensacola and Tallahassee to the east. I-65 runs northeast out of the city to Montgomery. Battle areas of the Mobile campaigns (naval- and land-based) are nearly all outside the city proper; Spanish Fort and Fort Blakely are across Mobile Bay just off I-10 East, and Forts Morgan and Gaines are south of the city on the Gulf of Mexico coastline.

The two existing coastal forts offer an interesting journey in turn. We suggest you follow AL 193 south out of the city (intersection with I-10 West at exit 17) about 20 miles to Dauphin Island. Turn left at the stop sign (end of AL 193) onto Bienville Road and travel about a mile to Fort Gaines. After your visit there, backtrack about one-quarter mile to the car ferry landing, near the fishing boat ramps. A privately run car ferry runs about every 90 minutes across the bay to Pleasure Island and Fort Morgan State Park (251-861-3000). The ferry has a range of prices from $5 to $35, depending on your mode of transportation, and some discounts are offered for round-trip passages. Both forts are (barely) within walking distance of the ferry landing, providing the weather cooperates and you are in reasonable shape.

Traveling east out of Fort Morgan State Park, the small town of Gulf Shores is 22 miles away on AL 180. Turn left onto Baldwin CR 59 in the main business district, which intersects I-10 about 25 miles north at exit 44. Fort Blakely and Spanish Fort are about 8 miles west and Mobile is 15 miles west on the interstate from this intersection, allowing an interesting, if lengthy, roundabout tour of the battle areas.

Originally located roughly near where AL 193 crosses Grant's Pass before it enters Dauphin Island, Fort Powell no longer exists, but the tour brochure at Fort Gaines points out its location, barely visible from one bastion.

POINTS OF INTEREST

Admiral Raphael Semmes Statue
Government St. at Water St.
Mobile, AL

The admiral was the famed commander of the CSS *Alabama*, the most successful Confederate commerce raider, which sank 57 Union ships before being shot to pieces and sunk by the USS *Kearsarge* off the coast of France.

Fort Conde Welcome Center
150 S. Royal St.
Mobile, AL
(251) 208-7304

While all of the Civil War actions took place outside the city of Mobile proper, there are still some worthwhile sights there for the dedicated buff. For a complete listing of this historic city's sights and attractions, most of which lean toward the antebellum, contact the welcome center, which can also supply maps (absolutely necessary here).

Fort Gaines Historic Site
51 Bienville Blvd.
Dauphin Island, AL
(251) 861-6992
www.dauphinisland.org/fort.htm

This well-preserved and lovingly cared-for fort was used as a coastal defense outpost during the Spanish-American War and both world wars, and later as a Coast Guard base, modified to suit each new role. Now owned and operated by the Dauphin Island Park and Beach Board, it is very well preserved and managed and an absolute delight to visit. An excellent brochure outlines the self-guided tour, and one of the "disappearing" gun mount magazines has been converted into an unusual but well-presented museum of uniforms, weapons, maps, photos, and documents spanning the 140-year history of the fort.

The old guardhouse next to the main sally port (entrance) contains a rather extensive collection of souvenirs as well as a nice collection of books, and some of the former garrison would no doubt be amused to note that their former commandant's office on the other side of the sally port now houses the restrooms. The tour brochure notes the location of Fort Powell, which no longer exists.

The fort is located near the end of Bienville Road, about 2 miles east of the intersection with AL 193 and about a quarter-mile east of the car ferry port.

Fort Morgan State Historical Site
51 AL 180 West
Gulf Shore, AL
(251) 540-5257

The basic shape and masonry walls of Fort Morgan still exist more or less intact, but the post was heavily modified for service in the Spanish-American War and both world wars. Now operated by the Alabama Historical Commission, the site includes several postwar buildings used as part of a radically expanded post at the turn of the 20th century, several artillery pieces from various periods of the post's history, and a self-guided tour of the partially restored fort.

As a general rule, we have found that the lower the level of ownership and management of a historic site (i.e., federal is high, local historical commission is low), the more informed, helpful, and friendly the staff is, and accordingly the more pleasant the visit is. Unfortunately, Fort Morgan is not a good example of this rule. On past visits, we have encountered incorrectly labeled or attributed signs and markers, a very confusing arrangement for paying entrance fees, poorly maintained and dangerous stairwells, and a distinct shortage of basic amenities. Reluctantly, we must recommend that perhaps the best visit of the fort and battle area can be taken in while just offshore aboard the Mobile Bay Ferry.

Group rates are available. You are supposed to pay your entrance fee about a half-mile east of the site at the same gate where you pay your fee for the Mobile Bay Ferry (which is only collected on the Fort Morgan side for trips either way), although there are no signs to indicate this, and you must inform the fee collector of your intentions. There is a single set of restrooms on-site next to the main parking lot and a single soft drink machine in a tiny, unmarked brick building next to the fort's sally port (under the flagpoles). A small museum with maps, photos, and artifacts shares space with a large gift shop near the main entrance. The fort is open daily.

Historic Blakeley State Park/Spanish Fort
34745 AL 225
Spanish Fort, AL
(251) 626-0798
www.blakeleypark.org

This 3,800-acre park is the site of the last major battle of the war, in April 1865. Although none of the earthworks or entrenchments still exists, there are several paths through the woods that run through the battle area, and two observation platforms overlooking the Tensaw River, where Battery Huger and Battery Tracy were located. A battle reenactment is held here the first weekend in Apr each year. Nearby Spanish Fort is now a heavily built-up suburb of Mobile; no trace of the old fort remains. The park is open daily.

The Museum of the City of Mobile
111 S. Royal St.
Mobile, AL
(251) 208-7569
www.museumofmobile.com

This museum houses a truly massive collection of artifacts detailing the long history of Mobile. A nice Civil War–era exhibit contains a small but well-presented weapons display.

USS *Alabama* Battleship Memorial Park
2703 Battleship Parkway (Highway 90/98)
Mobile, AL
(251) 433-2703
www.ussalabama.com

No, this isn't Semmes's famed warship, which lies in the murky depths 3 miles off the coast of Cherbourg, France. This is the equally famous WWII battleship, now nicely preserved as a floating museum. The decks, massive main-gun turrets, mess rooms, berthing compartments, bridge, and officers' quarters are open for tours. Also in the encompassing 100-acre park is the USS *Drum,* a WWII fleet submarine also open for tours, as well as a rather eclectic selection of combat aircraft, including a B-52D, B-25 Mitchell, P-51D Mustang, F4U Corsair, and even an A-12 (the interceptor version of the super-secret SR-71 Blackbird).

This attraction has absolutely nothing to do with the Civil War history of Mobile, but it is nearly irresistible to the historical traveler and an absolute must for any military buff. Park hours vary by season. The park is across the Mobile River from the downtown area; take I-10 east to exit 27 and follow the signs.

ACCOMMODATIONS

There are very few lodgings available near either fort, and those on the two islands tend to be the very high-priced resort variety with lengthy minimum stays required. We recommend you look for more reasonably priced establishments a few miles north in the metro Mobile area, particularly near the I-10 intersections, and we have noted a few of the better choices.

✴ ✴ ✴ ✴ ✴ ✴ ✴ ✴ ✴ ✴ ✴ ✴ ✴ ✴ ✴ ✴

Gulf Breeze Motel $–$$
1512 Cadillac Ave.
Dauphin Island, AL
(251) 861-7344
(800) 286-0296
http://gulfinfo.com/gulfbreezemotel/index.html

While most facilities on the Gulf Coast area of Mobile are expensive resorts, this small motel is a significant exception. The two-story, blue-and-white facility houses 31 fairly good-size units, each of which contains a refrigerator as well as the usual amenities. Less than 2 miles from Fort Gaines (turn right instead of left at the water tower, where AL 193 ends on the island), Gulf Breeze is just up the street from the beaches and an 18-hole golf course; a boat launch and slips are on the grounds. A bit unusual is the 48-hour cancellation notice needed for reservations (so your credit card is not charged for a night's stay), and the check-in time is quite early, at 1 p.m. The island is very pleasant, so if you wish to stay for a week, one night of your stay is free. Rates vary with the season and accommodations.

The Gulf Shores Plantation $$–$$$$
805 Plantation Rd.
Gulf Shores, AL
(251) 540-5000
(800) 211-5053
www.gulfshoresplantation.com

If you want to go whole hog in an upscale resort, this is the place to do it. Located very conveniently between Fort Morgan and Gulf Shores along a rather long and mostly deserted island road, this full-service resort has 325 rooms arranged as two- to five-bedroom condos and is rated three-diamond by AAA. All the rooms feature kitchens. There are six swimming pools on the property, as well as a golf course, lighted tennis courts, a sauna and Jacuzzis, and a game room for the kiddies. No pets are allowed. Most restaurants on this stretch of Gulf Shores are few and far between, but there is a Pizza Hut on the property as well as a beachside cafe. Isolation has its advantages, as the beach is practically a private one.

RESTAURANTS

As for the lodgings, we recommend looking for dining establishments off the two islands, as the ones nearest the two forts tend to be overpriced and not really superior to those closer to the city, with one significant exception.

Lighthouse Bakery $
919 Chaumont Ave.
Dauphin Island, AL
(251) 861-BAKE (2253)

This small bakery and sandwich shop is fairly well hidden away on a side street across from the Ship and Shore Store and facing the Baptist church. It appears sparkling new and caters to both the resort and fishing crowds. The best time to visit is at breakfast, when the pleasant staff has fresh, large

cinnamon rolls, danishes, and muffins ready (well before most historians of our acquaintance have their eyes cranked open!), as well as a variety of ever-changing daily specials.

Cajun roast beef, smoked turkey, and turkey pastrami sandwiches are available for dinner or early suppers, as well as a variety of other meat, cheese, and salad sandwiches. This is a "for-real" bakery, and fresh breads and rolls are available daily. Try to visit on a Thursday, when the to-die-for pepperjack cheese rolls are offered. The popularity this bakery has already engendered is reflected in the notice that you must call ahead to reserve one of the French bread loaves, available on Saturday.

Another highlight is the freshly ground and properly prepared coffees—a hearty espresso or "real" cappuccino is highly recommended.

Other Alabama and Mississippi Battlefields

Darley.

With the exceptions of the Vicksburg-Jackson, Mobile, and Shiloh-Corinth campaigns, the Civil War actions in Alabama and Mississippi largely consisted of smash-and-grab cavalry raids and small militia engagements. These two states, the very heartland of the Southern Confederacy, ironically came through the war nearly unscathed, as the major battles raged in their neighboring states to the east. Even where major battles did occur within their borders, as at Vicksburg and Mobile, the combat action stayed relatively close geographically to those cities, leaving the surrounding countryside mostly unmolested.

In this chapter we will concentrate on one relatively small but very significant battle in Mississippi and try to point out some of the other significant landmarks in both states. For a more in-depth discussion of the major campaigns fought in these states, please turn to the specific chapters on Mobile, Vicksburg, and Shiloh.

✦

ALABAMA

*A*labama was perhaps the Confederate state least directly affected militarily by the war. The fourth state to secede from the Union, the "Cradle of the Confederacy" served as the first national capital, was the home and first office for President Jefferson Davis, and remained throughout the war an important munitions and iron manufacturer and supplier to the Southern armies, but no grand campaigns marched through her until the very end, when nearly all resistance had faded away. Accurate records are very difficult to obtain or evaluate, but somewhere in the neighborhood of one-fifth of the entire population of the state enlisted in the military forces (about 100,000 men out of 500,000). About half of these men were killed or wounded during the war.

The population of Alabama was by no means unanimous in their support for the war, as in most other states both North and South. The mountainous northern sections were particularly noted for their strong pro-Union

stance; in one there was a very serious attempt to "secede" from the state of Alabama and form an independent, county-size, and pro-Union sovereign nation. The Free State of Winston died in its planning stages, but both sides took note of the seeming anti-Confederate fever there and tried in their own ways to exploit it. Their efforts failed, for just as in mountainous regions all over the world, the local population wanted to be left to their own devices and not to be involved in "flat-lander" squabbles.

Even this independent train of thought had its limitations. Part of a Union cavalry—the 1st Alabama Cavalry—was raised in Randolph County (on the southeastern edge of the independence-minded area), but the same county sent men to fill out in whole or in part some 30 artillery, cavalry, and infantry regiments for the Confederacy, not to mention a whole host of local militia and home guard units.

Union Raid into Central Alabama

Although the Union controlled most of northern Alabama by the second year of the war, it was not able to mount an offensive deep into the state until the strong Confederate garrisons in Mobile were eliminated. It was not until the last two months of the war, with Mobile safely under Union control and most of the other Alabama garrisons killed, captured, or scattered, that a raid deep into the state aimed at eliminating the strong arsenal at Selma and as many other manufacturing facilities and supply warehouses as could be safely captured or reduced. To this end, Major General James Harrison Wilson gathered more than 14,000 cavalrymen in extreme northwestern Alabama, just east of Corinth, Mississippi, in the early spring of 1865, preparing to mount a massive raid through the industrial heartland of Alabama and Georgia.

Wilson's Raid to Selma, as it was originally known, was the largest single operation of its kind during the war, and one of the most successful, but to be perfectly blunt, it could not have succeeded at any objective if Confederate resistance was not collapsing everywhere just as it kicked off. The only combat forces available to resist during this 28-day raid were three seriously decimated brigades of Brigadier General Nathan Bedford

Forrest's cavalry command, along with small remnants from Brigadier General James Ronald Chalmers's Mississippi and Brigadier General William Hicks "Red" Jackson's Tennessee Cavalry Divisions, and a small detachment from Brigadier General Philip Dale Roddy's Alabama Cavalry Brigade. In a few places this pitiful force was joined by local militia, but at no point did Wilson face a force stronger than 5,000 Confederates. Forrest claimed that he had a total force available of some 12,000 men in early March, but it is much more likely that he had somewhere around half that number actually still sticking around.

Major General James Harrison Wilson

Wilson's Raid Sets Off

Wilson's force concentrated at Eastport, Alabama, just across the border from northeastern Mississippi and left on its great raid on March 22. With only scattered resistance from bands of Forrest's cavalry and small groups of infantry, they moved quickly in three columns southeast through the state, aiming straight for Selma. Forrest attempted to make a stand just north of Plantersville, 18 miles north of Selma, with a hastily assembled force of about 2,000 cavalrymen and militia. On the morning of

April 2, Wilson's vanguard on the Randolph-Plantersville Road (now Alabama Highways 139 and 22), the 72nd Indiana Mounted Infantry, encountered rail barricades set up by Roddey's cavalry across the road. The Union force immediately attacked, forcing most of the Confederate cavalrymen to abandon their positions and fall back, while the rest covered their retreat. Wilson ordered his men to keep the pressure on, and a sort of "leapfrog" running battle soon ensued. The Confederates continued to fall back but kept up a hot fire as they did (this is a tactic known as a "fighting retreat").

Forrest had deployed the rest of his small force about a mile behind Roddey's position, and the Union force finally ran into his main line about 4 p.m. Believing they could just blow through Forrest's thin line, the men of the 17th Indiana Mounted Infantry charged, led by Captain Frank White. Wilson had described White as a "berserker of the Norseman breed," and the captain did his best to live up to that description. Charging into the line, into the very teeth of Forrest's only battery of artillery, a vicious hand-to-hand combat broke out with the for-once superior numbers of Confederate infantry. Forrest himself joined in the fray, soon wounded by a saber blow from Captain James D. Taylor, but he killed his assailant moments later with his pistol. White and his men were soon hurled back with significant losses.

Wilson ordered another attack to begin at once, this time with a brigade-wide front of dismounted cavalry and infantry, well supported by a heavy attack on the right of the Confederate line. That part of Forrest's line was held by the untrained and untried Alabama State Troops under Brigadier General Daniel Weisiger Adams. The militiamen soon caved in under the brutal attack, exposing Forrest's whole line and within a few minutes forcing him to pull his command south into Selma. Although a relatively short affair, one Union soldier called the fight, "a right smart little skirmish."

> *There is many a boy here today who looks on war as all glory, but boys, it is all hell. You can bear this warning to generations yet to come. I look upon war with horror.*
>
> —Major General William T. Sherman, Union Army, in an address to a Grand Army of the Republic convention, 1880

The Battle of Selma

A 5-mile-long series of earthworks and redoubts had been established in a semicircle around Selma, anchored on both ends to the Alabama River that flows across the south side of town. The most likely avenue of attack was from the north, the very direction Wilson was coming from, and the strongest parts of the line were here. In front of the trench line ran a parapet 6 to 8 feet tall, 8 feet thick at the base, and with a 5-foot-deep, 5-foot-wide ditch in front. While the fortifications were formidable, the garrison manning them was not. By the time Wilson closed in, Forrest's command was so small that he had to space them nearly 10 feet apart to cover the entire line (the standard was something more like elbow distance apart, ideally). Again, an exact figure as to the strength of this force is impossible to ascertain, but somewhere between 4,000 and 8,000 men manned the line, a bad mixture of hardened veterans of the Army of Tennessee alongside civilian preachers hastily "recruited" from the city churches.

The battle at Selma was almost anticlimactic from the start. Wilson's men moved south quickly on the morning of April 2, and by 3 p.m. they were just outside the city defenses and moving in line ready to assault. A little after 4 p.m. one of Wilson's divisions (Brigadier General Eli Long's 2nd Cavalry) stormed the northwestern ramparts astride the Summerfield Road, clearing the formidable obstacle in one great charge. The Confederate defenders put up a mighty defense during the assault—as Long and his staff rode forward, one was killed by a sharpshooter and four were wounded, including Long himself, who was shot in the head. Major General Emory Upton's 4th Cavalry Division had launched into the northeastern ramparts at nearly the same time, easily pushing over the parapet and encountering less resistance than Long suffered. As darkness fell, all Confederate resistance in the city broke, leaving Wilson his prize.

Wilson rested briefly in the small Alabama town and then gathered his force and headed east, toward his fateful rendezvous with the Confederate president himself.

MISSISSIPPI

The second state to declare secession (January 9, 1861), Mississippi was so enthusiastic as a whole to the new Confederacy that it somehow managed to contribute more fighting men to the Southern cause than the total number of white males it had in its 1860 census. More than 80,000 men served, mostly outside the state's borders, although Mississippi was a heavily fought-over battleground most of the war. Less than one-fourth of that number were still present in their regiments at war's end. While cavalry raids and operations ranged over most of the state repeatedly between 1862 and 1865, most large combat operations were concentrated in two areas: northeastern portions of the state around Corinth and Tupelo and the triangle between Vicksburg, Natchez, and Jackson (see the chapter on Vicksburg for a more thorough study of that campaign).

Corinth

This small town in extreme northeastern Mississippi came into prominence far out of proportion to its size during the war for two reasons—the Memphis & Charleston and Mobile & Ohio Railroads, which crossed in town. It was critical for the Confederacy to maintain control of these rail lines in order to maintain a cohesive and easily reinforceable front across the Western Theater, and it was equally critical for the Union to control them to prevent that very same thing.

After the disastrous fall of Forts Henry and Donelson in northern Tennessee in early 1862 (see the chapter on Other Tennessee Battlefields for a discussion of these battles), Western Department commander General Albert Sidney Johnston moved his headquarters to Corinth and tightened his lines of defense. As his western armies were badly outnumbered by the Union armies still assembling, Johnston decided to make the roads linking Memphis to Charleston his main line of resistance; he pulled troops away from Arkansas,

Map of the Battle of Corinth showing the lines of entrenchments made and routes followed by the U.S. forces under the command of Major General Halleck

Charleston, Savannah, Mobile, and most of Florida; and he initially abandoned plans to retake Kentucky. His strategy was to gather his forces in northern Mississippi, wait until the Union armies collected in Tennessee, and then strike hard and try to destroy their fighting capability before they could recover. While an excellent (and classic) strategy, it relied heavily on surprise and massive force, both of which were difficult to manage given the battlefield tactics and transportation methods of the day.

Johnston gave General Pierre Gustave Toutant Beauregard overall responsibility for assembling the scattered forces at Corinth and making them ready for battle. As Beauregard set about his task, Major General Henry Wager Halleck (commander, Department of the Mississippi) was sending his combined armies south to attack and take Corinth and Jackson, thus (hopefully) splitting the Confederate Western Theater neatly in half. Starting in early March 1862, Union forces started arriving in Savannah, Tennessee, to establish their forward base of operations for the move to Corinth, 30 miles to the south. Learning of the Union presence, Johnston decided to move out and strike the enemy force before it could fully deploy, even though a major portion of his own army had not yet arrived.

Johnston led about 40,000 men of his newly minted Army of the Mississippi north to the place where Union forces were landing for their own invasion—a small riverboat landing called Pittsburg Landing and better known for the local small country church, Shiloh (see the chapter on Shiloh for a discussion of this battle). After a two-day fiercely contested fight on April 6 and 7, which included the death of Johnston himself, Beauregard withdrew the battered army back to Corinth and dug in, while the Union Army was too exhausted and battered itself to pursue immediately.

Background to the Battle

Even before Johnston ordered the army out to Shiloh, work was under way to fortify Corinth. First begun as a series of simple breastworks on the north and east sides of town, after Beauregard brought the army back to town on April 8, 1862, work began in earnest to expand and improve the line. Work was complicated by the fact that hospitals, churches, and ordinary homes were filled to overflowing with Confederate wounded, as many as 8,000 by several accounts. Major General Earl Van Dorn's Army of the West had finally arrived from Arkansas, along with a division under Brigadier (later Major) General Sterling "Pap" Price, joining General Braxton Bragg's Army of the Mississippi, fresh back from Shiloh, to give Beauregard nearly 66,000 combat troops in the small city.

Halleck moved his great Northern army very slowly south, starting out on April 29 and taking nearly a month to move the 20 miles to the outskirts of Corinth. His nearly 130,000-man army was composed of Brigadier (later Lieutenant) General Ulysses S. Grant's Army of Tennessee, Major General Don Carlos Buell's Army of the Ohio, and Major General John Pope's Army of the Mississippi, the very combined Union force that had so worried Johnston.

Johnston had only had to worry about Grant's army the first day at Shiloh, and his successor Beauregard had been pushed off the field of battle when Buell's army showed up the next day. As the three great Union armies slowly moved into an encompassing siege position around the city, it was obvious that there was no way the smaller Confederate force could win in open battle and to stay would be a slow starvation after the supply lines were cut. Beauregard decided to evacuate his forces while he still had the chance and hopefully work his armies into a position where they could take out the superior Union forces piecemeal.

On May 29 most of the sick and wounded, along with most of the available supplies, were moved down the Mobile & Ohio Railroad line south to Tupelo, while regimental and brigade commanders shuffled their commands around the city to give the Union force the idea that they were about to try a breakout attack. "Quaker guns" (logs painted black) replaced the artillery in their redoubts, and buglers blew their calls in deserted camps while the infantry quietly slipped out the unguarded back door, following the trains to Tupelo. During the night what was left of the cavalry slipped out just as quietly, leaving startled Union pickets to see only a deserted line of earthworks and redoubts guarding an equally deserted town when the dawn broke. Some historians state that this withdrawal was the beginning of the end for the western Confederacy, as it left the Union Army in a strong position with a large force deep in the Southern lines of communication.

The Battle of Corinth: Act 1

With Beauregard's army safely out of the city, Halleck's men cautiously entered Corinth, fully expecting some sort of trap or ambush. When a thorough search of the area turned up no sign of gray-clad infantry, Halleck undoubtedly breathed a sigh of relief—and then set about strengthening the city's fortifications for an expected attack. Over the next few months, a series of artillery batteries ringed by infantry emplacements were built on the south side of town (called Batteries A through F), soon joined by an inner ring of five more such batteries, called the College Hill line.

By late summer 1862, the main focus of activity started moving away from Mississippi into Tennessee and northern Georgia. Bragg had replaced Beauregard as overall commander, but he soon moved with his Army of Tennessee to Chattanooga to counter an expected Union move against that transportation and manufacturing center. Van Dorn was given command of the District of Mississippi and moved his headquarters and most of his command southwestward to Vicksburg, while Price shifted his reduced Army of the West into Iuka, Mississippi, to keep an eye on the Union movements east.

There had been several command changes in the Union Army at Corinth as well. Halleck had been recalled to Washington to serve as the latest in a continuing series of unsuccessful commanding generals of all the Union armies, the very position his lieutenant Grant would successfully fill some time later. Grant set about preparing his army to move east into central Tennessee, while the beloved but inept Major General William Starke "Old Rosy" Rosecrans, a divisional commander during the brief siege, took over command of both the Army of the Mississippi and the Department of Corinth.

Iuka

Ordered to prevent any of the three Union armies in Corinth from traveling east to attack Bragg in Tennessee, Price was in a bad position. He had 14,000 men strung across a wide line in northeastern Mississippi, really more of a guard and early-warning force than any significant combat threat; his only reinforcements lay on the other

side of the Union positions, several hundred miles away in Vicksburg; and Grant appeared determined to move his armies through his position. Grant was also worried that Price might move his force north to join Bragg and resolved to attack the Confederate force before he could do so. As one might imagine, Civil War–era generals spent a lot of time in their tents worrying, usually about the most unlikely of things. On September 16, 1862, Grant ordered Major General Edward Otho Cresap Ord to take his 2nd Division (Army of Tennessee) and Rosecrans to take his Army of the Mississippi and assault Price's force in a coordinated attack on the morning of September 19.

The attack at Iuka did not come off as planned, to say the least. Ord's order to attack at a given time was changed to an order to move in when he heard Rosecrans's attack start, the intention being to better coordinate the two-pronged assault. Price had learned of Ord's movement against him from the northwest around dusk on September 18, although not of Rosecrans's from the southwest, and telegraphed Van Dorn with the news. The Confederate commander ordered Price to pull his troops out of Iuka, join his force now moving out of Vicksburg, and threaten Grant's armies from Tennessee. As Price's men moved out of town on the afternoon of September 19, they ran straight into Rosecrans's force, the Union movement to attack having been delayed by poor navigation skills.

While Rosecrans's and Price's troops rapidly deployed and launched into a vicious fight, Ord's force stayed unmoving on the north side of town. He later claimed that he heard no gunfire all the rest of the day, a claim supported by his command staff, but Grant remained suspicious ever after that he had simply decided to let Rosecrans do all the fighting. This is perhaps one of the better-known examples of a phenomenon known as "acoustic shadow," where someone many miles away may hear the noise of battle, but someone close in might hear nothing.

Price's northernmost battlefield commanders had warned him about Ord's presence, but when he did not join in Rosecrans's attack, the Confederate commander decided his force was just a ruse to try to get him to split his small command. However, when the Union attack was unsuccessful in breaking his own lines by nightfall, Price decided that, ruse or not, Ord was bound to join

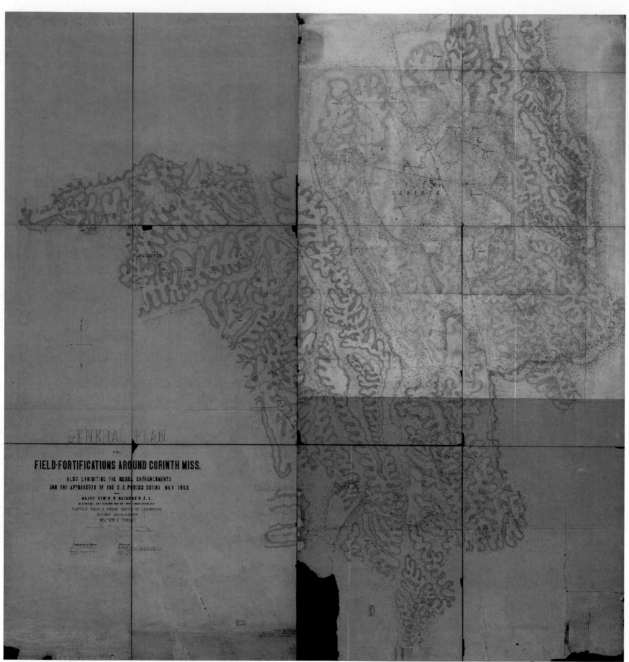

Field fortifications around Corinth

in the continued assault the next morning. Just before dawn on September 20 Price led his men safely south out of the besieged town, heading to join Van Dorn's force bearing north out of Vicksburg. Rosecrans initially ordered his men to pursue, but fearful of getting lost again and facing a strong rearguard action from Price's men, he soon called off the chase.

The Battle of Corinth: Act 2

With Price and Van Dorn both now safely out of his immediate area of concern, Grant moved north to Jackson, Tennessee, with most of his army, leaving Rosecrans with only four divisions to garrison the town and protect the northern Mississippi supply lines. Van Dorn knew that Corinth was a key town for either side to control and, with most of the Union armies now gone, determined to attack it. On the first of October, the 22,000 men of the combined Confederate armies in Mississippi moved north from their base near Ripley, 22 miles southwest of Corinth, in an attempt to take the fortified town from the northwest and by surprise.

By the very next day, the element of surprise was lost when the Confederate infantry skirmished with Union cavalry scouts at the Hatchie River Bridge on the outskirts of Corinth. Alarmed, Rosecrans concentrated his forces in the strong north and west fortification positions and waited for Chewalla, Tennessee, less than 8 miles from Corinth.

On the early morning of October 3, Major General Mansfield Lovell's, Brigadier General Dabney H. Maury's, and Brigadier General Louis Hebert's divisions burst out of the woods and stormed the northwesternmost line of outer defenses, easily driving in the Union pickets and advancing through the line of works with few casualties. As they dressed ranks again in preparation for assaulting the city's inner defenses, three small earthquakes shook the ground under them, frightening the men and shattering their confidence. Van Dorn ordered an hour's halt to give the men time to eat, drink, and rest before what he assumed would be a final assault. This delay only granted Rosecrans the time he needed to strengthen his line of inner defenses.

RENEWED ATTACKS

About noon Van Dorn ordered the men up and in line of battle again, but repeated assaults the rest of the afternoon failed to crack the Union line. At dusk Van Dorn ordered a halt to the battle, and plans were made with his division commanders for the next morning's assault. Hebert was to lead the attack by a strong assault on the Union right, followed in close order by Maury in the center and Lovell hitting the Union left flank. A predawn heavy artillery barrage was planned to help screen the infantry movements into line and reduce the Union defenses.

At 4 a.m. the Confederate artillery batteries opened up to "soften" the Union fortifications for the assaulting infantry, but they were soon silenced by very effective Union counter-battery fire. Just before he was to move out on assault, Hebert suddenly fell ill and was replaced by Brigadier General Martin E. Green, who wasted a precious hour trying to get reorganized. Maury had started his assault in the meantime, allowing Rosecrans to concentrate his artillery fire and troop strength on his small part of the assault line. For some unknown reason, Lovell never ordered his men to attack.

Battle of Corinth, Mississippi, October 4, 1862 (Currier & Ives lithograph)

When Green's men finally came into line, the two Confederate divisions succeeded in blowing through the Union defenses and into the city itself. At the height of the battle, several brigades managed to fight their way to the rail crossroads in the center of town, while Colonel William P. Rogers led his 2nd Texas Infantry Regiments up and over the ramparts of Battery Robinett, the last line of Rosecrans's defenses. However, since Lovell had failed to support the attack, Union troops from the south side of the city were able to move forward and hit the Confederates on their flank, violently breaking up the attack. Rogers was killed and his force shattered before they could consolidate their gain. Within two hours the Confederates were forced to withdraw from the city, and Rosecrans once again had full control of his lines. Van Dorn was forced to order a general retreat, which Rosecrans was unable to pursue, possibly out of fear of becoming lost once more.

For a relatively short fight, casualties were staggeringly high on both sides. Rosecrans reported that he had lost 315 killed and 1,812 wounded, with another 232 missing or captured (out of 21,147 engaged) during the two-day battle, while Van Dorn reported a loss of 1,423 killed, 5,692 wounded, and another 2,268 missing and presumed captured (out of his approximately 22,000-strong command). Corinth remained either occupied or under Union control for the rest of the war, and no Confederate army tried again to retake it.

TOURS

Alabama Sites

We suggest a visit to significant Alabama sites as part of a larger tour of the battle areas in Georgia, Tennessee, and Mississippi; accordingly, we list these areas from east to west, and from the northern part of the state to the southern half.

Jacksonville

Scene of a small cavalry raid in 1862, this small town north of Anniston is best known today as the home of Jacksonville State University. Just off the main square next to city hall is the First Presbyterian Church, one of a handful of antebellum structures still in existence in the city. This church, built in 1861, was used as a hospital during and after the short battle here; it is still in use and does not offer formal tours.

In the city cemetery 2 blocks south, at the corner of South Church and Mays Streets, is the resting place of General Robert E. Lee's "boy artillerist," Major John Pelham. A tall, well-sculpted statue of the young officer looks west out of the Confederate section of the cemetery (at the very edge of the cemetery, at the cross streets given above). Pelham had resigned from West Point after his home state of Alabama seceded, just a few weeks before he was due to graduate. Assigned to Lee's Army of Northern Virginia, Pelham displayed an amazing skill at gunnery, particularly with his fast-moving "horse artillery" battery.

Pelham was a good-looking and rather dashing sort and a favorite of the equally dashing cavalry officer Brigadier General James Ewell Brown ("Jeb") Stuart, who took Pelham along on his many cavalry raids. Officially just a casual observer, Pelham joined in on a mass charge of the 3rd Virginia Cavalry at Kelley's Ford on March 17, 1863. Struck on the neck by a bursting artillery shell, he was quickly taken to the nearby home of his fiancée, Bessie Shackelford, where he died that same night. He was just 24 years old.

Jacksonville is just off the (very) well-beaten path between Anniston and the shopping mecca of Boaz, about 15 miles north of I-20 (exit 185) on AL 21. Both Anniston and Gadsden, a few miles to the northwest on US 431, have plentiful food and lodging establishments.

Addison

The center of the onetime Free State of Winston, this tiny northwest Alabama community was ground zero for the anti-secessionist movement. The center of all this activity was in a roadside stopover, Looney's Tavern, which stood just outside town. The original building is long gone, but the site has a historic marker and can be found on Winston County Highway 41 about 2 miles north of its intersection with US 278, on the eastern edge of town. This road is very poorly marked; watch for the road sign pointing toward Decatur just before you start into the business district of the small settlement.

This area was seriously pro-Union during the war, as a few known statistics bear out. Not only was the little-known 1st Alabama Cavalry raised in this area (and went on to march with Sherman through Georgia), but an estimated 2,000 local citizens joined this and other Union regiments during the war. Another estimated 10,000 "Tories" lived in northern Alabama, actively assisting Confederate deserters and helping Union raiders. Three thousand of these Unionist citizens met at Looney's Tavern on July 4, 1861, to draft documents formally protesting Alabama's secession and to explore ways their county could secede from the state. In the end nothing ever came of the attempt.

Decatur

Located at an extremely strategic point on the Tennessee River served by the newly built Tuscumbia Railroad (known during the war as the Memphis & Charleston), this small town became an important transportation and supply center during the war. Although the target of both sides as "ownership" changed hands relatively early in the war, no pitched battles were fought in or around the town.

Immediately after the Union victory at Shiloh (April 7, 1862), Brigadier (soon Major) General Ormsby McKnight Mitchel was directed to take a reinforced division of about 8,000 men and take Huntsville and Decatur for the North at his earliest opportunity. This would cut the Confederate supply lines through north Alabama and south-central Tennessee, while providing a good base to use for a planned invasion of Montgomery and Mobile, as well as a nod of protection for the Unionist Tories who populated the surrounding area. On April 12 the lead brigades of Mitchel's force entered Decatur unopposed and immediately sent out reconnaissance parties farther west toward Florence and Tuscumbia.

The Union kept control of Decatur the remainder of the war, suffering only isolated and brief cavalry attacks on its garrison for the next two and a half years. In late October 1864, General John Bell Hood's decimated Army of Tennessee camped just outside the city for three days, "making demonstrations" against the Union garrison to keep them bottled up inside the city until the rest of his force had safely passed to the west. It is highly unlikely that he actually sought any battle, which did not come in any stead, as his target was badly needed supplies he expected to find at Tuscumbia.

Decatur is located west of Huntsville, just off I-65. US 72 Alternate connects the town with I-65 at exit 340, about 5 miles east of downtown. Although little military action occurred here, there are three interesting stops in the town.

Hines-McEntire Home
120 Sycamore St.
Decatur, AL

This two-story brick mansion on the Tennessee River bank was a headquarters for both sides during the war. Local legend holds that General Albert Sydney Johnston of the Confederacy planned his Shiloh campaign here and that, for the Union, General Ulysses S. Grant and Major General William Sherman met here for strategic discussions after the Vicksburg campaign.

A good view of the house can be obtained from the street. Sycamore Street runs north off Wilson Street/US 72 west of the Keller Memorial Bridge over the Tennessee River and just past a small bridge over the railroad tracks.

The Old State Bank
925 Bank St. NE
Decatur, AL
(256) 341-4818
www.decaturparks.com/statebank.asp

Built in 1833, this large, impressive Greek Revival building originally housed one of the three first branches of the Bank of the State of Alabama. Legend has it that then President Martin Van Buren attended the dedication ceremony. During the war it served as a hospital and supply depot (which Hood would no doubt have loved to get his hands on) and is reportedly one of only five structures left standing in town after the war. The huge columns gracing the front porch have damage that is claimed to be from some of the Confederate cavalry raids.

Now restored to its bank-era appearance (the state bank system in Alabama died in 1846), the Old State Bank stands on a beautifully landscaped downtown park and is open as a city museum. Hours vary; the staff advises that you call ahead to check. Additional hours are available by request. Admission is free.

Parham's Civil War Relics and Memorabilia
721–723 Bank St.
Decatur, AL
(256) 350-4018
www.rparhamsrelics.com

This small shop upstairs over an antiques store is a short walk from the Old State Bank and offers an interesting variety of small artifacts for sale, as well as books and modern memorabilia concerning the war. Owner Robert Parham is a local authority on the Civil War era and a good conversationalist; be prepared to stay awhile if you really want to know what happened here!

Some of the larger, better-known "relic" shops we have visited could take some lessons from Parham; he runs a tidy shop with artifacts priced for the average collector, concentrates on his immediate area, and has a refreshing lack of "the very bullet that killed A. S. Johnston" style of labels and identifications.

Wheeler

General Joe Wheeler Plantation
12280 AL 20
Hillsboro, AL
(256) 637-8513
www.wheelerplantation.org

Although most maps point to this location 15 miles west of Decatur as a "town," it really consists of one thing alone: the plantation and last home of Major General Joseph "Fighting Joe" Wheeler of the Confederate Army. Perhaps one of the best combat cavalry officers produced during the war, Wheeler fought primarily with the Army of Tennessee under Bragg, Johnston, and Hood, and commanded what was for all practical purposes the only unit resisting Sherman's Georgia Campaign of fall 1864. He led his cavalry in more than 500 skirmishes and 127 pitched battles, lost 16 horses shot out from under him, had 36 of his staff officers wounded, and was himself wounded three times. Although he and the equally famous Major General Nathan Bedford Forrest of the South loathed each other, they were both past masters at the art of employing cavalry to disrupt enemy lines of communication. Wheeler went on to a successful postwar career as a cotton planter and U.S. congressman, and during the Spanish-American War, he became the only Confederate general officer to regain his U.S. commission as a general officer.

During the Santiago Campaign (Spanish-American War), U.S. Major General Wheeler commanded the cavalry division that included Teddy Roosevelt's Rough Riders. Perhaps showing his advancing age (he was 62 at the time) or just hearkening back to a happier time, upon seeing the Rough Riders storming up Kettle Hill (not San Juan Hill, as is so often erroneously attributed), he allegedly turned to his aide and remarked, "Just look at them! They got the Yankee sons-of-bitches on the run!"

The main house has been restored to its original condition, most furnishings are period and original to the house, and another 13 buildings round out what is a close approximation of a postbellum working plantation. The main house contains a selection of personal and professional artifacts from Wheeler's long and fascinating life.

The plantation is most decidedly not the easiest place to find; take the four-lane AL 20/US 72 Alternate 15 miles west from the Decatur square, and watch carefully for a historic marker to your left (south) in a small parking lot—it is directly in front of the plantation entrance. There is no sign on the westbound route that we could see (there is one showing the evacuation route for the nearby Brown's Ferry Nuclear Power Plant!), but there is one on the eastbound side to direct you in. Call ahead to schedule a tour.

Florence

This city dates its founding from a year before Alabama even became a state (1818) and was an important trade and commerce center when this was the "western frontier." Although right smack in the middle of Union offenses aimed at Corinth to the west and Decatur to the east, and violently taken over by both sides several times during the war, it came through the war relatively unscathed. Today it is the home of the University of North Alabama and has retained its status as a trade and commerce center for industrial traffic on the adjacent Tennessee River.

Civil War sites are hard to find in this heavily urbanized city, but it can boast at least one gem of the era.

Pope's Tavern Museum
203 Hermitage Dr.
Florence, AL
(256) 760-6439

Originally a stagecoach stop built in 1811 in the middle of a dense wilderness, this small building in the midst of an equally dense urban neighborhood now houses a museum of Civil War–era and early pioneer artifacts. The tavern was used as a hospital for both Confederate and Union troops during and after the local skirmishes and the nearby Battle of Elk River, and as a supplemental hospital for the wounded from the Battle of Franklin (Tennessee).

Selma

Better known in modern times for its pivotal role in the civil rights movement, Selma was a very important manufacturing and supply center during the war, with several gun factories, foundries, warehouses, and a large armory. The Selma Naval Works produced rams, including the CSS *Tennessee,* and during the last two years of the war, nearly half the barrels and nearly two-thirds of the cartridge ammunition used by the armies in the Western Theater were produced here. The small town survived most of the war untouched, due in no small part to its isolated location deep in west-central Alabama.

Selma is about 40 miles west of both Montgomery and I-65, on US 80. Take exit 167 off I-65 on the south side of town, and go west on US 80 for a straight shot to the city.

While almost all of the town was destroyed either during the battle or burned by Wilson's men as they left a week later, there are a handful of extant structures. Just off US 80 on the north part of town, on Broad Street at the Trinity Lutheran Church, is a marker about the battle and a small section of breastworks, the only remaining part of the line.

John Bell Hood

Of all the hard-luck cases who were living examples of the Peter Principle (that everyone eventually rises to his or her level of incompetence), John Bell Hood tops the list. Hood was born in Owingsville, Kentucky, in 1831 and secured a berth at West Point by virtue of his uncle, congressman Richard French. He graduated after an undistinguished career at the military academy in 1853, ranked 44th out of 52. The custom at that time was to "brevet" newly minted officers (i.e., to give them the rank but not the pay, position, or real responsibility of a certain rank), and Hood was brevetted a 2nd lieutenant and sent to California soon after his graduation. In 1855 he was commissioned in the same rank and reassigned to the 2nd Cavalry in Texas, joining future Confederate and Union generals Robert E. Lee, William J. Hardee, Albert Sydney Johnston, and George H. Thomas. While there, he suffered the first of his many combat injuries in skirmishes with hostile Indians.

With the outbreak of war in 1861, Hood resigned his U.S. commission and was almost immediately granted a Confederate one to the rank of 1st lieutenant. By March of 1862 he had been promoted to brigadier general and placed in charge of the Texas Brigade (soon afterward named Hood's Texas Brigade, in the fashion of the day), under the overall command of Colonel John B. Magruder at Yorktown, Virginia. Five months later he was promoted to major general and given command of a division in Lieutenant General James Longstreet's corps, Lee's Army of Northern Virginia. He developed a reputation there as a gallant and brave fighter, inspiring deep love and devotion among his own men. At Gettysburg, however, an ill-conceived plan forced Hood under protest to charge his division uphill into a well-positioned Union force. His division was decimated, and Hood suffered a crippling injury to his left arm.

After a brief recovery period, Hood traveled with Longstreet west to reinforce General Braxton Bragg's army, about to engage at Chickamauga, Georgia. In a nearly unbelievable stroke of luck, Longstreet's corps arrived on the field at the exact place and time a Union brigade had been mistakenly moved out of the way. Longstreet was able to exploit the breach most successfully, but Hood suffered another gunfire wound, this time resulting in the amputation of his right leg. While recuperating, Hood developed an addiction to the painkiller laudanum, which many historians believe led directly to the poor battlefield decisions he subsequently made.

Upon returning to the field, Hood was promoted to lieutenant general and given command of a corps in General Joseph E. Johnston's Army of Tennessee, just in time for their rolling defense against Major General William T. Sherman's 1864 invasion of Georgia. Hood ranted against Johnston's careful hoarding of his strength while slowly giving way before Sherman, preferring the charging attack over the static defense, and said as much in a series of letters to Bragg, then President Jefferson Davis's military chief of staff, as well as to Davis himself. Davis was equally unhappy with the strategy Johnston had adopted, and on June 17, 1864, replaced him with Hood, with orders to attack Sherman. Three days later he ordered an all-out attack on the Union positions at Peachtree Creek, which failed at the cost of nearly one-fourth of his command. Two days later, after a forced, nightlong march through the city of Atlanta, he attacked Sherman's positions again, this time on the eastern outskirts of the city. This attack failed as well, and follow-up attempts at Ezra Church on the western outskirts and at Jonesboro to the south accomplished nothing but reducing his available force to less than half its original strength. Forced to abandon the city on September 1, Hood soon led what was left of his army on a hare-brained campaign, designed, he said, to lure Sherman out of the strongly fortified city and north into open ground, where the vastly larger Union Army could be destroyed. More than one grizzled veteran of the Army of Tennessee started saying openly that Hood had gone mad but, as good soldiers, they followed his commands.

This plan resulted in nothing more than making a portion of Sherman's available force chase Hood all up through northern Georgia before they were recalled to prepare for Sherman's march to Savannah. Hood concocted another hare-brained plan, this time to storm north through Tennessee, seizing the Union supply headquarters at Nashville, and then continue north through Kentucky, threatening Cincinnati, Ohio, and eventually moving east to join Lee's army at Petersburg, where they would join forces and crush the huge Union Army commanded by Lieutenant General Ulysses S. Grant. Davis, very reluctantly this time, agreed to Hood's idea and allowed him to proceed. Moving through very scattered and light resistance at first, Hood soon ran into a rapidly retreating force at Franklin, Tennessee, on November 30 and ordered the attack with only two of his three divisions in position and only two hours of daylight left. The attack was an unmitigated disaster, with Hood being only 1 of 2 alive and uninjured generals (out of 12) at the end of the fight. Still he pressed on, finally washing the remnants of his army up on the shores of Union ramparts at Nashville in December 1864.

With his army nearly completely destroyed, Hood tendered his resignation quietly, which was wisely accepted. Hood spent his postwar years in New Orleans as a modestly successful businessman and vehemently defended his war record to anyone who would listen—including readers of his own book of experiences, the aptly named *Advance and Retreat*, and his writings in the monumental *Battles and Leaders of the Civil War*. His bad luck plaguing him to the end, Hood, his wife, and his eldest daughter died in a yellow fever epidemic in 1879, leaving behind 10 orphaned children.

Old Dallas County Courthouse
(Smitherman Historic Building)
109 Union St.
Selma, AL
(334) 874-2174

The courthouse is a large, impressive Greek Revival building well restored and kept up, which was used as a hospital and military school during the war. Now used as a museum, it houses a small but rather impressive collection of Civil War artifacts and antiques, as well as a sample of the goods that Selma's factories produced for the war effort.

Old Depot Museum
4 Martin Luther King Jr. St.
Selma, AL
(334) 874-2197

The former Tennessee & Alabama River Railroad depot, nearly destroyed during the battle, has been restored and serves as the Selma–Dallas County Museum of History and Archives. Emphasis is equally divided between Civil War, railroading, and civil rights–era exhibits, and a very nice archival room is available. Additional displays cover the Native American history of the area, WPA murals, and a selection of very rare photos showing African Americans at work on a postbellum local plantation.

Old Live Oak Cemetery
AL 22 South (West Dallas Ave.)
Selma, AL

A great number of Confederates who died in the battle are buried here in the cemetery's Confederate section, graced by a large monument. Lieutenant General William Joseph Hardee is also buried here, as is navy captain Catesby ap Roger Jones, executive officer of the CSS *Virginia* (usually and erroneously identified as the *Merrimac*) and commander of the ironclad during the fight with the USS *Monitor,* later commander of the Selma Iron Works. Open during daylight hours.

Montgomery

Montgomery saw no combat during the war, thanks to her position deep in the state well away from the major battle areas, but her position in Confederate lore was established even before the first shots were fired. This was the home of the first Confederate capital, before it was moved to Richmond, Virginia, and the place where President Jefferson Davis took his oath of office. Wilson's Raid came through and took the city, a transportation and supply hub, without resistance a little more than a week after Selma fell. While this

capital city is a large and bustling metropolis, there are a few reminders about the war to be found.

Alabama State Capitol
600 Dexter Ave.
Montgomery, AL
(334) 242-3935
www.visitingmontgomery.com

The State Capitol was built in 1851 in a style very similar to the U.S. Capitol. A bronze star mounted on the west portico marks the very spot where Jefferson Davis took his oath of office. Forty-five-minute guided tours are given of the building. Make sure to see the impressive three-story, self-supporting double-spiral staircase built by former slave Horace King, a postbellum legislator. The capitol is open for self-guided tours; admission and tours are free. All guided tours must be prearranged.

First White House of the Confederacy
664 Washington Ave.
Montgomery, AL
(334) 242-1861
www.firstwhitehouse.org

The home of Jefferson Davis and his family during the first months of the Confederacy is right across the street from the capitol building and is now restored and open as a museum. The house is furnished with Davis's own furniture from his home in Mississippi, and the second floor is kept just the way it was when he was in residence. A small collection of Confederate relics and artifacts as well as some of Davis's personal belongings are on display. Admission is free, but donations are accepted and appreciated.

Mississippi Sites

Corinth

Corinth is a bit off the beaten path, which in this case is a very good thing—there simply hasn't been enough "progress" there to erase much of its past. The town is 89 miles east of Memphis, 226 miles southwest of Nashville, 168 miles west of Birmingham, and 218 miles north of Jackson; it helps the traveler to remember that getting there is half the fun! Corinth lies in extreme northeastern Mississippi very close to the Alabama border, at the crossroads of US 72 between I-65 (exit 340) and Memphis, and US 45 between I-40 at Jackson, Tennessee (exit 82), and Tupelo. If you are approaching from the east, we heartily recommend US 72, as it goes through Florence, Wheeler, and Decatur, Alabama—all interesting Civil War–related stops.

Corinth is without a doubt the most Civil War–oriented town we have visited, at least in the Western Theater. Information on its preserved houses, buildings, entrenchments, and museums could literally fill a good-size book. We strongly advise that you contact the Corinth Area Tourism Promotion Council (www.corinth.net) and ask for its excellent package of information before starting your trip.

Battery F
Davis Street
Corinth, MS
(662) 287-9273

One of several original and well-preserved earthworks in and around town, this was the one through which Confederate forces successfully assaulted on October 3, 1862. It is a redoubt of the type called a "lunette," with mountings for four guns and several surrounding infantry rifle pits. Well outside the main part of town, take Smith Bridge Road west across US 45, turn right onto Kimberly Road, and then left onto Davis Street.

Battery Robinette
102 Linden St.
Corinth, MS
(662) 287-9273

Also known as Fort Robinette (or Robinette), the earthworks here were the center of Corinth's inner defenses and then scene of some of the heaviest fighting. They were rebuilt to the original specifications in 1976. A small park surrounding the earthworks, display cannons, and monuments is open daily from dawn to dusk. There is no admission fee.

Corinth Area Tourism Promotion Council
602 East Waldron St.
P.O. Box 2158
Corinth, MS
(662) 287-8300
(800) 748-9048
www.corinth.net

While these folks do have a visitor center in downtown Corinth, most of the information they provide can be obtained at some of the venues and attractions as well as a new satellite visitor center on the west side of town at US 45. However, we strongly suggest you call or write them to get their free mail-out package, as this is one of the best presentations we have seen from any city of any size. The devotion this town has to the Civil War historian or traveler is truly astonishing and makes the visit here an absolute must.

Corinth Civil War Interpretive Center
501 W. Linden St.
Corinth, MS
(662) 287-9273
www.nps.gov/shil

The Civil War Interpretive Center once was a small building behind the Curlee House. In July 2004 a $9.5 million, 12,000-square-foot replacement opened its doors, ready to educate visitors about Corinth's importance during the war. The multi-acre site highlights the 1862 Siege and Battle of Corinth as well as 16 historic landmarks in and around town.

Corinth National Cemetery
1551 Horton St.
Corinth, MS
(901) 386-8311

This cemetery was established in 1866 as the 16th National Cemetery, just three-quarters of a mile from the railroad intersection that was the focus of so much of the fighting here. Union dead were gathered here from the battlefields of Corinth, Iuka, Parker's Crossroads, and some 17 other battle and skirmish areas, as well as hospitals and camps across Mississippi and Tennessee. There are 1,793 known and 3,895 unknown Union soldiers buried in this still-active cemetery, where more than 7,000 veterans of subsequent wars also have been laid to rest. National cemeteries are usually shrines to the Union cause, but this one is unusual: Three Confederate soldiers were buried here, too, just under the flagpole. Admission is free.

Crossroads Museum
221 N. Filmore St.
Corinth, MS
(601) 287-3120
www.crossroadsmuseum.com

This small museum should be your very first stop in town. Although it is quite small physically, this is one of the finest museums of its type that you will ever step into. Largely the result of efforts by Margaret Greene Rogers, this museum relies on its highly knowledgeable and informative staff to supplement the well-laid-out displays of letters, paintings, models, and relics.

The displays themselves are rather eccentric, with a mixture of fossils from the Paleozoic and Cretaceous periods next to Chickasaw Indian relics, which are next to turn-of-the-20th-century photos of Corinth alongside battlefield-dug Civil War relics. A separate room contains a selection of largely 19th-century household items, and a small research room contains a rather impressive amount of local history books and publications, with a heavy emphasis on the Civil War era.

Do not let this eccentricity and the relatively small size of the museum fool you; we fully expected to make this a "10-minute in and out" when we first visited and ended up spending well over an hour just talking with the staff about some of the more unusual items on display. This is most decidedly not the sort of place where you see the same "bullets-'n'-belt buckles" that so many small-town museums seem to have in common (to the point that most are hard to distinguish from one another), and we not only highly recommend a visit here but insist that this is a crucial stop for any visit to the town. Admission is free. Please help this small gem stay open, however, by giving a donation or making a purchase from the unusually small selection of "stuff for sale."

The Historic Verandah Curlee House
705 Jackson St.
Corinth, MS
(800) 748-9048

This 1857 home just off US 45 Business was the headquarters for both Bragg and Halleck and is one of the 16 National Historic Landmarks in Corinth. Central to the campaigns that were waged here, the home also houses the Corinth Civil War Interpretive Center on its grounds (see above) and offers tours of its well-restored and elegant interior. Tours are by appointment only, and may be scheduled by calling the house.

ACCOMMODATIONS

There are a few chain hotels and motels, but these tend to fill up on weekends, so be sure to make reservations well in advance. In addition to hotels, there are numerous RV parks and a few smaller lodging establishments.

Franklin Cruise $$$–$$$$
515 Cruise St.
Corinth, MS
(662) 287-8069
www.franklincruise.com

Franklin Cruise is a restored historic downtown building in the heart of Corinth. The suites are filled with fine antique furnishings, Oriental rugs, full kitchens, and even a washer and dryer. The suites are located above the antiques shop and showroom.

RESTAURANTS

Taylor's Escape $
1401 US 72 West
Corinth, MS
(662) 286-2037

Don't judge a book by its cover. This corrugated steel building may not look like much, but the food is good and the value is there also. The catfish platter is always a favorite with the locals, but bring an appetite if you order the large platter. You'll get seven fillets with baked potato, coleslaw, and hush puppies. This family-run, humble establishment is also known for its barbecue and steaks.

DAY TRIPS

Beauvoir
2244 Beach Blvd.
Biloxi, MS
(228) 388-4400
www.beauvoir.org

The restored last home of the only president of the Confederacy, Beauvoir was the seaside estate of Jefferson Davis. A National Historic Landmark, Beauvoir was built in the mid-1800s, and its 74-acre landscaped grounds and handsome buildings are open to visitors. In addition to the furnished presidential residence, there is a Confederate museum and cemetery where the Tomb of the Unknown Confederate is located. The beautiful grounds contain large oaks, magnolias, pines, gardens, and a lagoon.

It was at this spacious house facing the Gulf of Mexico that President Davis, after his release from a federal prison, wrote *The Rise and Fall of the Confederate Government.* Here's an interesting anecdote about Jefferson Davis: According to local legend, Davis was visited at Beauvoir by the Union soldier who had captured him. The man had no money, so Davis loaned him enough to get back home and gave him this suggestion: "If you ever meet any of our boys in want, relieve them if possible." The Davis family showed their appreciation for Confederate veterans even after Davis died in 1889. His widow refused to sell Beauvoir and the surrounding property to a hotel developer for $100,000; instead she sold it to the Sons of Confederate Veterans for $10,000.

In 2005, Beauvoir and the Jefferson Davis Presidential Library suffered heavy damage from Hurricane Katrina. Many of the outbuildings were completely destroyed, but the house and library have been restored due to the generosity and kindness of donors and volunteers.

Brices Cross Roads
607 Grisham St./MS 370
Baldwyn, MS
(662) 365-3969
www.bricescrossroads.com

In late spring 1864, with Sherman raging through northern Georgia and the entire Confederacy threatened with being cut in half, Major General Nathan Bedford Forrest received orders to hit Sherman's supply and communications lines in Tennessee and try to make him slow down or even withdraw from the Deep South. Moving out of his base at Tupelo with 3,500 cavalrymen, Forrest soon learned that a column of more than 8,500 Union cavalry and infantry under Brigadier General Samuel D. Sturgis was en route from Memphis with orders to stop him. As usual for the fiery cavalry commander, he turned his columns west and made all speed to Sturgis's force to surprise and destroy him before he was ready for battle.

On June 10, 1864, the rapidly advancing Confederate cavalry encountered the first Union patrols along the Baldwyn Road, about 1 mile east of the small settlement of Brices Cross Roads. Immediately launching into a strong attack, Forrest's men were upon the Union patrols almost before they had made it back to their main column. Union reinforcements were hastily brought up, but by mid-afternoon the Confederate force had completely smashed the Union lines and sent Sturgis's command in a panicked rout back to Memphis. The small Confederate command not only took the field and scattered their aggressor, but also managed to capture more than 1,500 Union soldiers!

The Brices Cross Roads site today is a very small park with a single monument and some good interpretive signs, but the drive to the site off US 45 features several roadside historic markers that give a good visualization of the action here. Adjacent to the small historic park is a cemetery containing the remains of 99 Confederate soldiers; all but one are unidentified.

Aside from the usual collection of scattered mobile homes, the surrounding area seems little changed from the war, which adds to the historic flavor. We highly recommend a visit here, which does not add very much to the travel time from Corinth to Tupelo. The grounds are open during daylight hours.

Recently, the nearby town of Baldwyn has opened the Brices Cross Roads National Battlefield and Visitor Center (662-365-3969), on MS 370 and across US 45 from the actual battlefield. The site has a small collection of artifacts, some good displays about the battle, and a very friendly staff.

Tupelo National Battlefield Site
MS 6
Tupelo, MS
(800) 305-7417
www.nps.gov/tupe

This small park within the city limits of Tupelo commemorates a rare unsuccessful attack by Forrest against a superior Union force here on July 13, 1864. Although the Union column did withdraw from the area after the three-hour battle and Forrest's cavalry followed in a sort of low-intensity running battle, the Union force managed to get its column through the area more or less intact (which was their original intention). The grounds are open daily during daylight hours. For more information visit the Parkway Visitor Center at Milepost 266, 6 miles north of the monument.

Vicksburg:
Sealing the Confederacy's Fate

Map of the Union forces arrayed against the Confederate stronghold of Vicksburg

Nearly before the first shots on Fort Sumter ended, visionary general officers of the Union Army foresaw that this would not be any "90-day struggle," as the Washington bureaucrats and woefully inadequate top army brass claimed. Not only were the very cream of the prewar U.S. Army officer corps resigning their commissions in order to serve their Southern home states, but the level of rhetoric coming from the near-fanatical secessionist politicians ensured that once separate, it would be a long, hard climb to reconstruct the whole nation.

The de facto leader of this visionary group was none other than General Winfield Scott, the aged veteran of the War of 1812 and the Mexican-American War (not to mention his less heroic involvement in the southeastern Native American removals of the 1820s and 1830s). Despite his ill health and dated military strategies, he insisted that not only was the nation headed for a long war, but that the South could only be defeated by a long, grinding campaign aimed at cutting its lines of supply and communication. His grand scheme, dubbed the Anaconda Plan, called for an absolute blockade of the entire Southern coastline by the U.S. Navy to prevent resupply from friendly foreign countries and stop waterborne reinforcement of the Confederate armies, followed by the capture and use of the Mississippi River from Illinois to the Gulf of Mexico to cut the Southern Confederacy in half and allow it to die from lack of supplies.

"Old Fuss and Feathers" Scott's plan was seriously derided at first, as few Union politicians or generals saw the need to do anything so drastic. The widely held belief on both sides was that one big battle would be all that was needed to send the opposing army fleeing from the field and resolve the conflict instantly. The laughter stopped, however, after the shocking Union defeat at the First Manassas (First Bull Run) battle in Virginia; and even as Scott was being replaced as general in chief by Major General George Brinton "Little Mac" McClellan, essential elements of the Anaconda Plan were being expanded into the overall Union strategy for the war.

SPLITTING THE SOUTH

The Union strategy during the war had three parts: first, the total naval blockade of the Southern coastline, envisioned by Scott; second, an overland campaign to capture the Confederate capital of Richmond, Virginia; and third, control of the Mississippi River and all the port towns along it. Brigadier General (later General in Chief) Ulysses S. Grant opened the third part of this grand strategy in early February 1862 with the assault on and capture of Forts Henry and Donelson on the Tennessee and Cumberland Rivers in northern Tennessee. With the way cleared toward Nashville and other points south in Tennessee, Grant then turned west along the Ohio River toward the Mississippi, swung around and isolated a strong Confederate garrison at Columbus, Kentucky, and then turned inland to move toward Corinth, Mississippi. Memphis fell soon afterward, after another short, fierce naval battle, completely opening the northern stretches of the Mississippi to Union control.

Major General John Pope successfully moved his Union Army of the Mississippi against fortified Confederate positions at Island Number 10 and New Madrid on the Mississippi, well supported by Union gunboats, and opened the northern stretches of the great river to Union control by early April 1862. Later that same month Flag Officer (later Admiral) David Glasgow Farragut and Major General Benjamin Franklin Butler captured New Orleans after a short naval battle, opening up the southern stretches of the river. By early spring 1862, only Port Hudson, Louisiana, and Vicksburg, Mississippi, remained in Confederate hands and prevented a complete Union domination of the river.

BACKGROUND TO THE BATTLE

*T*he Vicksburg Campaign was an unusually long and costly operation for both sides. From the earliest assault attempts in December 1862 to the final surrender on July 4, 1863, only the horrible siege at Petersburg, Virginia, from June 1864 to May 1865, was longer or more destructive in lives to both soldiers and civilians. As the best defensive ground of any port between Memphis and the Gulf Coast, Vicksburg was an obvious target that the Union commanders wasted little time in attacking.

Most histories of the Vicksburg Campaign concentrate on the famous siege of the small town, which lasted from April 29 to July 4, 1863, but in fact the battle for this critical river port started many months earlier.

Grant had been given the task of completely clearing the Mississippi of any Confederate threat when he assumed command of the newly formed Department of Tennessee on October 16, 1862. Under his command were some 43,000 men, reinforced to about 75,000 as the campaign wore on. Two days earlier Lieutenant General John Clifford Pemberton had assumed command of the Confederate Department of Mississippi and East Louisiana, which for all practical purposes simply meant the area immediately surrounding Vicksburg. The number of men he commanded has been the subject of countless debates since the war: While the force probably numbered in the 40,000 range, Grant claimed he faced well over 60,000, while Pemberton himself stated he had only 28,000.

Chickasaw Bluff

With his victory at the Battle of Shiloh and the fall of Corinth, Mississippi, assuring his dominance over western Confederate armies, Grant immediately set about moving against Vicksburg, which he considered one of the most vital targets in the entire Western Theater. He split his command into two great columns; led by Major General

William Tecumseh Sherman, the westernmost column was to move south with 32,000 men on transport barges down the Mississippi River from Memphis to directly attack Vicksburg. To keep Confederate forces divided and unable to concentrate on the city's defense, Grant personally led 40,000 men overland south along the Mississippi Central Railroad tracks from Grand Junction, Tennessee, 35 miles west of Corinth.

Grant moved south on November 26, 1862, slowly moving his large force through northern Mississippi. Passing through Holly Springs and Oxford, he established forward supply bases in both towns and left small garrisons to guard against expected Confederate raids. His major problem during the march south was that his supply lines back to Columbus, Kentucky, were growing longer and more vulnerable. On December 20, just as the vanguard of Grant's column was approaching the small town of Granada, a 3,500-man Confederate cavalry force under Major General Earl Van Dorn captured and destroyed his supply base at Holly Springs. At about the same time, another cavalry

Murfreesboro, Tennessee, vicinity; men repairing single-track railroad after Battle of Stones River

force under Brigadier General Nathan Bedford Forrest stormed through western Tennessee and southern Kentucky, destroying more than 60 miles of the critical railroad lines supplying the Union overland campaign. Grant was forced to call off his part of the attack and move northwest into Memphis.

The same day Grant lost his base at Holly Springs, Sherman and his men boarded a naval flotilla in Memphis and cast off toward Vicksburg. The infantrymen were loaded onto 59 transport ships and barges, escorted by 7 gunboats. A message about Grant's defeat reached Sherman the next day, but he decided to continue on, risking that his strong surprise assault might be enough to carry the coming battle. On Christmas Eve the Union flotilla arrived at Milliken's Bend, Louisiana, just north of Vicksburg, and prepared to start disembarking the troops.

DECEMBER 24, 1862, VICKSBURG

*V*icksburg had been an island of relative calm at this point, a safe harbor from the vicious naval battles that ranged north and south along the Mississippi. Social life went on, little changed from antebellum times, with frequent parties, cotillions, and afternoon barbecues—the major difference being that the men wore Confederate gray dress uniforms instead of their civilian garb. Dr. William Balfour and his wife, Emma, had prepared a grand Christmas Eve ball in their house on Crawford Street, inviting the local garrison's officers to join the society elite in an elaborate party. As the band played and couples danced, mud-splattered Private Philip Fall burst through the door searching for the ranking officer present, Major General Martin Luther Smith, carrying the startling news that Sherman and his force were nearly upon them at that very moment. Signaling for the band to stop playing, Smith addressed

the crowd, "This ball is at an end—the enemy are coming down the river, all noncombatants must leave the city." With that, Smith and his officers immediately departed, calling out the garrison to man the defenses while still in their dress uniforms.

Aware that Sherman was coming from the north, area commander Pemberton (who arrived on December 26 from his position at Grenada) placed the majority of his men in a northeast-to-southwest line at the foot of the Walnut Hills on the north side of town (nearly directly atop present-day US Business 61 on the north side of the military park), facing northwest toward where Sherman's troops were expected to approach. Pemberton had about 25,000 men total (including reinforcements brought in during the battle) divided into two divisions to stand against Sherman's four divisions with 30,000 men (some sources state 33,000). The Confederate lines were formidable, with several lines of entrenchments well supported by artillery emplacements and fronted by a thick tangle of abatis made of felled trees that also gave the infantry a well-cleared field of fire.

The Assault on Chickasaw Bluff

The Union troops disembarked starting in late afternoon on December 26 and by the next day were pushing inland toward Vicksburg, led by Colonel John F. DeCourcy's 3rd Brigade (3rd Division). As the infantry advanced slowly on the road past Mrs. Anne E. Lake's house, they came under heavy fire from advance Confederate pickets in the nearby woods. This advance to contact ended after a brief but heavy firefight; DeCourcy pulled his men back to camp and the pickets retired within the Confederate line. Other actions took place over the next two days, while Sherman tried to figure out where Pemberton's weakest spot was.

Finding no part of the Confederate line notably weaker than any other, Sherman decided to try a massive head-on assault. At 7:30 a.m. on December 29, his artillery opened a heavy fire on Pemberton's line, answered quickly by counter-battery fire from massed Confederate guns on the bluff above them. About 11 a.m., Union infantry officers ordered their men into line of battle—Brigadier General Frank Blair's brigade on the left, DeCourcy's and Brigadier General

John M. Thayer's brigades in the center, and Brigadier General Andrew Jackson Smith leading both the 1st and 2nd Divisions on the right, all arrayed to strike the Confederate line at about the same time.

Under heavy and accurate rifle fire as soon as they exited the woods, DeCourcy's and Blair's brigades stormed across the bayou and managed to push through the entangling defenses and take the first line of rifle pits. Soon joined by the 4th Iowa Regiment of Thayer's brigade (the only one to make it across the open fields), the Union infantrymen attempted to keep their assault moving and push back through the layers of defensive entrenchments, but they were soon stopped by murderous rifle and artillery fire. As they started to pull back and retreat to their encampment, General Stephen Dill Lee ordered his rebels forward in a counterattack. The 17th and 26th Louisiana Infantry Regiments surged forward, overrunning the hapless Union infantry, and soon returned with their prize: 21 officers, 311 enlisted men, and four regimental battle flags.

This scene was repeated all down the line. Although Smith's two divisions managed to make it literally within spitting distance of the Confederate lines on the right, they were not able to carry the works even after five assault attempts. As darkness fell, the Union troops abandoned what little gains they had made and returned to their encampments. That night, during a drenching and chilling rainstorm, Sherman made plans to assault again the next day, this time aimed at taking the artillery emplacements atop the bluff, but finally he canceled the attack after deciding that it would be too costly an attempt. Another planned attack, this time against Confederate fortifications on nearby Snyder's Bluff on New Year's Day, was canceled when a thick fog prevented easy movement.

> For twenty months now I have been a sojourner in camps, a dweller in tents, going hither and yon, at all hours of the day and night, in all sorts of weather, sleeping for weeks at a stretch without shelter, and yet I have been strong and healthy. How very thankful I should feel on this Christmas night! There goes the boom from a cannon at the front.
>
> —John Beatty, 3rd Ohio Infantry Regiment, Union Army

Late on the afternoon of January 1, 1863, Sherman ordered his men back aboard the transport ships and barges and set sail down the Yazoo River to its mouth on the Mississippi. The next day he was placed under the command of Major General John A. McClernand, who decided to carry the battle away from Vicksburg for the time being. Sherman's report of the battle, and his failure, is a model of terseness: "I reached Vicksburg at the time appointed, landed, assaulted and failed." His failure cost 208 dead, 1,005 wounded, and 563 captured or missing. Despite the personal responsibility he seemed to take in his report for the failed assault, in letters and his postwar memoirs he blamed a lack of fighting spirit in his own infantry for the failure, most notably DeCourcy's brigade, which had ironically advanced the farthest into the Confederate entrenchments. Pemberton reported a loss of 63 killed, 134 wounded, and 10 missing after the battle.

The landing at Vicksburg in 1863

ATTEMPTS TO BYPASS VICKSBURG

*G*rant waited a few weeks, building up his army before attempting to reduce Vicksburg again. His major tactical problem, underscored by Sherman's failure, was that the town was built on a steep bluff footed by swamps and the Yazoo and Mississippi Rivers, making any assault from the east, north, or south a near-suicidal venture. The only approach that might have worked was from the east, along the spine of ridges that arced nearly 200 miles above and below the town. This favorable approach had its own set of problems, most notably, how to get his troops in position atop the eastern bluffs. To add to all these problems, the winter rains that year had been unusually heavy, increasing the flooding problems and widening the rivers.

Grant's problems can be illustrated by the near-desperate attempt he had his engineers make, digging a 1½-mile-long canal across one of the peninsulas below Vicksburg, known locally as De Soto Point, which would hopefully allow his troop and supply ships to bypass the powerful artillery batteries and land unmolested south of the city. Now known as Grant's Canal, work continued through March of 1863, when early spring flooding destroyed some of the works and covered the peninsula and the Confederate defenders moved some of their artillery batteries to cover both ends of the canal.

Meanwhile, Major General James Birdseye McPherson was attempting to bring his XVII Corps in to reinforce Grant and hit the city from the south by cutting and blasting a passage through the labyrinth of swamps and small rivers from Lake Providence, 75 miles north of Vicksburg, to a point in the Mississippi River some 200 miles south of the city. A 400-mile-long route was mapped and partially prepared before the entire project was scrapped as unworkable.

A third attempt to gain the eastern bluffs was mounted by blasting through a natural levee at Yazoo Pass, 320 miles north of Vicksburg, and plotting a waterborne route south to the city. Before they could make much progress, Major General William W. Loring's division rushed north to stop the Union raid. About 90 miles north of Vicksburg, the Confederate troops hastily built an earthwork and cotton bale post (dubbed "Fort Pemberton") and engaged the onrushing Union gunboats on March 11. The Union infantry could find no way to assault the fort in the swampy terrain, and this expedition soon turned away in defeat. Less than a week later a fourth and last attempt to sail through the bayous north of the city, known as Steele's Bayou Expedition, ended in both defeat and the near capture of all the Union gunboats.

THE BATTLE OF GRAND GULF

*W*ith every attempt to bypass the Vicksburg defenses proving unsuccessful, Grant decided to take the head-on approach. McClernand had just been placed under Grant's overall command, and he was ordered to have his command build a road to move down the western bank of the Mississippi River to a forward base directly across from the Confederate outpost at Grand Gulf, 60 miles south of Vicksburg. Planning to try an amphibious assault under fire against the Confederate fortifications, Grant also directed McClernand to have his gunboats and troop transports run past the Vicksburg Mississippi River batteries and meet up with his Army of Tennessee at a point ironically named Hard Times. On the night of April 16, 1863, eight gunboats and three transports set sail downriver under the direct command of Commodore William David Porter, each specially prepared to meet the expected hot Confederate fire. The port (left) side of each ship, which would face the Confederate batteries, was piled high with cotton and hay bales, and small coal scows and supply barges were lashed to each side of the ships.

Just before midnight the small flotilla approached Confederate outposts just north of Vicksburg, which promptly raised the alarm. Artillery crews raced in to man their guns, and within minutes a furious firefight broke out along the river. Porter reported later that every one of his ships was hit in the exchange, some multiple times, but he also stated that his own broadsides into the town could not help but do great damage to the city, as they were firing at near point-blank range. One sailor reported that they were so close that falling bricks from buildings struck by the Union cannon could clearly be heard.

Despite the heavy and accurate Confederate fire, only one transport was sunk, and the other ships limped down to join the infantry at Hard Times. Another flotilla ran the same gauntlet on the night of April 22—six transports towing 12 supply barges—but this time Confederate gunners managed to sink one transport and six of the barges.

Grant had planned to use the transports and barges to bring 10,000 infantrymen across the Mississippi to a landing point at Grand Gulf, at the mouth of the Big Black River. Porter's gunboats opened fire on the Confederate fortifications at Grand Gulf on April 29 but failed to inflict any serious damage or silence their guns after nearly six hours of continuous bombardment. To add to Grant's problems, return fire from Confederate gunners inflicted serious damage to the Union gunboat fleet. Grant reconsidered his plan and decided to move his men downriver to a "cooler" landing zone. The next day, in the largest amphibious operation mounted by an American army until World War II, Grant crossed the river and landed at Bruinsburg with 24,000 troops and 60 cannon. After months of campaigning, Grant at last had a toehold on the east side of the river close to Vicksburg.

THE BATTLE OF PORT GIBSON

*W*hile Grant was crossing the river downstream, Sherman had mounted a strong demonstration against Haine's Bluff, while Colonel Benjamin Henry Grierson moved his Union cavalry south out of Tennessee and mounted another demonstration against the railroad lines between Meridian and Jackson before turning south toward Baton Rouge. Grant's men began moving north almost as soon as they reached dry land, aiming for the town of Port Gibson. By late in the afternoon of April 30, more than 17,000 Union troops were ashore and moving out rapidly, with several thousand more still en route across the river.

Two Confederate brigades had already marched south from Grand Gulf to oppose the Union assault: Brigadier General Edward D. Tracy's and Brigadier General Martin E. Green's, which by nightfall were astride the Bruinsburg and Rodney Roads directly in the path of the Union advance. Starting about midnight the advance skirmishers of the Union column met up with the Confederate pickets, and a lively firefight broke out. The firing died down about 3 a.m. but picked up again with vigor about the first light of dawn (about 5:30 a.m.).

The Confederate lines held well until about 10 a.m., when Green's brigade was pushed back up the road about 1½ miles by a heavy Union assault. There they were reinforced by two other brigades hastily dispatched from Grand Gulf: Brigadier General William E. Baldwin's and Brigadier General Francis M. Cockrell's, which helped shore up a strong line along the Rodney Road. Tracy's men managed to hold up well in their position on the right, despite losing Tracy himself, who was killed early in the fighting. Although several vicious counterattacks were mounted that managed some limited success, the Union assault was simply overwhelming, and all the Confederate commanders began retiring from the field about 5:30 p.m.

The daylong battle cost Grant 131 killed, 719 wounded, and 25 missing or captured, while the Confederate commanders reported a loss of 60 killed, 340

J. C. Pemberton

wounded, and 387 missing or captured. Accounts vary, but the total Confederate force in the field amounted to about 8,000, while Grant had an estimated 23,000 engaged in the fight by late afternoon. Confused by the Union attacks toward Vicksburg seemingly coming from all directions, Pemberton ordered Grand Gulf evacuated and all the troops to move within the defenses of Vicksburg, instead of confronting and attacking Grant's bridgehead.

THE BATTLE OF RAYMOND

*R*ather than directly move in and seize Grand Gulf, Grant decided to move northeast and cut the Southern Railroad lines between Jackson and Vicksburg, Pemberton's only remaining line of communications, supply, and retreat. Similar to Sherman's later march through Georgia, Grant set his forces in a three-corps-abreast formation, with McClernand's XIII Corps on the left, Sherman's XV Corps in the middle, and McPherson's XVII Corps on the right. Grant planned to move nearly directly northeast toward Jackson, then turn right and cut the rail line somewhere east of the small settlement of Edwards. On May 7 the three corps moved out, a total of 45,000 Union soldiers moving deep into the very heart of the Confederacy and dangerously far from their own base of supplies.

Pemberton guessed correctly what Grant was up to and sent word to his garrison in Jackson to move out and confront the Union advance, while he moved part of his own force in Vicksburg out to strike the Union line from the west. Brigadier General John Gregg moved his 3,000-man brigade out of Jackson promptly, arriving in Raymond on May 11 and setting up pickets along the west and south roads into the town. For artillery support Gregg could boast a single battery, the three guns of Captain Hiram Bledsoe's Missouri Battery.

At dawn on May 12, Gregg's pickets sent word that the Union vanguard was approaching their position along the Utica Road (today known as MS 18). The Confederate commander hastily deployed his men to strike what he thought would be the right flank of a small Union force, along both the Utica and Gallatin Roads, and placed the Missouri Battery atop a small hill commanding the bridge crossing Fourteenmile Creek. As the first regiments of McPherson's column moved into the small valley of Fourteenmile Creek, Gregg ordered volley fire into their flank.

The sudden burst of fire shattered the front Union ranks, and Gregg ordered his men to keep up a hot fire. After about two hours of volleys, Gregg ordered up his Tennesseeans and Texans in line of assault, planning to roll up the Union line and finish up the day. As the Confederates advanced into the dry creekbed and through the easternmost Union formations, they ran smack into the newly reorganized division led by Major General John A. Logan, who was leading his men into battle with "the shriek of an eagle." By 1:30 p.m., with Union regiments and brigades piling onto the field, Gregg finally realized that he was facing a full Union corps and started ordering his units to pull back. The battle had become a confused swirling of Union and Confederate units nearly invisible to their commanders in the thick, choking dust, and it took most of the rest of the afternoon for both commanders to get a complete grasp of their own positions and issue appropriate orders.

Gregg attempted to break contact and retreat, but McPherson's troops kept a running battle going until they reached Raymond itself. The Confederates hurried past townspeople who were preparing a "victory" picnic for them, before stopping for the night at Snake Creek. McPherson's men broke off the pursuit in Raymond, where the Union troops helped themselves to the picnic dinner. The next morning Gregg moved his brigade back into Jackson, reporting a loss of 73 killed, 252 wounded, and 190 missing or captured. McPherson reported to Grant that he had faced a force "about 6,000 strong" but emerged victorious, at the cost of 68 killed, 341 wounded, and 37 missing or captured.

The Battle of Jackson

Surprised at the strong show of force so far east of Vicksburg, Grant decided that he would have to take Jackson before he could safely turn back west toward "Fortress Vicksburg." On May 13 he ordered his army forward once again—McPherson north from Raymond along the Clinton Road, Sherman northeast through Raymond toward Mississippi Springs, and McClernand's corps arrayed in a defensive line from Raymond to Clinton to guard against any more unpleasant surprises. The same day, General Joseph Eggleston Johnston (commander, Department of Tennessee and Mississippi) arrived in Jackson by train to assume overall command of Vicksburg's defense. With Grant's army nearly knocking on Jackson's door, Johnston ordered an immediate evacuation of the city toward the north, with Gregg's brigade and parts of two other brigades remaining as long as possible to mount a rearguard action. After a heavy rainfall in the morning of May 14 briefly delayed their attack, Sherman's and McPherson's corps charged the weak Confederate defenses with bayonets fixed starting about 11 a.m., driving the Confederate defenders back after a bitter hand-to-hand struggle and capturing the outer defenses of the city without much loss.

Although strong Confederate artillery emplacements delayed the Union advance in the center, Sherman sent part of his command around the right flank and north along the railroad line into the heart of the city. With his left flank breached, Gregg ordered his brigades to move out of the city along the Canton Road to the north, while Union troops invested the city right behind them. By 3 p.m. the Stars and Stripes was being hoisted again over the State Capitol building. The few hours of combat resulted in about 300 Union soldiers killed, wounded, and missing and an estimated 850 Confederate casualties.

With Grant's army between him and Vicksburg, Johnston believed that he had arrived too late to do any real good, but he sent a series of messages to Pemberton urging him to march out of Vicksburg and join the 6,000 troops he had moved north out of Jackson in a battle to destroy Grant's force. Pemberton, a great believer in the use of fixed fortifications, was extremely reluctant to enter a campaign of movement and maneuver. He made it very clear that he wished to remain in his line along the Big Black River, but finally he agreed to move out. In a clear act of disobedience of orders, instead of moving to join Johnston, Pemberton decided on his own to strike against Grant's line of communication back to Grand Gulf, now occupied and a major supply center for the Union army.

On May 15 Pemberton initially moved his 23,000 men southeast to near Edward's Station, effectively moving farther away from Johnston and placing Grant's army between the two commands. Unknown to either Confederate commander, Grant's men had intercepted the series of orders and communications between them, and the Union commander was maneuvering his own forces to exploit the confusion. Johnston issued another order on May 16 to Pemberton to move northeast and join him, which for some reason he decided to obey, but by this time Grant was ready to strike.

The Battle of Champion Hill

As Pemberton moved northeast early on the morning of May 16 along the Ratliff road just south of Champion Hill, his three divisions strung out along the road for nearly 3 miles, a courier brought word that a large Union contingent was bearing down upon him from the Jackson road to the northeast. Pemberton immediately halted his march and arrayed in line of battle to protect the high ground of Champion Hill itself, as well as the crossroads leading to Edwards and Vicksburg. Major General William Wing Loring's division covered the Raymond road to the south, the right flank of Pemberton's line; Brigadier (soon after Major) General John S. Bowen's division deployed along the

Ratliff road to Loring's left; and Major General Carter Littlepage Stevenson's division covered the left flank and the crest of the small knob of Champion Hill.

Just before noon Brigadier General Alvin P. Hovey's and Logan's divisions of McPherson's corps attacked along the Jackson road against Stevenson's positions atop Champion Hill. Stevenson's men were soon forced off the crest under heavy fire, but Bowen's division shifted north and succeeded in regaining the hill. Grant ordered his artillery massed and directed all fire on the hilltop Confederate positions, quickly followed by renewed infantry assaults. About 1 p.m. Stevenson's and Bowen's men were forced to retreat under the crushing Union assault, escaping south along Baker's Creek to the Raymond road before turning west toward Vicksburg.

Brigadier General Lloyd Tilghman's brigade was ordered to act as a rear guard, to cover the escape "at all costs." Joined by Loring's men, they put up a fierce resistance but were cut off by massive artillery fire and forced to move farther south and east, eventually circling around north and meeting up with Johnston near Jackson. Tilghman himself was killed during the rearguard action.

Pemberton led his army's retreat west through Edwards before taking up a defensive position at the Big Black River for the night, while McClernand's corps moving in from the south entered and occupied Edwards about 8 p.m. Grant reported losses of 410 killed, 1,844 wounded, and 187 missing or captured, while Pemberton suffered 381 killed, 1,018 wounded, and 2,441 missing or captured, but the real damage was

Big Black River battlefield

the decisive defeat of the Confederate forces. Pemberton would eventually limp back into Vicksburg minus Loring's division, which never returned to his command, but Grant had succeeded in isolating Vicksburg to an island outpost completely cut off from any hope of resupply or reinforcement.

BIG BLACK RIVER BRIDGES

*P*emberton was unaware that Loring, who had circled around to the south and east to join up with Johnston at Jackson, was not following him back into Vicksburg. Instead of immediately moving all his forces back within Vicksburg's formidable defense, Pemberton ordered Bowen's division reinforced by Brigadier General John Vaughn's brigade to hold a defensive perimeter around the bridges over the Big Black River, in the hopes that Loring would soon show up and have a safe passage over the river. On the morning of May 17, with the rest of Pemberton's troops marching the 12 miles west to Vicksburg, McClernand's XIII Corps rapidly swept forward and engaged Bowen's small command.

Bowen had established a seemingly tight line of battle, well anchored on the river on the left and a waist-deep swampy area on the right, with 18 artillery pieces arrayed along the line to sweep a wide area of fire that any Union assault would have to march through. Even before McClernand's corps was fully arrayed for battle, Brigadier General Michael Lawler saw an opportunity to gain a quick Union victory and ordered his brigade to fix bayonets and hit the center of the Confederate line. In a hand-to-hand combat that lasted less than three minutes, Vaughn's brigade broke under the fierce assault and ran for the bridges, followed quickly by the rest of Bowen's command, as more and more Union infantry brigades fixed bayonets and followed Lawler's lead.

Many of the retreating Confederates drowned while attempting to cross the river, forced into the water by Pemberton's chief engineer, Major Sam Lockett, who had set fire to the bridges to keep them out of Grant's hands. There is no known surviving record of Confederate dead and wounded in the brief battle, but Grant reported capturing more than 1,700 prisoners and all 18 artillery pieces, while suffering a total of 279 dead, wounded, and missing out of his own commands.

Burning the bridges slowed Grant's advance less than a single day. His engineer threw up three bridges across the river by the morning of May 18, and the great Union Army quickly crossed and moved out toward Vicksburg.

FORTRESS VICKSBURG

Shortly after the fall of New Orleans in the spring of 1862, Flag Officer (soon afterward Rear Admiral) David Glasgow Farragut sailed his West Gulf Blockading Squadron north along the Mississippi River and captured Baton Rouge and Natchez without resistance. Joined just outside Vicksburg on July 1, 1862, by Flag Officer Charles Henry Davis's Western Flotilla, sailing south along the Mississippi after capturing Memphis and reducing the Confederate river fleet to a shattered remnant, the two powerful gunboat fleets had managed to take control of nearly the entire river for the Union after only a few months of campaigning. Now the only thing that stood in the way of complete and free Union transit of the river, other than the weaker Confederate bastion at Port Hudson across the river in Louisiana, was a few artillery batteries stationed high on a bluff next to the river in the small but very important port town of Vicksburg.

Farragut's fleet had passed Vicksburg several times, starting in late May, and had exchanged fire with the rapidly growing city defenses to no real effect. Before Davis's arrival, his own mortarboats and sloops had kept a steady bombardment of the town, irregularly at first, but growing in intensity as both sides brought more guns into action. After three weeks of numbing

and near-continuous fire, and after the intense heat and disease had rendered all but 800 of his 3,000 sailors unfit for duty, Farragut called off the operation and sailed south, while Davis returned his fleet to Memphis. Farragut reported that Vicksburg could only be successfully reduced by a combined army and naval force attacking from land and water simultaneously.

> *Confederate independence with centralized power without State sovereignty . . . would be very little better than subjugation, as it matters little who our master is, if we are to have one.*
>
> —Governor Joseph Brown of Georgia, in a November 1864 speech to the Georgia General Assembly

Even before the first Union assaults on the town, General Pierre Gustave Toutant Beauregard (commander, Department of the West) had prepared a plan of defense for the town after the defeat at Shiloh and sent engineer Captain D. B. Harris south from Fort Pillow to oversee the initial construction of a series of fortifications. Major (later Major General) Martin Luther Smith soon arrived from constructing the defenses of New Orleans to take over building the Vicksburg defenses and ended up commanding troops during the siege from behind his own line of fortifications.

In September 1862, following Farragut's failed attempts, this line of fortifications was extended to the inland side of Vicksburg, neatly surrounding the town with a powerful, near-unassailable, and continuous line of forts, infantry positions, and artillery emplacements. Within a few months the defense line ran from Fort Hill on the north side of town along the curving ridges some 9 miles south to South Fort, then back north along the river for some 4½ additional miles. The defensive line mounted about 115 heavy guns, with another 31 mounted in batteries alongside the river.

The only approaches into the city through the surrounding ridges were six roads and one railroad track that ran across natural bridges over rather steep ravines. To guard these natural avenues of attack, Harris's engineers had built nine well-constructed and powerful forts, some with walls nearly 20 feet thick. Each one of these forts was surrounded by a maze of interconnected

A map showing the Rebel defenses of Vicksburg

and interlocking rifle pits, artillery batteries, and communications trenches. In front of this line was a deep and wide ditch, and all the trees were cut down for quite some distance in front of the line to provide a clear field of fire, making any direct assault a suicidal venture at best. The town was now a massive fortified redoubt, nearly impregnable to reduction by weapons of the day, that could either prove a safe haven for its Confederate defenders or a deadly trap, depending entirely on what Grant chose to do.

First Assaults on Vicksburg

Grant believed he had Pemberton's 31,000 men demoralized and not fully prepared to make much of a fight after his two-week-long running battle from Port Gibson to the Big Black River, and he wanted to storm the Vicksburg defenses before they could recover. On May 19, with 50,000 men under his command but only 20,000 in position to strike, he ordered an immediate assault on the town.

Sherman's XV Corps was the only command in position to strike, and about 2 p.m. he ordered a general attack. Moving against the northeastern corner of the Vicksburg line, his men attempted to storm and reduce the powerful fort called Stockade Redan. Advancing under heavy and accurate Confederate fire, part of one regiment (the 13th U.S. Infantry) got close in enough to place their colors on the exterior sloping wall before being thrown back with heavy losses. This was the only "gain" Sherman managed before withdrawing; McPherson's XVII and McClernand's XIII Corps made some demonstrations against other parts of the line, but neither did any better than Sherman, who lost nearly 1,000 casualties to no gain.

Three days later Grant ordered another assault attempt, this time preceded by a four-hour-long artillery barrage against the Confederate line followed by a 45,000-man attack against a 3-mile front. Portions of all three corps managed to make it to the base of the Confederate defenses, but only one regiment penetrated the line. An Iowa regiment of McClernand's corps led by two sergeants shot their way into the Railroad Redoubt through a hole made by their artillery and in a fierce firefight managed to kill or drive out the Confederate

defenders. Before this regiment could be reinforced and the breach in the wall exploited, men of Colonel Thomas N. Waul's Texas Legion counterattacked and regained the fort. No other Union gain was made before the entire assault line was once against thrown back with heavy losses.

Pemberton had managed to rest many of his combat troops even during these assaults, using only about 18,000 of his men in the defense while inflicting a total of 3,200 Union casualties. Pemberton's casualties in these assaults are not recorded but were undoubtedly much less severe than Grant's. With his powerful assault forces turned aside without much difficulty, Grant changed his plans and settled in for a long siege of the fortified town, something Johnston had already warned Pemberton would be inevitable and disastrous if he pulled his forces back into the city as planned.

THE SIEGE

*G*rant officially began his siege operation on May 25 and, with the exception of two isolated events, made no further attempts to take Vicksburg by force. With all lines of supply, communications, or reinforcement successfully cut, Grant directed his engineers and infantry to begin construction of a series of siege trenches, designed to gradually grow nearer and nearer the Confederate positions. He had no intention of simply allowing Vicksburg to starve itself out, at least initially, but planned to try digging a series of mines (or tunnels) under the massive fortifications, pack them full of explosives, and literally blast his way through the walls into the city.

While the infantry was busy digging their way through Mississippi, Grant's artillery and Porter's naval flotilla set about making life miserable within the town. While the city had suffered sporadic shelling from Union gunboats on the river ever since the first days of the campaign, nearly constant incoming fire began soon after Pemberton brought his army inside the defenses and did not cease until the final surrender some 47 days later. It did not take long for Vicksburg's citizens to move out of their homes and into caves dug deep into the sides of the hills. It also did not take long to figure out when they could safely venture out to try to find food and water: 8 a.m., noon, and 8 p.m., when the artillerymen would cease firing to eat their meals. Grant continuously built up his siege artillery force, and by the end of June he had 220 guns of various sizes engaged around the city.

Within a relatively short time, the siege made life nearly untenable for civilians and soldiers alike within the city. Food supplies had not been abundant when the campaign began, and when all supply routes were cut, what few items were still available commanded premium prices. Flour sold for as high as $1,000 per barrel, molasses for $10 per gallon, spoiled bacon for $5 a pound, and what little cornmeal remained went for $140 per bushel. Beef, coffee, sugar, bread, and even horse or mule meat was nearly nonexistent. For a while a bread made of ground peas was available, for a price, but soon even this disgusting fare was gone. Some accounts even claim that the rat population of the city nearly disappeared by the middle of June, but this is undoubtedly an apocryphal tale. The truth, however, is just as stark: By late June the average soldier ration consisted of one biscuit, four ounces of usually rotted bacon, peas, and sometimes a little rice each day—less than half the normal combat ration.

One odd shortage that reared its head in June was that of cartridge bags for Pemberton's remaining heavy guns. These bags were made of flannel and held a measured charge of gunpowder, and not a single bolt of the cloth could be found anywhere in town. The soldiers were being asked to give up their outer shirts for the cause, and when the ladies of the town found out, they immediately volunteered their petticoats. A newspaperman in town later remarked that every outgoing shell from the city's 10-inch Columbiads was powered by these women's underwear.

Sherman Gets Impatient

Only two days after the siege operation began, Sherman displayed his usual impatience and requested help from Porter's naval flotilla to reduce the fortifications before him. The gunboat *Cincinnati* was reinforced with heavy logs and bales of cotton along her ironclad sides and then moved downriver to directly confront the river batteries below Fort Hill, clearing the way for the infantry to move in.

The *Cincinnati*'s captain, Lieutenant George M. Bache, brought her downriver on May 27 and turned close to shore on the north end of town to prepare to open a broadside fire on the Confederate batteries. However, before his guns could open fire, the swift river current caught his boat and spun it around, forcing Bache to unmask his stern batteries in order to maintain control. This was the weakest and least-armored section of the ironclad, and the Confederate gunners took full advantage. From atop Fort Hill and from the multiple batteries along the river, rains of 8- and 10-inch fire raked the Union gunboat, soon smashing through her stern and shooting away her steering gear. Within minutes the huge gunboat was an uncontrollable mess of smashed gun decks and wounded and dying men.

Bache attempted to run his boat aground on the far side of the river to allow his crew to escape safely, but the boat was too badly damaged to stay afloat that long. The *Cincinnati* went down in 3 fathoms of water, taking 40 of her men with her, her colors still flying from the blasted stump of a flagpole where they had been nailed during the brief but vicious battle.

The Mines

From the very start of the siege, Grant had planned to try to blast his way through the Confederate defenses by using mines, and by late June the first were ready to go. A tunnel had been dug under the 3rd Louisiana Redoubt, near the center of the arcing Confederate line, and filled with more than a ton of gunpowder. On June 25 the mine was ready, and Grant ordered every gun he had to open fire all along the Vicksburg line to prevent Pemberton from shifting his forces around. At 3 p.m. the powder was fired, and with a deafening roar the entire top of the hill was blown off, opening a crater 50 feet in diameter and 12 feet deep. With nearly 150 heavy guns and every infantry unit along the line supporting, two regiments led by Brigadier General Mortimer D.

Leggett charged into the breach, only to discover that the Confederates had discovered their mining attempt and moved back to a second fortified position.

From there, the Louisiana troops directed near-point-blank volleys of shot and canister into the Union infantry ranks, whose survivors were then soon joined in hand-to-hand combat by the 6th Missouri Infantry Regiment. The Illinois infantrymen attempted to stay in the crater, throwing up a hasty wall in front of them and forming in a double line of battle to keep up a continuous volley fire of their own. The Louisiana defenders responded by throwing hand grenades down into the crater, which Leggett later said did fearful damage to his surviving infantry. The firing died down after the Union infantry managed to pull back slightly and build a parapet across the crater for their own protection. Grant reported a loss of 30 men, but this is not thought to be accurate; his true loss in the short action was most likely between 300 and 400 killed or wounded. Pemberton reported a loss of 90 dead and wounded.

The next morning Pemberton's men exploded two mines of their own on the north side of the line, near where Sherman's troops were working on a mine near the Stockade Redoubt. No one was killed, but the Union mining operation there was destroyed. Another mine was started that day under the new position of the 3rd Louisiana Redan and fired off on July 1. This time a large number of Confederate defenders were killed or wounded in the explosion, which completely destroyed the large redoubt and blasted a hole 50 feet wide and 20 feet deep in the parapet walls. Colonel Francis Marion Cockrell led his Missouri regiment immediately forward to seal the breach, even though he was wounded by the explosion. Under extremely heavy artillery and rifle fire, the breach was gradually filled in and reinforced, although at a cost of more than 100 infantrymen during the six-hour-long operation. Grant never ordered an infantry attack forward to exploit this breach.

With mining operations continuing all along the Vicksburg line, Grant decided to hold his forces in place until all was ready, then fire all at once and assault in one huge wave over the line. By July 2 the siege trenches were so close to the Confederate positions that the defenders would only have time for one volley before the Union infantry would be on top of them. The only crimp in this plan was a possible attempt to relieve Vicksburg from Grant's rear.

Johnston had returned to Jackson after Grant's departure and had spent the intervening weeks building up his forces. In addition to the men he had pulled out of the capital in the face of the Union assault, he now commanded Loring's division, joining him after being cut off from Pemberton after the Battle of Champion Hill, as well as every militia unit, local defense command, home guard, or individual able man that could be scraped together from all around Mississippi. Johnston had appealed to both Bragg in Georgia and Davis in Richmond for more troops and supplies, but the building Chickamauga Campaign in north Georgia had taken up every spare man and all the available supplies. In Jackson he had nearly 30,000 troops, but the vast majority were green troops, totally untrained and ignorant of battle, with a curious collection of shotguns, muskets, and old rifles.

Despite the odds, Johnston was determined to do what he could and sent a message to Pemberton that he was on the way and would attempt to break through Grant's siege line, probably on July 7. Grant had intercepted this message and promptly shifted his forces around to face Johnston, who he feared far more than Pemberton, and requested immediate reinforcements from any command in the west. Several thousand men arrived from the Trans-Mississippi Theater and from Union armies in Tennessee later in June, and Grant sent Sherman to take control of the growing threat from the east.

In the end Johnston never did anything with the army he had raised, remaining in Jackson until June 28 and then hesitantly moving west. On July 4, still not in contact with Sherman's line at the Big Black River, he learned of Pemberton's surrender and immediately returned his army to Jackson.

July 4, 1863: The End

By early July nearly half of Pemberton's men were unfit to fight, suffering from malaria, dysentery, gangrene, and a host of other illnesses, and the rest capable of holding on but weakened by the severe food shortage. Nearly every building in the city had been hit by the ceaseless artillery fire, and most were reduced to blasted hulks. Snipers fired at any man who dared poke his head out of his trench or above the parapet of his redoubt; civilians were now living full-time in dug-out caves, many with ventilation so poor that candles wouldn't stay lit. The stench from blasted-apart horses and mules filled the air, and everyone was approaching complete exhaustion from the strain of the prolonged siege.

Pemberton knew that Grant was about to make a move against him and that his men probably wouldn't be able to stop it. Multiple communications begging Johnston to attack went unanswered or came back with replies saying the Jackson garrison needed more time to organize. In answer to Pemberton's predicament, a letter appeared in his headquarters on June 28, signed "Many Soldiers," praising his own inspired leadership but asking that he surrender. The letter went on to threaten a general mutiny if he did not. On July 1 Pemberton circulated a letter among his top commanders asking if their troops would be able to fight their way out of the siege, which came back with a decidedly negative answer. On July 2 he called a conference of all his officers and point-blank asked if they thought he should surrender the city. Only two disagreed but could offer no other feasible plan.

At 10 a.m. on July 3, 1863, white flags of truce were raised all along the Vicksburg line, and for the first time in weeks the guns fell silent. After some difficulty in discussing the terms of surrender, with Pemberton showing some late-stage theatrics and Grant calmly insisting upon unconditional surrender, a deal was finally struck late in the day. Confederate soldiers would surrender their weapons but would not enter prison camps, instead being paroled as soon as rolls could be made out. Grant wanted to avoid the expense and logistical nightmare of feeding and transporting 30,000 prisoners, and Pemberton found the offer quite acceptable, undoubtedly knowing that most of the men would soon return to the army anyway.

At 10 a.m. on July 4, 1863, the day after the great Union victory at Gettysburg, Pemberton ordered each of his divisions in turn to get out of their trenches, form up, and march under their own colors to the surrender point. Union regiments stood alongside the road watching silently as their beaten opponents passed, offering in a soldier's way a salute to the gallant defenders of Vicksburg.

With the Confederates stacking arms and tenderly laying down their colors, Major General John Alexander Logan led his 3rd Division into the town to occupy it, and soon one of his regimental flags and the Stars and Stripes were raised over the courthouse. The long campaign was at last over, and the end of the Confederacy in the West had begun.

> *Soldiering is a rough coarse life, calculated to corrupt good morals and harden a man's heart.*
>
> —Private Henry W. Prince, 127th New York Infantry, Union Army

Siege of Vicksburg, Surrender, July 4, 1863

THE COST

$\mathcal{B}$oth sides suffered terribly in the long campaign to capture Vicksburg, and, ultimately, the Mississippi River. There are fairly complete records for Grant's losses: 1,514 killed, 7,395 wounded, and 453 captured or missing. Confederate records are very spotty on this period, but during the siege operation alone Pemberton lost a reported 1,260 killed, 3,572 wounded, and 4,227 missing or captured. Union records indicate that a total of 29,491 surrendered on July 4, but this figure includes all the civilians left in town as well as the remnants of the Confederate defenders.

TOURS

Vicksburg

Vicksburg lies 45 miles due west of Jackson, Mississippi, easily accessible on I-20. The battlefield park lies just off I-20, exit 4; turn right at the bottom of the exit ramp (approaching from Jackson) onto Clay Street, and the well-marked entrance to the park is just ahead on your right. The main business district of Vicksburg is farther west along Clay Street, which is dotted with directional signs to guide you to all the prominent and most of the obscure sites and attractions. The Vicksburg Convention & Visitors Bureau Welcome Center is across the street on the left from the battlefield park entrance and is a must-stop for detailed directions, as well as the vast selection of brochures, discount coupons, maps, and other information on the local establishments and attractions. The staff is quite friendly and has demonstrated an outstanding willingness to go far out of their way to help meet visitors' needs.

MODERN TIMES AT CHICKASAW BAYOU

Almost all of the Chickasaw Bayou battlefield is now private property and not open to touring, but you can get a good view of the area from a highway that runs through the area and from certain points in the battlefield park. US 61 Business, also known in town as Washington Street, runs northeast out of town, and just past the boundaries of the battlefield park it passes over the remains of the Confederate line of defense. About 1½ miles north on US 61 Business is a turnoff to the left leading to an old Indian mound; this was the position held by the 31st Louisiana and 52nd Georgia Infantry Regiments, supported by a battery from the 1st Mississippi Light Artillery, which successfully held off five strong assaults by Union troops.

One of the best views of the general area can be had from Fort Hill, within the battlefield park (Stop 9 on the tour map). From the north ramparts, look straight ahead and a bit to your right: The bluffs you can see about 2 miles away are the positions of Confederate artillery during the battle. The Confederate infantry was in emplacements at the base of the bluffs, and the swampy area you can see a little to your left is where the Union troops assaulted through.

MODERN TIMES IN VICKSBURG

Today Vicksburg is a bustling small town, driven in about equal parts by Civil War–related tourism and the new boom in riverboat gambling. As you drive down the "main drag," Clay Street, you can't help but notice the extreme frequency of markers and monuments scattered among the fast-food restaurants and small businesses. Even many of the businesses completely unrelated to the Civil War make some reference to the long siege and battle in their names: the Battlefield Inn, Vicksburg Battle Campground, the Pemberton Square Mall, and so on. Although obviously the destination at the end of a well-worn path leading hordes of tourists from Jackson and other points east (and west and north and south), it is a surprisingly pleasant place to visit. Unlike our stops at a great number of other tourist and Civil War–related destinations, we did not have a single unpleasant encounter during our visits, and aside from a few government employees in the national park, we experienced nothing but the warmest and most gracious of welcomes wherever we went.

This no doubt was the result of Vicksburg's "other" and perhaps least obvious face: that it is ground zero for that most revered of all surviving Southern traditions, the Southern belle. Scarlett O'Hara of *Gone With the Wind* fame is the idea that most people not of the South have of belles, and in some ways it is an accurate portrayal. Belles are known here (and across the Old South) as an effective combination of sugar-sweet politeness covering the tenacity and effectiveness of a tank, women who would never think of being rude to a stranger any more than they would wear white shoes before Easter (or after Labor Day, for that matter). While some of their traditions seem a bit dated, such as never putting dark meat in a chicken salad or avoiding Miracle Whip like the plague ("real" Southern belles make their own, or at least buy Hellman's and add a little lemon),

it is an absolute delight to be in the presence of people who would never dream of making you feel uncomfortable or unwelcome. As opposed to the standards set by certain television talk shows and the average rush-hour commute, these ladies can think of no word stronger than "tacky" to describe the worst possible aspect of someone's behavior. And they would never, ever say that to their faces.

Old times are indeed not forgotten here, as the annual Spring and Fall Pilgrimages open the many antebellum homes for tours, the fees from which help keep many of them open and in the same family. Many of these homes claim rightfully to have survived the vicious fighting here, and several have visible damage to the structure as proof. While the main visitor center on Clay Street can give you maps and brochures of the even-dozen homes open year-round for tours, some of which are listed below, a casual drive around the small city takes you past many others that wear their scars from the war as badges of honor.

One last word about touring Vicksburg before we recommend some specific sites and attractions: When you go (and you must!), prepare to stay awhile and let the charm of this Confederate mecca embrace you. This is not the sort of historic site that treats its history as a sideshow to help get you to empty out your wallet; these folks rightfully treat their town as hallowed ground, where the sacrifices of both sides are respectfully preserved and, for the most part, tastefully presented.

POINTS OF INTEREST

Anchuca
1010 First East St.
Vicksburg, MS
(601) 661-0111
(888) 686-0111
www.anchucamansion.com

Take a 30-minute tour through this grand mansion filled with magnificent period antiques and gas-burning chandeliers. Built in 1830, Anchuca was one of the city's first mansion-type homes. Additions were made from 1840 to 1845. After his release from serving 2½ years in prison, President Jefferson Davis went to Anchuca to visit his oldest brother, Joe, who was living in the mansion, and made a speech from Anchuca's balcony. In addition to the two-story main house, Anchuca visitors can see the original slave quarters, also built in 1830, and the turn-of-the-20th-century guesthouse. There is a five-minute video before the self-guided tour begins.

The Duff Green Mansion
1114 First East St.
Vicksburg, MS
(601) 636-6968
(800) 992-0037
www.duffgreenmansion.com

A former hospital for Confederate and Union soldiers, this three-story mansion, built circa 1856, offers 30-minute tours daily on the hour. Visitors will see what is considered to be one of the finest examples of Palladian architecture in the state. The mansion was built by Duff Green, a wealthy merchant, for his bride, Mary Lake, whose parents donated the property as a wedding gift. In a cave near the mansion, she gave birth to a son during the siege of the city and named him, appropriately, Siege Green. Before the war, the 12,000-square-foot home was the site of many lavish parties. Now it offers bed-and-breakfast accommodations. Open daily for tours, except during private functions.

Vicksburg National Military Park and Cemetery
3201 Clay St.
Vicksburg, MS
(601) 636-0583
www.nps.gov/vick

This 1,858-acre park is called the best-preserved Civil War battlefield in the nation. A trail more than 16 miles long carries one through the major sites of the long campaign here. We suggest you start out in the visitor center in order to view the 18-minute film, *Vanishing Glory,* and see the life-size exhibits and artifacts telling the story of the campaign. This will give you a much better bearing over the complex actions than if you simply try to drive through the park and get a feel for it yourself. After your visit to the visitor center (and be sure to walk over and see the replica artillery emplacements next to the parking lot), drive through the park's rolling hills, past markers and monuments recounting the military campaign. The driving tour goes through the Vicksburg National Cemetery, where nearly 17,000 Union soldiers are buried. Also in the north section of the park are the remains of the Union gunboat USS *Cairo* and its adjacent museum. Hours vary by season.

RESTAURANTS

The main road through town and its intersection with I-20 has just about every major national chain restaurant, but for a real Vicksburg experience, we recommend you try one of the numerous local establishments dotted around town; check at the city visitor center for an up-to-date listing.

Gregory's Kitchen $
815 US 61 N. Bypass
Vicksburg, MS
(601) 634-0208
(877) 634-0208
www.gregoryskitchen.net

This family-owned restaurant features all-you-can-eat Mississippi pond-raised catfish and rib-eye steaks. The menu is handwritten, and the atmosphere is homey. You haven't lived until you've tried their fried dill pickles. The restaurant is open only on Thurs, Fri, Sat, and Sun.

Rusty's Riverfront Grill $–$$
901 Washington St.
Vicksburg, MS
(601) 638-2030
www.rustysriverfront.com

You may have to get here early, as people stand in line to try the fried green tomatoes topped with lump crabmeat at this locally run establishment. The restaurant is considered one of Vicksburg's best-kept secrets (until now).

Walnut Hills $–$$
1214 Adams St.
Vicksburg, MS
(601) 638-4910
www.walnuthills.net

Walnut Hills's round tables filled with down-home cooking are well known and for good reason. A typical menu features some of the best fried chicken found anywhere, plus country-fried steak, fried corn, snap beans, okra and tomatoes, corn bread, and blackberry cobbler.

DAY TRIPS

Grand Gulf Military Monument Park
12006 Grand Gulf Rd.
Port Gibson, MS
(601) 437-5911
www.grandgulfpark.state.ms.us

Grand Gulf Military Park is dedicated to the former town of Grand Gulf and to the Civil War battle that took place there. The park is 8 miles northwest of Port Gibson, off US 61, and consists of approximately 400 acres that incorporate Fort Cobun, Fort Wade, the Grand Gulf Cemetery, a museum, campgrounds, picnic sites, hiking trails, an observation tower, and a number of restored buildings. The museum contains Civil War memorabilia plus antique machinery and an assortment of horse-drawn vehicles. Day visitors to the park must come into the museum to pay the admissions fee.

The Manship Museum
420 E. Fortification St.
Jackson, MS
(601) 961-4724
http://mdah.state.ms.us

The Gothic Revival house built in 1857 and called a "cottage villa" will be forever known as the home of the Jackson mayor who surrendered the town to Union Army general W. T. Sherman during the Civil War in 1863. Not that the mayor had much choice, since Sherman was wont to ride his fiery trail through the South, wreaking havoc in his wake. Mayor Manship's house-museum uses photos, diaries, and letters to interpret family activities and events of the 1800s. The Manship Museum is administered by the Mississippi Department of Archives and History. Admission is free.

Old Capitol Museum
100 S. State St.
Jackson, MS
(601) 576-6920
http://mdah.state.ms.us

Mississippians are very proud of this museum. Called the Old Capitol Museum, it was built in the late 1830s and restored in 1961, and what a grand Greek Revival structure it is. It houses award-winning exhibits spanning the early days of the state's colorful history through the civil rights movement and beyond. Plan to spend awhile here for there's much to see and do, including a free guided tour. There's also a bookstore and gift shop.

Ruins of Windsor
MS 552
Port Gibson, MS

All that remains today of this gracious mansion 10 miles southwest of Port Gibson is 23 columns. A flight of metal stairs found intact here is now at the Oakland Chapel at Alcorn State University. The mansion, completed in 1861, was a Confederate observation post. After the Battle of Port Gibson, it was turned into a hospital to treat Union soldiers. The grounds are generally open year-round during daylight hours. If the gate is locked, you can walk the 150 yards from the road to the ruins, but keep an eye out for hunters during deer-hunting season (late Nov through late Jan). There have been a few isolated instances of illegal hunting near the ruins, and illegal hunters aren't mindful of tourists. Admission is free.

New Orleans and Port Hudson:
The River War

Darley.

Soon after the first shots of the war had been fired, an overall Union strategy based on a gradual strangulation of the South was adopted. Based on the previously derided Anaconda Plan first proposed by General in Chief Winfield Scott of the U.S. Army, the multiphased strategic plan relied on one basic and yet crucial component for success: the control and free transit of the Mississippi River by the Union Army and Navy, splitting the Confederacy in half and denying an important route of supplies to the blockaded states from ports in Texas and Mexico.

As this was in many ways still a frontier area with few roads (and even fewer that could be used to support an army), the task of wresting control of the great river was given in equal parts to army and navy commands. One combined command was established in Cairo, Illinois, and given the task of clearing out Confederate outposts along the river moving to the south, and another was formed at Ship Island, Mississippi, and given the task of fighting their way upriver to join the Cairo-based squadron in taking complete control of the river. Given command of the assembling fleet at Ship Island was a highly experienced naval captain, Tennessee-born but Union loyalist David Glasgow Farragut.

BACKGROUND TO THE BATTLE

The fact that military operations would have to be conducted on relatively shallow inland rivers that were choked with debris and had poorly charted and ever-shifting ship channels, and with enemy artillery and infantry emplacements literally only feet away from the ship channel, meant that some serious rethinking in ship design and naval tactics would have to be done. The U.S. Navy possessed 90 ships of all types when the war began, but only 42 were listed "in service" at spots all around the globe, and not a single warship would suffice for river warfare. Although other navies had experimented with metal-clad armored warships, and the

French had used several to good success in the Crimean War, almost every U.S. ship was both wooden and sail-powered.

On the other hand, the fledgling Confederate Navy had not a single ship at the outbreak of hostilities and a host of problems to overcome. Another part of the Union strategic plan called for a tight blockade of the Southern coastline and ports, which the Confederate Navy would be charged with either breaking or at least preventing from totally closing down the most critical ports. It was obvious that the Mississippi River was going to be a major area of conflict, and suitable ships for port defense there were needed as well. The final and greatest problem was where these ships would come from, as nearly every major shipyard and heavy industrial facility was located in the North.

THE TARGETS

Aside from a series of strong Confederate river forts and outposts from Memphis northward along the Mississippi, the major points of concern for the Union Navy were New Orleans, Port Hudson, and Vicksburg. New Orleans would be the immediate problem; the largest city in the Confederacy, it had the greatest number of shipbuilding and other industrial facilities of any other single area of the South, and to leave it untouched was to guarantee a strengthened Confederate military. However, it was located on a curve of the Mississippi surrounded by swamps and marshy lowlands that precluded an overland campaign and was well protected from attack by sea by two powerful forts 70 miles downstream just above the Head of the Passes, Forts Jackson and St. Philip.

The two masonry forts were originally ordered constructed by Andrew Jackson in 1822 following his victory over the British force in the area in 1814. Fort Jackson was the larger of the two, roughly star-shaped and positioned on the western bank of the river, manned

The Mississippi River route from New Orleans to Vicksburg

by about 700 troops and mounting 74 guns, including several 10-inch Columbiads, the largest gun in the Confederate inventory at the time. A smoothbore cannon, the Columbiad was capable of throwing a 128-pound shell over 1,800 yards with deadly accuracy. It was more than capable of destroying any of the U.S. Navy's wooden ships of the day. Fort St. Philip was across the river on the opposite bank, about a half-mile farther upstream, and was an unusual construction of thick brick walls covered by dirt ramparts in a sort of "squished" star arrangement, also manned by about 700 troops and mounting 52 guns. Both forts were well located in a bend in the river that any ship would have to slow down to navigate, making any attempt to "blow by" the posts unlikely.

To add to the riverborne defenses, a third ancient fort, Fort Chalmette, just upstream, was also garrisoned and armed. This was the site where Andrew Jackson fought the British during the War of 1812 (a battle that was fought more than two weeks after the war was officially over). No one thought it really necessary to man this old post, but it provided some insurance in case an enemy fleet managed to get past the two forts downstream. Between Forts Jackson and St. Philip, heavy chains holding several old ship hulks were placed across the river and strongly anchored, blocking the river passage.

THE NAVIES

The defense at Forts Jackson and St. Philip was further backed up by the fledgling Confederate Navy's western gulf fleet, consisting of four ships of the line: the *McRae*, the ironclad-ram *Manassas*, and the ironclads *Louisiana* and *Mississippi*. These were backed up by two ships of the Louisiana Navy, the *Governor Quitman* and the *Governor Moore*, and a group of converted riverboats mounting a single gun each and rather grandiosely called the River Defense Fleet: the *Breckenridge, Defiance, Stonewall Jackson, General Lovell, Warrior,* and *Resolute.* Records are incomplete, but the ships probably mounted a total of about 100 guns.

Plan of the attack on New Orleans

> *A Baptist. And always have been.*
>
> —Old civilian woman in north Georgia, when asked by Union troops if she was "secesh" or a Union supporter

By the end of March 1862, Farragut had assembled two small fleets to take on the enormous task of opening up the lower Mississippi: an 18-ship gunboat fleet led by his own flagship, the *Hartford*—a 2,900-ton screw sloop 225 feet long and 44 feet wide that had a top speed of just under 14 knots. The 2 frigates, 5 sloops, and 11 ironclad gunboats mounted a total of 243 guns. A second fleet known as the Mortar Flotilla, commanded by Commander David Dixon Porter, Farragut's own foster brother, consisted of 22 two-masted sail-powered schooners roughly 100 feet long each, mounting a single 13-inch mortar that fired a 200-pound shell up to 4,000 yards, landing nearly vertical and easily lobbed over fortification walls. These mortar schooners sailed under their own power while at sea but were towed upriver by their own assigned support fleet of 8 gunboats and unarmed towboats.

On April 8, 1862, Farragut moved all but one of his ships across the shallow passes and sandbars that marked the entrance to the Mississippi River at the Head of the Passes. A few days later he was followed by a large troopship fleet bearing Major General Benjamin Franklin Butler and his 18,000-man army command, and both began moving upriver on their campaign to take New Orleans.

THE BATTLE OF FORT JACKSON AND FORT ST. PHILIP

*F*arragut decided to let Porter's mortar flotilla handle the problem of the powerful Confederate forts before he brought his own fleet into firing range. On April 18, the 22 mortar schooners were towed into position just south of a bend in the river below Fort Jackson and commenced a heavy bombardment of the two posts. Over the next five days, about 17,000 rounds of ammunition were fired, which slightly damaged the forts but failed to kill many men of the garrisons or destroy any of their gun emplacements.

Farragut, displaying his usual impatience, decided to cancel the bombardment (which was not doing much good anyhow), send his fleet in to directly attack the Confederate stronghold, and as quickly as possible get past it upriver—his main goal being to capture New Orleans as soon as possible. The first of several obstacles in his way were the chained-together old ships across the river below the two forts, and he assigned Lieutenant Charles H. S. Caldwell, captain of the *Itaska,* to find a passage through.

After several failed attempts to blast through the line of obstacles by cannon fire and explosives, Caldwell decided to simply ram his way through. Bringing his gunboat up to full speed, he hit the chains about mid-channel and swiftly parted them, leaving a clear passage for the rest of the fleet. Farragut arranged his gunboats into three divisions and then signaled for them to move out at 2 a.m. on April 24.

The first division was led by the large gunboat *Cayuga,* in front of two screw sloops, two corvettes, and three more gunboats strung out in a single column. The small task force was not seen until nearly upon Fort Jackson, but then the Confederate gunners opened up with every available cannon. The *Cayuga* was raked by fire not only from the forts but also from three of the Confederate gunboats lying anchored nearby. All three gunboats were quickly sunk by the lead Union ship and two others that rapidly closed in.

The second division, led by Farragut's own flagship *Hartford,* soon entered the growing fight and was nearly immediately attacked by a Confederate ship pushing a fire raft, which struck and nearly threatened to set ablaze the Union ship. Farragut calmly ordered the fire to be doused and the enemy ship sunk, both of which occurred in rapid succession, and then he just as calmly turned his attention to the rest of the battle.

A wild naval melee had broken out by now, with the Confederate ram *Manassas* attacking the Union ships *Mississippi* and *Brooklin,* both of which escaped with little damage, before moving downstream toward the rest

A map of the fortifications at Fort Jackson near New Orleans

of the Union fleet. Before the *Manassas* could mount another attack, the *Mississippi* turned on her and forced the Confederate ship aground under a near blizzard of shot and shell. The crew barely escaped with their lives while the boat was shot to pieces on the bank. While this drama was unfolding downstream, the Louisiana Navy steamer *Governor Moore* attacked the onrushing Union fleet led now by the corvette *Varuna*. Each ship raked the other with concentrated fire, inflicting heavy casualties on both, while the *Governor Moore* actually shot its own bow away in order to place point-blank fire into the Union gunboat. After a follow-up ramming attack, the Union corvette sank near the far bank, taking most of her crew with her. The *Governor Moore* did not have much time to celebrate; moments later, as she turned away from the sinking Union ship, exposing her sides to the rest of the Union fleet, a heavy blast of fire from several ships exploded her magazine and sent her burning to the bottom with almost all her crew.

Seeing the burning and wrecked Confederate ships drifting past his schooners just downstream, Porter ordered his mortars to renew their fire on the forts. The fort's gunners were forced to stop their own fire on the Union fleet, but once again, little physical damage was done to the two Confederate outposts. However, the real damage was already done, as Farragut's fleet was now safely past the two forts, having wrecked the Confederate naval fleet at the cost of 37 dead, 149 wounded, one ship sunk, and two ships damaged. Farragut signaled Butler to bring his troopships upriver and bypass the forts, which would be allowed to simply starve themselves out when New Orleans was taken and their supplies cut off.

THE END OF THE BATTLE FOR NEW ORLEANS

As soon as Butler had moved his troopships above the two Confederate forts, Farragut ordered his fleet to set sail once again toward New Orleans. Nearing old Fort Chalmette, he noticed that the Confederate defenders had installed river batteries on both banks, threatening his passage. The *Brooklin* opened fire on both sides with her swivel-mount 80-pounder Dahlgren gun, sending only about 20 shots into the batteries before their gunners broke and ran, leaving the river passage open. This action was probably the best showing of the entire war for that particular model of Dahlgren gun, as most 80-pounders had a tendency to burst after a few rounds.

Watching Farragut's actions from a levee nearby, New Orleans garrison commander Major General Mansfield Lovell at once ordered his 4,000-man command to destroy what supplies they could, along with the tons of cotton bales sitting on the docks ready for shipment, and then pulled out of the city before Farragut's ships approached.

On the morning of April 25, Farragut's fleet sailed into the New Orleans port and docked without a single shot being fired, although his gun crews were standing by at the ready. The civil authorities of the city reacted with ill-thought-out impudence at first, actually daring Farragut to "try and take the city," but they finally bowed to the obvious and formally surrendered the city on April 29. The commanders of Forts Jackson and St. Philip originally intended to hold fast to their posts,

During the opening of the lower Mississippi and the capture of New Orleans, mortar steamers attacked the water battery of Fort Jackson.

but the men mutinied and demanded the forts be abandoned. On April 28 the forts' guns were spiked, and the officers formally surrendered their posts to Butler's men. The short action had cost the Confederates only 12 dead and 40 wounded, but they lost one of the most critical ports in the entire Western Theater.

NEW ORLEANS AFTER THE BATTLE

With the Big Easy rather easily taken, Butler was placed in charge of the occupation force, and Farragut soon moved out to points upriver. Butler, an unpleasant and rather corrupt administrator, managed to outrage the local populace to the point that even his own commanders in Washington were soon debating his judgment. He soon earned the nickname "Spoons" for his habit of raiding local plantations and wealthy estates, where he "confiscated" the silverware and other valuables. Several sources claimed he had a habit of doing this at dinner parties. Only a day after assuming his post, he began issuing a series of imperial-sounding edicts, including harsh pronouncements demanding the civilian population treat his men and the national flag with the utmost reverence at the threat (and delivery) of harsh punishments.

A local gambler, William Mumford, was arrested for pulling down a Union flag that one of Farragut's men had placed over the Old Mint Building before Butler even arrived. Mumford was tried for treason, quickly convicted, and just as quickly hanged on June 7. On May 15 Butler issued his General Order Number 28, which became better known as his "Woman Order." In short, this order stated that any lady of the town that dared treat any Union soldier with contempt in any way would be immediately assumed to be a prostitute and arrested as such. Newspapers as far away as London condemned this act, which ultimately helped lead to Butler's removal from his command in December, but curiously, the order was never revoked or changed.

LAST GUARDIAN OF THE RIVER: PORT HUDSON

With New Orleans and Memphis successfully taken, only two last Confederate outposts remained in the way of complete control of the river by the Union Navy—the heavy batteries controlling access between Port Hudson, Louisiana, and Vicksburg, Mississippi. Worse for the success of the grand Union strategy, this stretch of Confederate-controlled river included the mouth of the Red River, giving a clear waterborne supply and communications route to the Trans-Mississippi Theater.

Port Hudson is about 120 miles by air south of Vicksburg but more than 200 miles by the meandering Mississippi River; it served primarily as a tiny cotton port before the war. Settled by small farmers early in the 19th century, the small town never "caught on" with the large landowners and was in danger of disappearing when the war began. What the town lacked in amenities it more than made up for in abundance of good terrain for defense of the river passage. Eighty-foot-high bluffs lined the river to the west of the small settlement, where the river curves around nearly upon itself, making a high-speed passage impractical. Swamps, ravines, and nearly impenetrable woods surrounded Port Hudson on three sides, making the only practical land approach one from due east.

Despite this very favorable position and the urging of then Western Theater commander General Pierre Gustave Toutant Beauregard, the town remained without a significant garrison or serious fortifications until after nearby Baton Rouge was occupied in May 1862. Major General Earl Van Dorn, Vicksburg area commander, realized nearly too late the vital nature of this position and sent a 5,000-man force under Major General John C. Breckinridge to attack and try to retake the state capital in order to gain time to reinforce and build up Port Hudson.

Map illustrating the defenses of Port Hudson, Louisiana

Baton Rouge

$\mathcal{N}$ow a forward base for Farragut's fleet attacking Vicksburg, Baton Rouge was garrisoned by a 2,500-man force under Brigadier General Thomas Williams, supported by a varying number of naval gunboats. Breckinridge's command moved south in late July 1862, preparing to assault and retake the capital, but ran into several delays caused primarily by some unspecified disease sweeping through the camps. Although the Confederate commander received some reinforcements from a small outpost 60 miles north of Baton Rouge, by early August he was in position to attack with only about 2,600 effective combat troops. To reinforce his attack, Van Dorn had ordered a small naval task force south, led by the ironclad *Arkansas.*

Breckinridge arrived just outside town on the afternoon of August 4 and divided his decimated command into two weak divisions led by brigadier generals Daniel Ruggles and Charles Clark. Lieutenant Henry K. Stevens was having serious engine trouble with his *Arkansas,* adding to the growing problems with the Confederate attack, but Breckinridge gave the order to attack at 4:30 a.m. on August 5.

The plan was to attack with the two divisions nearly line-abreast against the Union line running parallel to the river, while the gunboats moved in and neutralized the Union gunboat threat. As was almost the usual during this war, nothing went off as planned. A thick fog prevented a coordinated movement of the two divisions; heavy skirmishing on the Union right confused the two division commanders, who moved their units in such a manner that several actually ended up firing on one another; and Stevens's problems with his gunboat delayed his entry into the battle until nearly the end. Despite this, the Union line caved in rather quickly, sending the blue-clad troops scurrying to the relative safety of their own gunboats' covering fire, while Ruggles and Clark moved forward into the town, fighting house to house and street to street with the scattered Union commands.

As the town was being overrun, Stevens moved into position and prepared to attack the three Union gunboats at the dock, when his engines suddenly seized up again, and the naval battle ended before it had even really begun. Reorganizing a hasty defense under the covering fire of the gunboats, Williams personally led a failed counterattack, dying in the attempt, and his scratch force once again fled to the cover of the gunboats. With no naval support coming, Breckinridge held the town until about 10 a.m. and then pulled out and marched north to Port Hudson. As the Confederate troops pulled out, Colonel Thomas W. Cahill assumed overall command for the North and moved his remaining force back into their original positions. Union losses in the brief fight were 84 dead and 299 wounded or missing, while Breckinridge reported a loss of 84 dead and 372 wounded, missing, or captured, including a seriously wounded Clark, left on the battlefield and later captured. Two weeks later, Butler ordered the city evacuated, looted, and razed to the ground and the garrison returned to New Orleans. His officers made sure the finest furniture, art, silver, and anything else of value went south safely in their own possession. As a final act, Spoons Butler ordered the inmates at the Louisiana State Prison at Baton Rouge released but involuntarily enlisted into Union service.

The Defense of Port Hudson

$\mathcal{N}$early the moment his rebel troops entered Port Hudson, Ruggles put them to work building defensive works and gun emplacements for the coming assault. The lines soon extended nearly 8 miles in a wide semicircle around the small settlement and mounted 10 heavy guns by the end of August. Two attempts by Farragut's fleet to bypass the fortifications afterward met with a hot and accurate fire, leading the newly promoted admiral to set aside his plans to attack Mobile and concentrate on building up a land and naval force to attack the remaining Confederate river strongholds.

By early March 1863 both sides had built up impressive forces in the area. Major General Franklin Gardner had assumed command of the Confederate garrison, now reinforced to four brigades with nearly 16,000 men manning 11 pentagonal gun emplacements mounting 21 heavy guns along 3 miles of the river, as well as another 5 miles of infantry entrenchments and gun emplacements guarding the inland approaches. In total, 107 heavy guns, field pieces, and mortars guarded the lines from 25 separate batteries, ranging from relatively small field howitzers up to three 9-inch naval Dahlgren guns and seven 30-pounder Parrott rifles.

Farragut had prepared a squadron to run the Port Hudson batteries and join the gathering force assaulting Vicksburg, consisting of his flagship *Hartford,* three other heavy seagoing ironclads, three smaller "river" ironclads,

---

The Song of the South

"Dixie" was a song written in 1859 by an Ohio musician, Daniel Decatur Emmett, while he was living in New York City. Emmett had never traveled through the South at the time and had only thirdhand or worse knowledge of what the area was actually like. However, he was under pressure to compose a new song for a failing minstrel show. The show folded shortly thereafter, but his song became a surprising hit. Originally entitled "I Wish I Were in Dixie's Land," it became the unofficial song of the Confederacy after being played at President Jefferson Davis's inauguration. Many Southerners objected to a proposal to make it the official anthem, as it was not considered "dignified" enough. In April 1865, just after receiving the news that General Robert E. Lee had surrendered his troops in Virginia, Lincoln stepped out of the White House and walked up to an army band that was playing nearby. He asked them to play "Dixie" for him, and when his shocked aides commented on the seemingly strange request, he remarked that it was the "finest tune I ever heard."

---

and the side-paddle ironclad *Mississippi,* along with six mortar boats. After dark on March 14, 1863, he ordered the squadron forward, trying to slip past the Confederate batteries under cover of darkness. *Hartford* and the smaller ironclad *Albatross* managed to get past the first set of batteries before the Union ruse was discovered and Confederate gunners opened a near point-blank fire.

A thunderous fire from the Confederate batteries raked the Union ships, pounding through the thick iron plating and destroying engines and steering gear. Two hours later, only Farragut's two lead ships had managed to pass the batteries more or less unscathed, while the rest of his fleet was nearly wrecked. All managed to limp back south, except for the *Mississippi,* which fought alone while grounded on a mud bank for nearly an hour until an onboard fire grew out of control. Her crew abandoned ship about 1 a.m.; an hour later she slipped free and drifted south, finally ending her life in a massive explosion about 5:30 a.m., when the fire finally reached her powder magazine. Farragut had managed to get two ironclads past the defenses and on to Vicksburg at the cost of 26 killed, 38 wounded, and 64 missing, as well as one ship destroyed and the rest seriously damaged. Confederate losses amounted to 3 killed and 22 wounded.

ASSAULT ON PORT HUDSON

*W*ith Farragut's failure to blast through the Confederate river defenses, it became obvious that a land attack to neutralize the position would be necessary. Major General Nathaniel P. Banks's Army of the Gulf, with nearly 35,000 men, was assigned the task of storming and taking the strong Southern position. Most decidedly a "political" general (he had been the Speaker of the U.S. House before the war and won his commission by pulling strings), Banks was not viewed as exactly the Confederacy's worst enemy; in the Shenandoah Campaign against Major General Thomas Jonathan "Stonewall" Jackson during late 1861, his command suffered so many defeats and huge amounts of captured supplies that the delighted Confederate troops nicknamed him "Commissary" Banks.

Despite the expressed feeling that his 35,000-man force was "inadequate" to take the Confederate stronghold, Banks moved out in mid-May 1863 with only a portion of his men to take it. The rest were left to garrison Baton Rouge, New Orleans, and several other smaller posts. Encircling the Confederate position by May 23 with roughly 15,000 (some accounts say 20,000) men and a handful of Union gunboats, Banks made his first attempt to assault on May 27. An ill-coordinated attack limped off at dawn on the Union right, followed hours later by attacks along the rest of the line.

This battle featured the first use of large numbers of African-American troops, including two regiments of Louisiana Native Guards—almost all former slaves. Although Banks outnumbered his Confederate opponents nearly four to one at nearly every place along the line, the attack was a dismal failure. The greatest Union advance was the advancement into the outer trench lines at a few points, all of which were quickly retaken and the attacks blunted. Total casualties for the failed attack were about 2,000 Union soldiers and about 250 Confederates.

A little over two weeks later, Banks attempted another assault. As in the May 27 attack, a nearly hour-long heavy bombardment preceded the attack, followed by a formal call for the Confederate garrison to surrender. When they refused, the bombardment was resumed and a general assault against the center of the Confederate line was prepared. At 4 a.m. on June 14, with only three hours to organize and prepare their men for the attack, a three-division front assaulted three points on the Confederate line, centered on a large fort known as the Priest Cap. The uncoordinated attack fared no better than the earlier attempt and gradually petered out before noon. The two attacks had cost Banks a total of 708 killed, 3,336 wounded, and 319 captured or missing, to gain nothing. Confederate losses amounted to 176 killed and 447 wounded, with none reported missing or captured.

Banks settled down into a tight siege of the Confederate garrison, which was running low on supplies even as the campaign began. As at Vicksburg, Union engineers and infantry cut a series of siege trenches growing ever closer to the Confederate line, while sappers attempted to mine under the line and blow it up. This

Pickets of the First Louisiana "Native Guard" guarding the New Orleans, Opelousas and Great Western Railroad

last attempt was foiled by the Confederates' own countermining efforts, while sharpshooters kept everyone's head down in the trenches and occasional firefights lit up the line. This siege, the longest in American history, lasted 48 days. Many accounts confirm that after the regular rations, horses, and mules were all gone, the men turned to eating dogs and rats until they, too, were all gone.

Banks had planned another general assault for July 7, which was postponed due to poor weather. Before it could be rescheduled, news arrived about the fall of Vicksburg; when informed, Gardner decided he could not hold out alone against additional Union forces surely heading his way. Formal surrender of the garrison took place on July 9, with 5,500 prisoners walking into captivity. With this act, the Mississippi River was at long last once again under full Union control, and the Confederacy had suffered a devastating breach from which it would never recover.

TOURS

New Orleans

New Orleans is in extreme southeastern Louisiana, not far from the Mississippi state line and easily accessible via I-10 from the east or west, I-55 south from Jackson, Mississippi, or I-59 south from Hattiesburg, Mississippi. Fort Jackson still exists, although most of the other forts and locations mentioned either disappeared under the meandering flow of the great river or long ago fell into disrepair and neglect. Fort Jackson is near the small town of Buras; south of New Orleans, take LA 23 south from US 90 on the south side of town, and follow it about 53 miles south to the marked historic site. It is very hard to get lost here, as it is the only major hardtop road in the vicinity! Still, you need to watch carefully for the turnoff (on the left going south), as the fort itself is on the other side of both a rather high levee and a sports complex.

Very little remains in the Big Easy from Civil War times, including any of the few fortifications constructed for its defense. A few houses noted for being Butler's headquarters or various Union officers' residences dot the city, but the dearth of really historic sites can be illustrated by the Cable House, whose claim to fame is that it was the residence of a California poet, Joaquin Miller, who was denied the use of the mail in the 1880s for his pro-Southern views. The most significant sites in the area are Fort Jackson and the Chalmette National Historic Park.

POINTS OF INTEREST

Please be aware that although Hurricane Katrina occurred in 2005, the rebuilding is still in progress throughout the state of Louisiana and the Gulf Coast area.

Chalmette Battlefield and National Cemetery
(part of Jean Lafitte National Historic Park and Preserve)
8606 W. St. Bernard Hwy.
Chalmette, LA
(504) 1281-0510
battlefield number: (504) 281-0511
www.nps.gov/jela/chalmette-battlefield.htm

Six miles southeast of the French Quarter, still within the metropolitan New Orleans area and surrounded by the gigantic Shell Oil Arabi facility, this area gained its highest fame as the site of General Andrew Jackson's victory over the British during (or more accurately, several days after) the War of 1812. During the New Orleans campaign, earthwork batteries mounting 10 32-pounder guns provided the last-ditch defense of the city. The 141-acre park is now a memorial to the 1812 battle and Jackson, with very little information presented about the Civil War use of the site, although the remaining earthworks are the original Confederate gun emplacements. For access information to the cemetery call (504) 589-3882.

Fort Jackson National Historical Monument
LA 23
Buras, LA

Sixty miles southeast of New Orleans, this fort survived both the encounters with Farragut's fleet and the Union occupation and was used as a training base during World War I, only to almost disappear due to flooding and the incredibly humid environment. The fort was restored but was still in very poor condition, despite constant efforts by the staff and a protective surrounding levee. Fort Jackson then suffered extensive structural damage from Hurricanes Katrina and Rita. In addition, many historic exhibits were destroyed.

Jackson Barracks Military Museum
6400 St. Claude Ave.
New Orleans, LA
(504) 278-8000
www.la.ngb.army.mil

Originally built in 1833, this was the main defense barracks for the New Orleans area until the end of World War I, and a host of high Confederate officers called this place home during their service as young U.S. Army officers before the war. Originally the barracks consisted of four two-story brick buildings with walls 20 inches thick, surrounded by a brick wall with four towers mounting cannon at each corner. This restored museum now houses weapons and artifacts from every American war through the 1991 Persian Gulf War, and has a nice collection of flags, personal equipment, cavalry and artillery artifacts, and ammunition from the Civil War era. Realistic tableaus set up throughout the museum give an intimate look at what life was really like for American soldiers during different periods. Admission is free. Saturdays are for groups and by appointment only.

Louisiana Civil War Museum at Confederate Memorial Hall
929 Camp St.
New Orleans, LA
(504) 523-4522
www.confederatemuseum.com

A very nice collection of Civil War relics, concentrating on those from Louisiana regiments. The flag collection is unusual and well presented, as are a nice weapons collection, some period currency and documents, and displays of personal effects of Jefferson Davis and Robert E. Lee. There are limited hours so call ahead. Admission is free. Across the street is the National D-Day Museum, also highly recommended. There is on-street parking at parking meters, as well as free and pay parking lots within a block of the museum.

ACCOMMODATIONS

New Orleans is a major convention and tourism destination, so reserving a room at pretty much any given price is not terribly difficult. However, finding that room might be. We heartily suggest that you contact the New Orleans Metropolitan Convention & Visitors Bureau before your trip, for both a map of this sometimes-confusing city and an updated list of available hotels. The staff is exceptionally helpful and pleasant and can be called at (800) 672-6124; information is also available on the Web at www.neworleansonline.com.

There are literally dozens of hotels in the metro area, an unusually high percentage of which are the usual and expected chains. However, there are a few establishments that we feel are worthy of special mention.

Hotel Monteleone $$$$
214 Rue Royale
New Orleans, LA
(866) 338-4684
www.hotelmonteleone.com

Many people say the French Quarter begins in the lobby of the Hotel Monteleone. It is one of the most historic properties in the French Quarter and is also supposedly haunted. There are 600 newly renovated rooms, plus 25 meeting and reception rooms available. Many notable authors have stayed here, and it is even designated as a literary landmark. Be sure to stop in at the Carousel Piano Bar and Lounge, even if you don't stay the night at one of New Orleans's most luxurious hotels.

Royal Street Courtyard $$$
2438 Royal St.
New Orleans, LA
(504) 943-6818
(888) 846-4004
www.royalstcourtyard.com

This nine-room guesthouse is an 1850s Greek Revival–style home that is now a bed-and-breakfast. It features four-poster beds in some rooms, with a private bath. It is far enough from the hustle and bustle of Bourbon Street to still have some quiet, yet only six blocks away, which makes it close enough to walk. The innkeepers are Phillip Lege and David M. Smith.

Soniat House $$$$
1133 Chartres St.
New Orleans, LA
(504) 522-0570
(800) 544-8808
www.soniathouse.com

A relatively small, 33-room hotel in a restored 1830s-era mansion at the edge of the French Quarter, the Soniat is one of the most elegant and beautiful hotels in the city. The sort of place where locals send someone they wish to impress, the exquisitely restored mansion is filled to the brim with fine antiques, the staff is exceptionally pleasant and attentive, and a high degree of attention to detail is obvious in everything we observed. The only drawbacks are the three-night minimum stay required during parts of the year and the outrageous prices for parking.

RESTAURANTS

New Orleans is a town devoted to the finer things in life, most notably, food. A comprehensive list of the good, non-chain restaurants here would fill a good-size book; we refer you to *Insiders' Guide to New Orleans* for a more complete listing. Here are a few of our favorites, where we can honestly say we have never had a bad meal (possibly because we have never had a bad meal anywhere in New Orleans, excepting the fast-food places!).

Antoine's $$$–$$$$
713 Rue St. Louis
French Quarter
New Orleans, LA
(504) 581-4422
www.antoines.com

This institution is as inseparable from New Orleans as the Mississippi River and nearly as ancient. First opened in 1840, it is the oldest continuously operating restaurant in the United States and has one of the largest wine cellars, with well over 30,000 bottles on hand at any given time. This is a place where tradition lives on both in the quality of its food and the experience and longevity of its staff. A regular haunt of the New Orleans society class, during Mardi Gras the Carnival Kings take over their own private dining rooms, and reservations are almost exclusively the domain of the "permanent table" variety.

More than 130 dishes adorn the Creole menu; specialties include Huîtres a la Foch (fried oysters served on toast, covered with pâté de foie gras), Oysters Rockefeller (invented here), Oeufs Sardou (poached eggs covered with artichoke hearts and hollandaise sauce), and even Portage Alligator au Sherry. Be sure to consider the Omelette Alaska Antoine for dessert, which can be ordered at the beginning of dinner. Reservations are for all practical purposes mandatory and should be made well in advance.

Bayona $$$$
430 Rue Dauphine
French Quarter
New Orleans, LA
(504) 525-4455
www.bayona.com

Bayona is housed in an unexpectedly romantic, more than 200-year-old cottage nestled along a lesser traveled avenue in the northern part of the French Quarter. Chef Susan Spicer tends toward well-considered game dishes, such as braised rabbit, and is noted for her signature cream of garlic soup. The menu also has delicacies such as mushroom gnocchi and escarole ragout. The service is understated but perfect in execution, and the wine list is extensive, very well selected, and unusually inclusive of both moderate and higher-range European and California vintages. The dessert list is equally extensive and inclusive, ranging from fine cheese plates to cakes, tarts, sweet roulades, ice creams, pies, and the best sorbets we have experienced on this side of the Atlantic.

In short, Bayona is the sort of place that justifies a short vacation trip in and of itself and is absolutely not to be missed when you find yourself anywhere in the region. Reservations are a must. The dress code is casually elegant or business casual.

Brennan's $$$
417 Royal St.
New Orleans, LA
(504) 525-9711
www.brennansneworleans.com

The building that houses Brennan's Restaurant was a bank at one time and also the private residence of the Gordon Family. The Gordons entertained General Andrew Jackson, who was the guest of honor at many parties. Unfortunately, the Gordons met with financial ruin and their home was sold at auction to Judge Alonzo Morphy. Morphy's son was Paul Charles Morphy, the celebrated American chess master. He died in the home in 1884.

Brennan's opened in this spot in 1954, and many famous dishes have originated from its legendary kitchen, such as Eggs Benedict and Bananas Foster. This is also a hot spot for celebrities when they are in New Orleans. Be sure to set a few hours aside for a meal here. It isn't just a meal, it is definitely an event.

Baton Rouge/Port Hudson

Baton Rouge is about 80 miles northwest of New Orleans on I-10, which also connects the state capital with Lafayette to the west. I-12 runs east out of Baton Rouge to connect with I-55 at Hammond and I-10 and I-59 near Sidell, close to the Mississippi state line. Port Hudson is about 12 miles north of Baton Rouge, just off US 61.

POINTS OF INTEREST

Centenary State Historic Site
3522 College St.
Jackson, LA
(225) 634-7925
(888) 677-2364
www.crt.state.la.us/parks/icentenary.aspx

Located north of Baton Rouge and Zachary, Centenary State Historic Site was originally the College of Louisiana in 1826. It passed hands throughout the years. It closed for the duration of the Civil War, as did most Southern colleges, and the buildings were used by both Conferederate and Union troops. The dormitory became a hospital in 1862, and during the Battle of Port Hudson, Union troops used the main academic building as area headquarters. There is also a Confederate cemetery on the grounds. Guided tours are offered daily.

Historical Homes

There are numerous historical homes from the antebellum period in West Feliciana and East Feliciana Parishes. It would not be fair to list just one or two when so many are available for viewing.

Pentagon Barracks
State Capitol Drive at River Road
Baton Rouge, LA

This site is not open to the public but is worth passing by for a look if one is in the area. The fort was a U.S. military post from 1779 until 1861, when it was seized and captured by the State of Louisiana. Operations were then turned over to the Confederacy. In 1862, Federal troops reclaimed it during the Battle of Baton Rouge. After the Civil War, in 1884, the General Assembly of Louisiana passed a resolution granting full usage of the barracks to Louisiana State University. Today it houses the offices of the lieutenant governor and private apartments for state legislators.

Port Hudson State Commemorative Area
236 US 61
Jackson, LA
(225) 654-3775
(888) 677-3400
www.crt.state.la.us/parks/ipthudson.aspx

This 650-acre park encompasses the northern portion of the Confederate lines and represents one of the better-preserved battlefields of the war. The town was basically destroyed during the battles and siege and abandoned by its civilian population after the war, so little has changed in either the remaining fortifications or earthworks. An unusual feature of the park is the three 40-foot observation towers that give an excellent view of the rugged terrain of the battlefield. An interpretive center on-site has displays about the battle as well as a few artifacts and an excellent display featuring a 20-pounder Parrott rifle and limber. Several other outdoor displays illustrate the artillery positions, including one original gun used during the battle, an 8-inch siege howitzer originally manufactured at West Point in 1841. An extensive trail system winds through the park, passing both original and reconstructed earthworks.

Getting to the park is a bit tricky: Take I-110 north out of Baton Rouge until it ends at US 61. Turn right and go about 12 miles north until you see the rather small sign for the Port Hudson State Commemorative Area.

ACCOMMODATIONS

Baton Rouge is a medium-size city with typical hotel chains located in all areas. Zachary, the closest city to Port Hudson, has only one hotel, a Best Western that is usually full. St. Francisville is the best choice for historical lodging in the area, and is located 25 minutes north of Baton Rouge on US 61.

The Cottage Plantation Antebellum
Tours and Lodging $$–$$$
10528 Cottage Lane
St. Francisville, LA
(225) 635-3674
www.cottageplantation.com

The Cottage Plantation has almost all of the original outbuildings, dating from the early 1800s, remaining in good condition. It provides a wonderful representation of a working plantation from the pre–Civil War era. The accommodations are clean and comfortable in a peaceful setting. There's even a swimming pool for those sultry summer days in the South. Daily tours are offered, should you just want to look and not stay the night. This plantation will really take you back into history.

The Myrtles Plantation $$$
7747 US 61
St. Francisville, LA
(225) 635-6277
(800) 809-0565
www.myrtlesplantation.com

This home was built in 1796 by General David Bradford. There are guided history and mystery tours, as it is said there were numerous murders here over the years (including a Civil War soldier). It is considered to be one of America's most haunted houses. Operated year-round as a full-service bed-and-breakfast inn, there are six rooms available in the main house with private baths, air-conditioning, heat, and direct TV. Cottage accomodations are also available. The on-site restaurant, the Carriage House, is open every day except Tues.

The stories here will entertain and educate visitors about the history of the area. There are several tours available. Tours of the grounds are given daily, beginning every hour and half-hour. Mystery tours are every Fri and Sat. Reservations are required.

RESTAURANTS

You really can't go wrong eating anywhere in Baton Rouge and the surrounding area. If you plan on spending the day at Port Hudson, a great idea would be to stop at Tony's Seafood Market and Deli (5215 Plank Rd., North Baton Rouge; www .tonyseafood.com), for a po'boy or plate lunch to take along with you. Here are just a few choices in the Zachary and St. Francisville areas.

The Magnolia Café $–$$
5687 Commerce St.
St. Francisville, LA
(225) 635-6528

This casual restaurant is located in the historic district of St. Francisville. People go out of their way to stop at this place

for lunch. Everything on the menu is good. It is housed in a modified 1930s tourist cabin. The best seats in the house are on the screened-in porch.

Sammy's Grill $–$$
20335 Old Scenic Hwy.
Zachary, LA
(225) 654-5355
www.sammysgrillonline.com

This is a popular establishment that serves steak, seafood, and burgers. They offer daily lunch specials and have an on-site sports bar. Their seafood-stuffed potato is a favorite with locals.

Florida: More Troops than Voters

Darley.

In 1860 Florida boasted a population of 78,686 free citizens and 61,753 slaves, the smallest population by far of any of the soon-to-be Confederate states. In terms of simple statistics, Florida fought and bled more than any other Confederate state in relation to its small population. By 1865 more than 15,000 troops would come out of this meager populace, most of which left the state by mid-1862, contrasted with about 14,000 registered voters in the entire state. One in 11 served; one-third of those did not return. About 5,000 of these soldiers died in action or as a result of disease during the war. Compared with today's population, it is the equivalent of Florida providing 1.4 million soldiers and losing 465,000!

Florida had only been in the Union for 16 years, after 300 years of being passed back and forth from Spanish to English to American control, when it voted for secession on January 10, 1861. Different sources claim either widespread opposition to or equally widespread enthusiasm for secession, but the simple fact was that Florida was more a liability than an asset to the Confederacy. The relatively few troops it provided did help the critical manpower shortage, but the state legislature could earmark only $100,000 for arms and equipment, soon exhausted in the inflated wartime market and leaving most of the men still unarmed.

Appeals to the Confederate government in Richmond for funds to equip the troops only revealed that there was no money to be had and that Florida would have to somehow equip the soldiers it was requested to provide. Additionally, the very troops requested by the national government would not be accepted for service until somehow properly equipped at the state's own expense. As late as mid-1862, official calls were asking civilians to provide what "shot guns, double and single barrel rifles, and muskets" that they had available.

As additional liabilities, Florida had more than 6,000 miles of difficult-to-defend shoreline, a scarce and widespread population at least partly sympathetic to the Union, and an interior easily penetrated by the multiple large river outlets. Despite all this, the state could not be ignored by the newly formed Rebel government, as it was a valuable source of cotton, turpentine, and beef, as well as a port and haven for blockade-runners.

BACKGROUND TO THE BATTLE

The populated areas of 1861 Florida were concentrated in the northern reaches, as were nearly all the ports and railroads. Ironically, the second-largest city was Key West, with a population of 2,832 (including 591 slaves), but it was isolated from the mainland by the lack of connecting roads or railroads.

The railroad network was still in the process of building up across the state when war broke out; as a result, no line connected Pensacola (the largest city) with the eastern portions, nor did any line connect eastern Florida with Georgia or Alabama. Forts originally built by the Spanish or by the U.S. government starting in the 1840s guarded the most critical approaches to Pensacola, Fernandina, St. Augustine, and the Keys. Both sides recognized that besides these major approaches, the capital at Tallahassee, the railroad crossroad town of Baldwin, and the river towns of Jacksonville, New Smyrna, St. Marks, Appalachicola, Cedar Key, and Tampa all were strategic locations to the control of the state.

There never seems to have been a grand strategy for control of Florida by the Union Army, nor was there a concerted effort by the Confederate government to provide for its defense. After Florida seceded, the Union all but surrendered all but three of the coastal forts with little or no resistance. Most of the troops called up in the state left for either the Army of Northern Virginia or Army of Tennessee, leaving a bare 2,000 for home defense throughout most of the war.

The Civil War in Florida can be divided into three phases: first, the seizure or defense of coastal fortifications early on; second, a withdrawal of Confederate forces from the eastern coast followed by a long period of uncontested garrison by Union forces in these abandoned positions; and finally, a short but intense period of combat for control of the northern reaches toward the end of the war, ironically all won by the Confederates.

A Civil War–era map of the Fernandina region of Florida

FERNANDINA

*F*ernandina, on (and sometimes referred to as) Amelia Island, is at the very northeastern tip of Florida, just across Cumberland Sound and the St. Marys River from Georgia's Cumberland Island and adjacent town of St. Marys. Guarding the mouth of the river that separates the two states (for a few miles, at least), the island was a Spanish-held haven for pirates and smugglers before the United States took over in 1821. To guard the water-borne approach and the new port town, construction of a fort began on the northernmost tip in 1847.

Most local publications trumpet that this was the only U.S. location to have been under eight flags in its history: French, Spanish, British, "Patriots," Green Cross of Florida, Mexican Rebel, U.S., and Confederate. The Patriot flag flew for the shortest time, when the U.S.-backed Patriots of Amelia Island overthrew Spanish control and declared their own territory, only for the day of March 17, 1812. The next day they raised the U.S. flag, but soon afterward the island was returned to Spanish control.

A Real Pirate Story

The most unusual flag, almost certainly unique in American history, was the Mexican Rebel flown while the pirate Luis Aury controlled the island from September to December of 1817. The island, where pirates, smugglers, and assorted riffraff roamed freely, had been a black-market haven since the 1808 U.S. embargo on slave importing. Aury was a Frenchman who was allowed to fly the Mexican flag and roam under its protection so long as he sent Mexico a percentage of his plunder. Using a secret act passed by Congress in 1811 as an excuse, the United States sent military forces under Captain J. D. Henley and Major James Bankhead to seize the island with its valuable port from Aury on December 23, 1817. The island was "held in trust" for the Spanish until formally ceded in 1821.

FORT CLINCH

*F*ort Clinch was named for General Duncan Lamont Clinch of Second Seminole War fame. The land was purchased in 1842 on the north end of Amelia Island, and construction began about 1847 but progressed very slowly; by the onset of war only two of the five planned bastions, two walls, the guardhouse, and a prison building were complete. A few other smaller buildings were in various stages of construction, but no cannon of any caliber had been mounted, and the post was only a military stronghold in the most liberal sense of the word.

Florida militia took over the fort without a struggle in May 1861, as the Union garrison had either already withdrawn or was simply at another fort. Over the next six months, several sand dune batteries were constructed around the island to supplement the unfinished fort, and a total of 33 artillery pieces were brought in and mounted. No real effort was made by the Confederate garrison to continue any of the work on the fort itself.

General Robert E. Lee, newly appointed commander of the Department of South Carolina, Georgia, and East Florida, had by this time changed his coastal defensive strategy from one of static, fort-based defense to one of mobile infantry and artillery strike forces, preferably arranged near railroad lines so as to be able to move quickly against enemy threats. Lee made two

brief inspections of the fortifications at Fernandina in November 1861 and January 1862 and found that despite the best efforts of the Florida troops, the defenses were inadequate at best. He ordered naval officers from Savannah to help mount the cannon and train the gunners and the 24th Mississippi Infantry Regiment to the fort as reinforcements.

Before the fort could be placed into full operation, Union seizure of barrier islands in Georgia and South Carolina showed just how vulnerable the isolated and lightly manned post was to an attack of any significant strength. Lee ordered evacuation of forces on both Cumberland and Amelia Islands in late February 1862. The Mississippi and Florida troops abandoned Fort Clinch by February 29, just as Union gunboats sailed up into Cumberland Sound and began shelling the fortifications. The Confederate troops were able to withdraw only 18 of the artillery pieces before the gunboats showed up; the other 15 were captured and left in place to serve their new masters.

Confederate sympathizers abandoned Fernandina along with the combat troops, leaving only a tiny, windswept, bug-infested island for the Union garrison to enjoy. No shots were fired in combat from the rude fort by either side during the entire war, the action soon shifting away from the coastline up to the north and west. Despite the decisive demonstration at Fort Pulaski a little over a month later that the era of masonry forts was over, the garrison spent the rest of the war and early postwar period working on the walls and emplacements. By 1867 the fort was nearly complete when abandoned once again, this time for more than 30 years.

ST. AUGUSTINE

*T*he nation's oldest city remained a Confederate-held town for just a little over 1 year of its 430-year history, and endured 3 years of sometimes hostile Union occupation, but supplied both fighting men and a well-protected harbor to the fledgling nation. Originally founded in 1565 by the Spanish, the town has been continuously inhabited ever since by the ebb and flow of one empire after another.

Civil War Times in the Ancient City

After only 16 years as part of a full-fledged state and "24 years of territorial vassalage," as one secessionist agitator charged, St. Augustine embraced the idea of secession and the new nation with gusto. Following Lincoln's election in 1860, when not a single vote for him was recorded in the entire state of Florida, the only debate seemed to be whether to secede immediately or to wait a bit. With their representatives voting solidly along with the vast majority for the ordinance of secession in Tallahassee on January 10, 1861, the town held a mighty independence celebration. On the fall of Fort Sumter in Charleston Harbor, another joyous celebration was held under the new flag of rebellion in the town plaza.

With secession fever rising in 1860, the town raised a militia unit for defense known variously as the Florida Independent Blues or St. Augustine Blues. They were soon joined by another infantry unit, the Milton Guards, and by the Marion Artillery in January 1861. The only U.S. fortification in the area, Fort Marion (formerly and today known as the Castello de San Marcos), was manned by a "garrison" of a single U.S. Army ordnance sergeant, who gave up the post several days before the secession vote with only verbal resistance and a demand for a receipt.

Despite the seeming invincibility of the old Spanish-built fort, competent military engineers realized early in the war that the town was vulnerable and would be difficult to adequately defend. General Robert E. Lee, during one of his Fernandina inspection trips, commented that "the small force posted at Saint Augustine serves only as an invitation to attack" and ordered that only the essential harbors of Charleston, Savannah, and Brunswick were to be fortified and defended. By February 1862, with the situation deteriorating in Tennessee, most of the town's defenders marched off to duty with the Confederate Army of Tennessee.

For all intents and purposes, Florida was left to her own devices without regular army troops for defense through most of the rest of the war. Newly elected Florida governor John Milton lamented that he "almost despaired of protection from the Confederate Government." In St. Augustine, a Union naval blockade in place since December 1861 had reduced the town almost to the point of governmental collapse. The prewar tourist industry had come to a complete halt, business could only be conducted at the most elemental level, and very few citizens were able to pay their taxes.

Sally port of Fort Marion

The Occupation

Almost as a blessing, a Union assault force arrived off the coast of St. Augustine, and on March 12, 1862, Commander C. R. P. Rogers arrived at the seawall to request the town's surrender. He was greeted there by friendly politicians and local Unionists; the offer was quickly accepted, and in short order the Stars and Stripes once again flew over Fort Marion.

With such an easy transition, the occupying Union garrison at first assumed the town was full of Northern sympathizers. Rogers received a rude awakening on his first walk around town, where he was greeted with loud comments of disapproval from some of the town's ladies. Another group of women chopped down the town plaza flagpole so that he would not be able to hoist the U.S. flag upon it.

Although there never was any concerted effort to regain the city, after the discovery of several Confederate Army deserters in town and the assassination of several Unionists nearby, all Southern sympathizers still living in St. Augustine were ordered expelled. Many had already left to live with friends or family in the Confederate-held interior, and most of the male population had entered military service.

Confederate Sympathizers Are Forced Out

The first forced expulsion began in September 1862, consisting of all those who had refused to take an oath of allegiance and agree to report on "subversive" activities. In typical military bureaucratic style, an order countermanding the removal arrived just as a shipload of women and children was on its way out of the harbor. Most of the women had been forced to give up their homes and possessions before boarding the ship and thus had no place left to stay. A few remained, but most went into the interior with the blessing of both townspeople and Union authorities, happy to reduce the number of mouths to feed.

A more orderly evacuation commenced in January 1863, apparently consisting primarily of those ladies who particularly irked the Union officials. The official decree was for those with "husbands and sons in the rebel army," but that could be applied to just about anyone left in town. Mrs. Victoria Williams was rather outspoken in her assessment of the situation and those in charge of it, to the extreme discomfort of their guards. By the time their ship reached Fernandina, she and her family were put off and given over with thanks to the Confederate authorities just outside the island town. Other families were put off in small groups at a number of other Southern ports.

Throughout the rest of the war, other individuals and small groups would be expulsed from town, mostly into the Confederate-held interior. Presumably many returned after hostilities ceased, but there is no consistent record of this.

Soldier Life in the Ancient City

The only real military opposition to the continued Union occupation was by a small Confederate cavalry force commanded by Captain J. J. Dickison. Mostly confining his activities to patrolling the west bank of the St. Johns River to warn of any Union offensive, Dickison occasionally raided the outskirts of town, inflicting a few casualties and capturing some unlucky Union soldiers. Even with this threat, the Union soldiers and authorities became complacent in their relatively comfortable post, to the point that Colonel William H. Noble (who had replaced Rogers) was himself captured in December 1864, while riding with his aide to Jacksonville. Even with this serious loss, Union authorities failed to change their security procedures, and two more groups of soldiers were taken prisoner within the next month.

Before the war, St. Augustine had been both a tourist destination (as it is very much today) and a wintertime health resort for sickly Yankees. In the fall of 1863, it resumed one of these roles when the Union Army decided to make the town into a convalescent camp and hospital.

Slowly but steadily, the town's population grew with the arrival of more Unionists and soldiers and with growing numbers of disenchanted Confederate Army deserters. By the end of the war, the town was nearly back to its prewar norm, with the federal courts reopened, the churches nearly filled to capacity, and trade with Northern cities restored. Even news of the Confederate Army commander in chief General Robert E. Lee's surrender in Virginia failed to change life to any great degree.

As in so many other Southern cities, the great emotion of the Confederate loss gradually changed into a wistful nostalgia for the Lost Cause. In 1872 the United Daughters of the Confederacy, locally headed by Anna Dummett, erected a tall stone obelisk in the central plaza as mute testimony to the 44 local men killed in the war. This monument still stands in the Plaza de la Constitution at the end of King Street, directly across from the Bridge of Lions downtown, guarded by 8-inch "Rodman" Columbiad artillery pieces and a nearby 10-inch seacoast mortar, part of the wartime Fort Marion defenses.

✦

THE INVASION OF NORTHEAST FLORIDA

The largest battle in Florida began as nothing more than yet another occupation of Jacksonville, the fourth in half as many years. In overall command was Brigadier General Truman A. Seymour, charged with securing the small port town for the Union once again and then moving westward into the interior area between the St. Johns and Suwanee Rivers with four goals in mind: first, to cut the railroads and stop the northward flow of food and supplies to the Confederate Army of Tennessee, several hundred miles north in Georgia; second, to capture the valuable store of cotton, turpentine, and lumber for the Union Army's own use; third, to "free" and recruit blacks for the increasing numbers of "colored" regiments; and lastly, and possibly least important, Seymour was to "inaugurate measures for the speedy restoration of Florida to her allegiance."

With some advance preparation by the Union garrison already at Fernandina, and with some difficulty passing through the sandbar-choked entrance to the St. Johns River, troop transports guarded by gunboats started upriver at daybreak on February 7, 1864. Seymour had under his command a force of about 7,000 men organized into 10 infantry regiments, 1 cavalry battalion, and 3 artillery batteries. One of the infantry regiments present was the all-black 54th Massachusetts (of Battery Wagner fame, as featured in the movie *Glory*).

The movement of Union troops toward the northeast Florida coast had not gone unnoticed by the Confederates, who quickly began scouting for a suitable place to mount a proper defense. In command of the Department of East Florida was Brigadier General Joseph Finegan, with a mere 1,200 men at his disposal, all widely scattered in small groups across the interior portions of the state from Fernandina to Tampa. Alerted to the danger, General P. G. T. Beauregard, Department of South Carolina, Georgia, and Florida (who had replaced Lee), immediately sent word to Finegan that help was on the way, to hold the Union forces at bay as best he could, and to "prevent capture of slaves."

Jacksonville

Meanwhile, the Union flotilla proceeded up the St. Johns River, pausing only long enough to engage and pursue a small number of Confederate pickets just below Commodore's Point, less than 2 miles from the wharves of Jacksonville itself. (Commodore's Point contains no marker or sign that we were able to locate, but lies at the northern base of the Isaiah D. Hart Bridge on US 1 Alternate, the Commodore Point Expressway. The area is now largely industrial.)

With little resistance, the flotilla of Union transports tied up to the Jacksonville docks at about 3:40 p.m. on February 7, and the troops began off-loading immediately. There was very little to secure in town, as three previous Union invasions and departures over the past two years had reduced most of the houses and shops to unreconstructed rubble. Nearly 3,000 people had lived in town in 1860; when Seymour arrived on the *Maple Leaf,* there were fewer than 200 remaining, almost all women and children, who assured the invaders that they were "Union."

By nightfall Seymour's troops had full command of Jacksonville, digging in for the night in an existing defensive position on the west side of the city, and he passed on orders for them to prepare to move rapidly toward the inland rail junction at Baldwin at dawn. For some unknown reason, this dawn assault did not take place; instead, after an uneventful night the men moved out in three columns at about 3 p.m. on February 8, their objective being the South Prong of the St. Marys River about 35 miles due west.

The Move West

The deliberate movement was the result of changed orders. Instead of a quick attempt to seize and cut the railroads,

Seymour apparently desired a somewhat deeper and more thorough disruption of the Confederate-held territory, tearing up what rails they could, destroying stockpiles of supplies, and reconnoitering the Confederate positions and emplacements. The troops were still only supposed to march about 35 miles inland, but there was no order or suggestion to avoid contact with any Confederate forces.

The three Union columns consisted of Colonel W. B. Barton's brigade (47th, 48th, and 115th New York Infantry Regiments) marching straight up the Lake City–Jacksonville road (roughly following the route of present-day US 90, paralleling I-10); Colonel Guy V. Henry's Mounted Brigade (40th Massachusetts Mounted Infantry, the Independent Battalion of Massachusetts Cavalry, Langdon's Light Artillery Battery, Elder's Horse Artillery Battery, and Batteries B and C of the Third Rhode Island Artillery) on a parallel road to the left; and Colonel J. R. Hawley's Brigade (7th Connecticut and 7th New Hampshire Infantry Regiments, and the 8th U.S. Colored Troops) on another road to the right. These three roads converged about 3 miles from Jacksonville, and Seymour expected Confederate opposition before that point.

Camp Finegan

Instead of making contact, the men marched on through the growing darkness before stopping for the night at the road junction. Henry's mounted troops continued before finally encountering an abandoned picket outpost about 5 miles down the road. Easing through the woods, the Union men quietly came upon a small manned outpost and seized it with a rapid assault. Quickly remounting and riding on for another 10 minutes, they soon came upon a major Confederate outpost known as Camp Finegan. (The exact location of Camp Finegan cannot be definitely placed, but it should be approximately in the area known as West Jacksonville, near the intersection of Lane Avenue and Beaver Street [US 90], about 1 mile east of the I-10 and I-295 intersection. The CSX Railroad track through this area runs over the roadbed of the Civil War–era tracks.)

Observing about 200 heavily armed Confederate defenders waiting in the camp (Lieutenant Colonel Abner McCormick's 2nd Florida Cavalry), Henry elected to bypass the camp and travel another 4 miles west to attack a reported artillery camp at Twelve Mile Station. Finding the camp manned but unguarded and the Confederates in the process of cooking and eating, Henry ordered a sudden, loud assault. Most of the artillerymen took off for the surrounding woods at the first notes of the Union bugles. The Confederates lost 18 men and 45 horses and mules, but the hardest blow was the loss of five critically needed artillery pieces.

Meanwhile, the Union infantry columns abandoned their plans for encamping at the road junction and began moving west through the thick, dark woods. Encountering Camp Finegan, they began to surround the camp before assaulting. Although they quietly captured all the Confederate pickets, something warned the men inside, and the Confederates deserted the camp before the Union attack could be mounted. After briefly searching the surrounding woods the next morning for deserters, the Union infantrymen moved out toward Baldwin, 15 miles to the west.

Baldwin

Henry's men left Twelve Mile Station at 4 a.m. on February 9, riding the 10 miles in to Baldwin and tearing up the rail tracks as they went. Baldwin itself was taken without resistance by 7 a.m., and in just this short time most of Seymour's objectives had been met. Major General Quincy Adams Gillmore, in overall command of the Union operation and now in Jacksonville, ordered more regiments forward for support and directed Seymour to continue inland. Henry ordered his men to move out once again on the morning of February 10.

Barber's Ford

Riding west of Baldwin and capturing occasional stocks of food and supplies along the way, no resistance was met until the bridge over the South Prong of the St. Marys River at a place known as Barber's Ford. There, the bridge had been burned and the 2nd Florida Cavalry waited in ambush. The lead Union pickets were gunned down as they approached the burned-out bridge, but the Confederates melted away with the loss of only four men as the Union Independent Battalion charged their position. Union losses were set at 17 dead and wounded. (The bridge over the South Prong of the St. Marys River was destroyed before the skirmish, and no period structure remains there today. No sign of Barber's Ford could be located, but the skirmish took place between Macclenny and Glen St. Mary on US 90; the CSX Railroad bridge just south of the road over the river is the historic site.)

Lake City

Seymour received additional orders from Gillmore that same day directing him to push his forces as far west as the Suwanee River and advising that additional infantry support was headed his way. At the same time, Finegan, in Lake City, was hurriedly concentrating all his forces to meet the Union invasion force.

Moving out from Barber's Ford about 1 p.m. on February 11, Henry's mounted force soon entered Sanderson, only to find three large warehouses full of supplies set afire only 15 minutes beforehand by the last departing Confederate train. After a short rest, the mounted troops continued westward through the night, arriving 3 miles east of Lake City by mid-morning.

Slowly advancing through a thick morning fog, Henry's troops suddenly encountered Confederate infantry already drawn up in line of battle. Due to the thickness of the fog and the noise discipline exercised by both sides, neither saw each other until they were fewer than 100 yards apart, and both sides then immediately opened fire. The 1st Georgia Regulars, under the command of Lieutenant John Porter Fort, withstood the initial Union assault led by the 40th Massachusetts and the Independent Battalion and soon forced the Union line into retreat. With food and ammunition running short, and the main body of infantry support more than 30 miles to their rear, Henry decided to retreat all the way back to Sanderson before halting.

The sometimes dubbed "Battle of Lake City" took place just east of the main commercial district of Lake City, approximately where Price Creek Road intersects US 90, just to the west of the airport. The Confederate line was reported to be a mile in length, running north and south across US 90 and the adjacent CSX Railroad track.

Olustee

For 10 days after ordering his forces to retreat back to the relative safety of Sanderson and Barber's Ford, Seymour marked time by slowly reinforcing his garrison and limiting his offensive actions to a single raid on Gainesville and another to the Georgia-Florida border area. Finegan wasted no time building up his small force, sending every available unit from western and southern Florida into his line east of Lake City, and appealing to Confederate authorities for more infantry and artillery.

By the afternoon of February 19, Seymour had consolidated a force of eight infantry regiments, one mounted infantry regiment, three batteries of artillery, and a cavalry battalion, numbering just over 5,400 men and 16 artillery pieces. Swinging once again into the offensive, he ordered his men west along the Jacksonville–Lake City road, with the intention of confronting the Confederate forces at Lake City, driving through them, and destroying the railroad bridge over the Suwanee River.

Finegan remained at his headquarters in Lake City, placing command of the Confederate force on Colonel Alfred H. Colquitt. He had moved his main body of troops a few miles east of Lake City to a tiny settlement named Olustee Station. By nightfall on the 19th, Finegan had collected some eight full infantry regiments, parts of two other infantry battalions, four artillery batteries, and two cavalry regiments, numbering about 5,200 men. Committed to holding a line of defense at Olustee Station, he ordered his men to construct a line of hasty emplacements and prepared to meet the expected Union assault.

Colquitt soon chose a good ground to make a stand; with a large lake to his left and a dense swamp just to the right, the railroad tracks and adjoining road ran through a narrow patch of high ground that would be much easier to defend than the usual flat, wide-open terrain of northern Florida. Ironically, although both sides were nearly evenly matched, both commanders believed they were facing a superior force, and neither ordered their cavalry force forward to scout the opposing army.

Learning about the Confederate position at Olustee during the night of February 19, Seymour hastily gave orders for his force to march out and confront it in the morning. Leaving Sanderson and Barber's Ford about 7 a.m. in road march formation, once again the mounted forces under Henry rapidly pulled ahead of the main body of infantry. There was apparently little or no concern about encountering a major Confederate force anytime soon, as neither flankers nor skirmishers had been deployed, no order to load and prepare the artillery for action had been given, and most of the infantrymen had not yet loaded their guns or otherwise prepared for imminent action. The Union cavalry casually rode down the road at a trot, expecting to simply scatter whatever enemy force they chanced upon, as they had been doing for weeks.

Encountering a small group of Confederate pickets, Henry's men returned their fire until they broke for the rear. Feeling a bit more prudent, Henry decided to wait a bit until the infantry could catch up with him. About 2 p.m. the vanguard of the Union infantry arrived, led by the 7th Connecticut Infantry, and were immediately ordered up front to probe for the main Confederate line. With the Confederate force still coming into line and Union infantry rapidly marching up the road, contact was not long in coming.

As the 7th Connecticut advanced slowly forward deployed as skirmishers, they came under increasingly heavy but still sporadic fire from Confederate skirmishers falling back. Seymour ordered a "reconnaissance by fire" from one of the cannon just arriving on the field, and the response was swift. As the line of Union infantry broke out of the pinewoods into the railroad track clearing, they discovered a line of heavy entrenchments manned by no fewer than four full infantry regiments (the 6th, 8th, 19th, and 64th Georgia Infantry). Soon under fire from three directions, Seymour ordered the Connecticut men to fall back a few yards to a cleared area next to a small pond.

Within a few minutes, five other Union infantry regiments rushed up into line of battle (the 7th New Hampshire; 8th U.S. Colored Troops; and the 47th, 48th, and 115th New York), while the four Georgia regiments moved out of their entrenchments and deployed into a three-quarter-mile line of battle directly facing the field.

Under intense fire from the Confederate line, one by one the Union infantry retreated farther to the rear, with one notable exception. Well-drilled for dress parade but totally untrained for combat, the 8th Colored Troops were rushed into line of battle with still-unloaded rifles and then deployed and attempted to load and make ready while under intense and accurate fire from the Georgia line. At first the troops wavered and hesitated, threatening to break and run, but soon they loaded up and began to return a steady, if inaccurate, fire. Refusing to be pushed back, the troops ended up losing more than 300 of the 550-man command in the withering Confederate fire.

As the fighting intensified, more units rushed in on both sides. Three more Georgia regiments (the 1st, 23rd, and 32nd Georgia Infantry) deepened and extended the Confederate line while the 6th Florida Infantry Battalion dressed the right of the line, slightly overlapping the Union line and enabling them to pour a galling fire on the now-exposed flank of the Florida men. As the men came into line, Colquitt ordered a general advance on the weakened Union position. As the attack mounted, two more Union infantry regiments (the 54th Massachusetts and the 1st North Carolina Colored) rushed into the growing battle at the double-quick.

As the two lines of battle slammed together, a near-impenetrable volume of fire erupted from the Georgians. Between bullets and mixed grape and canister shot from the handful of Confederate cannon newly arriving on the field, the 115th New York lost 296 officers and men dead, wounded, or missing in action. To their far left, the newly baptized-by-fire 8th Colored Troops had three successive regimental flag bearers shot down, while the fourth lost an arm in the intense fire but held on to the flagstaff and carried it off the field.

Despite the arrival of the two fresh black regiments, the Union line could hold only a few more minutes. By 2:30 p.m. their line was in full retreat, with the 54th Massachusetts and 1st North Carolina Colored Troops slowly pulling back, still dressed in ranks, and keeping up a steady fire to protect their fleeing comrades. The Confederate line surged ahead, fully intending to stay close on the heels of Seymour's broken command. By 3 p.m. their own charge ended, not by Union resistance but by lack of ammunition for rifles and cannon.

Resupplying from the filled ammunition pouches of the Union dead and some supplies newly moved up by rail, the Confederate line managed to shortly resume pursuit, completely chasing the Union units off the field by dusk. By Sunday night the shattered remnants of all the Union regiments were in or near Jacksonville,

A map of Pensacola Bay showing topography of the coast, Fort Pickens, the U.S. Navy Yard, and other fortifications

having burned both supplies and bridges behind them, while the Confederates seemed contented just to ransack the abandoned Union equipment rather than engage in any serious pursuit.

PENSACOLA

The First Shots

Lieutenant Adam J. Slemmer was in charge of a small garrison of Union troops in Fort Barrancas when news of Florida's secession came in. Quickly consolidating weapons and ammunition in Fort Barrancas, Slemmer ordered his men into the fort, gun batteries to be prepared for action, and drawbridges to be raised. The young Union officer had foreseen that combat was imminent, and he was not going to surrender without a good fight. Just before midnight on January 8, 1861, Union sentries spotted movement outside the fort. Issuing a challenge that went unanswered, the guard force opened fire without drawing blood. These were the first real shots fired in anger of the Civil War; about five hours later the bombardment of Fort Sumter in Charleston Harbor began.

Realizing that his small force had no real chance of withstanding a strong land-based attack from the rapidly growing Confederate forces in the area, Slemmer spiked

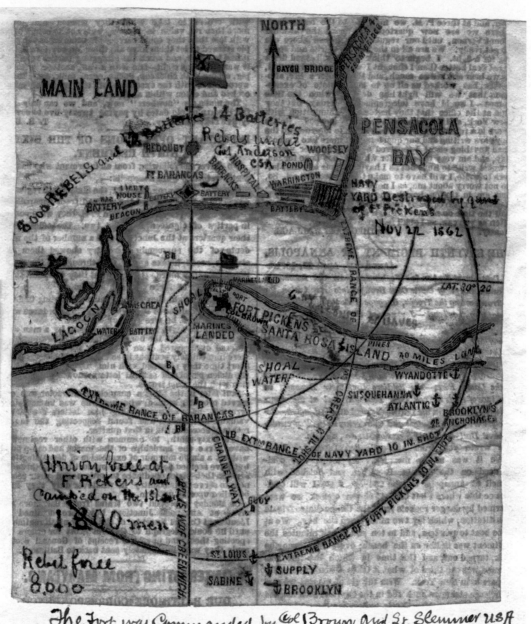

Color coding indicates the positions of the two sides around Fort Pickens.

his guns, destroyed powder stores in another nearby small fort, and evacuated his force to Fort Pickens. The next day, seven companies of infantry from Florida and Alabama took over the newly abandoned posts and immediately demanded Slemmer's surrender.

Fort Pickens

The southernmost and largest of the Pensacola Bay fortifications, Fort Pickens was named for American Revolution brigadier general Andrew Pickens of South Carolina. The large masonry fort was originally designed in 1829 as part of an interlocking band of forts around Pensacola Bay. Fort Pickens sat within 200 yards of the ship channel as it existed then and was intended to serve as defense against attacks coming only from seaward.

Completed late in 1834, the fort was a massively complex project, requiring 21.5 million locally made bricks, 26,000 barrels of lime from Maine, large quantities of granite from New York, lead for waterproofing from Illinois, and copper drains from Switzerland. Most of the construction was done by slaves sent from New Orleans, all under the direction of William Henry Chase, area supervisor for the U.S. Army Corps of Engineers.

The five-sided fort was designed to resist attack from any angle, including close-in infantry attack. Each corner had a bastion with cannon positions arrayed to enable fire right alongside the walls, the walls themselves rose some 40 feet above the surrounding dry moat, and positions were originally included for 200 24- to 32-pound cannon, 20 mortars, and 28 carronade on two levels. This number changed through the years, peaking at a recommendation for 221 guns in 1855, including 42 8-inch and 4 10-inch Columbiads. As a sort of "last-ditch" defense, each bastion had three "mine" chambers filled with explosives, which could be selectively set off to wipe out an occupying force if one should gain control of the structure.

Chase took a liking to the pleasant climate of Pensacola and moved back there after retiring from the army, shortly before the outbreak of hostilities. Following Florida's secession, Chase was given a commission as a colonel in the Florida army, and his first mission, ironically, was the capture or destruction of the fort he had built.

The Union Defenses Build Up

Having moved his men safely from Fort Barrancas and spiking the guns he could not remove, Slemmer refused a total of three demands for his surrender, believing that the massive fort could safely harbor his small command until reinforcements could be landed. Although reinforcements soon arrived in Pensacola Bay via the U.S. steam sloop of war *Brooklyn,* high-level politics between outgoing U.S. president James Buchanan and Florida senator Stephen R. Mallory forged an agreement that as long as Fort Pickens was not reinforced, it would not be attacked.

Slemmer had reason to be concerned about the delay in reinforcements. Although the fort had been designed for up to 1,200 soldiers manning well over 200 cannon, he had only 88 soldiers and sailors and 40 cannon in place. While the truce was under way, his men managed to mount another 14 cannon, but the majority of casements remained empty. To add to his headaches, although the fort did have defensive positions all around its perimeter, it had originally been designed to resist a naval push into the bay from the southwest, while simultaneously defending against a land-based push from the east. With the Confederates holding Fort Barrancas to the north and the small Fort McRee to the west, the lighter-built north and west walls, containing two of the three powder magazines, would be most vulnerable.

Confederates Attack

Eight days after newly elected U.S. president Abraham Lincoln took office, he ordered the *Brooklyn* to go ahead and land her troops to reinforce Fort Pickens. During the night of April 11, these troops entered the fort without opposition or answer from the surrounding Confederate positions. More troops arrived on April 16 and again landed without opposition on the seaward side of the fort.

After the formal organization of the Confederacy in February 1861, tensions ran very high in Pensacola, although, astonishingly, Slemmer was still permitted to buy food in town and use the local post office without fear of arrest or harassment. A handful of relatively minor raids and skirmishes prevented the Confederates from fully utilizing the deepwater harbor and eventually led to a determination to violently take over Fort Pickens.

On the morning of October 9, 1861, a landing force of just over 1,000 men under command of General Dick Anderson arrived on Santa Rosa Island about 4 miles east of the fort (roughly where the main commercial area today begins) and split into three groups to strike the fort from three sides. Within two hours, the assault force had overrun a small Union picket post but was soon forced to retreat under heavy fire from infantry and artillery. Without getting any closer than a mile from the fort itself, the Confederates sailed back off the island leaving behind 87 dead, wounded, or captured.

This was the only serious attempt to capture Fort Pickens during the war, but it did not go completely unanswered. A few weeks later, on November 22 and 23, 1861, joined by the Union gunboats *Niagara* and *Richmond* with their 24- and 32-pound guns, Slemmer ordered a massive bombardment of the Confederate positions. Five thousand outgoing shells badly damaged and silenced Fort McRee, destroyed most of the small village of Warrington and the Pensacola Navy Yard, and did some relatively minor damage to Fort Barrancas. The Confederates managed to return fire, lobbing some 1,000 shells at Fort Pickens and the gunboats, without serious effect on either.

A second bombardment on January 1 and 2, 1862, succeeded in exploding Fort McRee's powder magazine, rendering the post useless, and raked what was left of the Navy Yard with shot and shell. Fort Barrancas's defenders managed to return an intermittent fire toward Fort Pickens, again without effect.

While Slemmer and his command had absolute control over the entrance to the harbor and the immediate shoreline, their now-reinforced garrison was far too weak to assault the Confederate positions overland. A Union invasion of west and central Tennessee a few weeks later proved the deciding factor, however, with the subsequent withdrawal of more than 8,000 Confederate troops from Pensacola to fight with the Army of Tennessee. A small garrison remained behind, but when U.S. Navy commander David Farragut's fleet anchored just outside Mobile Bay on May 7, 1862, about 40 miles to the west, the remaining Confederates pulled out to help Mobile's defense, burning most of the military installations and supplies left behind.

Pensacola was formally surrendered by mayor Dr. John Brosnaham to Lieutenant Richard Jackson on the morning of May 10, 1862. For the remainder of the war the port city remained in Union control and was used primarily as a staging base for small raids into southern Alabama and western Florida.

TOURS

Reasoning with Hurricane Season

Weather experts say that hurricane seasons peak and ebb in relative strengths and numbers of major hurricanes, and that the East and Gulf Coasts can expect high levels of both in years to come. It is strongly suggested that you call just before your trip to make sure that the roads are passable and that your hotel is open, and it pays to monitor weather conditions during the hurricane season (roughly June through Nov, peaking in late Aug and Sept).

Amelia Island/Fernandina Beach

Fernandina is an easy drive from I-95—get off on exit 373 (SR A1A) just south of the Georgia state line and travel east about 10 miles. Both the historic district and Fort Clinch are just off SR A1A a few miles farther. Turn left on Centre Street to go to the district and left into the fort; park just before SR A1A reaches the beaches. Be sure to watch carefully for the turn, as the signs are parallel to the road and nearly hidden in the thick vegetation.

Modern Times at Fort Clinch

After the Civil War, this forlorn outpost was relegated to "caretaker" status, meaning that while no troops garrisoned it, and no upkeep or maintenance was done, the army intended to still claim it as insurance against a future crisis. That emergency did not come until the early spring of 1898, when the post was activated for service in the Spanish-American War. Abandoned again in September of that same year, the still-unfinished fort lay dormant for another 43 years until activated one last time for use as a watch station in World War II. Today Fort Clinch still stands as the centerpiece of 1,121-acre Fort Clinch State Park, a narrow peninsula with more than 2 miles of shoreline on the Atlantic Ocean and Cumberland Sound.

Fort Clinch State Park
2601 Atlantic Ave.
Fernandina Beach, FL
(904) 277-7274
www.floridastateparks.org/fortclinch

The still-unfinished fort is in a remarkable state of preservation, considering that wind, tide, and storms have been battering its earthen walls for more than 150 years. A small, tidy museum with a small number of well-presented artifacts begins your tour, and be sure to purchase your admission tickets in the gift shop before heading outside; rangers do occasionally check for receipts, as it is relatively easy to just walk in from the beach side. Make sure to ask for the pamphlet, "History of Fort Clinch," which gives a good capsule history and map of the fortifications.

The brick museum, constructed in 1934 by the Civilian Conservation Corps, is open every day. There is also a new visitor center/gift shop that sells souvenirs and books on the Civil War and Florida's natural and cultural history; an unusual collection of educational videotapes; and a large assortment of patterns for historic dress.

A short path leads from the museum to the main gate of the fort, just through a tall earthwork glacis and across a narrow drawbridge. Inside are several brick buildings containing replica period furnishings, and occasional outlines of foundation stones reveal what portions were never completed. Atop the earthwork rampart are several large replica artillery pieces, 10-inch Rodman Columbiads, which were capable of firing a 128-pound shot well over 5,500 yards at full charge.

These replicas cannot be fired, as the gun tubes are actually made of concrete, not iron. Also on top are mounts for several 15-inch Rodmans, for which there is no record of ever actually being mounted before the post was abandoned. Just outside the glacis next to the entrance path is an actual 15-inch Rodman, the only period piece at the fort.

Forts of this type had a multilayered array of artillery, with the large Columbiads upstairs typical of those used for long-range defense. Smaller pieces would have been mounted in the downstairs curtain wall for close-in defense, and different shot charges would be on hand to handle tasks from setting ships afire to wrecking sails and rigging to stopping close-in charging infantry.

The first full weekend of every month features an extensive living-history program of a typical day in the lives of a Union garrison. First Weekend Union Garrisons take place on Sat and Sun. Don't talk to these folks about anything post–Civil War, as they are quite realistically "in character" and will simply stare at you. A full-garrison encampment of Union troops is held one weekend in May, and a full-Confederate encampment is held the last full weekend in Oct.

All of these encampments show quite effectively how the typical soldier lived and worked. Artillery crews are usually on hand at these times and demonstrate the firing of a replica 3-inch ordnance rifle. Candlelight tours of the post are scheduled periodically, usually the first Sat evening of the month, with the exception of Dec; check with the visitor center for dates and details.

The surrounding state park is very interesting and enjoyable in its own right, featuring shelling, hiking trails, beaches, very nice bicycle paths, and picnicking and camping sites. Nature trails wind through a coastal hammock, where a wide variety of wildlife from egrets to alligators thrives. Call ahead for prices, hours, and closures.

OTHER POINTS OF INTEREST

Amelia Island/Fernandina Beach and Jacksonville

AIFBY Chamber of Commerce and Welcome Center
961687 Gateway Blvd., Suite 101 G
(at SR A1A and Amelia Island Railway)
Amelia Island, FL
(904) 261-3248
www.aifby.com

For a complete list of local businesses, contact the friendly people at the Amelia Island-Fernandina Beach-Yulee Chamber of Commerce, housed in the old railroad station at the end of the "main drag" near the shrimp-boat docks.

Two Web sites give a good overview of businesses and attractions: Amelia Now at www.amelianow.com and Amelia Island Destinations at www.ameliaisland.com.

Amelia Island Museum of History
233 S. Third St.
Fernandina Beach, FL
(904) 261-7378
www.ameliamuseum.org

"Florida's Only Oral History Museum" is an exceptional experience. The museum covers the history of the local area from the time of Timucuan Indians through the French, Spanish, English, and American periods, climaxing with Amelia Island's "golden age" in the late 19th century. Walking and docent-led tours are scheduled regularly each day. A guided Eight Flags Tour of various sites is scheduled each day too. A popular Ghost Walking Tour meets at St. Peter's Episopal Church, 801 Atlantic Ave., every Fri. Ghost Walks last for one hour. Tickets may be purchased online. Special tours for groups of four or more are available as well. The museum offers a well-stocked research facility containing local publications and documents on the second floor.

Fort Caroline National Monument
12713 Fort Caroline Rd.
Jacksonville, FL
(904) 641-7155
www.nps.gov/foca

The largest city in the United States (in area if not in population) has its own Civil War history, unfortunately nearly completely obscured by urban sprawl. Taken and occupied

a total of four times during the war by Union troops, both sides recognized that Jacksonville represented both a valuable protected port and a gateway into the northeastern interior of the state.

Fort Caroline is a rare reminder of the past here, consisting of a two-thirds-scale reconstruction of a fort built by French Huguenots in 1562, approximately at this site. Somewhere along the river bluffs nearby stood a reinforced Confederate artillery battery under the command of Lieutenant Colonel Charles F. Hopkins; the exact location could not be precisely located by any source we consulted.

On September 30, 1862, 1,500 troops under the command of Brigadier General John M. Brannon departed Hilton Head Island, South Carolina, with orders to challenge this battery and other Confederate defenses and to free the approach to Jacksonville on the St. Johns River. On October 1, now joined by six naval gunboats led by Commander Charles Steedman, Brannon's men began disembarking at Mayport Mills, about 5 miles to the rear of the Confederate emplacement. As the Union infantry approached overland and the gunboats sailed downriver to catch him in a two-pronged assault, Hopkins abandoned his position as untenable. This battery never came under fire or fired its guns in combat.

Fort Caroline itself is an interesting park, with a large area of pristine wilderness along the river, shell mounds left by the original inhabitants, a small but nice visitor center with videos and publications on area wildlife, and guided tours of the fort and nature preserve on Saturday. Admission is free. Pets are allowed in outdoor areas as long as they are on a 6-foot leash. The park service recommends calling or visiting the Web site before visiting as closures from flooding or construction can occur at any time.

Kingsley Plantation
11676 Palmetto Ave.
Jacksonsville, FL
(904) 251-3537
www.nps.gov/timu/historyculture/kp.htm

Just south of Amelia Island, on Fort King George Island north of the Mayport ferry dock, stands one of the oldest antebellum structures in the state. The plantation house is currently closed for structural work, but visitors can explore the grounds, which include the kitchen house, barn, slave quarters, waterfront, and part of one of the original gardens.

Zephaniah Kingsley purchased and began construction of the large plantation in 1814, which still exists today in nearly unchanged form. While not specifically related to the war, the exhibits and ranger-guided tours give an unblinking view of what life was really like on Southern plantations; it rarely resembled Tara of *Gone with the Wind* fame.

Slave quarters are tiny and resemble jail cells more than residences—mute testimony to the plantation owner's treatment of those who toiled in his cotton, sugarcane, and cornfields. Twenty-three of these cabins remain.

Kingsley Plantation is owned and operated by the National Park Service. A tour includes the kitchen house, barn, and the ruins of 25 of the original slave cabins. A bookstore is located at the visitor center. Admission is free, but donations are accepted. NOTE: Some historic buildings may be closed occasionally for ongoing structural work, but the park and grounds will remain open daily. Call ahead for more information.

ACCOMMODATIONS

Amelia Island/Fernandina Beach is a decidedly unusual mixture of upscale vacation destinations with overtones of shrimping, timber, and paper-mill industries. Two very high-end resorts grace the south end of the island: the Ritz-Carlton Resort and the Amelia Island Plantation. Several very nice bed-and-breakfast inns dot the old town, and there is ample boutique shopping available for long-suffering "Civil War widows."

Amelia Hotel at the Beach $$$
1997 S. Fletcher Ave.
Amelia Island, FL
(904) 206-5200
www.ameliahotel.com

This family-owned, ocean-view hotel is great for family or business travelers. The rates are reasonable for the location and all rooms have a mini-fridge and microwave and complimentary HBO and Wi-Fi access. Rooms are luxurious and spacious. The hotel is close to the historic downtown.

Ritz-Carlton Resort–Amelia Island $$$$
4750 Amelia Island Pkwy.
Amelia Island, FL
(904) 277-1100
(800) 241-3333
www.ritzcarlton.com

This Ritz-Carlton has everything you could possibly want in a resort, and then some. Each of the 444 rooms and suites has its own private balcony; twice each day the rooms are cleaned and primped; there is 24-hour room service, 1½ miles of exclusive beachfront, and the overall quality of impeccable service that is a Ritz-Carlton trait.

Four restaurants on the premises serve nearly anything you desire, from afternoon tea to cocktails and cigars to macrobiotic cuisine to multicourse gourmet meals. To work off all this, there are nine tennis courts, an 18-hole golf course, a well-appointed fitness center with steam and sauna, an indoor lap pool and whirlpool, an outdoor pool and whirlpool, and our personal favorites, plush terry robes and really comfortable chairs.

RESTAURANTS

Brett's Waterway Cafe $$–$$$
Fernandina Harbor Marina
1 S. Front St.
Fernandina Beach
Amelia Island, FL
(904) 261-2660
www.brettswaterwaycafe.com

This dockside restaurant is surprisingly upscale, given the sometimes grubby shrimp-boat dock alongside. Just

across the railroad tracks from the visitor center at the very end of Centre Street, Brett's offers a good selection of fresh Florida seafood, steaks, chicken, and an interesting assortment of specials.

The food here is very good, the prices (for this area) are quite reasonable, and the waitstaff is attentive and friendly, but the overall atmosphere is dampened a bit by some frosty greetings we witnessed and received. Be forewarned: They are quite serious about "casual resort wear" being expected of patrons. Reservations are accepted for parties of six or more.

St. Augustine

St. Augustine is in northeastern Florida, about 35 miles south of Jacksonville and 10 miles east of I-95. The easiest route into the historic part of town is via FL 16 off I-95 (exit 318); go east about 11 miles to where FL 16 ends at San Marco Avenue (not US 1), turn right, and the old city gate is about a mile down the road. For a more scenic route, take SR A1A down from Amelia Island; it is a long trip but well worth it for the view and salt air. Be careful not to miss the sharp turn into the parking lot at the Mayport Ferry, where SR A1A goes over the water, or you'll end up in one of the most confusing urban interstate highway tangles we have ever seen.

St. Augustine has regained its prewar reputation as a premier tourist attraction with a vengeance; on warm summer afternoons it can be hard to get through the throngs on St. George Street and San Marco Avenue. This is an incredibly pleasant place and one of our favorite destinations, even if its very real and important Civil War history is downplayed in favor of the rather longer Spanish era. Most sights and attractions are within walking distance of one another in the downtown area, which is bisected by the pedestrian-only St. George Street.

The historic zone roughly outlines the Civil War–era city limits, running from the old city gate on Orange Street, across from the old Spanish fort, east to the Matanzas Bay seawall, south to St. Francis Street, and west to the San Sebastian River. Most modern shops and conveniences are just to the west of this area, running north and south along US 1. Just south and east on SR A1A over the Bridge of Lions (named for the two white marble lion statues guarding the prominent 1926 Mediterranean Revival–style drawbridge over Matanzas Bay) are Anastasia Island and St. Augustine Beach, one of the cleanest, nicest, and least-crowded beach towns in all Florida.

Contact the St. Augustine Visitor Information Center before you travel and ask them to send you their large packet of information on local attractions, restaurants, motels, shops, and events (904-825-1000). As soon as you arrive in town, go by the center at 10 Castillo Dr., across the street from the Ripley's Believe It or Not! Museum and just up the street from the Castillo de San Marcos. This is one of the best-put-together visitor centers we've seen, with a nicely designed building, small museum, film on the history of the city, gift shop, and literally thousands of booklets, brochures, and maps free for the asking. Behind the center is a large parking lot that is relatively easy to get into and out of.

POINTS OF INTEREST

Castillo de San Marcos National Monument
1 S. Castillo Dr., SR A1A and US 1
St. Augustine, FL
(904) 829-6506
www.nps.gov/casa

Old Fort Marion, relabeled with its Spanish-era name in 1942, is the oldest masonry fort in the United States and the only 17th-century fort still standing in the United States. Replacing nine previous wooden forts dating back to 1565, construction of the large structure began in 1672 and took 27 years to complete. The Castillo is primarily made of an unusual material called coquina, a type of masonry block consisting of a compressed mixture of oyster shells and lime.

There are remnants of nearly every era of the fort's history still visible, and a large number of actual Spanish-era cannon are mounted on the upstairs gun deck. In front of the seawall, next to the ravelin (main entrance) are a number of Florida Territory–era (circa 1842) cannon laid on the ground. Original powder magazines and storerooms under the gun deck have been converted to small museums detailing nearly every aspect of the more-than-300-year-old fort.

Operated by the National Park Service, the fort is open for "wandering," four ranger presentations per day, frequent cannon-firing demonstrations, and self-guided tours every hour starting at 10 a.m. A video is shown every hour in the visitor center. It is 25 minutes long and features cannon- and musket-firing sequences as well as an outline of the Castillo's complex history.

Fort Matanzas National Monument
8635 SR A1A South
St. Augustine, FL
(904) 471-0116
www.nps.gov/foma

Although this 250-year-old structure lacks any Civil War connection, it is still well worth a visit. Fourteen miles south of St. Augustine on SR A1A, the small coquina structure was built to protect the southern approaches of the city at Matanzas Inlet. An unusual feature of the small park is that you must ride across the Matanzas River on a (free) ferry to tour the fort itself. The ferry to the fort leaves the visitor center dock, weather and water conditions permitting, every hour at half past the hour, from 9:30 a.m. to 4:30 p.m. The ferry is first come, first served.

Never used in full-scale combat, the fort is tower-shaped, with a second-floor gun deck containing two original artillery pieces, restored barracks room, and a third-story officers quarters.

A small visitor center contains a handful of artifacts, some good maps and brochures, a short film on the fort's history, and exceptionally friendly rangers. The park is administered by the National Park Service. Admission is free.

Gonzales-Alvarez House
(also called the Oldest House)
14 St. Francis St.
St. Augustine, FL
(904) 824-2872
www.oldesthouse.com

This structure claims, with some justification, to be the oldest house in America, dating from the early 17th century and continuously occupied ever since. The house was a noted tourist attraction even in Civil War times, and there are several documents from the era that complain of Union soldiers damaging the house by picking off pieces of wood and coquina—a masonry block made of oyster shells and lime—as souvenirs. The complex includes Florida's oldest house, two museums, a changing exhibition gallery, an ornamental garden, and a store. Ticket purchases are good for entry to all facilities.

Government House Museum
48 King St.
St. Augustine, FL
(904) 825-5079
www.staugustinegovernment.com

A museum covering almost exclusively the early Spanish and British history of the area, this house was used as the U.S. Provost Guard House during the Union occupation, and the exterior is nearly unchanged in appearance from that time.

ACCOMMODATIONS

St. Augustine is also well blessed with an abundance of decent chain and privately owned motels and bed-and-breakfast establishments. Most of the chain motels are clustered around the Old Town section on both San Marcos Avenue and US 1 just west of the main part of town; a few others are located on St. Augustine Beach. Please note that nearly every establishment charges extremely high rates during "special events," which are not confined to those taking place in St. Augustine itself. Daytona Beach, 60 miles to the south, hosts a series of racing and motorcycle events for several weeks in February and early March each year; unless you are attending these events, we strongly suggest you pick another time to visit this area. We can recommend the following independent establishment.

Inns of Elegance $$$
St. Augustine, FL
www.innsofelegance.com

Choose from this collection of five romantic bed-and-breakfast inns that are located in the heart of the historic district of St. Augustine. They all have a certain standard to follow and each has a history unto itself. Choose from St. Francis Inn, Bayfront Wescott House, Inn on Charlotte Street, Bayfront Marin House, or the supposedly haunted Casablanca Inn.

RESTAURANTS

Beachcomber Restaurant $–$$
2 "A" St.
St. Augustine, FL
(904) 471-3744

This is hands-down our favorite place for breakfast. Perched on a small dune literally on the beach, Beachcomber features a large open deck that hangs out over the sand, where you have salt water, sun, and surfers along with your bacon and eggs. There is a large U-shaped bar as well as tables for those who don't care for alfresco dining. Diners are advised to watch the weather as the indoor seating is very limited. Open now for more than 50 years, Beachcomber offers the standard American breakfast menu and features fresh seafood, fried shrimp, oysters, burgers, and bar-type finger food the rest of the day. A nice selection of domestic and imported beers and wines helps make their deck a popular "locals" attraction in the evenings.

Beachcomber is hidden away in a largely residential beachfront neighborhood and a bit difficult to find. Travel down SR A1A and carefully watch the cross-street signs, which go down in number from north to south. "A" Street is just past First Street, behind the A Street Surf Shop and Sharkey's Shrimp Shack.

Bistro de Leon $$–$$$
12 Cathedral Place
St. Augustine, FL
(904) 810-2100
www.bistrodeleon.com

The three-course lunch is the best way to enjoy the fare from restaurateur Jean-Stephane Poinard, a fifth-generation chef. This cozy cafe makes diners think they are sitting in a cozy French town such as Lyon. Everything is homemade, including the bread, the pastries, and the ice cream.

Kingfish Grill $$
252 Yacht Club Dr.
St. Augustine, FL
(904) 824-2111
www.kingfishgrill.com

Located on the docks of Camachee Cove Marina, this waterfront dining restaurant takes you on a global culinary adventure for lunch or dinner. They offer everything from fine seafood to casual cuisine.

Olustee

Olustee has returned to its prewar status as a sleepy roadside settlement, though the local major industry is staffing two large nearby state prisons instead of farming cotton. The battlefield itself is in a state of remarkably good preservation, kept up primarily for the annual re-enactment that takes place every February, and a Civil War Expo is planned each year in late summer. A mile-long trail has interpretive signs describing the events of the battle. To the rear of the center is a large, striking monument to the Confederate victory at Olustee, flanked by two cannon and two historic markers. There is a small museum, a walking trail, and a picnic area. Admission to the park and all facilities is free.

POINTS OF INTEREST

Natural Bridge Battlefield State Historic Park
7502 Natural Bridge Rd.
Tallahassee, FL
(850) 922-6007
www.floridastateparks.org/naturalbridge

Both the place of the second-largest battle in Florida and the site of the "last gasp" of the Confederacy, Natural Bridge today is a tiny park 15 miles southeast of Tallahassee, about 120 miles west of Olustee.

In early 1865 Tallahassee was the last unoccupied state capital in the Western Theater and a tempting target for overly confident Major General John Newton of the Union Army. From his poorly made topographic maps of the area, Newton convinced himself that it would be a relatively easy task to sail from his base at Key West to the mouth of the St.

Marks River, march quickly overland, and take the capital by surprise.

Joined in his quest by navy commander William Gibson, their flotilla sailed up from the Keys, landing in Apalachee Bay on March 3, 1865. That same day 300 sailors and marines stormed ashore and captured the East River Bridge 4 miles up the St. Marks River and prepared to advance their gunboats upriver toward the Confederate-held capital. Meanwhile, Newton's infantry had landed and was rapidly advancing overland toward Tallahassee.

As Newton attempted to sail upriver the next morning, all his boats ran aground in the shallow, sand-choked water. He was observed by townspeople nearby, and a message was sent to the capital warning of the assault force. A hastily assembled force under Lieutenant Colonel George Scott headed toward the only place to cross the St. Marks River without getting wet, at Natural Bridge, a natural phenomenon where the river runs underground for a short distance.

Scott's force could most charitably be called eccentric. The fewer than 700 men represented recuperating wounded veterans, local militia, home guards, and civilian volunteers from the surrounding counties. From Quincy came a group of some elderly men called the Gadsden Grays, mostly made up of veterans of the Seminole Wars. Rounding out the command were 24 teenagers from West Florida Seminary, ages 14 to 18, each going off to battle with a note of permission from his mother.

Unaware of Gibson's problems downstream and still expecting his gunboats for support, Newton moved rapidly overland toward the river crossing. The 700 men of the 2nd and 99th U.S. Colored Infantry Regiments closed in on the area just before dawn, apparently unaware of any hostile force ahead. Scott's force had arrived just a few hours before, hastily throwing up earth and log breastworks in a crescent shape on the west bank of the natural bridge.

As dawn peeked through the piney woods on March 6, the Union advance guard made contact. A well-aimed volley of fire from the Confederate works both opened the battle and threw the Union infantry back temporarily. All through the rest of the day, the Union tried to crack the Confederate line with a series of both major assaults across the narrow bridge and flanking movements through the surrounding swamplands. All attempts to dislodge the irregular defenders failed, and by nightfall Newton ordered a hurried retreat back to the still-grounded gunboats several miles to the south.

Today, there is only a tiny park with one set of three memorials and two sets of reproduced log breastworks to mark the site of the small but significant battle. An interpretive marker explains the setting of the battle.

To access the site, take I-10 west from Olustee/Lake City to exit 203, turn right on SR 61 and then almost immediately right again onto US 319/Capital Circle Road, and go south about 10 miles to SR 363/Woodville Highway. Travel south about 15 miles to Woodville, and turn left just past the elementary school onto Natural Bridge Road (also called CR 2192). The park is about 6 miles down this very lightly traveled country road. Park hours are 8 a.m. to sunset. Admission goes in an honor box.

Olustee Battlefield State Historic Site
P.O. Box 40
Olustee, FL
(386) 758-0400
www.floridastateparks.org/olusteebattlefield

The Olustee Battlefield is about 45 miles west of Jacksonville and 15 miles east of Lake City in a partially cleared area just north of the railroad tracks. Easy access is via US 90 that runs between Lake City and I-10 just east (and north) of the battlefield. The tiny village of Olustee is about 2 miles west of the battlefield. The occasionally used alternative name for this conflict, Ocean Pond, refers to a fair-size round pond just west of the battlefield.

ACCOMMODATIONS

There are no amenities at Olustee itself, but just about anything you need can be obtained 15 miles west in Lake City. This is a major stopping-off point for the large numbers of tourists headed for Disney World (150 miles to the southeast), so nearly every chain restaurant and motel has a presence here. However, the sheer numbers of tourists passing through tend to fill up the available rooms and seats rapidly, so we would advise you to plan your travel through here during nonpeak seasons (Jan through Apr, except during spring break season, or the fall until just before Christmas). The majority of motels and restaurants can be found on the western side of town, straddling the intersection with I-75.

Pensacola

Pensacola lies at the extreme western end of the Florida panhandle, accessible by I-10 from either Tallahassee or Mobile, Alabama. Most of the sites of interest are situated directly adjacent to Pensacola Bay, which lies at the south and east side of town. The easiest, if not the most direct route, is via I-10 South at exit 12. The major attractions are fairly well marked; to go to Fort Pickens, stay on I-10 until the end (where it becomes US 98 and later SR 399), and follow the signs to Pensacola Beach, finally turning right on Fort Pickens Road. Although there is really only one east-west road on the narrow beach area, the turn is in the middle of a built-up beach town area and is easily missed (it is just beyond the Tourist Information office).

The other significant sites are within Pensacola Naval Air Station. Take SR 295 West off I-110, and travel about 7 miles until you reach the main gate. This route is called Fairfield Drive, Warrington Road, and Navy Boulevard at various times along its length.

Fort Barrancas and Fort Pickens were used for a variety of purposes until the end of World War II. But their only real claim to fame in these later years was that Geronimo and 14 other Apaches were confined at Fort Pickens from October 1886 to May 1888, when they were moved to another post in Alabama. These Native Americans sparked the first tourist boom in the area. Hundreds of sightseers crossed the bay by boat to see the famous Apache chief, and the garrison was briefly reinforced to protect the public from these "dangerous" prisoners.

At the end of the 19th century, during the Spanish-American War era, Fort Pickens was reinforced with modern gun emplacements both inside and alongside the old brick walls. Abandoned again just after the turn of the 20th century, these emplacements saw their last military service as observation and coastal defense stations during WWII.

Fort McRee guarded the western end of the entrance to Pensacola Bay, on the eastern tip of Perdido Key. It was of a very unusual design, resembling a long, slightly bent aircraft wing with rounded ends, possibly the only one of this design ever built. Walls 35 feet high, 150 feet wide, and 450 feet long faced the ship channel, with mounts for 128 cannon in two tiers. The entire fort was surrounded by a dry moat 60 feet wide with a 3-foot glacis just outside it. The fort was originally planned to hold up to 500 soldiers. Construction began in 1840 and took three years to complete, using some 15 million bricks in the process. Unfortunately, no trace of this post remains. Having been battered by wind and wave for many years, the old walls finally crumbled away in the hurricane of 1906.

Today Fort McRee is completely gone, lacking even a historic marker to indicate where it stood, but Forts Pickens and Barrancas were restored and opened for touring by the National Park Service. Fort Pickens, however, sustained a lot of damage from hurricanes Ivan, Dennis, and Katrina. Hours vary by season. Self-guided tours are available during the week and ranger-guided tours on the weekend. Just inside the main fort entrance is the visitor center. In the clump of green-and-white buildings near the fishing pier, you'll find the Fort Pickens Museum (same hours as the fort) and the Fort Pickens Auditorium, which shows a movie or provides some kind of program on the fort, island, weather, local history, marine life, or the like at scheduled times during the year. There is an entry fee to the fort, which is valid for only seven days. The old fort is easy to locate: Go west on the only east-west road on Pensacola Beach, Fort Pickens Road, about 8 miles west of its intersection with SR 399/Pensacola Beach Road.

Fort Pickens (www.nps.gov/guis/planyourvisit/fort-pickens.htm; 850-934-2600), part of the Gulf Islands National Seashore, lies at the far end of a rather sizable National Park Service natural preservation area, about a 4-mile drive from the commercial zone of Pensacola Beach. This area was used for defensive fortifications from 1829 until the mid-1940s and still houses a number of fortification emplacements, batteries, and command and control bunkers dating from different war eras during these years. Fort Pickens itself is a low-ranging, two-story masonry fort oriented northeast-southwest; a number of WWII–era buildings used by the Park Service are arrayed on the Pensacola Bay side. Call (850) 934-2600 for hours and guided tour times. Outside the visitor center, a ranger does a program on artillery.

The 65 acres surrounding the forts contain oak and pine forests, a picnic area, and a nature trail. Fort Barrancas is on the grounds of Pensacola Naval Air

Tribute to a Major General

'Tis old Stonewall the Rebel that leans on his sword,
And while we are mounting prays low to the Lord:
"Now each cavalier that loves honor and right,
Let him follow the feather of Stuart tonight."

CHORUS: Come tighten your girth and slacken your rein;
Come buckle your blanket and holster again;
Try the click of your trigger and balance your blade,
For he must ride sure that goes riding a raid.

Now gallop, now gallop to swim or to ford!
Old Stonewall, still watching, prays low to the Lord:
"Good-bye, dear old Rebel! The river's not wide,
And Maryland's lights in her window to guide." (CHORUS)

There's a man in the White House with blood on his mouth!
If there's knaves in the North, there are braves in the South.
We are three thousand horses, and not one afraid;
We are three thousand sabres and not a dull blade. (CHORUS)

Then gallop, then gallop by ravines and rock!
Who would bar us the way take his toll in hard knocks;
For with these points of steel, on the line of the Penn
We have made some fine strokes—and we'll make 'em again. (CHORUS)

—A tribute song to Major General James Ewell Brown Stuart of the Confederate Army, sung to the tune of the old Scottish air, "Bonnie Dundee."

Station and is free to the public. The fort was constructed between 1829 and 1859, along with three other masonry forts surrounding Pensacola Bay. This large masonry and earthwork post stands on the site occupied by two previous forts, built by the English and Spanish beginning in 1763. The name is a reflection of this heritage, recalling the original post title of San Carlos de Barrancas. Six million bricks are in the surprisingly small structure, built primarily by slave labor contracted from New Orleans. The 300- by 330-foot structure contained mounts for 8 large howitzers and 33 smaller artillery pieces, but on the eve of hostilities in 1861 it actually contained 13 8-inch Columbiads, 2 10-inch mortars, and 24 smaller cannon. Hours vary by season. Fort tours last for 45 minutes. Visitors interested in the tour should meet at the fort at the Pensacola Naval Air Station. A 12-minute video about Fort Barrancas is shown daily.

POINTS OF INTEREST

Civil War Soldiers Museum
108 S. Palafox Place
Pensacola, FL
(850) 469-1900
www.cwmuseum.org

This gem of a museum is a perfect example of why you should not judge a museum by its entrance. What looks like a fairly unassuming storefront in the Pensacola historic district opens up to reveal a wonderfully presented, 4,200-square-foot facility with professional-quality displays and mountings. Based around the extensive collection of local gastroenterologist Dr. Norman W. Haines Jr., the collection (naturally) has a distinct leaning toward the rarely seen medical aspects of the war.

The museum chronicles every facet of the war to one degree or another, with a special emphasis on letters, diaries, quotes, and photographs to bring a human element to the four years of suffering. The whole period of struggle is documented by paintings, photos, and artifacts from John Brown and Frederick Douglass to the last Civil War veteran. The Pensacola Room records the significant people and events of the immediate area and includes a 23-minute video presentation, *Pensacola and the Civil War*.

One side of the two-room display is devoted entirely to medical equipment and procedures—primitive surgical equipment, early attempts at field anesthesia (including a minié ball with teeth marks!), amputations, and many photographs of the results.

Although relatively small, this fine museum is well worth a few hours' visit and includes a small bookstore, which (thankfully!) avoids the usual tacky "Rebel" souvenirs in favor of quite a nice selection of more than 700 related titles. We admit we have a weakness for locally produced history books and pamphlets, and this bookstore had a very nice selection. We cannot emphasize enough how highly we recommend this small museum; it is in itself worth a trip to Pensacola.

Pensacola Convention and Visitor Information Center
1401 E. Gregory St.
Pensacola, FL
(850) 434-1234
(800) 874-1234
www.visitpensacola.com

This very nicely laid-out and managed visitor center at the base of Pensacola Bay Bridge (on the mainland side) should be your first stop. The staff is exceptionally friendly and helpful, and there are literally thousands of maps, flyers, newspapers, and brochures on area attractions, amenities, and services.

ACCOMMODATIONS

Holiday Inn Express Pensacola Beach $$$–$$$$
333 Fort Pickens Rd.
Pensacola, FL
(850) 932-3536
(888) 465-4329
www.holidayinn.com

Formerly the Dunes, this Gulf-front hotel offers a free hot breakfast daily, clean rooms, a health/fitness center and an outdoor pool, and free high-speed Internet access.

The Pensacola area is always popular with visitors, but mainly during the summer months when school is out. If you plan on visiting the area during that time, make reservations well in advance. Don't just limit yourself to Pensacola proper. Fort Walton and Santa Rosa Island, as well as Destin, are all within driving distance and offer numerous lodging and dining choices. For more information see www.visitpensacola.com.

RESTAURANTS

McGuire's Irish Pub
600 E. Gregory St.
Pensacola, FL
(850) 433-6789
www.mcguiresirishpub.com

$$–$$$

This award-winning restaurant, established in 1977, serves steak, seafood, burgers, and Irish food. They serve generous portions in a fun atmosphere. Ales, porters, and stouts are brewed on the premises in their traditional oak and copper brewery. Enjoy live Irish entertainment while you eat. McGuire's is open seven days a week. Lunch and dinner are served and a kids menu is available.

Glossary

The Civil War, and the military in general, produced such a set of specialized terminology and phrases that it almost constitutes a separate language. While we attempted to write this book in as clear and ordinary a style as possible, on many occasions there was simply no way to avoid the use of specialized terms. Here is a selection of terms used in the book.

Abatis or abattis: A defensive "wall" made of cut trees, usually arrayed in a thick, interconnected tangle, which would not completely stop a charging enemy attack but would slow it, giving the defenders additional time to bring heavy fire to bear on the points affected.

Amphibious: An attack launched from transports at sea or on a river; implies a coordinated army-navy attack, although this was not always the case.

Assault: A concentrated attack on a specific target or area; implies the maximum use of force that will fit into a given quadrant of the battlefield. It also implies an all-out attack that does not stop until the objective is taken or the attacking force is destroyed, but the term is used frequently as a synonym for any attack.

Battle flag: The flag used by each regiment on both sides for unit identification and signaling. Most battles during this period tended to break down into mass chaos and confusion unless the commander kept firm control of his men, and the battlefield was far too noisy to hear a spoken order or even a bugle call. Soldiers were trained to recognize their regimental flag and to always follow it wherever it went. The flag bearer was given both a high honor and a great responsibility: He had to stay right by his commander at all times, he was usually not armed, and he could not break and run no matter how bad the situation was, as his whole regiment would then follow him to the rear. The casualty rate among flag bearers was appalling.

Bayonet: A long spike or thick knife blade with mountings to attach to the muzzle end of a rifle, enabling the soldier to stab his enemy at more than an arm's length away. Both the Enfield and Springfield bayonets were 18 inches long and triangular in section, which would cause a ghastly wound that usually would not heal properly and frequently caused a fatal infection in those who lived through the initial event. The "spirit of the bayonet" is a hallowed tradition for even modern infantrymen, although its use in battle has been greatly exaggerated. Most "hand-to-hand" combat actually involved the use of the butt end of the rifle, swung like a club, or even just fists, rocks, and heavy sticks. The bayonet-equipped rifle is a lethal and intimidating-looking weapon, but it took great skill and discipline to effectively employ it in the heat of combat. Soldiers usually used their issued bayonets for other purposes, as skewers to cook their meat or rammed into trees or walls to serve as coat hooks. Quite often they were heated and bent into hook shapes to drag the dead bodies of their comrades off the battlefield.

Blockade: To cut off and isolate a position or area from any resupply or reinforcement. During the Civil War this almost always referred to the Union Navy's blockade of the entire southern Atlantic and Gulf coastlines, preventing most supplies from England and France from coming into the Confederacy.

Blockade-runners: Civil War–era privateers, almost always civilians, who earned huge profits through great risk in sneaking their ships loaded with cargo through the Union Navy's coastal blockade. Although usually from the ranks of the lower classes and ordinary seamen before the war, they were the toast of Southern society as well as a major source of critical supplies for the embattled Southern armies. Northern newspapers universally decried them as the utter scourge of mankind.

Bomb-proof: A heavily reinforced, usually underground structure designed and built to protect the occupants—either civilians in an area under siege or troops in a combat area—from nearby artillery fire. Rarely would these structures protect from a direct hit by a large-caliber weapon.

Break contact: To pull back from a combat engagement, either to retreat or to shift the direction of a given assault. This is sometimes used as a polite way of saying that the men involved simply ran away.

Breastworks: A defensive barricade wall made of whatever materials were immediately available, usually logs, rocks, or fence rails. When placed in front of trench lines, they usually were covered with the excavated earth itself, piled up, and formed into steep-faced walls. By the second year of the war, "spades is trumps" as Private Sam Watkins said, and nearly every time troops on either side stopped for more than a few minutes, their officers would put them to work constructing defensive works. On most battlefields today, these works are the only remaining evidence of the war.

Casements: Refers to the lower areas in a masonry fort where the main artillery is mounted. These are usually some of the strongest parts of the fort's walls, built-up areas of stone or brick surrounding a narrow port or slit through which the cannon would fire.

Casualties: The losses for a unit, including deaths, injuries, captured or "missing" (usually from desertion), as well as losses from sickness or disease, by far the biggest killer of all during the war. On occasion the reports include losses resulting from discharge.

Chevaux-de-frise: Somewhat like an early version of barbed wire, these barricades were in effect and construction very similar to abatis, with the exception of being somewhat portable. These were constructed by taking a log or (more rarely) a piece of iron post 9 to 15 feet long, drilling holes through it every 6 to 12 inches and through both angles, and inserting sharpened stakes about 4 to 6 feet long through the post. From an end view they looked like a crude cross, while from a frontal view they vaguely resembled a large version of an aerator used today on lawns. Many of these would be constructed and placed in front of other static defenses, sometimes fastened together, and always in the direct line of fire from the defenders. Although they could be moved by a squad or less of men, they slowed down infantry attacks long enough to provide an effective "kill zone" where they were placed.

Color bearer: The man assigned to carry the colors of the regiment. As the flag was usually large and unwieldy, he would most usually be unarmed, and as the rest of the regiment followed his actions to the letter (at least in theory), he must be a very brave and trustworthy man, unlikely to bolt and run from the battlefield. He would always be found standing very close to the regimental commander. Casualties were very high among color bearers; at Shiloh six color bearers from three Wisconsin regiments were all shot and killed in the first few hours of battle on the first day.

Colors: The distinctive flag unique to each regiment. As most of the soldiers of this time were illiterate, and the smoke and noise of battle precluded effective use of shouted orders, the men were taught to recognize their own colors (in a formal ceremony, still done in today's army, called "parading the colors") and to follow them wherever they went on the battlefield.

Column: A road march formation of troops, usually in company or regimental order and as long as 3 to 9 miles. When these columns were ambushed or otherwise surprised by an enemy force, it took quite some time to get the force arrayed into a combat formation, allowing plenty of time for "hit and run" attacks to succeed in delaying the column and inflicting casualties with relatively little risk to the attacker.

Counterattack: To aggressively assault an attacking force, to try to turn the momentum from the offensive to the defensive side.

Deploy: To move into either an offensive assault formation or to man defensive positions. Occasionally used to indicate simply being sent somewhere.

Doctrine: The established way of doing a particular mission or task; doing it "by the book." Most of both the Confederate and Union general officer staffs had trained at West Point, and early in the war it was clear who had done their homework better, as tactics and strategies used were nearly identical. Later in the war the doctrine of the Confederate armies was to maintain their forces intact even at the cost of positions and territory, while Union doctrine was to bring the heaviest mass possible of men and supplies into every given situation.

Earthwork/sand-work: A fort with outer defense walls made from earth or sand rather than some sort of masonry. Ironically, although these forts were made of local materials due to supply or cost problems, they turned out to be much better at handling incoming artillery fire than the massive, expensive masonry forts.

En barbette: Guns or cannon mounted on a low platform on the top floor of a fort, able then to fire over the top of the parapet without any firing slit or cutout needed. This was a very exposed and dangerous position for the artillerymen.

Enfilade: Attacking an enemy force from a sharp angle, the side, or the rear. This usually implies the direction of fire, rather than an assault or such action.

Envelopment: To attack the sides and/or rear at the same time, usually requiring a high level of command coordination. Many well-planned attacks of this nature turned into disasters when the attack went in piecemeal, allowing the defenders to concentrate their forces as needed rather than spread them out to face multiple attacks.

Flanks: The sides or rear of a formation or position, usually one of the weakest points for an attacker to hit given the "line of battle" tactics of the day. The emphasis throughout most of the war was for an attacking force to maneuver into a position where they could hit the enemy's flanks; Grant and Lee in Virginia and Sherman and Johnston in Georgia provided classic examples of this.

Fleet: A group of warships and/or transports under a single commander, usually detailed for a general mission or task. A "flotilla" is generally a smaller grouping of the same sort, used for a single specific action or task.

Garrison: The body of troops assigned to a single fixed position, usually for a prolonged length of time and normally used only for guard duty or action from that one position. Just as the war began, many U.S. forts along the Atlantic and Gulf coasts in the South had a garrison of just one man (an ordnance sergeant), while by the fall of 1864 Atlanta had a Union Army garrison consisting of a full corps.

Gun deck: On a ship, the main deck where cannon or guns are mounted; in a fixed fortification, any of the positions where artillery is mounted.

Ironclads: Special warships armored with iron plating, usually enough to deflect both rifle and smaller cannon fire. Early in the war these were just standard wooden naval vessels hastily outfitted with crude armor, but by the second year of the war, ships were being designed from the hull up to be steam-powered armored warships. The USS *Monitor* is the most familiar example of this genre, a low-freeboard hull mounting a single movable turret housing two large guns.

Lunette: A special type of earthwork fort consisting of an angled, L-shaped wall, with the rear completely exposed. These were used primarily as outlying artillery positions.

Militia: Prewar local defense groups organized originally in colonial days for protection from Indian attacks. Later used as the core of the Continental Army and organized extensively in the South after the Revolutionary War to guard against slave insurrections. As the United States had only a tiny "professional" standing army well into the 20th century, the militias were relied upon to provide a trained cadre of fighting men that could be called up quickly in times of war (this is the "well-regulated militia" spoken of in the Second Amendment to the Constitution). By the 1840s the militias had become a sort of social culture, with many units dressing in all sorts of outlandish uniforms and drilling primarily for show in parades and such. These militias were quickly absorbed into the regular Union and Confederate armies after the start of the war and their stylish uniforms soon packed away.

Palisade: The steep outer walls of an earthwork or masonry fort.

Parapets: A low wall or fence along the top of a fort's ramparts, to provide some protection for the gunners manning en barbette positions. It now serves in existing forts to help keep the tourists from falling off the upper gun decks and ramparts.

Picket: A guard or sentry for either a fixed position or mobile force, these were usually placed well outside friendly lines or the head of the column, where they could best look for or hear any enemy movement. They were almost always the first to fight in any engagement and suffered appallingly high casualties. This duty would usually rotate from company to company in a regiment. During times of battle, they would work in conjunction with skirmishers and vedettes.

Quick-time: To walk in step at 120 steps per minute—the standard pace for infantry on the march. "Double-quick time" is 180 steps per minute, which means you are moving at a sort of jog, but still in step with the men around you in a formation. "Charge" means to run flat out at whatever lies ahead; obviously, calling for a faster pace or to run should only be done when nearly in contact with the enemy, as otherwise you have a bunch of worn-out infantrymen able to do little but gasp for breath.

Rampart: The top of a position's palisade, usually flattened so that artillery may be mounted and men may move about for guard and combat duties. To "take the ramparts" means the position has been breached by an enemy force that now holds the high ground and thus the tactical advantage.

Redoubt: Another term for a reinforced protective shelter, usually made of logs covered with earthwork, but implies that this is a fighting position as well, as opposed to the bomb-proof, which implies simply a hideout or isolated shelter. This term is also used frequently as a reference to any defensive trench work or earthwork.

Refuse: A line of battle or wall of fortifications that is angled sharply back from the main enemy advance or attack. This helps prevent the enemy force from attacking the flank of a formation or position.

Reinforcements: Troops brought into the battle either from an already-established reserve force or from other commands moved into the area.

Reserve: Troops kept back away from the main battle area to use to exploit any breach in the opponent's line, to replace casualties in the main battle force, or to use as the last line of defense. The rule of thumb is 2:1, keeping two parts of your command on the line of battle and one back as a reserve. There were some Civil War commanders who prided themselves on never using their reserves, no matter the situation, and others who would plug them in at the slightest sign of trouble.

Salient: A part of a defensive line or fortification that juts out from the rest of the line toward the enemy. Before the war this was taught to be something desirable, as it would naturally break up any enemy line of attack (and in theory allow the defender to fire straight into the flanks of an attacker on either side), but during the war most attacks focused on this feature to the distress of the defender. The "Dead Angle" at Cheatham's Hill (Kennesaw Mountain Campaign in Georgia, 1864) is an excellent example of what can go wrong with a feature in the line of this sort.

Sapper or Sappier: A specially assigned soldier, charged with the construction of mines and associated structures, usually aimed at the destruction of an enemy's works.

"See the elephant": An expression used to refer to engaging in combat. A soldier who has just lived through his first battle has "seen the elephant." While it is debatable (and fiercely argued over in some circles) where this expression came from, the most plausible explanation is that it refers to the circus. During a time when the vast majority of the population was cloistered on farms,

rarely going more than 20 miles from home in their entire lifetime, seeing the exotic animals in a circus was one of the highlights of their lives.

Shrapnel: Listed under Artillery section (see p. 434).

Siege: To surround and cut off an enemy position from resupply or reinforcement and then "starve them out." The earliest known military histories (Homer's *The Iliad,* for one) mention this kind of warfare, which is brutally effective if one is facing an enemy position without hope of a strong relief effort and if one is very patient. During the Civil War a siege was usually accompanied by bombardment from heavy artillery manufactured and brought in for this specific situation. Vicksburg, Atlanta, and Petersburg are the three most often-cited examples of this during the war.

Skirmishers: Troops, usually of company strength or less, assigned to protect the head and flanks of a main battle formation. These infantrymen fought very much as modern infantrymen do, using cover, concealment, and individual maneuvers to "pick away" as much as possible from the main enemy force before withdrawing into their own lines. During times of battle, they would work in conjunction with pickets.

Squadron: A naval formation, usually consisting mostly of gunboats and other armed vessels, and usually assigned to a given geographic area. Sometimes used as an alternative term for fleets or flotillas.

Staging bases: Main bases usually well removed from the battle areas where men and supplies are funneled out to the necessary commands. This is where the main supply depots would be located, as well as training camps for the men.

Strategy: The overall plan for conducting the war, or even just a single battle. A good example is the "Anaconda Plan," the grand overall plan for conducting the war against the Confederacy. Army commands and above would deal with plans on this level, leaving the specifics of exactly how to carry out these objectives to the lower commands.

Tactics: The specifics of how a particular strategy will be carried out on the battlefield. For example, Sherman's strategy was to drive southeast from Chattanooga and take Atlanta, but his tactical plans included details on which specific commands would move where and when. There are some sources in military science and theory circles that claim a distinction between strategy and tactics is ridiculous, as both talk about more or less the same thing, but we believe it is a useful distinction to mean you are talking about the grand strategies of politicians and top generals versus the battle tactics of field commanders and soldiers.

Theater: The general area of combat or a large area covered by a single command. For example, "theater armies" means all the combatant forces in a given major geographic area. The "theater armies" referred to at Resaca (during the Atlanta Campaign) meant all four armies commanded by Sherman as well as the three corps commanded by Johnston—all the troops they had immediately available to them. A "theater" can also mean something such as the "Western Theater," which included everything in the South from the Carolinas to the Mississippi. This book concentrates on this theater of the war.

Transports: Unarmed ships attached to fleets or flotillas, carrying army troops to use in assaults or amphibious invasions.

Trench work: A line of dug-out ditches, providing both cover and concealment for infantrymen who fought from inside them. Depending on how long the troops had been in their position before being attacked, these could be as crude as a shallow, scratched-out series of "foxholes" or a deep and elaborate series of interconnected ditches, bomb-proofs, and redoubts.

Vanguard: The forward-most elements of a command or column. In modern military parlance, this is the "point element," the troops most vulnerable to a sudden ambush or attack.

Vedette or vidette: A mounted guard or sentry, who otherwise did the same duty as a picket. During times of battle, vedettes would work in conjunction with pickets and skirmishers.

Volley fire: A line of infantry all firing at the same time on command. A central element of the Napoleonic tactics used throughout the war, massed infantry firing volleys was the only way that smoothbore muskets of limited range could gain a real advantage on a fluid battlefield; the infantrymen would form three lines slightly offset one behind another, and each would fire in turn on the order of their officer. By the time the third line fired, the first would be reloaded, so a near-continuous volume of outgoing fire could be maintained so long as the ammunition held out. As Civil War–era rifles had

ranges 3 to 10 times longer than Revolutionary War–era muskets, could be reloaded a bit faster, and had a much more lethal ammunition load, the same close-in volley fire tactics resulted in appalling casualties.

ARTILLERY

Artillery had its own specialized language; the following list is a sampling of the most commonly used terms.

Barrage: To use multiple guns firing on a single target or to saturate an area with as heavy a rate of fire as possible.

Battery: The basic organization of artillery units, which contained four, five, or six guns of single or multiple type, which usually worked together in a combat action. Occasionally batteries were broken up into two-gun sections for use in special circumstances.

Bombardment: The use of artillery to reduce either a military or civilian target to rubble. Atlanta withstood nearly six weeks of a high rate of fire from some of the heaviest guns the Union possessed; some sources claim that it is the "heaviest bombarded" city in North America. Other sources claim the same for Vicksburg, Port Hudson, Charleston, Petersburg, etc.

Caisson: The ammunition wagon and container for an artillery piece. Usually the piece and the caisson were hauled together by a single team of horses, called the caisson team. As these wagons were very sturdily built and had flat tops, they were often used as ambulances and even as hearses. The U.S. Army still uses caissons in formal military funerals; the 3rd Infantry, the "Old Guard" at Arlington National Cemetery, is often seen using caissons to haul the coffins of the honored dead to their final rest.

Canister/grapeshot: A tin can similar to a coffee can filled with either 27 or 48 iron balls, designed to burst open right after it left the muzzle and spray the area in front of the piece like a giant shotgun. Grapeshot is a slight variation that uses nine larger iron balls either sewn together in a cloth sleeve or held together in a light iron frame. The size of these balls varied with the caliber of the gun. This round was useful out to about 300 yards but was more usually employed at much closer range, including at point-blank range. When things were really bleak for the artillery crews, they would load up with "double canister," knocking the powder bag off the rear of the second round and ramming it in on top of the first. This cut the range roughly in half, but doubled the effectiveness up close. This was a deadly weapon to use against closely packed infantry charges and would result in the lines being literally blown apart, creating huge gaps.

Cannon: A generic term for a piece of artillery, not specific as to the type or size.

Columbiad: A very heavy-barreled, smoothbore weapon originally introduced in 1811, which could fire either shot or shell from either flat or high trajectories, giving it the combined characteristics of guns, howitzers, and mortars. For many years these were the backbone weapon of coastline defense, and nearly every coastal fort featured them at the outbreak of war. Early Columbiads could fire a 50-pound solid round shot about 1,800 feet. A variation of this gun, known as a Rodman, was manufactured in a way that created an exceptionally strong barrel, giving the improved guns the ability to fire shells that weighed up to 320 pounds out to nearly 3 miles away.

Counter-battery: To use artillery fire against an enemy artillery position to try to knock their guns out of the fight.

Dahlgren: A very heavy-barreled weapon, very similar in look to a Columbiad. These were used primarily on board naval vessels (the USS *Monitor* mounted two 11-inch Dahlgrens in its turret) and came in both smoothbore and rifled varieties. They were built in sizes ranging from 12-pounders to 150-pounders, as well as 9-inch to 20-inch calibers, with the 15-inch smoothbores being the most popular.

Friction primer: The "match" that was used to set off a cannon. It consisted of two short pieces of copper tubing soldered together at right angles, with one tube filled with mercury fulminate and the other, slightly longer tube filled with gunpowder. After the charge had been loaded and the gunpowder-filled charge bag torn open by a vent prick, the friction primer was inserted into the vent hole, directly over the now-opened charge bag, and attached to a lanyard. The mercury-filled tube had a short, twisted wire inserted that, when pulled out rapidly, created a friction spark with the mercury fulminate. This caused the gunpowder in the other tube to flash and, in turn, caused the pricked charge bag inside the tube to detonate, expelling the round from the tube.

Fuse: A length of flammable cording inside a plug that burned at a known rate and that was used to cause an explosive shell to go off at a given time after firing. A gun crewman cut the fuse to the length (time) desired and then inserted the fuse and plug assembly into a shell before handing it off to be loaded into the piece. The firing of the piece ignited the fuse, and artillery officers were well trained in the mathematics of figuring out exactly when a shell would arrive over a given target at a given range. The advantage of this was the ability to do "air bursts," which spread the lethal shrapnel over a much wider arc than if the shell had hit the ground before bursting.

Gun: A generic term for any artillery piece, although, to be precise, it really refers only to rifled cannon.

Hot-shot: Solid shot heated to red-hot in special ovens and then quickly loaded and fired at flammable targets: ships and their rigging, wagons and caissons, wooden palisades, abatis, etc.

Lanyard: A 12-foot-long rope with a wooden handle on one end and a hook on the other that was attached to a small loop in the wire of a friction primer. Used to fire the artillery piece.

Mortar: A short, very heavy-barreled artillery piece that used exceptionally heavy powder charges in order to loft solid shot or shell nearly vertically. These were extremely useful in lobbing charges over a walled enemy position or trench work that was resistant to direct fire.

Parrott rifle: A rifled, muzzle-loading cannon, ranging in size from a 3-inch (or 10-pounder) to a 10-inch (300-pounder). These are some of the easiest cannons to identify, having a thick band attached around the rear of the barrel, used to help withstand the tremendous pressures rifled cannons build up during firing. These rifled guns fired oblong "bolts," cucumber-shaped solid shot and explosive shells, that had brass rings attached to the base that "grabbed" the rifling during firing. Many accounts of soldiers on the wrong end of Parrott rifles firing talk about the particular "whiffling" shrill noise these bolts made when flying overhead. A deadly accurate weapon found in both armies in every theater of the war.

Piece: Another generic term for a cannon, although usually used to indicate a specific or singular gun.

Shell: A hollow round filled with gunpowder, which would burst either from striking a target or by the action of a timed fuse.

Shot: Solid round balls or oblong "bolts," usually used against masonry structures or other such heavy, solid objects. However, cannoneers had absolutely no qualms about using solid shot against infantry formations; one of author John McKay's great-grandfathers lost a leg to just such a round at South Mountain, Maryland.

Shrapnel: Red-hot, jagged bits of metal flying about at high rates of speed, produced by the exploding casing of a bursting shell. A shell bursting in the air above an infantry formation could produce many times the casualties of a solid shot blasting through the line.

Spike: To render a cannon unable to fire, usually by driving a soft iron nail through the vent hole and cutting off the protruding end. This would be done, if possible, when an enemy force was about to overrun an artillery position and the guns could not be withdrawn. There were frequent occasions, especially late in the war, when Union gunners simply shot all their caisson horses when on the verge of being overrun and left the guns intact, knowing that the Confederates would lack the horses needed to take the guns when they retreated. Then the Union gunners could simply move back in and resume their firing with little fuss.

Trails: The rear "legs" of the gun carriage, which had a short pole (called a trail handspike) attached for ease of aiming by moving the gun left and right. This is also where the cannon was attached to the rear of the caisson, being hauled tube pointed backward.

Tube: Sometimes used as a generic term for cannon, it is the heavy iron or bronze casting that is the barrel of the gun. It is attached to the gun carriage by means of two trunnions cast on either side, near the barrel's center of gravity, and raised up and down by means of various attachments to the knob and neck cast on the rear of the barrel.

Index

Second St., 115
Secret Six Tavern, 23
Selma (AL), 358–60
Selma (AL), Battle of, 350
Seven Days' Battle Sites, 112
1789 (country inn), 81
Sharpsburg (VA)/Monocacy (MD), xii–12
    accommodations, 10–11
    Battle of Antietam, 1–4
    Battle of Ball's Bluff, 6–8
    Battle of Monocacy, 4–6
    historic sites, 8–10
    restaurants, 11–12
Shenandoah Valley/Skyline Drive, 30
Shepherdstown (WV), 6–8
Sheraton-Raleigh Hotel, 163
Sheridan, Philip, 14, 17, 18, 27–29, 98, 126, 241, 242
Sherman, William Tecumseh
    advance through North Carolina, 152–55
    Atlanta campaign. See Atlanta (GA); Dalton to Jonesboro (GA) Atlanta campaign
    Atlanta citizen controversy, 303–4
    Battle of Allatoona Pass and, 190–91, 305–6
    Battle of Jackson and, 374
    biographical sketch, 227–28
    on burning of Atlanta, 307–8
    Chattanooga and. See Chattanooga (TN), Battle of
    Chickasaw Bluff and, 368–70
    end for Charleston and, 180
    Hood marching northward and, 188, 190, 192–94, 303, 306–7
    Johnston and, 247
    last of Army of Tennessee and, 151
    March to the Sea. See Atlanta to Savannah (GA) March to the Sea
    monument, 75
    moving south from Atlanta, 192–93, 306–7
    perspective on war, 349
    photographs, 270, 318
    presenting Savannah to Lincoln, 318
    reputation of, 312
    Shiloh and. See Shiloh (TN), Battle of
    Vicksburg attack, 378, 379, 380
Sherman's "great raid," 289–90
Shields Tavern, 115
Shillings on the Square, 300
Shiloh (TN)
    accommodations, 231
    getting to, 229–30
    points of interest, 230–31
    restaurants, 231
Shiloh (TN), Battle of, 216–31
    April 5, 1862 (night before battle), 220–21

April 6, 1862 (first day), 221–26
April 6–7, 1862 (night), 226–28
April 7, 1862 (second day), 228–30
Bloody Pond, 224–25, 260
Bragg's assault, 222
buildup, 219–21
change of Confederate command, 224
Confederate advance, 220
Confederate defense and retreat, 229–30
Confederate situation going into, 217
deployment of Union forces, 219–20
first night, 226–28
ghost stories, 260
Grant's last line of defense, 225
gunboat support, 217, 219, 225, 226, 228
Hardee's assault, 222
Hornets' Nest, 223, 225
last charge of April 6, 225–26
Peach Orchard, 223–24
photographs, 219, 221
plan, illustrated, 218
second Union line, 222–23
Union complacency, 220
Union situation going into, 217
Shiloh National Military Park, 230–31
Shriver House Museum, 42
Sidewalk Café, 122–23
Siege Museum, 128
Sigel, Franz, 25–26, 98
Signal Hill, 56
Smith, Andrew Jackson, 370
Smith, Charles Ferguson, 217, 219–20, 248, 251
Smith, Giles A., 286, 287
Smith, Gustavus, 282, 308, 310–11
Smith, Martin Luther, 369, 376
Snodgrass Hill (GA), 265–66
Soldier's National Museum, 42
Soniat House, 399
Sonny's Waterfront Restaurant, 166
Sope Creek (GA), 296
South Carolina, 168–86
    accommodations, 185
    background to war in, 169–70
    54th Massachusetts Infantry Regiment and, 178–80
    Morris Island attack, 177–78
    points of interest, 181–84
    restaurants, 185–86
    secession of, 169–70
    See also Charleston (SC); Fort Sumter; Secessionville (SC)
South Court Inn Bed & Breakfast, 32
South Mountain State Battlefield, 10–11
Southern Kitchen, 33
Southern Museum of Civil War and Locomotive History, 296
Southside 815, 91

Spanish Fort, 341–44
Spanky's Pizza Gallery & Saloon, 323
Spices Asian Restaurant & Sushi Bar, 81
Spotsylvania County Museum, 103
Spotsylvania Court House, 103
Spotsylvania Court House (VA), Battle of, 100–101. See also Fredericksburg/Spotsylvania (VA)
Spring Grove Farm Bed and Breakfast, 134
Spring Hill (TN), 194
St. Augustine (FL), 406–9, 420–22
St. Mary's Church, 87–88
Stafford House, 89
Stanton, Edwin M., 38, 71
Staunton (VA). See New Market/Staunton (VA)
Staunton Choral Gardens Bed and Breakfast, 32
Stone Mountain Park, Georgia's, 294
Stones River National Battlefield, 199, 243, 253
Stones River (TN), Battle of, 239–45
    advance to Murfreesboro, 240–41
    afternoon battle (December 31, 1862), 243–44
    background to, 239
    bitter stalemate, 244
    Confederate assaults, 242, 244–45
    getting to site (today), 243
    Morgan's raid on Hartsville, 240
    night before, 238 39
    preparing for battle, 241–42
    reorganization of Bragg's Army of Mississippi, 240
    Union responses, 242–43, 244–45
Stonewall Jackson Inn, 32
Stonewall Jackson Museum at Hupp's Hill, 30
Stonewall Jackson's Headquarters Museum, 20
Stuart, James Ewell Brown (Jeb), 15, 36, 40, 96, 109, 423
Sully Plantation, 88
Sunflower Vegetarian Restaurant, 91
Sunset Grill, 201
Surf Rider Restaurant, 115
Sweetwater Tavern, 58–59

T
Tallula, 91
Tasting Room, 12
Taylor's Escape, 362
Tennessee, 232–54
    categories of battles, 233
    first to secede, first to return, 233
    lodging. See accommodations
    points of interest. See points of interest and attractions
    restaurants. See restaurants
    See also Chattanooga (TN), Battle of; Knoxville (TN); Nashville/Franklin (TN); Rivers campaign (TN); Shiloh (TN), Battle of

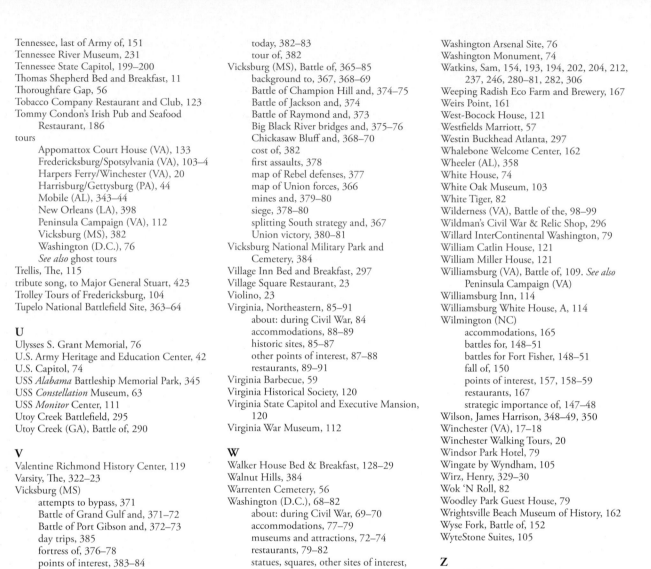